Historical Dictionaries of Ancient Civilizations
and Historical Eras
Series editor: Jon Woronoff

Historical Dictionary of Byzantium

John H. Rosser

Historical Dictionaries of Ancient Civilizations and Historical Eras, No. 4

The Scarecrow Press, Inc.
Lanham, Maryland, and London
2001

SCARECROW PRESS, INC.

Published in the United States of America
by Scarecrow Press, Inc.
4720 Boston Way, Lanham, Maryland 20706
www.scarecrowpress.com

4 Pleydell Gardens, Folkestone
Kent CT20 2DN, England

British Library Cataloguing in Publication Information Available

Library of Congress Cataloging-in-Publication Data

Rosser, John H. (John Hutchins), 1942–
    Historical dictionary of Byzantium / John H. Rosser.
    p. cm.—(Historical dictionaries of ancient civilizations and historical eras ; no. 4)
    Includes bibliographical references.
    ISBN 0-8108-3979-2 (alk. paper)
        1. Byzantine Empire—History—Dictionaries. I. Series.
    DF552 .R67 2001
    949.5'02—dc21   00-053334

⊖™ The paper used in this publication meets the minimum requirements of
American National Standard for Information Sciences—Permanence of
Paper for Printed Library Materials, ANSI/NISO Z39.48-1992.
Manufactured in the United States of America.

DEDICATED

to

Adam and Arrye, and to their children

Felix qui potuit rerum cognoscere causas.

(Virgil, *Georgics*)

CONTENTS

EDITOR'S FOREWORD

Once there were two empires. The Holy Roman Empire in the West was neither holy, nor Roman, nor really an empire. Byzantium in the East really was an empire, with a long succession of emperors. Its links with ancient Rome and Greece were much stronger. As the center of Orthodox Christianity, it could claim a considerable degree of holiness. In addition, it was a great center of learning and culture with exceptional achievements in art, architecture, and literature. And it held sway over vast lands and numerous peoples. Nonetheless, the West tended to look down on, and be suspicious of, its great neighbor centered in Constantinople. When Byzantium finally fell, it was due partly to its eastern enemies, but also due to the meddling and incredibly destructive "assistance" of supposed saviors from the West. Still, Byzantium left an enduring legacy in the Orthodox churches, and in such successor states as Russia, Greece, and Serbia.

The West has never fully understood those successor states of former Byzantium. So even more efforts must be made to understand this part of the world, and an examination of Byzantium and its legacy is one way of achieving that understanding. For this reason this *Historical Dictionary of Byzantium* is particularly useful. It adds to numerous other works, which cumulatively may have the desired effect. The Byzantine Empire, its genesis and development, its rise and fall, are first summarized in the chronology and explained in the introduction. The dictionary then presents significant persona (e.g., emperors, popes, generals, writers, and theologians) and outstanding events (e.g., wars and coups, councils and treaties) as well as important aspects of the economy, society, culture, and especially religion. A substantial bibliography shows how much has already been written about Byzantium, including books that readers would do well to peruse for further details.

This volume in our series of *Historical Dictionaries of Ancient Civilizations and Historical Eras* was written by John H. Rosser. Dr. Rosser has in a sense been preparing for the task for some three decades, starting with studies of Byzantine history at Rutgers University and continuing as a faculty member of the Department of History, Boston College, since 1971. He has also been active in Byzantine archeology;

his field research has resulted in numerous articles and an edited volume. But it was nonetheless a daunting challenge to compile such a book, summarizing as it does so many different aspects of Byzantium. The result is a work that profits from the integration of a single author, one that will provide an introduction to those beginning their study of Byzantium, and to those more advanced as well.

Jon Woronoff
Series Editor

ACKNOWLEDGMENTS

A single-volume encyclopedia such as this must necessarily select and compress from a great deal of material. It can make no claim to originality, other than the selection process, most important of which has been my desire to state the most salient assessments at the beginning of each entry. Such judgments the author takes responsibility for. However, the information itself is derived from the selected bibliography. Some works were consulted more than others; some areas of the bibliography were consulted infrequently, especially those areas having to do with civilization and culture: for this book is chiefly about important people, places, and major events.

For dictionary entries that have to do with people and events, much of the information is quite basic and available from a variety of sources (see I. A. Introductions, in the Bibliography), as well as being ingrained in memory from my years of teaching the history of Byzantium. However, information on places was sometimes another matter. Without the work of C. Foss, I would have had a much more difficult time locating basic information about a number of cities and regions in Asia Minor. Biographical and other dates were sometimes questionable; when in doubt, I relied on the *Oxford Dictionary of Byzantium*, 3 vols. (New York, Oxford, 1991), by A. P. Kazhdan, A.-M. Talbot, A. Cutler, T. E. Gregory, N. P. Ševčenko (eds.). I also depended on this work for a number of definitions having to do with titles and offices. For the 11th and 12th centuries, I was relieved to have the guidance of two recent works by M. Angold and P. Magdalino. Among the other scholars whose various works I consulted with some frequency are P. Brown, D. Geanakoplos, W. Kaegi, A. P. Kazhdan, A. Laiou, C. Mango, and I. Ševčenko. Any errors in the book, of course, are my own.

I would like to think that the dictionary is relatively free of personal or scholarly bias. Only two biases I am conscious of. One concerns the Crusades. Byzantinists take a fairly dim view of the Crusades, in particular the Fourth Crusade. The second has to do with the wide scope of the dictionary entries. Only a wide panorama can, in my opinion, do justice to Byzantium. Those who we call "Byzantines" would certainly have acknowledged the uniqueness of their civilization, but they would have also professed its magnetic power to attract peoples from well beyond Byzantium's borders. It is this magnetism, the charismatic quality of Byzantine civilization, that the author acknowledges.

The photograph of Saint Neophytos between the Archangels Michael and Gabriel, as well as the photograph of the interior of Hagia Sophia, are used with the permission of Dumbarton Oaks, Washington, D.C. All other photographs are by the author. The following plans and sections are used with the permission of Dufour Editions, Inc.: Plan of Constantinople; Section through the Theodosian Land Walls; Plan of Hagia Sophia; and Hagia Sophia: Section through nave, facing east. The map entitled the Byzantine Empire in 565 is used with the permission of Oxford University Press and the University of Chicago Press. The maps entitled the Byzantine Empire in 1265 and the Byzantine Empire and Ottoman Turks in 1355 are used with the permission of University Press of America and University of Chicago Press.

NOTE ON TRANSLITERATION

The transliteration of Greek names and terms can be done by two systems, and variations thereof: one that latinizes the Greek, and another that uses phonetic Modern Greek. Thus, the latinized Alexius Comnenus of the first system becomes Alexios Komnenos when transliterated into phonetic Modern Greek in the second system. With both systems one often finds familiar anglicized names unchanged, e.g. Constantine, Michael, John, Athens.

In this work the system chosen for dictionary entries is similar to that of the *Oxford Dictionary of Byzantium*, since this work is the next logical resource for students seeking additional information about specific entries. There, traditional Latin and anglicized terms are used for Greek names and terms (e.g., Constantine, Michael, John, Nicaea), but otherwise Greek names and terms are transliterated as close to phonetic Modern Greek as possible. Thus, both systems are used. The only change I have made is to avoid all diacritical marks and accents in foreign words (e.g., in Armenian and Arabic) as much as possible so as to make such words easier for students to write. For example, haceks in medieval names have been changed by adding an *h* (thus, Dushan for Dušan). The maps in the book use the latinized system. By learning to adjust to both systems, and variations thereof, the reader will gain a useful familiarity that will be of help in exploring the works listed in the bibliography, the titles of which require a knowledge of both systems.

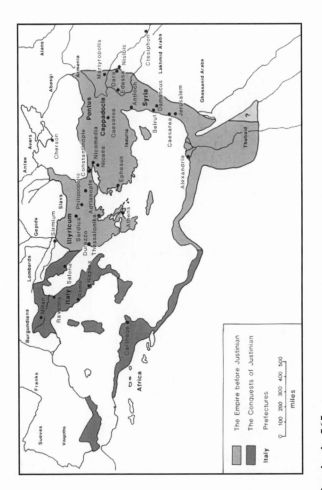

The Byzantine Empire in 565.
From D. J. Geanakoplos, *Byzantium: Church, Society, and Civilization Seen through Contemporary Eyes* (Chicago: University of Chicago Press, 1984), based on a map in N. Baynes and H. Moss, eds., *Byzantium: An Introduction to East Roman Civilization* (Oxford: Clarendon Press, 1961); by permission of Oxford University Press and University of Chicago Press.

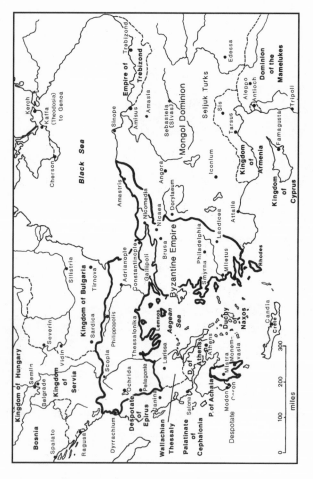

The Byzantine Empire in 1265.

From D. J. Geanakoplos, *Byzantium: Church, Society, and Civilization Seen through Contemporary Eyes* (Chicago: University of Chicago Press, 1984), based on *Shepherd's Historical Atlas*, 9th ed. (New York: Harper & Row, 1964); by permission of University Press of America and University of Chicago Press.

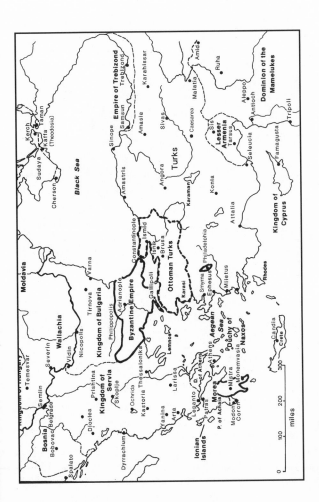

The Byzantine Empire and Ottoman Turks in 1355.
From D. J. Geanakoplos, *Byzantium: Church, Society, and Civilization Seen through Contemporary Eyes* (Chicago: University of Chicago: Press, 1984), based on *Shepherd's Historical Atlas*, 9th ed. (New York: Harper & Row, 1964); by permission of University Press of America and University of Chicago Press.

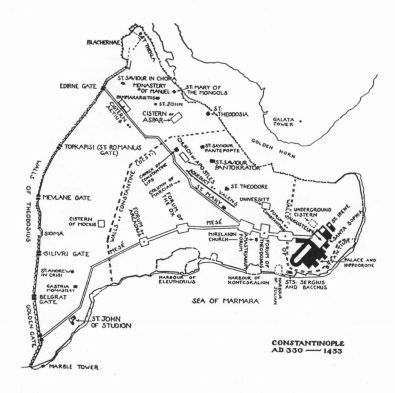

BLACHERNAE

ST THYRA

EDIRNE GATE

ST SAVIOUR IN CHORA
MONASTERY
"OF MANUEL"

ST MARY OF
THE MONGOLS

PAMMAKARISTOS

ST JOHN

CISTERN
AETHIUN

CISTERN of
ASPAR

ST.
THEODOSIA

GALATA
TOWER

TOPKAPISI (ST ROMANUS
GATE)

GOLDEN HORN

ST SAVIOUR
PANTEPOPTE

CHURCH of APOSTLES

WALLS of CONSTANTINE (POSEN)

ST SAVIOUR
PANTOKRATOR

MEVLANE GATE

CHURCH OF
CONSTANTINE
LIPS

COLUMN OF
MARCIAN

FORUM OF
THE OX

AQUEDUCT of ST VALENS

ST MARY

ST THEODORE

UNIVERSITY

UNDERGROUND
CISTERN

FORUM OF CONSTANTINE

ST IRENE

SANTA SOPHIA

AUGUSTEUM

CISTERN
OF MOCIUS

FORUM OF ARCADIUS

MESÉ

MESÉ

MIRELAION
CHURCH

FORUM OF
THEODOSIUS

FORUM OF JULIAN

MILLION FORUM

GOLDEN GATE

SIGMA

SILIVRI GATE

ST ANDREW
IN CRISI

GASTRIA
MONASTERY

BELGRAT
GATE

ST JOHN
OF STUDION

HARBOUR OF
ELEUTHERIUS

HARBOUR OF
KONTOSKALION

HARBOUR OF
JULIAN

STS SERGIUS
AND BACCHUS

PALACE AND
HIPPODROME

SEA OF MARMARA

WALLS OF THEODOSIUS

MARBLE TOWER

CONSTANTINOPLE
AD 330 —— 1453

Plan of Constantinople.

From J. E. N. Hearsey, *City of Constantine, 324–1453* (Philadelphia, 1966), by permission of Dufour Editions, Inc. Constantine I founded this imperial residence and eastern capital in 330 on the site of the ancient city of Byzantion. It was called "New Rome," though it was soon called Constantinople ("City of Constantine"), after its founder. The city must have been chosen for its strategic location: situated on a promontory where the Sea of Marmara meets the Bosporos, midway along the waterway that leads north from the Aegean Sea to the Black Sea, where Europe meets Asia. Constantinople retained many features of an imperial Roman city. One sees this in its monuments, which included a hippodrome, an aqueduct, reservoirs and cisterns, forums, baths, and imperial palaces. One entered the Theodosian walls through one of several public gates (some of which are designated by their Turkish names on the plan). The gate reserved for the emperor was the Golden Gate. The emperor traversed the thoroughfare called the Mese to reach his residence, the Great Palace, at the end of the promontory.

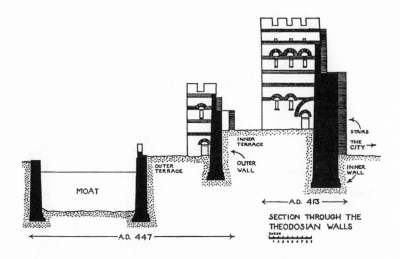

Section through the Theodosian Land Walls.

From J. E. N. Hearsey, *City of Constantine, 324–1453* (Philadelphia, 1966), by permission of Dufour Editions, Inc. These were the most formidable urban fortifications of the Middle Ages. Their historic role was to preserve Byzantium's capital intact against its foes. They accomplished this with a triple defense of ditch (which could be flooded by piped-in water to become a moat), outer wall, and higher inner wall. This arrangement extended from north to south across the entire six kilometers from the Sea of Marmara to the Golden Horn. The highest, innermost wall was built in 412/413; it is 11 meters high, with 96 towers (square or polygonal in plan) at intervals of about 70 meters. In 439 a single wall interspersed with towers was built along the Golden Horn (entrance to which could be obstructed by a great chain) and the Sea of Marmara. An outer wall and ditch were constructed later, in 447. The ditch alone was a significant impediment some 20 meters wide, and quite deep. By the mid-fifth century the city was virtually impregnable. Moreover, would-be assailants needed to besiege Constantinople both by land and sea, which relatively few of Byzantium's foes were capable of. Even the great Arab siege of 674–678 failed to breach these defenses. Yet two foes did succeed: the knights of the Fourth Crusade in 1204 and the Ottomans in 1453. The Ottomans did so with the aid of an enormous army and new gunpowder technology that included huge cannons.

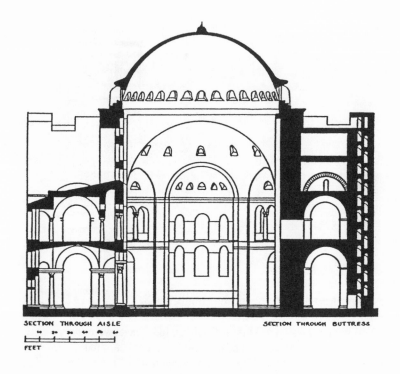

SECTION THROUGH AISLE   SECTION THROUGH BUTTRESS

FEET

Hagia Sophia. Section through nave, facing east.

From J. E. N. Hearsey, *City of Constantine, 324–1453* (Philadelphia, 1966), by permission of Dufour Editions, Inc. Hagia Sophia demonstrated what previously had been thought impossible: a huge dome (31 meters in diameter) was placed over a square space defined by four arches. Foremost among the problems was the fact that the ring-base of the dome's base had to be fully supported. To solve this problem, Hagia Sophia's two architects, Anthemios of Tralles and Isidore of Miletos, used curved triangular segments of masonry called pendentives between the gaps in each corner of the four arches. With four pendentives the base of the dome was provided with a circular support of masonry. In effect, the pendentives allowed the circular base of the dome to be placed on a square. Outward thrust from the dome was counteracted somewhat by a series of half-domes and semi-domes on the east and west, and by external buttresses on the north and south. Nevertheless, the first dome was too shallow and collapsed in 558. The dome that replaced it was higher, and, thus, more stable.

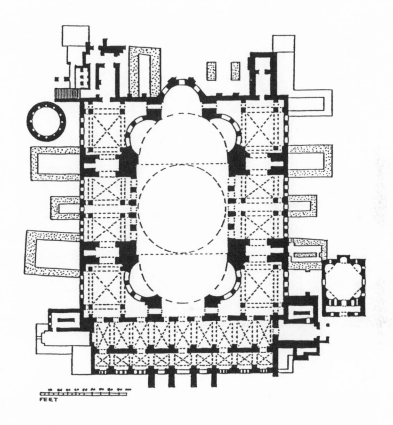

FEET

Plan of Hagia Sophia.
From J. E. N. Hearsey, *City of Constantine, 324–1453* (Philadelphia, 1966), by permission of Dufour Editions, Inc. As an architectural experience, Justinian I's great church appears complex, even baffling, like a puzzle incapable of solution. However, a brief glance at this plan appears to solve the puzzle. What one sees (going from west to east, from the bottom to top of the plan) is a domed basilica with two entrance vestibules—i.e., an exonarthex and a narthex—a main nave, and an apse. On either side of the apse are aisles with galleries above. Buttresses adorn the north and south sides. A baptistery is situated just south of where one enters the church. But what is difficult to comprehend from this plan is how the main dome is fully supported; four arches alone are hardly sufficient to support the dome. It is the triangular segments at each corner, called pendentives, that are the unnoticed heroes.

CHRONOLOGY

Byzantium endured from 324–1453. It began with the foundation of Constantinople by the emperor Constantine I in 324. It ended with the conquest of Constantinople by the Ottoman Turks on 29 May 1453. Between those dates are many important events, undoubtedly more than can be fit into this brief chronology. Attempts at periodization are interpretative, the simplest being three basic phases: Early (324–ca. 650), Middle (ca. 650–1071), and Late (1071–1453). For 1071, the date of the battle of Mantzikert, some might substitute 1204, the year the Fourth Crusade conquered Constantinople. In any case these phases, elaborated on in the introduction, are conventional ones. The reader will encounter others, including the one suggested in section V of the bibliography.

324–337	Reign of Constantine I as sole ruler
324	Foundation of Constantinople
325	First Ecumenical Council (at Nicaea)
330	Dedication of Constantinople
337–361	Reign of Constantius II, with Constantine II (337–340) and Constans (337–350) as augusti.
ca. 343	Council of Serdica
353	Defeat of Magnentius
359	Persians capture Amida
361–363	Reign of Julian
363–364	Reign of Jovian

364–378	Reign of Valens, with western emperors Valentinian I (364–375) and Gratian (375–383)
376	Visigoths cross the Danube
378	Battle of Adrianople
379–395	Reign of Theodosius I, with western emperor Valentinian II (ruled with Gratian 375–383; sole western emperor 383–392)
381	Second Ecumenical Council at Constantinople
391	New laws prohibit the offering of pagan sacrifices; all temples ordered closed
395–408	Reigns of Arkadios in the East, with western emperor Honorius in the West (reigned 395–423)
400	Massacre of Goths in Constantinople
402	Honorius's court retreats from Milan to Ravenna
408–450	Reign of Theodosios II in the East, with western emperor Honorius (until 423) and Valentinian III (reigned 425–455)
410	Rome sacked by the Visigoths
413	Theodosian land walls completed at Constantinople
425	University of Constantinople reorganized
429	Vandals and Alans cross over to North Africa
431	Third Ecumenical Council at Ephesus
438	Codex Theodosianus issued
439	Vandals capture Carthage
449	"Robber Council" at Ephesus

533–534	Vandalic War
534	*Corpus Juris Civilis* issued
535–554	Ostrogothic War
537	Hagia Sophia dedicated
540–545	War with Persia
545–550	Five-year truce with Persia (renewed 551, 556)
ca. 550	Southeast Spain occupied by Byzantine forces
553	Fifth Ecumenical Council at Constantinople
562–572	Peace treaty with Persia
565–578	Reign of Justin II, with Tiberios as caesar (574–578)
568	Lombards invade Italy
572–591	War with Persia
578–582	Reign of Tiberios I
ca. 578–585	Slavs settle in Greece in great numbers
582–602	Reign of Maurice
586	First siege of Thessalonike by Avars and Slavs
602–610	Reign of Phokas
603	War with Persia resumes (to 628)
610–641	Reign of Herakleios
611–622	Persian attacks on Asia Minor
626	Avars and Persians besiege Constantinople

695–698	Reign of Leontios
698	Arabs capture Carthage
698–705	Reign of Tiberios II
705–711	Reign of Justinian II (again)
711–713	Reign of Philippikos
713–715	Reign of Anastasios II
715–717	Reign of Theodosios III
717–741	Reign of Leo III
717–718	Arab siege of Constantinople
730	Leo III bans all religious images
740	Battle of Akroinon
741–775	Reign of Constantine V
742–743	Revolt of Artabasdos
751	Lombards capture Ravenna
754	Iconoclastic Council of Hiera
775–780	Reign of Leo IV
780–797	Reign of Constantine VI
787	Seventh Ecumenical Council at Constantinople
797–802	Reign of Irene
800	Coronation of Charlemagne
802–811	Reign of Nikephoros I

963	Great Lavra monastery founded on Mount Athos
963–969	Reign of Nikephoros II Phokas
969–976	Reign of John I Tzimiskes
976–1025	Reign of Basil II (with co-emperor Constantine VIII)
988	Baptism of Vladimir I, prince of Kiev; defeat of Bardas Phokas
996	Legislation restricting acquisition of land by wealthy magnates from the poor
1014	Basil II defeats the Bulgars; death of Tsar Samuel
1025–1028	Reign of Constantine VIII
1028–1034	Reign of Romanos III Argyros
1034–1041	Reign of Michael IV Paphlagon
1040	George Maniakes captures Syracuse
1041	Revolt of Peter Deljan suppressed
1041–1042	Reign of Michael V Kalaphates
1042	Reign of Zoe and Theodora
1042–1055	Reign of Constantine IX Monomachos
1043	Rus attack Constantinople; rebellion of Maniakes
1045	Kingdom of Ani annexed
1046	University of Constantinople refounded
1047	Revolt of Leo Tornikos suppressed; Pechenegs cross the Danube and plunder Thrace
1054	Schism between the churches

1095–1099	First Crusade
1108	Treaty of Devol
1118–1143	Reign of John II Komnenos
1126	Venetian commercial privileges reaffirmed
1127–1129	Victories over the Serbs and the Hungarians
1132–1137	Victories over the Danishmends and the Rubenids in Asia Minor
1137	Antioch submits to John II
1143–1180	Reign of Manuel I Komnenos
1147–1198	Second Crusade
1147	Normans seize Kerkyra (retaken in 1149) and plunder Corinth and Thebes
1171	Venetians arrested and their property seized throughout the empire
1176	Battle of Myriokephalon
1180–1183	Reign of Alexios II Komnenos
1182	Latins massacred in Constantinople
1183–1185	Reign of Andronikos I Komnenos
1184	Cyprus falls to Isaac Komnenos
1185	Normans capture Thessalonike
1185–1195	Reign of Isaac II Angelos
1186	Second Bulgarian Empire founded
1187	Revolt of Alexios Branas

1328–1341	Reign of Andronikos III Palaiologos
1330	Battle of Velbuzd
1331	Ottomans capture Nicaea
1341–1391	Reign of John V Palaiologos
1341–1347	Second civil war (between John V and John Kantakouzenos)
1342–1350	Zealot revolt in Thessalonike
1347–1354	Reign of John VI Kantakouzenos
1348–1349	Black Death ravages Constantinople
1354	Ottomans occupy Gallipoli
1355	Death of Stefan Urosh IV Dushan
1366	Amadeo VI of Savoy recovers Gallipoli
1369	John V's journey to Rome
1376–1379	Reign of Andronikos IV Palaiologos
1382	Ottomans conquer Serdica (Sofia)
1387	Ottomans conquer Thessalonike
1389	Battle of Kosovo Polje
1390	Reign of John VII Palaiologos
1391–1425	Reign of Manuel II Palaiologos
1393	Ottomans conquer Bulgaria
1394	Ottomans capture Thessalonike again
1399–1403	Manuel II's journey to the West

INTRODUCTION

No state ever existed that called itself either "Byzantium" or the "Byzantine Empire." These are modern, conventional terms for the Roman Empire from 324–1453: from the foundation of Constantinople (formerly called Byzantium) to the conquest of the city by the Ottoman Turks in 1453. The "Byzantines" always called themselves Romans (*romaioi*), and referred to their emperor as Emperor of the Romans (*basileon ton Rhomaion*). After 324 the orientation of the Roman Empire became more eastern, partly because Constantinople (also called New Rome; modern Istanbul), founded by Constantine I the Great, lay in the East. From the seventh century onward the heartland of Byzantium lay in Asia Minor, in what now comprises modern Turkey, and Byzantine possessions in the West were reduced to southern Italy. One can understand why some have called it the "Eastern Roman Empire." What is important to realize is that "Byzantium" refers to the Roman state after 324.

Byzantium was a Christian empire. To understand how this happened, one must turn again to Constantine I, who himself became a Christian in ca. 312, the first Roman emperor to do so. Constantine actively supported the church, and participated in church affairs, including the Council of Nicaea in 325, which declared Arianism a heresy. The emperor's role in the church established the emperor as God's viceroy on earth, the 13th apostle, as it were. Constantine's program of church construction laid the foundations for Christian architecture. Subsequently, Byzantine art developed as a religious art. Thus, not only did the Roman Empire change by virtue of its new capital and eastern orientation but also it became the chief supporter of the Christian church.

Byzantium was gradually transformed by these changes. The perception of Byzantium as lacking vitality, as exotically ritualized and conservative in its court and administration, and as perpetually in decline, even corrupt, reflects a western medieval viewpoint that persisted into modern times. The truth is quite the opposite. Byzantium showed a vitality unmatched by any medieval state. Rather than perpetual decline, one finds periodic renewal, even after Byzantium was destroyed by the Fourth Crusade in 1204. That it was the only medieval empire of long duration is proof of its vitality, of its ability to transform itself in the face of serious external threats.

Byzantine history can be divided into three basic phases: Early, Middle, and Late. The first phase, Early Byzantine (essentially Late Antiquity), dates from the foundation of Constantinople in 324 until ca. 650, by which time the Arab expansion emerged as a serious threat. The second phase can be called Middle Byzantine, lasting from ca. 650 to the battle of Mantzikert in 1071, which opened up Asia Minor, the heartland of medieval Byzantium, to Turkish settlement. (Some scholars might replace 1071 with 1204, the year when Constantinople was conquered by the Fourth Crusade.) The Late Byzantine phase lasted from 1071 until the fall of Constantinople to the Ottoman Turks on 29 May 1453.

After 324, Byzantium was gradually separated from its western provinces. This process was due chiefly to massive incursions of Germanic peoples in the late fourth and fifth centuries. The failure of the wars of reconquest launched by Justinian I (527–565), as well as the Slavic settlements in the Balkan Peninsula, were decisive in this respect. After the seventh century, knowledge of Greek, the common language spoken by Byzantines, declined precipitously in the West. Differences in church ritual and doctrine in subsequent centuries contributed to the schism between eastern and western churches in 1054. As mentioned previously, the western knights of the First Crusade who gathered in Constantinople in 1097 represented the first large number of westerners to travel to Constantinople across the Balkan Peninsula in centuries.

When the First Crusade arrived in Constantinople, the differences that had accrued over the centuries became apparent. Byzantium became envied for its riches, was perceived as foreign, as untrustworthy, and possibly heretical. The First Crusade posed a great threat to the city, as did the Second Crusade, which also passed through the city. Finally, the axe fell when the Fourth Crusade conquered Constantinople in 1204. Byzantium was effectively destroyed until 1265, when its virtual state-in-exile, the Empire of Nicaea, reconquered Constantinople. Threats continued to appear from the West, including those from the Catalan Grand Company, and from Charles of Anjou. However, it was the Turkish threat from the East, by the mid-14th century in the form of the Ottoman Turks, that proved fatal.

The Byzantine emperor governed a vast bureaucracy that minted coins, collected taxes, regulated commerce, and maintained large standing armies. The emperor could intervene in church affairs, although most emperors knew that replacing bishops and archbishops was acceptable, but meddling in theology was not. There were notable exceptions, such as Justinian I and Leo III, both of whom posterity has labeled "caesaropapist." Imperial ceremonials (e.g., acclamations, processions, audiences), all carefully scripted, formatted much of the emperor's public life. Much of it was in monumental settings like Hagia Sophia, the Great Palace, and the Hippodrome, and it was always intended to glorify the majesty of the imperial office. The great reception hall called the Magnaura, adjacent to the Great Palace, was where foreign ambassadors were received. Ambassadors were ushered into the emperor's presence with two gold organs playing, golden lions roaring, and mechanical birds twittering. The great throne there, called the throne of Solomon, contained a mechanism that could suddenly lift the seated emperor to the ceiling, which is what Liutprand of Cremona, ambassador for king of Italy Berenar II in 949, reports seeing. Ushered into the presence of Emperor Constantine VII, Liutprand did obeisance three times with his face to the ground. When he lifted his head for the third time the emperor had somehow changed his raiment and was high up near the ceiling.

Byzantine society was characterized by ethnic diversity. Greeks, Armenians, Slavs, Georgians, and other ethnic minorities were fully accepted, as long as they themselves accepted Orthodox Christianity. There were Armenian emperors; one Slav contender for the imperial throne, Thomas the Slav, almost became emperor. Jews, who did not meet this qualification, were nevertheless allowed to live in virtually autonomous communities where they practiced their religion freely. They engaged in numerous trades; Jewish doctors were popular with Jews and non-Jews alike. Western merchants and mercenaries were prominent in Constantinople from the 11th century. An example is Harold Hardrada, a Viking from Rus who commanded the elite Varangian Guard in Constantinople. He returned to Norway to become its king and died fighting King Harold of England in 1066 at Stamford Bridge. After 1066, the Varangian Guard recruited the Anglo-Saxon warriors whom William the Conqueror defeated at Hastings. There was even a mosque in Constantinople from the 10th century onward.

Byzantium made a profound influence on its neighbors, especially on the fledgling Slavic states. Indeed, there existed a kind of "Byzantine Commonwealth" of Slavic states, which included, above all, Kievan Rus, Serbia, and Bulgaria. To them Byzantium bequeathed its literature and art, indeed its distinctive alphabets, the Glagolitic and Cyrillic. This legacy continued even after Constantinople fell to the Ottomans. Moscow began to refer to itself as the "Third Rome," the inheritor of Byzantium, the second Rome. However, it is the larger centrality of Byzantium to medieval European civilization that may surprise the beginning student. For one cannot understand the Middle Ages without understanding Byzantium, the only true empire medieval Europe ever knew.

Today, access to Byzantine civilization is largely through its surviving art and architecture. Byzantine art may perhaps be best understood through its icons, which remain a living tradition within Orthodox churches. However, Byzantine architecture, including Byzantium's greatest church, Hagia Sophia, in Constantinople, is not so easily understandable. Like much of Byzantium, Hagia Sophia needs to be studied to be understood. The same is true of Byzantine history, which is often not taught at all, or poorly taught. Even if one travels to Greece, the modern heir of the Byzantine religious tradition, the non-Greek tourist will find a tourist industry that caters to an overwhelming interest in ancient, not Byzantine, Greece.

One must be prepared to sail to Byzantium on one's own, so to speak. Within the comfort of one's home one can access significant bibliography in English. One can admire Byzantine art in most major museums, including the museum at Dumbarton Oaks, in Washington, D.C., home to the famous research center devoted to Byzantine studies. One can visit its extant monuments, including the monasteries of Meteora, the restored town of Mistra, and, of course, Hagia Sophia in Constantinople.

Even today, modern Istanbul, despite its development as a Turkish city since 1453, contains impressive Byzantine monuments. First-time visitors, if offered a choice, should approach Constantinople for the first time by sea, as did the western knights of the Fourth Crusade, many of whom were stunned by their sight of the city. Geoffrey de Villehardouin describes this moment:

"I can assure you that all those who had never seen Constantinople before gazed very intently at the city, having never imagined there could be so fine a place in all the world. They noted its high walls and lofty towers encircling it, and its rich palaces and tall churches, of which there were so many that no one would have believed it to be true if he had not seen it with his own eyes, and viewed the length and breadth of that city which reigns supreme over all others." M. R. B. Shaw (trans.), *Joinville and Villehardouin: Chronicles of the Crusade* (Harmondsworth: Penguin, 1963), 58–59.

Readers who approach Byzantium for the first time may soon consider it is the best vantage point from which to view the entire historical landscape of the Middle Ages. The view of the Middle Ages from Constantinople, "that city which reigns supreme over all others" is truly Olympian. It connects the reader with all parts of the medieval Islamic world, the kingdoms bordering the Black Sea, the tribes of the Eurasian steppe, Kievan Rus and the Slavic states of the Balkan Peninsula, and the Latin West. The diversity of important foreigners that one encounters in the history of Byzantium illustrates this. They include Attila the Hun, Michael the Slav, Vladimir of Rus, Harold Hardrada, Bohemund, Roger Flor, Alamundarus, Alp Arslan, Amadeo VI of Savoy, Aspar, Asparuch, Bayezid, Bela III of Hungary, Vladimir of Rus, Boniface of Montferrat, khan Boris, Boucicaut, Charles I of Anjou, Chosroes I, Enrico Dandalo, Gagik II, Gainas, Gaiseric, Harun al-Rashid, Hervé Frankopoulos, Humbert, Jaroslav the Wise, John Italos, Krum, Liutprand of Cremona, Louis VII, Mamun, Manfred, Otto III, Ricimir, Robert Guiscard, Stefan Urosh II Milutin, Stilicho, Svjatoslav, and Vigilius. One could go on. Arguably no other vantage point—not Baghdad, not Cordoba, not Rome, not Palermo, and certainly neither Paris nor London—provides such a high hill from which to view the diversity of the Middle Ages.

From that high hill, one's assumptions about the preeminence of the Latin West from Late Antiquity to the Renaissance begins to diminish. Greco-Roman antiquity does not appear as a broken reed, with centuries of discontinuity leading to eventual Renaissance. Rather, continuity and transformation are the operative words. By studying the history of how "Byzantine" history was created in modern times, one begins to understand how great was the impact of Renaissance and Early Modern European scholarship on our present values and historical perspective. Add to this the fact that in our own times the decline of the great European empires has made it difficult to understand any of the great empires of the past, whether Aztec, Ottoman, or Byzantine.

Among the many reasons to study Byzantium, there is an important one that should be emphasized: Irrespective of its relationship with neighboring peoples, irrespective of its relationship to its Greco-Roman past, Byzantium was a unique world civilization that deserves to be considered on its own terms.

THE DICTIONARY

ABBASID CALIPHATE. The Abbasids, descended from Muhammed the Prophet's (q.v.) uncle Abbas, came to power in 749 in a revolt against the Umayyad Caliphate (q.v.). From their capital in Baghdad (q.v.), they held the caliphate (q.v.) from 750–1258. The early caliphate was noted for its cultural brilliance, especially under caliph (q.v.) Harun al-Rashid (786–809) (q.v.) and his son Mamun (813–833) (qq.v.). In arts and literature, Persian cultural influence on the Abbasids was great, but so was that of ancient Hellenic learning. Mamun founded a research center called the House of Wisdom, a library, academy, and center for the acquisition, translation, and study of ancient Greek manuscripts on science and philosophy. The works of Galen, Hippocrates, Euclid, Ptolemy, Archimedes, Plato, and Aristotle (qq.v) were particularly prized. Because Byzantine towns and monasteries were repositories of such manuscripts they became special targets for looting on Abbasid military campaigns. Diplomatic missions were further vehicles for this transmission. Mamun sent an embassy to Emperor Leo V (q.v.) to acquire Greek manuscripts. The emperor Theophilos (q.v.) sent his patriarch (q.v.), the learned John the Grammarian (q.v.), to Mamun. Mamun invited the most brilliant scientist of Theophilos's court, Leo the Mathematician (q.v.), to Baghdad, but Leo refused. In the early ninth century Abbasid raids into Asia Minor (q.v.) culminated in 838 in the sack of Amorion (q.v.), the paternal city of Theophilos. The slow decline of the caliphate began soon thereafter, marked by periods of disorder as the influence of Turkish mercenaries grew stronger. The Mongols (q.v.) finally ejected the Abbasids from Baghdad in 1258.

ABCHASIA. Region just south of the Caucasus Mountains (q.v.) on the eastern coast of the Black Sea (q.v.). It was made part of the kingdom of Lazica (q.v.) in the fourth century. Its strategic importance was apparent in the sixth century, especially from 549–557, during the Byzantine-Persian war over Lazika (qq.v.). Justinian I (q.v.) made Abchasia a Byzantine protectorate, suppressing a revolt in 550 that sought to invite the Persians in. Justinian also abolished

1

the region's trade in eunuchs (q.v.). Byzantine influence waned in the seventh century, despite the presence of two fortresses, Pityus and Sebastopolis, that maintained Byzantine interests. In the 10th century the region came under the control of the Bagratids (q.v.).

ABD AL-MALIK. Umayyad caliph (qq.v.) from 685–705. Until 692, he was preoccupied with internal rebellions. Justinian II (q.v.) took advantage of this by unleashing on Syria (q.v.) the Christian bandits called Mardaites (q.v.), and by sending an army under Leontios (q.v.) into Armenia (q.v.). The resulting treaty of 688 was favorable to Byzantium (q.v.), requiring the caliph to pay tribute and dividing with Byzantium the revenues from Cyprus, Armenia, and Georgia (qq.v.). In 692 the caliph was able to turn his attention to military expansion. He defeated Justinian II in Asia Minor (q.v.) in 693, forcing the emperor (q.v.) to abandon Armenia (which the Arabs [q.v.]) subsequently conquered in 703). In the West, the Arabs conquered Carthage (q.v.) in 698, extinguishing what was left of Byzantine authority in North Africa (q.v.). The caliph tried to remove vestiges of Byzantine influence within the caliphate (q.v.), e.g., by issuing the first purely Arab coinage without Greek inscriptions or imagery, and by making Arabic the official language. Nevertheless, in Jerusalem (q.v.) he used Byzantine mosaicists to decorate the great Dome of the Rock (q.v.).

ABU BAKR. The first caliph (q.v.). From 632–634 he administered the political state created by Muhammed the Prophet (q.v.). Abu Bakr organized the first concerted attacks on Byzantine territory in 633 and 634, winning victories in Syria and southern Palestine (qq.v.), while Muslim forces under the great general Khalid (q.v.) defeated Persian forces in Iraq. These early successes, harbingers of greater successes to come, were made easier by the exhaustion of Persia and Byzantium (qq.v.) following the conclusion in 629 of their own lengthy war.

ABU MINA. Important Egyptian pilgrimage (q.v.) site near Alexandria (q.v.) from the late fourth century. It consisted of the tomb of St. Menas (q.v.), over which was a *marytrion* (q.v.), which Justinian I (q.v.) renovated as a *tetraconch* (q.v.). Immediately to the east was a large late fifth-century basilica (q.v.) of the cross-transept type, its design and decoration influenced by church architecture in Constantinople (q.v.). To the west of the basilica was a baptistry, and around Abu Mina are the remains of other basilican churches. A great number of clay souvenir pilgrim flasks (q.v.) called "Menas flasks," once filled with miracle-working water from near the shrine, have been found throughout the former Byzantine empire. In general, the site illustrates the popularity of pilgrimage sites in the fifth and sixth centuries, as well as their imperial support.

ABYDOS. City and naval base at the entrance to the Hellespont (q.v.). Its custom house, established by Justinian I (q.v.), provided one of the most important sources of revenue to the Byzantine state, levying import and export duties on shipping going to and from Constantinople (q.v.).

ABYSSINIA. *See* **AXUM.**

ACACIAN SCHISM. *See* **AKAKIAN SCHISM.**

ACACIUS. *See* **AKAKIOS.**

ACADEMY OF ATHENS. Famous pagan school of philosophy in Athens (q.v.) that was closed by Justinian I (q.v.) in 529. In the fourth century its students included Basil the Great, Gregory of Nazianzos, and the future emperor Julian (qq.v.). The great philosophers of Neoplatonism (q.v.), including Proklos and Damaskios (qq.v.), taught there. Justinian's action can be seen as a symbolic attack on paganism. Nevertheless, it extinguished a tradition of learning that reached back to the time of Aristotle (q.v.) and ushered in the decline of Athens as a center of culture.

ACCIAJUOLI. Florentine merchant family that played a great role in Greece (q.v.) in the second half of the 14th century. They acquired Corinth (q.v.) in 1358, ruling it until 1397. They held Athens (q.v.) from 1358–1397, and from 1404–1446, when future emperor Constantine XI acquired it for Byzantium (qq.v.). They ruled Thebes (q.v.) from 1378–1456. In addition they held extensive lands in the Peloponnesos (q.v.), then called the Morea (q.v.).

ACHAIA. A late Roman province that included southern and central Greece (q.v.) south of Thermopylae (q.v.). Its capital was at Corinth (q.v.). Later Achaia was incorporated into the late seventh-century theme of Hellas (qq.v.). William I of Champlitte and Geoffrey (I) Villehardouin (qq.v.), knights of the Fourth Crusade (q.v.), established the principality of Achaia (1205–1430). Their successor

William II Villehardouin (q.v.) created impressive strongholds at Maina, Mistra, and Monemvasia (qq.v). However, beginning in 1262 Byzantine power slowly reconquered the southern part of the Latin principality, and in 1349 John VI Kantakouzenos (q.v) consolidated this Byzantine territory into the despotate of Morea, administered from Mistra (qq.v.). The intervention of the Navarrese Company (q.v.) into Achaia in the late 14th century served to weaken resistance to the Ottomans, who conquered the principality of Achaia in 1430.

ACHAIA, PRINCIPALITY OF. *See* **ACHAIA; MOREA; WILLIAM I CHAMPLITTE; WILLIAM II VILLEHARDOUIN.**

ACHEIROPOIETA. Greek term that refers to objects "not made by human hands." It more specifically refers to holy images of Christ and Mary that appeared miraculously. One of the most famous was a miraculous icon (q.v.) of the Virgin in the fifth-century Acheiropoietos Church at Thessalonike (q.v.). The *mandylion* of Edessa (q.v.) is another example.

ACHILLEIS. *See* **ROMANCES.**

ACRE. *See* **THIRD CRUSADE.**

ADRIANOPLE. The most important Byzantine city in Thrace (q.v.). Its position astride the main military road from Belgrade to Constantinople (qq.v.) meant that it was often besieged by invaders from the north, including Avars, Bulgars, Serbs, and Pechenegs (qq.v.). At the famous Battle of Adrianople (378), Goths killed the emperor Valens (qq.v.) and routed his army. The city's vulnerability to attacks from Bulgaria (Krum [q.v.] occupied the city briefly) turned it into a strategic center for military expeditions against Bulgaria (q.v.). Frederick I Barbarossa (q.v.) seized Adrianople briefly in 1190 during the Third Crusade (q.v.), and after the Fourth Crusade (q.v.) Baldwin of Flanders (q.v.) was defeated there (1205). John III Vatatzes (q.v.) occupied the city from 1242–1246. It was finally lost to Byzantium (q.v) around 1369 when the Ottomans (q.v.) captured it. Soon thereafter it became their capital, and it remained such until the Ottoman conquest of Constantinople in 1453.

ADRIATIC SEA. Situated between Italy (q.v.) and the coast of Dalmatia (q.v.), it was the most important east-west trade route prior to the 11th century. Byzantine domination of the Adriatic was tested after 827, when Muslim raiders began their conquest of Sicily (q.v.), launching attacks on coastal towns along the southern Adriatic. In 840 they captured Bari (q.v.), and in 866–867 they besieged Dubrovnik (q.v.), which was saved only when a fleet sent from Constantinople (q.v.) appeared. It was probably in response to such attacks that the theme (q.v.) of Dalmatia was created. However, by the late 11th century Byzantine control slipped away to the Venetians, partly due to a favorable treaty the Venetians signed in 1082 with Emperor Alexios I (q.v.). In return, Alexios got Venetian help against expansion by the Normans (q.v.) in the southern Adriatic (described by Anna Komnene [q.v.] in Book Six of *The Alexiad*). The growing power of Venice (q.v.) in the Adriatic was further enhanced by the partition of Byzantium after the Fourth Crusade (q.v.). In the 13th century the coastal towns along the Adriatic became a kind of national market for Venice, which, in turn, became the foundation for Venice's further expansion in the eastern Mediterranean (q.v.).

ADVENTUS. Latin for "arrival," referring to the ceremony required when an emperor, bishop (qq.v.), high officials, relics (q.v.) of a saint, or an imperial *fiancée,* was welcomed into a city. For example, in the case of an emperor returning to Constantinople (q.v.), a delegation that included city officials and the bishop met the emperor outside the city at a prescribed distance with acclamations (q.v.), incense, and golden crowns or wreaths. Then they accompanied the emperor along the Mese (q.v.), the great processional boulevard, into Constantinople. In 508 this ritual resonated in the barbarian West when Clovis (q.v.) created an imperial *adventus* into Tours to celebrate the status of honorary consul that emperor Anastasios I (qq.v.) had conferred upon him.

AEGEAN SEA. Situated between Greece and Asia Minor (qq.v.), interspersed with numerous islands and an indented coastline, the Aegean was crucial to the economic prosperity of Byzantium. Constantinople (q.v.) needed free access to the Aegean for its food supplies and for trade, which provided important customs duties through Abydos (q.v.). Some of the islands, such as Crete (q.v.), supplied grain to Constantinople. Defense of the Aegean evolved from the seventh-century naval command of the theme of Karabisianoi (qq.v.) to inclusion in the eighth-century theme of Kibyrrhaiotai (q.v.). In the ninth and 10th centuries there was further administrative development aimed at preventing Arab raids into the Aegean from Crete, which the Arabs (q.v.) seized around 828. However, by the end of the 11th century, Venetian economic power dominated, and after 1204 it was assured by their control of Crete, Euboea, Andros, and Naxos (qq.v.), as well as ports on the Hellespont and the Sea of Marmora (qq.v.). The Aegean spoils of the conquest of Constantinople by the Fourth Crusade (q.v.) made possible a Venetian colonial empire in the East.

AETIOS. Arian theologian (qq.v.) who taught at Antioch and Alexandria (qq.v.). He and his disciple Eunomios (q.v.) were exiled by Constantius II (q.v.), and recalled by Julian (q.v.). He rejected the view of *homoousios,* even that of *homoiousios* (qq.v.), in favor of the view that the created Son was unlike God the Father, having a completely different essence, nature, even will. He died in Chalcedon (q.v.) soon after the 366 rebellion of Prokopios (q.v.), which he may have supported.

AETIOS. *See* **IRENE.**

AETIOS OF AMIDA. *See* **MEDICINE.**

AETIUS. Most powerful general in West *(magister militum)* from 433 until his death in 454. His greatest opponent was Attila (q.v.) and his greatest victory was the defeat of a Hunnic army under Attila in 451 at the battle of the Catalaunian Fields (q.v.). As a young man he spent years as a hostage to the Huns (q.v.), forming a friendship with King Rugila, Attila's uncle and predecessor. His most reliable troops in the defense of Gaul against the Germans were Huns, and, moreover, Aetius himself married a German bride. Valentinian III (q.v.) assassinated him in 454, despite his loyal service. Such were the ironies of Aetius's career, ironies that reveal the complexity of Germano-Roman relations in the fifth-century West.

AFRICA. The term referred to only the western half of the northern coast (not the entirety) of the continent. The eastern half of that coast was referred to as Egypt. The desert wastes of the Sahara were like an impenetrable sea, which is why the interior remained largely unknown. Africa was penetrated by Vandals under Gaiseric (qq.v.), who invaded Africa from Spain in 429. Justinian I (q.v) sent a successful naval expedition against them in 533, led by Belisarios (q.v.). The Vandal kingdom collapsed within a year, but a revolt by the native Moors (q.v.) went on until 548. During the reign of Maurice (q.v.) Byzantine possessions around Carthage were consolidated into the Exarchate of Carthage (qq.v.). In the early seventh century, the Persians occupied Egypt from 618 until 629, when Herakleios (q.v.) vanquished Persia. After their capture of Egypt in 640–642, the Arabs (q.v.) began a westward march that ended at the shores of the Atlantic Ocean at the beginning of the eighth century. The Arab conquest extinguished the Exarchate of Carthage, the last vestige of Byzantium (q.v.) in Africa.

AFSHIN. *See* **DAZIMON.**

AGAPETOS. Deacon, most likely of Hagia Sophia (q.v.), and author of a work entitled *Ekthesis* (Exposition), a manual of advice to Justinian I (q.v.) on how to govern. The emperor is presented as God's earthly viceroy, whose piety and good works express God's will. The impact of this work on subsequent Byzantine political thought was enormous. Even after the fall of Byzantium, the importance of the work can be seen in the political ideology of Muscovy, and of the 17th-century French monarchy. Louis XIII (1601–1643) had the *Ekthesis* translated into French. During the reign of his son, Louis XIV (1643–1715), the *Ekthesis* influenced court ceremonial and political propaganda, making Louis, "Le Roi Soleil" (the Sun King), a living embodiment of Deacon Agapetos's ideas.

AGAPETUS I. Pope (q.v.) from 535–536 when Justinian I (q.v.) began his campaign to reconquer Italy from the Ostrogoths (qq.v.). Justinian's need of papal support allowed Agapetus a certain latitude in religious matters. When Agapetus arrived in Constantinople in 536, complaining about the conciliatory policy toward the adherents to Monophysitism (q.v.) by Anthemos I, patriarch of Constantinople (qq.v), the emperor allowed Agapetus to depose Anthemos. However, once Rome (q.v.) was reconquered Justinian treated Agapetus's successor Pope Vigilius (q.v.) in a cavalier manner, which some modern commentators have viewed as an example of the emperor's "caesaropapism" (q.v.).

AGATHIAS. Lawyer, poet, historian. In his own day he was known mainly as a successful Constantinopolitan lawyer and poet. Today he is best known for his history entitled *On the Reign of Justinian,* which continues the work of Prokopios of Caesarea (q.v.) in its coverage of the years from 552–559.

AGHLABIDS. Arab emirate in North Africa (q.v.) that conquered Sicily from Byzantium (qq.v.). The Aghlabids gained their independence ca. 800 from the Abbasids (q.v.), during the reign of Harun al-Rashid (q.v.). Centered in Tunis, the emirate's powerful fleet was well positioned to menace Byzantine Sicily (q.v.), beginning in 826. They achieved effective control over the island with the conquest of Taormina (q.v.) in 902. They captured Malta (q.v.) in 870, and they repeatedly attacked Sardinia (q.v.) as well as cities along the coast of Italy (q.v.), threatening Rome (q.v.) in 846. Their capture of Bari (q.v.) in 841 allowed them to dominate Apulia (q.v.) for the next three decades until German emperor Louis II (q.v.) reconquered it in 871.

AGNES OF FRANCE. Daughter of Louis VII (q.v.) of France who in 1180 married Alexios II, the son and heir of Manuel I (qq.v.), taking the name of Anna. As a part of Manual's diplomacy with the West, the marriage helped to mend relations with France, strained since Louis's earlier alliance with Roger II of Sicily (qq.v.). However, the marriage had grievous personal consequences for Anna. In 1183 she was forced to marry her husband's murderer, the new emperor Andronikos I (q.v.), then aged about 65. She was 13. After the death of Andronikos I in 1185, she lived her remaining years in Constantinople (q.v.), refusing overtures from the leadership of the Fourth Crusade (q.v.) after their conquest of the city.

AGRICULTURE. The Byzantine economy was primarily an agricultural economy comprised of small landowners, as well as large estates owned by monasteries and members of the aristocracy (q.v.). Grain (wheat, barley, rye) production predominated, along with such traditional agricultural products as olives, wine, flax, and a variety of fruits and vegetables. The state took an interest in maintaining the grain supply to major cities like Constantinople (q.v.), as well as in settling barbarian peoples on vacant lands, and maintaining the *stratiotika ktemata* (q.v.). Foreign invasions (e.g., of the Seljuks [q.v.] in 12th-century Asia Minor [q.v.]) were particularly disruptive, often resulting in burned crops and the dislocation of villages.

AIX-LA-CHAPELLE (AACHEN). *See* **CHARLEMAGNE.**

AKAKIA (Greek for "without guile" or "goodness"). Name given to a small bag of purple silk carried by the emperor in his right hand on ceremonial occasions. The dust inside was meant to encourage humility by reminding the emperor of his own mortality.

AKAKIAN SCHISM. The first schism (484–519) between the churches of Rome and Constantinople (qq.v.). Akakios (q.v.), for whom the schism was named, was patriarch (q.v.) of Constantinople. He supported Zeno's *Henotikon* (qq.v.), the "Edict of Unity," which unfortunately pacified neither the adherents to Monophysitism (q.v.) nor those who supported the 451 doctrinal statement of the Council of Chalcedon (q.v.). The schism illustrates how intertwined were religion and politics in the late fifth century, and how opposed were the claims of eastern emperors and popes (qq.v.) with regard to religious dogma. The divide between Chalcedonians and Monophysites was seen especially in the strife-ridden bishopric of Alexandria (q.v.). This religious problem became the chief internal issue of Zeno's reign.

AKAKIOS. Patriarch of Constantinople (qq.v.) from 472–489, whose name is attached to the first schism between the churches of Rome and Constantinople (qq.v). His opposition to the emperor Basiliskos's (q.v.) support of Monophysitism (q.v.) was resolved when Daniel the Stylite (q.v.) came down from his pillar and forced Basiliskos to reconcile with Akakios. However, Akakios's own attempt to pacify the Monophysites of Alexandria (q.v.) provoked the wrath of Pope (q.v.) Felix III, as did the further attempt at compromise, the *Henotikon* (q.v.). Felix III's excommunication of Akakios resulted in the Akakian Schism (q.v.), which lasted from 484–519.

AKATHISTOS HYMN. *See* **MUSIC; ROMANOS THE MELODE.**

AKINDYNOS, GREGORY. Monk and theologian who succeeded Barlaam of Calabria (qq.v.) in 1341 as leader of the opposition to Hesychasm (q.v.) and to its chief proponent Gregory Palamas (q.v.). His correspondence is important for understanding the opposition to Hesychasm. He was condemned in 1347, the same year John VI Kantakouzenos (q.v.), who supported the Hesychasts, came to power. Akindynos died in exile the following year.

AKOIMETOI. The "sleepless ones," referring to the so-called sleepless monks of the monastery of the *Akoimetoi* in Constantinople (q.v.), said to have been founded by Alexander the Akoimetos in 405. *Akoimetoi* monks observed absolute poverty, but they did no manual labor. Instead, they devoted themselves to perpetual prayer, praying ceaselessly in eight-hour shifts. Alexander was an unpopular and controversial figure in the capital who was condemned for

Messalianism (q.v.). One of his immediate successors as archimandrite (q.v.), Markellos the *Akoimetos,* was equally embroiled in controversy. In addition to being accused of Messalianism and Nestorianism (qq.v.), he led a public protest in the Hippodrome (q.v.) ca. 470 against the elevation of Aspar's (q.v.) son, an Arian (q.v.), to the rank of *caesar* (q.v.). The monastery of the *Akoimetoi* appears to have ceased functioning in the 13th century, during the period of the Latin Empire (q.v.).

AKOLOUTHOS. *See* **VARANGIAN GUARD.**

AKRITAI. Civilians and soldiers who defended the extremities (the core meaning of the Greek term) of Byzantium's eastern frontier. In the Byzantine epic poem *Digenes Akrites* (q.v.), the term refers more specifically to those who lived near the Euphrates (q.v.). Later, during the period of the Empire of Nicaea (q.v.), the *akritai* guarded the mountain passes in northwestern Asia Minor against the Seljuks (qq.v.).

AKROINON, BATTLE OF. Located near Amorion in Phrygia (qq.v.), Akroinon was where Leo III (q.v.) defeated an Arab army in 740, forcing the Arabs (q.v.) to withdraw from western Asia Minor (q.v.). This ended a phase of Arab-Byzantine warfare that began with the siege of Constantinople (q.v.) in 717–718, and which had threatened the very existence of Byzantium (q.v.).

AKROPOLITES, GEORGE. High official under Theodore II Laskaris and Michael VIII Palaiologos (qq.v.), teacher and writer. He conducted the negotiations at the Council of Lyons (q.v.) in 1274 that resulted in the union of the churches (q.v.). A pupil of Nikephoros Blemmydes (q.v.), he taught philosophy, particularly Aristotle (qq.v.), science and literature at a school of higher education (q.v.) founded by Michael VIII (qq.v.) in Constantinople. He was also tutor to the heir to the throne, Theodore II Laskaris (q.v.). His history (q.v.), a major source for the period 1203–1261, opens with a description of the attack of the Fourth Crusade (q.v.) on Constantinople. Thereafter, it concentrates on the fortunes of the Empire of Nicaea (q.v.), which he served as *logothetes tou dromou* and *megas logothetes* (qq.v.).

ALAMANIKON. *See* **ALEXIOS III ANGELOS; HENRY VI.**

ALAMUNDARUS (AL-MUNDHIR III). Arab ruler of the Lakhmids (q.v.) from ca. 505–554. He threatened Byzantium (q.v.), beginning in the reign of Anastasios I (q.v.), repeatedly raiding Byzantine territory in support of Persian king Kavad (qq.v.). Justin I (q.v.) was forced to seek peace with him in 524. However, his raids resumed in the reign of Justinian I (q.v.), despite opposition from Byzantium's client-state, the Ghassanids (q.v.).

ALAMUNDARUS (AL-MUNDHIR). Ruler of the Ghassanids (q.v.) from 569–582. His Arab (q.v.) troops fought as allies (*foederati* [q.v.]) of Byzantium against Persia (qq.v.), and against the Arab allies of the Persians, the Lakhmids (q.v.). In 580 al-Mundhir (the Byzantines called him Alamundarus) conquered the Lakhmid capital of Hira, for which he was honored by Tiberios I in a state visit to Constantinople (qq.v.). His adherence to Monophysitism (q.v.) aroused the suspicion of Maurice (q.v.), who had him exiled.

ALANS. A barbarian people who fled westward when the Huns swept across southern Russia (qq.v.) in the late fourth century. In 406 they crossed the Rhine (q.v.), and devastated cities in Gaul (q.v.) before crossing into Spain (q.v.) in 409. In Spain their king was slain and they were conquered by the Visigoths (q.v.). They served in various Byzantine, German and Hunnic armies, including those of Attila (q.v.). The most famous Byzantine general of Alan descent, Aspar (q.v.), had enormous influence in the eastern court in the mid-fifth century. In the early eighth century, Justinian II (q.v.) sent an embassy to the Alans of the northern Caucasus. In the 10th century Alania, as Byzantine sources refer to it, was the object of Byzantine diplomacy and church missions. Constantine IX (q.v.) fell in love with a young hostage from Alania, described (in the *Chronographia,* Book Six) by Michael Psellos (q.v.) as being the daughter of the Alanian king. However, Maria of Alania (q.v.), who figures so prominently in Anna Komnene's (q.v.) *Alexiad,* was actually Georgian. Anna Komnene also refers to Alan mercenaries as great fighters (*Alexiad,* Book 12). However, in the early 14th century they proved unsuccessful in fighting against the Turks and against the Catalan Grand Company (qq.v.), which annihilated them in 1306.

ALARIC. Chieftain of the Visigoths (q.v.) from 395–410. He revolted against imperial rule in 395 and led a marauding expedition through Thrace (q.v.), briefly threatening Constantinople (q.v.) itself before invading Thessaly and the Peloponnesos (qq.v.) in 396–397. He invaded Italy (q.v.) in 401, was repulsed by Stilicho (q.v.) in 402, then returned to besiege Rome (q.v.) in 408, retreating only when the senate negotiated his withdrawal. However, after Stilicho was executed by Honorios, Alaric invaded Italy for a third time, besieging Rome, which his forces pillaged in 410. The fall of Rome shocked the civilized world, prompting Augustine (q.v.) to write his *City of God*. Alaric marched to southern Italy, where his plans to sail to Africa (q.v.) were thwarted by a storm that destroyed his fleet. His death (410) concluded a series of disastrous consequences that resulted from the imperial decision to allow the Visigoths to cross the Danube (q.v.) in 376.

ALBANIANS. Probably the descendents of the ancient Illyrians who settled along the Adriatic coast from Epiros to Pannonia (qq.v.). They may have become pastoralists when the Slavs (q.v.) invaded the Balkan Peninsula (q.v.) in the late sixth century. First mentioned in Byzantine sources in the late 11th century, they were subjugated thereafter by the despotate of Epiros, the Second Bulgarian Empire, the Empire of Nicaea, and by Charles of Anjou (qq.v.). In the 14th century they migrated southward in great numbers into Thessaly, subsequently settling in the Peloponnesos (qq.v.) as well. After the death of Skanderbeg (q.v.) in 1468, they were subjugated by the Ottomans (q.v.).

ALBERT OF AACHEN. Author of the *Jerusalem History (Historia Hierosolymitana),* written ca. 1130; it is one of the three chief accounts (the other two are those of Fulcher of Chartres and Raymond of Aguilers [qq.v]) of the First Crusade (q.v.) and its aftermath. Although Albert seems to have collected information from returning soldiers and pilgrims (he never visited the East), his account is by far the longest, most detailed, most colorful, and perhaps most impartial of the major historical sources for this Crusade. His work was used extensively by William of Tyre (q.v.).

ALBIGENSIANS. *See* **BOGOMILS; PAULICIANS.**

ALBOIN. *See* **LOMBARDS.**

ALCHEMY. *See* **SCIENCE.**

ALEMANNI. Germanic people who first attacked the upper Rhine and lower Danube (qq.v.) in the third century A.D. Julian defeated them at Strasbourg in 357. After being defeated by Clovis (ca. 495) many settled in Raetia (q.v.). In 507 Theodoric (q.v.) settled others in Pannonia (q.v.). In 553 they invaded Italy (q.v.) with a host of allied Franks (q.v.). Narses (q.v.) annihilated them near Capua (q.v.).

ALEPPO. *See* **BERROIA.**

ALEXANDER. Bishop of Alexandria (313–328) (qq.v.), who attempted to suppress the Melitian and Arian schisms (qq.v.). At the Council of Nicaea (q.v.) in 325 Alexander was aided in his opposition to Arianism by the young priest Athanasios (q.v.), who succeeded him as bishop of the city.

ALEXANDER OF TRALLES. Sixth-century physician and brother of the famous co-architect of Hagia Sophia (q.v.), Anthemios of Tralles (q.v.). His 12-volume encyclopedia of medicine (q.v.) depends on Galen (q.v.), like the work of his contemporary Aetios of Amida (q.v.). However, his knowledge of pharmacology is much more practical, even original, including remedies from the Far East that the author may have gotten from Kosmas Indikopleustes (q.v.).

ALEXANDER THE AKOIMETOS. *See* **AKOIMETOI.**

ALEXANDRIA. Chief city of Byzantine Egypt (q.v.). As a cultural center, it had no peer in the East, rivaling Constantinople (q.v.) in every respect. Its university was renowned, and the famous Alexandrine library (destroyed by fire in 476) was the greatest library of the Late Roman world. Its theological school, which emphasized the divinity of Christ, supported the heresies of Monophysitism and Montheletism (qq.v.). The church of Alexandria (q.v.) produced strong bishops, such as Cyril and Athanasios (qq.v.), who often came into conflict with Jews and pagans in the city, as demonstrated by the death of Hypatia (q.v.). The Persians (q.v.) conquered Alexandria briefly in 618 and then again in 629. In 642 it was permanently lost to Byzantium when the Arabs (q.v.) captured it.

ALEXIOS I KOMNENOS. Emperor (q.v.) from 1081–1118. He is often viewed as one of Byzantium's great emperors, in part because of the memorable impression of his reign in the *Alexiad,* written by his daughter Anna Komnene (q.v.). He found the empire beset by foreign enemies, which he successively defeated, or at least neutralized. The greatest threat by far was from the Normans (q.v.). For the first four years of his reign he fought the Normans under Robert Guiscard and Bohemund (qq.v.), whose attack on Dyrrachion (q.v.) was intended as a prelude to an attack on Constantinople (q.v.). From 1085–1091 he concentrated on defending the northern frontier from incursions by the Pechenegs (q.v.), who Alexios annihilated at the battle of Mount Lebounion in 1091. After 1091 he turned his attention to the Seljuks of Asia Minor (qq.v.), sending appeals for mercenaries to the West. The response was the First Crusade (q.v.), which sent thousands of unruly Crusaders to Constantinople, among whom was a Norman contingent led by Alexios's former enemy Bohemund. Alexios's handling of the First Crusade was masterful, as seen in his acquisition of Nicaea (q.v.) in 1097. His internal policy consisted of reforms of both court titles and coinage, which included the gold *hyperpyron* (q.v.). He defended Orthodoxy (q.v.) by persecuting the Bogomils and John Italos (qq.v.) and supporting monastic establishments on Mount Athos and Patmos (qq.v.). However, Alexios's brilliance staved off decline in the short term. Moreover, his granting of unrestricted trading privileges to Venice (q.v.) in 1082, in return for Venetian help against the Normans, undermined future long-term recovery.

ALEXIOS I KOMNENOS. *See* **TREBIZOND, EMPIRE OF.**

ALEXIOS II KOMNENOS. Emperor (q.v.) from 1180–1183, but, in reality, little more than a tragic footnote to the growing hostility between East and West during the early Crusades (q.v.). Son of Manuel I and Maria of Antioch (qq.v.), he was too young to rule in his own right after his father died. Maria of Antioch, a westerner, became empress-regent, while real power lay in the hands of Maria's favorite, Alexios Komnenos (the late emperor's nephew). Alexios II became a mere figurehead. The regency's favoritism toward westerners, especially the Italian merchants, engendered popular hatred, also a successful revolt led by Andronikos I Komnenos (q.v.) in 1182, followed by a massacre of Latins in Constantinople (q.v.). After Andronikos Komnenos forced Alexios to condemn his mother to death, he had Alexios strangled in secret. His corpse was consigned to the sea.

ALEXIOS III ANGELOS. Emperor (q.v.) from 1195–1203 who came to the throne by blinding and imprisoning his brother Isaac Angelos II (q.v.). Weak and ineffectual at a time when the empire was disintegrating, Alexios was threatened by Serbia, Bulgaria (qq.v.), and by the German emperor Henry VI (q.v.), whose brother Philip of Swabia (q.v.) was married to Irene, daughter of the deposed and blinded Isaac II. In 1197 Alexios was reduced to stripping imperial tombs of their ornaments to pay the so-called German tax *(Alamanikon* [q.v.]), a tribute demanded by Henry VI. In 1203, when the Fourth Crusade (q.v.) arrived at Constantinople to restore Isaac II, Alexios III fled the city. His wandering ended only in 1211 when he was captured by Theodore I Laskaris (q.v.) and forced to retire to a monastery.

ALEXIOS III KOMNENOS. *See* **PANARETOS, MICHAEL.**

ALEXIOS IV ANGELOS. Emperor (q.v.) from 1203–1204, who conspired with the Fourth Crusade (q.v.). He was the son of deposed emperor Isaac Angelos II (q.v.). Alexios escaped to the West, where the leadership of the Fourth Crusade took him to Constantinople (q.v.) to reinstate his father. However, once on the throne Alexios IV could neither fulfill the vows of money and material aid to the Crusaders that he had agreed to nor gain the promised formal submission of the Byzantine church to the pope (q.v.). His cooperation with the Fourth Crusade made him unpopular in Constantinople, so much so that his overthrow and execution by Alexios V Doukas (q.v.) were welcomed by the citizenry of the capital.

ALEXIOS V DOUKAS ("MOURTZOUPHLOS"). Emperor (q.v.) who briefly in 1204 opposed the Fourth Crusade's siege of Constantinople (qq.v.). He had been a *protovestarios* under Alexios IV (qq.v.); his nickname *Mourtzouphlos* (Bushy-Browed) referred to his prominent shaggy eyebrows. He overthrew Alexios IV Angelos (q.v.) in a popular revolt while the Fourth Crusade threatened the city from its encampment outside the walls of Constantinople. For a few months Alexios V provided an energetic defense of the capital, but when the Crusaders gained entrance to the city by assault on April 12, Alexios fled, only to be captured, blinded, and executed some months later.

ALFONSO V. King of Aragon and Sicily (q.v.) who succeeded to the throne of Naples (q.v.) in 1435, an event that reconstituted both the old kingdom of the Two Sicilies, and Charles of Anjou's (q.v.) dream of leading a Crusade eastward to reestablish the Latin Empire of Constantinople (qq.v.). However, Alfonso died in 1458, five years after the Ottomans (q.v.) captured Constantinople, his plan never having been realized.

ALLECTUS. *See* **BRITAIN; CONSTANTIUS CHLORUS.**

ALLELENGYON. The *allelengyon* ("mutual pledge") was the collective tax obligation introduced by Basil II (q.v.) in 1002 that required wealthy landowners to pay the tax arrears of their poorer neighbors. The law was unpopular with the powerful landed magnates (the *dynatoi* [q.v.]), including the monasteries. Romanos III (q.v.) yielded to pressure from the church and abolished the tax in 1028.

ALOUSIANOS. Son of Bulgarian Tsar (q.v.) John Vladislav, co-ruler with Peter Deljan (q.v.) in the abortive Bulgarian revolt of 1040–1041. After besieging Thessalonike (q.v.) unsuccessfully, the ringleaders fell out with one another. With the revolt sputtering, and Michael IV (q.v.) marching out against them, Alousianos decided to betray Peter Deljan to the emperor. For this Alousianos was rewarded with the title of *magistros* (q.v.).

ALP ARSLAN. Seljuk sultan (qq.v.) from 1063–1073 who defeated Emperor Romanos IV (q.v.) at Mantzikert (q.v.) in 1071, one of the decisive battles in Byzantine history, a battle that opened up Asia Minor (q.v.) to Seljuk conquest.

ALTAR OF VICTORY. *See* **GRATIAN; SYMMACHUS.**

AMADEO VI. Count of Savoy (1343–1383) and cousin of John V Palaiologos (q.v.) who seized Gallipoli from the Ottomans (qq.v.). He was planning to join Pope (q.v.) Urban V's Crusade against Egypt (q.v.) in 1365, but sailed instead the following year to aid John V by forcing the Ottomans to withdraw from Gallipoli. When he learned that John V was being refused passage through Bulgaria, he attacked Varna, then seized Sozopolis and Mesembria (qq.v.), forcing the Bulgarians to relent. Amadeo tried to convince his cousin that conversion to the Roman faith would result in further military assistance from the West. When John V refused, Amadeo threatened to restore Gallipoli to the Turks. Nevertheless, in 1369 John V journeyed to Rome (q.v.) where he professed his personal allegiance to the pope. However, the hope of significant military help from the West proved as much an illusion as the pope's hope that the entire Byzantine church would follow John V's example.

AMALASUNTHA. Daughter of Theodoric, the Ostrogothic king of Italy (qq.v.). She was regent for her son Athalaric (526–534), then

queen and joint ruler with her husband Theodahad, who murdered
her in 535. Justinian I (q.v.), who was on good terms with her, used
her death as a pretext to invade Italy (q.v.). Her daughter Matasuntha
married Justinian I's general Germanos (q.v.).

AMALFI. Seaport on the southwest coast of Italy between Naples and
Salerno (qq.v.). Like Gaeta (q.v.), Amalfi belonged nominally to the
Byzantine duchy of Naples, but it constituted an independent merchant republic after 839 with close political, economic, and artistic
ties to Byzantium (q.v.), as the great Byzantine bronze doors of the
cathedral of Amalfi illustrate. However, the occupation of Amalfi in
1073 by the Normans (q.v.), as well as the increasing dependence of
Byzantium on Venice (q.v.), rapidly diminished those ties.

AMALRIC I. King of Jerusalem (q.v.) from 1163–1174 whose foreign
policy was dominated by the Crusader assault on Egypt (q.v.). To
this end, his alliance with Manuel I (q.v.) was essential. Despite the
assistance of a Byzantine fleet in 1169 he attacked Damietta (q.v.)
unsuccessfully. He visited Constantinople (q.v.) in 1171 and was
planning another attack on Egypt, with Byzantine aid, when he died
in 1174.

AMASEIA. Capital of the theme of Armeniakon (qq.v.), located on the
Lykos River in Pontos (q.v.). The strength of the city lay in its natu-
rally fortified citadel, which, except for a brief occupation in the
early eighth century by the Arabs (q.v.) under caliph Walid I (q.v.),
resisted foreign enemies until the Danishmendids (q.v.) occupied it
in 1071 after the battle of Mantzikert (q.v.). The Arabs renamed it
Amasya, the name it still bears.

AMASTRIS. City on the south coast of the Black Sea (q.v.) that was an
important port in the theme of Paphlagonia (qq.v.) from the early
ninth century. The local saint, George of Amastris (q.v.), was appointed bishop by the patriarch Tarasios around 790. The saint's *vita*
(q.v.) describes an undated attack by Rus (q.v.) on the city.
Theophilos (q.v.) assigned the troops of Theophobos (q.v.) to quarters in Amastris, where they remained until they revolted in 837.
Theodore I Lascaris (q.v.) seized it in 1214, but by the early 14th
century it was under the control of the Genoese.

AMBO. *See* **BEMA.**

AMBROSE. Bishop of Milan (qq.v.) from 374–397, whose multiple roles as chief opponent of Arianism (q.v.), advisor to western emperors, eloquent preacher, arranger of hymns and psalms, developer of the cult of relics, and erudite author, only hint at the enormous influence he exerted over church and state in the West, and at the originality of his life and career. Born into the highest social class, he was a respected provincial governor when the entire city acclaimed him bishop. He went from unbaptized Christian to bishop in eight days. More than any previous bishop, he played an important role in the politics of his day, as illustrated by his excommunication of Theodosios I (q.v.) after that emperor massacred thousands of civilians in Thessalonike (q.v.) in reprisal for the murder of some German troops garrisoned there. Theodosios was forced to yield to the penance Ambrose imposed on him, and, thus, yield to Ambrose's insistence that the church is independent from the state, and even superior to it in questions of faith and morals. He exerted a great influence on Augustine (q.v.), who writes (in the *Confessions,* Book Five, Chapter 13) of Ambrose's kindness, generosity, erudition, and eloquence.

AMBULATORY. A corridor around the core space of a building. In a church an ambulatory allows worshippers to move unimpeded around the central space of the church. An ambulatory-church plan consists of a domed central bay with ambulatories attached to the north, west, and south sides.

AMBULATORY CHURCH. *See* **AMBULATORY.**

AMIDA. Fortress in Mesopotamia (q.v.) along the Byzantine frontier with Persia (q.v.) that frequently changed hands. The Sassanians (q.v.) conquered it in 359; Ammianus Marcellinus's (q.v.) eye-witness account of the siege of 359 is a remarkable account. Julian (q.v.) reconquered it in 363. Kavad (qq.v.) captured it again in 502, but Byzantium recaptured it again two years later. Persia conquered it for the last time in 602. Herakleios (q.v.) recovered it in 628, and in 640 the Arabs (q.v.) seized it.

AMMIANUS MARCELLINUS. The greatest Latin historian of the fifth century, and the last great historian of Rome. His continuation of Tacitus, a history of the Roman Empire from 96–378 entitled *Res Gestae* (Deeds), survives only for 353–378, years for which Ammianus was a contemporary. A Syrian Greek born into a noble family of Antioch (q.v.), he served as a staff officer in Gaul (q.v) and in the East. He accompanied the emperor Julian (q.v.) on his Persian campaign in 363. His account of this campaign, and of the earlier Persian siege of Amida (q.v.) in 359, which he barely escaped from, reads like the first-hand account of a modern war correspondent. Equally impressive are his character portraits of Constantius II, Gallus (qq.v.), and especially Julian.

AMMONIOS. *See* **PHILOSOPHY.**

AMORION. Strategic city in Phrygia (q.v.). Because of its location on the main road from the Cilician Gates to the Asiatic suburbs of Constantinople (q.v.), it was the object of many Arab attacks in the seventh and eighth centuries. It was also the paternal home of Emperor Michael II (q.v.), who founded the Amorion dynasty (820–867), and capital of the Anatolikon theme (q.v.). The Abbasid caliph Mutasim (q.v.) conquered the city in 838, carrying away the entire population, an event that made a deep impression on contemporaries; recent archeological excavations have demonstrated how destructive the attack was. The story of the 42 Martyrs of Amorion (q.v.) became famous in hagiography (q.v.) and art.

AMORION DYNASTY. *See* **AMORION.**

AMPHIPOLIS. *See* **STRYMON.**

ANASTASIOS. Patriarch of Constantinople (qq.v.) who in 730 was chosen by Emperor Leo III (q.v.) to replace Patriarch Germanos (q.v.) after the latter refused to support Iconoclasm (q.v.). During the reign of Leo III's successor and fellow-Iconoclast Constantine V (q.v.), Anastasios switched sides again, this time to the usurper Artabasdos (q.v.), who briefly restored the veneration of holy icons (q.v.). After Constantine V regained power in 743 he humiliated Anastasios by having him whipped and led around naked astride a donkey. Forced to return to his support of Iconoclasm, Anastasios was allowed to remain as patriarch until he died in 754.

ANASTASIOS I. Emperor (q.v.) from 491–518 whose reign is often seen as a prelude to the age of Justinian I (q.v.). Despite his relative obscurity as a court attendant *(silentarios),* the empress Ariadne (q.v.) chose him to succeed her husband Zeno (q.v.). The choice proved to be a good one for the internal administration of the empire. His new large *follis,* along with smaller coins of lesser value, corrected the previous poor quality of copper coins in circulation. He also reformed the way taxes were collected, and he abolished the hated *chrysargyron* (q.v.), which unduly burdened urban populations. At the same time he replaced local officials with state-appointed tax collectors. These and other financial reforms enhanced state revenues, so much so that upon Anastasios's death the treasury held a surplus of 320,000 pounds of gold. Less successful was his religious policy. The *Henotikon* (q.v.) resulted in the Akakian Schism (q.v.) between Rome and Constantinople (qq.v.), which ended only in 519. His subsequent support of Monophysitism (q.v.) provoked periodic unrest in Constantinople and became a pretext for the revolt of Vitalian (q.v.). Besides a hostile relationship with the papacy (q.v.), he had hostile relations with the ruler of Italy, Theodoric (qq.v.). Bulgar (q.v.) attacks from the north prompted his famous, but ineffective, Long Wall in Thrace (qq.v.), and in East Persia (q.v.) he briefly captured the important frontier fortress of Amida (q.v.).

ANASTASIOS II. Emperor (q.v.) from 713–715, toward the end of a period of troubles that began in 695 and ended only in 717. He was brought to power by an army revolt that overthrew the emperor Philippikos, a supporter of Monotheletism (qq.v.). Anastasius II reversed that policy, and appointed a new patriarch, Germanos I (qq.v.). Anticipating an Arab attack on Constantinople (q.v.), he provisioned the capital, restored its walls, and launched a naval expedition to disrupt Muslim preparations. However, the naval expedition revolted on Rhodes, sailed back to the mainland, and raised up Theodosius III (q.v.) as a rival emperor. A six-month civil war ensued, which ended only when Anastasios voluntarily abdicated the throne and became a monk.

ANATOLIA. *See* **ASIA MINOR.**

ANATOLIKON. First in rank of the first four themes organized in Asia Minor (qq.v.) in the seventh century, it extended from the Aegean Sea east to Cappadocia (qq.v.), and south to Seleukia (q.v.). Its capital was Amorion (q.v.). It played a great role in defending Asia Minor against Arab (q.v) raids.

ANAZARBOS. *See* **RUBENIDS.**

ANCHIALOS. City in Thrace (q.v.) on the coast of the Black Sea (q.v.) fought over by Byzantine and Bulgarian armies. At Anchialos in 763, Constantine V (q.v.) handed Teletz, khan of the Bulgars (qq.v.), such a resounding defeat that Teletz was overthrown and Bulgaria (q.v.) weakened by internal revolts until the accession of khan Telerig (q.v.) ca. 770. In 917 at Achelous (near Anchialos) Tsar Symeon (qq.v.) destroyed a Byzantine army and reoccupied the city, which remained in Bulgarian hands until it was retaken by John V (q.v.) in 1364. In early 1453, before the fall of Constantinople (q.v.), Karadja Beg, general of Mehmed II (q.v.), captured the few remaining Byzantine cities on the Thracian coast of the Black Sea still in Byzantine possession, including Mesembria (q.v.) and Anchialos.

ANCHORITE. Greek for "withdrawal," "forsaking," referring to a monk who has withdrawn from the world to live the life of a hermit (*eremite* [q.v.]), in prayer, silence, and rigorous asceticism (q.v.). This kind of monasticism (q.v.) can also refer to a monk who has withdrawn to a separate dwelling (cell [q.v.]) under strict confinement within a *koinobion* (q.v.).

ANCONA. Italian port-city located on a promontory along the coast of the Adriatic Sea (q.v.). Like Croton (q.v.) it remained in Byzantine hands during the long wars with the Ostrogoths during the reign of Justinian I (qq.v.), resisting a determined siege by Totila (q.v.) in 551. In the ninth century it became semi-independent, recognizing the nominal authority of the papacy (q.v.). In 1155 Manuel I (q.v.) used Ancona as a base of operations against the Normans (q.v.). Merchants from Ancona carried on an active trade with Byzantium (q.v.). One such merchant, Cyriacus of Ancona, wrote an account of his travels throughout Byzantine lands from 1412 to 1454.

ANDREW OF CRETE. Saint and writer of hymns who lived from 660 to 740. He is usually credited with changing the entire form of church hymns from the *kontakion*, a kind of sermon in verse, to the *kanon*, a more creative and elaborate kind of hymn (q.v.) that was richly developed in subsequent centuries.

ANDRONIKOS I KOMNENOS. Emperor (q.v.) from 1183–1185, whose reign has remained controversial. He was a fascinating, complex, and unscrupulous personality, and a cousin and rival to Manuel I (q.v.), from whose suspicions he fled. He spent most of Manuel's reign seeking refuge in the courts of Muslim and Russian princes.

Finally pardoned, Andronikos became governor of Pontos, on the shores of the Black Sea (q.v.), in 1180, the same year Manuel died. The pro-Latin regency for Manuel's son Alexios II (q.v.), headed by Manuel's wife Maria of Antioch (q.v.), proved unpopular and Andronikos saw his chance. Styling himself the protector of the young Alexios II, he marched on Constantinople (q.v.) in 1182, which provoked a vicious massacre of Latins there. Andronikos forced young Alexios II to sign his mother's death warrant, and he was crowned co-emperor with the boy in September 1183. Two months later he had Alexios II strangled and married his widow, Agnes-Anna of France, who was just 13 (Andronikos was then about 65). His ruthlessness now turned against corrupt tax collectors in the provinces, and against those who plundered wrecked ships. This gained him popular acclaim, but a vendetta against the landed aristocracy and the provincial towns, which supported his immediate predecessors, created turmoil. Soon his popularity faded. His dependence on Venetian (q.v.) naval power, was one reason. Cyprus (q.v.) was lost to Isaac Komnenos (q.v.), Hungarians and Serbs (qq.v.) invaded Byzantine territory, and the Normans (q.v.) captured Dyrrachion and Thessalonike (qq.v.). When the Normans began to advance on Constantinople (q.v.) a popular revolution overthrew Andronikos. He was tortured to death by a mob in the streets of the capital.

ANDRONIKOS II PALAIOLOGOS. Emperor (q.v.) from 1282–1328, during whose long reign Byzantium's (q.v.) final decline began. Andronikos's first problem was to heal the wounds opened by his father Michael VIII's union of the churches (qq.v.). Despite his renunciation of the Council of Lyons (q.v), which had effected that union, despite his removal of Patriarch John XI Bekkos (q.v.) and the reinstatement of Patriarch Joseph I (q.v.), despite even the release from prison of those who had opposed union, the Arsenite (q.v.) extremists were not satisfied. Failure to heal the wounds within the church was mirrored by other failures at home and abroad. The coinage, the *hyperpyron,* continued to be devalued, and the monies saved by reducing the size of the navy were not enough to alleviate the general economic distress. Instead, the empire was forced to rely on the Genoese. As a result, he was drawn into a war between Venice (q.v.) and Genoa that lasted from 1296–1302. The rest of his foreign policy consisted of concentrating on protecting Byzantine territory in Asia Minor (q.v.) while using diplomacy to ward off Serbia and Bulgaria (qq.v). The advancing Serbs (q.v.) were bought off by the marriage of Andronikos's five-year-old daughter Simonis to Stefan Urosh II Milutin (q.v.), in addition to Byzantine acceptance of Serbian seizure of Skopje in Macedonia (qq.v.). However, the Ottoman advance in Asia Minor (q.v.) was relentless after the Byzantine defeat at Bapheus (1302), culminating in the capture of Prousa (q.v.) in 1326. Andronikos hired the Catalan Grand Company (q.v.), who won some successes against the Ottomans in 1304. That same year they joined forces with some Alan (q.v.) mercenaries, but they soon fell out with them; the Alans decided to pillage Thrace (q.v.) instead. When Catalan commander Roger de Flor (q.v.) was assassinated in 1305, the Catalans themselves went on a rampage in Greece (q.v.) that ceased only in 1311 when they established the duchy of Athens and Thebes (qq.v.). Thereafter, until 1321, there was a lull in military activities, giving the empire a breather. However, from 1321–1328, the final years of Andronikos II's reign, a tragic civil war occurred with his grandson, who finally overthrew him to become Andronikos III (q.v.). Perhaps Andronikos II is best remembered as a lover of the arts and of scholarship, a patron of men such as Theodore Metochites and Nikephoros Gregoras (qq.v.).

ANDRONIKOS III PALAIOLOGOS. Emperor (q.v.) from 1328–1341. The real power behind the throne was John Kantakouzenos (q.v.), who had helped dethrone Andronikos II (q.v.). Andronikos III proved to be a good general, winning victories against lesser foes in Thessaly and Epiros (qq.v.), and in the Aegean (q.v.), where a small Byzantine fleet (which he rebuilt) ejected the Genoese from Chios (q.v.). However, the Serbian advance in Macedonia (q.v.) was checked only when the Bulgars defeated the Serbs (qq.v.) at the battle of Velbuzd (q.v.) in 1330. Despite Andronikos's alliance with Venice (q.v.) and some of the small Latin states, the Ottoman (q.v.) advance was relentless. Under Sultan Orhan, Nicaea (qq.v.) was captured in 1331 and Nikomedia (q.v.) in 1337. When Andronikos died, he left behind a nine-year-old son, John V (q.v.), tended by his second wife, Anna of Savoy (q.v.), both poorly equipped to deal with the dangers that faced them, including a civil war with John (VI) Kantakouzenos (q.v.) that would further cripple the empire.

ANDRONIKOS IV PALAIOLOGOS. Emperor (q.v.) from 1376–1379 who came to the throne by overthrowing his father John V with Ottoman (qq.v.) help. For this, Sultan Murad I (q.v.) was given Gallipolis (q.v.). However, although Andronikos had gained Constantinople (q.v.), he was still a pawn of the Ottomans, a fact made clear when John V escaped from prison and persuaded Murad I to support him. With the aid of Murad I and the Venetian fleet, John V regained the throne again in 1379.

ANEKDOTA. Literally *Unpublished Things,* which is how the work is titled in *Souda* (q.v.), where one finds the earliest reference to it. The popular conventional title in English is *Secret History.* This scurrilous diatribe against Justinian I, Theodora, Belisarios, and Antonina (qq.v.) was apparently written by the official historian of Justinian I's reign, Prokopios of Caesarea (q.v.). The premise of the work is that Justinian I and Theodora were demons in disguise who delighted in trying to destroy the empire. The contrast with Prokopios's other major works, the *Wars* and *The Buildings,* is so striking that some scholars have rejected it as coming from the pen of Prokopios. Nevertheless, an analysis of the style of the *Anekdota* has made it clear that Prokopios is indeed its author. He may have written the work to express in private the anger that he could not express in public. Despite the work's bias, there is much useful information in the *Anekdota.*

ANGELOS DYNASTY. Ruled Byzantium (q.v.) from 1185–1204. The family came from obscure origins, but they advanced when Constantine Angelos married the younger daughter of Alexios I Komnenos (q.v.). After that, their family's ascent was assured, culminating in three successive emperors, Isaac II, Alexios III, and Alexios IV (qq.v.). Hardly "angels," as their family name suggests, they might at least have been competent leaders. Especially serious were the numerous regional rebellions that went unchecked (e.g., the rebellion of Isaac Komnenos in Cyprus [qq.v.]). The Fourth Crusade (q.v.) can be viewed as the culmination of a process of political fragmentation to which the Angelos dynasty contributed.

ANGLO-SAXONS. *See* **VARANGIANS.**

ANI. City in northeast Asia Minor (q.v.) that in 961 became the capital of Armenia under the Bagratids (qq.v.), and, after 1045, capital of the theme of Iberia (qq.v.). Despite its fortifications, which included a great citadel, it was captured by the Seljuks under Alp Arslan (qq.v.) in 1064, its garrison having been depleted by Constantine X's (q.v.) economizing.

ANKYRA. One of the great cities in central Asia Minor (q.v.); capital of the theme of Opsikion (qq.v.). Strategically located on a main military road, it was threatened by Persian and Arab (qq.v.) attacks. The Persians captured it in 622, and it was seized briefly by caliph Mutasim (qq.v.) in 838. It fell to the Seljuks (q.v.) in the late 11th century.

ANNA, PRINCESS OF KIEV. Sister of Emperor Basil II who was married to Vladimir I of Kiev (qq.v.) in 988. She was a reward to Vladimir I for sending Varangians (q.v.) to aid Basil II in suppressing the revolts of Bardas Phokas and Bardas Skleros (qq.v.). However, Basil II stipulated that Vladimir convert, and, thus, Anna's marriage led to what is arguably the most significant single event in Russian history, the conversion of Vladimir I and of the Rus (q.v.).

ANNA COMNENA. *See* **KOMNENE, ANNA.**

ANNA OF SAVOY. Daughter of Count Amadeo V of Savoy, and wife of Emperor Andronikos III Palaiologos (qq.v.), she played a major role in the civil war of 1341–1347 that concluded with the triumph of John VI Kantakouzenos (q.v.). Anna fought to protect the interests of her young son, Emperor John V (q.v.), for whom she was regent. She had strong supporters in Patriarch (q.v.) John XIV Kalekas and in Alexios Apokaukos (q.v.), and gained the support of the Serbian ruler Stefan Urosh IV Dushan (qq.v.). She even submitted to the pope (q.v.) in order to solicit western help, and pawned the crown jewels to Venice to purchase mercenaries, but all for naught. The crown jewels were never redeemed. Apokaukos died; she deposed the patriarch and was forced to accept John VI Kantakouzenos (q.v.) as co-emperor with her son.

ANNONA. *See* **TAXATION.**

ANONYMOUS VALESIANUS. *See* **EXCERPTA VALESIANA.**

ANTAES. A nomadic tribe of obscure origins that was assimilated with the Slavs (q.v.) in the fifth and sixth centuries. Prokopios of Caesarea (q.v.) describes the Antaes as looking like Slavs and speaking the same language. They attacked across the Danube (q.v.) in the reign of Justin I (q.v.), but after Justinian I (q.v.) settled them as *foederati* (q.v.) they defended the Balkan Peninsula against the Bulgars (qq.v.). Justinian's immediate successors, including Maurice (q.v.), found them useful opponents to the Avars (q.v.).

ANTHEMIOS. *See* **RICIMER.**

ANTHEMIOS. *See* **ARKADIOS; THEODOSIOS I.**

ANTHEMIOS I. *See* **AGAPETUS I.**

ANTHEMIOS OF TRALLES. Co-architect, with Isidore of Miletus, of Justinian I's (qq.v.) great church of Hagia Sophia in Constantinople (qq.v.). Anthemios was also a theoretical and practical scientist who wrote treatises about unusual mechanical devices. He apparently built some of them, including curved reflectors he called burning-mirrors.

ANTHYPATOS. *See* **MAGISTROS.**

ANTIOCH ON THE ORONTES (Modern Antakya, in Turkey). Chief city of Byzantine Syria (q.v.) and one of the great cities of the eastern Mediterranean (q.v.) until its sack by the Persians (q.v.) in 540. It was a cultural, religious, and administrative center, seat of one of the great eastern patriarchs (q.v.), resplendent with magnificent public architecture and impressive fortifications. Ammianus Marcellinus and Libanios (qq.v.) came from Antioch. The theological school was renowned. It was also a military base from which military expeditions against the Persians (q.v.) originated. The emperor Julian (q.v.) spent much of his reign there, preparing for his Persian campaign while railing against its pleasure-seeking citizenry. The Arabs (q.v.) seized it in 637. The First Crusade (q.v.) conquered it in 1098, after which it became a bone of contention between its Latin rulers and Byzantium (qq.v.), beginning with Bohemund (q.v.). At various times its technical submission to Byzantium was gained, e.g., Raymond of Poitiers (q.v.) submitted the city to John II (q.v.) in 1137. The Mamluks (q.v.) sacked it in 1268.

ANTONINA. *See* **BELISARIOS; PROKOPIOS OF CAESAREA.**

ANTONY OF NOVGOROD. *See* **NOVGOROD.**

ANTONY THE GREAT. Saint and a founder of eremetical monasticism (qq.v.). He lived for over 90 years as a hermit, and died at the age of 105 in 356. According to his biography (*vita* [q.v.]), ascribed to Athanasios (q.v.), bishop of Alexandria (qq.v.), Antony provided Athanasios with help against the Arians (q.v.). Whether this is true or not, there can be no doubt about the broad influence of the biography. For example, it made a deep impact on Augustine (q.v.) and his group of friends when they chanced to read it (the *Confessions,* Book Seven, Chapter Six).

APAMEA. *See* **SYRIA.**

APHRODISIAS. Capital city of Caria in southwest Asia Minor (qq.v.). Famous in Roman times for its production of sculpture, the city's excavated remains include many impressive public structures from the fourth through sixth centuries. The city never recovered from an earthquake in the early seventh century.

APHTHARTODOCETISM. Greek for "to appear incorruptible," referring to the radical variation of Monophysitism (q.v.) promoted by Julian of Halikarnassos, who believed that Christ's human body underwent no change and had been free of all passions since the moment of conception. Julian's ally, Severos of Antioch (q.v.), eventually distanced himself from this doctrine by accepting that Christ possessed a corruptible body while on earth. However, after Julian's death in 527 Justinian I (q.v.) adopted his views as a way to please the Aphthartodocetists, who had become the largest sect of Monophysites in Egypt (q.v.). Opposition came from the patriarch of Constantinople, Eutychios (qq.v.), but Justinian deposed him in early 565. After Justinian I's death the sect declined.

APLEKTON. A military base. There were a series of them on the main road across Asia Minor to the Arab (qq.v.) frontier. They were often located in or near important cities where troops could be provisioned, or where they could gather from neighboring themes (q.v.).

APOKAUKOS, ALEXIOS. *Mega doux* of the navy (qq.v.) under Andronikos III (q.v.); chief supporter of Anna of Savoy (q.v.) in the civil war of 1341–1347 with John VI Kantakouzenos (q.v.). Although he repaired the walls of the capital and commanded the fleet, he incurred hostility by his harsh persecution of John VI's supporters. Only after his murder (while he was inspecting a new dungeon he had ordered constructed) in 1345 by some political prisoners did resistance to John VI begin to unravel.

APOKAUKOS, JOHN. Bishop of Naupaktos in central Greece (qq.v.), noted for his correspondence, which illuminates the legal and social history of the late 12th and early 13th centuries. Learned and cosmopolitan, he was also a strong supporter of the Despotate of Epiros (q.v.), as were Demetrios Chomatenos and George Bardanes, the metropolitan of Kerkyra (qq.v.).

APOPHTHEGMATA PATRUM *(Sayings of the Fathers).* Title given to collections of sayings of the early *eremites* of Egypt (qq.v.). The sayings are a rich source for early asceticism (q.v.), and for the social and cultural history of the fourth century. Their more immediate impact in the fifth and sixth centuries was as inspirational reading that propagated the ideals of early monasticism (q.v.), e.g., in *The Heavenly Ladder* of John Kilmachos (q.v.).

APPANAGE. During the Palaiologan period, a system of imperial grants of territory to members of the ruling family. Such grants were revocable, and they helped to tie important provincial holdings (e.g., Thessalonike, the Morea [qq.v.]) to the capital through the loyal administration of imperial family members.

APPOLONIA. *See* **VIA EGNATIA.**

APSE. A semi-cylindrical niche covered by a semi-dome (conch), located in church architecture at the end of a nave (q.v.). The apse belonged exclusively to the clergy, who sat on a *synthronon,* a semicircular stepped bench around the curved wall of the apse, surmounted by the bishop's throne *(cathedra).*

APULIA. The heel-shaped, southeastern part of the Italian Peninsula, bordered by the mountainous Garagano Peninsula in the north and the Strait of Otranto in the south. Bari and Brindisi (qq.v.) were its chief towns. Apulia was a battleground between Justinian I's troops and the Ostrogoths (qq.v.). The Lombards (q.v.) overran it in the late sixth century, making it part of the Duchy of Benevento (q.v.). Subsequently it was attacked by Arabs (q.v.), and by Louis II (q.v.), but Basil I (q.v.) reconquered much of the region for Byzantium (q.v.) in the ninth century. In the 11th century, control shifted to the Normans under Robert Guiscard (qq.v.), who set up the Duchy of Apulia. Byzantium (q.v.) was ejected from Apulia in 1071 when the Normans took Bari (q.v.). This date resonates ominously in Byzantine history, for in 1071 the Seljuks won their important victory at Mantzikert in Asia Minor (qq.v.).

AQUINAS, THOMAS. Dominican (q.v.) theologian (1224–1274). Among his voluminous works is the *Summa theologica,* which systematically expounds theology using the philosophical thinking of Aristotle (q.v.). This became the foundation of western scholasticism (q.v.), which influenced such Byzantine writers as Demetrios Kydones, Prohoros Kydones, and Gennadios II Scholarios (qq.v.). Aquinas himself was influenced by the eastern theologian John of Damascus (q.v.).

ARABIA. The Arabian Peninsula, the largest peninsula in the world, home of the Arabs of Himyar (qq.v.) and of the prophet Muhammad (q.v.). It was the expansion of Islam (q.v.) after Muhammad's death in 632 that brought Arabia out of its isolation and into conflict with Byzantium and Persia (qq.v.). Thereafter, its political importance decreased as centers of Islamic power developed outside the peninsula.

ARABS. Inhabitants of the Arabian Peninsula and Syrian desert since long before the rise of Islam (q.v.). Before the fourth century, the caravan trade to Syria (q.v.) gave rise to the Nabataean kingdom with its capital at Petra (q.v.), succeeded by the kingdom of Palmyra (q.v.), whose Arab queen Zenobia was conquered by the emperor Aurelian in 273. Roman policy focused on protecting the empire's Syrian border against raids of nomadic Bedouins (Arabic for "desert dwellers"). To this end, frontier fortifications (*limes* [q.v.]) were erected in Syria, and Arab client states were cultivated as allies of the empire. In the sixth century, the Ghassanids (q.v.) of Syria were the most important Arab *foederati* (q.v.). Under the banner of Islam (q.v.) in the seventh century, the Bedouin tribes burst through the Syrian frontier, conquering most of Byzantium's eastern possessions, including Egypt (q.v.) and North Africa. In Asia Minor (q.v.) the Byzantine-Arab struggle began in 646 and went on for centuries. In the process the Arabs created a world civilization under the Umayyad and Abbasid caliphs (qq.v.), and they transmitted ancient Greek science, medicine and philosophy (qq.v.) to the West.

ARBOGAST. German officer in the West who proclaimed himself *magister militum* (q.v.) in 388. He crushed the rebellion of Maximus (q.v.) the same year, a deed that recommended him to Theodosios I (q.v.). For four years Theodosios I allowed Arbogast to be the power behind the throne of Valentinian II (q.v.). However, when Valentinian II died under mysterious circumstances, Arbogast, unable to rule in his own name, raised up a puppet emperor named Eugenius (q.v.). Both were defeated by Theodosios I in 394.

ARCHBISHOP. Literally "chief bishop" in Greek. The title first referred to metropolitans (q.v.) of great importance, e.g., those of Rome and Alexandria (qq.v.). From the fifth century the title was given to the five patriarchs (q.v.). It also came to apply to the heads of autocephalous (q.v.) churches, e.g., to the patriarch of the church of Cyprus (q.v.).

ARCHIMANDRITE. Administrator (also called a *hegoumenos*) of one or more monasteries (e.g, the group of monasteries on Mount Athos [q.v.]). *Archimandrites* of monasteries in or near Constantinople (q.v.) could be politically influential. For example, John (VII) Grammatikos (q.v.) was *archimandrite* of the monastery of Sergios and Bakchos (q.v.) in Constantinople.

ARCHRUNI, SENEKERIM. *See* **SEBASTEIA; VASPURAKAN.**

ARDABOURIOS. *See* **ASPAR; LEO I.**

ARDASHIR I. *See* **SASSANIANS.**

ARETHAS OF CAESAREA. Archbishop of Caesarea (qq.v.); important scholar, theologian, bibliophile, and literary figure of the early 10th century. Some of his more formal works are unoriginal, including his commentary on the Apocalypse, as well as many of his notes ("scholia") in the margins of the manuscripts of ancient authors he collected. His notes in the margin of a manuscript containing the brief chronicle of the patriarch Nikephoros (qq.v.) follow closely the Chronicle of Monemvasia (q.v.), and figure prominently in modern arguments about the veracity of that chronicle (q.v.). Other marginal notes, as well as his letters and pamphlets, are invaluable sources for contemporary affairs, including the *tetragamy* of Leo VI (qq.v.). His polemical writings include attacks on Leo Choirosphaktes and on Leo VI's (qq.v.) chief minister during the early part of his reign, Stylianos Zaoutzes.

ARGOS. *See* **SGOUROS, LEO.**

ARGYROPOULOS, JOHN. Scholar of ancient Greek philosophy who taught at the University of Florence (q.v.) in the mid-15th century. Like Manuel Chrysoloras (q.v.) before him, he helped to initiate the Florentines to a systematic study of Greek philosophy. He was part of the Byzantine delegation at the Council of Ferrara-Florence (q.v.) in 1438–1439. He studied at the University of Padua and returned to Florence in 1456 to teach Aristotle and Plato (qq.v.). An excellent command of Latin, and of western philosophy (q.v.), insured his success. His teaching of Plato, especially of Plato's dialogue the *Meno,* fired the imagination of his pupils, among whom was Lorenzo de' Medici. He died in Rome (q.v.), where he spent the final years of his life translating and teaching.

ARGYROS. Lombard (q.v.) soldier of fortune from Bari (q.v.); *magistros* and *doux* of Italy (qq.v.) from 1051–1058. His father Melo rebelled against Byzantium (q.v.). So did Argyros in 1042 when the Normans (q.v.), along with the militia of Bari, proclaimed him prince and duke of Italy. However, he negotiated his loyalty with Byzantium for the promise of a future title, and once in Constantinople (q.v.) he helped defeat Leo Tornikios (q.v.) in 1045. Constantine IX (q.v.) made Argyros *magistros* (q.v.), and *doux* and sent him back to southern Italy to fight the Normans. To do this he formed an anti-Norman alliance with Pope Leo IX (q.v.), but the Normans defeated them separately in 1053. When Humbert (q.v.) excommunicated Patriarch Keroularios (q.v.) the following year, Patriarch Michael Keroularios (qq.v.) blamed Argyros for contributing to the circumstances that made the schism of 1054 (q.v.) possible.

ARIADNE. Daughter of Emperor Leo I (q.v.) and Verina (q.v.), wife of emperors Zeno and Anastasios I (qq.v.). Her importance lay in her marriages. The first was to Zeno, sealing the alliance between this Isaurian chieftain and Leo I. She bore Zeno a son, Leo II (q.v.), who reigned briefly in 474 before his death that same year. At the death of Zeno in 491 she was allowed to choose and marry his successor, Anastasios I.

ARIANISM. The great fourth-century heresy (q.v.), originated by Arius, a presbyter in the church of Alexandria (q.v.). Arius postulated that Christ was created by God from nothing, from which he reasoned that the Son is not co-equal and co-eternal with the Father, but is subordinate to God, and a changeable creature. First condemned by Arius's bishop Alexander (qq.v.), it was also condemned in 325 at the Council of Nicaea (q.v.), where Alexander's deacon Athanasios (q.v.) led the opposition to Arius. The council rejected the view that Christ was *homoiousios,* "of like substance" with the Father, in favor of the word *homoousios* (a term first conceived of by Origin [q.v.]), "of the same substance" with the Father, implying full equality. Arianism continued to be a potent force, in part because the emperor Constantine I (q.v.) reversed his position and recalled Arius in 328. The emperor was baptized by an Arian bishop on his death-bed. His son Constantius II (q.v.) was an Arian, so Arianism received state support during his reign (337–361). The failure of the local Council of Serdica (q.v.) in ca. 343 to find a solution to the Arian controversy demonstrated how intractable the problem had become. The emperor Valens (364–378) (q.v.) was the last Arian emperor. After his death, Theodosius I (q.v.), a fervent supporter of the Nicene Creed, used the Council of Constantinople (q.v.) to condemn Arianism yet again (in 381). Thus, Arianism further intertwined church-state relations, and it compelled the church to define its most fundamental theology (q.v.).

ARISTOCRACY. A landed aristocracy existed throughout Byzantine history. However, the basis of landholding changed from the more familiar pattern of Late Roman times, with its large estates and numerous *coloni* (q.v.), peasants bound to the soil, to the estates of military officials who derived their authority from the theme (q.v.) system. The latter became the military aristocracy, the so-called *dynatoi* (q.v.), of Asia Minor (q.v.) in the 10th century, powerful families that produced the likes of Bardas Skleros, Andronikos Doukas, and Bardas Phokas (qq.v.). The ability of these families to foment rebellion brought Basil II (q.v.) into armed conflict with them. After Basil II's death in 1025, a struggle ensued between the military aristocracy and the civil aristocracy (which comprised the state bureaucracy). The accession of Alexios I Komnenos (q.v.) as emperor in 1081 was a victory of the military bureaucracy, which triumphed as long as the Komneni remained in power. The Palaiologan (q.v.) dynasts were themselves aristocrats who ruled with the aid of other chief aristocratic families, giving them grants of *pronoia,* as well as appanages (qq.v.). Thus, beginning in the 10th century the power of the aristocracy was intertwined with imperial power, both as a restraint and a means of access to the imperial office.

ARISTOTLE. *See* **EUSTRATIOS OF NICAEA; METOCHITES, THEODORE; MICHAEL OF EPHESOS; PHILOSOPHY.**

ARIUS. *See* **ARIANISM.**

ARKADIOS. Emperor (q.v.) in the East from 395–408. He and his brother Honorios (q.v.), who ruled in the West, shared power jointly after the death of their father Theodosius I (q.v.). Arkadios was dull-witted and clearly incompetent to rule alone. Thus, imperial power was exercised through a succession of regents, including Rufinus, Eutropios, Arkadios's wife Eudoxia, and Anthemios (qq.v.). The Germans were a major problem during his reign. Alaric (q.v.) revolted and his Visigoths menaced Greece and Italy (qq.v.). Only after the suppression of Gainas (q.v.) in 400 did the German problem ameliorate in the East. However, the Germans continued to play an important role in the army, from which they could hardly be expelled completely, although this was recommended by the writer Synesios (q.v.). Another influential figure was the fiery Patriarch John Chrysostom (q.v.), who Arkadios exiled on more than one occasion. Arkadios's reign can be viewed as a stage on which more powerful personalities played all the leading roles.

ARLES, COUNCIL OF. City in southern Gaul (q.v.), where Constantine I (q.v.) summoned bishops to condemn Donatism (q.v.). The council convened on 1 August 314, and in retrospect it has the appearance of a dress rehearsal for the Council of Nicaea (q.v.) in 325. Constantine's intervention in church affairs set a precedent that subsequent emperors would follow.

ARMENIA. The kingdom of Armenia. The term also refers to the region of Armenia, which comprised a buffer zone in eastern Asia Minor (qq.v.) between Cappadocia and the Tigris River (qq.v.). From the early fourth century, Armenia was Christianized; in the fifth century Armenians created an alphabet and began translating Greek and Syriac texts. Divided between Byzantine and Persian (q.v.) spheres of influence in 387, Armenia was fought over during the Byzantine-Persian war of the late sixth and early seventh centuries, only to accept Arab (q.v.) suzerainty in 693. Not until 884, under the Bagratid dynasty (q.v.), did it regain much of its independence. Beginning in the 10th century, Byzantium (q.v.) was able to annex it piecemeal. By 1045 this annexation was complete. However, after the battle of Mantzikert (q.v.) in 1071 Armenia fell under Seljuk (q.v.) domination. Beginning in the sixth century, Armenians emigrated to Byzantium in great numbers, becoming the most assimilated of any ethnic group, while, at the same time, maintaining their distinct literature, religion, and art. Thousands of Armenian soldiers served in imperial forces, and a number of important military leaders and civil administrators were Armenian, including emperors Leo V, Basil I, Romanos I Lekapenos, and John I Tzimiskes (qq.v.). This illustrates the larger point that Byzantium was a multiethnic society that throughout its history welcomed people of talent and ability. Like other immigrants, Armenians became, in effect, Byzantines.

ARMENIAKON. One of the earliest and most important of the themes (q.v.), due to its size and location in northeastern Asia Minor (q.v.). In rank second only to the theme of Antaolikon (q.v.), it bordered the Black Sea from Sinope (qq.v.) to a point just to the east of Trebizond, extending south of Tyana (qq.v.). Most likely in existence by the mid-640s (but not fully attested to in historical literature until 667), it played a great role in defending Asia Minor against Arab (q.v.) raiders.

ARMY. Byzantium (q.v.) was continuously at war, and without its army it would not have survived. The key to the army's success was its ability to change, as the face of the enemy changed. The fourth century saw the first change, in response to the greater mobility of German invaders. The army, composed of indigenous and federate troops (*foederati* [q.v.], recruited from barbarian allies) used frontier militias (*limitanei* [q.v.]) to protect the borders, while mobile troops (*comitatenses* [q.v.]) commanded by the emperor, with his elite imperial bodyguard, gave chase to intruders. At least this is how it was meant to work in theory. In practice the response of mobile field forces was not always quick enough, and some units became stationary residents of areas for long periods of time. Moreover, emperors of the fourth and fifth centuries increasingly left campaigning to a German *magister militum* (q.v.), some of whom, like Aspar (q.v.), proved to be unreliable, even treacherous. In any case, even greater mobility was required to deal with the Persians and Avars (qq.v.), each of whom relied on cavalry and archery. This prompted the organization (beginning in the seventh century) of vast military districts called themes (q.v.), whose armies were meant to provide a defense-in-depth against invaders. The soldier-farmers of thematic armies were supported by the revenues supplied by small estates (*stratiotika ktimata* [q.v.], literally "soldiers' properties"), given in return for hereditary military service. Thematic armies were slow to mobilize and their commanders (*strategoi* [q.v.]) were so often involved in revolts in the eighth century that their effectiveness is questionable. In any case, against Arab raiders more mobility was needed, hence the development of mobile field forces (*tagmata* [q.v.]) stationed around Constantinople (q.v.). Cavalry was an important part of the *tagmata*. Their role was to follow the Arab raiders, dogging their every move, delaying them until the combined *tagmata* and thematic troops could strike. Nikephoros II Phokas (q.v.) developed a form of heavy cavalry called *kataphraktoi* (q.v.), covered with mail or lamellar coats, and with iron helmets; their horses were protected as well. They operated in flying wedges, followed by the regular cavalry, which could disintegrate an opponent's ranks. If this sounds well thought out, it was. Strategy and tactics in Byzantium were the object of scientific study, as indicated by the military manuals (*strategika* [q.v.]) that have survived. From the 10th century down to the end of Basil II's (q.v.) reign in 1025, the army, although much reduced in numbers from fourth-century totals, was superior to any in the western world. The decline of the army began before 1025 with the growth of large estates in Asia Minor at the expense of soldier-farmers who were the backbone of the thematic armies. The military aristocracy (the *dynatoi* [q.v.]) were among the chief offenders, and they included the likes of Baradas Skleros and Bardas Phokas (qq.v.), whose revolts almost unseated Basil II. The struggle between the central government and the military magnates intensified after Basil II's death, continuing until 1081, just as new threats were appearing. Basil II's successors, including Alexios I Komnenos (q.v.), were forced to rely chiefly on massive numbers of mercenaries, as the old *tagmata* and thematic armies shrunk to insignificance. One exception to this were the "Macedonians," indigenous troops from the western provinces, levied largely in Thrace (q.v.). Beginning with Alexios I, the importance of the Varangian Guard increased, as numerous western soldiers-of-fortune appeared, like Hervé Frankopoulos and Roussel de Bailleul (qq.v.). In addition to westerners there were soldiers from the steppe (q.v.), e.g., Pechenegs, Cumans, and Uzes (qq.v.), many of whom may have been hired for individual campaigns rather than maintained continuously in the army. From the Balkan Peninsula (q.v.) other mercenaries were recruited, e.g., Serbs, Hungarians, Alans, and Vlachs (qq.v.). Alexios I created from this ethnic mix an effective army that campaigned for over 30 years. John and Manuel Komnenos (qq.v.) inherited this new army, and they combined it with an aggressive program of fortification in areas endangered by enemy attacks. Field armies were then used chiefly to besiege fortified places in enemy hands, and garrison them once they were conquered. As Byzantium was further weakened by the Crusades (q.v.), its ability to purchase mercenaries declined. Use of *pronoia* (q.v.) grants increased accordingly. By the late 14th century the Ottomans (q.v.) were fielding huge armies, much larger than Byzantine forces, pitifully small by comparison, could resist.

ARPAD. *See* **HUNGARY.**

ARSENIOS AUTOREIANOS. Patriarch of Constantinople (qq.v.) from 1254–1260 and again from 1261–1265, who became a center of church opposition to Michael VIII Palaiologos (q.v.). He crowned Michael VIII co-emperor with John IV Laskaris (q.v.) in 1259, but when, in 1261, Michael VIII crowned his infant son Andronikos II Palaiologos (q.v.) co-emperor and had John IV blinded, Arsenios excommunicated Michael VIII. In 1265 Arsenios was implicated in a plot to overthrow the emperor, and Michael VIII had Arsenios deposed. His supporters, the so-called Arsenites (q.v.), refused to recognize Arsenios's successor Joseph I (q.v.) as patriarch. The Arsenites remained a dissident faction within the church until 1310.

ARSENITES. Supporters of Patriarch Arsenios Autoreianos (qq.v.), who was deposed in 1265 by Michael VIII Palaiologos (q.v.) for excommunicating the emperor (for his blinding of John IV Laskaris [q.v.]). The Arsenites remained an influential minority in the church, adamantly refusing to accept Arsenios's replacement, Joseph I (q.v.), as well as subsequent patriarchs. Only in 1310, after the patriarch Athanasios I (q.v.) had been deposed to satisfy the Arsenites, did the schism end.

ARTA. Capital of the despotate of Epiros, located in western Greece (qq.v.) on the Ambrakian Gulf just north of the Gulf of Arta. From 1259, until Stefan Urosh IV Dushan (q.v.) conquered it in 1348, the city was captured and lost many times by imperial Byzantine forces. Thereafter, it came under Albanian, then Florentine control. The Ottomans (q.v.) captured it in 1449.

ARTABASDOS. *Strategos* of the Armeniakon (qq.v.), later count of the Opsikion (q.v.), who usurped power in 742–743 from Constantine V (q.v.). He captured Constantinople (q.v.), was crowned by the patriarch Anastasios (qq.v.), and restored the holy icons (q.v.). In the provinces the revolt was supported by troops from the themes of Opskikon and the Armeniakon (qq.v.). Constantine V defeated each of them in turn, regained the capital, and blinded Aratabasdos and his two sons in the Hippodrome (q.v.), where the patriarch Anastasios was publicly humiliated by being led around naked on a donkey.

ASCETICISM. (Greek for "training," "exercise"). An ascetic is a monk who practices a rigorous and disciplined self-denial, often as a solitary hermit (*anchorite* [q.v.], or *eremite* [q.v.]). The earliest monks of the third and fourth centuries were hermits, such as Antony the Great (q.v.), who lived in the desert. This kind of monasticism (q.v.) contrasts with the communal monasticism of the *koinobion*, even of the *lavra* (qq.v.).

ASEKRETIS. An imperial secretary. The *asekretis* of Constantine VII (q.v.), for example, was the poet Constantine of Rhodes (q.v.). By the 12th century the term was replaced by *grammatikos* (q.v.).

ASEN I. He and his brother Peter (q.v.) founded the Second Bulgarian Empire in 1185 with its capital at Turnovo (q.v.). Whether the brothers were Vlachs, Cumans, Bulgars, or Russians (qq.v.) has been much debated. Niketas Choniates (q.v.) suggests that they were Vlachs. What is clear is that they wrested control of Bulgaria (q.v.) away from Byzantium (q.v.), which had held it by force since 1018. In 1196 Asen I was murdered by his nephew Ivanko (q.v.), but the Bulgar threat to Byzantium continued during the reign of Asen I's younger brother Kalojan (q.v.).

ASIA MINOR. The heartland of medieval Byzantium (q.v.). Geographically, it constitutes a huge peninsula at the extremity of western Asia that extends toward Europe. It is also called Anatolia and is roughly synonymous with the Asian part of Turkey. Asia Minor extends from the Aegean Sea to the Euphrates River (qq.v.), and it is dominated by a large, central plateau, some 1,000–2,000 meters in elevation, with peripheral mountain ranges that include the great Taurus (q.v.) range in the southeast. Asia Minor's peace and prosperity remained intact until the destructive Persian (q.v.) raids of the early seventh century. These were closely followed by Arab (q.v.) raids that went on relentlessly for the next two centuries, despite the theme (q.v.) system, which provided a kind of defense-in-depth. During these centuries, cities were reduced in size and heavily fortified. Michael III (q.v.) launched an offensive in 856 that began to turn the tide. Subsequent military action, taking advantage of Muslim weakness, created peaceful conditions that lasted until the advent of the Seljuks (q.v.) in the middle of the 11th century. The battle of Mantzikert (q.v.) in 1071 opened the floodgate to Seljuk expansion. Final Byzantine efforts to maintain some control in Asia Minor were dashed at the battle of Myriokephalon (q.v.) in 1176.

ASINOU. *See* **CYPRUS.**

ASOT I. *See* **BAGRATIDS.**

ASOT II. *See* **BAGRATIDS.**

ASOT III. *See* **BAGRATIDS.**

ASPAR. Alan (q.v.) general who exerted great influence over Marcian and Leo I (qq.v.). Under Theodosius II (q.v.) he rose to become *magister militum* (q.v.), holding the rank of *patrikios,* then consul (qq.v.) in 434. He was a capable general who defeated the usurper John in 425, as well as Vandals and Huns (qq.v.). His name is still attached to a cistern he built in Constantinople (q.v.). Although his Arianism (q.v.) and barbarian background precluded him from ever aspiring to the throne, he nevertheless sought to dominate the eastern court. His influence was so great at Marcian's death that he nominated the next emperor, Leo I (q.v.). As a counterweight to Aspar and the Germans, Leo I promoted Isaurians in the army (qq.v.), resulting in a power struggle in which Aspar and Ardabourios were slain. This struck a blow against the German threat in the East, but at the same time it produced a new internal threat in the Isaurians.

ASPARUCH. Bulgar khan (q.v.) and son of Kuvrat (q.v.). He led the Bulgars south of the Danube (qq.v.) to establish the first Bulgarian state. It was the first kingdom in Byzantine territory that Byzantium (q.v.) recognized as independent. By force of arms against Constantine IV (q.v.), Asparuch wrested a treaty from Byzantium (q.v.) in 681 that paid the Bulgars an annual tribute and gave them possession of the Byzantine territory they occupied. Tradition has it that it was Asparuch who established Pliksa as the first capital of Bulgaria (qq.v.).

ASTROLOGY. Form of divination based on the belief that the position of the planets relative to each other, and to the signs of the zodiac, determines events. Despite its condemnation by the church it was widely believed in. However, in educated circles it remained controversial, although there were always prominent believers, e.g., Manuel I Komnenos (q.v.). Alexios I Komnenos (q.v.) ridiculed it, as did Anna Komnene (q.v.), who thought it nonsense. In the Palaiologan period, as Byzantium lost control of its destiny, interest in astrology increased, as illustrated by the career of John Abramios (q.v.), who founded a school of astrologers, and who cast horoscopes for Andronikos IV Palaiologos (q.v.) and his son John VII Palaiologos (q.v.).

ASTRONOMY. Byzantine astronomy consisted primarily of commentaries on Ptolemy of Alexandria (qq.v.), the greatest of ancient astronomers. The works of other ancient astronomers were known, and, beginning in the 11th century, Islamic star catalogs were translated. Latin and Hebrew astronomical texts were translated in the 14th and 15th centuries. In practice astronomy often degenerated into astrology (q.v.), even speculative cosmology (e.g., in the writing of Kosmas Indikopleustes, and of Michael Italikos [qq.v.]).

ATAGEG. *See* **NUR AL-DIN; ZANGI.**

ATHANASIOS. Archbishop of Alexandria (qq.v.); theologian, archopponent of Arianism (q.v.); proponent of the Nicene Creed and of monasticism (q.v.). Athanasios was secretary to archbishop Alexander (q.v.), with whom he traveled to the Council of Nicaea (q.v.) in 325. He succeeded Alexander in 328, working tirelessly for the Nicene party, promoting the Nicene term *homoousios* (q.v.), meaning "of one substance," to describe Christ's relationship to God the Father. He introduced monasticism (q.v.) to the West during his periods of exile there. His *vita* of Antony the Great (qq.v.) was very influential, as witnessed by the impact it had on Augustine (q.v.) and his circle of friends.

ATHANASIOS I. Patriarch of Constantinople (qq.v.) from 1289–1293, and again from 1303–1309. He was also a writer whose correspondence and sermons provide information on political, religious, and social issues of his day. His deposition in 1309 helped to bring an end to the Arsenite (q.v.) schism.

ATHANASIOS OF ATHOS. Monk who revolutionized monasticism on Mount Athos (qq.v.) by founding the Great Lavra (q.v.) in 963 with the financial support of Nikephoros II (q.v.). It became the prototype for subsequent monasteries on Mount Athos, all of which were ecclesiastically independent and built on a lavish scale with imperial or aristocratic support.

ATHANASIOS OF METEORA. Monk from Mount Athos (q.v.) who fled ca. 1340 for Thessaly (q.v.) to escape Ottoman (q.v.) attacks on the Athonian peninsula. He founded the Great Meteoron (late 14th century), the most important of the breathtaking monasteries atop the massive rock pedestals of Meteora (q.v.) at the northern end of the plain of Thessaly (q.v.).

ATHAULF. *See* **VISIGOTHS.**

ATHENAIS-EUDOKIA. Wife of Theodosios II (q.v.). Highly educated by her father Leontios, a pagan philosopher from Athens (q.v.), she was chosen by Pulcheria (q.v.) to be the wife of her brother, Theodosios II (q.v.). Athenais became a Christian, took the name Eudokia, and was married in 421. She journeyed to Antioch and Jerusalem (qq.v.) in 438 with noted Saint Melania the Younger, where her charm and erudition gained her great popularity. Later Athenais-Eudokia was accused of adultery (which she denied) and was forced to spend the last years of her life in Jerusalem (q.v.), where she endowed churches, monasteries, and hospices. She composed some religious poems, fragments of which survive.

ATHENS. Celebrated ancient city on the plain of Attica in east-central Greece (q.v.). It declined in the Byzantine era, beginning in 267 with a raid of barbarian Heruls that did great damage to the city. More damage occurred when Alaric (q.v.) occupied the city briefly in 396. Nevertheless, Athens remained a center of learning, where great minds like Julian, Basil the Great, and Gregory Nazianzos (qq.v.) studied. In the fifth century Athenais-Eudokia (q.v.), the daughter of a pagan philosopher from Athens, was chosen as bride for Theodosios II (q.v.). The closing of the famed Academy of Athens (q.v.) in 529 by Justinian I (q.v.), as well as the Slavic migrations into Greece, accelerated Athen's decline. Nevertheless, it remained in Byzantine hands until the aftermath of the Fourth Crusade (q.v.), when it was incorporated into the duchy of Athens and Thebes under Othon de la Roche (qq.v.). In the early 14th century it was taken over by the Catalan Grand Company (q.v.), after which it was ruled successively by Florentines, Venetians, and Byzantines from 1446–1456, when it fell to the Ottomans (q.v.).

ATHINGANOI. *See* **PHRYGIA.**

ATHOS, MOUNT. The rugged and picturesque peninsula, easternmost of the three promontories of Chalkidike (q.v.), where the famous Athonian monasteries are located. At present there are 20 monasteries, of which 17 are Greek, one is Russian (Panteleemon Monastery), one is Serbian (Hilandar Monastery [q.v.]), and one is Bulgarian (Zographou Monastery). At the end of the peninsula is Mount Athos, hence the name (called *Ayion Oros* [Holy Mountain], in Greek). When monasticism (q.v.) began on Athos is debated, but certainly by the ninth century monks were living there as hermits (q.v.), and in groups. Euthymios the Younger founded the first *lavra* (q.v.) during the reign of Michael III. In the reign of Basil I (q.v.), Kolobou, the first monastery, was founded. The construction of the Great Lavra (q.v.) in 963 by Athanasios of Athos (q.v.) was a major event, for it was the first large-scale *cenobitic* (q.v.) monastery founded, and it had an imperial benefactor, Nikephoros II Phokas (q.v.). This set the pattern for subsequent imperial support and protection. By the 11th century the number of monasteries had multiplied to over 40. Monks from all over the Orthodox world came, including Georgians (who founded Iveron [q.v.] in 979), Armenians, Serbs, Italians, Russians, and Bulgarians. The independence of the monasteries increased along with their wealth, which was aided by acquiring properties outside of Athos. It survived Latin rule, the raids of the Catalan Grand Company (q.v.), and conquest in 1430 by the Ottomans (q.v.), who confirmed the peninsula's independence in return for an annual tribute. The Athonian monasteries continue to thrive, as a living legacy of Byzantium (q.v.) to the modern world.

ATRIKLINES. *See* **PHILOTHEOS, KLETOROLOGION OF.**

ATROA, MONASTERY OF. *See* **LYMPOS, MOUNT.**

ATTALEIA. Modern Antalya, situated in Pamphylia (q.v.) on the south coast of Asia Minor (qq.v.). Its harbor was an important center of trade that facilitated commerce and communication with Cyprus and Cilicia (qq.v.). The city was also capital of the theme of Kibyrrhaiotai (qq.v.) and had a major naval base. Its fortifications helped to keep it in Byzantine hands until the early 13th century, when, in 1207, it fell to the Seljuks (q.v.).

ATTALEIATES, MICHAEL. Historian and jurist, and a younger contemporary of Michael Psellos (q.v.), who wrote an eyewitness account of the period from 1034–1079. His description of the last Macedonian (q.v.) emperors, and of the period of troubles that preceded the reign of Alexios I Komnenos (q.v.), is an invaluable companion to the *Chronographia* of Michael Psellos (q.v.). To some extent it is also a corrective, since Attaleiates defends Romanos IV and Nikephoros III (qq.v.), both of whom he served under. His work is dedicated to Nikephoros III, whom he praises.

ATTILA. Famous "king" of the Huns (q.v.) from 434–453, whose court is described by the historian Priskos (q.v.). Theodosios II (q.v.) paid him tribute, but in 450 Marcian (q.v.) refused payment. Attila invaded Gaul (q.v.) the next year under the pretext of claiming as his bride Honoria, the sister of Valentinian III (q.v.). He was defeated by Aetius (q.v.) at the battle of the Catalunian Fields (q.v.) in 451. Attila invaded Italy (q.v.) in 452 but withdrew after meeting with Pope Leo I (q.v.). He died on his wedding night in 453. Under Attila, the Huns were a major power to be reckoned with and the Hunnic empire reached its greatest extent. After his death the Hunnic empire disintegrated.

AUGUSTA. *See* **EMPRESS.**

AUGUSTAION. A large enclosed area in Constantinople (q.v.), perhaps part of a previous forum called the Tetrastoon (the Four Stoas). Constantine I (q.v.) remodeled it and named it in honor of his mother, the augusta Helena (qq.v.). He placed a statue of her there on a column. Around the area were grouped the most important buildings of the city. On the north side was the great church of Hagia Sophia (q.v.). On the east side was the Senate House. On the south side was the main entrance to the Great Palace (q.v.), adjacent to the Baths of Zeuxippus. One entered the Augustaion from the west, where the Milion (Milestone) was located. From this point the mileage of roads connecting Constantinople (q.v.) with its European provinces was measured. From the Milion one entered the Mese (q.v.), or Middle Street, the main thoroughfare through the city. Justinian I (q.v.) remodeled the Augustaion, rebuilding the Senate House, which had been destroyed in the Nika Revolt (q.v.). He also added an equestrian statue atop a column, referred to as Justinian's column, in front of which was a sculptural group of three barbarians offering tribute.

AUGUSTINE. Saint, theologian, bishop of Hippo Regius in Africa (q.v.) from around 396 until his death in 430. His theology, which had a great impact on the western church, developed chiefly from his opposition to three major heresies: Manichaeanism, Donatism, and Pelagianism (qq.v.). It was also a product of his personal experience of conversion, which he describes in his celebrated *Confessions*. His *City of God* was prompted by the fall of Rome to Alaric (qq.v.) in 410 and by pagan criticism that Christianity was responsible for the decline of Rome. Augustine's response was to remind Christians that they are citizens of the heavenly City of God, and only temporary sojourners in the earthly city, whose decline and destruction they should accept. The influence of this viewpoint can be seen in Orosius's (q.v.) *History against the Pagans*.

AUGUSTUS. *See* **CONSTANTINE I THE GREAT; TETRARCHY.**

AURELIUS VICTOR, SEXTUS. Latin historian who was a contemporary of Julian, Eutropius, and Ammianus Marcellinus (qq.v.). Julian appointed him governor of Lower Pannonia (q.v.). In 389 he was the urban prefect (q.v.) of Rome (q.v.). His brief survey of Roman history from Augustus to Julian (360) is in the form of imperial biographies.

AUTOCEPHALOUS. In a general sense the term describes a characteristic feature of every bishopric, namely, that it elects its own primate, or head, and is self-governing (*auto,* in Greek, means "self," and *kephale* means "head"). More specifically, the term is used to describe bishops who are made independent of any higher church authority, including that of a patriarch (q.v.), either by imperial decree or by an ecumenical council (q.v.). It can also refer to bishops who depend on a patriarch independent of an intermediate metropolitan (q.v.). The term can even apply to entire churches, like those of Cyprus and Bulgaria (qq.v.), which are self-governing. Relations between autocephalous churches and bishoprics were determined by a hierarchy headed by the "ecumenical patriarch" of Constantinople (q.v.), considered first among equals. This contrasts with the western church, whose organization was influenced by the principle of papal primacy (q.v.).

AUTOKRATOR. Greek term meaning "absolute ruler." It was equivalent to the Latin *imperator,* or emperor (q.v.). After the Persians (q.v.) were defeated in 629 the emperor was called *basileus* (q.v.), and *au-*

tokrator declined in significance. Nevertheless, it was still used to designate the senior emperor (the *megas basileus*) from his co-emperor(s). In the 10th century the title revived in importance when the tsars of Bulgaria (qq.v.) expropriated the title of *basileus*. Under the Palaiologan (q.v.) dynasts it distinguished not only the reigning emperor but also the heir-presumptive among the co-emperors.

AUTOMATA. *See* **MAGNAURA.**

AVARS. A Turkic people from the Asia steppe (q.v.) who settled in the plain of Hungary in 568, wresting away from Byzantium (q.v.) much of the Balkan Peninsula (q.v.). Strong allegiance to a single ruler, the khagan (q.v.), helped to create an empire in central Europe that was a solid base from which to launch attacks on Byzantium. Mastery on horseback gave them mobility, and their use of the iron stirrup (which they introduced to the West), often gave them the edge in battle. Their knowledge of siegecraft was such that city after city fell to them. Finally the Slavs (q.v.), who the Avars dominated and used in their raids, ended up settling in great numbers in the Balkan Peninsula, changing much of its ethnic composition. The Avars were particularly threatening in the reign of Herakleios (q.v.), when in 626 they coordinated with the Persians a massive assault by land and sea on Constantinople (q.v.). After that their empire declined. They were finally destroyed by Charlemagne (q.v.) between 791 and 795.

AVITUS, EPARCHIUS. Western emperor (q.v.) from 455–456. In 436, when Avitus was Preatorian Prefect of Gaul under Aetius (qq.v.), he concluded peace with Theodoric (q.v.) and obtained Theodoric's help against Attila (q.v.) in 451. In 455, after the deaths of Valentinian III and Petronius Maximus (qq.v.), and after the Vandals sacked Rome (qq.v.), Avitus was declared emperor. His son-in-law, the Latin writer Sidonius, showered him with accolades in poetic verse, but Marcian (q.v.) never confirmed him as emperor. This, as well as his inability to prevent further Vandal pillaging, and his failure to obtain enough grain for those starving in Rome (q.v.), forced him to flee the city. Ricimer and Majorian (qq.v.) conspired to depose him.

AVLON. *See* **EPIROS; OTRANTO.**

AXUM. The ancient kingdom (also called Abyssina) that stretched westward to the valley of the Nile and southward to the Somali coast, in what is today northern Ethiopia. Its capital city was also called Axum. Its port of Adulis, on the Red Sea (q.v.), was a market for African slaves, ivory (qq.v.), papyrus, and gold, as well as spices from India (q.v.). Like Byzantium (q.v.), it minted gold coins, and had a sophisticated court where Greek was spoken. Its economic and diplomatic influence extended to Arabia and Persia (qq.v.). Christianity was probably established during the fourth century, perhaps during the reign of king Ezana (q.v.). Its Monophysite (q.v.) church was dependent on the patriarch of Alexandria (qq.v.). Justin I persuaded king Elesboam to invade Himyar (q.v.), i.e., southern Arabia (Yemen), in 525, to counteract any Persian attempt to control the area. In 531, Justinian I (q.v.) sent an embassy to Axum to persuade the Ethiopians to destroy the Persian silk trade by transporting silk between Ceylon and the Red Sea ports. However, nothing came of this scheme. In the seventh centuries, Axum lost its Red Sea ports to the Arabs (q.v.), precipitating its decline. However, from the fourth to the seventh centuries, Axum was the greatest power in Africa (q.v.) after Byzantium.

AYDIN. Independent Seljuk emirate (qq.v.) on the coast of western Asia Minor (q.v.) that supported John VI Kantakouzenos (q.v.) during the civil war of 1341–1347. It reached the height of its power during the reign of Umur Beg, whose pirate fleet based in Ephesus and Smyrna (qq.v.) plundered Venetian islands and preyed on commercial vessels throughout the Aegean (q.v.). The emirate was conquered by the Ottomans (q.v.) in the 15th century.

AYN JALUT, BATTLE OF. *See* **MAMLUKS.**

AYYUBIDS. The Muslim dynasty founded in 1171 by Saladin (q.v.), son of Ayub, when he ended Fatamid rule in Egypt (qq.v.). Saladin's kingdom, which also included Syria and Palestine (qq.v.) became a base of operations from which he attacked the Crusaders, defeating them at the Battle of Hattin (q.v.) in 1187. Ayyubid power ended with the expansion of the Mamluks (q.v.). In 1250 the Egyptian Ayyubids were overthrown by the Mamluks. The Mamluks overthrew the Ayyubids of Syria in 1260.

AZYMA. The Greek term for unleavened bread used in the Eucharist (q.v.) by the Armenian church, and later by the Latin church. The

Byzantine church used leavened bread *(enzyma)*. An issue in the church schism of 1054 (q.v.), it was a further bone of contention at the Council of Lyons (q.v.) in 1274, and later in 1438–1439 at the Council of Ferrara-Florence (q.v.). To average Byzantines it came to symbolize just how irreconcilable were their differences with the West.

– B –

BABEK. *See* **KHURRAMITES; THEOPHOBOS.**

BAGHDAD. *See* **ABBASID CALIPHATE; CALIPH.**

BAGRATIDS. Armenian dynasty (884–1045) founded by Asot I ("the Great"). Under Asot II Erkat the Iron, who reigned from 914–928, taking the title King of Kings, Armenia (q.v.) consolidated its independence from both Byzantium and the Arabs (qq.v.). This was despite an expedition by Byzantine general John Kourkouas (q.v.) in 922 that bolstered the rival Armenian kingdom of Vaspurakan (q.v.). Asot III the Merciful, who reigned 953–977, transferred his capital to Ani, which became a center of Armenian civilization. The conquest of Ani in 1045 by Byzantine troops effectively ended the Bagratid dynasty. Armenia fell under the control of the Seljuks (q.v.) after the battle of Mantzikert (q.v.) in 1071.

BALADHURI, AL-. Arab historian (died ca. 892) of the early Arab (q.v.) conquests. Along with the history of al-Tabari (q.v.), Baladhuri is a chief source for the early Arab conquests, although his work is dependent on earlier Arab accounts.

BALDACCHINO. *See* **CIBORIUM.**

BALDRIC OF DOL. *See* **GESTA FRANCORUM ET ALIORUM HIEROSOLIMITANORUM.**

BALDWIN II. *See* **LATIN EMPIRE.**

BALDWIN OF FLANDERS. Baldwin I, first emperor (q.v.) of the Latin Empire of Constantinople (qq.v.) and one of the leaders of the Fourth Crusade (q.v.). He was crowned in 1204 and the next year was captured by the Bulgarian leader Kaoljan (q.v.) in a battle near Adrianople (q.v.). He apparently died in 1205 while imprisoned in Bulgaria (q.v.).

BALKAN PENINSULA. The southeasternmost peninsula of Europe, often referred to as the Balkans. On three sides it is bordered by seas: the Adriatic Sea, Ionian Sea, Mediterranean Sea, Aegean Sea, Sea of Marmora, and Black Sea (qq.v.). To the north, the Danube (q.v.) and Sava Rivers are its traditional northern limits. Maintaining control over the northern Balkans was essential for the protection of Greece and Constantinople (qq.v.). Nevertheless, geography and the peninsula's road systems conspired to make this difficult. The Danube was a boundary that could be penetrated. Once across the Danube, most mountain ranges run north-south, making invasion from the north relatively easy. Most road systems ran north-south as well, including the military road from the Danube (q.v.) frontier that ran from Belgrade to Nish (qq.v.), where it split into two branches: one going to Skopje and Thessalonike (qq.v.), the other in a more southeasterly direction to Serdica, then to Philippopolis, Adrianople, and Constantinople (qq.v.). The famous east-west highway called the Via Egnatia (q.v.) ran from Dyrrachion via Thessalonike to Constantinople (qq.v.). Thus, once the Danube was penetrated both geography and roads favored the invader. The history of the peninsula in Byzantine times can be viewed largely as a history of its invasions, e.g., by Visigoths, Avars, Slavs, Bulgars, Serbs, Rus, Pechenegs, Uzes, Crusaders, and Ottomans (qq.v.).

BALSAMON, THEODORE. *See* **CANON LAW.**

BANDON. A military unit, which by the 10th century consisted of 50–100 cavalry, or of 200–400 infantrymen, commanded by a count (q.v.). A *turm* was composed of five to seven *banda*.

BAPHEUS, BATTLE OF. *See* **ANDRONIKOS II PALAIOLOGOS; NIKOMEDIA; OSMAN.**

BARBARO, NICOLO. Author of an eyewitness account of the siege and fall of Constantinople to the Ottomans (qq.v.) in 1453. Barbaro was a Venetian ship-doctor who arrived shortly before the siege and was trapped inside the city. His account, notable for its sound chronology, is marred only by its bias against the Genoese (q.v.).

BARBERINI IVORY. *See* **IVORY.**

BARDANES, GEORGE. *See* **APOKAUKOS, JOHN.**

BARDANES TOURKOS. Military commander of five themes in Asia Minor (qq.v.) who rebelled against Nikephoros I (q.v.) in 803. The rebellion faltered within a month and Bardanes ended it by retiring to a monastery. Two young officers, Leo (V) the Armenian and Michael (II) the Amorion (qq.v.), both future emperors, were rewarded by Nikephoros I for deserting the rebellion.

BARDAS. Uncle and chief advisor of Michael III (q.v.); brother of Theodora and Petronas (qq.v.), who helped put Michael III on the throne by assassinating the regent Theoktistos (q.v.). This capable administrator, who held many titles (including caesar and *patrikios* [qq.v.]) organized the university at the Magnaura (q.v.), creating a faculty for it headed by Leo the Mathematician (q.v.). Bardas also played an active role in organizing the mission of Cyril and Methodius to Moravia (qq.v.), as well as in the baptism of khan Boris I of Bulgaria (qq.v.). Nevertheless, in 865 Michael III allowed the future emperor Basil I (q.v.) to assassinate Bardas.

BAR-HEBRAEUS, GREGORIUS. Syrian historian (1226–1286); last classical author in Syriac literature. His original name was Gregory Abu'l Faraj. He was bishop of the Jacobite (q.v.) church and author of a variety of works, including commentaries in Syriac and in Arabic on Aristotle (q.v.). His world *Chronicle* (q.v.) in Syriac, based chiefly on the *Chronicle* of Michael I the Syrian (q.v.), goes from Adam to the invasions of the Mongols (q.v.).

BARI. Fortified city in Apulia on the Adriatic Sea (qq.v.), and the center of Byzantine operations in southern Italy (q.v.) from the time of its reconquest by Basil I (q.v.) in 876 to 1071 when the Normans (q.v.) conquered Bari. The date 1071 is among the most ominous in the history of Byzantium (q.v.), for it was not only the year the Byzantines were ejected from Italy but also the year of the battle of Mantzikert (q.v.), which marked the beginning of Seljuk (q.v.) expansion in Asia Minor (q.v.).

BARLAAM AND IOASAPH. Popular Byzantine romance often attributed to John of Damascus (q.v.), but probably authored by a certain John of Mar Saba. The plot of the story is a version of the life of Buddha, but how it got to Byzantium (q.v.) is unclear.

BARLAAM OF CALABRIA. Monk, theologian, and chief opponent of Hesychasm (q.v.). Barlaam was a Greek from Calabria (q.v.) who taught in Constantinople (q.v.) and who had friends in high places. These included John Kantakouzenos, and Andronikos III (qq.v.), who sent him on a mission to the Avignon papacy in 1339 where he explained the Byzantine position on the union of the churches (q.v.). His sarcastic attacks on the Hesychast monks of Mount Athos (q.v.) as being superstitious drew a response from Gregory Palamas (q.v.), who engaged in a protracted theological argument with him. In 1341 Barlaam was condemned at a council in Hagia Sophia (q.v.), after which he returned to Italy. There, he taught Leontius Pilatus, who played an important role in the early phase of the Italian Renaissance. (Pilatus translated the *Odyssey* of Homer [q.v.] into Latin.) At Avignon, Barlaam met the great Italian humanist Petrarch, and he tried, rather unsuccessfully, to teach him Greek. Boccaccio, in his *Genealogy of the Gods,* refers to Barlaam as a man small in stature but enormous in breadth of knowledge.

BASIL I. Emperor (867–886) and founder of the Macedonian dynasty (q.v.), who came to the throne by murdering his benefactor Michael III (q.v.). He deposed the patriarch Photios (qq.v.) and reinstated Ignatios (q.v.), which helped to restore relations with the papacy (q.v.). His reign was preoccupied with war on several fronts against the Arabs (q.v.). Basil's goal of reconquering southern Italy (q.v.) from the Arabs was accomplished with the aid of Frankish emperor Louis II (q.v.). Arab attacks along the coasts of Dalmatia and Greece (qq.v.) were rebuffed, and Cyprus (q.v.) was occupied for seven years. The one serious setback was in Sicily, where Syracuse (qq.v.) fell to the Arabs. In the East, despite some defeats, a period of systematic advances against the Arabs began with victories in the region of the Euphrates River and against the Paulicians (qq.v.). Basil's internal policy included a plan to completely revise Justinianic law, but this was never realized beyond the introductory *Procheiron* and *Epanagogue* (qq.v.). His innovative church called *Nea Ekklesia* (New Church) has survived only in literary descriptions.

BASIL II. Called "Bulgar-Slayer" *(Bulgaroktonos),* he reigned from 976–1025 as the greatest of the Macedonian emperors (qq.v). This was not apparent at the beginning of his long reign. His first military expedition (in 986) against Samuel of Bulgaria (q.v.), ended in total defeat at a narrow pass called Trajan's Gate (q.v.). This encouraged two rebellions, those of Bardas Skleros and Bardas Phokas (qq.v.). Only with the help of 6,000 Varangians (q.v.) sent by Vladimir I of

Kiev (qq.v.) were the revolts suppressed. In return, Basil gave his sister Anna (q.v.) to Vladimir in marriage, requiring that he convert and be baptized, which he did. Basil II tried to curb the expansion of the landed estates of great landowners (including monasteries), the *dynatoi* (q.v.), in an effort to preserve peasant land, especially military holdings. Among his decrees (the first in 996) was one forcing the great magnates to pay the unpaid taxes (*allelengyon* [q.v.]) of their poorer neighbors. Basil further reduced the power of the provincial armies, the themes (q.v.), which the military magnates controlled, by commuting army service into a money payment. The revenues he used to create a standing army, the elite forces of which were his Varangian Guard (q.v.). With such troops, Basil II set out to subjugate the Bulgars (q.v.) while at the same time defending Antioch and Aleppo in Syria (qq.v.). Total victory against the Bulgars was achieved only in 1014, after a great victory in which Basil II captured 14,000 Bulgarian soldiers. Basil II blinded them and sent them back to Tsar Samuel (qq.v.), who was struck senseless and died two days later (on 6 October 1014). Former Bulgaria became a part of Byzantium (q.v.). Toward the end of his reign he intervened in Armenia (q.v.), annexing Vaspurkan and part of Iberia (qq.v.). At his death in 1025, there were no serious external threats on the horizon. Indeed, Byzantium seemed invincible. But Basil II was a hard act for future 11th-century emperors to follow, one that demanded harsh fiscal and foreign policies that few emperors could emulate.

BASILEUS. Title used for the Persian king until Herakleios (q.v.) conquered Persia (q.v.) and expropriated it. It was understood as "emperor," and became the chief imperial title, instead of *autokrator* (q.v.). It is not clear if demonstrable Persian influence was the reason for this change. After Charlemagne (q.v.) was recognized as *basileus* in 812, Byzantine emperors used the title *basileus ton romaion* (Emperor of the Romans). The Slavic translation for *basileus* is tsar (q.v.).

BASILICA. A type of Roman building that was used for the first great Christian churches built by Constantine I (q.v.). Previous Roman basilicas were used for a variety of public purposes, e.g., law courts, audience halls, and covered markets. The simplest basilicas were halls without adjacent aisles. More complex ones had a vestibule (called a narthex [q.v.]) leading to a central nave, with narrower side aisles, above which could be galleries. The nave could terminate in a rectangular or semicircular apse. The basic design, which is flexible and open to a variety of permutations of its individual components (e.g., the Domed Basilica [q.v.]), proved suitable for the development of the Christian liturgy. In a larger sense, the Christian basilica illustrates the interplay of continuity and transformation that in Constantine's reign began to reshape the Roman Empire into what is today referred to as Byzantium (q.v.).

BASILIKA. The law code (*Basilika* is Greek for "imperial laws") begun by a commission of lawyers under Basil I (q.v.) and completed under Leo VI (q.v.). It essentially updated the *Corpus Juris Civilis* of Justinian I (qq.v.). It also includes the *Novels* (q.v.) of Justinian and of his successors Justin II and Tiberios (qq.v.), as well as canon law. Despite the apparent disadvantage of reissuing, in effect, a scaled-down version of an old (and out-dated?) law code, there were advantages over the *Corpus Juris Civilis*. First of all, the *Basilika* is in Greek, the language of the East, as opposed to Latin. Second, it is divided into subjects, with the laws pertaining to each subject in one place, unlike the *Corpus Juris Civilis*. Because of these advantages, it soon superceded the *Corpus Juris Civilis* entirely.

BASILIKOI ANTHROPOI. Literally "imperial men," referring generally to imperial officials both high and low. This is the way the term is used in the *Kletorologion* of Philotheos (q.v.). By the 10th century there may also have been a military detachment with this name. The *De ceremoniis* of Constantine VII Porphyrogennetos (q.v.) and the Escurial *taktikon* (q.v.) mention a *katepano* (q.v.) of the *basilikoi*.

BASILISKOS. Brother of Zeno's wife Verina (qq.v.) who usurped the throne from 475–476 during Zeno's reign. Before this Basiliskos was noted chiefly for having led the disastrous naval expedition against the Vandals (q.v.) in 468. During his brief usurpation he supported the Monophysites (q.v.), which angered the patriarch Akakios (qq.v.), and prompted the pillar-saint Daniel the Stylite (q.v.) to lead a popular uprising in Constantinople (q.v.) against Basiliskos. This set the stage for Zeno's triumphant return to the capital, and for Basiliskos's exile.

BASIL THE COPPER HAND. He raised a revolt in Bithynia (q.v.) against Romanos I (q.v.) in about 932. He claimed to be Constantine Doukas (q.v.), who had been killed in 913 in an abortive revolt.

Basil was captured and punished by having his hand cut off. Back in Bithynia (q.v.) he made a copper hand for himself, and he stirred up a popular uprising of the poor, whose plight had worsened since the great famine of 928. He was captured and sent to Constantinople (q.v.), where he was put to death.

BASIL THE GREAT. Saint, and one of the three Cappadocian fathers (along with Gregory of Nazianzos and Gregory of Nyssa [qq.v.], Basil's brother), all great church fathers of the fourth century. They were opponents of Arianism (q.v.), including its chief proponent Eunomios (q.v.), at a time when the eastern emperor Valens (364–378) was promoting the heresy (q.v.). In 370 Basil became bishop of Caesarea in Cappadocia (qq.v.), from where he worked to deal Arianism a final blow at the Council of Constantinople (q.v.) in 381. In the process he helped to develop the concept of the Trinity and created the Basilian rule, a balanced regimen of work and worship for monks that had a tremendous impact on the development of monasticism (q.v.). His writings on theological topics reflect the erudition of his education (he was a pupil of Libanios [q.v.]). His many letters are a rich source for the cultural history of the period.

BASIL THE NOTHOS. High state official (*parakoimomenos* [q.v.]) under Constantine VII, John I Tzimiskes, and Basil II (qq.v.). Romanos II favored Joseph Bringas (q.v.) over him, and Basil hated Bringas for it. His revenge came when Nikephoras II Phokas (q.v.) overthrew Bringas in 963. Basil schemed against Nikephoros II and may have poisoned the next emperor, John I Tzimiskes. He administered state affairs for the young Basil II (q.v.) until Basil II exiled him in 985.

BAYBARS. *See* **MAMLUKS.**

BAYEZID I. Ottoman sultan (1389–1402), called "Thunderbolt." He sealed the conquest of Serbia, conquered Bulgaria (qq.v.), and fought the first battles on Hungarian soil, becoming the terror of central Europe. What was left of Byzantium (q.v.), except for the Morea (q.v.), lay chiefly behind the great walls of Constantinople (q.v.). John V Palaiologos and his successor Manuel II Palaiologos (qq.v.) were, in fact, little more than vassals of Bayezid, forced to endure one humiliation after another. When Byzantine appeasement failed Bayezid laid siege to Constantinople during the last eight years of his life. Unexpectedly, Bayezid was defeated and captured by Timur (q.v.) at the battle of Ankara in 1402, a turn of events that prolonged the life of Byzantium for yet another half century.

BEACON SYSTEM. A series of fire-signals that warned Constantinople (q.v.) of an Arab invasion into Asia Minor through the Taurus (qq.v.) mountain range. The first signal station was at the fort of Loulon, just north of the Cilician Gates (q.v.). The system was conceived of by Leo the Mathematician (q.v.), who also created synchronized water clocks that were placed at each end of the system. There were 12 specific messages, each of which could be indicated by lighting the first beacon at the particular hour associated with the intended message. The message was received at the final signal-station, located in the Great Palace at Constantinople (qq.v.).

BEDE. *See* **BRITAIN.**

BEDOUINS. *See* **ARABS.**

BEIRUT. *See* **BERYTUS.**

BELA III. King of Hungary (1172–1196), and, for a while, heir to the Byzantine throne. Manuel I Komnenos (q.v.) desired to unite Hungary with Byzantium (qq.v.), to which end he secured the engagement of his daughter Maria to Bela, who was given the Greek name Alexios, along with the title of despot (q.v.), which made him heir-apparent to the throne. However, with the birth of Alexios II (q.v.), Bela's engagement to Maria was rescinded.

BELEGEZITAI. *See* **DEMETRIAS.**

BELGRADE. Called Singidunum by the Romans, the city is strategically situated at the confluence of the Sava and Danube (q.v.) rivers. Moreover, the Belgrade-Constantinople highway was the most important trans-Balkan route from central Europe to Constantinople (q.v.). Captured by the Avars (q.v.) in the early seventh century, it emerged in the 10th century with a new Slavic name, Beograd ("White Fortress"). It was part of the First Bulgarian Empire until 1018, when it was incorporated into Byzantine territory. It went back into the hands of the Bulgars (q.v.) in 1040, during the revolt of Peter Deljan (q.v.). Subsequently, it was acquired by the Hungarians, and then by the Serbs (q.v.), who made it their capital in the 12th century. In 1427 the Hungarians took it, and in 1456 Hunyadi won a great victory over the Ottomans (q.v.), who had to break off their siege of the city. It finally fell to the Ottomans in 1521.

BELISARIOS. Justinian I's (q.v.) greatest general. His contributions to Justinian I's reign were considerable. Without him, Justinian I might have lost his throne in the Nika Revolt (q.v.) of 532. The reconquest of North Africa from the Vandals (qq.v.) in 533–534 and the early successes against the Ostrogoths (q.v.) from 536–540 were due in large part to his generalship. Against the Persians (q.v.), his success was mixed, but his role invaluable. In 559 he was called out of retirement to conduct an heroic defense of the capital against a raid by Cotrigurs (q.v.). The negative portrait drawn of him (and of the reconquest of North Africa) in Prokopios of Caesarea's (q.v.) *Anekdota* (Secret History) is unfair, whatever the truth about Belisarios's wife Antonina (q.v.). And it would be unfair to blame him for the Berber (q.v.) revolt in North Africa that dragged the war on there until 548, or unforeseen events in Italy (q.v.) after his departure that continued the Ostrogothic war until 554. However protracted and ephemeral Justinian's reconquests were in the West (e.g., much of Italy was lost to the Lombards [q.v.] in 568), at least for a time the empire regained much of its former territory. What Justinian envisioned and planned, Belisarios, often with limited resources, made possible.

BEMA. The chancel, i.e., the sanctuary of a Byzantine church, where the altar is situated, often enclosed by a chancel barrier called a *templon* (q.v.). From the *bema* a raised pathway (the *solea*) led to the pulpit *(ambo)*.

BENEVENTO. City in central Italy (q.v.) that suffered in the wars between Justinian I and the Ostrogoths (qq.v.). Totila finally destroyed its walls in 545. The Lombards (q.v.) occupied it from ca. 570, creating the duchy of Benevento, which included Capua and Salerno (q.v.) until the ninth century. Benevento became independent in 774, when Charlemagne (q.v.) destroyed the Lombard state. Thereafter, it switched acknowledgement of technical suzerainty from Charlemagne's successors to Byzantium (Leo VI [q.v.] reoccupied it briefly from 891–895, and again in 1042–1051), then to the Normans and to the papacy (qq.v.), as the situation demanded.

BENJAMIN OF TUDELA. Jewish traveler from Spain (q.v.) who visited Constantinople (q.v.) during the reign of Manuel I Komnenos (q.v.). His description of the city is invaluable, as are his other travel notes, including his description of his journey through central Greece (q.v.) in 1162 on his way to Constantinople.

BERBERS. *See* **MOORS.**

BERROIA. There were two important cities with this name. One is modern Aleppo in northern Syria (q.v.), which was seized by the Persians (q.v.) from 604–628, then captured by the Arabs (q.v.) in 636. It was recaptured by Nikephoros II Phokas (q.v.) from the Hamdanids (q.v.) in 962, becoming briefly a vassal state of the Byzantines. The attempts of Basil II (q.v.) to maintain control of the city ultimately failed. The other Berroia (Verroia) is the modern city of the same name in northern Greece (q.v.).

BERTHA OF SULZBACH. First wife of Manuel I (q.v.), who took the name Irene after her marriage in 1146. She was the sister-in-law of German king Conrad III (q.v.), who continued to oppose Roger II of Sicily (qq.v.). The marriage, arranged by John II (q.v.), was meant to strengthen Byzantium's (q.v.) anti-Norman alliance with Conrad III. Unfortunately for Manuel, the year after the marriage, in 1147, Conrad III went on the Second Crusade (q.v.), allowing Roger II to plunder Kerkyra, Corinth, and Thebes (qq.v.).

BERYTUS (BEIRUT). Important cultural center on the seacoast of Syria (q.v.), famous for its law school, silk factories, and production of purple dyes. Its decline began with a massive earthquake and tidal wave that leveled the city in 551, after which its law school was transferred to Sidon. Captured by the Arabs (q.v.) in 635, it was restored briefly to Byzantium (q.v.) during the reign of John I Tzimiskes (q.v.).

BESSARION. Metropolitan bishop of Nicaea (qq.v.) and pro-union participant at the Council of Ferrara-Florence (q.v.), he was a theologian, collector of Greek manuscripts, and scholar. The last attribute is the most significant, considering his influence on the Italian humanists of his day. In a sense he was a Greek who became a Latin. He emigrated to Italy (q.v.) after the Council of Ferrara-Florence, where he had a long and distinguished career as a cardinal (1439–1472) in the western church. His collection of Greek manuscripts he bestowed on the city of Venice (q.v.), where it formed the nucleus of the library of St. Mark, providing texts for the famous first editions of the Aldine press.

BIBLIOTHECA. *See* **PHOTIOS.**

BISHOP. The priest in charge of a city and its surrounding territory (i.e., the see [q.v.]) whose rank was below that of a metropolitan (q.v.). Since church organization paralleled that of the secular state, bishops and secular officials shared similar concerns and often overlapping responsibilities, e.g., the city's finances, construction projects, and food supply.

BITHYNIA. Province in northwest Asia Minor (q.v.). In the seventh century it was incorporated into the theme of Opsikion (qq.v.), and in the eighth century the part opposite Constantinople (q.v.) was given to the new theme of Optimatoi (q.v.). Its importance is explained by its close proximity to Constantinople, agricultural fertility, the military highways that traversed it, great monasteries, and important cities of Chalcedon, Nicaea, Nikomedia (its capital) Malagina, and Prousa (qq.v.). From 1206–1261 Nicaea was the capital of the Empire of Nicaea (q.v.).

BLACHERNAI. An area of Constantinople (q.v.) located in the northwest corner of the city where the sumptuous Blachernai palace, renovated and added on to by the Komnenoi emperors, was located. In the 12th century, it replaced the Great Palace (q.v.) as the home of the emperors. Robert of Clari (q.v.) describes the palace as having 200–300 rooms and 20 chapels, all decorated in gold mosaic and filled with precious treasures. The adjacent Blachernai church, restored by Romanos III (q.v.), was an important cult center dedicated to the *Theotokos* (q.v.).

BLACK SEA. Inland sea whose strategic importance had to do with its close proximity to Constantinople (q.v.), which was fed by shipments of grain and salted fish coming from the Black Sea. The Byzantine colony at Cherson, in the Crimea (qq.v.), was the place where Byzantium (q.v.) endeavored to monitor northern peoples such as the Khazars, Pechenegs, and Rus (qq.v.).

BLEMMYDES, NIKEPHOROS. The most eminent teacher and scholar of the Empire of Nicaea (q.v.); tutor of George Akropolites and Theodore II Laskaris (qq.v.). His writings include two autobiographies, written in 1264 and 1265, which are important historical sources for the period, as well as his letters to Theodore II Laskaris (q.v.).

BLUES. *See* **DEMES.**

BOEOTIA. Region of central Greece (q.v.) northwest of Athens (q.v.). It borders the Gulf of Corinth (q.v.) on its southwest, and the Strait of Europos on its east-northeast. Its metropolis was Thebes (qq.v.). The history of Byzantine Boeotia is closely related to its proximity to Athens (q.v.), which imported its grain and used it as a buffer against invasions from the north. Boeotia and Attica were part of one of the earliest themes of the Balkan Peninsula, the theme of Hellas (qq.v.), with its capital at Athens, first mentioned in 695. Among the Byzantine monuments of Boeotia is the church of the Panaghia (q.v.) at Skripou, near Orchomenos, dated to the late ninth century. Boeotia was part of the duchy of Athens and Thebes established by Othon de la Roche (q.v.) in 1205.

BOETHIUS. *See* **THEODORIC THE GREAT.**

BOGOMILS. Bulgarian dualists who denounced both the church and state as creations of an evil material world. The founder of the movement was a certain priest (*pop*) Bogomil, who began preaching during the reign (927–969) of Peter of Bulgaria (q.v.) that the world was created by the devil and must be avoided. His cosmological dualism owed much to the Paulicians (q.v.), and before that to a long tradition that stretches back to Manichaeanism (q.v.) and Gnosticism. However, unlike the Paulicians, who took up arms to defend themselves, Bogomil and his followers were pacifists who practiced civil disobedience. The movement can be viewed as a popular reaction against Byzantine cultural influence in Bulgaria (q.v.). Alexios I Komnenos (q.v.) had a Bogomil leader named Basil burned in the Hippodrome (q.v.) in an effort to suppress the movement in Constantinople (q.v.). Bogomilism spread to western Europe, where its adherents were known by many names, including Albigensians and Cathars.

BOHEMUND. Norman (q.v.) foe of Alexios I Komnenos (q.v.); son of Robert Guiscard (q.v.). He and his father directed Norman expansion eastward into Byzantine territories during the early years of the reign of Alexios I Komnenos (q.v.), capturing Dyrrachion (q.v.) in 1081. Alexios I and Bohemund fought over northern and western Greece (q.v.) until Robert Guiscard died in 1085, after which the Norman threat collapsed and Alexios regained Dyrrachion. Alexios I had every reason to be suspicious when Bohemund appeared at

Constantinople (q.v.) in 1097 as a leader of the First Crusade (q.v.). Nevertheless, Alexios I attempted to use him to Byzantine advantage, and Bohemund was inclined toward cooperation and readily took an oath of allegiance to Alexios. However, Bohemund not only refused to return Antioch (q.v.) to Alexios I, as promised, but returned to Italy (q.v.) in 1104 to organize a new Crusade, this time directed against Byzantium (q.v.). To this end he crossed the Adriatic Sea (q.v.) and besieged Dyrrachion in 1107. Bohemund's subsequent defeat by Alexios, and the allegiance he was forced to swear to the emperor (q.v.) as a result of the Treaty of Devol (q.v.), was so humiliating that he never returned to Antioch. He died in obscurity, probably in 1111. Anna Komnene (q.v.) has a memorable description of Bohemund in her *Alexiad*.

BOIOANNES, BASIL. Governor-general (*katepano* [q.v.]) of Byzantine possessions in Italy (q.v.) from 1017–1028, appointed by Basil II (q.v.). His energetic leadership helped to consolidate and defend those possessions against Lombard (q.v.) attacks and German intervention.

BONIFACE OF MONTFERRAT. Leader of the Fourth Crusade (q.v.), and subsequently marquis of the Kingdom of Thessalonike (q.v.). After the Crusaders captured Constantinople (q.v.) in 1204, Boniface seized Thessalonike and conquered Thessaly from Leo Sgouros (qq.v.), adding substantially to the territory of his new kingdom. Boniface died in 1207 in a battle against the Bulgars (q.v.), after which the Kingdom of Thessalonike found itself under assault by Theodore Komnenos Doukas of the Despotate of Epiros (qq.v.), who captured Thessalonike in 1224.

BOOK OF THE EPARCH. A manual of trade regulations, probably issued by Leo VI (q.v.). It would have served as a guide for the eparch (q.v.) of the city, whose duty it was to regulate the commercial life of the capital. Its purpose was to protect the guilds of Constantinople (qq.v.) from competition while at the same time protecting the state's right to regulate the guilds. The guilds discussed are diverse, from jewelers to sellers of soap. It is apparent that each was carefully regulated in order to protect the consumer and the state. In the case of goods such as high-quality silks, export was strictly controlled. Control of markets, production, prices, and profits was accompanied by protection and security for all guild members. No one could compete with other members of his guild, or join another guild. The net result was to stifle competition, making it almost impossible to amass the large amounts of capital needed to develop large enterprises. Secret trading activities and accumulations of capital were made difficult since all sales, even in one's own home, had to be reported to the eparch. Liutprand of Cremona (q.v.), ambassador of Otto I (q.v.), discovered this when he tried to export prohibited merchandise. The customs officials had already been informed of his purchases.

BORIS I. Khan of the Bulgars (qq.v.) from 852–889 who received baptism from Byzantium (q.v.) in 864. He took the name of Michael, after his godfather Michael III (q.v.). However, he did this only after Michael III moved an army and fleet to the borders of Bulgaria (q.v.), threatening invasion if Boris did not receive baptism. Boris renounced his alliance with the Franks (q.v.), and invited Byzantine missionaries into Bulgaria. Immediately Boris had to suppress a revolt by his nobility that aimed at restoring paganism. Deep concerns about what it meant to be a Christian prince and about the impact of Christianity on Bulgarian customs together with his desire for a separate and independent church prompted Boris's inquiries to Pope Nicholas I (q.v.), and to the Franks (in 866). Nevertheless, Boris's baptism brought Bulgaria within the ecclesiastical and cultural orbit of Byzantium, and further work in Bulgaria by disciples of Cyril and Methodios (qq.v.) helped to insure the success of the new religious experiment.

BOSPOROS. City on the Black Sea (q.v.). Along with Cherson (q.v.), it was an important center of trade where Byzantium (q.v.) traded for furs, leather, and slaves with the barbarian peoples north of the Black Sea. Located on the easternmost projection of the Crimea (q.v.), the city was ruled by the Huns (q.v.) until it sought the protection of Justin I (q.v.) in 522. In 528 its king Grod came to Constantinople (q.v.) and was baptized, whereupon Justinian I (q.v.) sent a garrison of soldiers to Bosporos and fortified its walls. However, from 576 onward Byzantium controlled Bosporos intermittently until the Mongols (q.v.) captured it (by 1240).

BOSPOROS. Strait that links the Black Sea with the Sea of Marmara (qq.v.). Constantinople (q.v.) is located where the Sea of Marmara and the Bosporos meet. The strategic importance of the Bosporos is illustrated by the fact that when Mehmed II (q.v.) prepared to besiege Constantinople, his first act was to construct in 1452 a huge fortified enclosure now called Rumeli Hisar on the west bank of the Bosporos. Its cannons were able to control all sea traffic between Constantinople and the Black Sea, hence its Turkish name at the time, Boghaz-kesen ("the cutter of the strait").

BOUCICAUT. French marshal sent by French king Charles VI in 1399 to help raise the Ottoman siege of Constantinople (qq.v.). He fought his way to the city, despite the attempt of Sultan Bayezit I (q.v.) to prevent his small fleet from passing through the Hellespont (q.v.). He brought with him 1,200 soldiers, most of them archers. He stayed there for the remainder of the year, raiding the eastern coast of the Bosporos and Sea of Marmara (qq.v.), but he achieved nothing of importance. He then encouraged Manuel II (q.v.) to seek further military aid from the West, and on 10 December 1399 Manuel II and Boucicaut left for France, where plans to send more French troops never materialized.

BOUKELLARION. Theme in Asia Minor (qq.v.) created in the eighth century from part of the theme of Opsikion (q.v.). Its capital was Ankyra (q.v.), and it derived its name from *boukellarioi,* hired private soldiers who served as bodyguards and private retainers. This reduction of the size of Opsikion was probably done by Constantine V (q.v.) in response to the revolt of Artabasdos (q.v.). Subsequently, Opsikion was further reduced by the creation of two more themes, Optimatoi and Paphlagonia (qq.v.), diminishing even more the capability of any single *strategos* (q.v.) to revolt.

BOUKOLEON. An area of Constantinople on the Sea of Marmara (qq.v.) east of the church of Sergios and Bakchos (q.v.), where the Boukoleon harbor was located, adjacent to a seaside palace whose remains are referred to as the "house of Justinian."

BOULGAROPHYGON. Site of Symeon of Bulgaria's (q.v.) major victory over a Byzantine army in 896, made possible by Symeon's previous defeat of the Hungarian troops allied with Byzantium (q.v.). The peace that resulted was contingent on Byzantium paying an annual tribute to Symeon.

BOURTZES, MICHAEL. General under Nikephoros II Phokas, John I Tzimiskes, and Basil II (qq.v.). His mostly distinguished military career (e.g., he and fellow general Peter Phokas captured Antioch [q.v.] in 969) was interspersed with treachery. He supported the murder of his benefactor Nikephoros II, later deserted Basil II for the rebel Bardas Skleros (q.v.), then did an about-face to fight with Basil II against the rebel Bardas Phokas (q.v.).

BOYAR. A member of the military aristocracy in Bulgaria or in Kievan Rus (qq.v.). Six great boyars advised the khan (q.v.) in Bulgaria. In Kievan Rus, boyars served in a prince's entourage and constituted his council.

BRACHAMIOS, PHILARETOS. *See* **GERMANIKEIA; MOPSUESTIA.**

BRANAS, ALEXIOS. Capable general who served Alexios II Komnenos, Andronikos I Komnenos, and Isaac II Angelos (qq.v.). His greatest victories were against the Normans (q.v.) in November of 1185, blunting their march toward Constantinople (q.v.) and forcing them to evacuate Thessalonike and Dyrrachion (qq.v.). In 1187 Branas revolted against Isaac II, aided by the provincial aristocracy. His siege of Constantinople ended unsuccessfully when Conrad of Montferrat (q.v.) organized a band of mostly Latin soldiery to defeat Branas's army. Branas himself was killed on the field of battle.

BRIDE SHOW. The first bride show was in 788 when the Empress Irene (q.v.) held one for her son Constantine VI (q.v.). Reminiscent of the mythic Judgment of Paris, the emperor (q.v.) presented a golden apple to the woman of his choice from several candidates previously selected with great care. Four other bride shows were held in the following century, the most famous being that of Theophilos (q.v.), who rejected Kassia in favor of Theodora (qq.v.).

BRINDISI. Important commercial port in Apulia (q.v.), and terminus of the Via Appia, the Roman road that went to Rome via Capua (qq.v.). Its chief strategic importance lay in the fact that it was a main point of embarkation for Dyrrachion (q.v.), across the Adriatic Sea (q.v.), where the Via Egnatia (q.v.) began. This fact explains the importance of Brindisi to the Normans (q.v.), and why they conquered it in 1071, making it a staging area for attacks on Dyrrachion.

BRINGAS, JOSEPH. Civil official who held various high positions for Constantine VII Porphyrogennetos and Romanos II (qq.v.). As *parakoimomenos* (q.v.) for Romanos II he managed the entire affairs of state. However, when Romanos II died an untimely death, his wife Theophano (q.v.) was caught up in a power struggle that pitted the unpopular Bringas against the famous general, Nikephoros (II) Phokas. Theophano sided with Nikephoros Phokas, as did the high civil official Basil the Nothos (q.v.). Bringas tried to defend the capital, but he had little support and was soon forced to retire to a monastery. It was a victory for the military aristocracy, one that made Nikephoros II Phokas (qq.v.) emperor, and Theophano his new wife.

BRITAIN. Roman province from 43–ca. 410, when Honorios (q.v.) informed Britain that it must see to its own defense against the Saxons, who had menaced the province's southern shore since the third century. Constantius Chlorus, father of Constantine I the Great (qq.v.), ruled Britain after defeating the usurper Allectus in 296. The decline began in 367–368 with what Ammianus Marcellinus (q.v.) calls the "barbarian conspiracy," simultaneous attacks by Picts, Scots, Attacotti, and Saxons. A Roman army from abroad was transported to Britain to restore order. In the last decade of the fourth century the raids of Picts and Scots were so sustained that Stilicho (q.v.) was forced to mount an expedition to Britain. Despite this, Honorios withdrew military forces from the island. Nevertheless, trade continued throughout the Early Middle Ages, as demonstrated by the Sutton Hoo Treasure (sixth or seventh century in date) from the ship-tomb of a king of East Anglia, consisting of exquisite silver objects of Byzantine manufacture. Byzantine cultural and religious influence persisted as well. Examples of this include Theodore of Tarsos (q.v.), archbishop of Canterbury (668–690), also Bede's *Ecclesiastical History of the English People* (731), which mentions events in faraway Constantinople (q.v.). Following the Norman conquest in 1066, Anglo-Saxon soldiers filled the ranks of the Varangian Guard (q.v.) and diplomatic activity increased. In 1400 Manuel II Palaiologos (q.v.) visited England in an attempt to secure aid against the advancing Ottomans (q.v.).

BROUSA. *See* **PROUSA.**

BRUMALIA. Pagan celebration in honor of Dionysos that continued to be celebrated in Byzantium (q.v.). It lasted for almost a month, from 24 November until the winter solstice. The carnival atmosphere included men and women in costumes and masks, dancing in the streets to songs in honor of the god. It was condemned at the Council of Trullo (q.v.) in 691–692, but Constantine V (q.v.) celebrated it at court in the following century.

BRYAS. Suburb of Constantinople across the Sea of Marmara (qq.v.), site of Theophilos's (q.v.) Bryas Palace, built around 837. Its design was based on the description of the Arab (q.v.) palaces that Patriarch John VII Grammatikos (qq.v.) had seen on his embassy to Baghdad (q.v.).

BRYENNIOS, NIKEPHOROS. Distinguished general, *doux* of Dyrrachion (qq.v.), and pretender to the throne during the reigns of Michael VIII Doukas and Nikephoros III Botaneiates (qq.v.). After failing to gain the throne in 1077 he refused to put down arms, was defeated by Alexios (I) Komnenos (q.v.), and blinded. His revolt was symptomatic of the chaotic period of decline that preceded Alexios Komnenos's own usurpation in 1081.

BRYENNIOS, NIKEPHOROS THE YOUNGER. Historian and general. He was the son (or grandson) of general Nikepheros Bryennios (q.v.), who rebelled in 1077. Nikephoros campaigned with Alexios I Komnenos (q.v.) and ended up marrying Anna Komnene (q.v.). He wrote a memoir that traces the family history of the Komneni; the most useful part of it concerns events from 1070–1079.

BUFFAVENTO CASTLE. *See* CYPRUS.

BULGARIA. Established in 681 by Asparuch (q.v.), Bulgaria became the first independent state on Byzantine soil to be recognized by Byzantium (q.v.). The Bulgars, with their capital at Pliska (qq.v.), ruled over a large indigenous population of Slavs (q.v.) and Greeks. By the 10th century Bulgars and Slavs had intermixed into a single people, referred to as Bulgarians. Bulgaria always remained a kind of third-world country on Byzantium's northern border, one that was dependent on the Byzantine economy, one subject to Byzantine cultural influences. It was also an intermittent military threat, especially under khan Krum (qq.v.), and tsars Symeon and Samuel (qq.v.). Byzantine cultural influence seemed to make headway when, in 864, khan Boris I (qq.v.) received baptism from Byzantium. This provoked a revolt of the Bulgar nobility, which defended Bulgar paganism against Byzantine encroachment. Boris suppressed the revolt, but it made him hesitant to place the Bulgarian church under Byzantine ecclesiastical administration. However, in 870 he did just that, after negotiations with Pope Nicholas I (qq.v.) broke down. In 885 Boris accepted four pupils of the brothers Cyril and Methodios (qq.v.) who provided him with a Slavonic-speaking clergy and with necessary liturgical texts. Boris struggled to preserve Church Slavonic (q.v.) as the language of the Bulgarian church in the face of Byzantine insistence on Greek. Nevertheless, resistance to Byzantine cultural and ecclesiastical hegemony remained strong in Bulgaria, as Bogomilism (q.v.) demonstrated. To some extent these contradictory forces were never resolved. "Peace" meant Byzantine occupation of the country from 1018–1185, after Basil II (q.v.) ended a series of campaigns in 1014 with a decisive victory over the forces of Samuel of Bulgaria (q.v.). Subsequently a revolt occurred in 1185, which by 1186 resulted in a new state referred to as the Second Bulgarian Empire. Its capital was at Turnovo (q.v.) and its early rulers were energetic men like Kalojan and John Asen II (qq.v.). The new state expanded into Thrace (q.v.), and, after the battle of Klokotnitsa (q.v.) in 1230, into western Macedonia (q.v.) as well. However, the growing power of Serbia (q.v.) threatened Bulgaria, and at Velbuzd (q.v.) in 1330 the Serbs destroyed a Bulgarian army. Within several decades after Velbuzd, Bulgaria's decline was made even more apparent by the Ottoman expansion into the Balkans. In 1373 Bulgaria became a vassal to the Ottomans (q.v.), and in 1393 Murad I (q.v.) conquered Bulgaria outright, burning Turnovo.

BULGARIAN TREATY. Not an actual treaty, but rather an anonymous speech dedicated to the signing of a treaty in 927 between Byzantium and Bulgaria (qq.v.). It contains some interesting but veiled allusions to an invasion by Symeon of Bulgaria (q.v.), his coronation by Nicholas I Mystikos (q.v.), and the elevation to the throne of Romanos I (q.v.). Various authors have been proposed, including Theodore Daphnopates (q.v.).

BULGARIANS. *See* **BULGARS.**

BULGARS. Pastoralists originally from central Asia, who migrated westward to the steppe (q.v.) north of the Caspian Sea, as did the Huns and the Avars (qq.v.). They must have been Turkic in origin because nearly a hundred proto-Bulgarian (i.e., pre-Christian) inscriptions survive in characters known to be Turkic. Their history in the fifth and sixth centuries is obscure, although it has been suggested that they were related to the Cotrigurs and Utigurs (qq.v.). The establishment of the Avars in Pannonia (qq.v.) by the late sixth century allowed the Bulgars to expand. One contingent aligned itself with the Lombards (q.v.), helping them to conquer Italy (q.v.).

Another contingent participated with the Avars and Slavs (qq.v.) in attacks on Thessalonike and Constantinople (qq.v.). However, most Bulgars lived north of the sea of Azov, where, in 632, one of their leaders, Kuvrat, formed a confederation of Bulgar tribes. After Kuvrat's death, the confederation disintegrated under the growing power of the Khazars (q.v.) to the east. Some Bulgars, led by Asparuch (q.v.), crossed the Danube River (q.v.), resisting an attempt by Constantine VI (q.v.) to oust them by force. In 680 they signed a treaty with Byzantium (q.v.), creating the first independent state that Byzantium recognized on its own soil. The region was already settled by Slavs, who were much more numerous, and who the Bulgars subjugated. By the ninth century, the Bulgars had virtually become Slavs, at which point this intermixed people are referred to as Bulgarians.

BURGUNDIANS. Germanic tribe that crossed the Rhine River (q.v.) in 406. In 413 the Burgundians founded the First Burgundian Kingdom (q.v.), located in Gaul (q.v.) with its capital at Worms (the setting for the great medieval German epic, the *Nibelungenlied*). In 443 a second kingdom was established south of Lake Geneva, after a defeat by the Huns (q.v.) that cost King Gundahar and 20,000 Burgundians their lives. Despite their adherence to Arianism (q.v.) until 516, when King Sigismund converted to Orthodoxy (q.v.), the Burgundians had good relations with their indigenous Roman subjects. Indeed, Roman influence was greater among the Burgundians than among any other Germanic people who settled in Roman territory, in part because of their close proximity to Italy (q.v.). However, Frankish expansion threatened the Burgundians; Clovis (q.v.) finally conquered them in 532–534.

BUSTA GALLORUM. Site in Italy (q.v.) of a famous Byzantine victory over Totila of the Ostrogoths (qq.v.) in 552. This battle was a serious blow to Ostrogothic resistance, and within two years the long Ostrogothic war was over. Narses (q.v.), the capable Byzantine general who had replaced Belisarios (q.v.) in Italy, sent the blood-stained garments of Totila to Constantinople (q.v.) as proof of his death.

BYZANTION. Byzantion was settled in the seventh century B.C. by Megarians under a leader named Byzas, hence the city's original name. Situated at the juncture of Europe and Asia, where the Sea of Marmara meets the Bosporos (qq.v.), it possessed an easily defensible topography that included a large natural harbor, the Golden Horn (q.v.). This strategic location may have influenced Constantine I's (q.v.) decision to establish in 324 at Byzantion a Christian capital for the Roman Empire; it was dedicated officially in 330. Called "New Rome," it was soon referred to as Constantinople (q.v.), i.e., "the city of Constantine." The modern terms "Byzantium," (q.v.) and "Byzantine Empire," derive from the fact that Constantinople (modern Istanbul) was formerly called Byzantion.

BYZANTIUM. The eastern Roman Empire, ruled from Constantinople from 330–1453; i.e., from the time Constantine I the Great (q.v.) dedicated his new imperial capital Constantinople (formerly called Byzantion [qq.v.]) to the conquest of Constantinople in 1453 by the Ottomans (q.v.). The term "Byzantium" is a creation of Hieronymus Wolf (1516–1580), librarian and secretary to the Fuggers in Augsburg, who published the works of Zonaras and Niketas Choniates (qq.v.). After 330, the Roman Empire evolved into a multi-ethnic, Christian, Greek-speaking state, one whose orientation after the sixth century was progressively eastward-looking. Nevertheless, the inhabitants of the empire continued to refer to themselves as Romans *(Romaioi),* and their state as *Romania.*

– C –

CAESAR. A title equivalent to emperor-designate during the tetrarchy of Diocletian (qq.v.). Subsequently it was assigned almost exclusively to the emperor's (q.v.) sons until the 11th century, after which time its conferral became more widespread (e.g., as an honorary title award to foreign rulers).

CAESAREA. Chief city of Cappadocia (q.v.). Basil the Great (q.v.), the great church father of the fourth century, was born in Caesarea and was one of the so-called Cappadocian church fathers, along with Gregory of Nazianzos and Gregory of Nyssa (qq.v.). Its strategic location astride a major road network explains its fate at the hands of Persian and Arab (qq.v.) invaders. Despite Justinian I's rebuilding of its walls, the Persians under Chosroes II (q.v.) captured and burned the city in 611. The Arabs captured it briefly in 646. In the 10th century Caesarea was the center of the Phokas family; two of them, Nikephoros II Phokas and Bardas Phokas (qq.v.), were proclaimed emperor (q.v.). The Danishmendids (q.v.) conquered the city in 1092.

CAESAREA MARITIMA. Port-city and major commercial and cultural center of northern Palestine (q.v.). It was rebuilt on a grandiose scale by Herod the Great, king of Judaea (37–4 B.C.). Caesarea Maritima still maintained its architectural and cultural splendor in the time of Eusebios (q.v.), historian of the early church, and bishop of Caesarea from 313 to his death in 339. The city was seized by the Persians (q.v.) in 604 and held by them until 628. It returned to Byzantine possession briefly before the Arabs (q.v.) conquered it around 640, after which it was not recovered.

CAESAROPAPISM. A term invented by 19th-century western European scholars to describe how the Byzantine emperor (q.v.) allegedly acted as both "caesar" (i.e., emperor) and pope (qq.v.). The term infers that, in effect, the Byzantine church was under the control of the state and that emperors could decide matters of church doctrine. This needs much qualification, but at its core is a conceptual truth, namely, how difficult it was for Byzantines to separate their church from the emperor. Emperors were conceived of as God's representatives on earth, with a duty to defend the faith and watch over the church. In practice, this often resulted in emperors appointing patriarchs (qq.v.), or forcing them to abdicate, calling church councils and occasionally confiscating church property. Nevertheless, few emperors attempted to pronounce on dogma, as did Justinian I (q.v.), and Justinian I was forced to call the Fifth Ecumenical Council to validate his Three Chapters (qq.v). Even Iconoclast (q.v.) emperors used church councils for this purpose. Emperors who defied the church at large, as happened at the Council of Lyons (q.v.) in 1274, and at the Council of Ferrara-Florence (q.v.) in 1438–1439, when the Byzantine church was subjected to the papacy (q.v.) for reasons of political expediency, faced popular opposition from both laity and clergy. If used at all, the term needs qualification, depending on the particular emperor and on the particular area of church-state relations.

CALABRIA. From about the middle of the seventh century the term no longer designated all of southern Italy (q.v.), but only the peninsula (Bruttium in antiquity) that forms the toe of the Italian "boot," separated from Sicily by the Strait of Messina (qq.v.). After the Arab conquest of Sicily in 902, Calabria was reorganized into a theme (q.v.), which continued to be threatened by Arabs and Lombards (qq.v.) in the 10th and 11th centuries. Norman (q.v.) expansion in southern Italy resulted in the conquest of Calabria by 1059. Norman suppression of the Greek rite in Calabria and Apulia (q.v.) was closely intertwined with the schism between the churches in 1054.

CALIPH. "Successor" in Arabic, the title given to the successors of the prophet Muhammad (q.v.). Caliphs had secular and spiritual authority, but not the prophetic authority of Muhammad himself. The first caliphs were Abu Bakr, Umar, Uthman (qq.v.), and Ali. The first caliphate was founded in 661 by the Umayyads (q.v.) with its capital at Damascus (q.v.). Its immediate successor was the Abbasid (q.v.) caliphate, which ruled from Baghdad.

CALIPHATE. See **CALIPH.**

CANON LAW. Canon law comprised church regulations combined with selected legislation from civil law (q.v.). Regulations issued by councils, including ecumenical councils (q.v.), comprised the core of canon law. Supplemental collections like the *nomokanones,* which included church regulations and excerpts from civil laws (e.g., from the *Corpus Juris Civilis*), were also important. Among the noteworthy later commentators were Theodore Balsamon, who defended the use of *charistikion* (q.v.), and Demetrios Chomatenos (q.v.).

CANTACUZENE, JOHN VI. See **JOHN VI KANTAKOUZENOS.**

CAPELLA PALATINA. See **ROGER II; SICILY.**

CAPITATIO-JUGATIO. Tax system inaugurated by Diocletian (q.v.) that lasted until the beginning of Justinian II's (q.v.) reign. It combined, in some fashion that is not entirely clear, both a land tax and a poll tax, as a way to assess the *annona* (q.v.) in an equitable way. Each *jugum,* a unit of land, was assessed along with each *caput* (person, livestock) who cultivated the land.

CAPPADOCIA. Region of central Asia Minor (q.v.) famous for the Cappadocian Fathers, Basil the Great, Gregory of Nazianzos, and Gregory of Nyssa (qq.v.). Its strategic importance from the seventh century onward lay in its close proximity to frontier passes through the Taurus Mountains (q.v.), from either Caesarea or Tyana (qq.v.).

The route from Tyana led to the famous Cilician Gates (q.v.). Attacks by Persians and Arabs (qq.v.) made it imperative that the theme (q.v.) system include Cappadocia, hence the themes of Anataolikon and Armeniakon (qq.v.). In the ninth century, the smaller themes of Charsianon, Cappadocia, and Kleisoura (qq.v.) were carved from these larger themes. By that time the Paulicians (q.v.) were a threat as well. Fortified refuges were built to protect the imperiled indigenous population, and Slavs (q.v.), Syrians, and Armenians were resettled to make up for civilian losses. Under these circumstances the military aristocracy increased its power, as reflected by the revolt of Bardas Phokas against Basil II (qq.v.). For a while, the extension of the eastern frontier by Basil II and his immediate predecessors took pressure off Cappadocia until the advent of the Seljuks (q.v.). The Seljuks sacked Caesarea in 1067. After the battle of Mantzikert (q.v.) in 1071 they annexed all of Cappadocia.

CAPUA. *See* **BENEVENTO.**

CARAUSIUS. *See* **CONSTANTIUS CHLORUS.**

CARIA. Region of southwest Asia Minor (q.v.). In the early fourth century it became a province whose capital and metropolis (q.v.) was the city of Aphrodisias (q.v.). In the seventh century it was incorporated into the theme of Kibyrrhaiotai (qq.v.).

CARTHAGE. The great African port-city in the Bay of Tunis that had no rival in the western Mediterranean outside Rome (qq.v.). It exported massive amounts of grain, oil, and other agricultural products, also fine pottery, including African Red Slip ware. Conquest by the Vandals (q.v.) in 439 seems to have done little to hinder its commercial exports. The Vandals made Carthage their staging area for piratical raids throughout the western Mediterranean, the pillage of Rome in 455 being the most famous of those raids. Its church suffered persecution by the Vandals, who were Arians (q.v.), but previous to the Vandals it was embroiled in controversy over Donatism (q.v.). Despite Justinian I's (q.v.) reconquest (533) and refurbishment of the city, and the subsequent creation by Maurice (q.v.) of the Exarchate (q.v.) of Carthage, the city declined in the seventh century. By the middle of the seventh century Arab raids were having an effect on the economy. In 698, Carthage fell to the Arabs (q.v.), and thus into the orbit of the new Islamic world.

CASPIAN GATES. Passes in the Caucasus Mountains north of Georgia (Iberia [q.v.]) used to defend against barbarians to the north of the Caucasus. Treaties between Byzantium and Persia (qq.v.) in 363, 422, and 442, respectively, provided for a joint defense of the passes, with Byzantium contributing a fixed sum to keep the fortifications in repair.

CASSIODORUS. Latin historian; senator and high official under Theodoric the Great (q.v.). Unfortunately, both his world chronicle (from Adam to 519) and his *History of the Goths* have not been preserved, except in an abridgment of the latter by the historian Jordanes (q.v.).

CATACOMB. An underground cemetery consisting of corridors, rooms (*cubicula*), and burial niches (*loculi* and *arcosolia*). The most famous catacombs are those around Rome (q.v.), which contain some of the earliest Christian art.

CATALAN DUCHY OF ATHENS. *See* **CATALAN GRAND COMPANY.**

CATALAN GRAND COMPANY. Soldier company of Spanish mercenaries hired by Andronikos II (q.v.). They were supposed to halt the Ottoman (q.v.) expansion in what little was left of Byzantine Asia Minor (q.v.); instead, they wreaked havoc on Byzantine territories from 1304–1309. Estimates of their numbers vary; they may have been as few as 2,000. Despite some initial success, relations with Andronikos II soon broke down, and in 1305 their leader Roger de Flor (q.v.) was assassinated. After this, the Catalans went on a rampage that eventually led them into Thrace and Macedonia (qq.v.), where they besieged monasteries on Mount Athos (q.v.), devastated Chalkidike (q.v.), and unsuccessfully besieged Thessalonike (q.v.) by land and sea. In 1309 they attacked Latin territories farther south, and in 1311 they took control of Athens, creating the Catalan duchy of Athens and Thebes (qq.v.), which lasted until 1388. The Catalan Grand Company was hardly unique as a fighting band. The Navarrese Company (q.v.) took over the Principality of Achaia (q.v.) in 1381. In 15th-century Italy such companies, led by professional generals *(condottieri),* were often employed by city-states, and just as often out of control.

CATALANS. *See* **CATALAN GRAND COMPANY.**

CATALAUNIAN FIELDS. Site of an important battle in Gaul (q.v.) in 451 between Attila and Aetius (qq.v.), Roman general of the West. Even though the armies fought to a standstill, Aetius won a strategic victory, since Attila was forced to withdraw his Huns from Gaul (q.v.).

CATHARS. *See* **BOGOMILS; PAULICIANS.**

CATHEDRA. *See* **APSE.**

CATHERINE, MONASTERY OF SAINT. Famous fortified monastery built by Justinian I (q.v.) at the base of Mount Sinai to protect the monks who tended a church on the site of the Burning Bush. Catherine of Alexandria, martyred in 305, became the monastery's patron saint in the 10th or 11th century. The walls were meant to protect against Bedouin raids, and its isolation helped to protect its icons (q.v.) and manuscripts from destruction by Iconoclasts (q.v.). It remains a repository of priceless manuscripts and icons.

CAUCASUS. Mountain system that extends 1,210 kilometers from the Black Sea (q.v.) to the Caspian Sea, acting as a divide between Asia and Europe. Through this divide were several passes, the most famous being the Caspian Gates (q.v.), which steppe (q.v.) peoples from the north could penetrate if left undefended. The defense of these passes was shared mutually by Byzantium and Persia (qq.v.) from 363–422, after which Byzantium arranged to subsidize the Persian defenses. The wars with Persia during the reign of Justinian I (q.v.) included fighting in Abchasia and Lazika (qq.v.), just south of the Caucasus (q.v.) along the Black Sea (q.v.) coast, with the aim of preventing the Persians from gaining access to the Black Sea. Justinian I (q.v.) also had an interest in the region as a way of connecting with northern trade routes to China (q.v.), thus circumventing Persian middlemen who controlled the silk (q.v.) trade.

CAVALRY. *See* **ARMY.**

CEFALÙ. *See* **ROGER II; SICILY.**

CELL. A monk's private room, or individual dwelling. The largest early Christian monastery in Egypt (q.v.), dating from the sixth to eighth centuries, was named "Kellia," which in Greek means "cells," for it was a collection of about 1,600 individual dwellings.

The *lavra* (q.v.) developed from this, as a clustering of individual cells under the direction of an archimandrite (q.v.), where monks lived solitary lives, assembling only occasionally during the week. The *koinobion* (qq.v.) was a more developed form of communal monasticism.

CEYLON. Modern Sri Lanka, called *Taprobane* by the Byzantines. The island was the focal point for goods in transit from the Far East, including pepper, cloves, silk, sandalwood, musk, and copper. Kosmas *Indikopleustes* (q.v.) describes Byzantine merchants trading there, but much of the trade was carried on by merchants from south Arabia, Axum (Abyssinia), and Persia (qq.v.). Direct Byzantine trade with Ceylon, always endangered by aggressive Persian merchants, ended in the early seventh century with the Arab conquest of ports along the Red Sea (q.v.) that had served to off-load goods destined for Byzantium (q.v.).

CHALCEDON. One of the chief cities of Bithynia (q.v.), where the important Council of Chalcedon (q.v.) was held in 451. It originated as a sister-city to Constantinople (q.v.), for both were founded by Megarian colonists in the seventh century B.C. across the Bosporos (q.v.) from each other. Persian and Arab (qq.v.) attacks on Asia Minor (q.v.) occasionally aimed at Constantinople. When they did, they inevitably imperiled Chalcedon. The Persians (q.v.) captured Chalcedon twice. It was attacked by the Arabs (q.v.) in the seventh century. In 1350 it was conquered by the Ottomans (q.v.).

CHALCEDON, COUNCIL OF. The Fourth Ecumenical Council, held in Chalcedon (q.v.) in 451. This council was presided over by the emperor Marcian (q.v.), and it marked a personal victory for his consort Pulcheria (q.v.). The 449 "Robber" Council of Ephesus (q.v.) was condemned, along with Eutyches and Dioskoros (qq.v.), and all others who supported Monophysitism (q.v.). The condemnation of Nestorianism at the Council of Ephesus (qq.v.) in 431 was reiterated, although the omission of three Nestorian writers in the condemnation would later embroil Justinian I (q.v.) in the so-called affair of the Three Chapters (q.v.). Nevertheless, the Council of Chalcedon was decisive in the formulation of Orthodoxy (q.v.), confirming the existence of Christ's dual natures, human and divine, united inseparably and unconfusedly in a single, unique Person *(hypostatis)*. It was also a serious blow to the prestige of the see of Alexandria (q.v.), which had supported Monophysitism (q.v.). This council raised the status of the patriarchate of Constantinople (qq.v.) by increasing its territory with the addition of the dioceses of Thrace, Asia, and Pontos (qq.v.), allowing it to consecrate regional metropolitans (q.v.) and hear appeals from them. It also placed under the see of Constantinople the jurisdiction of missionary areas to the north of these three provinces. In effect, Constantinople was elevated to the most powerful see in the East. Canon 28 confirmed Constantinople's ranking as second only to the see of Rome (q.v.), and increased the power of all bishops (q.v.) by putting monasteries under the authority of their local bishops.

CHALDIA. Theme (q.v.) created by Theophilos (q.v.) on the southern coast of the Black Sea (q.v.) with its capital at Trebizond. The theme of Paphlagonia (q.v.) seems to have been created at the same time. Both themes strengthened Byzantine control of the Black Sea. After 1204 it was incorporated into the Empire of Trebizond (q.v.).

CHALKE. The major ceremonial entrance to the Great Palace at Constantinople (qq.v.). The original structure was destroyed in the Nika Revolt (q.v.) of 532. It was rebuilt by Justinian I (q.v.) as an enclosed porch covered by a dome (q.v.) resting on the arches of four barrel vaults and their corner pendentives (q.v.). Its great bronze doors are probably why it was called "brazen" (*chalke*). Its dome was decorated with mosaics showing Justinian I with Theodora (q.v.) and an entourage of senators, and the emperor victorious over the Goths and Vandals (qq.v.). The exterior was replete with statues of emperors, of Belisarios (q.v.), as well as ancient statuary (four gorgon heads, two Athenian philosophers). However, it was the icon (q.v.) of Christ called Christ Chalkites that was most famous. Leo III's (q.v.) removal of this icon in 726 was the beginning of Iconoclasm (q.v.). When Iconoclasm was finally defeated in 843, the patriarch Methodios (qq.v.) asked the painter Lazaros to create a new icon of Christ to replace the one destroyed by Leo III.

CHALKIDIKE. Peninsula just southeast of Thessalonike (q.v.) that projects into the northern Aegean (q.v.). At its southernmost extremity are three smaller peninsulas, Kassandra, Sithonia (or Longos), and the easternmost one, Mount Athos (q.v.). In the 14th century Chalkidike was pillaged by the Catalan Grand Company (q.v.), then conquered by Stefan Urosh IV Dushan (q.v.), before falling prey to the Ottomans (q.v.).

CHALKOKONDYLES, LAONIKOS. Byzantine historian of the Ottoman (q.v.) conquest. Born in Athens (q.v.), he was a student of the humanist George Gemistos Plethon at Mistra (qq.v.). In his old age, sometime after 1480, he composed his magisterial history of the rise of the Ottomans, carrying it down to the capture of Lemnos (q.v.) in 1463. His sense of chronology (q.v.) leaves much to be desired, and the modern reader will not appreciate the contrived speeches (after the manner of Thucydides). However, he did use first-rate Turkish sources and his focus on an enemy of Byzantium (q.v.) is unique among Byzantine historians, of whom he was the last.

CHANCEL. *See* **BEMA.**

CHARISTIKION. The temporary leasing of a monastery's administration to a layman, or institution, by an emperor, patriarch (qq.v.), or some other state or church official. The origins of the practice are obscure; the period of Iconoclasm (q.v.) has been suggested. Nevertheless, by the 11th century the practice was well established. When it worked well, it benefited both the lay administrator and the monastery, for it promoted the economic development of monastic lands. However, some bishops complained about poor lay management, loss of revenues, and improper interference in church affairs. Patriarch Nicholas III Grammatikos (q.v.) supported these complaints, and he convinced Alexios I Komnenos (q.v.) to require that all such grants be registered with the patriarch so they could be monitored. A grant of *charistikion* differed from a grant of *pronoia* (q.v.) insofar as the former, unlike the latter, had no obligation of service.

CHARLEMAGNE. His coronation as emperor by Pope Leo III (qq.v.) at Rome (q.v.) on 25 December 800 provoked a major crisis with Byzantium (q.v.). There could be only one emperor; this everyone agreed upon. Thus, in Byzantine eyes Charlemagne was a usurper. In western eyes, he appeared differently. In 800 Irene (q.v.) sat on the throne of Byzantium, in contradiction to previous tradition that a woman could not hold sole imperial power. In effect, it could be argued that the throne was theoretically vacant. Moreover, Irene had come to power by blinding her son, Constantine VI (q.v.). Irene's support of icon (q.v.) veneration was attacked in the *Libri Carolini* (Books of Charles), issued ca. 793 by Charles's advisors to attack the Council of Nicaea (q.v.) of 787. Despite these justifications, Charlemagne attempted to improve his position by proposing marriage to Irene, but Irene was overthrown and exiled in 802 by

Nikephoros I (q.v.). Years of negotiations followed, until in 812 Charlemagne was granted the imperial title, though the Byzantines considered him emperor of the Franks (q.v.), not emperor of the Romans.

CHARLES I OF ANJOU. King of Naples and Sicily (qq.v.), the so-called Kingdom of the Two Sicilies, and brother of French king Louis IX, claimant to the Byzantine throne. Encouraged by Pope (q.v.) Clement IV to intervene in Italy for the purpose of destroying German control over the Kingdom of the Two Sicilies, Charles did so in 1266 by defeating Manfred (q.v.). The next year he was planning a Crusade, approved by Pope Clement IV, to conquer Byzantium (q.v.) and reunite the churches. After the death of Louis IX, who had disapproved of the project, Charles pressed ahead, capturing Dyrrachion (q.v.) and sending troops to the Peloponnesos (q.v.) to fight alongside William II Villehardouin (q.v.), Latin prince of Achaia (q.v.). However, when Michael VIII agreed to a union of the churches (q.v.) at the Council of Lyons in 1274 (q.v.) Charles was thwarted. Nevertheless, the election in 1281 of Pope Martin IV, a Frenchman and ardent supporter of Charles of Anjou, allowed Charles to renew his plans to attack Byzantium. These plans were spoiled in 1282 when the revolt of the Sicilian Vespers (q.v.), and intervention of Peter III of Aragon (q.v.), ejected the French from Sicily, ending the greatest threat to Byzantium in the second half of the 13th century. Charles died three years later in 1285.

CHARSIANON. The name of a fortress in Cappadocia (q.v.), subsequently of the *kleisoura* (q.v.) around it, then of the larger theme (q.v). The theme must have been created after 863, because Theophanes Continuatus (q.v.) still refers to it as a *kleisoura* in that year. By the end of the ninth century it is being called a theme; most likely it was raised to this status by Leo VI (q.v.).

CHARTOPHYLAX. A church or monastic archivist, responsible for official documents, letters, and other records. The secular counterpart was the *chartoularios* (q.v.). Alexios I Komnenos (q.v.) supported the right of the *chartophylax* of Hagia Sophia (q.v.) to preside over the patriarchal synod of Constantinople (qq.v.) in the patriarch's absence, something Patriarch Nicholas III Grammatikos (q.v.) opposed as an infringement of his own power. John XI Bekkos (q.v.) was a *chartophylax* before becoming patriarch under Michael VIII (qq.v.).

CHARTOULARIOS. Typically an archivist, or a bureaucrat responsible for keeping of records. The ecclesiastical counterpart was the *chartophylax* (q.v.). For example, the *chartoularios tou kanikleiou* (Chartulary of the Inkpot) kept the pen and purple ink used by the emperor to sign decrees, a position the eunuch Theoktistos held under Michael II (qq.v.). The term could also refer to the chief administrator of a government bureau (*sekreton* [q.v.]). From the 10th century onward some *chartoularioi* held military commands.

CHERSON. Byzantine port-city at the southwestern end of the Crimea (q.v.) that provided an important link to northern barbarian peoples, especially in terms of trade (e.g., furs, slaves, wax, honey, salted fish) and diplomacy. Its stout fortifications (rebuilt by Zeno and Justinian I [qq.v.]) and a deep natural harbor played a crucial role in relations with the Khazars and Kievan Rus (qq.v.). For example, Vladimir I (q.v.) may have been baptized in Cherson, and certainly clergy from Cherson played an important role in staffing Vladimir I's new church. It also was a place of exile for two important personages, Pope Martin I and Justinian II (qq.v.), and a place of refuge for monks fleeing Iconoclasm (q.v.). Theophilos created the theme (q.v.) of Cherson, guarded by a fortress called Sarkel (q.v.). After the Latin conquest of Constantinople in 1204, Cherson fell under the sway of the Empire of Trebizond (q.v.); its commercial importance declined when Genoa (q.v.) established trading colonies in the Crimea.

CHILIA. Port at the mouth of the Danube River on the Black Sea (qq.v.) that exported grain, honey, wax, wine, and slaves to Constantinople (q.v.). In the 13th century it changed control from the Mongols to Byzantium (qq.v.) and back again, only to pass to the Second Bulgarian Empire in the early 14th century, to Genoa (q.v.), and then to the princes of Moldavia (q.v.). The Ottomans (q.v.) captured it in 1484.

CHINA. China was known to Byzantium (q.v.) through ambassadors from the Turks (q.v.) of central Asia. It was presumably from them that in the early seventh century the historian Theophylaktos Simokattes (q.v.) obtained detailed information about Chinese culture and imperial Chinese ceremonial. Trade was also done through intermediaries. Chinese silk was imported from Persia (q.v.) until, according to Prokopios of Caesarea and Theophanes of Byzantium (qq.v.), Justinian I (q.v.) obtained its secrets from Nestorian (q.v.)

missionaries, who also managed to smuggle out some silkworm eggs. Nestorian communities were established in China, and in 1278 Andronikos II (q.v.) received an embassy of Nestorians from Beijing. Paper was a Chinese invention that found its way to Byzantium by the ninth century, via the Arabs (q.v.) who learned it from Chinese they captured in Samarkand in 751. Chinese awareness of Byzantium may have been chiefly through the Byzantine gold *solidus* (q.v.), which circulated in China, as well as through Byzantine glass, enamels, and other luxury items.

CHIONIADES, GREGORY. Astronomer (q.v.) who worked in Constantinople and Trebizond (qq.v.) until he died around 1320. He journeyed to Tabriz, capital of the Mongol ruler of Persia (q.v.), Ghazan Khan (1295–1304), where he studied Persian astronomy, and then returned to Trebizond to train students in it.

CHIOS. Island in the eastern Aegean Sea (q.v.), where the famous monastery of Nea Mone (q.v.) is located. Chios is several kilometers from the coast of Asia Minor (q.v.), and its history has often reflected the changing political fortunes of Asia Minor, and of the Aegean Sea. Thus, the Arabs (q.v.) made it one of their chain of stations on the way to their first siege of Constantinople (q.v.) in 674–678. By the end of the seventh century it was back in Byzantine hands, and in the ninth century it was included in the theme (q.v.) of the Aegean Sea. It stayed in Byzantine possession until 1204, when Byzantium was partitioned by the Fourth Crusade (qq.v.). It passed to Baldwin of Flanders (q.v.), but John (III) Vatatzes (q.v.) regained it. Although the Treaty of Nymphaion gave it to the Genoese in 1261, they lost it to a Byzantine fleet in 1329. In 1346 the Genoese reconquered Chios, and it remained in the hands of the Genoese until the Ottomans (q.v.) conquered it in 1556.

CHI RHO. Monogram of Christ's name (Christogram) used by Constantine I (q.v.). It consisted of an overlap of the first two Greek letters for *Christos,* the Chi (X) and a Rho (P). The monogram developed from the original *labarum* (q.v.), the military standard of Constantine I. The use of the monogram was *apotropaic,* which is to say to turn away evil, which is why it was used on the *labarum* (q.v.) of Constantine's armed forces.

CHITON. (Greek for "tunic".) The basic component of Byzantine dress, worn by both men and women. Chitons could be long or short, short-sleeved or long-sleeved. At court one's rank was visible by the kind of *chiton* one wore, e.g., the *kamision* indicated a lower rank than the *skaramangion* (q.v.).

CHLAMYS. (Greek for "garment".) Broadly speaking, a cloak worn fastened at the right shoulder. The great, full-length *chlamys* was a feature of the imperial court.

CHLEMOUTSI. *See* **MOREA.**

CHOIROSPHAKTES, LEO. Byzantine diplomat to the court of Symeon of Bulgaria (q.v.). His letters illuminate Byzantium's relations with Bulgaria (qq.v.) during the reign of Leo VI (q.v.). As a *magistros* under Basil I (qq.v.), and relative of Zoe Karbonipsina (q.v.), he had good connections in the imperial court. These may have helped him in 907, when he supported the revolt of Andronikos Doukas (q.v.), but they were not enough to save him in 913 when he helped Constantine Doukas (q.v.) attempt to gain the throne. He was forced into a monastery, and thus out of public life. In addition to his letters, he authored epigrams, hymns, and theological works. Arethas of Caesarea (q.v.) wrote a pamphlet attacking his alleged paganism. Altogether, he was one of the most interesting personalities of Leo VI's reign.

CHOMATENOS, DEMETRIOS. Archbishop of Ohrid (q.v.) from 1216–ca. 1236; jurist of canon law. Ohrid, situated in western Macedonia (q.v.), belonged to the despotate of Epirus in the first half of the 13th century. His literary works are the chief source for the internal history of the Despotate of Epiros (q.v.), for its relations with neighboring states during the first half of the 13th century, and for the revival of law. His coronation in Thessalonike of Theodore Komnenos Doukas as *basileus* and *autokrator* of the Romans (qq.v.) created a schism between the churches of the Despotate of Epiros and the Empire of Nicaea (q.v.) that lasted from 1228–1233. Germanos II, patriarch of Constantinople (qq.v.), condemned the coronation.

CHONIATES, MICHAEL. Metropolitan of Athens (qq.v.) from 1182–1204; pupil of Eustathios of Thessalonike and elder brother of historian Niketas Choniates (q.v.). He resisted Leo Sgouros (q.v.) during the latter's siege of Athens, but the conquest of Constantinople by the Fourth Crusade (qq.v.) forced his retirement in 1205. He is best known today for his letters, sermons, and speeches, which provide information about many topics relating to Athens and its larger environs. He paints a dismal picture of predatory tax officials, marauding pirates, greedy local magnates encroaching on peasant properties, and growing decline of agriculture in the years leading up to the Latin conquest.

CHONIATES, NIKETAS. One of the great historians of medieval Byzantium (q.v.), along with Psellos and Anna Komnene (qq.v.); he was the younger brother of Michael Choniates (q.v.). His *History* deals with the period from 1118–1206, when hostility between Byzantium and the West reached the breaking point. His work, which is particularly important for the reign of Manuel I Komnenos (q.v.) and his immediate successors, relies on eyewitnesses, including his own personal experience as a high official during the reign of Isaac II Angelos (q.v.). His treatment of the reign of John II (q.v.) may derive from the work of Kinnamos. He paints a tragic picture of the Crusader sack of Constantinople (q.v.) in 1204.

CHORA MONASTERY. *See* **CONSTANTINOPLE; METOCHITES, THEODORE.**

CHORIKIOS OF GAZA. Teacher of rhetoric in Gaza (q.v.) in the sixth century. He was a pupil of Prokopios of Gaza (q.v.), about whom he composed a funeral oration. Among his many works is a description of the church of Sts. Sergios and Stephen at Gaza, built prior to 536. The church is known only through this description.

CHOSROES I. Persian king (531–579) whose long reign was a glorious counterpart to Justinian I's (q.v.) reign. He was a reformer, like Justinian I, who revamped the internal administration of his kingdom, made the army (q.v.) more efficient and battle-ready, and patronized scholarly works. Yet it was his wars with Byzantium (q.v.) that overshadowed all else. His first war (527–532) resulted in an "everlasting" peace (requiring annual tribute to Persia [q.v.]) that allowed Justinian I the freedom to pursue his conquest of the West. However, war resumed in 540 when he invaded Syria and captured Antioch (qq.v.). A struggle over Lazika (q.v.) dragged on until a general treaty, pledging peace for 50 years, was signed in 561. Byzantine control over Lazika was confirmed, but there was little else to show for decades of intermittent warfare. War erupted in 572 when Justin II (q.v.) refused tribute to the Persians. The main theater of war was Armenia (q.v.), which Byzantium was unable to retain.

CHOSROES II. Persian king (590–628); the grandson of Chosroes I (q.v.). He inherited a war with Byzantium (q.v.) that was begun in 572 and fought mainly over control of Armenia (q.v.). The war ended in 591 after Maurice (q.v.) intervened in a civil war in Persia (q.v.) to put Chosroes II on the throne. The resulting treaty was advantageous to Byzantium, for it ended the annual tribute to Persia (q.v.), ceded to Byzantium much of Persian Armenia and eastern Mesopotamia (q.v.), and returned two important frontier towns, Dara and Martyropolis (qq.v.). However, war erupted again when Phokas (q.v.) overthrew Maurice in 602. Chosroes II invaded Mesopotamia, Syria, and Asia Minor (qq.v.), allegedly to revenge the death of Maurice. When Heraklios (q.v.) came to power in 610, the war continued in Persia's favor until Heraklios launched a counteroffensive in 622 that ended in the destruction of Persia's army at the battle of Ninevah in 627. Chosroes II was overthrown and murdered the following year.

CHRISTODOULOS OF PATMOS. *See* **PATMOS.**

CHRONICLE. A common format for the writing of history in Byzantium (qq.v.), in which events are recorded year by year. World chronicles, which begin with the creation of the world, were particularly popular, and they were often translated into Latin, Church Slavonic, and Georgian. The authorship and readership of world chronicles were most often monastic (e.g., the works of John Malalas, George Synkellos, George Hamartolos, Glykas, and the so-called *Chronicon Paschale* [qq.v.]), which extends from Adam to the year 628. However, there were other kinds of chronicles, including those that concentrate on a particular region, such as the Chronicle of Galaxeidi that focuses on the region around Galaxeidi, a town on the northern shore of the Gulf of Corinth [q.v.]), and the Chronicle of Monemvasia (q.v.) which deals with the Peloponnesos (q.v.). The conceptual difference between chronicle and history seems distinct to modern eyes, but to the Byzantines it was not.

CHRONICON PASCHALE. *See* **CHRONICLE.**

CHRONICON VENETUM. *See* **DANDALO, ANDREAS.**

CHRONOLOGY. Before the ninth century there were considerable differences in the chronologies used for the writing of history and chronicles (qq.v.). Some pre-ninth-century chronologies started with dates of regional significance, such as the beginning date of the Antiochene Era, 1 October 49 B.C. The Diocletianic Era was used only in Egypt (q.v.), and it began on 24 August 284. Only in 537, when Justinian I (q.v.) decreed that each new year would begin on 1 September, corresponding with each new Indiction (q.v.), was this matter resolved. Nevertheless, until the ninth century there was no agreed upon chronological system (based on the lunar cycle) for world chronicles. The chronicler Theophanes the Confessor (q.v.), writing in the early ninth century, used the Alexandrine reckoning, which placed Creation 5,494 years before the birth of Christ. After Theophanes, the Byzantine Era (5,508 years before Christ's birth for the age of the world) was widely accepted.

CHRYSAPHIUS. Eunuch and *praepositus sacri cubiculi* (qq.v.) who gained great influence in the court of Theodosios II (q.v.). A master of intrigue, he succeeded in removing from the palace the emperor's wife, Athenais-Eudokia, and his sister Pulcheria (qq.v.), and he made a pawn of the emperor (q.v.). He embroiled Theodosios II in a failed plot to murder Attila (q.v.), and he supported Eutyches (q.v.) by persuading the emperor to call the "Robber" Council of Ephesus (q.v.) in 449. Chrysaphius's influence ended with Theodosios II's death, when Marcian (q.v.) had him executed.

CHRYSARGYRON. A detested tax abolished in 498 by Anastasios I (q.v.) as part of his financial reforms. The loss to the treasury was made up by revenues from imperial estates, recently increased by the confiscation of property from Zeno and other Isaurians (qq.v.). In the fifth century, the tax was paid in gold and silver every four years by those doing business transactions (which included merchants, tradesmen, even beggars and prostitutes). The abolition of the tax was greeted with rejoicing in cities throughout the empire. It is not clear if Anastasios I introduced another tax, the *chrysoteleia* (q.v.) to replace the *chrysargyron*.

CHRYSOBERGES, MAXIMOS. Theologian, student of Demetrios Kydones (q.v.). He studied Kydones's translations of Thomas Aquinas (q.v.), converted to Catholicism and became a Dominican monk, as did his two brothers. In 1393, he left for the West, where Pope (q.v.) Boniface IX allowed him to celebrate the Dominican rite in Greek.

CHRYSOBERGES, NIKEPHOROS. *See* **PATRIARCHAL SCHOOL.**

CHRYSOBULL. Any important state document (e.g., treaties, laws, confirmation of privileges) affixed with the emperor's (q.v.) gold seal. The weight and size of the seal indicated the importance of the recipient. The emperor signed his own name in purple ink.

CHRYSOKOKKES, GEORGE. Fourteenth-century compiler of astronomical tables who studied in Trebizond (q.v.), where he had access to the works of Trebizond astronomer Gregory Chioniades (q.v.). He was of the generation before the most famous Palaiologan astronomers, among whom was John Abramios (q.v.). He should not be confused with the 15th-century humanist George Chrysokokkes, who taught Bessarion (q.v.).

CHRYSOLORAS, MANUEL. Diplomat and scholar during the reign of Manuel II (q.v.) who introduced to the Italian Renaissance the systematic study of Greek literature. His impact on the humanists of Florence, where he taught from 1397–1400, was immense. All of the leading Florentine humanists, including Guarino and Leonardi Bruni, were his pupils. He inculcated in them skills for translation and textual analysis and an enthusiasm for Greek literature. The texts they used came from Manuel's own library, which he brought with him. His skills as a diplomat were highly prized by Manuel II, who regarded him as a personal friend and advisor. He converted to the Latin rite, and toward the end of his life he spent two years in Rome (q.v.), dying in 1415 while attending the Council of Constance. In the Louvre Museum there is a charming portrait of Manual sketched by an anonymous 15th-century artist.

CHRYSOPOLIS. Called Scutari from the 13th century; one of the chief places to cross the Bosporos (q.v.) from Asia Minor to Constantinople (qq.v.). Inevitably any attack through Asia Minor, whether by Arabs or Turks (qq.v.), or by a rebellious thematic army, was drawn toward this Asiatic suburb of Constantinople. Not to be confused with the other Chrysopolis, a fortress in northern Greece (q.v.) near ancient Amphipolis.

CHRYSOTELEIA. The "gold tax" of Antasasios I (q.v.), the purpose of which is unclear. It may have replaced the *chrysargyron* (q.v.). Another alternative is that it commuted the *annona* (q.v.) into a cash tax, or that it may have been an irregular tax.

CHRYSOTRIKLINOS. Literally, the "Golden Hall," a circular audience hall in the Great Palace at Constantinople (qq.v.). Below its dome of 16 windows were eight vaulted niches opening to other rooms. Because important ceremonial receptions took place there, in the apse was a throne for the emperor, along with beautiful tables and chairs. A famous cabinet called the *pentapyrgion* displayed imperial treasures to further impress the guests.

CHURCH SCHISM OF 1054. This was the last of several church schisms that began with the Akkakian Schism (q.v.) of 484–519. This schism, despite its circumstantial appearance, can be seen as a culmination of a gulf between the churches that developed since the ninth century. The immediate events are the following. Humbert (q.v.), secretary and ambassador from Pope Leo IX (qq.v.) left an intemperate bull of excommunication on the altar of Hagia Sophia (q.v.) The bull was drawn up by Humbert himself, without authorization of the pope (who, in any case, had just died, making Humbert's authority technically invalid). It contained what had become the usual litany of complaints about Byzantine church doctrine and liturgical practices, e.g., Byzantine use of leavened bread in the Eucharist (rather than *azyma* [q.v.]), and a creed that did not contain the *filioque* (q.v.). That the schism was not healed has much to do with the stubborn resistance of Patriarch Michael I Keroularios (qq.v.), who reciprocated the excommunication. For the first time the Byzantine church learned of the Donation of Constantine (q.v.) and how it supported the doctrine of papal primacy (q.v.). That these differences in doctrine and liturgical practices proved enduring can be attributed in part to the Crusades. In particular the Fourth Crusade's (qq.v.) conquest of Byzantium (q.v.), which resulted in the forcible submission of Byzantine clergy to the papacy (q.v.) from 1204–1261, aroused widespread hostility against the western church. Further attempts to achieve a union of the churches (q.v.) at the Council of Lyons and at the Council of Ferrara-Florence (qq.v.) were on paper only, done to gain military aid from the West. Thus, Humbert's rash action mushroomed into something far more significant and enduring.

CHURCH SLAVONIC. The Slavonic liturgical and literary language. It includes Glagolitic (q.v.), which was invented by Constantine the Philosopher, whose monastic name was Cyril (q.v.). It also includes Cyrillic (q.v.), which may have been invented by Kliment of Ohrid (q.v.).

CIBORIUM. A free-standing domed or pyramidal canopy, resting on four or six columns, over an altar or tomb.

CILICIA. Region in southeast Asia Minor (q.v.), between the Mediterranean and the Taurus (qq.v.) mountain range whose strategic importance is related to the Cilician Gates (q.v.). From 703–965 the Arabs (q.v.) controlled Cilicia and were able to invade Asia Minor at will, despite the beacon system (q.v.) just north of the Cilician Gates that communicated to Constantinople (q.v.) the news of an Arab invasion. After the battle of Mantzikert (q.v.) in 1071, Armenians fleeing the Seljuks (q.v.) migrated to Cilicia, creating an Armenian state referred to as Lesser Armenia (ruled by the Rupenids [q.v.], then by the Hetumids from 1226–1341). John II Komnenos and Manuel I Komnenos (qq.v.) intervened in 1137 and 1159 to reestablish Byzantine control, but after the battle of Myriokephalon (q.v.) in 1176, all pretense of Byzantine control over Cilicia evaporated.

CILICIAN GATES. Narrow defile through the Taurus (q.v.) range that was the chief passage from the plain of Cilicia into Asia Minor (qq.v.). A beacon system (q.v.) at the west end signaled the appearance of Arab (q.v.) raiders. Cities situated near the Cilician Gates, such as Tyana (q.v.), were attacked repeatedly in the eighth and ninth centuries.

CIRCUS FACTIONS. Hippodrome (q.v.) factions (*demoi* in Greek, meaning "people"). They were comprised of racing fans loyal to the traditional four chariot colors: the Blues, Greens, Whites, and Reds. By the sixth century the most popular factions in Constantinople (q.v.) were the Blues and the Greens. They were noted for their tendency toward violence and hooliganism. The description of them in the *Anekdota* (Secret History) (q.v.) of Prokopios of Caesarea (qq.v.) makes them sound like thugs sporting gang colors. In addition to defending the walls of Constantinople in times of peril, they can be seen as having a political function, for they created the illusion of popular participation in government. Sometimes their riots expressed support for popular causes or were complaints against imperial abuses. This is what happened in the Nika Revolt against Justinian I (qq.v.) in 532. After the seventh century the circus factions in Constantinople were limited to strictly ceremonial functions.

CLARISSIMUS. The lowest of three senatorial ranks, the highest being *illustris* (q.v.), and the second-highest *spectabilis* (q.v.). By the middle of the sixth century *clarissimus* and *spectabilis* went out of use, in favor of new titles like *gloriosus* (q.v.) and *magnifici*.

CLAUDIAN. Claudius Claudianus (ca. 370–ca. 404), a Latin rhetorical poet from Alexandria (q.v.), who made a career for himself in the West writing panegyrics for prominent personages such as Theodosios I, Honorios, and Stilicho (qq.v.), who was Claudian's patron. Despite Claudian's great talent, and the many accolades by his contemporaries, much of his poetry seems like bombastic propaganda to modern eyes. Nevertheless, his poems are an important historical source for the first decade of Honorios's reign, including the revolt of Gildo (q.v.), the struggle between Rufinus and Eutropios, and the rise of Alaric (qq.v.).

CLERMONT, COUNCIL OF. *See* **CRUSADES.**

CLOISONNÉ. Enamel work in which the areas of colored glass are separated by thin strips (*cloisons,* in French) of gold. The term also describes a masonry technique used to decorate the exterior of churches by using bricks to frame small stone (ashlar) blocks.

CLOVIS. *See* **FRANKS; GREGORY OF TOURS.**

CODEX. "Book" in Latin. Books became popular in the fourth century, replacing the rolled manuscript. Their advantages were several. Unlike rolled manuscripts, both sides could be written on, and information could be retrieved quickly. (It is hard to imagine, for example, that the *Codex Justinianus* [q.v.] would have been as popular and useful a legal tool had it been issued in rolled manuscripts.) Once the folded pages, called quires, were stitched and bound, a book was also more durable than a rolled manuscript. Exquisite page illustrations (called illuminations or miniatures) and rich bindings could make it a thing of beauty, reflecting the owner's status. Pocket-sized *codices* of the Gospels, the Psalms (psalters [q.v.]), and biographies (*vitae* [q.v.]) of saints, encouraged meditation and prayer. Book illuminations, many with rich gold backgrounds, were highly prized and exerted a significant influence over the art of Byzantium's (q.v.) neighbors in the West, also in Armenia, Georgia, Bulgaria (e.g., the *Codex Suprasliensis*), and Rus (qq.v.). Much of what modern audiences perceive about Byzantium have come through exhibits and reproductions of its art, including illuminated books.

CODEX GREGORIANUS. A collection of imperial edicts from 196 to the reign of Diocletian (q.v.), surviving only in fragments. Nothing is known about its compiler except that his name was Gregory. It is not even clear where Gregory compiled the codex.

CODEX HERMOGENIANUS. A collection of imperial edicts, only fragments of which survive, containing chiefly edicts of Diocletian (q.v.). The author, Hermogenianus, is thought to be the same Hermogenianus who was a praetorian prefect (q.v.) in 304.

CODEX JUSTINIANUS. *See* **CORPUS JURIS CIVILIS.**

CODEX SUPRASLIENSIS. Discovered in the Suprasl monastery in Poland, this Cyrillic *menologion* (qq.v.) is the largest surviving *codex* in Old Church Slavonic (qq.v.). The original on which this copy is based is thought to date to the reign of Symeon of Bulgaria (q.v.), and it is representative of a large group of *codices* in both Cyrillic and in Glagolitic (q.v.) that originated in Bulgaria.

CODEX THEODOSIANUS. Issued jointly by Theodosios II and Valentinian III (qq.v.) in 438, and owing much to the previous *Codex Gregorianus* and *Codex Hermogenianus* (qq.v.), this collection of laws includes imperial edicts from the time of Constantine I the Great (q.v.). It is the most valuable single historical source for social conditions in Byzantium (q.v.) during the fourth and fifth centuries, and it was the basis for the later *Codex Justinianus* in the *Corpus Juris Civilis* of Justinian I (qq.v.).

COINAGE. Constantine I (q.v.) introduced the gold *nomisma* (Latin *solidus*) at 72 *nomismata* per pound of gold. The *nomisma* was used primarily by the state to pay its soldiers and bureaucrats, and in its relations with other states. Beyond that it served as a constant standard to which the other gold, silver, and copper coinage (whose types were inevitably less long-lived) were related. Thus, the gold *semissis* was half a *nomisma,* and the gold *tremissis* was a third of a *nomisma*; both types lasted until 878. The *tetarteron,* introduced by Nikephoros II Phokas (q.v.) was a quarter of a *tremissis.* The basic silver coin was the *miliaresion,* evaluated at 12 to the *nomisma.* The *follis* (q.v.), the chief copper coin introduced by

Anastasios I (q.v.), was calculated at 288 per *nomisma,* and 24 per silver *miliaresion.* Rigorous maintenance of an unadulterated *nomisma* of standard weight made it an international currency until the late 11th century, by which time it had been adulterated and was in need of reform. Alexios I Komnenos (q.v.) introduced a reformed *nomisma,* called the *hyperpyron* in 1092, an electrum worth a third of the new *nomisma,* which became the standard gold coin until the empire fell to the Ottomans (q.v.). It was much competed against by the foreign gold and silver coins that were increasingly used within the empire.

COLONUS. A hereditary tenant farmer whose status differed little from that of a slave. Though technically free and with some legal rights (e.g., they could not be ejected from their land), they were bound to the soil in perpetuity. Their freedom to marry was restricted, and they could not join the army. The origin of the *colonus* lies in the unsettled conditions of the second half of the third century. It was then that many free peasants sought the protection of wealthy landowners to whom they transferred the ownership of their land in return for physical protection and payment of their taxes. The state seems to have worked with magnates to make this informal process a legal one that made the *coloni* chattel who were tied to their land, all in the interest of securing a stable base of agricultural workers. *Coloni* were a fact of agricultural life throughout the empire from the fourth through the sixth centuries, their conditions varying from province to province. In the East, *coloni* disappear after the sixth century. In the West, the *coloni* became the serfs of the Middle Ages.

COMES. *See* **COUNT.**

COMITATENSES. Mobile field troops, as opposed to stationary frontier troops (*limitanei* [q.v.]). In practice, *comitatenses* were often based in one place so long that they became, in effect, garrison troops, like the *limitanei.* The idea of a select military retinue *(comitatus)* goes back at least to Diocletian (q.v), if not before. However, it was Constantine I the Great (q.v.) who gave the *comitatenses* a more final format, consisting of infantry and cavalry divisions, each under a *magister militum* (q.v.). Constantine I also disbanded the old Praetorian Guard, replacing it with the *scholae palatinae* (q.v.), elite troops consisting of five western and seven eastern regiments, each with about 500 soldiers. On campaigns, troops of the *scholae* *palatinae,* along with foreign auxiliaries, accompanied the *comitatenses.*

CONCH. *See* **TRICONCH.**

CONRAD III. German king (1138–1152), first of the Hohenstaufen dynasty. His alliance in 1140 with John II Komnenos against the Normans (qq.v.) was sealed with the marriage of Conrad III's sister-in-law, Bertha of Sulzbach (q.v.) to John II's son Manuel I (q.v.) in 1146. This alliance was the cornerstone of Byzantine policy in the West, a policy that aimed at destroying Norman power in southern Italy (q.v.). After 1130, when Roger II (q.v.) united Apulia and Sicily (qq.v.) into a single realm called the Kingdom of Sicily, Norman power increased substantially. Unfortunately, this policy unraveled when Conrad III advanced on Constantinople (q.v.) in 1147 with the Second Crusade (q.v.), diverting his attention from Europe, and allowing Roger II to seize Kerkyra (q.v.) and pillage Corinth, Thebes, and Euboea (qq.v.). Conrad returned from the Second Crusade too ill to carry out a combined Byzantine and German campaign against the Normans in Italy.

CONRAD OF MONTFERRAT. Caesar (q.v.) and general who defeated Alexios Branas (q.v.); famous defender of Tyre (q.v.) in 1187–1188 against the forces of Saladin (q.v.). Conrad's arrival in Constantinople (q.v.) in 1187 to marry the sister of Isaac II Angelos (q.v) grew out of Manuel I Komnenos's (q.v.) previous alliance with the Montferrat family (which dominated the region of Piedmont in northwest Italy [q.v.]) against their common enemy in Italy, Frederick I Barbarossa (q.v.). To seal the alliance, Conrad's brother Renier Montferrat married Manuel I's daughter Maria in 1180, and was given the title of caesar. When Isaac II Angelos (q.v.) came to the throne in 1185, he sought military support from all quarters, turning again to the Montferrat family, who suggested Conrad as a suitable general. Conrad's service to the empire was sealed in 1187 when he married Isaac II's sister Theodora. Soon after the wedding Alexios Branos (q.v.) revolted and Conrad's leadership was crucial in crushing the revolt. However, almost immediately after that he abandoned Byzantium (q.v.), sailing to Tyre to organize the defense of that city against Saladin (q.v.). His adventures made him famous in the West, as attested by the lengthy account of them in the work of Robert of Clari (q.v.)

CONSISTORIUM. An imperial council that advised the emperor on important legislation and policy. Created by Constantine I the Great (q.v.), its permanent members included a number of the highest officials in the central government, e.g., the *magister officiorum*, the *comes sacrarum largitionum*, and the *quaester sacri palatii* (qq.v.). Its normal duties included consultation with the emperor about legislation and policy matters. The term *silentium* (q.v.) was given to its meetings. There were also ceremonial ones that included the reception of foreign dignitaries, and judicial functions that included trying important cases such as treason. It played no serious role in matters of state beyond the reign of Justinian I (q.v.), who ended the *consistorium* as a select advisory council.

CONSTANS I. Youngest son of Constantine I the Great and Fausta (qq.v.); also emperor of the western half of the empire after 340, the year when his brother and co-ruler Constantine II (q.v.) was killed while invading Constans's territory. He was a firm supporter of the Nicene Creed and opponent of Arianism (q.v.). He was killed in 350 fighting against the usurper Magnentius (q.v.)

CONSTANS II. Called "Pogonatos" ("the bearded"), Constans II was emperor from 641–668, when Arab expansion was continuing at a dizzying pace. In 642 the Arabs captured Alexandria (qq.v.), the same year they attacked Armenia (q.v.). In 647 the Arabs entered Asia Minor (q.v.) in force, raiding Cappadocia and capturing Caesarea (qq.v.). In 649 they raided Cyprus, and they pillaged Rhodes, Crete (qq.v.), and Cos in 654. In the next year the Arabs defeated a Byzantine fleet in a sea battle in which Constans II escaped only because he changed clothes with a seaman (who died while taking the brunt of the Arab attack). As if by miracle, the Arab assault stalled from 656–661 due to a civil war in the caliphate between Muawiya (q.v.) and Ali, the son-in-law of Muhammad the Prophet (q.v.). The respite allowed Constans II to turn his attention to Greece (q.v.), where, in 658, he attacked "sklavinia" (q.v.) (perhaps Macedonia [q.v.]). The Slavs (q.v.) whom he captured he resettled in Asia Minor (q.v.), where they were enrolled as troops. This experiment had mixed success, considering that in 665 some 5,000 Slav soldiers deserted to the Arabs. In 663 he opened up an inconclusive campaign against the Lombards (q.v.), after which he went to Rome (q.v.) where he was received by Pope (q.v.) Vitalian, a successor to Pope Martin I (q.v.). Constans II had exiled Pope Martin to Cherson (q.v.) in 654 after the pope (q.v.) condemned the imperial edict *(Typos)* of

648 that sought to pacify the opponents of Monotheletism (q.v.). Maximos the Confessor [q.v.], who supported Pope Martin, was also exiled. He then retired to Syracuse in Sicily (qq.v.), whose defenses he intended to strengthen against Arab attacks, and where he considered moving the imperial capital. In 668 after having survived many rebellions, he was murdered by a member of his entourage.

CONSTANTIA (SALAMIS). *See* **CYPRUS; EPIPHANIOS.**

CONSTANTINE. Usurper who from 407–411 controlled Britain (q.v.), eastern Gaul (q.v.) (including Mosel, Trier, Lyons, and Arles), and who defended the Rhine River (q.v.) successfully from barbarian incursions. In 408 he occupied Spain (q.v.) and in 409 Honorios (q.v.), preoccupied by Alaric (q.v.), was forced to recognize him as a legitimate emperor (q.v.). However, Honorios's real intention was to destroy the usurper, which he did in 411 when he had Constantine assassinated.

CONSTANTINE I THE GREAT. First Christian emperor (q.v.), who reigned from 306–337. Proclaimed augustus (q.v.) in York in 306 by his dying father Constantius Chlorus (q.v.), Constantine gained control of the West by defeating Maxentius in Rome (qq.v.) at the battle of the Milvian Bridge in 312. In 324 he gained control of the entire empire when he defeated his eastern rival Licinius (q.v.) at Chrysopolis in Bithynia (qq.v.). He converted to Christianity (in 312 according to the famous story in the *Vita Constantini* [q.v.] by Eusebios of Caesarea [q.v.]), and he thereafter showed a favoritism to the Christian church (e.g., he constructed churches at state expense and allowed the church to accept bequests) that put Christianity on the road to becoming the state religion by the end of the fourth century. The role he played in church affairs, especially in the controversies over Donatism and Arianism (qq.v.), became a prototype for future church-state relations. This was seen especially at the Council of Nicaea (q.v.). The new imperial residence at Byzantion (q.v.), founded in 324, would soon acquire the name Constantinople (q.v.), the "city of Constantine," and become the capital of the eastern half of the empire. Constantine perfected the administrative reforms of Diocletian (q.v.) by dividing the empire into four prefectures (q.v.), each administered by a praetorian prefect (q.v.), whose duties were only civil. Dioceses and provinces (qq.v.) remained as before. However, he separated the civil and military functions in each prefecture (q.v.); now each praetorian prefect had a *magistri militum* (qq.v.) in charge of military forces. In 312, he disbanded the old Praetorian Guard, greatly enlarging the mobile field forces, the *comitatenses* (q.v.). He reformed the currency, issuing a gold *solidus* (q.v.) that remained the "dollar" of the Mediterranean (q.v.) for almost a millennium. He was baptized in 337 as he lay dying by Eusebios of Nikomedia (q.v.), having changed the Roman Empire more than any emperor since its founder Augustus.

CONSTANTINE II. Eldest son of Constantine I the Great (q.v.) and co-emperor in the West with his brother Constans I (q.v.) from 337 until 340. A staunch opponent of Arianism (q.v.), he ruled over Gaul, Spain, and Britain (qq.v.). In 340 he invaded Italy (q.v.), ruled over by Constans I, and he was killed in battle, leaving Constans I sole ruler in the West.

CONSTANTINE III. Co-emperor (641) with Heraklonas (q.v.). He was the son of Herakleios (q.v.) by the latter's first wife Eudokia, and father of future Constans II (q.v.). His stepmother Martina (q.v.) opposed him, favoring her own son Heraklonas (q.v.). He died on 25 May 641, apparently of tuberculosis, after reigning about three months.

CONSTANTINE III LEICHOUDES. Imperial counselor, patriarch of Constantinople (qq.v.) from 1059–1063. He directed state affairs as the chief administrator (*mesazon* [q.v.]) for Constantine IX (q.v.), aided by a small circle of brilliant friends who included John Mauropous, Michael Psellos, and John Xiphilinus (qq.v.). In 1059 Isaac I Komnenos (q.v.) made him patriarch, a move that failed to gain Isaac the control over the church that he desired, in part due to the enduring hostility of those who adored the previous patriarch Michael I Kieroularios (q.v.). As patriarch, Leichoudes's chief policy was a failed attempt to force the Syrian and Armenian Monophysites (q.v.) into communion with Constantinople.

CONSTANTINE IV. Emperor (q.v.) from 668–685. It was during his reign that the Arabs (q.v.) first besieged Constantinople (q.v.) from 674–678. At the siege "Greek fire" (q.v.) played an important role in defeating the Arab fleet. Failing to take the capital, and facing defeats in Asia Minor (q.v.), the caliph Muawiya (qq.v.) signed a 30-year peace treaty with Byzantium (q.v.). The siege (and the later one in 717–718) saved Byzantium, and perhaps all of European civilization, from Islamic conquest. Nevertheless, the Arabs continued to make steady advances along the coast of North Africa (q.v.), and Byzantium suffered considerably from other foes, including Asparuch, khan of the Bulgars (qq.v.), whose encroachments south of the Danube River (q.v.) Constantine IV was forced to recognize. In reality, the region the Bulgars occupied had long ago been settled by Slavs (q.v.) who were hardly under Byzantine control. Also of significance during his reign was the Sixth Ecumenical Council (q.v.), which condemned Monotheletism (q.v.) and reconciled the eastern and western churches.

CONSTANTINE V. Emperor (q.v.) from 741–775; ruthless proponent of Iconoclasm (q.v.) and military campaigner. His reign had scarcely begun when Artabasdos (q.v.), *strategos* of the Armeniakon (qq.v.), revolted, seizing Constantinople (q.v.) and restoring the veneration of icons (q.v.). After regaining power in November 743, he was preoccupied with campaigning against the Arabs (q.v.). From 746–752 he won a string of victories, aided by a civil war in the Umayyad Caliphate (q.v.) that ended in 750 when the new Abbasid Caliphate (qq.v.) came to power. In 754 at Hiera (q.v.) Constantine V officiated over a church council comprised of supporters of Iconoclasm, which condemned Iconophiles (q.v.) and the idolatrous worship of icons. A severe persecution began, aided by imperial officials like Michael Lachanodrakon (q.v.). Iconophiles were everywhere persecuted, but monasteries were especially singled out, and their properties confiscated and sold. Public religious images were destroyed, including those at the popular church dedicated to the Virgin at Blachernai (q.v.). Relics (q.v.) were also destroyed. Veneration was only allowed for the True Cross (q.v.). Much popular hatred was aroused, and a rumor circulated by his enemies that Constantine V had defecated in his baptismal font, resulting in his popular nickname *kopronymos* ("named in dung"). In 756 hostilies resumed with the Bulgars (q.v.), which continued until the end of his reign when he died on campaign against khan Telerig (qq.v.). However, despite his victories against the Arabs and Bulgars, Constantine V neglected Italy (q.v.) to his peril, for the Lombards seized Ravenna (qq.v.) in 751, extinguishing the Exarchate (q.v.) of Ravenna. It is no wonder that the papacy (q.v.), alienated by Iconoclasm and by the previous removal by Leo III (q.v.) of several of its western dioceses (q.v.) to the patriarchate of Constantinople (q.v.), looked to the Franks (q.v.) for protection. In 754, with a Lombard army threatening Rome (q.v.), Pope (q.v.) Stephen II journeyed north across the Alps to confirm Pippin III as king of the Franks and to award him with the rank of Exarch of Ravenna, a title which only the emperor had previously conferred. This set the stage for the subsequent papal coronation of Charlemagne (q.v.).

CONSTANTINE VI. Emperor (q.v.) from 780 to 797, mostly in name only. The son of Leo IV and Irene (qq.v.), he was only 10 when Leo IV died suddenly in 780. Irene and her chief advisor Staurakios (q.v.) ran the affairs of state; her chief goal was to restore the veneration of icons (q.v.). She did this, after much preparation, at the Seventh Ecumenical Council at Nicaea (qq.v.) in 787. Thereafter, the history of his reign was dominated by the conflict with Irene. The conflict came to a head in 790 when, with the aid of Michael Lachanodrakon (q.v.), Constantine forced Irene to leave the palace. However, once in power he became unpopular. His defeats by the Bulgars and Arabs (qq.v.) inspired conspiracies and rebellion in the army. He blinded his uncle, the caesar (q.v.) Nikephoros, who was at the center of one conspiracy. The blinding of Alexios Mousele, the *droungrios tes viglas* (q.v.), provoked another rebellion in the Armeniakon (q.v.). Constantine's position was further eroded by the so-called Moechian Controversy (q.v.), engendered by his marriage to his mistress Theodote after he divorced his wife Maria. By 797, Constantine was so unpopular that Irene was able to depose him, blinding him in the very purple room (the Porphyra) where he was born.

CONSTANTINE VII PORPHYROGENNETOS. Emperor (q.v.) from 945–959; writer and promoter of artistic and scholarly projects. He was co-emperor with Leo VI (q.v.) in 908, but then bypassed for almost 40 years. At first, due to his youth, his uncle Alexander (q.v.) ran the affairs of state. Subsequently there was a regency headed by Patriarch Nicholas I Mystikos (q.v.), then by the dowager empress Zoe Karbonopsina (q.v.), who was forced to yield to Romanos I (q.v.). As sole ruler, his external policy was dominated by warfare with the Arabs (q.v.), with mixed results. An attempt in 949 to dislodge the Arabs in Crete (q.v.) failed. Germanikeia (q.v.) was captured in the same year, only to be recaptured in 953 by Sayf al-Dawla (q.v.). Generals (and future emperors) Nikephoros (II) Phokas and John (I) Tzimiskes (qq.v.) won victories from 954 to 958, the year Tzimiskes captured Samosata (q.v.). Constantine VII did not significantly modify the basic thrust of Romanos I's (q.v.) agrarian policy. For example, he required the *dynatoi* (q.v.) to restore all peasant lands acquired since 945 without compensation, and he commanded that soldiers' properties not be alienated. However, for land sales made between 934–945, peasants had to repay the purchase price, which was a concession to the magnates. He received various foreign embassies of note, including one from Olga, princess of Kiev (qq.v.). Embassies were exchanged with the court of Otto I the Great (q.v.), and with the Muslim court at Cordoba (q.v.). Constantine VII is best known for his own literary works, which include *De administrando imperio, De thematibus,* and *De cerimoniis* (qq.v.). Also worth noting is his support of the minor arts (e.g., manuscript illustration and carved ivories), and for scholarly compilations and encyclopedias like the *Geoponika* (q.v.), for his chief interest was cataloging and sorting information. Even his own *asekretis* (q.v.), Constantine of Rhodes (q.v.), described the Church of the Holy Apostles in Constantinople (qq.v.) by cataloging its elements. However, it is particularly in the realm of historical writing, which had declined during the preceding century, that he created an enduring legacy. Genesios, Theodore Daphnopates, and the author of an anonymous historical work, called "Theophanes Continuatus" (qq.v.), were among the historians associated with his court. Other luminaries he appointed as state officials, or as professors in the palace school. Constantine VII remains Byzantium's preeminent scholar-emperor, as well as one of its great patrons of scholarship. However, not among his legacies is the palace in Constantinople referred to as Tekfur; it is now dated to the Palaiologan (q.v.) period.

CONSTANTINE VIII. Emperor (q.v.) from 1025–1028. His brother and predecessor Basil II (q.v.) set a high standard that Constantine VIII failed to emulate. Constantine was interested in little beyond chariot racing in the Hippodrome (q.v.). His legacy, so to speak, lay in his two daughters, Theodora and Zoe (qq.v.). Both played important roles in the Byzantine court for the next quarter century, especially Zoe.

CONSTANTINE IX MONOMACHOS. Emperor (q.v.) from 1042–1055. Later Byzantine (and modern) historians have condemned his disbandment of the border theme of Iberia (qq.v.). He is seen as having further undermined the themes by limiting the civil authority of military governors in favor of appointed judges. His two serious military revolts, by generals George Maniakes and Leo Tornikios (qq.v.), owed something to dissatisfaction over these changes in policy. Nevertheless, Constantine IX was a reformer of the empire's internal administration. He desired a more professional civil bureaucracy, to which end he founded a new school of law, headed by future patriarch John (VIII) Xiphilinos (qq.v.). Xiphilinos was one of a circle of intellectuals who graced Constantine's court who included Michael Psellos, John Mauropous, and yet another future patriarch Constantine (III) Leichoudes (qq.v.). Whatever his good intentions, neglect of the armed forces, indeed their systematic reduction, was foolhardy. The acquisition of Ani from Gagik II (qq.v.) and the defeat of the Rus (q.v.) fleet sent against Constantinople (q.v.) in 1043 by Jaroslav of Kiev (qq.v.) were small victories compared to the threat of new enemies on the empire's borders. In the West, the Normans (q.v.) began their conquest of southern Italy. In the East, the Seljuks under Tughrul Beg (qqv.) raided eastern Asia Minor. In the Balkan Peninsula (q.v.) the Pechenegs (q.v.) crossed the Danube (q.v.) in 1048 and pillaged Thrace (q.v.). The portrait of Constantine IX and Zoe (q.v.) drawn by Michael Psellos in his *Chronographia* is of an emperor who thought of imperial position as an opportunity for rest and relaxation. He spent lavishly on new monastic endowments (e.g., on the *Nea Mone* [q.v.]), on his mistress Skleraina (q.v.), and on gifts to curry favor with the great families. Money was obtained by reducing funds for the army (q.v.), and by debasing the *nomisma* (q.v.). In the church schism of 1054 (q.v.), Constantine had hoped for compromise, for he needed a papal alliance against the Normans in southern Italy. His capitulation to patriarch Michael I Keroularios (q.v.), who resisted any compromise, illustrates Constantine's weakness before the power of the church. Although he tried to be an idealist and reformer, his efforts largely turned to dust when faced with the power of the church and of powerful aristocratic families (*dynatoi* [q.v.]). All the while, new enemies gathered strength along the borders of Byzantium (q.v.).

CONSTANTINE X DOUKAS. Emperor (q.v.) from 1059–1067, whose incompetent administration and neglect of the army (q.v.) opened up Asia Minor and the Balkan Peninsula (qq.v.) to new invaders. His accession, engineered by Michael Psellos (q.v.), can be seen as a reaction against the reforms of the previous emperor, Isaac I Komnenos (q.v.). He utterly neglected the army, while spending lavishly on his court, on the civil service, and on gifts to monasteries and to foreign rulers. Meanwhile, under Robert Guiscard (q.v.), the Normans (q.v.) by 1059 had conquered all of southern Italy (q.v.); by the time of Constantine X's death in 1067 they were four years away from conquering Bari (q.v.). When Uzes (q.v.) invaded Byzantine Macedonia (q.v.) in 1064–1065 Constantine X could only raise 150 soldiers to oppose them. Fortunately, the plague did to the Uzes what Byzantine arms could not do. However, in the East the military situation was grave. In 1064 the Seljuks under Alp Arsan (qq.v.) invaded Armenia (q.v.), capturing Ani (q.v.), whose garrison had been depleted by cutbacks. The defenses of Asia Minor began to crumble with the Seljuk sack of Melitene (q.v.) in 1058. In effect, Constantine X's neglect of the army laid the foundation for the Seljuk victory at Mantzikert (q.v.) in 1071.

CONSTANTINE XI PALAIOLOGOS. Byzantium's last emperor (q.v.) (1449–1453), who died when the Ottomans captured Constantinople (qq.v.) on 29 May 1453. He was a man of energy and integrity who did what he could to stave off the Ottomans. Previous to his coronation at Mistra (q.v.) in 1449, he ruled the Morea as despot (qq.v.), with his brothers Theodore II and Thomas Palaiologos (qq.v.). He rebuilt the Hexamilion (q.v.) in 1444, which the Ottomans had destroyed in 1423. He then seized Athens and Thebes (qq.v.). These actions provoked a response from Sultan Murad II (q.v.), who invaded the Morea in 1446, making Constantine XI his tributary. Once emperor, Constantine XI had no choice but to beg the western powers for military aid. Knowing that the prerequisite for this was the union of the churches (q.v.), on 12 December 1452, in Hagia Sophia (q.v.), the Roman mass was celebrated and the previously rejected decrees of the Council of Ferrara-Florence (q.v.) were reaffirmed, though not in any way implemented due to popular hostility. The western powers were too divided to offer serious help and Mehmed II (q.v.) captured Constantinople after a siege of six weeks. Constantine XI was last seen fighting near the Gate of St. Romanos, where the battle was most intense, having discarded his imperial insignia so that his body might not be identified and made an Ottoman trophy.

CONSTANTINE BODIN. King of Zeta (Diokleia [q.v.]); proclaimed tsar of Bulgaria (qq.v.) in 1072. He was the grandson of Stefan Voislav (q.v.), who had rebelled against Byzantine control around 1034, and son of Michael Voislav, whose anti-Byzantine policy along the south Adriatic (q.v.) coast culminated in 1077, when his Serbian kingdom was recognized by the papacy (q.v.). In 1072 Bodin joined the Bulgar rebellion of George Voitech, and he was acclaimed tsar at Prizren. However, Alexios I Komnenos (q.v.) soon reestablished Byzantine power and captured Bodin. Eventually he escaped and returned to rule over Diokleia (around 1082). From

1085–1094, Alexios I waged war against Diokleia, capturing Bodin again and annexing Zeta.

CONSTANTINE OF RHODES. Poet, and *asekretis* of Constantine VII (qq.v.). His poetical description of the Church of the Holy Apostles in Constantinople (qq.v.) is of some importance, given the church's utter destruction by Mehmed II (q.v.).

CONSTANTINE THE PHILOSOPHER. *See* **CYRIL AND METHODIOS.**

CONSTANTINE TICH. *See* **IVAJLO.**

CONSTANTINOPLE (Modern Istanbul). Capital of Byzantium (q.v.) from 324–1453, except for 1204–1261 when it was the capital of a Latin Empire founded by the Fourth Crusade (qq.v.). Constantine I (q.v.)'s motives in establishing the new capital in 324 (dedicated in 330) are not known. He may have viewed it initially as a new imperial residence, similar to those in Milan and Nicomedia (qq.v.). He may have seen it as a Christian capital, untainted by Rome's (q.v.) long association with paganism. In any case, he called it "New Rome," though people preferred Constantinople (literally "City of Constantine"), the name that stuck. Certainly its strategic importance must have been obvious to him, for it lay at the end of the Via Egnatia (q.v.) where one crosses from Europe to Asia Minor (q.v.). From Constantinople one had access north through the Bosporos to the Black Sea (qq.v.), and south through the Hellespont to the Aegean Sea (qq.v.). Once fortified with a land wall, which Constantine did, the city was difficult to take, for it had to be besieged by sea as well. It has a superb natural harbor called the Golden Horn (q.v.), which itself was fortified by means of a chain across its entrance. The massive land walls of Theodosios II (q.v.), stretching some six kilometers, were the most impressive urban fortifications of the Middle Ages. Its triple-defenses involved a deep ditch, with successive outer and inner walls. Indeed, the developed city had no real western competitors in terms of its size, fortifications, sumptuous churches, and public monuments. This explains Geoffrey Villehardouin's (q.v.) description of his fellow Crusaders being struck dumb at their first sight of Constantinople (in 1203). Robert of Clari's (q.v.) description betrays this same sense of wonderment at a city whose population may have been ca. 300,000. Venice (q.v.), the largest city in the West at the time, may have had a population of around 80,000 (Paris not more than around 20,000). What Robert of Clari describes is a city without parallel in Christendom, one filled with both Christian and ancient monuments. Its central street, the Mese, ended at the Great Palace (qq.v.), around which were situated the Hippodrome, the Augustaion (qq.v.), the baths of Zeuxippus, the underground Basilike cistern, and the churches of Hagia Sophia, St. Irene, and Sts. Sergios and Bakchos (qq.v.). Elsewhere in the city, at every turn, were monasteries and churches, e.g., the Stoudios Monastery, the Chora Monastery. Constantinople's importance to every aspect of the history of Byzantium cannot be overemphasized. The city was a bastion of resistance against Arab expansion, in which regard the history of European civilization might have been dramatically different had the Arab sieges of Constantinople in 674–678, and in 717–718, succeeded. Ironically, the most destructive siege of Constantinople came in 1204, when Christian knights of the Fourth Crusade (q.v.) sacked Constantinople and partitioned Byzantium. Constantinople's preeminent role in preserving ancient Greco-Roman civilization lasted until the city's final conquest by the Ottomans (q.v.) on 29 May 1453.

CONSTANTINOPLE, FIFTH ECUMENICAL COUNCIL AT. Ecumenical council (q.v.) convened by Justinian I (q.v.) in 553 to condemn the Nestorianism (q.v.) of the Three Chapters (q.v.). Justinian's ulterior motive was to attempt to gain Monophysite (q.v.) adherence to the previous Council of Chalcedon (q.v.). In this he failed. Justinian's actions in these matters, which include his treatment of Pope Vigilius (qq.v.), can be seen as an example of caesaropapism (q.v.).

CONSTANTINOPLE, SIXTH ECUMENICAL COUNCIL AT. Held in 680–681, the ecumenical council (q.v.) condemned Monotheletism (q.v.), and the related heresy of Monoenergism (qq.v.). The subsequent Council in Trullo (q.v.) completed the work of this council in 691–692.

CONSTANTINOPLE, UNIVERSITY OF. *See* **EDUCATION; THEODOSIOS II.**

CONSTANTIUS II. Son of Constantine I the Great and Fausta (qq.v.), caesar (q.v.) from 324–337, augustus (q.v.) after 337, and sole emperor (q.v.) from 353–361. After Constantine I's death, Constantius ruled with his two brothers. Constantine II (q.v.) died in 340, and

Constans I (q.v.) was killed in 350 fighting the usurper Magnentius (q.v.). Constantius II became undisputed emperor after defeating Magnentius in 353. He raised Gallus (q.v.) to caesar in 351, but executed him in 354. His promotion of Julian (q.v.) as caesar in 355 proved his undoing, for Julian rebelled against him. Constantius died in Cilicia (q.v.) in 361 while marching against Julian. To some extent his reign is most noteworthy for his promotion of Arianism (q.v.).

CONSTANTIUS CHLORUS. Member of the tetrarchy (q.v.); father of Constantine I the Great (q.v.). A career army officer, he fought in Syria (q.v.) under Aurelian, was governor of Dalmatia (q.v.), and by 288 was praetorian prefect in Gaul (qq.v.) of the emperor (q.v.) Maximian. In 289 he had married Maximian's daughter Theodora, divorcing his previous wife Helena, the mother of the future Constantine I the Great (q.v.). In 293 Diocletian (q.v.) made him caesar (q.v.) and part of the tetrarchy. Constantius demonstrated his generalship by driving the usurper Carausius from Gaul (q.v.), and then reclaiming Britain (q.v.) from the rebel Allectus in 296. In 305, when Diocletian abdicated, Constantius was elevated to augustus (q.v.) of the West, with Spain (q.v.) added to his jurisdiction. He venerated *sol invictus* (the unconquerable sun), but he did not persecute Christians during the Great Persecution (q.v.) of 303–311. He died in York in 306, with his son Constantine by his side. Constantine was proclaimed by his troops as the new augustus of the West, in response to Constantius's last request.

CONSUL. In the Roman Republic, two annual consuls were the chief magistrates of the Roman state. By the time Justinian I (q.v.) allowed the office to lapse (in 542) it had been an obsolete honorific title for centuries. It was an office that only the very wealthiest citizens could afford to accept, because each consul was expected to spend huge sums on public spectacles like Hippodrome (q.v.) races, banquets, and gifts of silver and gold. Numerous examples of one such kind of gift, the consular diptych (q.v.), have survived.

COPTIC. The term can refer to the language of the Copts (q.v.) as well as the script in which it is written. Coptic originated in the first century A.D., using the Greek alphabet supplemented by seven signs from the demotic. Today Coptic is used only in the liturgy of the Egyptian Christian church. The term can also refer to the entire culture of Christian Egypt (q.v.).

COPTS. The indigenous population of Egypt (q.v.) who spoke Coptic (q.v.). The term derives from an Arabic corruption of the Greek word for Egyptian *(Aigyptioi)*. In Byzantine times most of the Copts were Monophysites (q.v.) belonging to the Coptic church, which never subscribed to the decrees of the Council of Chalcedon (q.v.).

CORDOBA. City in southern Spain (q.v.) that was home to bishop (q.v.) Hosios, the most influential member of Constantine I's (q.v.) entourage. Attacks on the city by the Visigoths (q.v.) began in 550, prompting Justinian I (q.v.) to send an expeditionary force to southern Spain. Nevertheless, Cordoba fell to the Visigoths in 572. It was subsequently conquered by the Arabs (q.v.) in 711 when they conquered the Visigothic kingdom of Toledo. From 756–1031 it was capital of the caliphate (q.v.) of Cordoba, which received embassies from both Theophilos and Constantine VII (qq.v.). Uprisings against the caliph resulted in the expulsion of 15,000 of its citizens to Alexandria (q.v.) in 815; in 827 they were ejected from Alexandria by a general of the caliph Mamun (q.v.). The exiles chose Crete (q.v.), which they wrested from Byzantine control. Byzantine embassies to Cordoba were sent by Theophilos (q.v.) in 830, and by Constantine VII (q.v.) in 949.

CORFU. *See* **KERKYRA.**

CORINTH. One of the chief cities of medieval Greece (q.v.), situated in the northeast Peloponnesos (q.v.) on the Gulf of Corinth, overlooked by a powerful *kastron* (q.v.) called Acrocorinth. The city's location, near the Isthmus of Corinth, coupled with its two harbors, made it a center of commerce; e.g., in the 12th century it had a large textile industry (of silk, cotton, linen). It was also the object of attack for invaders of the Peloponnesos, e.g., the Visigoths under Alaric (qq.v.) in 396, and Roger II (q.v.) in 1147.

CORIPPUS. African poet; author of the *Johannis,* an epic poem in eight books of Latin hexameters that extols the deeds of John Troglita against the Moors (qq.v.) in 546–548. The *Johannis* is the chief source for Troglita's campaign, besides including interesting information about the Moors. Corippus wrote another Latin panegyric composed in 565 and dedicated to Justin II (q.v.), important for its description of court ceremonial.

CORPUS JURIS CIVILIS *(Corpus of Civil Law)*. The collective legislative work of Justinian I (q.v.). It consists of the Codex *(Codex Justinianus)*, the Digest *(Digestum,* or *Pandectae)*, the Institutes *(Institutiones)*, and the Novels (qq.v.) *(Novellae Consitutiones,* meaning New Laws). The work was begun by a commission of 10 legal experts assembled in 528 and headed by the greatest legal mind of the day, Tribonian (q.v.). They worked with astonishing speed. In 529 they issued the *Codex Justinianus,* the collection of 4,562 imperial edicts from Hadrian to Justinian I that replaced the older *Codex Gregorianus, Codex Hermogenianus,* and *Codex Theodosianus* (qq.v.). It was subsequently revised, in the light of further work by Tribonian, and reissued in 534. The Digest, a compendium of legal opinions by famous Roman jurists, was issued in 533, as was the Institutes, a handbook to help guide law students through the Codex and Digest. The Novels, the final part of Justinian I's work, consist of those imperial edicts issued after 534, down to the end of Justinian's reign in 565. Unlike previous legal works that were written in Latin, the Novels were issued in Greek, the language of the East. The *Corpus Juris Civilis* not only preserved Roman law but provided the basis of law for emerging European nations. Its influence on western civilization is probably greater than any other book, except, of course, the Bible.

CORSICA. *See* **VANDALS.**

COSMOLOGY. *See* **KOSMAS INDIKOPLEUSTES; MICHAEL ITALIKOS.**

COTRIGURS. A Turkic people from Central Asia who migrated westward across the steppe (q.v.), settling west of the Black Sea (q.v.) by the end of the fifth century. Justinian I (q.v.) tried to check the threat of Cotrigur raids by cultivating another Turkic people, the Utigurs (q.v.), who lived to the east of the Sea of Azov. In 551, when some 12,000 Cotrigurs, encouraged by their allies, the Geipids (q.v.), crossed the Danube (q.v.) on a plundering expedition, Justinian I incited the Utigurs to attack them and they were forced to withdraw. In 558 a Cotrigur chieftain named Zabergan invaded Thrace (qq.v.), sending one part of his forces into Greece (q.v.) as far as Thermopylae (q.v.). Another part moved against Constantinople (q.v.), which Belisarios (q.v.) defended heroically. Justinian I again stirred the Utigurs to attack the Cotrigurs, which they did once the Cotrigurs withdrew across the Danube. In the second half of the sixth century, the Cotrigurs were subjugated by the Avars (q.v.), who forced some to accompany them to Pannonia (q.v.). Other Cotrigurs were incorporated into Bulgaria (q.v.) in the seventh century.

COUNT (COMES). An honorary term attached to various state offices, first used by Constantine I the Great (q.v.) and translated loosely into English as "count," e.g., the Count of the Private Estates *(comes rerum privatarum)*, who administered the imperial domains, and the Count of the Sacred Largess *(comes sacrarum largitionum)*, who administered the central treasury, as well as all state-run industries, the mint, and customs. The term also refers to certain military officers, e.g., the Count of the Tent, who was the chief aide of a *strategos* of a theme (qq.v.). The chronicler Marcellinus Comes served under Justinian I (qq.v.).

CRETE. Island in the eastern Mediterranean (q.v.) located almost equidistant from mainland Greece and Africa (qq.v.). Its capital was Gortyna. The island was raided by the Goths in 268, the Vandals in 457, and the Slavs in 623. Arabs (q.v.) occupied it briefly in 674, and in ca. 827 thousands of Arabs who had originally been expelled from Cordoba (q.v.) and who had resettled in Alexandria (q.v.), were ejected from there and made their way to Crete. They conquered the island, establishing Chandax as their capital. Crete became a base of operations for raids throughout the Aegean (q.v.) until 961, when it was reconquered by Nikephoros (II) Phokas (q.v.). The island remained in Byzantine possession until the Fourth Crusade's conquest of Constantinople (qq.v.) in 1204, when it was awarded to Boniface of Montferrat (q.v).

CRIMEA. The Crimean Peninsula, separating the Black Sea (q.v.) from the Sea of Azov, was the locale where Byzantium (q.v.) traded and conducted diplomacy with its northern neighbors at Cherson and Bosporos (qq.v.). Cherson, located on the Crimea's southwestern tip, was Byzantium's northernmost outpost. The interior of the peninsula was occupied by Khazars (q.v.) from the seventh to 10th centuries, prompting Theophilos (q.v.) to create the theme of *Klimata* (qq.v.) around 832 with its center at Cherson.

CRISPUS. Son of Constantine I the Great (q.v.) and Minervina; pupil of Lactantius (q.v.). He was made caesar (q.v.) in 317 and was entrusted with Gaul (q.v.), where he won victories over the Franks (q.v.) and Alemanni. He commanded the fleet that defeated the flotilla of Licinius (q.v.) in 324. His brilliant career was cut short in 326 when he was executed by his father for reasons that remain unclear. Hostile writers claim that it was because his stepmother Fausta (q.v.) falsely accused him of attempted rape.

CROATIA. A Slavic state in the northwest of the Balkan Peninsula (q.v.). The origins of the Croatians have been the subject of much controversy. According to Constantine VII's *De administrando imperio* (qq.v.) the Croats emigrated to the Balkan Peninsula (qv.) at the invitation of Herakleios (q.v.), who sought their aid against the Avars (q.v.). Having defeated the Avars, they were themselves settled by Herakleios, were converted to Christianity, and they became the nominal subjects of Byzantium (q.v.). The overlordship of Charlemagne (q.v.) was accepted in 803, but in 879, by which time Frankish power had declined, the Croats switched their loyalty to the papacy (q.v.), and, in effect, became independent. However, when it was advantageous to do so, Croatia allied itself with Byzantium, e.g., as prince Tomislav (q.v.) did in opposition to Symeon of Bulgaria (q.v.). Byzantine influence declined in Croatia after 1060, when the liturgy in Church Slavonic (q.v.) was prohibited. By this time Croatia's orientation had shifted decisively to central and western Europe, as seen in 1102 when Croatia and Hungary were united.

CROSS-DOMED CHURCH. Church whose core consists of four barrel-vaults radiating from a central bay surmounted by a dome with the north, south, and west sides of the core enveloped by aisles and galleries. Haghia Sophia in Thessalonike (q.v.), perhaps early eighth century in date, is an example.

CROSS-IN-SQUARE CHURCH. Also called a *quincunx,* this church plan is the most common Byzantine church plan from the 10th century until 1453. It has a core of nine bays, the central bay consisting of a dome (q.v.) over a large square resting on four columns. The corner bays can be either domed or groin-vaulted. Examples include the church dedicated to the *Theotokos* at Hosios Loukas (qq.v.), and the Church of St. Panteleemon at Nerezi, near Skopje (qq.v.), built ca. 1164. A variant of this design is the Late Byzantine five-domed church plan, with a central dome and four minor domes over the four corner bays between the arms of the cross. Examples include Gračaniča in Serbia (qq.v.), begun ca. 1311, and the Church of the Holy Apostles (ca. 1329) in Thessalonike (q.v.).

CROTONE. Fortress-city in Calabria (q.v.), important during the long war with the Ostrogoths in Italy (qq.v.). Like Ancona (q.v.), Crotone remained in Byzantine hands throughout the war, despite a determined effort by Totila (q.v.) to conquer it in 551–552. Justinian I (q.v.) sent a fleet to reinforce the city; according to Prokopios of Caesarea (q.v.) he also sent the garrison at Thermopylae (q.v.) to Crotone.

CRUSADES. The crusading movement began when Pope Urban II (qq.v.) called the First Crusade (q.v.) at the Council of Clermont in 1095. The object was to regain Jerusalem (q.v.) from the forces of Islam (q.v.), and to aid the eastern church in the process. The conquest of Jerusalem by the First Crusade in 1099, its subsequent loss after the battle of Hattin (q.v.) in 1187, and further attempts to reconquer Jerusalem comprise the chief historical theme of the early Crusades. However, less obvious, but arguably more historically significant in the long run, is the threat that the Crusades posed to Byzantium (q.v.). For the first time in centuries, large numbers of westerners passed through Constantinople. Many viewed the Byzantines as heretics who had previously been condemned in the church schism of 1054 (q.v.). The First Crusade, which contained a contingent of Normans (q.v.), well-known enemies of Byzantium, were viewed as a menace by emperor Alexios I (qq.v.). Indeed, the Normans took advantage of the Second Crusade (q.v.) to attack Corinth and Thebes (qq.v.). The Third Crusasde (q.v.) resulted in the capture of Cyprus (q.v.) in 1191. With the Fourth Crusade (q.v.) the peril to Constantinople was realized. The conquest of the city in 1204 resulted in the *Partitio Romaniae* (q.v.), a triumph for the long-term commercial interests of Venice (q.v.), resulting in the destruction of Byzantium and the division of its empire among Venice (q.v.) and its partners. In sum, what the Crusades had attempted to support they ended up destroying; only in 1261 were forces from the Empire of Nicaea (q.v.) able to regain Constantinople. However, restored Byzantium never fully recovered from the destruction wrought by the Fourth Crusade. Other Crusades followed the Fourth Crusade, but in hindsight it can be argued that chief among the results of the entire crusading movement was not the conquest of Jerusalem in 1099, but the conquest of Christian Byzantium in 1204. In a much larger historical context, the Crusades, especially the Fourth Crusade, can be seen as prototypes for later European expeditions for plunder and conquest. For example, in 1521 Hernán Cortés viewed his *conquista* of Mexico as the culmination of a glorious

Crusade comprised of *milites Christi* ("Knights of Christ") who waged a just *guerra santa* ("holy war") against the hated "infidel."

CTESIPHON. *See* **SASSANIANS.**

CUMANS. Turkish-speaking nomads from central Asia who served as standing troops for Byzantium (q.v.) in the 12th–13th centuries. They moved into the south Russian steppe (q.v.) in the mid-11th century, driving the Pechenegs across the Danube (qq.v.), and attaching themselves to Byzantine armies as mercenaries. Their most memorable service to Byzantium (q.v.) was in 1091, when Alexios I Komnenos (q.v.) used them to annihilate the Pechenegs at the battle of Mount Lebounion. In the 12th century they were enrolled into the army in substantial numbers, where their skill as mounted archers was renowned. They also began to settle in Byzantine territory, where some were given *pronoia* (q.v.) grants. However, even while some Cumans served Byzantium, other Cumans remained intermittent threats, or served other masters. Manuel I Komnenos (q.v.), for example, turned back a Cuman raid across the Danube in the aftermath of the Second Crusade (q.v.). Cumans played a role in the revolt of Peter and Asen I (q.v.) against Byzantium in 1186. They served in the army of Kalojan (q.v.) that in 1205 destroyed a Latin army, capturing Baldwin of Flanders (q.v.). They were decisive in the victory of John Asen II at Klokotnitsa (qq.v.) in 1230. Around 1241 the Mongols (q.v.) defeated the Cumans, forcing many to flee to Byzantine territory. Some were settled along the frontiers of Thrace and Macedonia (qq.v.), and in Asia Minor (q.v.) in the Meander valley and in Phyrgia (q.v.). Some fled to Hungary and Bulgaria (qq.v.), while others became Mamelukes (q.v.). The Cumans played an important role in the army of Michael VIII Palaeologos (q.v.), including his victory at the battle of Pelagonia (q.v.) in 1259.

CURIA. The council of the urban elite that ran municipal affairs. Each *curia* chose new members, called *decurions,* or *curiales.* They were inevitably composed of wealthier citizens drawn from the local senate, because their duties were burdensome. They had to maintain all public services, including such services that one might have expected the central government to shoulder (e.g., the horses and mules for the imperial post). They were also responsible for maintaining the public infrastructure, and for the collection of taxes. It is this latter burden that was particularly onerous, for if collected taxes were insufficient the *curia* was expected to make up the difference from its members, which could impoverish them. This was one of the reasons Anastasios I (q.v.) relieved urban councils of collecting the *annona* (q.v.). Curias declined in the sixth century, but they were officially abolished only during the reign of Leo VI (q.v.).

CURRENCY. *See* COINAGE.

CYPRUS. Island in the eastern Mediterranean (q.v.) whose Roman capital was Salamis, renamed Constantia following the earthquakes of the mid-fourth century. The island's historical importance lies in its strategic location near the coasts of Syria and southern Asia Minor (qq.v.). Beginning ca. 647 the island was raided by the Arabs (q.v.), resulting in the abandonment of some coastal cities, including Kourion. A treaty of 688 with Abd al-Malik (q.v.) made Cyprus a neutral zone with tax revenues divided between the Abbasids and Byzantium (qq.v.), and Justinian II (q.v.) resettled a number of Cypriots at Kyzikos (q.v.). Basil I (q.v.) reconquered the island for several years, but only with the conquest of Nikephoros II Phokas (q.v.) in 965 was it brought securely into Byzantine possession. Its close proximity to the Holy Land made it a source of food and supplies for the Crusader principalities. However, that same proximity allowed Reynald of Châtillon to plunder it in 1157. In 1184 the self-proclaimed ruler of the island, Isaac Komnenos (q.v.), declared Cyprus independent. However, in 1191 Isaac was captured when Richard I Lionheart conquered Cyprus during the Third Crusade (q.v.). Thereafter, Cyprus remained in Crusader hands under the Lusignans until 1489, when the Venetians acquired it. The Ottomans (q.v.) conquered it from the Venetians in 1571. The Byzantine monuments of Cyprus are numerous and renowned. They include important Christian basilicas (q.v.) at Kourion, Lythrankomi, Salamis/Constantia, and Paphos. An extraordinary wall mosaic of the Virgin and Christ child, thought to date from the sixth or seventh century, survives from a basilican church at Kiti. Among the later Byzantine monuments is the 12th-century monastic cell (q.v.), called the *enkleistra*, of the hermit (q.v.) Neophytos. The frescoes (q.v.) that decorate his dwelling (one shows him between archangels) are excelled only by those of the contemporary churches at Asinou and Lagoudera. Alexios I Komnenos (q.v.) is thought to have constructed the defenses that guarded Cyprus's northern coast, including the castles of St. Hilarion, Buffavento, Kantara, and Kyrenia.

CYRENAICA. A province in North Africa (q.v.) that included the east coast of Libya. Under Diocletian (q.v.) it was divided into two provinces, Libya Superior (Pentapolis) and Libya Inferior. The Arabs (q.v.) conquered the region ca. 643.

CYRENE. *See* SYNESIOS.

CYRIL. Patriarch of Alexandria (qq.v.) from 412–444, and arch-opponent of Nestorianism (q.v.). He opposed Jews (q.v.) and pagans, indeed any rival to his ecclesiastical authority, and he was inclined to resort to violence and intrigue to overcome his opponents. Until 428 the scope of his ambition was Alexandria itself, where he became locked in a power struggle with the civil governor, a pagan named Orestes who was friends with the brilliant pagan philosopher Hypatia (q.v.). Cyril's henchmen included 500 monks from the Nitrian desert (q.v.), and hundreds of lay brothers, some of whom assassinated Hypatia, chopping her body up and burning it. In 428 Cyril's ambition moved to a larger struggle with Nestorius (q.v.), bishop of Constantinople (qq.v.), whose rivalry with Alexandria went back to 381, when the Second Ecumenical Council (q.v.) ranked the see (q.v.) of Constantinople above that of Alexandria. Moreover, Cyril was a theologian who had wrestled with the nature of Christ's human and divine natures. He disagreed with Nestorius's view that the Virgin Mary had given birth only to the man Jesus, and could not, therefore, be called *Theotokos* (q.v.), meaning Mother of God. In 431 at the Council of Ephesus (q.v.) Cyril engineered the condemnation of Nestorius, with the help of street violence and 1,500 pounds of gold used to bribe members of Theodosius II's (q.v.) court. Ironically, Cyril's own theological views about Christ inspired Monophysitism (q.v.), which Cyril's successor Dioskoros (q.v.) embraced. Condemnation of Monophysitism in 451 at the Council of Chalcedon (q.v.) was a stinging humiliation for the see of Alexandria.

CYRIL AND METHODIOS. Saints, apostles to the Slavs (q.v.), creators of the Glagolitic (q.v.) alphabet. Cyril was the monastic name taken by Constantine, sometimes referred to as Constantine the Philosopher because of his fame as a teacher of that subject. Cyril and his brother Methodios (q.v.) grew up in Thessalonike (q.v.) and they spoke the dialect that Slavs around the city spoke. Methodios had been a governor *(archon)* of a Slav principality in Macedonia (q.v.). Cyril was a brilliant linguist who had previously been sent on a diplomatic mission to the Khazars (q.v.). Their mission to Moravia (q.v.) in 863 was requested of Michael III (q.v.) by prince Rastislav. Cyril, with the help of Methodios, invented a Slavonic (Glagolitic [q.v.]) alphabet, which he used to translate the liturgy of John Chrysostom (q.v.) and the New Testament. Ultimately, the Moravian mission failed in the face of intensive pressure from the Frankish clergy in Moravia, and because of Cyril's premature death in Rome in 869. However, Methodios continued the work of translation, and his disciples in Bulgaria (q.v.) invented another alphabet for the Bulgars called Cyrillic (qq.v.), adapted from the Greek alphabet. Most important is the long-term effect of their work in attracting much of the Slavic world to Byzantine Christianity, and, thus, to Byzantine culture and civilization.

CYRILLIC. The oldest manuscripts in Church Slavonic (q.v.) are in two different scripts, Glagolitic (q.v.) and Cyrillic. Cyril and Methodios (q.v.) invented the former, but the latter script, which incorrectly bears Cyril's name, is thought to be an invention of the disciples of Methodios, perhaps Kliment of Ohrid (q.v.). It uses a Greek-based script for the Slavonic language, one based on Greek miniscule (q.v.). Thus, while Glagolitic is a highly original script, Cyrillic is adapted from the Greek alphabet. Versions of the Cyrillic script are used for the Russian, Bulgarian, Serbian, and Macedonian (qq.v.) alphabets.

CYRIL OF SKYTHOPOLIS. He and John Moschos (q.v.) are the most important sixth-century writers of hagiography (q.v.). Born in Palestine (q.v.), he pursued the monastic life first as a hermit (q.v.), then in the monastery of St. Euthymios the Great (q.v.) at Jericho, and, finally, from 557 until his death, in the famous Great Lavra of St. Sabas (q.v.). He planned to write a large collection of Palestinian monastic biographies, but did not, probably because he died prematurely. However, several of his biographies survive, including the life *(vita)* of St. Sabas (qq.v.). The biographies contain a wealth of accurate details, making them a rich source for the social history of the sixth century.

CZECHIA. Czechia, or Bohemia, was a vassal of Moravia (q.v.), when Cyril and his brother Methodios (qq.v.) arrived in Moravia in 864. According to Czech tradition the first known Christian duke, Borivoj of Prague, was baptized by Methodios. Borivoj and his wife Ludmila, and their grandson Saint Wenceslas, continued with the liturgy and priesthood bequeathed to them by Byzantium (q.v.). For some two centuries, this tradition flourished in Czechia, centered at the Benedictine abbey of Sazava, near Prague. However, by the late 11th century this began to change when, in 1096, Church Slavonic (q.v.) was banned. Although 12th-century king Vladislav of Bohemia referred to himself as a vassal of Manuel I Komnenos (q.v.), his link with Byzantium was tenuous. Byzantium was too far away to compete with influences emanating from Germany and Hungary (qq.v.).

– D –

DACIA. Region north of the Danube (q.v.) that corresponds roughly to modern Romania. It was conquered by Trajan in two hard-fought wars that ended in 106, and abandoned in the middle of the third century. It was inhabited by indigenous Daco-Getans, some of whom became the Vlachs (q.v.). Its capital was Serdica (q.v.). Its other major city, Naissus (q.v.), was the birthplace of Constantine I the Great (q.v.).

DALASSENE, ANNA. Influential mother of Alexios I Komnenos (q.v.), whose ambition was instrumental in his rise to power. She encouraged her son's revolt against Nikephoros III (q.v.) in 1081 and, to judge from the comments of her granddaughter, Anna Komnene (q.v.), she handled all affairs of state and was the emperor's chief advisor. In fact, an imperial edict of 1081 granted her powers equal to those of Alexios I. She was the driving force in the Komneni family, an embodiment of all the family's resourcefulness, a brilliant woman who did not shrink from the necessities of power, as illustrated by her blinding of Nikephoros Diogenes in 1095 for plotting revolution. Her piety was renowned. Shortly before her death she retired to the Pantepoptes Monastery (q.v.), which she founded.

DALMATIA. The eastern coast of the Adriatic (q.v.) and its hinterland, from the region of Istria to Kotor, bounded by the Dinaric range, which runs parallel to the coast. It was a Roman province until the fourth century, when it became a diocese (q.v.). Although briefly occupied by Odoacer (q.v.), then by the Ostrogoths (q.v.), it was one of the few parts of the western empire that escaped the expansion of Germanic peoples in the fifth century. The invasions of Slavs and

Avars (qq.v.) in the early seventh century destroyed older inland cities like Salona (q.v.), and gave new importance to the major coastal cities of Zara, Split, Dubrovnik, and Dyrrachion (qq.v.), which retained their Romano-Italian character throughout the Middle Ages. However, political and ecclesiastical control was unstable, reflecting the gradual decline of Byzantine power in the West. Byzantine hegemony was overturned briefly by Charlemagne (q.v.), but after the Franks (q.v.) restored Dalmatia to Byzantium (q.v.) in 812, it was attacked by Muslims from North Africa (q.v.). Dubrovnik, for example, was rescued in 868 from an Arab (q.v.) siege by a Byzantine fleet. Sometime toward the end of the ninth century much of Dalmatia was incorporated into the theme of Longobardia (qq.v.); Dyrrachion, the most important base of Byzantine power on the Adriatic coast, became the capital of its own theme. The growing influence of Venice, Hungary, and Bulgaria (qq.v.) is evident during the 10th century. Tsar Samuel (qq.v.) held Dyrrachion until Basil II (q.v.) reconquered it in 1005. The 11th century saw the added threats of Croatia (q.v.), and especially of the Normans (q.v.), who seized Dyrrachion briefly in 1081. In the 12th century Byzantine control collapsed. Venice expropriated the northern part of the coast, Croatia and Hungary (united in 1102) the middle part, and Byzantium held on, intermittently, to Dubrovnik, until that city was taken by the Venetians in 1205. Venice ruled Dalmatia until 1358 when, except for Dubrovnik (self-governing from 1358–1526), Dalmatia came under the control of Hungary, which held it until the early 15th century.

DAMASCUS. Capital of the Umayyads (q.v.) from 661–750, situated between the eastern and western parts of this first Islamic caliphate (q.v.). The city, located in southwest Syria (q.v.) on the eastern edge of the Anti-Lebanon Mountains, was in Byzantine possession until 612, in Persian hands from 612–628, and back in Byzantine possession until the Arabs (q.v.) conquered it in 635. A center of Muslim arts and learning under the Umayyads. Damascus contained the greatest Muslim building of the eighth century, the Great Mosque, adorned with wall mosaics that were probably produced by Byzantine artisans. John I Tzimiskes (q.v.) forced the city to pay tribute in 975, the year of his campaign in Syria. In the 12th century the city was the stronghold of Nur al-Din, also of Saladin (qq.v.), who died there, and whose coffin is still displayed.

DAMASKIOS. One of the last great Neoplatonist (q.v.) scholars of the Academy of Athens (q.v.). After Justinian I (q.v.) closed the academy in 529, he went to the court of Persia (q.v.), along with six other famous philosophers. They were welcomed by Chosroes I (q.v.), but in 532, homesick, they returned. In his treaty of 532 with Justinian I, Chosroes required that the emperor (q.v.) not persecute them.

DANDALO, ANDREAS. Doge of Venice (q.v.) from 1343–1354; chronicler. Byzantium (q.v.) progressively tottered on the brink of collapse while he was doge. His response was to loan Byzantium yet more money (30,000 ducats), for which Anne of Savoy (q.v.), regent for the young John V (q.v.), pawned the crown jewels as security. He continued to wage war in Byzantine waters against arch-rival Genoa (q.v.), which dominated trade in the Black Sea (q.v.). In 1352 an indecisive battle was fought in the Bosporos (q.v.) between the two foes, with John V providing 14 ships to help the Venetians. Dandalo's chronicle (q.v.) begins with the foundation of Venice (q.v.) and goes down to 1354. Up to 1008 it relies on the *Chronicon Venetum* (q.v.), the oldest history of Venice. But thereafter its importance as an historical source increases, especially for the years Dandalo was in power. As one might expect, he idolizes his ancestor, doge Enrico Dandalo (q.v.).

DANDALO, ENRICO. Doge of Venice (q.v.) from 1192–1205 who led the Fourth Crusade (q.v.) that conquered Constantinople (q.v.) in 1204. Niketas Choniates (q.v.) and some modern historians view him as a villain who plotted the capture of the city. Whether plotted for or not, through the *Partitio Romaniae* (q.v.) Dandalo established Venetian economic hegemony in the eastern Mediterranean (q.v.).

DANELIS. Wealthy widow and patron of future emperor Basil I (qq.v.). When Basil was in the Peloponnesos (q.v.) on a mission for Theophilitzes, an official in the service of Michael III (q.v.), he met Danelis, who had vast estates in the region of Patras, making her perhaps the wealthiest person in Greece (q.v.). Convinced by a monk's prophecy that Basil would one day become emperor, she became his patron, and he became a spiritual brother to her son. Her wealth, which was enormous, included vast estates and slaves (q.v.). Modern scholars have suggested that the source of her wealth lay in textile production, perhaps the weaving of silk (q.v.), or of woolen goods.

DANIEL THE STYLITE. Pillar saint at Anaplous on the Bosporos (q.v.) from 460 until his death in 493. His anonymous *vita* (q.v.) provides information about emperors Leo I and Zeno (qq.v.), as well as the usurper Basiliskos (q.v.). He is seen as the successor to Symeon the Stylite (q.v.), who bequeathed him his leather tunic. Daniel had influential patrons, including Leo I, for whom he acted as occasional mediator. Daniel's power was illustrated by the popular uprising in Constantinople (q.v.) that occurred when he descended from his pillar to mediate between the patriarch Akakios (q.v.) and Basiliskos. This, and other examples from his biography, illustrate the important role of holy men in fifth-century Byzantine society.

DANISHMENDIDS. Emirs of Cappadocia (qq.v.), and rivals of the Seljuks in Asia Minor (qq.v.). Emir Danishmend established his domain in Sebasteia (q.v.) around 1086, and extended it to the north as far as Ankara (q.v.) and Neokaisareia; in 1101, he conquered Melitene (q.v.). The Danishmendids existed by plundering neighboring regions. They fought against John II Komnenos (q.v.), but they became allies with Manuel I Komnenos (q.v.) against the Seljuks. However, that alliance came to naught when the Seljuks defeated Manuel I's army at Myriokephalon (q.v.) in 1176. Two years later Melitene fell to the Seljuks, and by 1180 the Seljuks had put an end to the Danishmendids.

DANUBE. The great river (2,850 kilometers long) that traverses the Balkan Peninsula (q.v.), ending in a large delta before entering the Black Sea (q.v.). Along with the Rhine River (q.v.), at least until the Rhine defenses were abandoned in 406, it comprised the northern border for the Roman Empire (q.v.), and subsequently for Byzantium (q.v.) as well. As a boundary between barbarism and civilization, and a major route of transport, it was guarded by a series of fortresses, yet was hardly an impregnable obstacle for invaders from the north. Nevertheless, the defense of Byzantium's European provinces was closely connected to the defense of the Danubian frontier. After the death of Justinian I (q.v.) in 565, the Danube River was crossed almost at will by Avars and Slavs (qq.v.), who settled south of the river. In 680 the Bulgars (q.v.) settled in the Dobrudja (q.v.), and Byzantium was forced to recognize its independence. The conquest of Bulgaria (q.v.) in 1018 reestablished Byzantine hegemony south of the Danube for a while, but during the 11th and 12th centuries these defenses broke down before the determined assaults of Uzes, Pechenegs, and Cumans (qq.v.).

DAPHNI. *See* **GREEK CROSS-DOMED OCTAGON CHURCH; MOSAICS.**

DAPHNOPATES, THEODORE. Writer; eparch of Constantinople (qq.v.) during the reign of Romanos II (q.v.). His correspondence is an important source of information about Byzantine domestic and foreign affairs, including relations with Symeon of Bulgaria (q.v.). He wrote biographies of several saints, compiled excerpts from the writings of John Chrysostom (q.v.), and may have authored the last part of the chronicle of Theophanes Continuatus (qq.v.), as well as the Bulgarian Treaty (q.v.).

DARA. Frontier fortress-town in upper Mesopotamia (q.v.); also called Anastasiopolis. It was built by Anastasios I (q.v.) to counteract the nearby Persian fortress of Nisibis (q.v.). The battle of Dara in 530, described in detail by Prokopios of Caesarea (q.v.), was won by Belisarios (q.v.) against the forces of Kavad of Persia (qq.v.). However, the Persians conquered and held it from 573–591, and again from 604–628. It was conquered by the Arabs (q.v.) in 639. John Kourkouas (q.v.) recaptured it in 943.

DARDANELLES. *See* **HELLESPONT.**

DAVID I KOMNENOS. *See* **JOHN IV KOMNENOS.**

DAZIMON. Site of a major battle on 22 July 838 between Theophilos (q.v.) and Afshin, general of caliph Mutasim (q.v.). Theophilos's defeat at Dazimon allowed Mutasim to seize Ankara and Amorion (qq.v.). Dazimon is in Pontos (q.v.) and has been variously located at Dazmana, and at Tokat, where a fortress commands the eastern road that ran from Constantinople to Sebasteia (qq.v.).

DE ADMINISTRANDO IMPERIO. *On the Administration of the Empire* (De administrando imperio), written by Constantine VII (q.v.), is a handbook for rulers and diplomats written in the 950s. It deals chiefly with neighboring peoples, their customs, strengths, and weaknesses, and how, if necessary, to overcome them by diplomacy and arms. Its historical value lies in the wealth of information it provides (some of it admittedly old) about Byzantium's (q.v.) neighbors, including the Pechenegs, Uzes, Rus, Bulgars, Khazars, and Hungarians (qq.v.).

DE CEREMONIIS. *On the Ceremonies of the Byzantine Court* (De ceremoniis aulae byzantinae), written by Constantine VII (q.v.), is a compilation of materials pertaining to the required court rituals for various occasions, e.g., the reception of foreign ambassadors, baptism, marriage, the burial of emperors (q.v.), coronations, proper etiquette in the Hippodrome (q.v.), and processions on feast days. The work may have been intended as an archive (e.g., the work of Peter the Patrician [q.v.] is included) for a future manual on court ritual. For historians it is a gold mine for the study of Byzantine diplomacy, for how the Great Palace (q.v.) was laid out, for historical events such as the reception of Olga (q.v.), and for the offices and dignities of the Byzantine court. This work illustrates how integral and pervasive was court ritual to all aspects of Byzantine government. As Liutprand of Cremona (q.v.) and every foreign ambassador learned, court ritual served as a constant reminder of one's place in relation to Byzantine imperial power.

DEESIS. Greek for "entreaty," referring to an image of intercession in Byzantine art. This can include the image of a donor presenting a gift, but typically it is an image of the *Theotokos* (q.v.) and John the Baptist in poses of intercession on either side of Christ. The scene expresses the honor given to the *Theotokos* and John as the first to acknowledge Christ's divinity, as in the mosaic of the *Deesis* in Hagia Sophia in Constantinople (qq.v.). If the Twelve Apostles and saints are added to the Virgin and John, it is called a Great *Deesis* scene.

DELJAN, PETER. Self-proclaimed son of Samuel of Bulgaria (q.v.) who engendered a brief revolt from 1040–1041 against Byzantine domination of Bulgaria. The revolt was provoked by the ruthlessness of Byzantine tax-collectors, made worse in 1040 by a decision of John the Orphanotrophos (q.v.) to demand cash instead of payment in kind. Insurgents who seized Belgrade, Nish, and Skopje (qq.v.) soon had the support of troops from the themes of Dyrrachion and Nikopolis (qq.v.). Dyrrachion was captured, as was Nikopolis, Serdica, and Demetrias (qq.v.). However, the attempt to seize Thessalonike (q.v.) failed and in 1041 the ringleaders fell out with each other. The revolt ended when Alousianos (q.v.), co-ruler with Peter Deljan, betrayed his partner to Michael IV (q.v.).

DEMES. *See* **CIRCUS FACTIONS.**

DEMETRIAS. Main port of Thessaly (q.v.), located near modern Volos. The city's maritime connections looked eastward to Constantinople (q.v.), to the coast of Asia Minor, even to Egypt (qq.v.). It survived a nearby settlement of Slavs (q.v.), called Belegezitai, in the seventh and eighth centuries, but in 901 or 902 Demetrias was sacked by Arabs (q.v.) led by the Greek renegade Damianos. The army of rebel Peter Deljan (q.v.) sacked it again in 1040. After the conquest of Constantinople by the Fourth Crusade (q.v.), it was given to empress Euphrosyne Doukaina Kamatera (q.v.), then in 1210 to the widow of Boniface of Montferrat (q.v.). The Melissenoi family controlled the city from 1240 until the end of the 13th century, when Venice and Byzantium (qq.v.) struggled to possess it. The Catalan Grand Company (q.v.) conquered it in 1310 and it remained in Catalan possession until 1381. The Ottomans (q.v.) conquered it in 1393.

DEMETRIOS, ANGELOS DOUKAS. Despot of Thessalonike (qq.v.) from 1244–1246. He was the last ruler of the Despotate of Epiros (q.v.) to rule Thessalonike, which fell to the Empire of Nicaea (q.v.) in 1246.

DEMETRIOS, MIRACULA OF SAINT. *See* **THESSALONIKE.**

DEMETRIOS PALAIOLOGOS. Despot of the Morea (q.v.) from 1449–1460, son of Manuel II (q.v.). The black sheep of the sons of Manuel II, he possessed a restless ambition combined with an unscrupulous character. With his brother John VIII (q.v.) he attended the Council of Ferrara-Florence (q.v.) in 1438–1439, although he styled himself as a champion of the anti-union party. He established connections with the Ottomans (q.v.) and in 1442 he attacked Constantinople (q.v.) with the help of Ottoman troops in a vain effort to depose his brother. Despite being forgiven by John VIII, when Manuel II came to the throne Demetrios was shipped off to govern Selymbria on the Black Sea (qq.v.). In 1449, he left to administer the despotate of the Morea (q.v.) with another brother, Thomas Palaiologos (q.v.), with whom he quarreled incessantly. In 1460 he was forced to surrender Mistra (q.v.) to the Ottomans, but he continued to be treated favorably at the sultan's (q.v.) court in Adrianople (q.v.), where he died as a monk in 1470.

DEMETRIOS TRIKLINIOS. *See* **EURIPIDES; THOMAS MAGISTROS.**

DEREAĞZI. *See* **LYCIA.**

DE REBUS BELLICIS. Late fourth-century military treatise by an anonymous Latin writer. The treatise is addressed to the reigning emperors (q.v.), perhaps Valentinian I and Valens (qq.v.). The author considers himself a reformer, but the reforms he recommends vary from commonsensical to bizarre. He also recommends new military technology, the illustrations of which include inventions that seem a bit far-fetched.

DE RE MILITARI. *On Warfare,* an anonymous military treatise apparently written in the late 10th or early 11th century. It was added to the *Taktika* of Leo VI (q.v.), and is similar in style to another anonymous text entitled *De velitatione* (q.v.), dated to about 975. The author is a man of extensive military experience, and his concerns center on how to conduct a campaign across the northern frontier against Bulgaria (q.v.).

DESERT FATHERS. *See* **APOPHTHEGMATA PATRUM.**

DESPOT. A title *(despotes)* created by Manuel I Komnenos (q.v.) in 1163 for Bella III (q.v.), heir-apparent to the Byzantine throne until the birth of Alexios II (q.v.). The Palaiologan emperors (qq.v.) used the title for rulers of important appanages (q.v.), e.g., of Thessalonike and the Morea (qq.v.). It was awarded in 1282 to John II Komnenos of Trebizond (qq.v.). In the 14th century it was used for the independent rulers of the despotate of Epiros (q.v.).

DE THEMATIBUS. Constantine VII Porphyrogenitos's (q.v.) treatise (translated as *The Book of the Themes,* or *On the Themes*) on the geography and history of the themes (q.v.), written sometime between 952–959. Much of its information is taken from the sixth-century works of Stephen of Byzantium, and of Hierokles (qq.v.).

DE VELITATIONE. *On Skirmishing,* by an anonymous author who wrote the work at the instruction of Nikephoros II Phokas (q.v.), using the late emperor's (q.v.) own notes. Probably finished before the death of John I Tzimiskes (q.v.) in 976, the work offers details on how to counter Arab raids by use of guerrilla tactics.

DEVOL. More properly Diabolis, a stronghold and episcopal see (q.v.) situated on the Via Egnatia (q.v.). It was apparently the first stop after Ohrid (q.v.), judging from the *Alexiad* of Anna Komnene (q.v.). However, its exact location is still unknown. In 1108 Alexios I Komnenos forced Bohemund (qq.v.) to sign the Treaty of Devol, which ended for a time the Norman (q.v.) threat to Byzantine European possessions.

DEVSHIRME. *See* **GLABAS, ISIDORE; JANISSARIES.**

DIAKONIKON. A storage chamber in Byzantine churches used as a sacristy (thus, *skeuophylakion,* meaning a place to keep vessels), and as a place to store gifts brought to the church. Deacons were responsible for it, hence its name. In early basilicas (q.v.) it could be a separate building, but most often it is the southern of two chambers (called *pastophoria*) flanking the apse. The other flanking chamber is called the *prothesis* (q.v.).

DIGENES AKRITAS. Epic romance, whose setting is the Byzantine-Arab frontier, written in the second half of the 11th century (or in the 12th century). The poem derives from a previous oral tradition (ninth or 10th century in date) about a legendary hero named Basil who is subsequently called *Digenes Akritas. Digenes* means "born of two peoples," for in the poem Basil's father is said to have been an Arab emir (q.v.), and his mother the daughter of a Byzantine general of the Doukas family. An *akritas* (q.v.) was an inhabitant of the eastern frontier (that included Cappadocia [q.v] and the region between Samosata and Melitene [qq.v.]). Much of the story concerns Basil's exploits along this frontier. In the poem his fame reaches the emperor (q.v.), who rides to the Euphrates River (q.v.) to honor him. Some of Digenes's foes have been identified as leaders of the heretical Paulicians (q.v.). Emir Monsour, for example, his father in the tale, must refer to the real-life Omar of Melitene, an ally of the Paulicians. In the description of Digenes's palace (including its ceilings covered in glittering mosaic with scenes from Homer's *Iliad* and *Odyssey,* from the life of Alexander the Great, and from the Old Testament), one gains an understanding of how splendid were the residences of wealthy landowners (the *dynatoi*) in Asia Minor (qq.v.). When the poem was written (during the half century or so after the Seljuk [q.v.] victory at Mantzikert [q.v.]) such families had already left the eastern frontier for more secure surroundings at the Byzantine court in Constantinople (q.v.). Thus, the poem can be viewed as a romantic retrospective of the recent past.

DIGEST. A compendium of previous legal opinions, also called the Pandects, published in 533 as part of the *Corpus Juris Civilis* (q.v.), and arguably the most important part of Justinian I's (q.v.) legislative work. Much credit goes to Tribonian (q.v.), the great jurist who headed a commission of 16 lawyers who undertook the daunting task of reviewing about 2,000 books of judicial interpretation amounting to over 3,000,000 lines. The commission reduced it all to 150,000 lines by omitting obsolete and duplicate opinions, and resolving contradictions. The legal opinions that remained were gathered into 50 books arranged according to subject. The result is a harmonious body of judicial interpretation, much of it drawn from second and early third century jurists like Ulpian, Paul, Papinian, Pomponius, and Gaius. The Digest remains the chief record of this earlier Roman jurisprudence.

DINOGETIA. Byzantine fortress on a small island near the mouth of the Danube (q.v.), built sometime from the fourth to sixth centuries as part of the defenses (*limes* [q.v.]) of Scythia Minor (q.v.). Damaged by a Cotrigur (q.v.) raid in 559, it lay deserted until restored and garrisoned by John I Tzimiskes (q.v.), as part of his effort to defend the Dobrudja (q.v.). It remained occupied through the reign of John II Komnenos (q.v.).

DIOCESE. Diocletian (q.v.) reorganized the empire's provinces (q.v.) into 12 secular dioceses, each governed by a vicar. The dioceses were subsequently grouped into four larger prefectures (q.v.). The system lasted until the seventh century. Church organization followed suit, each ecclesiastical diocese having the same territory as its secular counterpart. In the same manner, church dioceses were subdivided into episcopal provinces. Each bishop of a diocese had the title of exarch (not to be confused with a secular exarch [q.v.]), later that of patriarch (q.v.). The only exception to this was the bishop of Constantinople (qq.v.), who was a patriarch without a diocese.

DIOCLETIAN. Emperor (q.v.) from 284–305 whose reign is associated with certain important administrative and other reforms. Provincial governors were stripped of their military authority and provinces (q.v.) became smaller by increasing their number from 57 to almost a hundred. Provinces were grouped into 12 dioceses (q.v.), each governed by a vicar (q.v.), who, like the provincial governors he supervised, were responsible for justice and taxation, but had no military authority. At the highest level of administration was the tetrarchy (q.v.). The net result was to decentralize authority in such a way as to enhance imperial authority. For example, now provincial governors were responsible only for civil administration, while military authority was separated into the hands of a *doux* (q.v.). Diocletian's financial reforms included an attempt to reform the coinage, an Edict on Prices (q.v.), and a new method to assess the *annona* (q.v.) called the *capitatio-jugatio* (q.v.). This necessitated an increase in the number of tax officials in the provinces. Other reforms included the new collections of imperial edicts, the *Codex Gregorianus* and *Codex Hermogenianus* (qq.v.). Some of Diocletian's work failed. The tetrarchy collapsed soon after Diocletian's retirement in 305. The Edict on Prices proved ineffectual, and the Great Persecution (q.v.) of 303–311 failed. However, his administrative reforms, augmented by those of Constantine I (q.v.), lasted until the seventh century.

DIOKLEIA. Originally the name referred to a fortress in Illyricum (q.v.) destroyed by the Avars (q.v.) in the seventh century. Subsequently the name came to refer to the region along the Adriatic coast from Dyrrachion (qq.v.) to Kotor in the north, coinciding with modern Montenegro. In the 10th century a Slavic (q.v.) principality arose, comprised chiefly of Serbs (q.v.). It was conquered by Samuel of Bulgaria (q.v.) in 997, but with the conquest of Bulgaria (q.v.) in 1018 it became a dependency of Byzantium (q.v.). After the 10th century it was called Zeta (q.v.).

DIONYSIOS OF TELL MAHRE. Jacobite patriarch of Antioch (qq.v.) from 818–845, alleged to be the author of a lost church chronicle (q.v.) that was used by later writers, including Michael I the Syrian and Gregory Abul-Faraj (qq.v.). That lost chronicle was mistakenly identified with an anonymous work of the late eighth century, the *Chronicle of pseudo-Dionysios of Tell Mahre,* which incorporates the chronicle attributed to Joshua the Stylite (q.v.), and makes use of other sources as well, including the *Church History* of John of Ephesus (q.v.).

DIONYSIOS THE AREOPAGITE, PSEUDO-. Allegedly Dionysios, a member of the Athenian Areopagos who was converted by Saint Paul and who authored mystical theological writings. However, Dionysios is only a pseudonym for an unknown author who wrote in the late fifth or early sixth century, sometimes borrowing from the

Neoplatonic philosopher Proklos (q.v.). Various names have been suggested for the author, including Peter the Fuller (q.v.), Peter the Iberian, John Scholastikos, and Severos of Antioch (q.v.). The theology (q.v.) shows a fusion of Christian thought and Neoplatonism (q.v.) that views God's relationship to believers as expressed through a set of celestial and ecclesiastical hierarchies, rather than as real and immediate. The *Ecclesiastical Hierarchy,* supposedly authored by Dionysios, presents the liturgy (q.v.) as an earthly mirror of heavenly reality, an intermediary between the individual Christian and God. Dionysios's insistence on the unity of God made his writings popular among believers in Monophysitism (q.v.). Nevertheless, his writings were recognized as Orthodoxy (q.v.) in the seventh century by Maximos the Confessor (q.v.). The ninth-century translator Johannes Scotus Eriugena was responsible for introducing Pseudo-Dionysios to the West, where he had a great and enduring influence on medieval philosophy. In Byzantine monasticism (q.v.) his writings had less impact, in part because his mysticism was too intellectualized for the likes of Symeon the New Theologian, Gregory Palamas, and the Hesychasts (qq.v.).

DIOSKOROS. Monophysite patriarch of Alexandria (qq.v.) from 444 –451, succeeding Cyril (q.v.). Under his guidance the 449 "Robber" Council of Ephesus (q.v.) condemned Flavian, Patriarch of Constantinople (qq.v.), restored Eutyches, and declared for Monophysitism (qq.v.). Theodosios II (q.v.) ratified the decisions of the council, but those decisions were overturned in 451 at the Council of Chalcedon (q.v.), which deposed and exiled Dioskoros.

DIPTYCH. Two tablets, usually of wood or ivory, joined by hinges. Consular diptychs (examples survive from 428–541) were presented to senators, friends, and relatives by each of the annual consuls (q.v.) to commemorate their year in office. Each consular diptych contains the name and portrait of the consul. Imperial diptychs were given as presents to high civil officials and clergy upon their taking office. Sacred diptychs, commemorating the names of important laymen and clergy, living and dead, were placed on the altar and read aloud during the celebration of the Eucharist (q.v.). To erase the name of an emperor, bishop, or pope (qq.v.) from a sacred diptych was tantamount to excommunication. Conversely, as Michael VIII (q.v.) was preparing to depart for the Council of Lyons (q.v.) in 1274, he ordered that the pope's name be added to the diptychs read aloud during the liturgy (q.v.). This signified to the Greek clergy his intention to restore communion with the western church.

DNIEPER. The main river of southern Russia, and one of the longest rivers in Europe, originating near Moscow and flowing past Kiev into the Black Sea (qq.v.). It was the route by which the Rus (q.v.) of Kiev attacked Constantinople (q.v.). Its links to other main river systems, including the Volga, made navigation possible to northern Europe as well. The lower Dnieper was controlled by the Cumans (q.v.) from the mid-11th century until the mid-13th century, when the Mongols (q.v.) invaded the region.

DOBROMIR CHRYSOS. *See* **IVANKO.**

DOBRUDJA. Region between the lower Danube (q.v.) and the Black Sea (q.v.). The Romans called it "Little Scythia" (Scythia Minor); in the fourth-sixth centuries its metropolis was Tomis (qq.v.). Largely agricultural, it became in the Middle Ages a magnet for nomadic peoples from the Eurasian steppe (q.v.) who sought a more settled life south of the Danube. In 578 the Avars (q.v.) crossed the Danube and marched through the Dobrudja. In 680 Asparuch (q.v.) gained Dobrudja through treaty with Byzantium (q.v.), by which time it had been settled by Slavs (q.v.). In 967 it was occupied by Svjatoslav of Kiev (qq.v.), but in 971 John I Tzimiskes (q.v.) defeated him, forcing Svjatoslav to withdraw. Thereafter, John I and Basil II (q.v.) strengthened the defenses of the Dobrudja, which included restoring the fortress of Păcuiul lui Soare. Nevertheless, in the 11th century the Dobrudja suffered from Pecheneg (q.v.) raids. From the 12th through the 14th centuries, Byzantine control of Dobrudja's ports was lost to the Venetians and Genoese, while the interior was claimed by proto-Romanian and Slavic rulers who acknowledged Byzantine sovereignty. The region fell into the hands of the Ottomans (q.v.) after the battle of Varna (q.v.) in 1444.

DOME. In Byzantine architecture, a hemispherical ceiling (vault) over a square space defined by four arches, supported at the corners by pendentives or squinches (qq.v.). The impression made by Justinian's domed churches in Constantinople (q.v.), especially Hagia Sophia (q.v.), helped to establish the dome as the most characteristic feature of Byzantine church architecture.

DOMED BASILICA. A church of basilican (q.v.) plan with a dome (q.v.) over the central part of the nave (q.v.). The first domed basilica was the church at Meriamlik on the south coast of Asia Minor (q.v.), dating to 471–494. One of the most famous is St. Irene in Constantinople, built by Justinian I (q.v.).

DOMED OCTAGON CHURCH. A church of basilican (q.v.) plan with a dome (q.v.) over a square bay in the center of the nave (q.v.). The dome rests on an octagon base, created by a squinch (q.v.) at each corner of the square bay. Examples include the *katholikon* at Hosios Loukas (qq.v.) and the Nea Mone church on Chios (qq.v.). The Greek cross-domed octagon church (q.v.) makes use of this basic design.

DOME OF THE ROCK. *See* **ABD AL-MALIK; JERUSALEM.**

DOMESTIKOS. A term widely used to indicate military commanders and important civil and ecclesiastical officials. The most prominent military *domestikoi* were those who commanded the *tagmata,* including the *hikanatoi* (qq.v.), as well as the *domestikos ton scholon* who commanded the *scholae palatinae* (q.v.) and occasionally the entire field army. *Domestikoi* who were civil officials were important functionaries, some of them close to the emperor (q.v.), such as the *domestikoi* of the *sekreton* (q.v.). There were also ecclesiastical officials with this title.

DOMINICAN ORDER. Western monastic order founded by the Spanish priest Saint Dominic. It was sanctioned by Pope (q.v.) Honorius III in 1216 as an order whose special mission was to preach and teach. During the Latin occupation of Constantinople (q.v.) Dominicans fluent in Greek established a convent in Pera (q.v.) where they were active on behalf of controversial issues that divided the churches, e.g., papal primacy and the *filioque* (qq.v.). The *Summa Theologica,* the great work of the Dominican theologian Thomas Aquinas (q.v.), influenced several Byzantine writers, including Demetrios Kydones (q.v.), who translated it into Greek.

DONATION OF CONSTANTINE. A document apparently forged by the papacy (q.v.) in the eighth century to bolster its claims of political and ecclesiastical supremacy. It states that after Constantine I (q.v.) was baptized by Pope (q.v.) Silvester I (314–335), Constantine moved his residence to Constantinople (q.v.), leaving the pope with full authority over the church and over the western provinces of the empire. The document proved useful as a justification of papal policy toward the Franks (q.v.), including the papal coronations of Frankish ruler Pippin in 751 and of Charlemagne (q.v.) in 800. In the 11th century, it figured in the dispute between Patriarch Michael I Keroularios and Humbert (qq.v.) that resulted in the church schism of 1054 (q.v.). The Renaissance humanist Lorenzo Valla proved that the document was a papal forgery.

DONATISM. Reminiscent of Novatianism (q.v.), the Donatists of North Africa (q.v.) argued that the sacraments given by priests who had compromised the faith during the Great Persecution (q.v.), including sacraments given by priests who had been ordained by such priests, were invalid. The controversy began with the refusal of the Donatists in 311 to recognize Caecilian as bishop (q.v.) of Carthage because he had been ordained by a bishop accused of having surrendered liturgical items during the Great Persecution. They consecrated Donatus in his place. The controversy refused to go away, even after Constantine I (q.v.), and a commission headed by Pope Miltiades, rejected the Donatist claims, a decision confirmed by the Council of Arles (q.v.) in 314. Donatism grew to be a separatist church of great proportions, a native church that rejected the state-supported church, which it viewed as foreign, as imposed, as a kind of anti-church. Despite the opposition of Augustine (q.v.), who affirmed the principle that the validity of the sacraments are not dependent on the moral character of the priest administering them, despite every attempt to persecute them, the Donatists maintained their church as an underground movement up to the Arab conquest of the seventh century.

DOROSTOLON. City on the right bank of the Danube (q.v.) that Justinian I (q.v.) refurbished and that helped to defend Byzantium's (q.v.) northern frontier. It was conquered by the Bulgars (q.v.), recaptured by John I Tzimikes in 971, and, after the Byzantine conquest of Bulgaria (q.v.) in 1018, it was the chief city of the region of Paristrion (or Paradounavis). In the 11th century the Pechenegs (q.v.) captured it, Alexios I Komnenos (q.v.) recaptured it, and in 1186 it was incorporated into the Second Bulgarian Empire. It surrendered to the Ottomans (q.v.) in 1388.

DOROTHEOS OF GAZA. Sixth-century writer on the ascetic (q.v.) life. Before he founded his own monastery near Gaza (q.v.), he lived in another monastery near the city. He may have been forced to leave that monastery because of his support of the ideas of Evagrios Pontikos (q.v.), who was condemned for following Origen (q.v.). Dorotheos's *Didaskaliai* (Instructions) are a collection of spiritual instructions for monks that became quite popular, to judge from the various translations that survive.

DORYLAION. A major military base *(aplekton)* in Asia Minor (qq.v.) on the road to the eastern frontier. Located in the theme of Opskikion (qq.v.), at an important road junction, it was the gathering point for troops from the themes of Thrakesion (q.v.) and Opsikion. Its warm springs were famous. The Arab writer Ibn Khurdadhbeh (q.v.) describes them as consisting of seven great basins, all roofed, each basin able to accommodate a thousand men. The Seljuks (q.v.) captured it in the late 11th century. It was recaptured and rebuilt by Manuel I Komnenos (q.v.) in 1175, only to fall again to the Seljuks after the battle of Myriokephalon (q.v.) the following year.

DOUKAS. Byzantine historian who wrote a history that covers the years 1341–1462, describing events from the accession of John V to the siege of Mytilene by the Ottomans (qq.v.). The work begins with a brief survey of world history until 1341; after 1389 it becomes even more detailed. Doukas was a Greek from Asia Minor (q.v.) who spoke Italian and Turkish, and spent much of his life in the service of the Genoese, both as an envoy and as a secretary. In his capacity as envoy, he made several visits to the sultan Mehmed II's (qq.v.) court at Adrianople (q.v.). He also served the Gattilusio (q.v.) family, the Genoese family who controlled Lesbos (q.v.). He was a supporter of the union of the churches (q.v.). His history is especially invaluable for aspects of Mehmed II's reign about which he had personal knowledge, or was told about by his Genoese friends. Though not an eyewitness to the conquest of Constantinople (q.v.) by the Ottomans, his account of this event is considered reliable.

DOUKAS, ANDRONIKOS. Famous military commander whose revolt against Leo VI (q.v.) in 906 was provoked by the intrigues of the courtier Samonas (q.v.). Samonas tricked Andronikos into disobeying an imperial order to join the expedition of Himerios against the Arabs (qq.v.). In fear of his life, Andronikos defected to Baghdad (q.v.), where he was well received. However, when Samonas informed the Muslims of Leo VI's letter of pardon to Andronikos, Andronikos was thrown into prison and forced to convert to Islam (q.v.). He seems to have died shortly afterward.

DOUKAS, CONSTANTINE. Son of Andronikos Doukas (q.v.), and, like his father, a famous military commander under Leo VI (q.v.). Also like his father, his career ended tragically. He was a *strategos* (q.v.) of Charsianon, and subsequently *domestikos ton scholon* (q.v.). Ironically, it was he who arrested Samonas (q.v.), the man whose intrigues had forced his father to flee to the Arabs (q.v.). However, when Alexander (q.v.) died in 913, Constantine marched his troops into Constantinople (q.v.) and claimed the throne with broad popular support. Patriarch Nicholas I Mystikos (qq.v.), who at first seemed to support him, suddenly withdrew his support, and Constantine was killed by the imperial guard at the very gates of the Great Palace (q.v.). His dying words were a curse on the patriarch. Leo Choirosphaktes (q.v.) and other supporters among the aristocracy (q.v.), including relatives of Constantine, were punished. Constantine's fame lived on in the revolt of Basil the Copper Hand (q.v.) and in praise offered to him in the *Digenes Akrites* (q.v.).

DOUKAS, CONSTANTINE. Son of Michael VII Doukas and Maria of Alania (qq.v.), born around 1074. He was betrothed to the daughter of Robert Guiscard (q.v.), Helena, but these marriage plans were overturned when Nikephoros III (q.v.) came to power. When Alexios I Komnenos (q.v.) became emperor he favored Constantine, betrothing him to Anna Komnene (q.v.). Constantine had every right to expect that one day he would inherit the throne. But this arrangement was nullified when Alexios produced a male heir in John II (q.v.). It has also been suggested that Constantine may have developed a disease that made his prospects untenable. In any case, Constantine retired to his estates and died sometime not long after 1094, having been a pawn all his life in the politics of marriage alliances.

DOUKAS, CONSTANTINE X. *See* **CONSTANTINE X DOUKAS.**

DOUKAS, JOHN. Brother of Emperor Constantine X Doukas (qq.v.) who held the title of caesar (q.v.). He was involved in many important events from 1057–1081. He was a trusted advisor and *strategos* (q.v.) who helped to put down a conspiracy in 1061. When Romanos IV (q.v.) was captured by the Seljuks at the battle of Mantizkert (qq.v.), he forced the empress Eudokia Makrembolitissa (q.v.) into a monastery. With the help of Michael Psellos (q.v.) he engineered the enthronement of Michael VII (q.v.), and the blinding of Romanos IV. However, a palace eunuch (q.v.) named Nikephoritzes (q.v.) plotted the fall of John Doukas. This was accomplished by sending him with an army against the forces of Roussel de Bailleul (q.v.), who had rebelled in Asia Minor (q.v.). Roussel captured John and proclaimed him emperor (and alleged supporter), but soon John was captured by the Turks (q.v.) and ransomed by Constantine X. John wisely decided to become a monk to avoid punishment. John's final historical role was to arrange the marriage of his granddaughter Irene Doukaina to the future Alexios I Komnenos (qq.v.), and to help engineer Alexios's accession to the throne. In the *Alexiad,* Anna Komnene (q.v.) relates how John, dressed as a monk, and standing with Alexios and his army below the walls of Constantinople (q.v.) in 108l, was mockingly referred to as "the abbot" by the Varangian Guard (q.v.) on the walls above, and how John advised Alexios not to attack these troops but to befriend them. It was advice that gave Alexios entrance to the capital, and hence the throne. He remained an esteemed advisor to the new emperor until his death in about 1088.

DOUX. Under Diocletian and Constantine I the Great (qq.v.) a *doux* (*dux* in Latin) commanded the military forces of each province. With the introduction of the theme (q.v.) system the office changed considerably. A governor of a theme became a *strategos* (q.v.), to whom the *doux* held a subordinate position. After about 960 larger districts, e.g., Mesopotamia, even Bulgaria (qq.v.), could be administered by a *doux,* as could large cities like Thessalonike and Adrianople (qq.v.). Under Alexios I Komnenos (q.v.) and his dynastic successors, the term applied to all the governors of themes, each of whom had both civil and military powers. They also had a subordinate *katepano* (q.v.). *Doux* could also refer to the *domestikos ton scholon* (q.v.), and the term *megas doux* (q.v.) referred to the commander of the fleet.

DROMON. The standard Byzantine warship that employed both sails and oars. A typical 10th-century dromon had two banks of oars employing 200 rowers, in addition to a battering ram on the prow, and enough heavily armored marines to board an enemy ship if necessary. In other words, it looked and acted very much like the *bireme* of classical Greece. However, from the late seventh century on, the prow was a bronze-tipped siphon for discharging Byzantine napalm, the famous Greek Fire (q.v.) that proved decisive in so many battles. Hides and lead sheathing protected the ship's sides against enemy incendiaries. Also new was a wooden tower amidships that allowed catapults and archers to launch stones, arrows, and other antipersonnel devices.

DROMOS. The imperial postal and transportation system, consisting of a series of road stations where pack animals rested and goods were collected. It was administered by the praetorian prefect (q.v.), and, later, by the *logothetes tou dromou* (q.v.).

DROUGOUBITAI. A tribe of Slavs (q.v.) who, with several other Slavic tribes, took to the seas in the early seventh century to pillage the coast and islands of Greece (q.v.). Shortly thereafter, they participated in a siege of Thessalonike (q.v.) that was led by the Avars (q.v.). Eventually, they were settled as farmers in two regions, the first around Thessalonike, extending as far as Berroia (q.v.), and the other around Philippopolis in Thrace (qq.v.). They were subject to Byzantium (q.v.), but perhaps not until after 658 when Constans II (q.v.) subjected "sklavinia," a region of Slavs somewhere in Greece, probably in Macedonia (q.v.). In any case, the Drououbitai had their own "king," which indicates a certain degree of autonomy.

DROUNGARIOS. In the provinces, a high-ranking military officer who commanded a *droungos* within a theme (qq.v.). There was also a Droungarios of the Watch *(droungarios tes viglas),* who commanded the Watch (q.v.), or *vigla,* that guarded the emperor (q.v.), and a Droungarios of the Fleet *(droungarios tou ploiou),* who commanded the imperial fleet stationed at Constantinople (q.v.).

DROUNGOS. District subdivision of a theme (q.v.), consisting of a thousand men, commanded by a *drungarios* (q.v.). A *droungos* was larger than the *bandon,* but smaller than a *turma* (qq.v.).

DUBROVNIK. Called Ragusa in Italian, this prosperous port and stronghold on the coast of Dalmatia (q.v.) was founded in the seventh century by refugees from Dalmatian Epidauros who had fled the assault of Slavs and Avars (qq.v.). In 868 Basil I (q.v.), answering an appeal from the city, relieved an Arab (q.v.) siege that had lasted two years, after which the city provided ships for a counter-attack on Muslim conquests in Apulia (q.v.). Probably at this time the theme (q.v.) of Dalmatia was organized to provide security for the region. Thereafter, rule over Dubrovnik went back and forth between Byzantines, Venetians, and Normans (q.v.). The Venetians held it from 1205–1358, after which time it became a protectorate of Hungary (q.v.) until 1526, when it came under Ottoman (q.v.) domination.

DUCHY OF ATHENS AND THEBES. *See* **ATHENS; OTHON DE LA ROCHE; THEBES.**

DUIN. Capital of that part of Armenia (q.v.) under Persian rule in the fifth and sixth centuries. It was conquered by Herakleios (q.v.) in

623, but it was lost to the Arabs (q.v.) in 640. Byzantine attempts at reconquest (the last in 1045) were unsuccessful. A church council at Duin in 505 accepted the *Henotikon* (q.v.), and a second council in 554 rejected the Council of Chalcedon (q.v.), breaking with the Byzantine church.

DUSHAN, STEPHEN. *See* **STEPHEN DUSHAN.**

DUX. *See* **DOUX.**

DYNATOI. "The powerful" (in Greek), a term used in the 10th and 11th centuries, chiefly to designate powerful landed aristocracy (q.v.) of eastern Asia Minor (q.v.), some with familiar names like Phokas, Skleros, and Doukas. More generally, the term refers to powerful office holders, even monasteries, whose power derived from large landholdings. The problem for the government was partly financial, since such large estates tended to increase at the expense of smaller peasant properties. Tax revenues declined accordingly, since the magnates often evaded taxes through grants of *exkousseeia* (q.v.). A series of emperors (q.v.) from Romanos I through Basil II (qq.v.) legislated against them because the growth of large estates decreased the state's revenues and its *stratiotika ktemata* (q.v.). Basil II, for example, made the *dynatoi* pay the *allelengyon* (q.v.) of their poorer neighbors. This ultimately failed; by the 12th century large estates proliferated throughout the empire at the expense of independent villages. The Palaiologan period (1261–1453) was the golden age of the *dynatoi,* as state authority over the provinces waned.

DYRRACHION. Port-city in Dalmatia (q.v.) on the coast of the Adriatic (q.v.), important chiefly because it was the western end of the Via Egnatia (q.v.). Anyone seeking to attack Byzantium from Italy (qq.v.) had to conquer Dyrrachion in order to use the Via Egnatia to get to Thessalonike and Constantinople (qq.v.). Anastasios I (q.v.), who was born in Dyrrachion, fortified the city with three lines of concentric walls. In the ninth century its importance as a base of Byzantine sea power was recognized when the city and its hinterland were organized into a special theme (q.v.). Each attempt by the Normans (q.v.) to invade Byzantium began with an attack on Dyrrachion. Their first attempt in 1081 succeeded in capturing the city; they controlled it until the death of Robert Guiscard (q.v.) in 1085. Subsequent Norman assaults were less successful. Other invaders from Italy included William II of Sicily (qq.v.), who sacked the city in 1185, and Charles of Anjou (q.v.), who seized it briefly in 1274. Venice (q.v.), whose power in the Adriatic was overwhelming by the 14th century, had control of Dyrrachion from 1392–1501. Attacks from the interior of the Balkan Peninsula (q.v.) were fewer, but no less important. For example, the Serbs (q.v.) under Samuel of Bulgaria (q.v.) seized the city for several years until Basil II (q.v.) reconquered it in 1005, and in 1501 the city fell to the expanding military might of the Ottomans (q.v.).

– E –

ECLOGA. A legal handbook issued by Leo III (q.v.) in 741. It was intended as an abridged and updated substitute for the *Corpus Juris Civilis* (q.v.), which was outdated, and incomprehensible to those unacquainted with Latin. It also intended to introduce Christian principles to the law, making the law more humane by substituting mutilation (e.g., cutting off the nose, tongue, or hand, and blinding) for the death penalty, a prevalent punishment in Justinian's *Corpus*. The *Ecloga* also served as a manual for the teaching of law, replacing Justinian I's (q.v.) *Institutes*. Its usefulness is attested to by its revisions by an Arab adaptation, an Armenian translation, and various Slavonic translations. It was not replaced in Byzantium (q.v.) until the *Epanagogue* (q.v.), and its revision, the *Prochiron* (q.v.), issued in the following century.

ECONOMY. Byzantium's (q.v.) economy was based chiefly on agriculture (q.v.), for most citizens of the empire were farmers. By the ninth century, farmers were free peasants (as reflected in the Farmer's Law [q.v.]), and remained such until the growth of the *pronoia* (q.v.) system in the 12th century. Most revenues from state taxation (q.v.) were derived from taxes on land, which is why land-grabbing by wealthy aristocracy in Asia Minor (qq.v), the so-called "powerful" (*dynatoi* [q.v.]), threatened the economic health of the state. Taxes and assessments for the army were paid largely in coinage (q.v.), for Byzantium had a monetary economy. Nevertheless, there was a parallel barter economy in the countryside, and in cities one could find some services and salaries being paid in kind. Constantinople (q.v.) and other cities of the empire, most of them situated along the coastline of the Mediterranean and Aegean (qq.v.) were emporiums of trade. Trade on land and by sea was strictly controlled and taxed. For example, Abydos (q.v.) collected taxes on shipping going to and from Constantinople. The state also controlled manufacturing by controlling the guilds, and by reserving certain manufacturing (e.g., in silk) for itself. Nevertheless, private enterprise did exist, as illustrated by the story of the widow Danelis (q.v.), and, in the late 13th-century, by the career of Goudeles Tyrannos (q.v.). In general, the health of the Byzantine economy was much dependent on the state's ability to control its borders. Attacks on Asia Minor by Arabs, and subsequently by Seljuks (qq.v), eroded the agricultural heart of the Byzantine economy. Byzantine control of its maritime economy was eroded by inroads from the Italian republics, especially Venice (q.v.), despite the attempt by Alexios I (q.v.) to create a more flexible monetary system, one suited more to commercial markets. Venice especially made inroads into the Byzantine economy. This culminated most dramatically in the conquest of Constantinople in 1204 by the Venetian-led Fourth Crusade (q.v.).

ECUMENICAL COUNCILS. The seven ecumenical (i.e., universal) church councils accepted by the eastern church. Most councils were convened to deal with attacks on Orthodoxy (q.v.). The First Ecumenical Council at Nicaea (q.v.) in 325 condemned Arianism (q.v.). The Second Ecumenical Council at Constantinople (q.v.) in 381 condemned the *Pneumatomachoi*, who believed that the Holy Spirit was a created being. The Third Ecumenical Council at Ephesus (q.v.) in 431 condemned Nestorianism (q.v.). The Council of Chalcedon (q.v.) in 451 condemned Monophysitism (q.v.). The Fifth Ecumenical Council at Constantinople in 553 condemned the Three Chapters (q.v.). The Sixth Ecumenical Council at Constantinople in 680–681 condemned Monotheletism (q.v.). The Seventh Ecumenical Council at Nicaea in 787 condemned Iconoclasm (q.v.) and restored the veneration of icons (q.v.).

ECUMENICAL PATRIARCH. *See* **PATRIARCH.**

EDESSA. Ancient city in upper Mesopotamia (q.v.), on the edge of the Syrian desert. The legend that king Abgar V, a contemporary of Christ, converted and that Christ sent him a towel (the *mandylion*) with a likeness (*acheiropoietos* [q.v.]) of Christ's face, was widely believed. Allegedly, the holy towel was accompanied by a letter promising that the city would never be taken by an enemy. In reality, the Abgar who converted was a later king, Abgar IX (179–216), but the legend was widely believed, and it proved an inspiration to the city's citizenry. Those counting themselves Christians at Edessa included not only followers of the Council of Chalcedon (q.v.), but adherents to Monophysitism and Nestorianism, as well as Maronites (qq.v.). The city was a center for Nestorianism (q.v.), until its famous theological school was destroyed during the reign of Zeno (q.v.). Nestorians were welcomed into Persia (q.v.), where they were allowed to found a new school at Nisibis (q.v.). Edessa was the object of Persian attacks in the sixth century. Kavad (q.v.) besieged it unsuccessfully in 503, as did Chosroes II (q.v.) in 544. The Arabs (q.v.) captured it around 640, and it remained in Muslim hands until John Kourkouas (q.v.) recaptured it in 944, sending the famous *mandylion* back to Constantinople (qq.v.), where it was escorted through the capital by Romanos I (q.v.). Edessa was occupied again in 1032 by George Maniakes (q.v.), who took from the city its second relic, the apocryphal letter of Jesus to Abgar. The Crusaders seized Edessa in 1098, creating the County of Edessa, the first of the Crusader states in Syria (q.v.). It subsequently fell to Zangi (q.v.) in 1146, was recovered briefly by the Crusaders, only to be sacked by Nur al-Din (q.v.), who massacred its male citizens and sold its women and children into slavery. Until these final devastations, Edessa remained a commercial and intellectual center that boasted such famous writers as Joshua the Stylite (q.v.).

EDESSA. *See* **VODENA.**

EDICT OF MILAN. A modern term for an edict that was issued, allegedly, by Constantine I and Licinius (qq.v.) at a meeting in Milan (q.v.) in 313. It granted religious freedom to all, and ordered previously confiscated private buildings and churches of Christians to be returned. The original version does not exist. There is only a Latin rescript preserved by Lactantius (q.v.), and a Greek translation of the rescript by Eusebios of Caesarea (q.v.) in his *Ecclesiastical History*. It has been argued that there never was a specific Edict of Milan, only the edict of toleration issued by Galerius (q.v.) in 311. It has also been argued that it is an edict of Licinius that simply restates Galerius's edict. In any case, since Constantine had granted such toleration in 306, and Maxentius (q.v.) had followed suit in 311, the Edict of Milan, if there ever was one, appears redundant for the western provinces.

EDICT ON PRICES. Issued by Diocletian (q.v.) in 301, it consisted of a long list of specific goods and services, each appended with a maximum price. As an attempt to control runaway inflation, it failed. It was published in lengthy inscriptions, fragments of which survive from over 40 cities. However, none survive from the regions governed by Maximian and Constantius Chlorus (qq.v.), though their names are appended to the edict. Presumably they did not publish it, for whatever reasons. The edict failed, in part because it reveals a basic misunderstanding of inflation, attributing it solely to greed. Nonetheless, the serious consequence of inflation for the army (q.v.) was clearly understood. The edict's preamble points out that rapid inflation was impoverishing soldiers by wiping out their purchasing power. For the modern historian the edict is an important historical source for what it reveals about goods and services, trade and commerce, prices and coinage (q.v.).

EDIRNE. *See* **ADRIANOPLE.**

EDUCATION. Until the sixth century, education in Byzantium (q.v.) was the traditional Greco-Roman education, which emphasized grammar and rhetoric, i.e., the ability to speak and write Greek well. Primary and secondary education (chiefly for boys) was accomplished by tutors who introduced classical literature, especially Homer (q.v.). Higher education was available in certain cities, e.g., Alexandria, Athens, Constantinople (established by Theodosios II in 425), and Gaza (qq.v.). There was a famous law school in Berytus (q.v.). The higher school at Constantinople (not a university in the western sense) was organized to train students for the state bureaucracy. Inevitably, an education based on pagan literature created tension in a society that was increasingly Christian. This explains why Justinian I (q.v.) closed the pagan school in Athens in 529. Amid the turmoil that followed Justinian I's reign, cities declined and the other great centers of higher education disappeared altogether. Higher education resurfaced in the ninth century when caesar Bardas (qq.v.) created a school in the Magnaura (q.v.), staffed with teachers the caliber of Leo the Mathematician (q.v.). Secondary education was also reorganized for the purpose of providing administrators to staff the state bureaucracy. Constantine VII (q.v.) reinvigorated higher education in the 10th century bringing students and professors together under his own patronage. In 1046–1047 a school of law and philosophy was organized in Constantinople by Constantine IX (q.v.), with John (VIII) Xiphilinos (q.v.) as its president (*nomophylax* [q.v.]). Xiphilinos was part of a circle of intellectuals that included Michael Psellos (q.v.), whose career as a professor of Neoplatonism (q.v.) demonstrates the tension that remained between secular and religious studies. Higher education for the clergy was established in 1107 when Alexios I Komnenos created the Patriarchal School (qq.v.). Numerous private tutors, supervised by the state, offered instruction. The capture of Constantinope in 1204 by the Fourth Crusade destroyed these institutions. After Constantinople was recovered in 1261 Michael VII (q.v.) created a school of philosophy (q.v.) headed by George Akropolites (q.v.). However, most schooling in the Palaiologan (q.v.) period was done through private schools and tutors. As one can see, medieval Byzantium never developed a university on the western model of an independent, self-governing corporation.

EGERIA. Western nun who went on a pilgrimage to the Holy Land in 381–384. Her account, not all of which survives, is the first known description of a pilgrimage. It includes important information on the way in which the Holy Land had been transformed by Christian piety and church construction since Constantine I's (q.v.) conversion.

EGNATIA, VIA. *See* **VIA EGNATIA.**

EGYPT. One of Byzantium's (q.v.) most important provinces until its occupation by the Persians (q.v.) from 618/619–629, and its subsequent conquest by the Arabs (q.v.) in 640–642 (described by John of Nikiu [q.v.]). Its vital economic importance lay in the large supply of grain it provided. The earliest Christian hermits (q.v.) flourished in Egypt, and the heresy of Monophysitism (qq.v.) found fertile soil among the Copts (q.v.). The see of its capital, Alexandria (qq.v.), was among the most powerful in the empire, as illustrated by the career patriarch Cyril (qq.v.).

EISAGOGE. *See* **EPANAGOGE.**

EKTHESIS. Herakleios's (q.v.) futile attempt, by edict in 638, to find a formula that would reconcile the Monophysites (q.v.) with those who adhered to the teachings of the Fourth Ecumenical Council at Chalcedon (qq.v.). This had become a particularly important issue with the recovery of the eastern (chiefly Monophysite) provinces from the Persians (q.v.). Monoenergism (q.v.), the doctrine that

Christ had one active divine-human force *(energeia),* was a first attempt at compromise. Patriarch Sergios of Constantinople (qq.v.) supported this, but Sophronios, who became patriarch of Jerusalem (qq.v.) in 634, did not. Sergios dropped Monoenergism in favor of Monotheletism (q.v.), the doctrine that the human and divine natures in Christ were united in a single will *(thelema).* This had been first proposed to him by Pope Honorius I (625–638). Herakleios made this doctrine official in 638 with the publication of his *Ekthesis* ("statement of faith"). However, the futility of this was quickly apparent, for both sides rejected it, including Pope Honorios I's successor, Pope Severinus, who declared for two wills in Christ. Moreover, by 638 the Arabs conquered Syria and Palestine (qq.v.), and would soon conquer Egypt (q.v.), the very provinces that the *Ekthesis* was attempting to pacify. Constans II's *Typos* (qq.v.), issued in 648, aimed at patching up relations with the papacy (q.v.) by forbidding any discussion of wills and energies.

ELPIDIOS. *Strategos* (q.v.) sent by Irene (q.v.) to Sicily (q.v.) in 781. Accused of supporting a plot against her, and with the army (q.v.) in Sicily standing behind him, Irene was forced to dispatch a fleet to capture him. Soon after the fleet arrived, Elpidios fled to the Arabs (q.v.) of North Africa, where he declared himself emperor and was crowned by the Arabs. In 794 he appeared on a marauding expedition into Byzantine territory with Suleyman, son of Harun al-Rashid (q.v.); this is the last that is known of him.

EMESA. City in Syria ([q.v.]; modern Homs), west of Palmyra (q.v.). The Persians (q.v.) occupied it from 609–628, and it fell to the Arabs (q.v.) in 636, after the defeat of Herakleios at the battle of Yarmuk (qq.v.). Thereafter, it remained in Muslim possession, despite a brief Byzantine reconquest in 969. Byzantine armies sacked and burned the city on two other occasions in the 10th century (in 983 and in 999). Its most famous citizen was Romanos the Melode (q.v.).

EMIR. *See* **EMIRATE.**

EMIRATE. With the breakup of the Seljuk sultanate of Rum (qq.v.) in the 13th century, various *emirs* (Turkish military commanders) emerged to found small states in Asia Minor (q.v.). Among these emirates were those of Germiyan, Karaman, Karasi, and of the Ottomans (qq.v.).

EMPEROR. Title of the Byzantine sovereign. The precise terms used included *autokrator* (Greek for the Latin *imperator*), and, after the conquest of Persia by Herakleios, *basileus* (qq.v.). Fundamentally, the concept is Roman, for Byzantium (q.v.) was, in truth, the Roman Empire in the East down to the conquest of Constantinople (q.v.) in 1453. Once Christianity became established as the sole state religion, the emperor was viewed as God's viceroy on earth, from whom all political and military power flowed. This concept of emperorship, and the titles associated with it, Byzantine emperors protected as a copyright against any infringement by western emperors (e.g., Charlemagne [q.v.]). Authority was delegated to high officials who resided with the emperor, normally at the Great Palace of Constantinople (qq.v.) but also to administrators in the provinces. For this an emperor needed basic administrative and rhetorical skills. More important than even military leadership, the management of a vast empire required, above all, the skills needed to administer a court and vast bureaucracy.

EMPRESS. A title *(augusta, basilissa)* bestowed by the emperor (q.v.) on a female member of the imperial family, typically on his wife, but occasionally on a mother or sister. The significance of the title is shown by the fact that not every wife of an emperor was crowned empress. Until the eighth century it was granted only to imperial wives who produced a male heir to the throne. One of the most powerful empresses, Anna Dalassene (q.v.), was not an imperial wife, but the mother of Alexios I Komnenos (q.v.).

ENGLAND. *See* **BRITAIN.**

ENKOLPION. *See* **RELIQUARY.**

ENZYMA. *See* **AZYMA.**

EPANAGOGE. An introduction to the collection of laws called the *Basilika* (q.v.), which aimed at replacing the former *Ecloga* (q.v.). It was issued in 886, and replaced in 907 by the *Prochiron* (q.v.).

EPARCH, BOOK OF THE. *See* **BOOK OF THE EPARCH; GUILDS.**

EPARCH OF THE CITY. Governor of the city of Constantinople (q.v.) whose post was created in 359 on the model of the urban prefect of Rome (q.v.). As chief judge of the imperial tribunal, he was responsible for law and order in the capital, as well as for the maintenance of prisons. He also supervised building activity, spectacles and ceremonial, and commercial activity (described in the Book of the Eparch [q.v.]).

EPARCHIUS AVITUS. *See* **AVITUS, EPARCHIUS.**

EPHESUS. One of the great coastal cities of Asia Minor (q.v.) in classical antiquity; capital of the Roman province of Asia. A flourishing seaport, as well as a center of commerce and finance, made it one of the most prosperous of the major cities along the Aegean (q.v.) coast. It was also among the most splendid in terms of its public monuments, including the long, colonnaded street with marble paving slabs that ran from the harbor to the theater. It had two famous churches, the Church of St. John, and the Church of the Virgin, the basilica (q.v.) where the Council of Ephesus (q.v.) met in 431. The so-called "Robber Council" (q.v.) met in Ephesus in 449. Around 614 the city suffered catastrophic destruction, probably by the Persians (q.v.), and/or by earthquake, from which it never fully recovered; entire areas of the city had to be abandoned, and they were never reoccupied. In the eighth century its size was still considerable enough to make it the largest city (and perhaps capital) of the theme of Thrakesion (qq.v.), and later part of the maritime theme of Samos (q.v.), perhaps indicating its role as a naval base. Its continuing commercial importance is seen in the regional fair held there in the eighth century. However, by the ninth century the harbor had silted up, and the city's population had shrunk to a settlement around the harbor, and to a strongly fortified area surrounding the Church of St. John. On this reduced scale it survived, and from about the 10th century onward it revived and prospered. In the mid-13th century it attracted the great teacher and writer Nikephoros Blemmydes (q.v.), whose pupils included George Akropolites and Theodore II Laskaris (qq.v.). In the early 14th century the city was threatened by the Catalan Grand Company, and by the Ottomans (qq.v.), who conquered it in 1304.

EPHESUS, ECUMENICAL COUNCIL OF. The Third Ecumenical Council called in 431 at Ephesus by Theodosios II (q.v.) to settle a dispute between Nestorios, patriarch of Constantinople (qq.v.), and Cyril, patriarch of Alexandria (qq.v.), over the exact relationship of Christ's human and divine natures. Nestorios followed the theological school at Antioch (q.v.) which believed that although the two natures were in contact, they were essentially independent of each other. This led him to state that Mary was not, properly speaking, the *Theotokos* (q.v.), or " bearer of God," but the mother of a man, Christ. After all, Nestorios reasoned, how can one say that God, who is unchanging, was born and grew up? This attack on Mary aroused great passions within the church. When the council opened, the situation was chaotic, even disgraceful. Cyril borrowed 1,500 pounds of gold to bribe high officials at court. His supporters roamed the streets of Ephesus shouting and looking for trouble. Nestorios's house had to be guarded by soldiers for his protection. John I (q.v.), patriarch of Antioch, and Nestorios's main supporter, arrived three weeks late, which allowed Cyril to engineer Nestorios's condemnation. John I quickly responded by organizing a rival council on the spot to condemn Cyril, whom they declared deposed. At first Theodosios II let the two depositions stand, but Cyril's money and influence at court, including the support of Theodosios II's sister Pulcheria (q.v.), won the day, and he was allowed to resume his see (q.v.). However, Nestorios remained in exile in Egypt (q.v.). In 433 moderates on both sides agreed to accept the epithet *Theotokos* (q.v.) for Mary, and agreed to a compromise formula stating that Christ had two natures that existed in an unconfused union. Nestorios's followers retreated to Edessa (q.v.), and, after Zeno (q.v.) drove them from that city in 489, to Nisibis, in Persia (qq.v.). In terms of their ecclesiastical rivalry, the see of Alexandria had humiliated the upstart see of Constantinople.

EPHESUS, "ROBBER" COUNCIL OF. Later declared invalid by the Council of Chalcedon (q.v.), this council met in 449 to depose Flavian, patriarch of Constantinople (qq.v.) and to approve Monophysitism (q.v.). As with the Council of Ephesus (q.v.) in 431, theological controversy was mixed with ecclesiastical rivalry between the sees of Alexandria (q.v.) and Constantinople. Dioskoros, patriarch of Alexandria after Cyril (qq.v.), espoused the doctrine that after the Incarnation, Christ's two natures were united into one nature *(mono physis)*. This doctrine was taken up in Constantinople by the monk, Eutyches (q.v.), who was condemned by Flavian. However, Eutyches's godson Chrysaphios, a powerful court minister, convinced Theodosios II (q.v.) to call this so-called Robber Council in 449, dominated by Dioskoros. Flavian was deposed, and Eutyches was declared Orthodox (q.v.). Pope Leo I's (q.v.) opposition to Monophysitism was expressed in a letter that the council refused to accept. Thus, the see of Alexandria triumphed again, but its victory was short-lived, for two years later the Council of Chalcedon reversed its decisions.

EPHREM THE SYRIAN. Syriac writer, theologian, hymnographer, saint. Born in Nisibis (q.v.) ca. 306, he later moved to Edessa (q.v.) where he spent the last decade of his life, dying there in 373. Ephrem wrote an enormous number of works, mostly in verse, on a variety of topics, including polemics against the emperor Julian, Arius, and Mani (qq.v.). Their translation into Greek, Armenian, Latin, and Church Slavonic insured their lasting impact, especially on subsequent Syriac and Byzantine hymnographers like Romanos the Melode (q.v.).

EPHTHALITES. A Hunnic people (or peoples) who menaced Persia (q.v.) from 427–557. Referred to by Prokopios (q.v.) as "white" (hence the term White Huns [q.v.]), due to their fair complexion, their precise relationship to other Hunnic peoples is unclear. Their conquests of the lands between the Caspian Sea and the Indus River were completed by about 425, after which they turned their attention to Persia (q.v.). For over a century, intermittently, the Ephthalites distracted the Persians from frontier warfare with Byzantium (q.v.) and disrupted Persia's caravan trade with China (q.v.), prompting the Persians to insist that Byzantium continue to pay for the defense of the Caspian Gates (q.v.). In 427 hostilities erupted that resulted in a Persian victory, but the remainder of the fifth century was less fortunate to the Persians. In 469 the Persians were defeated, and in 484 the Ephthalites killed the Persian king Peroz. However, from 496–498 Kavad (q.v.) was in exile among the Ephthalites and it was they who reinstated him on the throne in 499. From 503–513 they suffered a series of defeats at the hands of the Persians, who ejected them from Persian territory. In 557 an alliance of Turks (q.v.) and Persians destroyed them.

EPIBOLE. A term meaning "impost" or "surcharge," referring to the state's practice of making the owners of productive land share mutually in taxation (q.v.) levied on fallow land. In this way the originally estimated taxes of an entire fiscal unit (usually a village) could be fulfilled. By the sixth century the procedures worked out to do this equitably took into account the previous assessments of all unproductive property, as well as the normal tax obligations of the fiscal unit. Only then was the tax surcharge distributed among the members of the unit. Basil II (q.v.) replaced the *epibole* with the *allelengyon* (q.v.).

EPIPHANIOS. Bishop (q.v.) of Salamis (Constantia) in Cyprus (q.v.) from 367–403, writer, and authority on heresy (q.v.). He was hostile to both religious art and to classical education. He is also remembered for his opposition to those defending the theology of Origen (q.v.). This is illustrated by how he was drawn into a controversy that pitted John Chrysostom against a supporter of Origen, Theophilos of Alexandria (qq.v.). His support of Theophilos took him to Constantinople (q.v.); on the return voyage he died. Among the writings is one entitled *Refutation of All the Heresies*.

EPIROS. A mountainous region in what is now southern Albania and northwestern Greece (qq.v.), separated from the rest of Greece by the Pindos (q.v.) mountain range. In the fourth century its administration was divided into the province of Old Epiros, with its capital at Nikopolis (q.v.), and New Epiros, farther north, with its capital at Dyrrachion (q.v.). The cities, the most important of which are located on coastal plains, like the port-city of Avlon, were affected by the raids of Vandals (q.v.). Nikopolis was briefly captured by the Vandals in 474. The region was also affected by barbarian raids in 517 and in 539–540, prompting Justinian I (q.v.) to build and refurbish fortifications in the region. These seem to have withstood an invasion of Ostrogoths (q.v.) in 551, but not the invasions of Avars and Slavs (qq.v.) in the 580s. By about 615 the cities were overrun and the region depopulated. Byzantine hegemony was reestablished slowly, beginning in the ninth century with the creation of the themes (q.v.) of Dyrrachion and Nikopolis. The region fell under the domination of the despotate of Epiros (q.v.) in 1204, and then (after 1264) by independent Greek despots (q.v.) until 1318. Thereafter, successive rulers included Italians (the Orsini and Tocco families), Albanians, and Serbs (qq.v.). For example, the Serb Thomas Preljubovic ruled over Ioannina (q.v.) from 1366–1384, defending it from Albanian attacks. The Ottomans (q.v.) conquered the region in the 15th century. Intermittent invasions and migrations of peoples created a diverse society that included not only Greeks but also Slavs, Vlachs, Albanians, Jews, Turks, and even Armenians (qq.v.).

EPIROS, DESPOTATE OF. Greek state in Epiros (q.v.) established after the Fourth Crusade conquered Constantinople (qq.v.) in 1204 and divided up Byzantium (q.v.). Until 1230 it appeared to have a much better chance of restoring the empire than the other two Greek states, namely, the Empire of Nicaea and the Empire of Trebizond (qq.v.). The pedigree of its founder, Michael I Komnenos Doukas

(1205–1215), was impeccable, including a connection to the Angelos (q.v.) family. His half-brother Theodore Komnenos Doukas (q.v.), who succeeded him, captured Ohrid in 1216, Thessalonike in 1224, and Adrianople (qq.v.) in 1225, by which time his empire extended from the Adriatic to the Aegean (qq.v.). Crowned emperor (q.v.), and refusing to recognize his rival John III Vatatzes (q.v.) as emperor at Nicaea, Theodore had every reason to expect that he would recapture Constantinople. But that hope was dashed at the battle of Klokotnitsa (q.v.) in 1230, where the Bulgar Tsar John Asen II (qq.v.) captured Theodore, defeated his army, then occupied Macedonia (q.v.) as far west as Dyrrachion (q.v.). In 1246 Thessalonike, which had eluded John Asen II, was captured by John III Vatatzes. By this time the former empire was reduced to calling itself a despotate, and its fortunes declined further after Michael II Komnenos Doukas (ca. 1230–ca. 1266) was defeated at the battle of Pelagonia (q.v.) in 1259. In the 14th century, the despotate effectively ceased with its occupation by the Orsini family from 1318–1337, then by Serbs (q.v.) under Symeon Urosh in 1348. The Ottomans (q.v.) conquered the region piecemeal in the first half of the 15th century. Arta (q.v.), the former capital of the Despotate of Epiros, fell to the Ottomans in 1449.

EREMITE. (In Greek, "hermit," derived from *eremia*, meaning "solitude," and *eremos*, meaning "desert.") A hermit who has withdrawn to some solitary place as an anchorite (q.v.) to practice rigorous asceticism (q.v.), in contrast to the communal monasticism (q.v.) of a *koinobion* (q.v.). The sayings of the early eremites of Egypt (q.v.) were compiled in anthologies that are referred to as the *Apophthegmata Patrum* (q.v.).

ERTOGHRUL. *See* **OTTOMANS.**

ESONARTHEX. *See* **NARTHEX.**

ESTOIRE D'ERACLES. The name given to a collection of works about the early Crusades (q.v.), the core of which is an Old French translation made in 1220–1223 of the Latin *Chronicon* of William of Tyre (q.v.), including also the various French continuations of his work beyond where William ended (in 1184). The continuations, which are of particular importance for the years 1184–1197, include such events as the fall of Jerusalem in 1187, the conquest of Cyprus during the Third Crusade (qq.v.), and events leading up to the Fourth Crusade (q.v.).

ETHIOPIA. *See* **AXUM.**

EUBOEA. Island in the Aegean Sea (q.v.) located close to the mainland of eastern Greece (q.v.), running almost parallel along the coast of Attica and Boeotia (q.v.), separated by a strait that contracts into a narrow channel called the Euripos. The opposite (eastern) coast that faces the Aegean Sea is so rugged as to be almost inaccessible. Historically this has meant that the fate of Euboea was usually tied to control of the opposite mainland. From the late seventh century until the conquest of Constantinople by the Fourth Crusade (qq.v.) in 1204 it was part of the theme of Hellas (qq.v.). After 1204 Venice (q.v.) controlled the island, which the Venetians called *Negroponte* (Black Bridge), referring to the bridge across the Euripos that connected the island to the mainland. Euboea was one part of a chain of islands and mainland ports that commanded the sea route from Venice to Constantinople. The island fell to the Ottomans (q.v.) in 1470.

EUCHAITA. A rural pilgrimage center in Pontos (q.v.), west of Amaseia (q.v.) on the road to Gangra (q.v.). Anastasios I (q.v.) enclosed it with walls in the early sixth century, and in the seventh century it became part of the theme of Armeniakon (qq.v.). One of the most famous commanders of the Armeniakon, the future Leo V (q.v.), was exiled there for a time in the early ninth century. The cult of St. Theodore Teron provided an important source of revenue for the city, and in the 11th century, according to its metropolitan John Mauropous (qq.v.), the city's annual festival for the saint coincided with a great fair that transformed the city from a wasteland to a bustling marketplace. Much of recent scholarly discussion about the town has focused on the extent to which, despite having been burned by the Persians (q.v.) in 615 and occupied briefly by the Arabs (q.v.) in 663–664, its survival was an exception to the more general rule of urban decline in Asia Minor (q.v.) in the seventh century. Nevertheless, by the eighth century the city seems to have shrunk from its Anastasian walls to a fortified acropolis, becoming more of a stronghold than an actual city.

EUCHARIST. *See* **LITURGY.**

EUCLID. His *Elements of Geometry,* written around 300 B.C., had a profound impact on Byzantine science, in part because Euclid's work was given such practical use in Byzantine astronomy, astrology (qq.v.), even architecture. For example, Anthemios of Tralles, architect of Hagia Sophia (qq.v.), wrote a work on conical sections and was an expert on projective geometry. Leo the Mathematician (q.v.), allegedly the inventor of the *automata* of the Magnaura (q.v.), was an expert on Euclid. The *Elements,* revised by the astronomer Theon of Alexandria, father of Hypatia (qq.v.), was also of interest to Neoplatonists such as Proklos (qq.v.), who were attracted to the 10th book of the *Elements,* which deals with irrational quantities, implying a thought-world where facts cannot be expressed in concrete terms.

EUDOKIA INGERINA. Mistress to Michael III (q.v.) and subsequently wife of Basil I (q.v.). Michael III's mother Theodora (q.v.) and the powerful minister Theoktistos (q.v.) forced Michael III to give her up. She was married to Basil I when he became co-emperor in 866. Her children included the future emperor Leo VI (qq.v.), whose father was probably Michael III and whose first wife Theophano (q.v.) Eudokia chose for him in a bride show (q.v.).

EUDOKIA MAKREMBOLITISSA. Niece of Patriarch Michael I Keroularios and empress of Constantine X Doukas (qq.v.). After his death in 1067 she was regent for her sons Michael VII (q.v.), Andronikos, and Constantine, promising Patriarch John VIII Xiphilinos (q.v.) that she would not marry again. However, continued inroads by the Seljuks (q.v.) forced the patriarch, and her chief advisors caesar John Doukas and Michael Psellos (qq.v.) to reconsider the need for an emperor experienced in military affairs. Xiphilinos released her from her oath, and she agreed to marry Romanos IV Diogenes (q.v.). Romanos IV achieved some success in 1068 and 1069, but he was captured at the battle of Mantzikert (q.v.) in 1071, a defeat caused by the retreat of Andronikos Doukas, son of caesar John Doukas. When, after his release by Alp Arslan (q.v.), Romanos IV attempted to regain his throne, caesar John Doukas forced Eudokia to enter a monastery, lest she support him. Michael VII was proclaimed sole emperor in his place. After the death of Michael VII, and no longer a political threat, she was allowed to return to Constantinople (q.v.).

EUDOXIA. Empress (q.v.) and wife of Arkadios (q.v.). Eudoxia was a beautiful, strong-willed woman who was easily offended. Her feud with Patriarch John Chrysostom (q.v.) produced the first major crisis in state relations with the church. In 399 when Eutropios (q.v.),

Arkadios's chief minister, offended her, she engineered his removal from office. John's references from the pulpit to Eudoxia as a Jezebel infuriated her, and she persuaded her husband to depose him, too. She was aided in this by John's adversaries within the church, including Theophilos, bishop of Alexandria, and Syrian bishop Severianos (qq.v.). However, John's popularity with the people produced such a crowd around Hagia Sophia (q.v.) that for three days imperial officials could not seize him. Finally, he surrendered, and he was exiled in 403. Recalled due to popular pressure, he was exiled again in 404. He died in 407 in a faraway place on the coast of the Black Sea (q.v.).

EUGENEIANOS, NIKETAS. Author of the 12th-century romance (q.v.) entitled *Drosilla and Charikles,* and probably of an anonymous work entitled *Anacharsis or Ananias.* He was a pupil of Theodore Prodromos (q.v.), another prominent writer of romances in the 12th century.

EUGENIKOS, JOHN. Writer and deacon who opposed the union of the churches (q.v.) at the Council of Ferrara-Florence (q.v.), as did his brother Mark Eugenikos (q.v.). He attended the Council of Ferrara-Florence, and, like his brother, he refused to sign its decree of union. For this he was exiled to the Morea (q.v.). In addition to a polemic against the decree of union, he wrote hymns (q.v.), sermons, and a poem of lament *(threnos)* commemorating the conquest of Constantinople (q.v.) in 1453.

EUGENIKOS, MARK. Metropolitan of Ephesus (qq.v.) and famous opponent of the union of the churches (q.v.) at the Council of Ferrara-Florence (q.v.); brother of John Eugenikos (q.v.). He attended the council, but he refused to sign the decree of union, for which he was imprisoned for two years. He was made a saint by the Orthodox Church in 1456.

EUGENIUS. Puppet emperor raised in 392 by Arbogast, *magister militum* (q.v.) in the West, after Valentinian II (q.v.) died under suspicious circumstances. Theodosios I (q.v.) marched against Eugenius and Arbogast in 394, defeating them near Aquileia. Arbogast committed suicide, and Eugenius was captured and put to death.

EUGENIUS III. *See* **SECOND CRUSADE.**

EUGENIUS IV. Pope (q.v.) from 1431–1447 who was architect of the Council of Ferrara-Florence (q.v.) in 1438–1439. He negotiated with John VIII Palaiologos and Patriarch Joseph II (qq.v.) to obtain their agreement to the union of the churches (q.v.). The pope also promoted a Crusade (q.v.) that ended disastrously at Varna (q.v.).

EUNAPIOS OF SARDIS. Greek historian who wrote a history of the years 270–414, which survives only in fragments. He wrote from Sardis (q.v.) for an audience of eastern intellectuals whose paganism matched his own. However biased, Eunapios's work was widely used by other historians, including Zosimus, Philostorgios, and So- zomenos (qq.v.). Whether Ammianus Marcellinus (q.v.) used Euna- pios, or vice versa, is unclear. Eunapios was friends with the em- peror Julian (q.v.) and he authored a short biography of Julian's physician Oribasios (q.v.).

EUNOMIOS. Chief proponent of a form of Arianism (q.v.) that taught that the Son was created as an intermediate divinity without a human nature, and with only a resemblance to God the Father. Eu- nomios was exiled by Constantius II (q.v.), recalled by Julian (q.v.), and exiled again by Theodosios I (q.v.). He was a disciple of the Arian theologian Aetios (q.v.).

EUNUCHS. Castrated males. In Byzantium (q.v.), from the reign of Constantius II (q.v.), they traditionally held high positions in the state civil and military administration and within the church. In theory, they were without family and totally dependent on the em- peror, which explains the great confidence and authority placed in them. The staff (called *koubikoularioi* [q.v.]) of the imperial apart- ments were eunuchs who prepared the emperor's bed and clothing, served his meals, and planned his personal schedule. Famous high- ranking eunuchs include Eutropios, Samonas, Joseph Bringas, and John the Orphanotrophos (qq.v.). In the court of Alexios I Kom- nenos (q.v.) alone, for example, there were 12 high-ranking eu- nuchs, a host of eunuch servants, in addition to the patriarch (q.v.) Eustratios Garidas. Other eunuch patriarchs include Germanos I in the eighth century, and Methodios I and Ignatios (qq.v.) in the ninth century. The most famous eunuch general was Narses (q.v.), who served Justinian I (q.v.). Not all eunuchs were as reliable as Narses. Many plotted and intrigued, such as John the Orphanotrophos who engineered his brother's accession to the throne as Michael IV (q.v.). Nikephoritzes (q.v.), who administered state affairs for Michael VII (q.v.), achieved great power but also great condemnation.

EUPHRATES RIVER. The Middle Euphrates river was a heavily fortified eastern frontier that bordered Sassanid Persia (qq.v.) until the Arab conquest of Byzantine Mesopotamia (q.v.) in 640. The Upper Euphrates, from the seventh through the ninth centuries, was a battleground between the Arabs and Byzantium (qq.v.). The fortresses of Kamacha and Keltzene formed the core of the theme of Mesopotamia (qq.v.) in the ninth century. In the 10th century, John Kourkouas, Nikephoros II Phokas, John I Tzimiskes, and Basil II (qq.v.) reestablished the empire's borders at the Euphrates once more. Melitene (q.v.) was reconquered in 934, Hierapolis was recaptured in 974, and Samosata (q.v.) once more fell under Byzantine dominion. However, by the end of the 11th century, the region was again lost, this time to the Seljuks (q.v.).

EUPHROSYNE, DOUKAINA KAMATERA. Empress (q.v.) of Alexios III Angelos (q.v.) from 1195–1203. Her intelligence and instinctive ability in handling affairs of state enabled her to dominate her husband, whose weak mind and character made him totally unsuited to rule. She engineered the return of Constantine Mesopotamites, who became the most powerful minister of state in league with the empress seeing their influence decline, jealous members of the imperial family, including Euphrosyne's own brother Basil Kamateros (q.v.), conspired to overthrow Mesopotamites by weakening his chief supporter, the empress. They accused her of adultery, for which Alexios III sent her to a monastery for six months (1197). Soon after her release, Mesopotamites was exiled, and her power waned. In 1203, when the Fourth Crusade seized Constantinople (qq.v.), Alexios III fled the capital, leaving Euphrosyne behind. She was arrested but subsequently fled with Alexios V (q.v.) in 1204, only to be ransomed by Michael I Komnenos (q.v.) and spend the rest of her days in Epiros at Arta (qq.v.).

EURIPIDES. Greek tragedian (480–406 B.C.), whose works were studied in Byzantium (q.v.), though probably not performed on stage due to their strictly pagan content. In the 11th century Psellos (q.v.) authored a comparison of Euripides and George of Pisidia (q.v.), who wrote epic eulogies of Herakleios (q.v.). Thereafter, interest in the work of Euripides never flagged, as seen in John Apokaukos's (q.v.) appreciation of Euripides. In the 14th century there was great interest in Euripides among philologists such as Maximos Planoudes, Thomas Magistros (qq.v.), and Demetrios Triklinios. Triklinios prepared new editions of the Greek tragedians, including the plays (some previously not taught, and thus not studied) of Euripides and of Sophocles. After the fall of Constantinople (q.v.), Greek refugee scholars used these editions to teach Euripides at Padua and Florence. At Venice (q.v.), Marcus Musurus edited Euripides for the Aldine press. In such ways, Euripides passed to the Italian Renaissance.

EURYTANEIA. Region in central Greece (q.v.) noted for its Alpine scenery and relative isolation. Besides its important post-Byzantine churches it also contains the ninth-century Church of the Dormition at Episkopi.

EUSEBIOS OF CAESAREA. Church historian and apologist; bishop of Caesarea Maritima (qq.v.), and biographer of Constantine I the Great (q.v.). His *Church History* is of inestimable importance for the history of early Greek Christianity. It describes in great detail, for example, the impact of the Great Persecution (q.v.) in Palestine under Maximinus Daia (qq.v.). The same can be said about his *Vita Constantini* (Life of Constantine [qq.v.]), which remains at the core of any attempt to understand an emperor (q.v.) whose reign Eusebios describes as the high point of all human history. In the *Vita Constantini* is found the famous story the emperor told Eusebios about a miraculous vision he saw in the sky of a luminous cross and the words "By This Conquer!" Eusebios's other works include the *Chronicle,* in which he demonstrates how deep into antiquity are the roots of Christianity, and two apologetical works, his *Preparation for the Gospel and Proof of the Gospel.* He tolerated Arianism, a heresy (qq.v) he was persuaded to renounce at the Council of Nicaea (q.v.) in 325. He died in 339.

EUSEBIOS OF NIKOMEDEIA. Arian bishop of Nikomedeia (qq.v.) and leader of the Arian party who was exiled in 325 for refusing to sign the decrees of the Council of Nicaea (q.v.). Recalled by Constantine I the Great (q.v.) in 327, he became a trusted advisor to the emperor (q.v.), baptizing him on his death bed. Constantius II (q.v.) made him bishop of Constantinople (q.v.) in 338, and it was during his tenure as bishop of the capital that he ordained Ulfilas (q.v.), the so-called bishop of the Goths. He died around 342, and, thus, did not live to see the failure of Arianism, or of his introduction of future emperor Julian (q.v.) to the Holy Scriptures.

EUSTATHIOS OF ANTIOCH. When he was chosen bishop of Antioch (qq.v.) in 324 the church there was in total disorder due to the controversy over Arianism (q.v.). At the Council of Nicaea (q.v.) in 325 Eustathios was a chief opponent of Arius, but when Arius was recalled from exile by Constantine I the Great (q.v.) in 327, Eustathios's position was soon undermined. A council of his Arian opponents in Antioch deposed him in 330, accusing him of Sabellianism, the view that God appears in different modes as Father, Son, and Holy Spirit. He was also accused of keeping a mistress. Constantine I sent him into exile. Despite being condemned at the Council of Gangra (g.v.) in 341, in 362 his supporters (called Eustathians) elected the priest Paulinos as bishop of Antioch, precipitating the Meletian schism (q.v.)

EUSTATHIOS OF THESSALONIKE. Scholar, writer, teacher, archbishop of Thessalonike (qq.v.), and the most celebrated teacher of the 12th century. For a while he taught rhetoric, grammar, and philosophy at the Patriarchal School (q.v.). His extensive and detailed commentaries on the *Iliad* and *Odyssey* of Homer (q.v.), on Aristophanes, Pindar, and John of Damascus (qq.v.), illustrates how 12th-century scholars were assimilating and reflecting on classical literature. However, it is his descriptions of contemporary life that modern historians find most useful, and a sheer delight to read. His style is naturalistic, immediate, like that of his predecessors Michael Psellos and Anna Komnene (qq.v.). His gripping account of the Norman (q.v.) siege and occupation of Thessalonike in 1185 is perhaps the best eyewitness account in Byzantine literature. His treatise on monasticism (q.v.) is scathing in its criticism of contemporary monks who swore, fornicated, engaged in trade, and acted no different from laymen. He also wrote panegyrics to Manuel I Komnenos (q.v.) and letters that include an enormous amount of useful details about 12th-century agriculture (q.v.). When he died in 1196 Byzantium (q.v.) lost an intellect and writer the likes of which had not been seen since Psellos (q.v.).

EUSTRATIOS OF NICAEA. Philosopher, theologian, metropolitan of Nicaea (qq.v.), whose trial for heresy (q.v.) was the chief event in the closing years of Alexios I Komnenos's (q.v.) reign. Eustratios was a pupil of John Italos (q.v.), but he escaped being condemned for heresy with Italos in 1082. Like Italos, Eustratios was a commentator on Proklos and Aristotle (qq.v.) who concluded that Christ reasoned like Aristotle. This immediately invited suspicion. He also seemed to devalue Christ's humanity. This opened him up to further charges, and in 1117 he was condemned (q.v.).

EUTHYMIOS. Patriarch of Constantinople (qq.v.) from 907–912 whose career became embroiled in the *tetragamy* (q.v.) controversy. He was appointed after the deposition of Patriarch Nicholas I Mystikos (qq.v.), who refused to recognize the *tetragamy* (q.v.), or fourth marriage, of Leo VI (q.v.). This created two parties within the church, one siding with the deposed Nicholas, the other with Euthymios. Just before his death, Leo VI recalled Nicholas and deposed Euthymios, who was sent into exile. In 920, three years after Euthymios's death, Romanos I Lekapenos (q.v.) attempted to reconcile the church through his Tome of Union (q.v.). His *vita* (.v) is an important historical source for the period from 886–917.

EUTHYMIOS OF SARDIS. Bishop of Sardis (qq.v.) and staunch Iconophile (q.v.) in the struggle over Iconoclasm (q.v.). His leadership at the Second Council of Nicaea in 787 did not save him from being deposed by Nikephoros I (q.v.), who accused him of supporting the rebel Bardanes Tourkos (q.v.). He was persecuted in the second period of Iconoclasm by Leo V (q.v.), who exiled him to Thasos (q.v.), and by Theophilos (q.v.), who exiled him to the island of St. Andrew in the Sea of Marmara (q.v.). There he died in 831 from a flogging he received.

EUTHYMIOS THE GREAT. Saint and famous ascetic (q.v.) who founded the first *lavra* (q.v.) in Palestine (q.v.) in 428. He was loyal to the decrees of the Council of Chalcedon (q.v.) and threw his support behind Patriarch Juvenal of Jerusalem (q.v.), helping him to regain his episcopal see from the usurper Theodosios. He also persuaded the empress Eudokia (Athenais-Eudokia [q.v.]), who was living in retirement in Jerusalem, to change her support from Monophysitism to Orthodoxy (qq.v.) decreed by the Council of Chalcedon in 451. After his death in 473, Euthymios's disciple Sabas (q.v.) continued his work in Palestine (q.v.).

EUTHMIOS THE YOUNGER. *See* **ATHOS, MOUNT; OLYMPOS, MOUNT.**

EUTROPIOS. Grand chamberlain *(praepositus sacri cubiculi* [q.v.]) for Arkadios (q.v.). He plotted with Stilicho (q.v.) to have Gainas (q.v.) assassinate their mutual archrival Rufinus (q.v.). (Claudian's [q.v.] *Against Rufinus,* an attempt to exonerate his patron Stilicho in this matter, is sheer propaganda.) With Rufinus out of the way, and the weak-willed Arkadios totally under the influence of Eutropios, the eunuch's (q.v.) powers increased enormously. He took personal command of an army in 398 that drove the Huns (q.v.) from Cappadocia and Pontus (qq.v.) back across the Caucasus (q.v.). Despite this success, he alienated the Gothic army commanders Tribigild and Gainas (qq.v.), who demanded that Arkadios depose him. The empress Eudoxia (q.v.) seconded this demand and Arkadios was forced to exile Eutropios to Cyprus (q.v.). Subsequently he was executed.

EUTROPIUS. Latin historian and imperial official who served in Julian's (q.v.) Persian campaign, as did another Latin historian, Sextus Aurelius Victor (q.v.). Eutropius wrote a survey *(Breviarium)* of Roman history to the death of Jovian (q.v.) in 364 that has some importance for the events for which he was a contemporary. His narrative of Julian's reign complements the work of Ammianus Marcellinus (q.v.). Eutropius is mentioned in connection with the treason trials at Antioch (q.v.) in 371. He was then proconsular governor of Asia, and he narrowly escaped the torture and execution meted out to Julian's other friends.

EUTYCHES. *Archimandrite* (q.v.) of a monastery outside Constantinople (q.v) who created the theological doctrine of Monophysitism (q.v.). Eutyches's godson, Chrysaphius (q.v.) was influential at court, but despite this, Patriarch Flavian (q.v.) had Eutyches condemned and deposed in 448. Chrysaphius responded by persuading Theodosios II (q.v.) in 449 to call a general church council at Ephesus (q.v.), at the so-called Robber Council of Ephesus (q.v.). There, Patriarch Dioskoros of Alexandria (qq.v.) supported Eutyches. The council reinstated Eutyches and deposed Flavian, but when Theodosios II died he was sent into exile again.

EUTYCHIOS. Patriarch of Constantinople (qq.v.) from 552–565, and again from 577–582. Justinian I (q.v.) hoped that Eutychios, who had supported Justinian I's Three Chapters (q.v.), would be as loyal as the previous patriarch Menas (q.v.). His immediate task was to gain a favorable outcome for Justinian I at the Fifth Ecumenical Council (q.v.) at Constantinople in 553, which he did, despite a condemnation (later reversed) from Pope Vigilius (q.v.). However, he could not agree with Justinian I's support of the doctrine of Aphthartodocetism (q.v.), and so the emperor deposed him, exiling him to a monastery at Amasea (q.v.). He was subsequently restored as patriarch during the reign of Justinian I's successor, Justin II (q.v.).

EUTYCHIOS. Last exarch of Ravenna (q.v.). Sent to Italy (q.v.) by Leo III (q.v.) around 728, he tried unsuccessfully to murder Pope Gregory II (q.v.), who had resisted Leo III's Iconoclasm (q.v.). Left to organize the defense of the exarchate (q.v.) on his own, he ended up seeking Gregory II's help, as well as the help of his papal successors Gregory III and Zacharias (qq.v.), all of whom negotiated with the Lombards (q.v.) on Eutychios's behalf. However, in 751 the Lombards captured Ravenna, putting an end to Byzantine authority north of Rome (q.v.).

EUTYCHIOS OF ALEXANDRIA. Melkite bishop of Alexandria (qq.v.) from 935–940 who wrote a world chronicle (q.v.) in Arabic from Adam to 938. It reports important Byzantine affairs (e.g., Byzantine Iconoclasm [q.v.]) and coordinates the chronology (q.v.) of Byzantine imperial reigns with those of the eastern patriarchs and caliphs (qq.v.).

EVAGRIOS PONTIKOS. One of the most interesting monastic thinkers and writers of the fourth century. His mentors were Basil the Great and Gregory of Nazianzos (qq.v.), from whom Evagrios acquired a passion for theology and monasticism (q.v.). His support of Origen (q.v.) led him to state that Christ was not the second person of the Trinity, but a pure intellect united to the Logos. His Origenism was later condemned at the Council of Constantinople (q.v.) in 553. Nonetheless, his writings on monastic spirituality were enormously influential, although they were circulated under pseudonyms like Neilos of Ankyra (q.v.) because they were so obviously influenced by Origenism. He conceived of monasticism as a mental prayer, as essentially contemplation, laying the basis for a mystical tradition in monasticism that Hesychasm (q.v.) was a later expression of. The last 16 years of his life were spent in the desert of Egypt (q.v.) at the great monastic centers of Nitria and Kellia (qq.v.), where he met Makarios the Great (q.v.) before he died in 399.

EVAGRIOS SCHOLASTIKOS. Church historian whose *Ecclesiastical History* in six books continues the ecclesiastical histories of Socrates, Theodoret, and Sozomenos (qq.v.), beginning with the Council of Ephesus (q.v.) in 431 and ending in 593. The work is of great value for secular history, as well as for church history. For example, Evagrios's work is one of only a few important sources for the penetration of Greece by Slavs and Avars (qq.v.) in the last quarter of the sixth century.

EXARCH. *See* **EXARCHATE.**

EXARCHATE. There were two of these new administrative units created by Maurice (q.v.). The first was the Exarchate of Carthage (q.v.), which defended Byzantine possessions in North Africa against the Moors (qq.v.). The second was the Exarchate of Ravenna (q.v.), which protected Byzantine possessions in Italy against the Lombards (qq.v.). Their creation was an indirect admission that the remnants of Justinian I's (q.v.) reconquests in the West were too far away to be governed from Constantinople (q.v.). The exarchates functioned almost autonomously, exercising both civil and military authority within their territories. The one in North Africa fell to the Arabs (q.v.) in the late seventh century. The Exarchate of Ravenna fell to the Lombards in 751.

EXCERPTA. A compilation of writings by various ancient and Byzantine authors done at the behest of Constantine VII (q.v.). Since many of these works exist only in these excerpts, this compilation is particularly valuable. For example, it preserves the account of Priskos's (q.v.) embassy to the court of Attila (q.v.).

EXCERPTA VALESIANA. A short biography of Constantine I (q.v.) written in the late fourth century by an anonymous pagan author. Compared to the fulsome praise of Eusebios of Caesarea (q.v.), the view of Constantine is surprisingly objective. The author even makes occasional use of the Christian history of Orosius (q.v.). The title derives from its ninth-century manuscript, published in the 17th century by Henri de Valois (Valesius). The manuscript also contains a later work about Ostrogothic Italy (q.v.) under Odoacer and Theodoric the Great (qq.v.).

EXEMPTION. Any form of immunity from taxation or other obligation to the state. Exemptions could be temporary or permanent. From the 14th century, permanent exemptions like *exkousseia* (q.v.) were granted by the emperor (q.v.) with increasing frequency to merchants, monasteries, and individuals. This practice was a factor in the decline of the Byzantine state.

EXKOUBITORES. Imperial guard created by Leo I (q.v.), commanded by a *comes* (q.v.) *exkoubitores,* later a *domestikos* (q.v.) *exkoubitores.* Such commanders wielded considerable power on occasion, as seen in the example of usurper Valentinus Arsakuni (q.v.) who engineered the downfall of Martina (q.v.). Unlike the largely ceremonial *candidatoi* (q.v.), the *exkoubitores* were one of several elite regiments (*tagmata* [q.v.]) that included the *scholae palatinae* and the *hikanatoi* (qq.v.).

EXKOUSSEIA. Tax exemption (q.v.) on land, *paroikoi* (q.v.), ships, buildings, and animals that appears in the 10th century, taken advantage of by powerful landed magnates (the *dynatoi* [q.v.]). It is interpreted variously as the equivalent to immunity in the Latin West, and thus a complete tax exemption, or as an exemption only from certain taxes. In the 14th and 15th centuries the term appears to cover any tax exemption.

EXONARTHEX. *See* **NARTHEX.**

EXPOSITIO TOTIUS MUNDI. Travelogue of the mid-fourth century. It was probably written by a Greek merchant, but it is preserved only in two Latin versions. It begins with a fictitious account of Eden, then moves westward with descriptions of India, Persia, Syria, Alexandria, Asia Minor, Thrace, Macedonia, Greece, Italy, Gaul, Spain, Africa, Cyprus, Crete, Sicily, and Britain (qq.v.). Its comments range from climate to commerce. Among the exports from Spain, for example, it lists oil, bacon, cloth, and mules; from Africa it notes oil, cattle, and clothing.

EZANA. King of Axum (q.v.) who was a contemporary of Constantine I (q.v.). He issued cross-inscribed gold coins at a weight equivalent to the *solidus* (q.v.). During this same period a certain Frumentius, consecrated by Athanasios (q.v.), became the first serious missionary to Axum.

EZERITAI. Tribe of Slavs in the Peloponnesos (qq.v.) in the Taygetos Mountains. The Ezeritai are mentioned in the *De administrando imperio* (q.v.) as living with the Melingoi (q.v.), another Slavic tribe. The Ezeritai revolted during the reign of Romanos I (q.v.) and were defeated. However, unlike other Slavic tribes who were assimilated, they continued to maintain their independence up to the conquest of the Peloponnesos by the Ottomans (q.v.).

– F –

FARMER'S LAW. Regional manual of agricultural law, generally dated to the seventh or eighth century, often to the reign of Justinian II (q.v.). Exactly what region (or regions) is described is debated by scholars. Among its 85 laws there are references to vineyards and fig trees, but none to olive trees, which would seem to exclude Greece and Dalmatia (qq.v.) as the region(s) it applied to. Macedonia and inland Thrace (qq.v.) seem more likely candidates, since both regions produce figs but no olives. The laws describe a countryside devoid of large estates, consisting rather of independent villages of free peasants and relatively few slaves, whose labor was divided between the cultivation of crops, vineyards, and gardens, and the raising of livestock. The portrayal of village life is descriptive, but what region does it describe? Without presuming that what is depicted are villages of Slavs (q.v.), the overall picture is of a countryside that emerged from the period of the Slavic invasions.

FATAMIDS. Muslim (Shiite) sect whose caliphs (q.v.) claimed descent from Fatima, daughter of the prophet Muhammad (q.v.), and acknowledged no Muslim authority in Islam (q.v.) other than its own. They founded a state in Tunis in 909, dominating northwest Africa, as well as Sicily (qq.v.). Their fleet was supreme in the western Mediterranean (q.v.), much as the Vandal fleet had been in the fifth century. By the mid-10th century, Malta, Sardinia, Corsica (qq.v.), and the Balearic Islands were in their possession. Fatamid power reached its apogee during the reign of their fourth caliph (q.v.), al-Muizz, who celebrated the conquest of Egypt (q.v.) in 969. Despite this advance, Nikephoros Phokas conquered Crete (qq.v.) in 961. In 973 the Fatamids moved their capital to Cairo, continuing their expansion with the conquest of Palestine (q.v.) and portions of Syria and western Arabia (qq.v.). Under caliph al-Hakim the Fatamids defeated a Byzantine fleet in 998, and they destroyed the Church of the Holy Sepulchre in Jerusalem (qq.v.) in 1009, events which created a state of hostilities with Byzantium (q.v.) until 1038, when a treaty was signed allowing Byzantium to rebuild the Church of the Holy Sepulchre. After al-Hakim's death in 1021 Fatamid power declined steadily throughout the remainder of the 11th century. The First Crusade (q.v.) conquered Palestine, including Jerusalem (q.v.) in 1099. The Fatamids were left with little more than Egypt, which Nur al-Din (q.v.) conquered in 1169, effectively ending Fatamid rule. The last Fatamid caliph died in 1171.

FAUSTA. Daughter of Maximian (q.v.); wife of Constantine I the Great (q.v.); mother of Constantine's three surviving sons Constantine II, Constantius II, and Constans I (qq.v.). Constantine murdered her (or forced her to commit suicide) in 326, allegedly when he discovered that Fausta had fallen in love with her stepson Crispus (q.v.) and had falsely accused him of rape when he refused her overtures.

FELIX III. *See* **AKAKIOS.**

FERRARA-FLORENCE, COUNCIL OF. Church council of 1438–1439 that achieved a union of the churches (q.v.) on paper, though not in reality. In return for accepting the papacy's (q.v.) position on such crucial doctrines as papal primacy, the *filioque,* and use of *azyma* in the Eucharist, Byzantium (qq.v.) expected effective military aid against the Ottomans (q.v.), which the papacy could not provide. The Crusade that Pope Eugenius IV (qq.v.) called met utter defeat at Varna (q.v.) in 1444. Emperor John V (q.v.) and his entourage, except for Mark of Ephesus (q.v.), who refused to sign the council's decrees, were subjected to relentless hostility upon their return. By comparison, the first union of the churches at the Council of Lyons (q.v.) in 1274 achieved more practical results. Patriarch Joseph II (qq.v.) escaped direct insult by dying in Florence, but Isidore of Kiev (q.v.) was deposed and imprisoned upon his return to Moscow (q.v.) in 1440.

FESTUS. Latin historian who wrote a summary *(Breviarium)* of Roman history from the founding of Rome (q.v.) to 369. He was born in the north Italian city of Tridentum, and despite his lowly birth, criticized by Ammianus Marcellinus (q.v.), rose to become proconsul of Asia. Ammianus also criticizes his cruelty in executing Maximos of Ephesus (q.v.) and other pagans connected with Julian (q.v.). He must have been a flatterer, judging from the dedication of his work to Valens (q.v.).

FEUDALISM. Term that denotes the political and social organization of much of the medieval West after the breakup of Charlemagne's (q.v.) kingdom. Feudalism never developed in Byzantium (q.v.), and attempts by some scholars to view appanages and *pronoia* (qq.v.) as inspired by western feudalism are not convincing. *Pronoia* was a fiscal and administrative institution under state control, unlike western fiefs, which were personal, territorial, and resulted in further fragmentation of estates (subinfeudation). However, in the 12th century, especially during the reign of Manuel I Komnenos (q.v.), knowledge of western feudalism had an impact on how the Byzantine state dealt with important western personages. For example, the loan word *lizios,* from the French liege, referring to a liege vassal, was first used by Alexios I Komnenos in the Treaty of Devol (qq.v.) to define Bohemund's (q.v.) subservience to the emperor.

FILIOQUE. Latin for "and from the Son," referring to a phrase inserted into the western credal statement in 589. It refers to the Holy Spirit proceeding not only from the Father (as stated in the eastern creed), but from Christ as well. This difference in the basic creeds of the eastern and western churches became an obstacle to the union of the churches (q.v.).

FIRST CRUSADE. The First Crusade was called by Pope (q.v.) Urban II in 1095 at the Council of Clermont, in France (q.v.). In support of an earlier appeal by Alexios I Komnenos (q.v.) for mercenaries to fight the Seljuks in Asia Minor (qq.v), the pope announced a yet broader project: an expedition of armed pilgrims to recapture Jerusalem (q.v.) from the forces of Islam (q.v.). The First Crusade's conquest of Jerusalem in 1099 was a great victory, but its passage through Constantinople (q.v.) in 1097 on the way to Jerusalem was greeted with skepticism by Alexios I. Peter the Hermit's (q.v.) followers were undisciplined, and among the contingents of knights that passed through the city (q.v.) were Normans under Bohemund (qq.v.), an arch enemy of Byzantium (q.v.). Bohemund's subsequent refusal to return Antioch (q.v.) to Byzantium was resolved only by the Treaty of Devol (q.v.). The conquest of Jerusalem was an obvious victory for the First Crusade, but thereafter relations between Byzantium and the West deteriorated significantly. In retrospect, Alexios I was correct to view papal-sponsored western armies with suspicion, in light of the harm done Byzantium by the Second, Third, and especially Fourth Crusades (qq.v.). The chief sources for the First Crusade include Albert of Aachen, Fulcher of Chartres, and Raymond of Aguilers (qq.v.).

FIVE MARTYRS OF SEBASTEIA. Saints martyred in Sebasteia (q.v.) during the reign of Diocletian (q.v.). According to the legend, collected by Symeon Metaphrastes (q.v.) and others, the martyrs included a priest, Auxentios, and soldiers inspired by the example of an officer named Eustratios.

FLAVIAN. Patriarch of Constantinople (qq.v.) from 446–449. His condemnation of Eutyches (q.v.) for heresy in 448 brought down on him the wrath of the powerful eunuch Chrysaphios (qq.v.), and of the patriarch of Alexandria, Dioskoros (qq.v.). At the "Robber" Council of Ephesus (q.v.) in 449, Dioskoros had Flavian deposed. He died while preparing to go into exile.

FOEDERATI. Term used in the fourth century for barbarian border tribes who were bound by treaty *(foedus,* in Latin) as allies, settled in imperial territory, and enlisted as troops. In the late fourth century, for example, the Ostrogoths (q.v.) were settled in Pannonia (q.v.) and the Visigoths in northern Thrace (qq.v.), where they were enlisted as *foederati* in the army (q.v.). In the fifth century the term became a political fiction used to sanction barbarian settlements in Italy, Gaul, and Spain (qq.v.), paving the way for the system of independent states that was to replace the empire in the West.

FOLLIS. The large copper coin introduced by Anastasios I (q.v.), with a value of 40 *nummi,* and inscribed with a M (= 40). Smaller copper coins of lesser value were also issued. This was done to alleviate the chronic shortage of smaller coins for the general populace and to stabilize all smaller units of currency. The value of the *follis* was 1/24th of a *miliaresion* (q.v.) and 1/288th of a *solidus* (q.v.). The weight of the *follis* was reduced in the seventh century, and in 1092 Alexios I Komnenos (q.v.) replaced the *follis* with a new coin, the *tetarteron* (q.v.).

FORTY MARTYRS OF SEBASTEIA. Saints killed in 320 in Sebasteia (q.v.) during the reign of Licinius (q.v.). According to the legend recounted by Symeon Metaphrastes and other hagiographers (qq.v.) they were Christian soldiers who refused to renounce their faith. They were stripped naked and herded onto a frozen pond, where most of them died of exposure. Those remaining were executed.

FORTY-TWO MARTYRS OF AMORION. Saints executed on 6 March 845 for refusing to convert to Islam (q.v.). According to the legend they were carried off after the capture of Amorion (q.v.) in 838 by the caliph Mutasim (q.v.) to his new capital on the Tigris (q.v.), Samarra. After seven years in prison they failed to convert and were beheaded. The story relates that their bodies were thrown into the river, but they miraculously floated to the top of the water.

This is Byzantium's (q.v.) last great legendary tale of group martyrdom.

FOURTH CRUSADE. The Crusade (q.v.) that destroyed Byzantium (q.v.) in 1204. The *Partitio Romaniae* (q.v.) divided up the territory of the empire as spoils among Venice (q.v.) and the other major participants of this Crusade. The Byzantine reconquest of Constantinople (q.v.) in 1261 by forces from the Empire of Nicaea (q.v.) reconstituted Byzantium, but the empire never recovered its former strength. The negative results of the 1204 conquest are, in any case, clearer than the question of how the Fourth Crusade was diverted to Constantinople in the first place. At the very least, a combination of self-interest and unfortunate coincidences played a role. That there was a conspiracy from the outset is alleged by Niketas Choniates (q.v.), who blames Venetian Dodge Enrico Dandalo (qq.v.). Other chief participants, including Philip of Swabia and Boniface of Montferrat (qq.v.), found advantage in the diversion. Modern historical opinions vary, but all are forced to rely chiefly on Geoffrey Villehardouin (q.v.), whose account—a clever apologetic—forms the principal historical source for the Fourth Crusade.

FRANCE. State that originated in 987, when Hugh Capet became king. During the next three centuries French knights played an important and tragic role in Byzantine affairs through the medium of the Crusades (q.v.). French knights made up leading contingents of the First Crusade (q.v.). Louis VII (q.v.) led a major army during the Second Crusade (q.v.). Manuel I Komnenos (q.v.) became enamored with French customs, which hardly enamored him with his subjects. The coup de grace of French influence, so to speak, came when French knights stormed the walls of Constantinople during the Fourth Crusade (qq.v.), effectively destroying Byzantium (q.v.). A French nobleman, Baldwin of Flanders (q.v.) became the first emperor of the new Latin Empire (q.v.). Ironically, much later, when a restored Byzantium (q.v.) lost territory to the Ottomans (q.v.), appeals were sent to France. Manuel II Palaiologos (q.v.) even journeyed to Paris in 1400 to beg Charles VI for aid.

FRANCISCANS. The Order of Friars Minor ("Little Brothers"), founded by St. Francis of Assisi (1181–1226), one of the most remarkable persons of the Middle Ages in the West. In 1210 Pope Innocent III (q.v.) allowed Francis to govern his followers as a religious order. Dedicated to serving the poor, the new order also turned its attention to missionary work in the East in an attempt to regain the Holy Land and bring about a union of the churches (q.v.). They established themselves in Constantinople during the Latin Empire (qq.v.) and soon the papacy (q.v.) found them useful as emissaries. In 1234 Pope Gregory IX sent a Franciscan mission to John III Vatatzes (q.v.) to discuss the union of the churches (q.v.). The most famous mission was by John Parastron, a Greek Franciscan, to Michael VIII (q.v.) to instruct the emperor (q.v.) in the theology (q.v.) of the Roman church prior to the Council of Lyons (q.v.). In this regard, the emperor also received Jerome of Ascoli, and Bonaventura da Mugello, the minister-general of the Franciscans, who negotiated the actual church union. The Council of Lyons only ratified what the Franciscans and Michael VIII had already agreed upon. The Franciscans continued as papal emissaries to Constantinople through the 14th century, maintaining a residence across the Golden Horn in Pera (qq.v.).

FRANKS. Group of Germanic tribes who by the third century were settled on the east bank of the lower and middle Rhine (q.v.). They were united under Clovis (481–511), who became an Orthodox (q.v.) Christian and founded a kingdom in Gaul (q.v.). Frankish power culminated in the year 800, with the coronation of Charlemagne (q.v.). After 843 Charlemagne's empire fragmented and was reconstituted in the following century as the western empire (essentially medieval Germany [q.v.]), and as the fledgling nation-state of France (q.v.).

FREDERICK I BARBAROSSA. Successor to Conrad III (q.v.) as king of Germany (q.v.) from 1152–1190; crowned western emperor in 1155. Frederick competed with Manuel I Komnenos (q.v.) for control over Italy and Hungary (qq.v.). Manuel I's invasion of southern Italy in 1155 failed in the face of stiff resistance by Norman king William I of Sicily (qq.v.). In 1158 Manuel I withdrew from Italy, signing a treaty with William I that recognized Frederick I as their mutual enemy. At this point, all Manuel could do was to try to keep Frederick I from annexing all of Italy. However, Frederick's intervention in northern Italy became a quagmire that ended in his defeat by the league of Lombard towns at the battle of Legnano on 29 May 1176. Frederick also attempted to control Hungary (q.v.), but Manuel I countered in 1163 by betrothing his daughter Maria to Bela III (q.v.), who was given the Greek name Alexios. Frederick's relations with Byzantium (q.v.) deteriorated further during the Third

Crusade, when Isaac II (qq.v.) made a treaty with Saladin (q.v.) to impede Frederick's army once it entered Byzantine territory. Frederick occupied Philoppopolis, then Adrianople (qq.v.), forcing Isaac II to cave in and transport Frederick and his troops to Asia Minor (q.v.). There, in Isauria (q.v.), Frederick drowned while crossing a stream.

FREDERICK II HOHENSTAUFEN. Emperor of Germany (qq.v.) from 1212–1250; he united Germany and the kingdom of Sicily (qq.v.) in 1198. Frederick's hostility to the papacy (q.v.) extended to all that the papacy (q.v.) supported, including the Latin Empire (q.v.). For this reason the emperor of Nicaea, John III Vatatzes (qq.v.), cultivated Frederick, hoping for help in recovering Constantinople (q.v.). In 1238 he sent troops to Italy (q.v.) to fight alongside those of Frederick, and John III married Frederick's daughter Constance of Hohenstaufen, who took the name Anna. Despite all this, John III gained very little from this alliance. When Frederick II died in 1250, his son Manfred (q.v.) reversed his father's policy and became an enemy to the Empire of Nicaea (q.v.).

FRESCO. A technique of painting on damp, fresh lime plaster, which, when dried, bonds the pigments with the wall. Decoration on church walls and ceilings was done either in fresco or mosaic (q.v.), the fresco technique being considerably less expensive.

FULCHER OF CHARTRES. French priest whose *Historia Hierosolymitana* (A History of the Expedition to Jerusalem) is among the three most valuable and reliable Latin sources for the history of the First Crusade (q.v.). (The other two sources are Albert of Aachen and Raymond of Aguilers [qq.v.].) He was present at the Council of Clermont when Pope Urban II (qq.v.) preached the First Crusade in 1095. He accompanied the troops of Stephen of Blois, Robert of Normandy, and Robert of Flanders to Jerusalem (q.v.), and, after the city's conquest in 1099 he remained in the Holy Land as chaplain to Baldwin of Boulogne. Other Latin chroniclers, including William of Tyre (q.v.), relied on his work for the years 1100–1127.

– G –

GABALAS FAMILY. *See* **RHODES.**

GABRIELOPOULOS FAMILY. *See* **THESSALY.**

GAETA. Seaport in central Italy (q.v.), between Rome and Naples (qq.v.). After the collapse of Byzantine rule in the Exarchate of Ravenna (q.v.) in 751, Gaeta was isolated, belonging nominally to the Byzantine duchy of Naples (q.v.). In reality, it was virtually independent like Amalfi (q.v.). Both were enclaves that found it profitable to maintain allegiance to Byzantium (q.v.). This situation persisted until Gaeta was conquered in 1032 by the Lombards (q.v.) of Capua. In 1064 it fell to the Normans (q.v.).

GAGIK I. King of Armenia (q.v.) from 989–ca. 1020, whose reign marked the high point of the kingdom of the Bagratids (q.v.). The disintegration of the kingdom after Gagik's death gave Basil II (q.v.) the opportunity to annex Vaspurkan (q.v.).

GAGIK II. Last Bagratid king (1042–1045) of Armenia (qq.v.); nephew of king John Smbat (q.v.). Induced to come to Constantinople (q.v.), he was forced to abdicate in return for estates in Cappadocia (q.v.), where he retired in 1045 with many distinguished Armenian families. His abdication allowed Byzantium (q.v.) to annex Ani (q.v.) and Smbat's entire kingdom, ostensibly to defend it (and Asia Minor [q.v.]) against Seljuk (q.v.) aggression. However, Constantine IX Monomachos (q.v.) failed to maintain adequate troops there, and the Seljuks conquered Ani in 1064.

GAINAS. Gothic (q.v.) general who briefly (399–400) endangered the throne of Arkadios (q.v.) and who seemed to personify the inherent danger of promoting Goths to high military commands. Arkadios (395–408) was a child-emperor, who, after the fall of Rufinus (q.v.), was dominated by his Grand Chamberlain Eutropios (q.v.) and by Gainas, who was his commander-in-chief *(magister ultriusque militiae* [q.v]) of the armies in the East. A crisis ensued when Gainas went over to the rebel Tribigild (q.v.), and the two of them forced Arkadios to execute Eutropios. With his main rivals gone, Gainas dominated Constantinople briefly (q.v.) until a spontaneous revolt on 12 July 400 resulted in the deaths of several hundred of his troops, forcing him to flee the capital with the remainder of them. Ironically, he was pursued by another Gothic general named Fravitta, who had remained loyal to Arkadios. The Hunnic chieftain Uldin captured Gainas and sent his head back to Arkadios.

GAISERIC. King of the Vandals (q.v.) from 428–477, and ablest Germanic leader of his time. Under Gaiseric the Vandals crossed from Spain to North Africa (qq.v.), establishing a capital at Carthage (q.v.). An adherent to Arianism (q.v.), Gaiseric began a persecution of his Orthodox (q.v.) subjects that his successors continued, which is vividly documented in the history of Victor of Vita (qq.v.). Gaiseric's craftiness in diplomacy is seen in his negotiations with Attila (q.v.), but it was as a naval strategist that he displayed brilliance. He created a fleet of small, light vessels, as perfectly suited for piracy as for sustained conquest. This fleet attacked Sicily, occupied Sardinia, Corsica (qq.v.), and the Balearic Islands; it menaced the coasts of Greece and Italy (qq.v.), and even pillaged Rome (q.v.) in 455. Leo I's (q.v.) great naval expedition against the Vandals in 468, led by Basiliskos (q.v.), failed, as did earlier attempts in 460 and 461 by the western emperor Majorian (q.v.). These failures only underscored Gaiseric's supremacy in the western Mediterranean (q.v.).

GALATA. Suburb of Constantinople (q.v.), located directly opposite Constantinople across the Golden Horn (q.v.). The fort on its shore protected the great harbor chain that could be hoisted to prevent entrance to the Golden Horn. Its Jewish quarter was destroyed by the Fourth Crusade (q.v.). In 1267 Michael VIII (q.v.) gave Galata to the Genoese, who subsequently turned it into a fortified colony called Pera (q.v.). By the reign of Andronikos III Palaiologos (q.v.) most incoming merchant ships, and their customs duties, went to Pera. It surrendered to the Ottomans (q.v.) in 1453.

GALAXEIDI, CHRONICLE OF. *See* **CHRONICLE.**

GALEN. Medical theorist born in Pergamon (q.v.) ca. 130 (died ca. 200) whose medical treatises were the basis of medicine in Byzantium (q.v.), indeed throughout the entire intellectual world of the Middle Ages. The secret of his success in Byzantium (though he had been a pagan) was his belief that everything in the human body was formed by a creator for a particular purpose. This fit in well with Christian theology. Thus, his theory of the four body-fluids called humours and their alleged relationship to different temperaments and diseases and his physiology, which had the blood ebbing and flowing (not circulating) through the expansion and contraction of the right side of the heart, were never challenged. The great Byzantine physicians, e.g., Oribasios, Aetios of Amida, Alexander of Tralles, Paul of Aegina, and John Aktouarios (qq.v.) only summarized and commented on his ideas.

GALERIUS. Member of the tetrarchy (q.v.). Diocletian (q.v.) chose him as caesar (q.v.) in 293, with jurisdiction over the Balkan Peninsula (q.v.) and the Danubian provinces. At Thessalonike (q.v.) are the remains of what may have been his palace, now the church of Hagios Georgios (q.v.). There is also a triumphal arch depicting Galerius's victory over the Persians (q.v.) in 297. When Diocletian retired in 305, Galerius became senior augustus (q.v.) of the tetrarchy. He chose Maximinus Daia as his caesar (qq.v.), and Licinius (q.v.) as augustus in the East, but he opposed the self-appointment of Maxentius (q.v.). Galerius may have been the driving force behind the Great Persecution (q.v.), which continued until he issued an edict of toleration shortly before his death in 311. The Edict of Milan (q.v.) was probably a reissuance of Galerius's edict.

GALLA PLACIDIA. Daughter of Theodosios I, sister of Honorios, and mother of Valentinian III (qq.v.). The Visigoths (q.v.) took her to Gaul (q.v.) after they sacked Rome (q.v.) in 410. There, in 414, she was married to Ataulf, successor to Alaric (qq.v.), and bore him a son, christened Theodosios, who died shortly after birth. When Atualf died soon thereafter, Galla Placidia was allowed to return to Honorios, who married her in 417 to the patrician Constantius against her wishes. She was crowned augusta, and the son born to them was the future Valentinian III. After Constantius's death in 421, Honorios accused her of treason and she fled to the court of Theodosios II (q.v.). When Honorios died in 423 she returned to the West, where she was regent for young Valentinian III, her rule uncontested for the first 12 years of his reign. When she died in 450 she was buried in a mausoleum in Ravenna (q.v.), which bears her name.

GALLIPOLI. Strategic port on the European shore of the Sea of Marmara (q.v.) at the northern end of the Hellespont (q.v.). From the Fourth Crusade (q.v.) onward, it was usually controlled by Byzantium's (q.v.) enemies. Venice (q.v.) held it from 1205 to 1235, when it was reconquered by John III Vatatzes (q.v.). It fell to the Catalan

Grand Company (q.v.) in 1304; they evacuated it in 1307. It was captured by the Ottomans under Orhan (qq.v.) in 1354, retaken for Byzantium by Amadeo VI of Savoy (q.v.) in 1366, but returned to Murad I (q.v.) in 1376 by Andronikos IV Palaiologos (q.v.) to ensure Murad I's continued support of his usurpation of the throne.

GALLUS. Half-brother of Julian (q.v.), caesar (q.v.) under Constantius II (q.v.), who executed him 354. He and Julian grew up on an isolated imperial estate in Cappadocia (q.v.) after Constantius II massacred most of their family members in 337. In 351 Constantius (q.v.) made Gallus caesar in the East, where he prepared to attack the Persians (q.v.) while Constantius II was in the West suppressing the revolt of Magnentius (q.v.). Ammianus Marcellinus (q.v.) paints a picture of Gallus's cruelty in Antioch (q.v.), especially in relation to the treason trials of 354, which Ammianus viewed as judicial murder. Whatever the truth of Ammianus's portrait, Constantius II came to view Gallus with suspicion, as he later did Julian. However, Julian escaped execution, whereas Gallus did not.

GANGRA. Metropolis of Paphlagonia (qq.v.), in Asia Minor (q.v.), site of a local council held around 341 to condemn extremist monks who followed the teachings of Eustathios of Sebasteia (q.v.). Gangra suffered attacks by Arabs (q.v.) in the eighth century, during the lifetime of Philaretos the Almsgiver (q.v.), who came from Amneia, a village dependent on Gangra. The Danishmendids (q.v.) conquered Gangra in 1075, but it was recaptured by John II Komnenos (q.v.) in 1136, along with the Danishmendid castle of Kastamonu, ancestral home of the Komnenoi. However, Gangra soon reverted to the Turks. The local saint was Hypatios, whose sixth-century *vita* (q.v.) describes how he killed a dragon that was living in the imperial treasury of Constantius II (q.v.).

GANGRA, COUNCIL OF. Local council held ca. 341 to condemn the followers of Eustathios of Sebasteia (q.v.). Eustathios's writings have not survived. However, since he became a metropolitan (q.v.) of Sebasteia subsequent to the council, it seems likely that he was more moderate in his beliefs than were his alleged followers. The Eustathians were condemned by the council for rejecting marriage and family life, rejecting a married priesthood, refusing to eat meat, fasting on the Lord's day, preaching that the rich would never enter Heaven, rejecting church rituals, and allowing women to dress like men. The records from the council's canons about these extremists provides the earliest information about monasticism in Asia Minor (qq.v.).

GARIGLIANO. River in southern Italy (q.v.), within the territory of Gaeta (q.v.). Around 882, Arabs (q.v.) from northwest Africa (q.v.) established a colony at a strategic position commanding the right bank of the Garigliano, near its mouth. This was not the only Arab colony in southern Italy, but it proved one of the more difficult to conquer. Finally in 915 a coalition of papal, Lombard (q.v.), and Byzantine forces attacked the colony. The Byzantine fleet, which still operated in these waters, sealed off their escape route to the sea, forcing the Arabs to flee to the mountains, where they were hunted down and killed.

GATTILUSIO. Family from Genoa who ruled Lesbos (qq.v.) from 1355–1462. Francesco Gattilusio was a Genoese buccaneer who had offered his services to John V Palaiologos (q.v.) and who helped the emperor (q.v.) seize Constantinople (q.v.) in 1354. For this, in the summer of 1355 John V gave him his sister Irene in marriage, and made him lord of Lesbos (q.v.). In 1366 Francesco joined Amadeo VI of Savoy (q.v.) in the recovery of Gallipoli (q.v.). The family's position was made secure by further imperial marriages. His son Francesco II (1384–1403) married his daughter Irene to John VII Palaiologos (q.v.), and Constantine XII Palaiologos's (q.v.) second wife was the daughter of Dorino Gattilusio. The family acquired other islands in the northern Aegean (q.v.) as well, including Ainos, Thasos, Samothrace, Lemnos, and Palaia Phokaia.

GAUFREDUS MALATERRA. Author of a history of the Normans of Sicily (qq.v.) from ca. 1038–1099, including an account of the campaign of George Maniakes (q.v.) against the Normans of southern Italy (q.v.), i.e., Calabria (q.v.), in 1042.

GAUL. Roman province south and west of the Rhine (q.v.), comprising what is now France (q.v.), Belgium, and Luxembourg, and parts of Germany (q.v.), Switzerland, and the Netherlands. The early career (355–361) of Julian (q.v.) illustrates the vigorous defense of Gaul in the fourth century. In the fifth century it was occupied by Visigoths, Burgundians, and Franks (qq.v.).

GAZA. City in southern Palestine (q.v.). Prior to its conquest by the Arabs (q.v.) in 635 it was a center of learning with a school of famous rhetoricians and poets. It was also a center of pagan worship until its bishop Porphyrios of Gaza (qq.v.) journeyed to Constantinople (q.v.) in 401 and convinced the empress Eudoxia (qq.v.) to support the demolition of the temple of Zeus Marnas, and the building of a church in Gaza, which was accomplished. Nevertheless, its school continued to flourish under such famous writers as Chorikios of Gaza and Prokopios of Gaza (qq.v.). The monastic writer Dorotheos of Gaza (q.v.) was also a native of the city, as was the church historian Sozomenos (q.v.). The city's port of Constantia was the terminus of an important trade in incense and spices from ports on the Indian Ocean through Mecca and Medina in the Arabian Peninsula.

GELASIOS OF CAESAREA. Bishop of Caesarea in Palestine (qq.v.) from ca. 367. An adherent to the Council of Nicaea (q.v.), he was ejected from his see (q.v.) during the reign of Valens (q.v.). His *Ecclesiastical History* is lost, but it seems to have been an important source for the fifth-century continuators of Eusebios of Caesarea (q.v.), e.g., Gelasios of Kyzikos, Sokrates, Sozomenos, Theodoret of Cyrrhus (qq.v.), and Rufinus of Aquileia, all of whom projected back onto the fourth century their own image of what the Constantinian church was like.

GELASIOS OF KYZIKOS. Fifth-century church historian who wrote a history of the church during Constantine I the Great's (q.v.) reign that survives to 335. It bears resemblance to the work of Eusebios of Caesarea (q.v.), as well as to the work of Eusebios's fifth-century continuators Sokrates, Sozeomenos, and Theodoret of Cyrrhus (qq.v.), all of whom relied on the lost church history of Gelasios of Caesarea (q.v.). He also wrote a *Syntagma,* a collection of the acts of the Council of Nicaea (q.v.) in 325, to demonstrate how far from the council were the views of the Monophysites (q.v.).

GELASIUS I. Pope (q.v.) from 492–496 who contributed to the idea of papal primacy (q.v.) by defining two powers, imperial and priestly. Priestly authority he considered superior to secular authority since priests he believed were ultimately responsible for the salvation of all men, even emperors (q.v.). He rejected the *Henotikon* of Zeno (qq.v.), and he excommunicated Patriarch Akakios (qq.v.) for supporting it, an act that inaugurated the first great schism in the church, the Akakian Schism (q.v.). He also rejected canon 28 of the Council of Chalcedon (q.v.), claiming the right for the papacy (q.v.) to pass final judgment on the canons of all church councils, and he refused to grant Constantinople (q.v.) the status of a metropolitan (q.v.) city. His theory of the two powers was fundamental to the thinking of later papal reformers.

GELIMER. Last king (530–534) of the Vandals (q.v.) whose inept military leadership contributed to the destruction of the Vandal state. His forces were caught by surprise and were ill-equipped to confront the forces of Justinian I, led by Belisarios (qq.v.). His defeat at the battle of Ad Decimum (Tenth Milestone) on 13 September 533 allowed Belisarios to enter Carthage (q.v.) unopposed. Belisarios seized Gelimer's throne and feasted on the food that Gelimer had ordered prepared in anticipation of his victory. Three months later Gelimer's army was crushed at the battle of Tricamarum. He fled, only to surrender in the spring of 534. That summer in Constantinople (q.v.) Gelimer was paraded in a triumph that culminated in the Hippodrome (q.v.), where he was stripped of his purple garments and forced to prostrate himself before Justinian and Theodora (q.v.)

GEMISTUS PLETHON. *See* **PLETHON, GEORGE GEMISTOS.**

GENESIOS. Chronicler whose work continues the chronicle of Theophanes (qq.v.), covering the years from 813–886. Constantine VII Porphyrogennetos (q.v.) commissioned his work. Despite various attempts to identify him, little is known about Genesios. What does seem certain is that either he copied from Theophanes Continuatus (q.v.), or they used a mutual source. Both works share the same poor understanding of events and have similar problems of chronology (q.v.).

GENIKON. *See* **LOGOTHETES.**

GENNADIOS I. Patriarch of Constantinople (qq.v) from 458–471. He was noted for his miracle-working and for his strict adherence to the doctrines of the Council of Chalcedon (q.v.) promulgated in 451. He continued the policies of his predecessor Flavian (q.v.), opposing Eutyches (q.v.), and allying himself with Pope Leo I (q.v.), with whom he worked to depose Timotheos Ailouros (q.v.), the Monophysite bishop of Alexandria (qq.v.). Leo I exiled him to Gangra (q.v.). Gennadios also obtained a decree of exile against Peter the Fuller, the Monophysite bishop of Antioch (qq.v.). His career must be seen within the larger framework of theological discord that occurred after the Council of Chalcedon.

GENNADIOS II SCHOLARIOS. First post-Byzantine patriarch of Constantinople (qq.v.) from 1454–1456, 1463, and again from 1464–1465. Born George Scholarios, he was a scholar who wrote on Aristotle (q.v.) and was versed in western scholasticism, including Thomas Aquinas (q.v.). When the Ottomans conquered Constantinople (qq.v.) in 1453, he had been living as the monk Gennadios, in a kind of exile as leader of the opposition against the union of the churches (q.v.). In January 1454, Sultan Mehmed II (q.v.) invested him with his insignia of office, as an emperor (q.v.) would have done, giving him complete authority over the *millet* of Rum (q.v.), as the Ottomans referred to the Orthodox (q.v.) community now under their dominion.

GENOA. Port-city in northwestern Italy that came into Byzantine hands around 540 when Justinian I conquered Italy (qq.v.). It fell into the hands of the Lombards (q.v.) a century later, but by the 10th century, it became a free commune, and its maritime power increased steadily. In the 11th century, aided by Pisa (q.v.), the Genoese drove the Arabs from Corsica and Sardinia (qq.v.). The Crusades (q.v.) made Genoa wealthy, and rivalry with Venice (q.v.) and Pisa for access to the lucrative Byzantine markets ensued. In 1155 Genoa was granted a market area and port facilities in Constantinople (q.v.). The Venetians triumphed in 1204, when the Fourth Crusade (q.v.) captured Constantinople, but the Treaty of Nymphaion (q.v.) in 1261 tied Michael VIII Palaiologos (q.v.) to Genoa in a permanent alliance. Within a month of the signing of the treaty Constantinople was recaptured, and Genoa's commercial position was preeminent. Genoa's defeat of Pisa in 1284 was a turning point; now she had no serious rivals. Her colonies grew in number, and most impressive were the northern ones in the Black Sea (q.v.), including Vinina and Chilia (q.v.), Kaffa and Sougdaia in the Crimea, and Trebizond (qq.v.). The alum mines at Phokaia (q.v.) were ceded to the Zaccaria (q.v.) family, who also gained Chios (q.v.) in 1304. By the mid-14th century the Genoese colony at Galata (q.v.) had become a kind of state within a state, levying duties on all shipping to the Black Sea, with a virtual trade monopoly in the Bosporos (q.v.), and in much of the northern Aegean (q.v.). However, a series of wars with Venice from 1292–1382, including a war over Tenedos (q.v.), weakened Genoese commercial hegemony, making Genoa vulnerable to the Ottomans (q.v.) in the 15th century.

GEOFFREY I VILLEHARDOUIN. Nephew of historian Geoffrey de Villehardouin (q.v.) who in 1205, in the service of Boniface of Montferrat (q.v.), and with the help of William I of Champlitte (qq.v), inaugurated the Frankish conquest of the Morea. From 1208, when William I returned to France (q.v.), Geoffrey became sole prince of Achaia (q.v.), organizing his conquests as a feudal kingdom. He died ca. 1230.

GEOFFREY II VILLEHARDOUIN. Son of Geoffrey I Villehardouin (q.v.), and Prince of Achaia (q.v.) from ca. 1230–1246. He was succeeded by his brother, William II Villehardouin (q.v.).

GEOFFREY DE VILLEHARDOUIN. Major participant and chief Latin historian of the Fourth Crusade (q.v.). Marshal of Champagne prior to the Fourth Crusade, his *Conquest of Constantinople* is a kind of official history of the Crusade, written from the point of view of someone who helped negotiate with Venice (q.v.) for the transport of the Crusade, and who subsequently participated in the important decisions that diverted the Fourth Crusade to Zara (q.v.) and then to Constantinople (q.v.). His bias clearly favors those who worked to keep the army together, including doge Enrico Dandalo of Venice (qq.v.), who is pictured as a wise and unselfish leader, contrary to Byzantine sources. Above all, Villehardouin values loyalty, living up to one's word, and fulfilling contractual obligations. Thus, he disdains those Latin knights who promised to sail from Venice but failed to show, and those who left the army as it made its way eastward. In a similar way, the failure of Alexios IV Angelos (q.v.) to fulfill his promises to the Crusaders, and the perfidy of Alexios V Doukas (q.v.) become a perfect rationale for the conquest of Constantinople, and destruction of Byzantium (q.v.), in 1204. After the conquest he was made Marshal of Romania, in Thrace (q.v.). He died around 1212.

GEOGRAPHY. Byzantium (q.v.) preserved and studied the great geographers from antiquity, including Strabo, Pausanius, and Ptolemy (qq.v.). However, nothing was added to the study of theoretical geography. The weight of classical scholarship seems to have been an impediment to fresh research, as indicated by Constantine VII's *De Thematibus* (qq.v.), which relies on ancient literature. Travel literature makes for more interesting reading, especially the sixth-century memoir of Kosmas, called *Indikopleustes* (q.v.). However, the expansive geographical curiosity of Kosmas yielded to a more restricted view of the world in subsequent centuries as Byzantium lost territory to foreign invaders, becoming itself more restricted in scope.

GEOPONIKA. An anonymous work on agriculture (q.v.). Its dedication to Constantine VII Porphyrogennetos (q.v.) dates it to 945–959, and its organization (a manual of fragments from ancient Greek writers) is typical of the compilations sponsored by this emperor (q.v.). Its section on viticulture was translated into Latin by Burgundio of Pisa in the 12th century.

GEORGE BRANKOVICH. Last ruler (1427–1456) of medieval Serbia (q.v.). The capture of Bayezid I (q.v.) at the battle of Ankara in 1402, and the resulting three decades of Ottoman weakness, gave Brankovich the opportunity to restore Serbian independence, symbolized by the new stronghold and capital Smederevo (q.v.). His territory expanded with the inheritance of his uncle Stefan Lazarevich, who died childless in 1427. While the Ottomans (q.v.) regrouped he found support in alliances with John VIII Palaiologos (q.v.). However, he was too weak to resist the Hungarians, who seized Belgrade in 1427, or the renewed vigor of the Ottomans under Murad II (q.v.). Murad II took Smederevo in 1439, and although it was recaptured with the help of Hunyadi (q.v.), the stunning victory of Murad II at the battle of Varna (q.v.) in 1444 brought Brankovich once more into Ottoman vassalage. When Mehmed II (q.v.) demanded troops for the siege of Constantinople (q.v.) in 1453, he complied. Brankovich died in 1456, and so did not live to see the Ottoman conquest of Smederevo in 1459, which ended medieval Serbia.

GEORGE HAMARTOLOS. His world chronicle (q.v.) from Adam to 842 is one of the few contemporary historical sources for the period 813–842. Nothing is known about him, except that he was a monk, referred to as George the Monk. He is also referred to as George Hamartolos (*hamartolos* means "sinner"). Certainly his major concerns have to do with issues affecting monasticism (q.v.) and the church, e.g., Iconoclasm and Islam (qq.v.). His chief sources for Byzantine affairs are Theophanes, Malalas, and Symeon Logothetes (qq.v.). A continuation of his chronicle, some versions of which extend to 1143, is often attributed to Symeon Logothete (q.v.).

GEORGE OF AMASTRIS. Saint, hermit, bishop of Amastris (qq.v.) in the late eighth century. His *vita* (q.v.), attributed to Ignatios the

Deacon (q.v.) on stylistic grounds, reports an undated attack of the Rus on Amastris (qq.v.).

GEORGE OF PISIDIA. Poet who wrote three epic eulogies about the wars of Herakleios (q.v.); he was a deacon at Hagia Sophia in Constantinople (qq.v.). The first eulogy deals with Herakleios's campaign against the Persians (q.v.), the second with the attack of the Avars (q.v.) on Constantinople in 626, and the third with the emperor's (q.v.) final victory over Persian king Chosroes II (q.v.). In the 11th century, Psellos (q.v.) compared the style of George of Pisidia to that of Euripides (q.v.).

GEORGE OF TREBIZOND. Humanist; one of the great translators of Greek texts into Latin. His parents were from Trebizond (q.v.), but he was born in Crete (q.v.) in 1395. He embraced Catholicism and emigrated to Venice (q.v.) in 1415 where he taught Greek and studied Latin. When Pope Nicholas V (q.v.) became his patron he attached himself to the papal academy, headed by Bessarion (q.v.), that translated Greek works into Latin. George translated 11 major Greek texts, some of them never before translated, in addition to other texts from a variety of authors, including Ptolemy, Aristotle, Plato (qq.v.), and the Greek church fathers. He authored a treatise on rhetoric (q.v.), which became the chief text on the subject for the Italian humanists, as well as a treatise on logic. He passionately argued the superiority of Aristotle over Plato, criticizing Bessarion, Plethon, and Theodore Gaza (qq.v.) for their contrary views. He supported the papacy (q.v.) at the Council of Ferrara-Florence (q.v.) and was an ambassador of Pope Paul II to Mehmed II (q.v.).

GEORGE THE SYNKELLOS. Author of a world chronicle (q.v.) that extends from the Creation to the reign of Diocletian (q.v.) in 284. He was *synkellos* of Tarasios (qq.v.), patriarch of Constantinople (qq.v.) from 784–806. George's work is of interest primarily because of its relationship to the more important *Chronographia* of Theophanes the Confessor (q.v.), which picks up in 284 where George leaves off and which may rely on notes that George provided to Theophanes.

GEORGE THE MONK. *See* **GEORGE HARMATOLOS.**

GEORGIA. *See* **IBERIA.**

GEPIDS. German barbarians related to the Goths (q.v.) who settled in northern Dacia (q.v.) in the fourth century. They were subject to the Huns (q.v.) in the fifth century, until the death of Attila (q.v.). In the sixth century, the Gepids were the most powerful of the Germanic peoples on the Danube (q.v.) frontier. Justinian I (q.v) benefited from the hostility between the Gepids and the Lombards (q.v.) by playing one off against the other. In 567, two years after Justinian I died, a major war between the two erupted in which the Lombards, supported by the Avars (q.v.), annihilated the Gepids. After this, the Gepids disappeared from history.

GERASA. City (modern Jarash, in Jordan) noted for its nine ruined churches, all extraordinary in size, dating from the fourth through the early seventh centuries. All are basilicas (q.v.) except for the centrally planned church of St. John the Baptist, and the cross-in-square church (q.v.) dedicated to the apostles, prophets, and martyrs. The city, once part of the province of Arabia (q.v.), was conquered by the Arabs (q.v.) in 634.

GERMANIKEIA. City situated at the foot of the Antitaurus mountain range, facing the plain of Mesopotamia (q.v.). Its history symbolizes the centuries-long frontier warfare between Byzantium and Islam (qq.v.). The Arabs (q.v.) conquered it in 637 and made it a base for their raids into Asia Minor (q.v.). Constantine V (q.v.) captured it in 746, dismantled its fortifications, and evacuated some of the population to Thrace (q.v.). The Abbasids (q.v.) reoccupied it in 768; Harun al-Rashid (q.v.) strongly fortified it. Theophilos (q.v.) recaptured it in 841, after which the city changed hands a number of times until it was taken by Nikephoros II Phokas (q.v.) in 963 while on expedition to Aleppo (q.v.). In the late 11th century it was briefly part of an Armenian principality under Philaretos Brachamios, but soon fell to the Seljuks (q.v.) before returning briefly to Alexios I Komnenos (q.v.). In 1104 the Crusaders regained it and made it part of the county of Edessa (q.v.). In 1152, after the fall of Edessa, Germanikeia was occupied by Nur al-Din (q.v.). Nestorios (q.v.) was born in Germanikeia, ironically so since it became a stronghold of Monophysitism (q.v.). Leo III (q.v.), an Isaurian (q.v.) according to Theophanes the Confessor (q.v.), actually came from Germanikeia.

GERMANOS. General and nephew of Justinian I (q.v.). He replaced Solomon in North Africa (qq.v.) in 536 and defeated the rebel Stotzas the following year. In 540 he unsuccessfully defended Antioch against Chosroes I (qq.v.), after which he fell into disfavor. He married Matasuntha (ca. 542), the daughter of Amalasuntha (q.v.), after the death of Vitiges (q.v.). At some unknown date he defeated an invasion of Antae into Thrace (qq.v.).

GERMANOS I. Patriarch of Constantinople (qq.v.) from 715–730. He opposed the Iconoclasm (q.v.) of Leo III (q.v.), and when the emperor (q.v.) convened a *silentium* (q.v.) in 730 to validate Iconoclasm, the patriarch refused and was deposed. His former *synkellus* Anastasios (qq.v.), who supported Iconoclasm, was made patriarch in his place.

GERMANOS II. Patriarch of Constantinople (qq.v.) from 1223–1240, residing in Nicaea (q.v.). He mounted a vigorous defense of his claim to be ecumenical patriarch, and he remained in contact with the citizens of Constantinople (q.v.), who lived under Latin domination. He also defended the claims of John III Vatatzes (q.v.) to be sole emperor (q.v.), despite Demetrios Chomatenos's (q.v.) coronation of rival Theodore Komnenos Doukas as *basileus* and *autokrator* (qq.v.) of the Romans. His negotiations with Pope Gregory IX (q.v.) concerning union of the churches (q.v.) resulted in the Council of Nicaea-Nymphaion (q.v.) in 1234, where he defended the Orthodoxy (q.v.) of the eastern Church against the arguments of papal delegates. In 1232 the church of Epiros (q.v.) came under his control, and three years later he recognized the church of Bulgaria as autocephalous (qq.v.). His active career included being mentor to Nikephoros Blemmydes (q.v.); in addition, he authored homilies and theological works.

GERMANY. The kingdom of the East Franks (q.v.), which became the nucleus of Germany after the division of Charlemagne's (q.v.) realm in 843. In 911 when the last of the Carolingian kings of Germany died, Conrad I was elected king, followed in 918 by Henry I of Saxony. In 962 his son Otto I the Great (q.v.) was crowned emperor of what was called the Roman Empire (much later referred to as the Holy Roman Empire). Byzantium (q.v.) eventually recognized Otto I as *basileus* (q.v.) of the Franks, but not of the Romans. Relations between the two empires were frequently tense, especially over conflicting territorial claims in Italy (q.v.). The passage of Frederick I Barbarossa (q.v.) through Byzantium during the Third Crusade (q.v.) was fraught with tension. Frederick I's son Philip of Swabia (q.v.) played a minor though important role in the diversion of the Fourth Crusade to Constantinople (qq.v.).

GERMIYAN. Turkish emirate (q.v.) established in western Asia Minor (q.v.) amid the ruins of the Seljuk sultanate of Rum (qq.v.). Its center was the former Byzantine city of Kotyaion (Kütahya). For much of the 14th century its power along the Aegean (q.v.) coast of Asia Minor exceeded that of the Ottoman (q.v.) emirate. However, beginning in the late 14th century it came under Ottoman control. Germiyan temporarily regained its independence in 1402 after Timur captured Bayezid I at the battle of Ankara (qq.v.); the Ottomans regained control of it in 1429.

GESTA FRANCORUM ET ALIORUM HIEROSOLIMI-TANORUM *(The Deeds of the Franks and other Jerusalemers).* This major source for the First Crusade (q.v.) was written, perhaps as a diary, by an anonymous Crusader who accompanied Bohemund to Antioch (qq.v.), and continued on to Jerusalem with Tancred (qq.v.). It ends with the battle of Askalon (q.v.) in 1099. It was the most popular of the contemporary accounts, in part because Bohemund, who the author obviously admired, publicized it. Other accounts of the Crusade, including those of Albert of Aachen, Fulcher of Chartres, Guibert of Nogent (qq.v.), Baldric of Dol, and Robert the Monk, depend heavily on the *Gesta Francorum*.

GHASSANIDS. Arab allies *(foederati* [q.v.]) of Byzantium (q.v.) who defended the frontier of Syria (q.v.) in the sixth century. Their greatest prince was al-Harith, called Arethas by the Byzantines. Justinian I (q.v.) awarded him the title of phylarch in the wars with Persia (q.v.), and with their Arab allies, the rival Lakhmids (q.v.). The Ghassanids professed Monophysitism (q.v.), which Justinian I tolerated, and which his empress Theodora (q.v.) supported, but Justinian I's successors did not. Nevertheless, the Ghassanids continued to be of service to Byzantium. In 580 al-Mundhir (Alamundarus [q.v.]; not to be confused with the Lakhmid ruler Alamundarus [q.v.]), son of Arethas, destroyed Hira (q.v.), capital of the Lakhmids, and the Ghassanids fought valiantly at the battle of Yarmuk (q.v.) in 636, after which they were resettled in Asia Minor (q.v.).

GILDO. Moorish rebel whose revolt (397–398) was suppressed by Stilicho (q.v.). Ironically, Gildo's rise to power was fueled by the rewards he received from Theodosios I (q.v.) for helping the emperor (q.v.) put down (in 379) a similar revolt by his brother Firmus. Like Firmus, Gildo sought to create a separate African kingdom. He sought to gain the political support of the eastern emperor Arkadios (q.v.) by offering to transfer the diocese of Africa (qq.v.) from Honorios (q.v.) to Arkadios. However, when he prevented the grain supply from reaching Rome (q.v.) Stilicho marched against him. Gildo was defeated in battle and killed. Despite this, the dream of a separate kingdom in Africa (q.v.) persisted among other barbarian peoples, among whom were the Vandals (q.v.).

GIUSTINIANI, GIOVANNI LONGO. Genoese commander who led the defense of the land walls during Mehmed II's (q.v.) siege of Constantinople (q.v.) in 1453. In January of that year he arrived with 700 troops recruited from Genoa, Chios, and Rhodes (qq.v.), placing himself and his soldiers at the service of Constantine XI (q.v.). Historical accounts of the siege stress his important role in repairing and defending the land walls until, in the final Ottoman (q.v.) assault, he was wounded and carried from the scene of battle. He died either at Galata (q.v.) or on Chios.

GLABAS, ISIDORE. Metropolitan of Thessalonike (qq.v.) from 1380–1396. He left the city during its siege (1383–1387) by the Ottomans (q.v.), but he returned in 1393 when it was under Ottoman control. His sermons and letters are an important source of information about the siege, and especially about what it was like under Ottoman administration, which lasted until 1403. In one of his sermons there is mention for the first time of the Ottoman *devshirme,* the forcible recruitment of Christian boys for service in the sultan's elite shock troops, the famed janissaries (q.v.).

GLABAS, MICHAEL TARCHANEIOTES. Byzantium's (q.v.) most able general (died ca. 1305) during the reign of Andronikos II Palaiologos (q.v.). He campaigned successfully against the forces of Bulgaria, Serbia, and the Angevins (qq.v.), in an effort to preserve what was left of the western possessions of the empire. His campaign in northern Epiros (q.v.) briefly recovered Ioannina and Dyrrachion (qq.v.), before he returned to Constantinople (q.v.) in 1293, events reported in the *Chronicle of Morea,* and later by the poet Manuel Philes. In 1298, he had the wisdom to recommend to Andronikos that peace be made with Stefan Urosh II Milutin (q.v.), rather than face a protracted war with Serbia. He is buried in the south *parekklesion* (q.v.) of the Church of Hagia Maria Pammakaristos in Constantinople.

GLAGOLITIC. The first alphabet of Old Church Slavonic (q.v.), invented by Constantine the Philosopher (q.v.) ca. 863 for his mission to Moravia (q.v.). It was a new and original alphabet, although some of the letters are derived from the Hebrew alphabet and others from Greek cursive writing (minuscule [q.v.]). It should not be confused with the Cyrillic (q.v.) alphabet, a later invention, created perhaps by Kliment of Ohrid (q.v.).

GLORIOSUS. In the sixth century this title replaced *illustris* (q.v.) as the highest title for members of the senate (q.v.). It was given to major administrators, including prefects (q.v.), the *magister militum,* the *magister officiorum,* and the *praepositus sacri cubiculi* (qq.v.).

GLYKAS, MICHAEL. Poet; author of a world chronicle (q.v.) from the Creation to 1118; imperial *grammatikos* (q.v.). The writing style of his poetry was influenced by the vernacular style of contemporary romances and poetry. In his world chronicle, he even enlivens his account of the Creation with animal fables from the ancient Greek bestiary entitled *Physiologos.* His style contrasts sharply with the more sophisticated chronicler Zonaras (q.v.). However, both shared a dislike of the Komnenoi. Glykas was blinded and imprisoned for his part in a plot against Manuel I Komnenos (q.v.).

GOLDEN GATE. *See* **ADVENTUS; MESE.**

GOLDEN HORDE. *See* **MONGOLS.**

GOLDEN HORN. *See* **CONSTANTINOPLE.**

GÖREME. Valley in Cappadocia (q.v.) renowned for its rock-cut churches and refectories (q.v.), some of them carved in cones of rock that create a landscape of the strangest beauty. There are no literary texts that survive about this site, but clearly they were once monasteries, probably numerous small ones, since some refectories appear to belong to particular churches. The wall-paintings (in fresco [q.v.] technique) date these monuments to the 10th and 11th centuries.

GOTHS. Germanic people whose impact on the empire was profound from the third century through the reign of Justinian I (q.v.). Their raids across the lower Danube (q.v.) in the third century were a major threat to the Roman state. In the fourth century they split into two groups, the Visigoths and Ostrogoths (qq.v.). Many were settled below the Danube and enrolled in the army as *foederati* (q.v.). There, they were promoted, often to the highest commands, especially under Theodosios I (q.v.). Occasionally this had dire results, as in the case of Gainas (q.v.). Both Visigoths and Ostrogoths ultimately founded states on imperial territory, preceded by pillage and conquest, best illustrated by Alaric's (q.v.) invasions of Greece and Italy (qq.v.) before the Visigoths were finally settled in Gaul (q.v.). Once settled, their Arianism (q.v.) continued to insure that they would never be fully integrated into the empire, something Synesios of Cyrene (q.v.) argued. However, the massacre of Goths in Constantinople in 400 (including the death of Gainas [q.v.]) solved the problem of the Goths in the East.

GOUDELES TYRANNOS. Byzantine capitalist of the late 13th century. His will of 1294, deeding his estate to a monastery in Constantinople (q.v.), is an inventory of assets in the region of Smyrna and Nymphaion (qq.v.). Included are textile factories, a bakehouse and bakery, vineyards, cattle and horses, half of a bathhouse, and various other properties. The diversity of his holdings, and the obvious wealth they represent, illustrate the free enterprise and relative lack of state control over the economy of this period.

GRAČANIČA. Monastery church built by Stefan Urosh II Milutin of Serbia (qq.v.). Its cross-in-square (q.v.) plan is of the late Byzantine type, with five domes (q.v.). Probably the architect and artisans were from Thessalonike (q.v.), but the church itself (begun ca. 1311), with its towering five domes and the decorative facade, excels any late Byzantine church in that city. In a larger sense, the church reflects the powerful Byzantine cultural influence on Serbia after Milutin made peace with Andronikos II (q.v.) in 1298, followed by Milutin's marriage to Andronikos's daughter Simonis (q.v.) the year after that.

GRAMMATIKOS. A secretary or scribe. In reference to imperial secretaries, the term replaced *asekretis* (q.v.) during the period of the Komnenoi emperors. More generally, an epithet of respect meaning learned teacher, e.g., as with John VI Grammatikos (q.v.).

GRAND CHAMBERLAIN. *See* **PRAEPOSITUS SACRI CUBICULI.**

GRAND KOMNENOI. *See* **TREBIZOND.**

GRATIAN. Western emperor (q.v.) from 367–383; elder son of Valentinian I (q.v.). He succeeded Valentinian I as western emperor in 375, with half-brother Valentinian II (q.v.) as his nominal colleague. He appointed Theodosios I (q.v.) as eastern emperor in 379, after the death of Valens at the battle of Adrianople (qq.v.). With Ambrose (q.v.) as an advisor, he attacked paganism, removing the Altar of Victory from the senate house in Rome (q.v.) in 383. He also seized the revenues of the Vestal Virgins and refused the pagan title of high priest (*pontifex maximus*). He was assassinated by the followers of Maximus (q.v.), who was eventually defeated and killed by Theodosios I in 388.

GREAT LAVRA. *See* **ATHANASIOS OF ATHOS; ATHOS, MOUNT; MONASTICISM.**

GREAT PALACE. The official imperial residence in Constantinople (q.v.), situated east of the Hippodrome (q.v.), to which its residential wing, the Palace of Daphne, was connected. The Augustaion (q.v.) was situated on its north side, where the palace's main entrance, the Chalke (q.v.), was situated. The palace, begun by Constantine I (q.v.), consisted of groups of reception rooms, audience and banquet halls, chapels, throne rooms, and residences, linked by covered corridors and porticos. Among its famous buildings were the Chrysotriklinos, the Nea Ekklesia, and the triconch of Theophilos (qq.v.). Constantine VII's *De ceremoniis* (qq.v.) describes the palace in sufficient detail to reconstruct much of its layout, but actual excavations have been insufficient to identify specific buildings. The Great Palace and adjacent Hippodrome figured prominently in the Nika Revolt (q.v.) of 532. Komnenian emperors (q.v.), beginning with Alexios I (q.v.), preferred to live in the Blachernai palace (q.v.). The decline of the Great Palace began in 1204 when it was made the residence of the Latin emperors. It further declined under the Palaiologan dynasty (q.v.)

GREAT PERSECUTION. The last empire-wide persecution of Christians by the Roman state. It lasted from 303–311, beginning during the reign of Diocletian (q.v.). However, the moving force behind it was Diocletian's caesar (q.v.), and fanatical pagan, Galerius (q.v.). This was a serious attempt to destroy the Christian church by arresting clergy, razing church buildings to the ground, burning the Scriptures, and stripping Christians of their right to plead in courts of law. There were numerous martyrs in Palestine under Maximinus

Daia (qq.v.), as reported by Eusebios of Caesarea in his *Ecclesiastical History,* and *Martyrs of Palestine.* However, outside Palestine decrees were unevenly enforced. In the West, for example, Constantius Chlorus, father of Constantine I the Great (qq.v.), seems to have enforced the decrees hardly at all. In 311 Galerius acknowledged the persecution's failure in an edict of toleration that became the basis of the Edict of Milan (q.v.).

GREECE. By Greece *(Hellas)* medieval writers usually refer to central Greece and the Peloponnesos (q.v.), in other words to regions south of Thermopylae (q.v.). The territorial extent of the late-seventh century theme of Hellas (qq.v.) is debated, but certainly it included the Peloponnesos and the eastern part of central Greece, which is to say Boeotia, and perhaps Thessaly (qq.v.). Byzantium (q.v.) twice lost control of much of Greece. The first time was when the Slavs (q.v.) settled throughout much of Greece in the late sixth century. Nikephoros I (q.v.) took the first significant steps toward restoration of Byzantine control. By the 11th century, urban and agricultural prosperity was restored. The second time was in the aftermath of the Fourth Crusade (q.v.), when Greece became divided into competing minor states that included the principality of Achaia (q.v.), the despotate of Epiros (q.v.), and the despotate of Morea (q.v.). The last part of Byzantium to fall was not Constantinople in 1453, but Mistra (q.v.) in 1460.

GREEK ANTHOLOGY. Modern title of two 10th-century collections of ancient and Byzantine epigrams: the *Anthologia Palatina,* and the *Anthologia Planudea* (compiled by Maximos Planoudes [q.v.]). Included are poems of Paul the Silentarios, Julian the Egyptian, Priscian, and Ignatios the Deacon (qq.v.). The value of these collections is that they preserve poetry that otherwise would not have survived.

GREEK CROSS-DOMED OCTAGON CHURCH. A church that makes use of the basic design of the domed-octagon church (q.v.), but with radiating barrel-vaulted arms emanating from the central bay, all enclosed within an outer square or rectangle. Examples include the *katholikon* at Daphni, outside Athens (qq.v.).

GREEK FIRE. Napalm-like substance that could be squirted under pressure from specially designed ships, used for the first time with devastating effect on the Arab fleet besieging Constantinople (q.v.)

in 678. Tradition attributes its invention to a Greek architect from Syria (q.v.) named Kallinikos. Though a closely guarded secret, the formula seems to have included crude oil, mixed with sticky resins and sulfur, which was heated and then discharged by a pump through a bronze tube. In effect, it was like a modern flame-thrower. From some distance it could cover an enemy ship with an adhesive fire that could not be quenched with water. It could also be used in grenades and in portable pumps to attack or defend land walls during sieges.

GREENS. *See* **DEMES.**

GREGORAS, NIKEPHOROS. If not the most brilliant writer of the 14th century (which he may have been), he was certainly the most versatile of scholars. He wrote on every subject important to the scholarship of his day, including history, logic, rhetoric, philosophy, astronomy, theology, and hagiography (qq.v.). His letters are important historical sources, and he himself was a most capable historian. His *Roman History,* covering the years 1204–1359, is particularly valuable for the events of his lifetime (ca. 1290–ca. 1360). He is biased against Palamism (q.v.), which he attacked after 1347, but favors John VI Kantakouzenos (q.v.), who he supported during the civil war of 1341–1347. The Palamite victory at a local council in Constantinople (q.v.) in 1351 included a condemnation of Gregoras, who was confined to his house, then to the Chora Monastery (q.v.) until 1354, when he was freed. He spent his remaining years denouncing his enemy Gregory Palamas (q.v.).

GREGORY. Exarch of Carthage (qq.v.) whose short-lived rebellion (646–647) against Constans II (q.v.) grew out of the opposition of Maximos the Confessor (q.v.) and the North African bishops to Monotheletism (q.v.). Gregory, a relative of Herakleios (q.v.), perhaps sought to imitate the late emperor's (q.v.) rebellion. In any case, Gregory fell victim not to the forces of Constans II, but to the westward advance of the Arabs (q.v.) in 647.

GREGORY I THE GREAT. Pope (q.v.) from 590–604 who is considered the greatest of the early medieval popes; saint. He refused to recognize the title of "Ecumenical Patriarch" that John IV "Faster" (q.v.), archbishop of Constantinople (qq.v.) proclaimed for himself. John was supported by Maurice (q.v.), whose overthrow in 602 Gregory welcomed. Maurice's successor Phokas (q.v.), however unpopular he was in Constantinople, was esteemed by Gregory, who erected a column in the Roman forum in his honor. Among Gregory's many achievements was the maintenance of papal independence against the Lombards (qq.v.), and his sending of St. Augustine of Canterbury to England (q.v.) to organize the church there.

GREGORY II. Pope (q.v.) from 715–731 who came into conflict with Leo III over Iconoclasm (qq.v.). Supported by Italy (q.v.) and the entire western church, he courteously rejected Leo III's order demanding acceptance of Iconoclasm. Leo III reminded the pope that he was both emperor (q.v.) and priest, but Gregory rejected this "caesaropapism" (q.v.), replying that church dogma was reserved for priests alone. At the same time, he tried to avoid a complete breach with the empire, threatened as it was with domination by the Lombards (q.v.). The conflict was bequeathed to the next pope, Gregory III (q.v.).

GREGORY III. Pope (q.v.) from 731–741 who inherited the dispute with Leo III over Iconoclasm (qq.v.). At a synod in Rome (q.v.) in 731, he denounced Iconoclasm and excommunicated the subservient patriarch Anastasios (qq.v.). In response, Leo III sent an armed fleet to Italy (q.v.), but the fleet was wrecked in a storm. Unable to enforce compliance, Leo III then diverted revenues from papal properties in Sicily and Calabria (qq.v.) to the imperial treasury, effectively ending papal jurisdiction over these papal patrimonies. He may have also transferred these ecclesiastical dioceses, as well as that of Illyricum (qq.v.), from papal authority to the patriarch of Constantinople (qq.v.). In effect, this made it impossible for the papacy (q.v.) to gain Byzantine help against the Lombards (q.v.). In 739, and again in 740, Gregory III appealed to Charles Martel, leader of the Franks (q.v.), for help against the Lombards. When Gregory died in 741, the Lombards were at the gates of Rome (q.v.), and the papal-Byzantine tie seemed stretched to the breaking point.

GREGORY VII. Reformist pope (q.v.) from 1073–1085 whose vision of the papacy (q.v.) included a great army to save Byzantium from the Seljuks (qq.v.) ; this vision was later realized by Urban II (q.v.) in the First Crusade (q.v.). Gregory VII's vision of a union of the churches (q.v.) following from such a venture did not happen until the disastrous and tragic Fourth Crusade (q.v.).

GREGORY VIII. *See* **THIRD CRUSADE.**

GREGORY X. Pope (q.v.) from 1271–1276 who presided over the Council of Lyons (1274), which achieved, on paper, the union of the churches (q.v.). In reality, Gregory X had required this of Michael VIII Palaiologos (q.v.) in return for pressuring Charles I of Anjou (q.v.) to postpone the expedition he was organizing to conquer Constantinople (q.v.). Gregory further conspired with Michael VIII to organize a Crusade that Charles would lead against the Seljuks in Asia Minor (qq.v.). However, these plans were still in the preliminary stage when the pope died.

GREGORY ABU'L-FARAJ. *See* **BAR-HEBRAEUS, GREGORIUS.**

GREGORY OF DEKAPOLIS. Saint (died ca. 841). His *vita* (q.v.), written by Ignatios the Deacon (q.v.), is an interesting historical source. Gregory spent a number of years as a monk before starting out on his travels in the 830s. First he went to Ephesus (q.v.), then to the Sea of Marmara, Thrace, Thessalonike, Corinth, Syracuse, Naples, and Rome (qq.v.), before returning to Thessalonike, from where he later traveled to Constantinople (q.v.). Among the information in this *vita* is a description of a revolt by Slavs near Thessalonike (qq.v.).

GREGORY OF NAZIANZOS. Fourth-century writer; saint; one of the "Cappadocian Fathers," along with Gregory of Nyssa and Basil the Great (qq.v.). Son of the bishop (q.v.) of Nazianzos in Cappadocia (q.v.), he became bishop of Constantinople (q.v.) in 380–381, and chaired the Second Ecumenical Council (q.v.) at Constantinople in 381, where he opposed the followers of Eunomios (q.v.). He was bishop of Nazianzos from 382–384, before his death ca. 390. His writings are varied, including sermons and polemics against heresy (q.v.). His chief historical role was that of defender of Orthodoxy (q.v.) at a time when Orthodoxy needed defending.

GREGORY OF NYSSA. Theologian; saint; one of the "Cappadocian Fathers," along with his brother Basil the Great and Gregory of Nazianzos (qq.v.). Appointed bishop of Nyssa (qq.v.) in 371, he was removed on false charges for two years (376–378), returning only after the death of Valens (q.v.). He defended Orthodoxy against Arianism (qq.v.) at the Council of Constantinople (q.v.) in 381, but he is remembered chiefly as a theologian of great originality. He wrote on topics ranging from the Trinity to the Resurrection, in addition to polemics against heretics like those who followed Eunomios (q.v.).

GREGORY OF SINAI. Founder of Hesychasm on Mount Athos (qq.v.). Originally a monk at Sinai (q.v.), he went to Mount Athos, where he introduced the so-called Jesus prayer ("Lord Jesus Christ, Son of God, have mercy on me"), repeated over and over again as one meditated with controlled breathing. Soon the Athonian monasteries became the center of Hesychasm. He left Athos ca. 1330 and settled at Paroria in Thrace (q.v.), where he enjoyed the patronage of Ivan Alexander, tsar of Bulgaria (qq.v.). Among his disciples were Kallistos, twice patriarch of Constantinople, and Theodosios of Turnovo (qq.v.).

GREGORY OF TOURS. Historian of the Franks (q.v.); bishop (q.v.) of Tours (573–594). His *Historia Francorum* (History of the Franks) covers the period from the Creation to 591, but it is of value chiefly for the period of his bishopric, which he writes about in detail. Frankish-Byzantine relations receive attention, including the alliance between Clovis and Anastasios I (qq.v.), and the participation of Frankish troops in Byzantine resistance to the Lombard invasion of Italy (qq.v.) in 568.

GREGORY SINAITES. *See* **GREGORY OF SINAI.**

GROTTAFERRATA. *See* **NEILOS OF ROSSANO.**

GUIBERT OF NOGENT. Latin historian of the First Crusade (q.v.). It is not clear if he was present at the Council of Clermont (q.v.), but it is certain that he did not go on the First Crusade. His history of the First Crusade *(The History That Is Called Deeds of God Done through the Franks),* covering the years 1095–1104, reworks the anonymous *Gesta Francorum* and Fulcher of Chartres's (qq.v.) work of the same name, adding some material gotten from participants. He knew Peter the Hermit (q.v.) but knew none of the Byzantine participants, including Alexios I Komnenos (q.v.), whom he rails against.

GUILDS. State-controlled corporations of traders and artisans. The *Book of the Eparch* (q.v.) illustrates how extensive was the guild system in Constantinople (q.v.) in the 10th century. State control of goods and services, including their quality and price, had as its first goal the proper provisioning of the capital. The scope was extensive, encompassing such diverse trades as soap merchants, butchers, silk-traders, gold merchants, and notaries. Regulatory oversight was administered through the eparch of the city (q.v.).

GUNTHER OF PAIRIS. Latin historian of the Fourth Crusade (q.v.). His *Historia Constantinopolitana* is biased against the Byzantines, and papers over the bloodshed of the sack of Constantinople (q.v.). Gunther glorifies the role of Martin, his abbot and chief informant, who threatened with death a Greek priest from the Monastery of the Pantokrator (q.v.) until he was shown a hoard of relics, which he took as booty back to France (q.v.).

GYNAIKEION. A place where women *(gynaiakes)* worked, typically a workshop for the weaving of textiles. There were imperial *gynaikeia* that produced luxury textiles, especially of silk. The term is not to be confused with *gynaikonitis,* the women's quarters in the Great Palace (q.v.).

– H –

HADRIAN I. Pope (q.v.) from 772–795. His appeal to Charlemagne (q.v.) for help against the Lombards (q.v.) resulted in the Frankish defeat of Lombard king Desiderius (qq.v.) and the conquest of northern and central Italy (q.v.) in 774. A considerable amount of conquered territory was turned over to the papacy (q.v.), and in gratitude Hadrian crowned Charlemagne king of the Lombards. Charlemagne became, in effect, the protector of the papacy, and in 781, Hadrian stopped dating his acts by the year of the reigning emperor. In effect, papal recognition of Byzantine dominion ceased, despite the subsequent condemnation of Iconoclasm (q.v.) by Byzantium at the Second Ecumenical Council at Nicaea (qq.v.) in 787.

HADRIAN II. Pope (q.v.) from 867–872. He was drawn into two struggles with the Byzantine church. The first concerned the election of Photios as patriarch of Constantinople (qq.v.), which Hadrian disapproved of. This was decided in the papacy's (q.v.) favor at the council at Constantinople in 869–870, where, with Hadrian's legates looking on, Photios was excommunicated. The second involved Hadrian's attempt to extend papal influence to the new Christian churches in Moravia and Bulgaria (qq.v.). In 870 Khan Boris I (qq.v.) requested a bishop (q.v.) from the papacy, which was the equivalent of inviting papal jurisdiction over Bulgaria. Hadrian also gave his approval to the Moravian mission of Constantine the Philosopher and Methodios (qq.v.). The two brothers appeared in

Rome in 867 with their pupil Kliment of Ohrid (q.v.). For a moment it looked as if the new Slavic churches might fall under papal jurisdiction. However, a council at Constantinople in 879–880 decided in favor of Byzantine jurisdiction over the Bulgarian church. In any case, by this time Khan Boris had turned once again toward Byzantium (q.v.), after Hadrian delayed sending a bishop to Bulgaria.

HADRIANOPLE. *See* **ADRIANOPLE.**

HAGIA IRENE, CHURCH OF. Domed basilica in Constantinople (qq.v.), adjacent to Hagia Sophia (q.v.), dedicated to the holy peace *(hagia irene)* of God. The present church was erected by Justinian I (q.v.) on the ruins of an earlier church that was burned down in the Nika Revolt (q.v.) of 532.

HAGIA SOPHIA. Justinian I's (q.v.) great church in Constantinople (q.v.), built from 532–537, dedicated to the holy wisdom *(hagia sophia)* of God. It was erected on the ruins of a fourth-century basilica burned down in the Nika Revolt (q.v.) of 532. Justinian's architects, Anthemios of Tralles and Isidore of Miletos (qq.v.), may have been inspired by the church of St. Polyeuktos, built the decade previous. They created a domed basilica of incredible size, resting on a square formed of four arches and further supported by four pendentives (q.v.) in the corners of the arches, 55 meters above the floor. The first dome was too shallow and collapsed in 558. Isidore the Younger (q.v.) replaced it with a steeper ribbed dome, 31 meters in diameter, which, despite partial collapses in 989 and 1346, has survived to the present day. Viewed from inside the church, the dome (840 square meters) seems to hover over the spectator, and one's eyes move restlessly to the amorphous space that expands beyond the dome into galleries, outer bays, half-domes, and apse. Its beauty was celebrated by the poet Paul the Silentiarios (q.v.) in a poem delivered in 563, which is the best contemporary account of its internal arrangements. Justinian himself, when viewing the completed church, is said to have boasted that he had outdone Solomon. Indeed, the monumentality of Hagia Sophia remained unique in Byzantine architecture.

HAGIOGRAPHY. *Aghios* in Greek means "holy" or "saint," and thus this modern term describes the vast number of biographies *(vitae)* of martyrs and of other saints, as well as collections of their sayings and accounts of their miracles. Most biographies of saints contain a wealth of important details about social conditions of the time, especially in rural areas of the empire often overlooked by more traditional historical sources. Occasionally, important information is revealed about significant political events. For example, the *vita* of Daniel the Stylite (qq.v.) informs us about the reasons for the disgrace of Aspar (q.v.), and how Zeno became known to Leo I (qq.v.).

HAGIOS GEORGIOS, CHURCH OF. *See* **THESSALONIKE**.

HAKIM, AL-. *See* **FATAMIDS; JERUSALEM; YAHYA OF ANTIOCH.**

HALMYROS. *See* **THESSALY.**

HAMDANIDS. Arab dynasty of Mosul and Aleppo (qq.v.) whose expansion from ca. 930 reflected the continued decline of the Abbasid Caliphate (qq.v.). Its greatest ruler, Sayf al-Dawla (q.v.), was a great adversary of John Kourkouas (q.v.), winning a victory over him in 938 on the Upper Euphrates, and staving off further Byzantine inroads into Syria (q.v.). However, Sayf al-Dawla's defeat by John I Tzimiskes in 958, and the pillage of Aleppo in 962 by Nikephoros Phokas (q.v.), ushered in the decline of the Hamdanids, enabling the Byzantines and Fatamids (q.v.) to carve up northern Syria by the end of the century. Hamdanid power effectively ended by 1016.

HARITH, AL-. *See* **GHASSANIDS.**

HARMENOPOULOS, CONSTANTINE. Jurist whose *Hexabiblos* (Six Books), completed in 1345, is the most important late Byzantine work of jurisprudence. It comprises a compendium of previous civil and criminal law, as well as earlier legal manuals, including the *Prochiron,* the *Epanagoge,* and the *Ecloga,* supplemented by the Farmer's Law (qq.v.). The *Hexabiblos* proved to be an enormously popular and long-lived work, one that Renaissance humanists studied. It continued to be used in Greece (q.v.) in the early 20th century.

HAROLD HARDRADA. King of Norway (1046–1066) who died fighting Harold of England at Stamford Bridge. He was also a Viking (q.v.) adventurer and hero of Scandinavian sagas. He served with the Varangian (q.v.) troops that fought with George Maniakes in Sicily (qq.v.) before fleeing to Kiev (q.v.) in 1042, after Constantine XI (q.v.) suspected him of supporting the rebellion of Maniakes. There he married the daughter of Jaroslav the Wise (q.v.). He returned to Norway, whose king he became, and he died at Stamford Bridge in 1066 in a vain attempt to defend his claim to the English crown.

HARUN AL-RASHID. Abbasid caliph (qq.v.) from 789–809, during whose reign the Baghdad (q.v.) caliphate reached the height of its glory. Harun al-Rashid was famous for his cultivated court and for the success of his expeditions into Byzantine Asia Minor (q.v.). In 798 his troops reached Ephesus (q.v.), and in 803 he captured Tyana and Herakleia (qq.v.). Harun cultivated Charlemagne (q.v.), that other great leader of the opening years of the ninth century, as a possible ally against the Umayyads of Spain (qq.v.).

HARUN IBN-YAHYA. Palestinian Arab author whose unique memoir, written ca. 900, is preserved in a later Arab anthology called the *Book of Precious Things*. Captured as a prisoner of war in Askalon, he was taken to Attaleia, then to Constantinople (qq.v.) where he spent some years, perhaps as a slave. His memoir is especially important for its detailed description of Constantinople. For example, he includes a description of the water clock, or *horologion* (q.v.), at Hagia Sophia (q.v.). His subsequent trip to Rome via Thessalonike (qq.v.) is likewise filled with useful information, including his report that it took 12 days to journey from Constantinople to Thessalonike and that all along the way he saw villages and cultivated land.

HATTIN, BATTLE OF. *See* **NUR AL-DIN; SALADIN; THIRD CRUSADE.**

HEBDOMEN. Suburb of Constantinople (q.v.) situated on the Sea of Marmara (qq.v.). Located on the Via Egnatia (q.v.), its importance also derived from its imperial palace and harbor, as well as from its splendid churches, including that of St. John the Baptist.

HEBROS. River in Thrace (q.v.), also called the Marica (or Maritsa), which originates in the Rila Mountains south of Serdica (q.v.), draining much of the plain of Thrace before exiting into the Aegean Sea near Ainos (qq.v.). Two important cities are situated on the Hebros, namely, Philippopolis and Adrianople (qq.v.). The Ottoman victory at the battle of Marica (q.v.) in 1371 ended the Serbian principality of Serres (q.v.) and prepared the way for the conquest of Serbia by the Ottomans (qq.v.).

HEGOUMENOS. *See* **ARCHIMANDRITE.**

HELENA. Mother of Constantine I the Great (q.v.); saint. She was a woman of humble origins, born ca. 250 in Bithynia (q.v.), who was a concubine, or wife, to Constantine's father, Constantius Chlorus (q.v.). She became a devoted Christian, founding churches in Rome, Constantinople (qq.v.), and in the Holy Land (e.g., the Church of the Nativity at Bethlehem, and a church on the Mount of Olives). Legend has it that she discovered the True Cross on a trip to Palestine (qq.v.). Whatever the truth of the legend, she made pilgrimage to the Holy Land fashionable. There is the suspicion that after Constantine's execution of Crispus (q.v.) she bore some responsibility for the murder (or suicide?) of Constantine's wife Fausta (q.v.).

HELIODOROS OF EMESA. *See* **PRODROMOS, THEODORE.**

HELIOPOLIS. Present-day Baalbek in Lebanon, and site of one of the great centers of pagan worship in the ancient world. Here, where a much older sanctuary to Ba'al had stood, the Romans built a gigantic complex of temples dedicated to Zeus, Dionysos, Aphrodite, and Hermes. The whole enterprise, which took two and a half centuries to build, was completed just as Christians received state support to tear it down, a process still incomplete at the time of the Arab conquest in 637.

HELLAS. *See* **GREECE.**

HELLESPONT. The Dardanelles strait, strategically situated between the Sea of Marmara and the Aegean Sea (qq.v.), and, thus, of vital importance to the security of Constantinople (q.v.). Its entrance was guarded by the island of Tenedos (q.v.). The two important cities along the Hellespont were Abydos and Gallipoli (qq.v.). Control of the Hellespont was a lifeline that enabled Constantinople to survive even if an enemy controlled northwestern Asia Minor (q.v.) and the city's European hinterland. The survival of Constantinople for a century after the Ottomans (q.v.) expanded into Europe can be attributed not only to the city's massive lands walls but also to its control of the Hellespont.

HENOTIKON *(Edict of Unity).* The edict was issued by Zeno (q.v.) in 482 in an effort to appease both the supporters of the Third Ecumenical Council at Chalcedon and the Monophysites (qq.v.) by avoiding any mention of the "one nature" or "two natures" of Christ. The edict's statement that Christ was of the same nature with the Father in Godhead and of the same nature with us in manhood, satisfied no one. Pope Felix III (q.v.) also condemned it, excommunicating Akakios, patriarch of Constantinople (qq.v.). The Akakian Schism (q.v.), the first schism within the church, resulted.

HENRY VI. Western emperor from 1191–1197; son of Frederick I Barbarossa (q.v.). By marrying the Norman princess Constance, daughter of Roger II of Sicily (qq.v.), in 1185, he inherited a claim to the throne of Sicily, which he took by force in 1194. After seizing Sicily, he seized the Norman dream of conquering Byzantium (q.v.). In 1195 he launched a Crusade that was nothing more than a veiled threat against Byzantium, offering to rescind the threat only if a large sum from Alexios III (q.v.) was forthcoming. Alexios III (q.v.) levied the *Alamanikon* ("German") tax in 1197 to meet this demand, but the collected funds were never sent, since in that same year news reached Constantinople (q.v.) of Henry VI's providential death.

HENRY OF HAINAULT. *See* **LATIN EMPIRE.**

HERAKLEIA. Three important cities bore this name. Herakleia in Cappadocia (q.v.) stood before the famous Cilician Gates (q.v.), and was, thus, a target of Arab raids. Herakleia in Paphlagonia (q.v.) was a splendid port-city on the south coast of the Black Sea (q.v.). Herakleia in Thrace (q.v.) was situated on the Sea of Marmara along the Via Egnatia (qq.v.).

HERAKLEIOS. Emperor (610–641); son of the exarch of Carthage (qq.v.), also named Herakleios. This younger Herakleios sailed from Carthage with a fleet that overthrew the tyrant Phokas (q.v.). During the first decade of his reign the Persians (q.v.) handed him a series of military reverses, including the capture of Jerusalem (q.v.) in 614, and in 618 the first stages of the Persian annexation of Egypt (which lasted unitl 629). Indicative of the general despair was Herakleios's proposal to return to Carthage, something the patriarch Sergios I (qq.v.) dissuaded him from doing. Finally, in 622 the emperor launched a series of heroic campaigns against Chosroes II (q.v.) that kept the emperor away from Constantinople for almost a decade. When the Persians and Avars (q.v.) attacked the city in 626, patriarch Sergios had to lead its defense. The following year Herakleios inflicted a crushing blow on Persian armies at Ninevah. The collapse of the Persian state in 630 and restoration of the Holy Cross (q.v.) ended four centuries of intermittent warfare between Byzantium and Persia (qq.v.). However, the fruits of Herakleios's great victory evaporated with the victory of the Arabs (q.v.) in 636 at the battle of Yarmuk (q.v.). When Herakleios died the Arabs controlled Syria, Armenia, Mesopotamia, and Egypt (qq.v.). Herakleios's final years were a dismal story of relentless Arab expansion and of court intrigues by his second wife (and niece) Martina (q.v.), who aimed at gaining succession for her son Heraklonas (q.v.). There were also vain attempts to pacify the adherents to Monophysitism, and to resolve controversies over Monoenergism, Monotheletism (qq.v.), and, finally, Herakleios's own *Ekthesis* (q.v.).

HERAKLONAS. Co-emperor (641) with his half-brother Constantine III (q.v.); he was briefly emperor (q.v.) the same year. His mother was Martina (q.v.), the second wife of Herakleios (q.v.). When Constantine III died, Heraklonas reigned alone, but Martina was the real ruler. Her support of Monotheletism (q.v.), and the occupation of Alexandria by the Arabs (qq.v.), made her unpopular. She and Heraklonas were overthrown in a revolt by Valentinos Arsakuni (q.v.) in 641. Her tongue was cut out and Heraklonas had his nose slit, the first instance of this kind of mutilation (as a punishment, and as symbol of unsuitability for holding office).

HERESY. Literally "sect" in Greek, a heresy is any sectarian belief or practice not considered Orthodoxy (q.v.) by accepted church councils. The first six ecumenical church councils (q.v.) condemned the major heresies of Arianism, Nestorianism, Monophysitism, Monotheletisim, and Monoenergism (qq.v.). These heresies concerned the place of Jesus in the Trinity and the relationship of Jesus's divine and human natures. The seventh ecumenical council at Nicaea (q.v.) condemned Iconoclasm (qq.v.). Regional and local church councils also played a role in condemning heresies.

HERMIT. *See* **ASCETICISM.**

HERMOGENES. *See* **RHETORIC.**

HERMONIAKOS, CONSTANTINE. *See* **HOMER.**

HERODIAN. *See* **THEOGNOSTOS.**

HERULS. *See* **ATHENS.**

HERVÉ FRANKOPOULOS. Hervé, called Frankopoulos ("son of the Frank"), commanded (ca. 1050) the Normans (q.v.) who served as mercenaries along the eastern frontier. Denied the title of *magistros* by Michael VI (qq.v.), he rebelled in 1057. Though defeated, he managed to flee to Isaac I (q.v.), to whom he gave support, causing other commanders to do likewise. For this Isaac I made him *magistros* and *stratelates* (commander) of the East. Hervé's successors Robert Crespin and Roussel de Bailleul (q.v.) were equally unreliable Norman commanders.

HESYCHASM. *Hesychia* ("quietude," or "tranquility" in Greek), a time-honored goal of solitary monks, became the basis of a 14th-century movement that was introduced to Mount Athos by Gregory of Sinai (qq.v.). Hesychast monks sought to achieve mystical communion with God by repeating over and over again the prayer "Lord Jesus Christ, Son of God, have mercy on me." Breathing was regulated and various physical postures were assumed to aid this process. When Barlaam of Calabria (q.v.) ridiculed the Hesychasts, a controversy ensued in 1336 that pitted him against Gregory Palamas (q.v.), the great defender of Hesychasm. Barlaam was condemned in 1341, but the controversy resurfaced in the social civil war of 1341–1347.

HESYCHIOS OF MILETOS. Sixth-century historian whose works survive in fragments in the works of Photios, and in the *Souda* (qq.v.). He wrote a chronicle (q.v.) from the period of ancient Assyria to the death of Anastasios I (q.v.) in 518. He also wrote a history (q.v.) of his own time, which focused on the reign of Justin I and the early history of Justinian I (qq.v.).

HETAIREIA. Regiments of the imperial bodyguard recruited largely from foreigners such as Rus and Khazars (qq.v.). After the 11th century it was comprised of aristocratic young men. *Hetairos* is Greek for "comrade."

HETUMIDS. *See* **CILICIA.**

HEXAMILION. Fortification wall across the Isthmus of Corinth (q.v.) that defended the narrow entrance to the Peloponnesos (q.v.). It was refurbished by Justinian I (q.v.) as part of his vast attempt to improve imperial defenses. It was restored again in 1415 by Manuel II (q.v.) to defend against the Ottomans (q.v.), who nonetheless managed to breach it in 1423, and again in 1446.

HIERAPOLIS. City in northern Syria (q.v.) that played an important part in the wars with Persia (q.v.). In 363, for example, Julian (q.v.) launched his Persian campaign by marching five days from Antioch (q.v.) to Hierapolis, where his fleet, which had come down the Euphrates from Samosata (qq.v.), assembled. In the sixth century, the city was noted as a center for Monophysitism (q.v.). It was taken by the Arabs (q.v.) in 637, but recovered by John I Tzimiskes (q.v.) in 974. It changed hands twice again in the 11th century before Malikshah (q.v.) captured it in 1086.

HIERIA. Suburb of Constantinople (q.v.), located on the Asiatic coast of the Bosporos (q.v.). An imperial palace located here was sometimes used for ceremonial purposes. The Council of Hiera (q.v.) took place here in 754.

HIERIA, COUNCIL OF. Convened by Constantine V (q.v.) in 754 to provide the dogmatic rationale for imperial decrees that ordered the destruction of icons (q.v.) and the excommunication of Iconophiles (q.v.). Constantine V packed the council with his supporters and provided it with its theology. Iconophiles were condemned as either representing only Christ's human nature (Nestorianism [q.v.], in effect) or merging the two natures (Monophysitism [q.v.]).

HIEROKLES. Author to whom is attributed the *Synekdemos*, a work listing the cities of the eastern part of the empire, organized according to provinces. The work is dated to the period of Justinian I (q.v.).

HIERON. Custom-house on the Bosporos (q.v.) from which tolls on the Black Sea (q.v.) were levied. Abydos (q.v.) was its counterpart on the Hellespont (q.v.). Irene (q.v.) gained popularity from eliminating these and other tolls in 801; her successor, Nikephoros I (q.v.), restored them. The castle located there appears to be Byzantine, perhaps built by Manuel I Komnenos (q.v.).

HIKANATOI. Cavalry regiment (*tagma* [q.v.]) of obscure origins mentioned in the *taktika* (q.v.) of the ninth and 10th centuries.

HILANDAR MONASTERY. Center of Serbian culture and spirituality on Mount Athos (q.v.), constructed in 1198 by Stefan Nemanja (q.v.), who retired there as the monk Symeon, shortly before his death in 1199. Its library is renowned for its hundreds of Greek and Church Slavonic (q.v.) manuscripts, its famous icons (q.v.), including one of the *Hodegetria,* and its *katholikon* (qq.v.), rebuilt in 1303 by Stefan Urosh II Milutin (q.v.) as a triconch (q.v.) church.

HILARION, CASTLE OF SAINT. *See* **CYPRUS.**

HIMATION. (Greek for "garment"). Long mantle worn over a *chiton* (q.v.), common in late antique and medieval portraits of Christ, the apostles, and prophets. The term can also refer to the dark cotton garment worn by monks and nuns.

HIMERIOS. *Logothetes tou dromou* (q.v.) and admiral under Leo VI (q.v.). His checkered career included his failure to prevent Leo of Tripoli (q.v.) from sacking Thessalonike (q.v.) in 904, a great victory ca. 906 over an Arab fleet in the Aegean (q.v.), and the failure of his expedition against the Arabs of Crete (qq.v.) in 912. These events comprised one part of the larger Byzantine effort to counter successful Arab naval operations in the Aegean.

HIMYAR. South Arabian kingdom, in what is today Yemen, that flourished from the fourth through sixth centuries. It exported frankincense and myrrh, but its wealth derived mainly from transporting goods from India and East Africa (qq.v.) to markets in Syria and Egypt (qq.v.). Axum (q.v.), its great rival, conquered Himyar from 525–575, after which the kingdom was ruled by Persia (q.v.) until 628, when it fell into the orbit of Islam (q.v.).

HIPPODROME. An arena for chariot racing. Long, narrow hippodromes like the Circus Maximus in Rome (q.v.) were common in major cities throughout the empire, and charioteers were popular figures. The Hippodrome in Constantinople (q.v.) was situated next to the Great Palace (qq.v.). From the imperial box *(kathisma)* the emperor (q.v.) viewed the chariots as they raced around the central *spina* seven times. Fans supported competing circus factions (q.v.), each with their respective racing colors; the Greens and Blues were popular in Constantinople in the sixth century. The circus factions frequently rioted; in 532 Belisarius (q.v.) put down the Nika Revolt (q.v.) by slaughtering thousands in the Hippodrome of Constantinople. The decline of racing in the seventh century paralleled the decline of cities, although in Constantinople the Hippodrome remained in use until the Fourth Crusade (q.v.) conquered the city.

HIRA. Capital of the Lakhmids (q.v.), who, before their conquest by the Arabs (q.v.) in 633, formed a powerful Arab state to the south of Babylon. The Lakhmids were allied with Persia (q.v.) while their rival Ghassanids (q.v.) were allied with Byzantium (q.v.). Hira had a large Nestorian (q.v.) community.

HISTORIA AUGUSTA. A collection of biographies of emperors and usurpers from Hadrian to the reign of Diocletian, thus 117–284 (with a gap for the years 244–259). The alleged authors are six biographers writing during the late third and early fourth centuries, but most modern scholars attribute the work to a single author writing in Rome (q.v.) in the late fourth century. The information for emperors from Hadrian to Caracalla is of value, but for subsequent third-century personages it is often of little value, and sometimes clearly fictional.

HISTORY. Genuine history as inherited from ancient Greek and Roman historians (e.g., of the sort written by Thucydides) declined after Prokopios of Caesarea (q.v.), to be replaced largely by the chronicle (q.v.). Nevertheless, the influence of classical models was never lost, as seen in the 11th-century works of Psellos and Anna Komnene (qq.v.). However, Psellos calls his *Chronographia* (q.v.) a chronicle, which points to a conceptual difference between history and chronicle that seems more apparent to us than it did to the Byzantines. The distinction between church history, as begun by Eusebios of Caesarea (q.v.), and secular history was maintained. Still, reference to divine intervention is not uncommon in secular histories. Psellos's *Chronographia* is unusual in this respect, for his analysis of events is focused on human motives and behavior.

HISTRIA. Ancient Istros, the first Greek colony, situated not far from the western shore of the Black Sea (q.v.) near the mouth of the Danube River (q.v.). It prospered in the Byzantine period up to ca. 580, when urban life declined dramatically, probably as a result of Avar (q.v.) raids.

HODEGETRIA. Greek for "she who points the way," referring to the representation in Byzantine art of the Mother of God (*Theotokos* [q.v.]) carrying the Christ Child, upright on her left arm. Her right hand points to the child as the way to salvation. An icon (q.v.) of *Theotokos Hodegetria*, thought to have been painted by St. Luke, was especially venerated in Constantinople (q.v.).

HOLOBOLOS, MANUEL. Poet; orator; panegyrist; victim of Michael VIII Palaiologos's (q.v.) reign of terror against those who opposed the union of the churches at the Council of Lyons (qq.v.). The works of Holobolos include a panegyric to Michael VIII, and poems to various members of the imperial court and high church officials. Despite the praise, Michael VIII flogged and exiled Holobolos for his anti-unionist sentiments. Only after Michael VIII's death was he able to return to Constantinople (q.v.), where he resumed his career under Andronikos II (q.v.). In an increasingly different political climate he also resumed his anti-unionist agitation. In 1285 he had the satisfaction of participating at the Council of Blachernae (q.v.), which condemned the union of the churches. He died around 1310.

HOLY APOSTLES, CHURCH OF THE. There are two famous churches with this name. The first was built by Justinian I in Constantinople (qq.v.). It was located on the site of an earlier fourth-century basilican (q.v.) church of the same name that housed the mortal remains of Constantine I (q.v.), considered a kind of 13th apostle. The second famous church with this name is the 14th-century Church of the Holy Apostles in Thessalonike (qq.v.).

HOLY CROSS. *See* **TRUE CROSS.**

HOLY SEPULCHRE. *See* **JERUSALEM.**

HOMER. Homer was an essential ingredient to Byzantine education. The oldest complete manuscripts of the *Iliad* and the *Odyssey* date from the 10th century, which is when Byzantine scholarly interest in Homer revived. In the 12th century Eustathios of Thessalonike and John Tzetzes (qq.v.) provided substantive commentaries. The poet Constantine Hermoniakos drew on the work of Tzetzes for his *Trojan War,* which attempted to rehash Homer for an early 14th-century audience. John Argyropoulos (q.v.), who taught at Florence in the mid-15th century, translated Homer into Latin, making his works more accessible to western readers.

HOMOIOUSIOS. *See* **AETIOS; ARIANISM.**

HOMOOUSIOS. *See* **AETIOS; ARIANISM; ORIGIN.**

HONORIUS I. *See* **MONOENERGISM; MONOTHELETISM.**

HONORIUS. First emperor (q.v.) of the West (395–423). His brother Arkadios (q.v.) became emperor of the East in the same year, at the death of their father, Theodosios I (q.v.). It was Theodosios I who created this administrative division. Honorius, who was a child of 10 years when he became emperor, was dominated first by Stilicho, his *magister militum* (qq.v.), and then by Constantius, husband of Honorius's sister Galla Placidia (q.v.). External affairs were dominated by Alaric's (q.v.) invasions of Italy (q.v.): in 401 and 408, and in 410 when Visigoths (q.v.) sacked Rome (q.v.). The threat of Alaric caused Honorius to move his capital in 402 from Milan to Ravenna (qq.v.), a city that offered greater natural protection from invasion. After Alaric's death in 410 the Visigoths continued to dominate external affairs as they moved first into southern Gaul (q.v.) and then (in 416) into Spain (q.v.). Honorius's reign also saw the Vandals (q.v.) and other Germanic peoples cross the Rhine (q.v.) in 406. In addition to these disastrous military events, Honorius withdrew military forces from Britain (q.v.), effectively abandoning the province.

HORMISDAS. Pope (q.v.) from 514–523 whose prolonged negotiations with Anastasios I (q.v.) to heal the Akakian Schism (q.v) came to fruition only when Anastasios's successor Justin I (q.v.) came to the throne. In 519 Hormisdas sent an embassy to Constantinople (q.v.), which produced a reconciliation between the churches that was as much desired by the papacy (q.v.) as by Justin I and his nephew, the future Justinian I (q.v.). The edicts of the Council of Chalcedon (q.v.) were reaffirmed, and Hormisdas emerged as a champion of Orthodoxy (q.v.) in the West.

HOROLOGION. Any device that measured time, from mechanized clocks like the one described by Prokopios of Gaza (q.v.) to the synchronized waterclocks *(klepsydra)* devised by Leo the Mathematician (q.v.) as part of the beacon system across Asia Minor (qq.v.) that warned of Arab (q.v.) raids. The term can also refer to any liturgical book of hours used by a monastery.

HOSIOS DAVID. *See* **THESSALONIKE.**

HOSIOS LOUKAS. Monastery dedicated to Loukas the Younger (q.v.), located in central Greece (q.v.) in the foothills of Mount Hellikon, not far from Delphi. The two churches there include a cross-in-square church (q.v.) dedicated to the *Theotokos* (q.v.), built between 946 and 955 by the *strategos* (q.v.) of the theme of Hellas (qq.v.). Next to it is the more sumptuous *katholikon* (q.v.), constructed ca. 1011 by an unknown patron. Noteworthy is the large dome (q.v.), almost nine meters in diameter, that rests on an octagonal base created by squinches (q.v.). The interior decoration of the *katholikon*, which is exceptionally rich in mosaics (q.v.) and in marble-revetted walls, is the oldest of any intact Middle Byzantine (10th–12th century) church.

HOSIOS DAVID. *See* **THESSALONIKE.**

HOSPITAL. *See* **MEDICINE; PHILANTHROPY.**

HOSPITALLERS. The Order of the Hospital of St. John of Jerusalem, recognized as a religious order by Pope Paschal II in 1113. Initially, its goal was to provide charitable aid to pilgrims in the Holy Land. However, after the First Crusade's (q.v.) conquest of Jerusalem (q.v.) in 1099, master Raymond du Puy reorganized the order along military lines, effectively turning its monks into soldiers. Thereafter, like the Templars, they were a mainstay of Crusader armies in the Holy Land. After the Crusaders were expelled from the Holy Land in 1291 the Hospitallers established a base on Rhodes (q.v.) from 1309 to 1522, the year when it was conquered by the Ottomans (q.v.). They had a house in Constantinople (q.v.). Manuel I (q.v.) used Hugo, prior of that house, as a diplomatic envoy. In 1390 the Hospitallers helped future Emperor Manuel II to restore his father John V (q.v.) to the throne, driving out John VII (q.v.). In 1399, Hospitallers aided Manuel II and Marshal Boucicaut (q.v.) in a joint expedition against the Black Sea (q.v.) fortress of Riva, held by the Ottomans. Lacking the resources to defend the Morea (q.v.), in 1397 Manuel's brother Theodore I Palaiologos (q.v.) negotiated the sale of Corinth (q.v.) to the Hospitallers, who then defended it against the Ottomans until 1403. The Hospitallers expanded their control as far as Mistra (q.v.) until popular resistance forced Theodore to buy back the entirety of Morea in the Treaty of Vasilipotamo in 1404. As stipulated by the treaty, the Hospitallers withdrew their forces. The Hospitaller attempt to create a base of operations in the Morea had failed.

HUGH OF VERMANDOIS. Brother of French king Philip I; participant in the First Crusade (q.v.). Shipwrecked near Dyrrachion (q.v.) in 1096, he was escorted to Constantinople (q.v.) by agents of Alexios I Komnenos (q.v.) to whom he swore an oath of fealty. Alexios then used him to obtain the same oath from Godfrey of Bouillon (q.v.). After the conquest of Antioch (q.v.) Hugh was sent on a mission to Alexios I, after which he returned to France (q.v.).

HUMBERT. Ambassador of Pope Leo IX (qq.v.) to Constantine IX and to Patriarch Michael I Keroularios (qq.v.). Humbert initiated the chief ecclesiastical event of the 11th century, the church schism of 1054 (q.v.). His bull of excommunication, left unceremoniously on the altar of Hagia Sophia (q.v.), condemned the omission of *filioque* (q.v.) in the Byzantine creed, the Byzantine church's failure to use unleavened bread *(azyma)* in the Eucharist (qq.v.), as well as other liturgical practices that differed from those of the western church.

HUNGARY. State founded in the late ninth century by the Magyars, a Finno-Ungric people from the steppe (q.v.). After the Pechenegs (q.v.) drove them beyond the Danube (q.v.), the Magyars settled in Pannonia (q.v.) under their prince Arpad. They quickly became allies of Byzantium (q.v.) in its war (894–896) with Bulgarian Tsar Symeon (qq.v.). The successors of Arpad expanded westward until stopped by Otto I (q.v.) at the battle of Lechfeld in 955. Byzantine missionaries arrived in Hungary in 953, but their influence declined radically when King Stephen (1001–1038) allied Hungary with western Catholicism. Nevertheless, Byzantine-Hungarian diplomatic relations continued to be active, especially after the betrothal of Manuel I's daughter Maria to Bela III (qq.v.), who gained the throne of Hungary with Byzantine help. Ottoman (q.v.) expansion into the Balkan Peninsula (q.v.) led to Byzantine pleas for military assistance. However, the Hungarians were preoccupied defending their own borders, and such help as Janos Hunyadi (q.v.) could offer ended in defeat at Varna (q.v.) in 1444.

HUNS. Nomadic people from Asia who appeared in the West in 375, defeating the Ostrogoths and driving the Visigoths (qq.v.) across the Danube (q.v.) in 376. Under their "king" Attila (q.v.), from 434–453, the Hunnic empire reached its greatest extent; after his death it disintegrated. The overall historical role of the Huns is controversial. It can be argued that the Huns helped to delay the breakup of the Roman Empire in the West by the control they exerted over Germanic peoples beyond the Danube, and that they served another valuable function in supplying mercenaries for imperial armies. It can also be argued that the Huns hastened the process of disintegration by driving the Germans, especially the Visigoths, deeper and far earlier into imperial territory. Another Hunnic people, the Ephthalites (q.v.), the so-called "White Huns" (due to their fair complexion), menaced Persia (q.v.) from 427–557.

HUNYADI, JANOS. *See* **BELGRADE; HUNGARY.**

HYDATIUS. Latin chronicler and Spanish bishop (q.v.). His *Chronicle*, which continues a chronicle by Jerome (qq.v.), covers the years 379 –469. It is authoritative for events in Spain (q.v.) during those years.

HYMN. *See* **MUSIC.**

HYPATIA. Renowned pagan teacher of Neoplatonism (q.v.) and mathematics at the University of Alexandria (q.v.), and the leading intellectual of her day. Her pupils included Synesios (q.v.). Her father was the famous mathematician and astronomer, Theon of Alexandria. She was murdered in 415 by a band of lay brethren who attended the sick, and who were supervised by Cyril (q.v.), the patriarch (q.v.) of Alexandria. His complicity in her murder was alleged, but never proven.

HYPATIOS. Nephew of Anastasios I (q.v.), whose unpopular administration as *magister militum* in Thrace (qq.v.) provided Vitalian (q.v.) with a pretext for revolt. Hypatios's army won some initial victories against the rebel in 513, but he suffered serious reverses the following year. He was briefly proclaimed emperor (q.v.) against his wishes during the Nika Revolt (q.v.) of 532. When Justinian I (q.v.) gained control of the revolt, he had Hypatios executed.

HYPATIOS, SAINT. *See* **GANGRA.**

HYPERPYRON. *See* **COINAGE.**

– I –

IAMBLICHOS. See **NEOPLATONISM.**

IBAS OF EDESSA. Bishop of Edessa (q.v.) from 435–449, when he was deposed by the "Robber" Council of Ephesus (q.v.). Reinstated at the Council of Chalcedon (q.v.) in 451, he continued to write polemics against Cyril of Alexandria (q.v.) until his death in 457. His critics claimed his theology (q.v.) leaned toward Nestorianism (q.v.), which resulted in his condemnation in 553 at the Fifth Ecumenical Council at Constantinople (qq.v.) in 553 during the Three Chapters (q.v.) controversy.

IBERIA. The term can refer variously to Spain (q.v.), or to Georgian Iberia in the Caucasus (q.v.), the sixth-century client state of Persia (q.v.). There was also a theme (q.v.) with this name created by Basil II (q.v.), which included Mantzikert (q.v.). After the battle of Mantzikert in 1071, the theme was overrun by the Seljuks (q.v.).

IBN AL-ATHIR. Arab historian (1160–1233) whose *Historical Compendium,* a history of the Muslim world from the Creation to 1231, is among the greatest historical works of the 13th century. It is particularly useful for Byzantine military affairs in Asia Minor (q.v.) in the second half of the 12th century, for the events of the Third Crusade (q.v.), and for the conquest of Constantinople by the Fourth Crusade (qq.v.).

IBN BATTUTA. Arab traveler (1304–1377) who journeyed extensively throughout the Islamic world, Asia Minor and the Crimea (qq.v.). His *Travels,* composed in 1355, is exceedingly useful for social and economic conditions in early 14th-century Asia Minor (q.v.). For example, he confirms that there were still considerable numbers of Christians in western Asia Minor. In Laodikeia (q.v.) he saw Greek textile workers still at work, and women wearing turbans. In Constantinople (q.v.) he had a personal audience with Andronikos III (q.v.) in late 1331.

IBN HAWQAL. Arab geographer whose 10th-century *Picture of the Earth* is an historical geography (q.v.) of Muslim and Byzantine lands that includes economic information not found in Byzantine historical sources, e.g., a description of commerce and taxation in Antalya (qq.v.). His maps indicate some Byzantine themes (q.v.).

IBN JUBAYR. Arab traveler, born in Spain (q.v.), whose *Travels* include a vivid description of the first (in 1183–1185) of his two journeys by sea to Mecca aboard ships from Genoa (q.v.). Among the valuable information he supplies are descriptions of the Norman court in Palermo (qq.v.), Crusader-occupied Acre (q.v.), as well as comments on Byzantine relations with the Genoese.

IBN KHURDADHBEH. Arab geographer (died ca. 912) whose *Routes and Kingdoms* (completed ca. 885) offers an important description of the theme (q.v.) system in the ninth century, along with details about thematic troop strengths and pay. The book also offers precise information on the cities, road system, and forts of Asia Minor (q.v.). For example, it provides details about the main road that went from the Cilician Gates (q.v.) to the fort of Lulun, and thence, in stages, across Asia Minor to the Sea of Marmara and Constantinople (qq.v.).

ICON. Greek for "image," referring to an image of a holy person (e.g., the image of Christ, the *Theotokos* [q.v.], a saint, archangel, or apostle). Today the term usually refers to an image painted on a portable wooden panel, but the term can also refer to an image created by other artistic mediums.

ICONOCLASM. Greek for the "breaking of images," referring to any attempt to destroy religious images (icons [q.v.]), and referring more specifically to the attempt by certain eighth and ninth-century emperors (q.v.) to cleanse Byzantium (q.v.) of what they perceived as religious idolatry. Hostility toward religious images was not new. Old Testament prohibitions against idolatry had a continuing influence on the church and probably account for church-supported Iconoclasm prior to 726, when Emperor Leo III (q.v.) ordered that the image of Christ above the Chalke of the Great Palace (qq.v.) be removed. What was new was imperial support of such prohibitions. A *silentium* (q.v.) in 730 ordered the general destruction of religious images. The Patriarch Germanos I (q.v.) was forced to resign, and Leo III, intent on demonstrating his control over the church, replaced him with the Iconoclast Anastasios (q.v.). Real persecution began during the reign of Constantine V (q.v.), who rejected the veneration of relics (q.v.), and who argued that the Eucharist was the only true image of Christ. Persecution declined during Leo IV's (q.v.) reign, and it was condemned in 787 at the Second Council of Nicaea (q.v.), convened by Irene (q.v.) to restore icons. With this the first period of Iconoclasm (726–787) came to a close. Its revival in the ninth century under Leo V and Theophilos (qq.v.) constituted a second period (815–843). Theophilos's widow Theodora and her minister Theotikstos (qq.v.) condemned Iconoclasm for the last time in 843. Thus, from 726–843 the Iconoclast movement was a potent and disruptive force in Byzantium. Usurpers and rebels like Artabasdos (q.v.), Michael Lachanodrakon, and Thomas the Slav (q.v.) championed the cause of images against Iconoclast emperors who stripped the church of its Iconophile bishops (qq.v.), persecuting those, like Euthymios of Sardis (q.v.) who resisted. During Constantine V's reign, it seemed as if the state was at war against the institution of monasticism (q.v.), which supported icon production and veneration. The last Iconoclast emperor Theophilos singled out monks for punishment, including the two icon-painters Theodore and Theophanes Graptos (q.v.). The failure of Iconoclasm was partly due to the widespread popularity of icons, expressed in the intense devotion of ordinary citizens, many of whom venerated small icons in private, as did Theophilos's own wife Theodora (q.v.). But monks suffered the most, had more cause for celebration in 843, and were themselves most celebrated in the history and hagiography (qq.v.) about Iconoclasm.

ICONODULES. *See* **ICONOPHILES.**

ICONOPHILES. From the Greek word that means "image-lovers," synonymous with iconodules, which means "image-servants." Both words refer to someone who venerates religious icons (q.v.). The terms date from the period of Iconoclasm (q.v.), and they were used to distinguish those who defended icons as sacred objects from Iconoclasts who sought to destroy them.

ICONOSTASIS. Greek for "image-stand," which can refer to free-standing constructions housing icons (q.v.). One sees these all over the countryside of modern Greece (q.v.), often erected for commemorative purposes (e.g., to mark the site of a former church). The term also refers to the tall wooden partition pierced by three doors, decorated with icons, that separates the bema from the naos (qq.v.) of a church. This partition developed from the earlier templon (q.v.), a low balustrade found in early Byzantine churches.

IGNATIOS. Patriarch of Constantinople (qq.v.) from 847–858, and again from 867–877; son of former emperor Michael I Rangabe (qq.v.). His struggle with Photios (q.v.) is complex in terms of both its causes and its consequences. It provoked an international crisis with the papacy (q.v.), created one of the most serious internal conflicts within the eastern church, and became part of the political controversy surrounding the murder of Michael III by Basil I (qq.v.). It began in 858 when Ignatios was deposed by Bardas (q.v.) (the true ruler of the state). Bardas's favorite, the scholar Photios (q.v.), was made patriarch. This immediately split the church into two opposing camps. The supporters of Ignatios protested Photios's uncanonical appointment to Pope Nicholas I (q.v.). The pope was intent on asserting his authority over the eastern church, and used this opportunity to convoke a council in Rome that demanded that Ignatios be reinstated. In turn, a church council was convened in Constantinople in 867 that condemned and anathematized Pope Nicholas I; it further condemned the western church's addition of the *filioque* (q.v.) to the creed. Relations between the eastern and western churches, already strained over their competition for the allegiance of new converts in Moravia and Bulgaria (qq.v.), only complicated matters. Then, in that same year (867) Basil I murdered Michael III and assumed the imperial throne. Because Basil needed papal support in Italy (q.v.), where Byzantine troops were operating against the Arabs (q.v.), the emperor (q.v.) reinstated Ignatios (867). He then convened a church council in Constantinople in 869–870, attended by papal legates of Pope Hadrian II (q.v.). This council formally condemned Photios and declared Ignatios reinstated. The final twist to this complex affair is that when Ignatios died, Photios was reinstated as patriarch.

IGNATIOS OF SMOLENSK. His journey from Moscow to Constantinople (qq.v.) in 1389, and his subsequent residence on Mount Athos and in Thessalonike (qq.v.), are recorded in three works of meticulously descriptive detail. Among the important information he provides is an account of the coronation of Manuel II (q.v.) in 1392.

IGNATIOS THE DEACON. Prolific ninth-century writer, whose works include the biographies (*vitae* [q.v.]) of patriarchs Tarasios and Nikephoros I (qq.v.), as well as those of Gregory of Dakapolis and George of Amastris (qq.v.). He also wrote poetry, a lampoon of Thomas the Slav (q.v.), letters, funeral elegies, and other works (including now lost ones) listed in the *Souda* (q.v.).

IGOR. Prince of Kiev (q.v.) from 912–945, succeeding Oleg (q.v.). Byzantium (q.v.) remembered him primarily for his expeditions against Constantinople (q.v.) in 941 and in 943 (or 944). In the first attack the Rus (q.v.) fleet was destroyed by Greek fire (q.v.). The second attack was met on the Danube (q.v.) with offers of a new commercial treaty (945), which the Rus agreed to. After Igor's death at the hands of Slavic tribesmen his wife Olga (q.v.) ruled Kiev during the minority of their son Svjatoslav (q.v.).

IKONION. City (modern Konya) in Pisidia (q.v.), on the Anatolian plateau of Asia Minor (q.v.). Frequently the object of Arab attacks, it became capital of the Sultanate of Rum (q.v.) after its conquest by the Seljuks (q.v.) in 1084.

ILLOS. Powerful Isaurian *patrikios* and *magister militum* (qq.v.) who helped Zeno (q.v.) recover his throne. The queen-mother Verina (q.v.) attempted to assassinate Illos, but she failed. Illos demanded that Verina be imprisoned, and Zeno complied. The empress Adriadne's (q.v.) own attempts to assassinate him also failed. These events prompted Illos to revolt in 484, gaining support from pagans and Orthodox (q.v.) alike, who were hostile to Zeno's pro-Monophysite (q.v.) policy. Defeated in battle, he held out for four years in an Isaurian fortress before being captured in 488 and beheaded.

ILLUSTRIS. The highest of three titles given to members of the senate (q.v.), and high administrators, from the fourth century onward. Below *illustris* (*illustres* is the plural) were the titles of *clarissimus* and *spectabilis* (qq.v.). When bestowed on officeholders, any one of these titles automatically guaranteed a place in the senate. From the middle of the sixth century, the *illustres* were raised to *gloriosi* (q.v.), and the *spectabiles* were raised to join the *illustres*.

ILLYRICUM. A fourth-century prefecture (q.v.) in the Balkan Peninsula (q.v.) comprising Pannonia, Macedonia, and Dacia (qq.v.). It was divided into two parts after 395. Justinian I (q.v.) transferred the capital of the prefecture to Justiniana Prima (q.v.), a city he built ca. 530 near his birthplace. However, after Justinian I's death in 565, Illyricum suffered invasion by Lombards, Avars, Slavs, Serbs, and Croats (qq.v.). In the seventh century many inland sites were abandoned, including Justiniana Prima. The ninth-century themes of Dyrrachion and Thessalonike (qq.v.) were created from what survived of the former prefecture.

IMAD AL-DIN. Historian; Abbasid (q.v.) diplomat. Friend of both Nur al-Din and Saladin (qq.v.), his works are among the most important contemporary sources for Saladin's career. He also wrote the earliest history of the Seljuks (q.v.), which offers detailed information about the first Seljuk conquests in Asia Minor (q.v.), including an account of the battle of Mantzikert (q.v.).

IMBROS. Island in the northern Aegean northeast of Lemnos (qq.v.), near the entrance to the Hellespont (q.v.). It was in Byzantine hands until 1204, when Venice (q.v.) obtained it. The Gattilusio (q.v.) family controlled it from 1354, but within a century it had reverted back to Byzantium (q.v.). It fell into the hands of the Ottomans (q.v.) after the fall of Constantinople (qq.v.) in 1453. Mehmed II (q.v.) gave the island as an appanage to Demetrios Palaiologos (qq.v.), his son-in-law, in 1460. The historian Michael Kritoboulos (q.v.) was a native of the island.

INDIA. Until the seventh century Byzantine trade with India was almost entirely in the hands of merchants from Persia, Axum, and Himyar (qq.v.), who conveyed spices, precious gems, and incense to Ceylon, ports along the Red Sea (qq.v.), and to Persia, by overland caravans. The Byzantine *solidus* (q.v.) was the preferred coinage (q.v.) for trade, according to Kosmas Indikopleustes (q.v.), a Byzantine merchant from Alexandria (q.v.) who offers the most detailed account of India, including trade with the country and its people. The fascination India held for the Byzantines is evident in another sixth-century work entitled *Indian Animals* by Timothy of Gaza (q.v.). The expansion of the Arabs (q.v.) in the seventh century ended Byzantine contacts with India, but Byzantine interest continued, as evidenced by the romance of Barlaam and Ioasaph (q.v.).

INDICTION. The term originally meant a levy of foodstuffs for the imperial government. From 1 September 312 onward it was used to refer to a 15-year tax cycle. From 537 all imperial documents were dated by the year of the indiction (first year, second year, etc.), although by itself this means little to modern historians unless the first year of the cycle can be related to a calendar year.

INFANTRY. *See* **ARMY.**

INNOCENT III. Pope (q.v.) from 1198–1216 whose efforts at church union (q.v.) reached an unforeseen conclusion in the Fourth Crusade's (q.v.) conquest of Constantinople (q.v.). Innocent lost control of the Crusade to the Venetians, who used the Crusade to capture the Christian city of Zara (q.v.) in 1202. For this, the pope excommunicated the Crusaders, including the Venetians. He then lifted the ban on the Crusaders in order to allow them to collaborate with the (still excommunicated) Venetians. Innocent's subsequent wait-and-see attitude seemed to bear fruit when the Fourth Crusade conquered Constantinople in 1204. Thereafter, despite attempts at persuasion and even the forcible inclusion of the Byzantine church within the Latin church, real union of the churches (q.v.) was never achieved.

INSTITUTES. Handbook of civil law for law students; part of the *Corpus Juris Civilis* (q.v.), with the authority of law. It was prepared by Tribonian (q.v.) and two other jurists, Theophilos and Dorotheos, while they were working on the Digest (q.v.). Essentially, it updated the Commentaries of Gaius, the great second-century jurist, in a way that made it a primer for the remainder of the *Corpus Juris Civilis*. The Institutes and the Digest were published in 533, necessitating a revision of the 529 *Codex Justinianus*, which was completed in 534.

IOANNINA. City in Epiros (q.v.) situated on a fortified promontory that juts into Lake Pamvotis, against the backdrop of the highest peaks of the Pindos (q.v.) range. Apparently founded by Justinian I (q.v.), it was captured by the Normans (q.v.) in 1082, then fell under the control of the despotate of Epiros (q.v.) from 1205–1318, after which it reverted to the Byzantines until around 1348 when it was conquered by Stefan Urosh IV Dushan (q.v.). In 1430 the Ottomans (q.v.) occupied it.

IONIAN SEA. That part of the Mediterranean Sea (q.v.) between Greece and Italy (qq.v.). It is connected to the Adriatic Sea (q.v.) by the Strait of Otranto. The seven principal Ionian islands include Kerkyra (q.v.), Paxoi, Levkas, Ithaka, Kephalonia, Kythera, and Zakynthos.

IRAN. *See* **PERSIA.**

IRENE. First empress (q.v.) to rule Byzantium (q.v.) in her own right (797–802); restorer of icons. In state documents she was referred to as "emperor" (*basileus* [q.v.]), not empress. She was regent for Constantine VI (q.v.) from 780–790, during which time she was aided by the eunuchs Staurakios, *logothetes tou dromou* (qq.v.), and Aetios. In 783 Staurakios launched an expedition against the Slavs in Greece (qq.v.), and in 787 he aided Irene in the restoration of icons at the Seventh Ecumenical Council at Nicaea (q.v.). In 790 Constantine VI removed Irene and her advisors, but they returned to the palace in 792 and plotted Constantine VI's overthrow (797). Her negotiations to marry Charlemagne (q.v.) in 802 were stymied by Aetios and resulted in her overthrow by Nikephoros I (q.v.) that same year.

IRENE DOUKAINA. Wife and empress (q.v.) of Alexios I Komnenos (q.v.) and mother of Anna Komnene, John II Komnenos (qq.v.), and seven other children. Anna Komnene describes her beauty as equal to the goddess Athena. Irene frequently attended Alexios I on military campaigns, but back in Constantinople (q.v.) her role was diminished by the influence of Alexios I's mother, Anna Dalassene (q.v.). She retired to a convent in 1118, when John II Komnenos succeeded his father.

IRENE-YOLANDA OF MONTFERRAT. She married Andronikos II Palaiologos (q.v.) in 1284, after the death of his first wife, Anna of Hungary (q.v.). By this marriage, the house of Montferrat surrendered its claims to the crown of Thessalonike (q.v.), which Boniface of Montferrat (q.v.) had originally held. Yolanda, who took the Greek name Irene, bore three sons, John, Theodore, and Demetrios. She also bore a daughter, Simonis (q.v.), who was married to Stefan Urosh II Milutin (q.v.). When Andronikos refused her request to divide the empire equally among his sons, including his first-born Michael (IX), she took her own sons and went to live in Thessalonike (q.v.). There she intrigued against her husband with Milutin, the Catalans, and Charles of Valois (qq.v.). She died in Thessalonike in 1317.

ISAAC I KOMNENOS. Emperor (q.v.) from 1057–1059. After overthrowing Michael VI (q.v.) his brief reign held the promise that Byzantium's (q.v.) military power might be restored. However, the rapid pace of his reforms alienated the civil bureaucracy, whose pensions and salaries were cut drastically. The new tax surcharges on the provinces and the collection of unpaid taxes did not make him popular. The Patriarch Michael I Keroularios (qq.v.) turned against him when he revived the anti-monastic legislation of Nikephoros II Phokas (q.v.), and he appointed Michael Psellos (q.v.) as his chief minister. Isaac removed Keroularios and appointed Constantine III

Leichoudes (q.v.) in his place, which alienated the church. Threats from the Pechenegs and Hungarians (qq.v.) were repulsed, but Isaac became increasingly isolated, and when he fell ill Psellos persuaded him to retire to a monastery.

ISAAC II ANGELOS. Emperor (q.v.) from 1185–1195, and again from 1203–1204. His general Alexios Branas (q.v.) repulsed William II's Normans (qq.v.) in 1185. However, thereafter his reign was characterized by drift and decline. While he sold state offices and renovated the Great Palace (q.v.), Alexios Branas revolted (1187), and had to be defeated by Conrad of Montferrat (q.v.). In that same year an expedition failed to recover Cyprus from Isaac Komnenos (qq.v.). The Vlachs and Bulgarians (qq.v.) revolted under Peter of Bulgaria and Asen I (qq.v.). In 1190 Isaac II vainly resisted the passage of Frederick I Barbarossa during the Third Crusade (qq.v.), in obligation to Saladin (q.v.). Frederick I's occupation of Adrianople (q.v.) brought Isaac to heel. In 1195 Isaac was overthrown and blinded by his brother Alexios III (q.v.). Eight years later he was placed briefly on the throne with his son Alexios IV (q.v.), only to be overthrown the following year by Alexios V (q.v.).

ISAAC KOMNENOS. Self-proclaimed "emperor" of Cyprus (q.v.) from 1184–1191. With forged papers, this great-nephew of Manuel I Komnenos (q.v.) gained control of the island and declared it independent from the government in Constantinople (q.v.). Without a fleet, Andronikos I Komnenos (q.v.) was unable to put down the revolt. In 1187 Isaac II Angelos (q.v.) sent a fleet to recover the island, but Margaritone (q.v.), admiral of Isaac Komnenos's ally William II of Sicily (qq.v.), defeated it. Isaac ruled Cyprus tyrannically until 1191, when Richard I Lionheart captured the island.

ISAURIA. *See* **ISAURIANS.**

ISAURIANS. The backward, near barbarian tribesmen of Isauria, a mountainous region in the southern interior of Asia Minor (q.v.). Isauria was the only part of the empire that could furnish large numbers of native, warlike soldiers, and Leo I (q.v.) recruited them in large numbers to counteract the German control of the eastern army in the guise of Aspar and the Ostrogoths (qq.v.). In 466 Leo married his daughter Ariadne (q.v.) to the Isaurian chieftain Tarasicodissa, who took the name Zeno (q.v.). During Zeno's reign (474–491) the ascendancy of the Germans was replaced by Isaurian influence.

When Zeno died, the Isaurians were suppressed by Anastasios I (q.v.). After the last of the rebel leaders were killed in 497, large numbers of Isaurians were transported to Thrace (q.v.) where they were settled in colonies.

ISAURIAN DYNASTY. Ruled Byzantium (q.v.) from 717–802. Theophanes the Confessor (q.v.) reports that the first Isaurian ruler, Leo III (q.v.), was an Isaurian (q.v.), though in reality he came from Germanikeia (q.v.). Nevertheless, the name has stuck for this dynasty, a dynasty so closely tied to Iconoclasm (q.v.) and to the struggle with the Arabs in Asia Minor (qq.v.).

ISIDORE I BOUCHEIRAS. Patriarch of Constantinople (qq.v.) from 1347–1350. He and his two successors (Kallistos I and Philotheos Kokkinos [qq.v.]) were fervent Hesychasts and friends of Gregory Palamas (qq.v.). Like Kallistos I, he was also a pupil of Gregory of Sinai (q.v.). In 1347 Isidore performed the second coronation of John VI Kantakouzenos (q.v.), who had been crowned first in Adrianople (q.v.) the previous year. This second coronation was carried out without the crown jewels, for they were still pawned to Venice (q.v.), and without the traditional setting of Hagia Sophia (q.v.), due to its dilapidated state. Such was the poverty of the Byzantine state at the time.

ISIDORE OF KIEV. Metropolitan of Russia (qq.v.) who signed the decree of the union of the churches at the Council of Ferrara-Florence (qq.v.) in 1439. A former Greek monk at Mistra (q.v.), Isidore had previously represented John VIII Palaiologos (q.v.) at the Council of Basil in 1434. Upon his return to Moscow (q.v.) in 1440 Grand Duke Basil II threw him into prison, rejecting both union with the papacy (q.v.), and any further ties with Byzantium (q.v.). Isidore escaped to the West, where he became a papal ambassador for Nicholas V (q.v.), in which capacity on 12 December 1452 he proclaimed church union in Constantinople (q.v.). When the city was captured by the Ottomans (q.v.) in 1453, he exchanged the red robes of a cardinal for the clothes of a beggar in order to escape death. He was later ransomed by a Genoese merchant.

ISIDORE OF MILETUS. Architect, engineer, and mathematician who taught physics at the universities of Alexandria and Constantinople (qq.v.), and who assisted Anthemios of Tralles (q.v.) in the planning and construction of Hagia Sophia in Constantinople (qq.v.), the great church commissioned by Justinian I (q.v.). Isidore is not to be confused with his nephew, Isidore the Younger (q.v.).

ISIDORE OF SEVILLE. Bishop (q.v.) of Seville (ca. 600–636) and compiler of the standard encyclopedia of knowledge for the West in the Middle Ages, the *Etymologies*. His *History of the Reigns of the Goths, Vandals, and Suevi* is a chronicle (q.v.) of events in Spain (q.v.) from the fourth to seventh centuries that includes some information about Byzantine affairs outside of Spain.

ISIDORE THE YOUNGER. Nephew of Isidore of Miletus (q.v.) who rebuilt the dome of Hagia Sophia in Constantinople (qq.v.) after it collapsed in 558, raising the height of the original dome by about seven meters. Although subsequently damaged (in 989 and in 1346) and repaired, essentially it is Isidore's dome that visitors to Hagia Sophia view today.

ISLAM. Arabic term meaning "submission" (to God), the essential message of the religion founded by Muhammad (q.v.) the prophet (ca. 570–632). A follower of Islam is called a Muslim (or Moslem), which means "one who submits." For Byzantines Islam remained the heresy of their Muslim opponents (initially the Arabs [q.v.]).

ISTRIA. Mountainous peninsula in the northern Adriatic Sea (q.v.) between the gulfs of Trieste and Fiume. The Ostrogoths (q.v.) seized it in 493. The forces of Justinian I (q.v.) reconquered it in 539. The Lombards (q.v.), who invaded Italy (q.v.) in 568, took over much of Istria by the end of the sixth century. Nevertheless, the coast remained under Byzantine control even after the fall of the Exarchate of Ravenna (qq.v.) in 751. In 788 Charlemagne (q.v.), having completed his conquest of Lombardy, extended his conquests farther to the east and seized Istria. In the ninth century Frankish domination was replaced by that of Venice (q.v.).

ITALY. Beginning with the tetrarchy (q.v.), the political importance of Rome (q.v.) and of Italy declined with the establishment of new imperial residences outside Rome (e.g., Maximian [q.v.] ruled from Milan [q.v.]). This process increased with the foundation of Constantinople (q.v.) in 330, and with the creation of eastern and western co-emperors later in the fourth century. Milan and, after 402, Ravenna (q.v.), were favored residences of the western emperors (q.v.). Invasion and conquest added to Italy's decline. Incursions by Alaric's Visigoths (qq.v.) culminated in their sack of Rome in 410. Italy suffered further depredation by the Vandals (q.v.), who again sacked Rome in 455. The overthrow of Romulus Augustulus (q.v.) in 476 and the conquest of Ravenna by the Ostrogoths (q.v.) in 493 created an Ostrogothic state. Justinian I (q.v.) reconquered Italy from the Ostrogoths in a long war that lasted from 535–562. What resulted was the devastation of Milan (q.v.), as well as the depopulation of Rome (q.v.) and of much of Italy. During the midst of this war, a force of Franks and Alemanni (qq.v) invaded Italy in 553–554; it was annihilated by Narses (q.v.). Not long after the war's conclusion, Justinian I's victory was overturned by the Lombard (q.v.) invasion of Italy in 568. Except for Ravenna and Venice (q.v.) in the north, Byzantium (q.v.) was relegated to southern Italy. After 568, Rome began to fend for itself under the leadership of the papacy (q.v.), while Byzantine possessions were reorganized as the Exarchate (q.v.) of Ravenna. However, in 751 the Lombards captured Ravenna, and not long after (in 787) northern Italy was conquered by Charlemagne (q.v.). Byzantine possessions in southern Italy were frequently endangered by Arab (q.v.) raids and Lombard revolts that required occasional military intervention, e.g., by Basil I, by *katepano* Basil Boiannes, and George Maniakes (qq.v.). However, it was the Norman (q.v.) expansion in southern Italy, beginning in 1016 and culminating in 1071 with the conquest of Bari, that ejected Byzantium from Italy.

IVAJLO. Tsar of Bulgaria (qq.v.) from 1278–1279. He overthrew Constantine Tich, and tried to save Bulgaria from the depredations of the Mongols (q.v.). He was victorious over the Mongols, but not over Michael VIII Palaiologos (q.v.), who intervened militarily to support the claim of his son-in-law John Asen III to the throne. When Ivajlo turned to the Mongols for aid, they murdered him.

IVAN III. Grand duke of Moscow (q.v.) from 1462–1505. He married Sophia Palaiologina (q.v.), who was daughter of Thomas Palaiologos (q.v.), last despot of the Morea (qq.v.), and niece of Byzantium's (q.v.) last emperor, Constantine XI Palaiologos [qq.v.]). He displayed the two-headed eagle on his seals, introduced Byzantine ceremonial to his court, and encouraged the view that Moscow had inherited the mantle of Byzantium (q.v.) as defender of Orthodoxy (q.v.).

IVAN ALEXANDER. Tsar of Bulgaria (qq.v.) from 1331–1371 who took advantage of the Byzantine civil war of 1341–1347 to enlarge his domains with Philippopolis (q.v.) and other towns. His alliances with the Ottomans (q.v.) and with Stefan Urosh IV Dushan (q.v.) had the similar aim of territorial gain at Byzantine expense.

IVANKO. Nephew of Asen I (q.v.) who assassinated Asen I in 1196. He tried to hold Turnovo (q.v.) against Asen I's brother Peter (q.v.), but when promised Byzantine support failed to materialize, he fled Bulgaria for Constantinople (qq.v.). There he married into the imperial family of Alexios III (q.v.) and was given Philippopolis (q.v.) to administer. Deserting Alexios III in 1198, he briefly set up an independent principality in Rhodope and central Thrace (qq.v.) before being captured in 1200 by a ruse and executed.

IVERON MONASTERY. Founded on Mount Athos (q.v.) in 979 for monks from Iberia (Georgia), hence the name. It became a center of Georgian culture with a renowned scriptorium. Its *katholikon* (q.v.), completed in 983 and contemporary with the *katholikon* at the Great Lavra (q.v.), is among the oldest churches on Mount Athos.

IVORY. Used extensively for diptychs, icons (qq.v.), book covers, and other objects, including furniture decoration, from the fourth through sixth centuries. The Arab conquest of North Africa (q.v.) seems to have curtailed Byzantine access to ivory, for it became much rarer after the sixth century. Some of the most memorable works of Byzantine art are in ivory, e.g., the famous Barberini Ivory in the Musée du Louvre in Paris that depicts Anastasios I or Justinian I (qq.v.), and the ivory panel in the Museum of Fine Arts in Moscow depicting Christ crowning Constantine VII (q.v.).

– J –

JACOB BARADAEUS. *See* **JACOBITES.**

JACOBITES. The Monophysites of Syria (qq.v.), who took their name from Jacob Baradaeus, the Monophysite bishop of Edessa (qq.v.) who organized the Monophysite church in Syria ca. 542. It was Jacob Baradaeus who ordained John of Ephesus (q.v.).

JANISSARIES. Turkish for "new troops," referring to the shock-troops of the Ottoman sultan (qq.v.). They were composed mostly of Christian boys taken in the *devshirme* (Turkish for "collection"), the levy exacted on non-Muslim male youths living in the sultan's domains. The boys taken in this manner converted to Islam (q.v.) and became the sultan's slaves for life. Some went into the civil administration, others were trained for the janissaries. The janissaries played a crucial role in the Ottoman conquest of Constantinople (q.v.) in 1453.

JAROSLAV THE WISE. Prince of Kiev (q.v.) from 1019–1054, son of Vladimir I (q.v.). Jaroslav continued the building program of his father, remaking Kiev into a city that recalled the imperial splendor of Constantinople (q.v.), with its own Golden Gate (q.v.) and Cathedral of St. Sophia that emulated Justinian I's Hagia Sophia (qq.v.). Jaroslav's attack on Constantinople in 1043 was the last Rus (q.v.) attack on the city. After Jaroslav's death the importance of the Rus in Byzantine affairs declined, due, in part, to the advance of the Pechenegs across the Danube (qq.v.).

JEROME. Biblical scholar, translator, saint, born ca. 342. His greatest achievement was his translation of the Bible into Latin (called the *Vulgate* Bible). His literary output includes many biblical commentaries, translations of various Greek works, as well as a paraphrase of the *Chronicle* of Eusebios of Caesarea (q.v.), a number of homilies of Origin (q.v.), and a world history (q.v.) from Abraham to 325 (continued by Marcellinus Comes [q.v.]). He also wrote polemics against Arianism (q.v.) and other heresies (q.v.). He spent several years as a hermit (q.v.) in the Syrian desert, and he was secretary to Pope Damascus from 382–385. He retired to Bethlehem in 386, where he died in 420.

JERUSALEM. The conversion of Constantine I (q.v.) and his mother Helena (q.v.) to Christianity transformed Jerusalem. When Helena visited the city in 326 she discovered a tomb she identified as the Holy Sepulchre of Christ, and a nearby rock she identified as Golgotha. Constantine I built a basilica (q.v.), the Church of the Holy Sepulchre, as well as a basilica on the Mount of Olives, and one in Bethlehem. Julian's (q.v.) attempt to rebuild the Jewish Temple was only a pause in the rapid transformation of the city into a center of Christian pilgrimage. Athenais-Eudokia (q.v.) was also a great benefactor, as was Justinian I (q.v.). In 451 at the Fourth Ecumenical

Council at Chalcedon (q.v.) the city became one of the five patriarchates (q.v.). In 614 the Persians (q.v.) captured the city and carried off the True Cross (q.v.). Herakleios (q.v.) recaptured the city and returned the relic (q.v.) in 629, but in 638 the patriarch Sophronios (qq.v.) was forced to surrender Jerusalem to the Arabs (q.v.). Thereafter, it remained in Muslim (q.v.) hands for over five centuries, becoming a major Muslim pilgrimage site with commemorative architecture that included the Dome of the Rock. The caliph al-Hakim (qq.v) destroyed the Church of the Holy Sepulchre in 1009. Later in the 11th century Jerusalem changed hands between the Seljuks and Fatamids (qq.v.) until the First Crusade (q.v.) conquered it in 1099. Thereafter, it became the capital of the Crusader Kingdom of Jerusalem. Saladin (q.v.) reconquered it for Islam (q.v.) in 1187. The Crusaders ruled it again from 1229–1243, after which it fell again to the forces of Islam.

JEWS. Jews comprised one of the most sizeable and important minorities in Byzantium (q.v.). Benjamin of Tudela (q.v.) describes Jewish communities in numerous cities, including many cities in Greece (q.v.). He mentions 2,000 Jews living in Thebes (q.v.), the largest Jewish community outside Constantinople (q.v.). Jews engaged chiefly in manufacturing and commerce, and they lived under various legal restrictions. For example, they were prohibited from holding slaves, proselytizing, holding governmental office, and attending public ceremonies. No wonder that they openly supported the empire's enemies on occasion. They supported the Vandals and Ostrogoths against Justinian I (qq.v.), also the rebels in the Nika Revolt (q.v.). When the Persians invaded Asia Minor and Palestine (qq.v.) in the early seventh century, Jews took the Persian side. When Jerusalem (q.v.) fell to the Persians in 614, the Jews of the city attacked Christians and their churches. The Arab conquests changed the situation dramatically by placing most of the empire's Jews under the caliphate (q.v.). For those who remained in Byzantine territory, intermittent imperial edicts (e.g., by Herakleios, Leo III, and Basil I [qq.v.]) ordered the baptism of Jews; these edicts failed. The general impression is that the Jews were mostly left to themselves, though segregated in their own urban quarters. Persecutions were infrequent, and some emperors (q.v.), such as Michael VIII and his son Andronikos II (qq.v.), were remarkably tolerant.

JOEL. Thirteenth-century author of a world chronicle (q.v.) that begins with the Creation and ends with the capture of Constantinople by the

Fourth Crusade (qq.v.) in 1204. Its brevity is such that it has little or no historical value.

JOHN I. Patriarch of Antioch (qq.v.) from 429–442. He supported Nestorios at the Council of Ephesus (qq.v.) in 431, but arrived late to the council after Cyril of Alexandria (q.v.) had engineered the condemnation of Nestorios. John immediately organized a rival council that condemned Cyril, creating a schism in the council that took two years to resolve. However, John agreed to a compromise in 433 that condemned Nestorios and accepted the term *Theotokos* (q.v.). The compromise also papered over specific differences of opinion about the relationship of Christ's two natures by stating vaguely that they existed in an unconfused union.

JOHN I. Pope (q.v.) from 523–526. Theodoric the Great (q.v.) forced him to undertake a mission to Constantinople (q.v.) to urge Justin I (q.v.) to lift restrictions against the Arians (q.v.) in the East. The implied threat was that otherwise there would be reprisals against Italian Orthodox (q.v.) believers. Justin I (q.v.), anxious to maintain good relations with the papacy (q.v.) after the end of the Akakian Schism (q.v.), received the pope warmly. Justin agreed to restore churches to the Arians, and permitted them to hold services. Despite this success, upon John I's return Theodoric threw him into prison, where the pope died a few days later on 18 May 526.

JOHN I DOUKAS. Ruled Thessaly (ca. 1267–ca. 1289) from Neopatras (qq.v.), following the death of his father Michael II Komnenos Doukas. He was a fierce enemy of Michael VIII Palaiologos (q.v.) who besieged Neopatras in 1272–1273, and who died campaigning against John in 1282.

JOHN I TZIMISKES. Emperor (q.v.) from 969–976. Born in Armenia (q.v.), he became a renowned general under Nikephoros II Phokas (q.v), who he assassinated in 969 with the aid of Nikephoros II's wife Theophano (q.v.). This proved a great victory for the church, for in return for the patriarch Polyeuktos's (q.v.) support Tzimiskes sent Theophano into exile. Tzimiskes also rescinded Nikephoros II's legislation against the growth of church and monastic estates. John I ejected Svjatoslav from Bulgaria (qq.v.) in 971, and the next year made an alliance with Otto I (q.v.) that softened the hostility engendered by Nikephoros II's relations with the German empire. In 972 the princess Theophano (q.v.), niece of John I, was betrothed to Otto

II (q.v.), and Otto I was recognized as *basileus* of the Franks (qq.v.). John spent much of his reign campaigning in Syria (q.v.), the Holy Land, and Mesopotamia (q.v.), in effect consolidating previous victories won under Nikephoros II, establishing Byzantium (q.v.) as the preeminent power in the Near East.

JOHN II KOMNENOS. Emperor (q.v.) from 1118–1143 whose capable leadership consolidated the successes of his father Alexios I Komnenos (q.v.). During the first part of his reign, John campaigned in the Balkan Peninsula (q.v.), first against the Pechenegs (q.v.), winning a decisive victory over them in 1122. In 1129 he forced Serbia (q.v.) to acknowledge Byzantine overlordship, and he checked the expanding power of Hungary (q.v.), Serbia's chief ally. Only after 1130 was he able to turn his attention to Asia Minor (q.v.), where he campaigned against the Danishmendids (q.v.). The Rubenids (q.v.) of Armenian Cilicia (Armenia Minor) he conquered in 1137, and in 1138 he besieged Antioch (q.v.), forcing Raymond of Poitiers (q.v.) to take an oath of fealty as a sign of his submission to Byzantium (q.v.). However, John was forced to reaffirm Venetian commercial privileges in 1126. His plans to restore Byzantine power throughout the Near East, as unrealistic they may have been, ceased abruptly with the emperor's death in a freak hunting accident with a poisoned arrow. There is a portrait of John II and his wife Irene in the mosaic (q.v.) panels in the south gallery of Justinian I's Hagia Sophia (qq.v.).

JOHN II KOMNENOS. Emperor of Trebizond (qq.v.) from 1280–1297. However, in 1282 Michael VIII (q.v.) persuaded him to relinquish his imperial title in favor of despot (q.v.), after first being rewarded with marriage to Michael VIII's daughter Eudokia. Despite this, John II's successors again assumed the imperial title.

JOHN III VATATZES. The most important emperor (reigned 1221–1254) of the Empire of Nicaea (qq.v.). He consolidated the work of his predecessor, Theodore I Laskaris (q.v.), whose daughter Irene he married. By 1225 he occupied all of the territory formerly claimed by the Latin Empire (q.v.), in addition to the islands of Lesbos, Chios, Samos, Icaria, and Rhodes (qq.v.). He marched on Thrace (q.v.), briefly occupying Adrianople (q.v.) before withdrawing in the face of Theodore Komnenos Doukas, despot of Epiros (qq.v.). However, Theodore was captured at the battle of Klokotnitsa (q.v.), and the tide slowly turned in favor of Vatatzes, especially after the death of John Asen II (q.v.) in 1241. Vatatzes captured Thessalonike (q.v.) again in 1246, and by the time of his death he had doubled the size of the Empire of Nicaea.

JOHN IV KOMNENOS. Emperor of Trebizond (qq.v.) from 1429–1459. He came to power by assassinating his father in 1429 and spent the rest of his reign defending Trebizond from Ottoman sultans Murad II and Mehmed II (qq.v.). A large-scale attack on the city in 1456 forced John to pay tribute to the Ottomans, and to organize a coalition of neighboring Turkish tribes to defend the city. However, none of this helped his successor, the final emperor of Trebizond, David I Komnenos (1459–1461), who was forced to surrender Trebizond to the Ottomans on 15 August 1461 after Mehmed II surrounded the city with a huge expeditionary force.

JOHN IV LASKARIS. Emperor of Nicaea (qq.v.) from 1258–1261. He reigned, but never really ruled. Born the son of Theodore II Laskaris (q.v.) in 1250, this child-emperor was at the mercy of Michael (VIII) Palaiologos after his father's death in August 1258. Michael murdered the regent George Mouzalon the following month and had himself crowned co-emperor with John in January 1259. In 1261, after the recovery of Constantinople (q.v.), Michael blinded John on Christmas Day and confined him to a prison, where he outlived Michael VIII, dying ca. 1305. Michael VIII's son Andronikos II (q.v.) visited John in 1284 and begged his forgiveness.

JOHN IV "FASTER." Patriarch of Constantinople (qq.v.) from 582–595. John was the first to use the title "Ecumenical Patriarch" (q.v.), which provoked hostile reactions from Pope Pelagius II and his successor Gregory I (q.v.), who was especially sensitive to any implied attack on papal primacy (q.v.).

JOHN V PALAIOLOGOS. Emperor (q.v.) from 1341–1391. In the early part of his long reign Byzantium (q.v.) was torn apart by two major civil wars (1341–1347 and 1352–1354) with John Kantakouzenos (q.v.). The Black Death ravaged the empire in 1348, and Venice and Genoa (qq.v.) fought a great naval battle in the Bosporos (q.v.) on 13 February 1352 for control of the Black Sea (q.v.). John's reign saw the steady advance of the Ottomans (q.v.), whose vassal John became after the battle of Marcia (1371). John attempted to gain support from the West by a personal conversion to Catholicism in 1369, but this only exacerbated his relations with the Byzantine church and with his citizenry. Toward the end of his reign there were two major rebellions (1373 and 1376–1379) by his son Andronikos IV (q.v.), and one by his grandson John VII (q.v.) in 1390. In 1391, the year of John's death, Byzantine territory was parceled out among his heirs, and Byzantium's fate seemed increasingly in the hands of the Ottomans.

JOHN VI KANTAKOUZENOS. Emperor from 1347–1354 and historian. His name is synonymous with two civil wars. The first (1321–1328) was against Andronikos II (q.v.) and put Andronikos III (q.v.) on the throne. John and his fellow conspirators, including the unscrupulous Syrgiannes Palaiologos, were amply rewarded, and John became the real power behind the throne. The second civil war (1341–1347) made John emperor, along with nominal emperor John V (q.v.). In 1349 John used Ottoman (q.v.) troops to force his way into Thessalonike (q.v.) to end the revolt of the Zealots (q.v.). Further use of the Ottomans introduced Orhan (q.v.) and his son Suleyman Pasha to Europe, where they established (1352) a base at Gallipoli (q.v.). Defeated in 1354 by John V, Kantakouzenos entered a monastery where he composed a history of his times in the form of a personal memoir (the *Histories*), covering the years 1320–1356. Despite his attempt in this work to justify his actions, it is hard to disassociate his name from the civil wars that weakened Byzantium (q.v.), opening it to further Ottoman expansion.

JOHN VII GRAMMATIKOS. Patriarch of Constantinople (qq.v.) from 837 (or 838) to 843. His Armenian family name was Morocharzianos; he was called Grammatikos (q.v.) out of respect for his learning. His career is intimately linked with the second period of Iconoclasm (815–843), for under Leo V (qq.v.) he helped to prepare the council of 815 that restored Iconoclasm. He became *archimandrite* (q.v.) of the monastery of Sergios and Bakchos in Constantinople (qq.v.), as well as tutor and influential advisor to Theophilos (q.v.). His combination of zeal and learning, in addition to his renowned debating skills, made him a formidable adversary of Iconophiles (q.v.) until his deposition and exile in 843, when veneration of icons (q.v.) was restored.

JOHN VII PALAIOLOGOS. Emperor (q.v.) briefly in 1390; oldest son of Andronikos IV (q.v.). He seized Constantinople (q.v.) in 1390 as a pawn of Bayezid I (q.v.), overthrowing his grandfather John V (q.v.). Manuel II (q.v.) soon regained control with the aid of the Hospitallers (q.v.), driving John from the city (17 September 1390), ending his brief reign. Nevertheless, Manuel II reconciled with John; when Manuel II journeyed to the West in 1399–1403, he allowed him to remain in Constantinople as his regent. John married Irene Gattilusio of Lesbos (qq.v.). Their child Andronikos died shortly before John VII's own death in 1408.

JOHN VIII PALAIOLOGOS. Emperor (q.v.) from 1425–1448, succeeding his father Manuel II (q.v.). His reign saw continued Ottoman (q.v.) advances against Byzantine European possessions. Thessalonike (q.v.) fell in 1430, and before his reign ended the Despotate of Morea (q.v.) began paying tribute to Murad II (q.v.). John's attempt to secure aid from the West required the union of the churches at the council of Ferrara-Florence (qq.v.) in 1438–1439. In response, Pope Eugenius IV (q.v.) preached a Crusade that was crushed by the Ottomans at Varna (q.v.) in 1444. Thus, the West found itself incapable of saving Byzantium (q.v.) while in Constantinople (q.v.) John VIII found himself unable to make church union anything more than a union on paper.

JOHN VIII XIPHILINOS. Patriarch of Constantinople (qq.v.) from 1064–1075, jurist; friend of Michael Psellos and John Mauropous (qq.v.). Prior to his appointment as patriarch he was the first president (*nomophylax* [q.v.]) of the law school created by Constantine IX (q.v.); then he fell out with the emperor (q.v.) and was forced to retire to a monastery. Constantine X (q.v.), followed the recommendation of Psellos and called him back to service as patriarch in 1064.

JOHN X KAMATEROS. *See* THEODORE I LASKARIS.

JOHN XI BEKKOS. Patriarch of Constantinople (qq.v.) from 1275–1282. He replaced Joseph I (q.v.), who Michael VIII (q.v.) deposed for refusing to agree to the union of the churches (q.v.) at the Council of Lyons (q.v.) in 1274. Though a tolerant and learned man (he was formerly *chartophylax* of Hagia Sophia [qq.v.]), he was forced to preside over the emperor's (q.v.) cruel persecution of anti-unionists. For this he paid dearly after Michael VIII's death. He was condemned as a heretic in 1283 and imprisoned from 1285 until his death in 1297.

JOHN ABRAMIOS. Astronomer and astrologer of the late 14th century and early 15th century. He founded a school that edited classical texts on astrology, medicine, and magic (qq.v.). He practiced magic and cast horoscopes for emperors Andronicus IV Palaiologos and his son John VII Palaiologus (qq.v.). His interest in astrology and magic demonstrates how pervasive such beliefs were throughout late-Byzantine society, even among its intellectuals.

JOHN ASEN II. Ruler of the Second Bulgarian Empire from 1218–1241. His victory over Theodore Komnenos Doukas at Klokotnitsa (qq.v.) in 1230 gravely weakened the Despotate of Epiros (q.v.) and made Bulgaria (q.v.) preeminent in the Balkan Peninsula (q.v.). John Asen II ruled over much of Thrace and Epiros (qq.v.), giving some foundation to his claim to be "Emperor of the Bulgarians and Greeks."

JOHN ASEN III. *See* **IVAJLO.**

JOHN CHRYSOSTOM. John the "Golden Mouth" *(Chrysostomos)*, eloquent bishop of Constantinople (qq.v.) from 398–404, whose previous fame as a preacher in Antioch (q.v.) attracted the notice of the emperor Arkadios (qq.v.). Once in the capital, he spoke his mind against the Gothic general Gainas (q.v.), and against the powerful court favorite Eutropios (q.v.). He also attempted to reform the morals of the clergy and court, which gained the ire of the empress Eudoxia (qq.v.). She took personally his insults about the dress and adornment of women. John's reference to her as "Jezebel" earned him his first banishment (403), something engineered as much by Eudoxia as by Theophilos, bishop of Alexandria (q.v.), and the Syrian bishop Severianos (q.v.), both adversaries of John. In 407 John died in Pontos (q.v.) during his second period of exile, while being moved to a remote location, despite pleas of exhaustion. However, his fame was such that 31 years after his death his body was returned to Constantinople, where it was buried in the Church of the Holy Apostles (q.v.).

JOHN ITALOS. Head of the school of philosophy in Constantinople (qq.v.) who was condemned for heresy (q.v.) in 1082. The driving force behind his condemnation was the new emperor Alexios I Komnenos (qq.v.), who seemed determined to root out suspected heretics, while his mother Anna Dalassene (q.v.) was turning the Great Palace (qq.v.) into something resembling a monastery. That Italos was born in south Italy of a Norman (q.v.) father, and was the pupil of Michael Psellos (q.v.), who himself barely escaped condemnation, must have aroused Alexios's suspicion. The condemnation illustrates the threat to Orthodoxy (q.v.) that the church and its supporters perceived in Psellos's revival of Platonic thought. More broadly, the condemnation was meant to reaffirm that theology (q.v.) was not a subdivision of philosophy.

JOHN KLIMACHOS. Author (died ca. 650) of *The Heavenly Ladder,* hence the epithet *klimachos* ("of the ladder"). The ladder is a metaphor for the spiritual life, in which one ascends to higher levels (30 "rungs") of spirituality. The *Apophthegmata Patrum* (q.v.) of the early eremites (q.v.) provided John with a rich source of advice, most often unorganized and obscure, but never prosaic. It was immensely popular over the centuries, and hundreds of icons (q.v.) exist showing monks treading upward on the ladder's rungs, while demons attempt to pull them off.

JOHN LYDOS. Author of a work entitled *On the Magistracies of the Roman State* that describes the bureaucracy of the empire in the mid-sixth century. John was a civil servant under Justinian I (q.v.), which gives his denunciation of John of Cappadocia (q.v.) particular credence.

JOHN OF ANTIOCH. Author of a chronicle (q.v.), surviving only in fragments, from Adam to the death of the emperor Phokas (qq.v.). It is not clear who this John was, though John I, Jacobite patriarch of Antioch (qq.v.) from 631–649, is sometimes suggested.

JOHN OF BRIENNE. *See* **LATIN EMPIRE.**

JOHN OF CAPPADOCIA. Chief financial minister and advisor of Justinian I (q.v.), denounced for his corruption and debauchery by Prokopios of Caesarea and John Lydos (qq.v.). Justinian complied with the demand in the Nika Revolt (q.v.) that John be removed from his post for fiscal oppression. He returned after the revolt was suppressed, only to fall victim to the scheming of the empress Theodora (qq.v.), who hated him and had him banished in 541.

JOHN OF DAMASCUS. Arab Christian born in Damascus (q.v.) who authored numerous works of theology, philosophy, polemics, history, hymns, and hagiography (qq.v.). Of particular importance is his *The Source of Knowledge,* which attempts a systematic study of all aspects of the Christian faith and dogma. For this he relied on the work of Theodoret of Cyrrhus (q.v.). Much later Thomas Aquinas (q.v.), the great 13th-century theologian of the Catholic church, used John's work as a model for his *Summa Theologica*. Also of importance is his development of the fundamental theory of icons (q.v.) and their proper veneration. Among John's other works are polemics against Iconoclasm (q.v.) as well as numerous sermons, *vitae* (q.v.) of saints, and hymns (q.v.). His brother was Kosmas the Hymnographer (q.v.). He died in 749 in the Lavra of St. Sabas (q.v.).

JOHN OF EPHESUS. Author of the *Church History,* a work in Syriac that extends from Julius Caesar to 585. Only the final part of the work, covering the years 521–585, survives. It provides a valuable narrative of the reign of Justinian I (q.v.) and its aftermath. The point of view is pro-Monophysite (q.v.), as seen in his favorable opinion of Justinian I's wife Theodora (q.v.). In 545–546 he made a name for himself in Constantinople (q.v.) by denouncing prominent persons as crypto-pagans.

JOHN OF NIKIU. Bishop of Nikiu in Egypt (q.v.) who authored a world chronicle (q.v.) going from Adam down to the early years of the reign of Herakleios (q.v.). It is particularly valuable for the Arab conquest of Egypt, and for the early Arab expansion generally. Unfortunately, the work survives only in fragmentary Arabic and Ethiopian translations.

JOHN OF RILA. Patron saint of Bulgaria (q.v.). He spent much of his life (ca. 880–946) as a hermit (q.v.), but toward the end of his life he founded the famous Rila monastery, a *koinobion* (q.v) in the Rila Mountains in southwest Bulgaria.

JOHN SMBAT III. Bagratid king of Armenia (qq.v.) who reigned ca. 1020–1042. The reign of his father Gagik I (q.v.) was the highpoint of the Bagratids, but Smbat's own reign was weakened by internal strife. Basil II (q.v.) used this weakness to demand that upon Smbat's death Byzantium (q.v.) would acquire the Armenian kingdom of Ani (q.v.), a demand to which Smbat agreed.

JOHN "THE ALMSGIVER." Patriarch of Alexandria (qq.v.) from 610–619; saint. He was a native of Cyprus (q.v.) and a simple layman before he was elevated to the rank of patriarch. He was renowned for his support of Orthodoxy (q.v.) against Monophysitism (q.v.), as well as for his charity. Both John Moschos, and

Sophronios (qq.v.), who lived in Alexandria at the time, subsequently wrote biographies (*vitae* [q.v.]) of the saint, as did a fellow Cypriot, Leontios of Neapolis. These works provide a vivid picture of life in early seventh-century Egypt (q.v.).

JOHN THE GRAMMARIAN. *See* **JOHN VII GRAMMATIKOS.**

JOHN THE ORPHANOTROPHOS. Eunuch (q.v.) who successfully conspired to help his brother, who became Michael IV (q.v.), gain the throne. He used his position as *orphanotrophos,* i.e., director of imperial orphanages, to gain even greater power during the reign of Romanos III (q.v.). While Michael IV was on the throne John was the most powerful person at court. Although he engineered the accession of Michael V (q.v.), Michael soon exiled him, and Constantine IX (q.v.) blinded him. Michael Psellos (q.v.) was an eyewitness to the blinding, and his account of it in his *Chronographia* is among the most dramatic passages in Byzantine literature.

JOHN TROGLITA. *Magister militum* of Justinian I (qq.v.) who won the war against the Moors (q.v.) after it had dragged on indecisively for a decade (536–546). Within the space of two years, from 546–548, Troglita managed to subdue the Moors. The African poet Corippus (q.v.) wrote a poem entitled *Johannis* to celebrate Troglita's victories.

JORDANES. Latin historian who wrote a history of the Goths down to 551. The work (entitled *Getica*) is largely dependent on a lost work of Cassiodorus (q.v.). It also makes use of a lost work by Priskos on the Huns (qq.v.) that includes a portrait of Attila (q.v.). Jordanes was born on the lower Danube in Moesia (qq.v.), but he spent most of his life in Ravenna (q.v.), where he served as a notary for Ostrogothic chieftain Gunthigis-Baza. He died in Ravenna in 552.

JOSEPH I. Patriarch of Constantinople (qq.v.) from 1266–1275, and again from 1282–1283. He pardoned Michael VIII (q.v.) for blinding John IV Laskaris (q.v.), something Joseph's predecessor, Arsenios Autoreianos (q.v.), had been unwilling to do. However, the Arsenites (q.v.), who considered Joseph I illegitimate, rallied around Joseph as a hero when he was deposed in 1275 for refusing to accept the union of the churches (q.v.) at the Council of Lyons (q.v.) in 1274. After Michael VIII's death in 1282 the pro-Unionist John XI Bekkos (q.v.) was deposed and Joseph I returned briefly as patriarch before his death in 1283.

JOSEPH II. *See* **FERRARA-FLORENCE, COUNCIL OF.**

JOSEPH THE HYMNOGRAPHER. *See* **MUSIC.**

JOSHUA THE STYLITE. Monk from Edessa (q.v.) who wrote a chronicle (q.v.) in Syriac covering the years 495–506. The original has not survived, except perhaps in an anonymous chronicle (extending to the year 775) with the attached pseudonym of Dionysios of Tell Mahre (q.v.). Another anonymous chronicle, entitled *The History of the Time of Troubles in Edessa, Amida, and all Mesopotamia,* which describes the wars between Byzantium and Persia (qq.v.) during the reign of Anastasios I (q.v.), may also have been authored by Joshua the Stylite. In any case, discussion about the authorship of these chronicles is much less significant than are the chronicles themselves, both of which are important sources for events along the eastern frontier in their respective periods.

JOVIAN. Emperor (q.v.) from 363–364, and before that an army commander and an ardent Orthodox (q.v.) Christian in the army of Julian (q.v.). He succeeded Julian after the latter's unexpected death while on campaign against the Persians (q.v.). In order to extricate the army from Persia, Jovian signed a treaty that surrendered much of Mesopotamia (q.v.), including Nisibis (q.v.) and other fortified places. He died soon thereafter in Asia Minor (q.v.), perhaps by carbon monoxide poisoning due to fumes from a charcoal brazier.

JULIAN OF HALIKARNASSOS. *See* **APHTHARTODOCETISM.**

JULIAN "THE APOSTATE." Emperor (q.v.) from 361–363 whose brief reign of 17 months captured the imagination of his contemporaries and of subsequent generations. His efforts to restore paganism borrowed some elements from the Christian church. Nevertheless his efforts failed, as his satire *Misopogon* ("Beardhater") makes clear. His edict excluding Christian teachers from teaching was condemned by pagans, including Ammianus Marcellinus (q.v.). Moreover, Maximos of Ephesus (q.v.), Julian's mentor, was something of a quack and hardly the best advertisement for a pagan revival. Also misguided was Julian's attack on Persia (q.v.) in 363, where he was killed in battle, by a Christian according to some sources.

JULIAN THE EGYPTIAN. *See* **GREEK ANTHOLOGY; PRISCIAN.**

JULIANUS "ARGENTARIUS." *See* **SAN VITALE, CHURCH OF.**

JULIUS NEPOS. Western emperor (q.v.) from 474–475. Nepos was the last western emperor to be recognized as legitimate in the East. He was deposed by his general, the *magister militum* (q.v.) Orestes, who elevated his son Romulus Augustulus (q.v.) to the throne. The death of Nepos in 480 removed any possibility of rivalry with Odoacer (q.v.), who ruled Italy (q.v.) since 476 after overthrowing Romulus Augustulus.

JUSTIN I. Emperor (q.v.) from 518–527; uncle of Justinian I (q.v.). The chief events of his reign included the restoration of good relations with the papacy (q.v.), exemplified by the end of the Akakian Schism (q.v.) in 519 and by the cordial visit of Pope John I to Constantinople (qq.v.) in 526. Hostilities with Persia (q.v.) erupted in 526, but otherwise there was peace with Persia during his reign. In the *Anekdota* (Secret History) (q.v.) he is derided by Prokopios of Caesarea (q.v.) as an illiterate dunce, completely under the sway of his nephew Justinian who succeeded him. His reign can be viewed as a preparation for the more significant reign of Justinian I (527–565).

JUSTIN II. Emperor (q.v.) from 565–578. He was nephew and successor of Justinian I (q.v.). His reign consisted of one military failure after another, beginning with the Lombard invasion of Italy (qq.v.) in 568. Justin II opened hostilities with Persia (q.v.) in 572; the following year the Persians captured the supposedly impregnable fortress of Dara (q.v.) on the frontier in Mesopotamia (q.v.). Raids of Avars and Slavs (qq.v.) south of the Danube (q.v.) began during his reign. Whatever the reasons for his madness, he did go mad, and his wife, the empress Sophia (q.v.), ruled behind the scenes. It was she who persuaded Justin II, in one of his sane moments, to raise his notary Tiberios (I) to the position of caesar (q.v.) in 574, and to co-emperor in 578 shortly before Justin II's death.

JUSTINIAN I. Emperor (q.v.) from 527–565. His accomplishments, even those that ultimately failed, rank him among the greatest of Byzantine emperors. His codification of Roman law, the *Corpus Juris Civilis* (q.v.) and the construction of Hagia Sophia (q.v.) are his enduring achievements. However, his reconquest of the West was eventually reversed. The war against the Ostrogoths (q.v.) dragged on until 552; three years after Justinian died much of Italy (q.v.) was conquered by the Lombards (q.v.). However, his conquest of the Vandals (q.v.) in 533, despite a long war with the Moors (q.v.)

from 536–548, lasted until the Arabs conquered Carthage (qq.v.) in 698. Intermittent war with Persia (q.v.) disturbed trade, forcing Justinian to create an indigenous silk (q.v.) industry on Byzantine territory. Altogether, the demands of war on two fronts created a ruthless fiscal policy that led to the Nika Revolt (q.v.). The emperor was fortunate to have great generals like Belisarios and Narses (qq.v.), and capable ministers like Tribonian and John of Cappadocia (qq.v.), hated though John was by Empress Theodora (q.v.) and the populace. He was not so fortunate in his historian, Prokopios of Caesarea (q.v.), whose *Anekdota* (Secret History) (q.v.) portrays Justinian and Theodora as virtual demons. The image Justinian chose for himself is seen on the mosaic panel at the church of San Vitale in Ravenna (q.v.), where Justinian appears enshrined with a halo as God's viceroy on earth, and the protector of Orthodoxy (q.v.) in the West. It is also the image of an emperor who closed down the Academy of Athens in 529, condemned the Three Chapters (q.v.), and called the Fifth Ecumenical Council at Constantinople (qq.v.).

JUSTINIAN II. Emperor (q.v.) from 685–695, and again from 705–711. He was a relentless antagonist of the Arabs (q.v.), and more ambitious in his colonization schemes than Constans II (q.v.). He resettled the Mardaites (q.v.) in various places, including the Peloponnesos (q.v.) and naval theme of Kibyrrhaiotai (qq.v.). He took Slavs (q.v.) from a region called "Sklavinia" in the Balkan Peninsula (q.v.) and resettled them in the theme of Opsikion (q.v.). He also repopulated Kyzikos (q.v.) with Cypriots, created the *kleisoura* of the Strymon (qq.v.) and most likely created the theme of Hellas (q.v.). Fervently Orthodox (q.v.), he persecuted the Paulicians (q.v.), condemned Monotheletism (q.v.), and convened the Council in Trullo (q.v.), after which he attempted to arrest Pope Sergius I for not accepting the council's edicts. He was overthrown in 695 by Leontios, *strategos* (qq.v.) of the theme of Hellas. Leontios slit Justinian II's nose (earning Justinian the epithet *rhinotmetos,* meaning "slit-nose") and exiled him to Cherson (q.v.). Nevertheless, with the assistance of Tervel of Bulgaria (qq.v.) Justinian returned to besiege Constantinople (q.v.) in 705, gaining entrance to the city by crawling through an aqueduct pipe. Leontios fled. Unfortunately, once on the throne again he aroused internal unrest by becoming a bloodthirsty tyrant. Taking advantage of the situation, the Arabs (q.v.) invaded Asia Minor (q.v.) with impunity from 709–711, the year Justinian II was dethroned and executed by Philippikos (q.v.).

JUSTINIANA PRIMA. *See* **ILLYRICUM.**

– K –

KABASILAS, NICHOLAS CHAMETOS. Mystic and Palamite theologian; writer and scholar. Despite being a friend and supporter of John VI Kantakouzenos (q.v.), he managed to survive the massacres in Thessalonike under Zealot (qq.v.) rule. His historical importance lies chiefly in the diversity of his writings and what they reveal about intellectual life in the 14th century. Among his most interesting literary works is a monograph on usury; another work criticizes the confiscation of monastic lands to finance the military needs of the state.

KAFFA. Tartar (q.v.) outpost in the Crimea (q.v.). It became the key to Genoese control over the Black Sea (q.v.) after the Treaty of Nymphaion in 1261 allowed Genoa (qq.v.) to establish a colony there. During the next century, from Kaffa the Genoese competed for the Black Sea trade in grain, fish, furs, and slaves. In some respects, Kaffa resembled the kind of trading posts that Europeans subsequently established on the west coast of Africa (q.v.). In 1475 Kaffa was conquered by the Ottomans (q.v.), by which time the trading outpost had grown into a substantial city.

KALLIKLES, NICHOLAS. *See* **TIMARION.**

KALLINIKOS. *See* **GREEK FIRE.**

KALLIPOLIS. *See* **GALLIPOLI.**

KALLISTOS I. Patriarch of Constantinople (qq.v.) from 1350–1353, and again from 1355–1363. He was one of three Hesychast (q.v.) monks to occupy the patriarchal throne (the other two were Isidore I Boucheiras and Philotheos Kokkinos [qq.v.]), all of whom were friends of Gregory Palamas (q.v.). Kallistos was also a disciple of Gregory Sinaites (q.v.). In 1351 he presided over a local council in Constantinople (q.v.), convened by John VI Kantakouzenos (q.v.), that condemned anti-Palamites. However, in 1353, he resigned rather than participate in the coronation of Matthew I Kantakouzenos (q.v.). He was replaced with Philotheos Kokkinos (q.v.), but he was recalled to office when John V (q.v.) regained his throne.

KALOJAN. Tsar of Bulgaria (qq.v.) from 1197–1207. Until 1204 he

was a fierce enemy of Byzantium (q.v.), along with Ivanko and Dobromir Chrysos (qq.v.). By treaty in 1202 with Alexios III (q.v.) his
territorial gains were ratified, and his position was further supported
when Pope Innocent III (qq.v.) crowned him king, for which he submitted the Bulgarian church to the papacy (q.v.). However, after
1204 when the Latin Empire (q.v.) threatened Bulgaria, Kalojan became the self-proclaimed restorer of Orthodoxy (q.v.). In 1205, with
help from his Byzantine and Cuman (q.v.) allies, Kalojan annihilated a Latin army sent against him and captured Emperor Baldwin
of Flanders (q.v.), who died in captivity. Kalojan himself was killed
in 1207 while besieging Thessalonike (q.v.). Arguably, his chief
legacy was to the Empire of Nicaea in Asia Minor (qq.v.), which he
saved by weakening Latin military power.

KAMINIATES, JOHN. Author of an alleged eyewitness account of
the Arab capture of Thessalonike (q.v.) in 904 entitled the *Capture
of Thessalonike*. He was a priest in the city at the time of the three-
day Arab siege by Leo of Tripoli (q.v.). A pillage and bloodbath followed the city's capture on 31 July 904. However, there are reasons
to believe that the work may not be genuine, but rather composed
much later, perhaps after the Ottoman (q.v.) sack of Thessalonike
(q.v.) in 1430.

KAMISON. *See* **CHITON.**

KAMYTZES, MANUEL. *See* **IVANKO.**

KANANOS, JOHN. Historian of an account of the unsuccessful siege
of Constantinople (q.v.) in 1422 by Murad II (q.v.). Written in a col-
loquial style, in the form of an essay, the account is surprisingly detailed in its description of events and precise in its chronology (q.v.).

KANDIDATOI. Cavalry troop of imperial bodyguards, like the
scholae palatinae and the *exkoubitoi* (qq.v.). *Kandidatoi* were
more an ornamental guard, recognizable on ceremonial occasions
by the white trappings they wore over gilded armor. During the
reign of Justin I, the future Justinian I (qq.v.) was a *kandidatos*.

KANDIDOS. Historian whose lost work, which covered the years
457–491, is summarized in the *Bibliotheca* of Photios (q.v.). Kandidos came from Isauria (q.v.). His work was most certainly written
during the reigns of Leo I and Zeno (qq.v.).

KANON. *See* **MUSIC.**

KANTARA CASTLE. *See* **CYPRUS.**

KAPNIKON. *See* **TAXATION.**

KARABISIANOI. *See* **KIBYRRHAIOTAI.**

KARAMAN, EMIRATE OF. First of the new emirates (q.v.) to emerge from the ruins of the old Sultanate of Rum (q.v.). Established ca. 1260 in Cilicia and in the Taurus (qq.v.) Mountains, by the early 14th century it had expanded as far as Ikonion, the Seljuk (qq.v.) capital. By the end of the 14th century it was the preeminent state in southeast Anatolia (q.v.). Its relations with Byzantium (q.v.) were minimal, but not so with the Ottomans (q.v.), who assaulted it repeatedly before conquering it in 1475.

KARASI, EMIRATE OF. Turkish emirate that in the early 14th century controlled an area from north of Smyrna up to the Hellespont (qq.v.). At first both the emirate of Karasi and the emirate of Saruhan (q.v) seemed more important than the emirate of Osman (q.v.), but by the mid-14th century the Ottomans (q.v.) had annexed Karasi; Saruhan they annexed later, in 1410.

KARIYE CAMII. *See* **CHORA MONASTERY, CHURCH OF.**

KASTORIA. City in western Macedonia (q.v.) founded by Justinian I (q.v.), situated on a promontory that reaches into Lake Kastoria. Its wealth as a regional commercial center is illustrated by the number of 10th- to 12th-century churches that have survived. Among its citizenry were a significant number of Jews (q.v.). The city was occupied by Tsar Samuel (q.v.) from 990 until Basil II (q.v.) recaptured it in 1018. The Normans under Robert Guiscard (qq.v.) occupied it briefly in 1093, before Alexios I (q.v.) reoccupied it that same year. In the first half of the 13th century it changed hands between the Despotate of Epiros and the Empire of Nicaea (qq.v.), before Michael VIII (q.v.) captured it in 1259 after the battle of Pelagonia (q.v.). It changed hands several times in the 14th century: from John II of Neopatras to the Gabrielopoulos family to Stephen Urosh IV Dushan and then to Symeon Urosh (qq.v), before falling to the Ottomans (q.v.) in 1385.

KASTRON. The Greek term (from Latin *castrum,* meaning fortress) refers to any fortified citadel, but most often to a fortified hill above a town or city. From the seventh century onward the term can refer to a provincial city. Asia Minor (q.v.) was defended against Arabs and Turks (qq.v.) by numerous *kastra,* many of which survive today in various states of ruin.

KATAKALON KEKAUMENOS. *See* **MICHAEL VI.**

KATAPHRAKTOI. A *kataphrakton* was a coat of mail. The *kataphraktoi* were cavalry whose horses and riders were heavily protected and capable of doing immense damage in a frontal assault on enemy lines. Riders were completely covered by chain mail, an iron helmet, and leg guards. They fought chiefly with an iron mace or saber. The horses were covered with thick felt or hides, so much so that only their eyes, nostrils, and lower legs were visible. They attacked in a triangular formation, at a steady pace, flanked by two lines of ordinary cavalry. Such armored cavalry was used by the Sassanians (q.v.), and by Byzantine armies as early as the reigns of Constantine I and Constantius II (qq.v.). They are mentioned in the *Strategikon of Maurice* (q.v.), and in the *Praecepta militaria* (q.v.) by Nikephoros II (q.v.), who devotes the third and fourth chapters of his work to the use of these mounted knights in battle.

KATEPANO. Title used variously in the ninth and 10th centuries for a number of military and civil officials, e.g., the *katepano* of the imperial workshops. In the 11th century a *katepano* was a military governor of a province or district, equivalent to a *doux* (q.v.). George Maniakes (q.v.) held the title in Italy (q.v.) in the mid-11th century. A civilian governor was called the *praitor* (q.v.).

KATHEDRA. The bishop's throne in a church, usually situated in the semicircular stepped bench *(synthronon)* reserved for the clergy along the curved wall of the church's apse.

KATHISMA. *See* **HIPPODROME.**

KATHOLIKON. Greek term for the main church in a monastery, customarily dedicated to the monastery's patron. A famous example is the *katholikon* of the monastery of Hosios Loukas (q.v.).

KAVAD. King of Persia (q.v.) from 488–531, and father of the greatest of all Sassanian kings, Chosroes I (qq.v.). Overthrown in 496, he was reinstated in 499 with the aid of the Ephthalites (q.v.). His support of Mazdak (q.v.) can also be viewed as a means to consolidate his power. He went to war with Anastasios I (q.v.) from 502–507 over the emperor's (q.v.) refusal to pay for the defense of the Caspian Gates (q.v.), and again from 527–531 due to rivalry over Iberia and Lazica (qq.v.).

KEDRENOS, GEORGE. Author of a world chronicle (q.v.) from the Creation of the world to 1057. The work is essentially derivative throughout, most obviously after 811, where Kedrenos reproduces the work of John Skylitzes (q.v.) almost word for word.

KEKAUMENOS. Author of a diverse collection of advice and stories known as *Strategikon* (Book of Advice). Little is known about the author except that he flourished in the 11th century and was perhaps a member of the military aristocracy (q.v.). He settled in Thessaly (q.v.) where he became a military governor. His advice, which is tailored to each civil and military office, is based on a profound pessimism about human nature. The information offered includes topics as diverse as Byzantine relations with the Arabs and the Vlachs of Pindos (qq.v.).

KERKYRA. Island in the Ionian Sea (q.v.), also called Corfu, that commands the entrance to the Adriatic Sea (q.v.). Its successive rulers during the period of the early Crusades (q.v.) reflected the political instability of the region. The Normans (q.v.) attacked it in 1081 and captured it in 1147, probably hoping to make it a base of operations against Byzantium's (q.v.) possessions in Greece (q.v.). However, in 1149 it surrendered to Manuel I Komnenos (q.v.). The Venetians conquered the island in 1204; then it fell to the Despotate of Epiros (q.v.) in 1214. Charles I of Anjou (q.v.) seized it in 1272. In 1386 it reverted again to Venice (q.v.).

KHAGHAN. Title used by the rulers of Bulgaria (q.v.), and by the rulers of other Turkish peoples from the central Asian steppe (q.v.), e.g., the Avars and Khazars (qq.v.). It is synonymous with khan, although khan is preferred by modern scholars for the pre-Christian rulers of Bulgaria (q.v.).

KHALID. Brilliant Arab commander who wrested Syria from Byzantium (qq.v.) during the reign of the caliph Umar (qq.v.). Superior mobility, made possible by forced camel marches through the desert, provided him with the element of surprise, as demonstrated by his sudden appearance in March 635 before Damascus (q.v.), which fell after a brief siege. On 20 August 636 in the valley of the Yarmuk River, the eastern tributary of the Jordan River, Khalid won his most famous victory by utterly destroying a Byzantine army. This victory assured Arab domination of Syria.

KHAN. *See* **KHAGAN.**

KHAZARS. Turkic tribe of the Caucasus (q.v.) who allied themselves with Herakleios (q.v.) to oppose the Persians (q.v.), and who provided subsequent help against the Avars and Arabs (qq.v.). In the ninth century the Khazars received a Christian mission (ca. 860) headed by Constantine the Philosopher (Cyril [q.v.]), by which time their khagan (q.v.) and upper echelons of Khazar society had converted to Judaism. Justinian II (q.v.) took refuge among the Khazars, and Leo VI "the Khazar'" (q.v.) was the son of Constantine V (q.v.) and a Khazar princess. The Khazar state was destroyed by Svjatoslav and Vladimir I (qq.v.) in the 10th century.

KHURRAMITES. Religious sectarians of Armenia (q.v.) and Azerbaijan, led by a certain Babek, who rebelled against the caliph Mamun (qq.v.). The rebellion was perhaps largely responsible for the cessation of military hostilities between the caliphate and Byzantium (q.v.) from 814–829. In 834 a large number of Khurramites led by Nasr (Theophobos [q.v.]), fled to Byzantine territory, where Theophilos (q.v.) enrolled them in the army (q.v.).

KIBYRRHAIOTAI. Naval theme (q.v.), first mentioned in the late seventh century. Its administrative center was Attaleia (q.v.). It evolved from the karabisianoi, the first permanent Byzantine fleet, but the name of the theme is derived from the small coastal town of Kibyrra, in Pamphylia (q.v.). The theme covered a large part of the southern coastline of Asia Minor (q.v.), including the regions of Caria, Lycia, Pamphylia, and portions of Isauria (qq.v.). Its chief function was to protect Asia Minor's southern flank against Arab naval attacks. It is last mentioned in 1043.

KIEV. Capital of the Rus (q.v.), established ca. 879 by Oleg (q.v.), successor to Rurik of Novgorod (q.v.), according to the *Russian Primary Chronicle*. Kiev was a center from which raids were launched down the Dnieper (q.v.) against Constantinople (q.v.), the purpose of which seems to have been the acquisition of formal trading privileges with Byzantium (q.v.). Oleg's raid on Constantinople in 907 was followed by a trading agreement in 911. Subsequent raids by Igor (q.v.) in 941 and 943 (or 944) produced a new treaty. The closer relationship between the Rus and Byzantium that developed from these treaties is seen in Olga's (q.v.) visit to Constantinople, in Svjatoslav's (q.v.) attack on Bulgaria (q.v.) in 968, and in the Varangians (q.v.), whom Vladimir I supplied to Basil II (qq.v.) in 988. After the conversion of Vladimir I, Byzantine influence in Kiev increased dramatically. This is especially seen during the reign of Jaroslav (q.v.), who attempted to rebuild Kiev in the image of Constantinople. Kiev flourished until it was pillaged by the Mongols (q.v.) in 1240; thereafter it declined. In the next century Moscow (q.v.) emerged as the true successor to Kiev, the center of all Russia, and the focal point for continued transmission of Byzantine civilization.

KILIJ ARSLAN I. *See* **MYRIOKEPHALON, BATTLE OF; NICAEA; RUM, SULTANATE OF.**

KILIJ ARSLAN II. *See* **RUM, SULTANATE OF.**

KINNAMOS, JOHN. Author of a history of the reign of John II Komnenos and Manuel I Komnenos (qq.v.), covering the years 1118–1176, thus continuing the work of Anna Komnene (q.v.). Kinnamos was a secretary (*grammatikos* [q.v.]) of Manuel I, who he obviously admired, for Manuel's heroic deeds are lauded in a eulogistic manner. Yet he was hardly just a panegyrist, although he is sometimes compared unfavorably to Niketas Choniastes (q.v.) in this respect. The final portion of Kinnamos's work (preserved in a single 13th-century manuscript), which concerns the last years of Manuel I's reign, is missing.

KITI. *See* **CYPRUS.**

KLEISOURA. Type of military district (literally "mountain pass"), that flourished from the eighth through the 10th centuries. It was smaller than a theme (q.v.) and was sometimes the forerunner of a theme.

KLETOROLOGION. *See* **TAKTIKA.**

KLIMENT OF OHRID. Missionary to the Slavs (q.v.), Bulgarian priest, teacher, writer, saint. He was a companion to Naum of Ohrid (q.v.) and a disciple of Cyril and Methodios (qq.v.), whom he accompanied to Moravia (q.v.) in 863. In 886 he was sent by Boris I to Macedonia (qq.v.), first to the region of Devol (q.v.), then (after 893) to Ohrid (q.v.), which soon became a center of Slavonic culture. He wrote numerous homilies, and quite likely authored the *vitae* (q.v.) of Cyril and Methodios. He may also have invented the Cyrillic (q.v.) alphabet, which soon competed with Glagolitic (q.v.).

KLOKOTNITSA. Battle in 1230 that established Bulgaria (q.v.) as the chief power in the Balkan Peninsula (q.v.). It halted the expansion of the Despotate of Epiros (q.v.), whose ruler Theodore Komnenos Doukas (q.v.) was captured by Tsar John Asen II (qq.v.), eliminating the despotate as a competitor in the race to seize Constantinople (q.v.), then held by the Latin Empire (q.v.).

KODINOS, PSEUDO-. *See* **TAKTIKA.**

KOIMESIS. The term refers to the feast of the Dormition ("falling asleep," i.e., death) of the Virgin, celebrated on 15 August, as well as to its image in art.

KOINOBION. Literally "communal living," the term refers to a monastery where monks live and work together, organized around the same daily schedule, administered by an abbot (*hegoumenos* [q.v.]). All property is owned in common. This type of monasticism (q.v.), first developed by Pachomios (q.v.), became the norm in Byzantine monasticism, as established by Basil the Great (q.v.). It contrasts with the ascetical (q.v.) life practiced by individual hermits (q.v.).

KOMENTIOLOS. General who played an active role in the campaigns of Maurice against the Persians, Avars, and Slavs (qq.v.). He replaced Philippikos (q.v.) in Persia in 588 and immediately won a stunning victory near Nisibis (q.v.). However, his return to the Balkan Peninsula (q.v.) proved his undoing. In 598 he and a fellow-general Priskos (q.v.) were defeated by the Avars, who then invaded Thrace (q.v.). Theophylact Simokattes (q.v.) reports that an embassy to Maurice from soldiers stationed in Thrace accused Komentiolos of treason, but somehow he survived imperial censure. However, when Phokas (q.v.) overthrew Maurice in 602 he had Komentiolos executed.

KOMNENE, ANNA. Historian; eldest daughter of Alexios I Komnenos (q.v.). Her *Alexiad,* which is a tribute to her father, encompasses the years 1069–1118, and it is a chief source for the 11th century. Until her brother John (II) (q.v.) was born, and subsequently recognized (in 1092) as heir to the throne, Anna was herself heir to the throne through her betrothal to Constantine Doukas, son of Michael VII (qq.v.). After Constantine's premature death, Anna married Nikephoros Bryennios the Younger (q.v.) and schemed with her mother, Anna Dalassene (q.v.), to make Bryennios emperor (q.v.). Nevertheless, after her father's death in 1118 her brother John became emperor and she was forced to retire to a monastery. There, embittered by her fate, she wrote the *Alexiad,* one of the great Byzantine historical works, and the only work of its kind written by a woman during the Middle Ages.

KONTAKION. *See* **MUSIC; ROMANOS THE MELODE.**

KOSMAS INDIKOPLEUSTES. Author of the *Christian Topography,* perhaps the most interesting and curious work of the first half of the sixth century. He was called *Indikopleustes,* meaning "sailor to India," because of his travels along the borders of the Indian Ocean. As travel literature and as a work of geography founded on personal travel, his descriptions of the Red Sea, Nile River, Axum, Nubia, Arabian Gulf, and Ceylon (qq.v.) are important. He was a merchant, probably from Alexandria (q.v.), also a Nestorian (q.v.) who wrote during the Three Chapters (q.v.) controversy. His work describes trade, but he mentions other things as well, including exotic animals (as does Timothy of Gaza [q.v.]). Most curious to the modern reader is his attempt to prove that the accepted cosmology of Ptolemy is erroneous; he argues that the universe is shaped like the tabernacle of Moses (thus, like a rectangular box). He was perhaps the greatest of Byzantine travelers, but certainly no Copernicus.

KOSMAS THE HYMNOGRAPHER. *See* **ROMANOS THE MELODE.**

KOSOVO POLJE, BATTLE OF. *See* **MURAD I; OTTOMANS.**

KOTYAION (KÜTAHYA). *See* **GERMIYAN; PHRYGIA.**

KOUBIKOULARIOI. *See* **PRAEPOSITUS SACRI CUBICULI.**

KOURION. *See* **CYPRUS.**

KOURKOUAS, JOHN. Brilliant general under Romanos I and Constantine VII (qq.v.) whose victories along the eastern frontier included the conquests of Melitene in 934 and Edessa (qq.v.) in 944. He sent he famous *mandylion* (q.v.) of Edessa back to Constantinople (q.v.) in triumph. His great Muslim adversary was the Hamdanid ruler Sayf al-Dawla (qq.v.).

KOUROPALATES. Title bestowed chiefly on members of the imperial family and on foreign princes. It was inferior only to caesar and *nobilissimos* (qq.v.) in the *Kletorologion* of Philotheos (q.v.). By the 11th century, when Byzantine titles had become less attractive to foreigners, it was refused by Robert Guiscard for his son, and refused by Roussel de Ballieul (qq.v.).

KRITOBOULOS, MICHAEL. Historian of the reign of Mehmet II (q.v.). His *History,* which covers the years 1451–1467, extols Ottoman sultan (qq.v.) Mehmet II as the new *basileus* (q.v.), the legitimate successor to the last Byzantine emperor Constantine XI (qq.v.). The work belongs with other works that deal with the end of Byzantium (q.v.), e.g., those of Doukas, Chalkokondyles, and Sphrantzes (qq.v.)

KRUM. Khan of the Bulgars (qq.v.) from ca. 802–814, and one of Byzantium's most fearful enemies. His army in 811 won a stunning victory over Nikephoros I (q.v.), who was killed. Krum made a drinking cup from the emperor's (q.v.) skull. In 812 Krum seized Mesembria (q.v.) and set about conquering towns in Thrace and Macedonia (qq.v.). The following year he marched unsuccessfully on Constantinople (q.v.), but he captured Adrianople (q.v.) and carried off its citizens to Bulgaria (q.v.). Fortunately for Byzantium he died the following year, in 814, while preparing another expedition against Constantinople.

KUVRAT. Khan of the Onogor Bulgars (qq.v.) who rebelled against the Avars (q.v.) ca. 635 with the support of Herakleios (q.v.). In 619 Kuvrat visited Constantinople (q.v.), was baptized a Christian, and awarded the title of *patrikios* (q.v.). The timing of the revolt was perhaps influenced by the defeats that Herakleios inflicted on the Avars and Persians (qq.v.) between 626–630. However, future emperors lived to regret Herakleios's support of this revolt, for under Kuvrat's son Asparuch (q.v.) a Bulgarian state was established in Byzantine territory.

KYDONES, DEMETRIOS. Leading statesman and intellectual of the 14th century, and one of the greater writers and theologians of the entire Palaiologan (q.v.) period. He was the chief minister (*mesazon* [q.v.]) of John VI Kantakouzenos (q.v.) until the emperor's abdication in 1354. In 1364 he resumed his political career in the court of John V Palaiologos (q.v.), and he helped arrange the emperor's conversion to Catholicism in 1369 on the steps of St. Peter's in Rome (q.v.). He was also an informal tutor and advisor to Manuel II (q.v.). Ardently pro-western, he was a convert to Catholicism who had an openness to Latin culture and civilization that he shared with a circle of like-minded intellectuals, who included his brothers Andrew and Theodore, also Maximos Chrysoberges (q.v.) and Manuel Kalekas. His devotion to translating the writings of Thomas Aquinas (q.v.), including sections of the *Summa theologica,* made him an ardent proponent of Thomism, and an opponent of the theology of Gregory Palamas (qq.v.). His voluminous correspondence with John VI Kantakouzenos, Manuel II, and many other leading personalities is of utmost significance for the cultural history of the 14th century.

KYDONES, PROCHOROS. Younger brother of Demetrios Kydones (q.v.); opponent of Palamism (q.v.). He was a monk at the Great Lavra on Mount Athos (qq.v.) until he was expelled from the monastery in 1367 and condemned for his views in Constantinople (q.v.) the following year. His historical legacy lies chiefly in his Greek translation of sections of the *Summa theologica* of Thomas Aquinas (q.v.), and in his use of Aquinas's arguments to combat Palamism.

KYRENIA CASTLE. *See* **CYPRUS.**

KYROS, PATRIARCH OF ALEXANDRIA. *See* **SOPHRONIOS.**

KYZIKOS. Strategic port-city on the south coast of the Sea of Marmara (q.v.), close to Constantinople (q.v.). Until the seventh century it was the capital of the province of Hellespont (q.v.); it was also metropolis of the ecclesiastical diocese (q.v.) of Hellespont. Kyzikos was situated on an easily defended peninsula (also referred to as Kyzikos) that the Arabs (q.v.) used when they attacked nearby Constantinople from 674–678. Justinian II (q.v.) resettled the peninsula in 688 with inhabitants from Cyprus (q.v.). The Grand Catalan Company (q.v.) occupied it in 1304, before moving on to Gallipoli (q.v.).

– L –

LABARUM. Christian symbol devised by Constantine I (q.v.) and used by his troops as a military standard. Its first use was at the battle of the Milvian Bridge (q.v.) in 312, where Constantine defeated Maxentius (q.v.). In descriptions of this battle the *labarum* is only vaguely described by Eusebios of Caesarea and Lactantius (qq.v.). Subsequently it appears as a Christogram, including the familiar Chi-Rho symbol comprised of the Greek letter Chi (X) overstruck with the Greek letter Rho (P). According to the *Vita Constantini* (q.v.), Constantine accorded it the power to bring him victory over his pagan enemies.

LACHANODRAKON, MICHAEL. *Strategos* (q.v.) of the theme Thrakesion (qq.v.) under Constantine V (q.v.) and feared Iconoclast. His name inspired fear among both Arabs and Iconophiles (qq.v.). He won a great victory over Harun al-Rashid (q.v.) in 782. His zealous support of Iconoclasm (q.v.) was translated into an attack on monasticism (q.v.) in Thrakesion. Monastic properties were confiscated, and he burned to the ground the famous Pelekete monastery on Mount Olympos (q.v.). After the death of Constantine V in 775 he served under Constantine VI (q.v.), helping him to depose Irene (q.v.) in 790. He died on campaign against the Bulgars (q.v.) in 792.

LACTANTIUS. Latin writer (died ca. 325) of Christian apologetics whose pamphlet *De mortibus persecutorum* (On the Deaths of the Persecutors) attempts to demonstrate how divine wrath was visited on those emperors who persecuted Christians, from Nero to the so-called Edict of Milan (q.v.). The work is an invaluable source for the Great Persecution (q.v.) of 303–311, and for the reigns of Diocletian, Galerius, and Maximinus Daia (qq.v.).

LAGOUDERA. *See* **CYPRUS.**

LAKHMIDS. Arab client state of Persia (q.v.) centered at Hira on the lower Euphrates (qq.v.), a location that made the Lakhmids a natural buffer between Persia and Byzantium (q.v.). Their greatest ruler, al-Mundhir III (ca. 505–554), called Alamundarus by the Byzantines (not to be confused with the Ghassanid [q.v.] ruler of the same name), was so great a threat to Byzantium that Justinian I (q.v.) was forced to develop the Arab Ghassanids as an opposing client state. The Lakhmids were conquered by the forces of Islam (q.v.) in 633.

LAODIKEIA. Two cities bore this name. One was the capital of Phrygia, in Asia Minor (qq.v.), in the theme of Thrakesion (q.v.). Captured by the Seljuks (q.v.) after the battle of Mantzikert (q.v.) in 1071, during the next two centuries Byzantine forces recaptured and lost it to the Seljuks several times. The second city with this name was the renowned seaport in northern Syria (q.v.). It was lost to the Arabs (q.v.) sometime around 640, recovered by Nikephoros II Phokas (q.v.) in 968, and it was then successively occupied by Seljuks and Crusaders until in 1108 the Treaty of Devol delivered it to Alexios I Komnenos (qq.v.). It was lost to the Crusaders later in the 12th century.

LARISSA. Chief city of Thessaly (q.v.), strategically situated in the middle of the plain of Thessaly on the right bank of the Peneios River, at a point where all of the region's major roads intersect. Thus, to control Thessaly one had to control Larissa. Inevitably, this meant that it fell prey to invasion. In the 10th century it was attacked by Bulgarians and Serbs (qq.v.). Tsar Samuel (qq.v.) captured it in 986, carrying off the relics of St. Achilleios, the first bishop of Larissa. (The city was metropolitan bishopric of Hellas [qq.v.] from the eighth century.) Bohemund (q.v.) unsuccessfully besieged the city in 1082. After 1204 Boniface of Montferrat (q.v.) parceled out Thessaly, giving Larissa to a Lombard gentleman who took the name Guglielmo de Larsa. However, by around 1220 it was in the hands of the Despotate of Epiros (q.v.), which held it until 1393, when it was taken by the Ottomans (q.v.).

LASKARID DYNASTY. Dynasty that ruled the Empire of Nicaea (q.v.) from 1205–1258. Its emperors included Theodore I Laskaris ([q.v.]; 1205–1221), who founded the Empire of Nicaea, and who staved off a Seljuk (q.v.) invasion in 1211; his son-in-law John III

Vatatzes ([q.v.]; 1221–1254), who expanded the empire into European territory; Theodore II Laskaris ([q.v.]; 1254–1258), who defended the empire's European possessions against the Bulgarians and despotate of Epiros (qq.v.); and John IV Laskaris ([q.v.]; 1258–1261), who was blinded by Michael VIII Palaiologos (q.v.), whose sole rule ushered in the Palaiologan dynasty (q.v.).

LATIN EMPIRE. The Latin Empire (1204–1261), called *Romania* by contemporaries, established after the Fourth Crusade (q.v.) conquered Constantinople (q.v.). The empire was immediately weakened by the terms of the *Partitio Romaniae* (q.v.), which divided the conquered territory of much of Greece (q.v.) into separate, virtually independent states that included the principality of Achaia, the duchy of Athens, and the kingdom of Thessalonike (qq.v.). When a Latin army was defeated by Kalojan near Adrianople (qq.v.) in 1205, the empire's future seemed in doubt. Latin emperor Baldwin of Flanders (q.v.) was captured in that battle, and he spent the rest of his life in captivity in Bulgaria (q.v.). Despite the threat from Bulgaria, the Latin Empire's greatest threat came from the Empire of Nicaea (q.v.). Once Baldwin's brother Henry of Hainault (1206–1216) had restored Latin rule over Thrace (q.v.), he attacked the Empire of Nicaea (q.v.), hoping to destroy it. But the Empire of Nicaea resisted Latin attacks, and a treaty of 1214 recognized something more like peaceful coexistence. After Henry's death, Peter of Courtenay, the husband of Henry's sister Yolande, was selected emperor (q.v.). Peter's capture in 1217 by the ruler of Epiros (q.v.), Theodore Komnenos Doukas (q.v.), left Yolande in charge until her death in 1219. Two years later her son, Robert of Courtenay (1221–1228), succeeded her, followed by Baldwin II (1228–1261). However, in 1231 the barons chose as co-emperor the titular king of Jerusalem (q.v.), John Brienne (died 1237). Baldwin II, who was the only Latin emperor born in Constantinople (and who adopted the Byzantine title *porphyrogenetos* [q.v.]), reigned over an empire that by 1237 was confined chiefly to the city of Constantinople. In retrospect, it seems apparent that the fate of the Latin Empire was sealed after the battle of Adrianople, especially by its inability to destroy the Empire of Nicaea. Theodore Komnenos Doukas (q.v.) took Thessalonike in 1224 and Adrianople in 1225, but any hopes that the Despotate of Epiros had of recovering Constantinople collapsed in 1230 when Theodore was captured by Bulgarian Tsar John Asen II (qq.v.) at the battle of Klokotnitsa (q.v.). After 1243 the Seljuks (q.v.) were weakened by Mongol expansion in Asia Minor (qq.v.), allowing the Empire of Nicaea to turn its full energies westward, further isolating Latin Constantinople. The city fell to a sudden assault in 1261 by the forces of Michael VIII Palaiologos (q.v.).

LATROS. One of the great monastic centers of Byzantium (q.v.), located around Mount Latros in Caria (q.v.). Settled first in the seventh century, Latros reached its peak in the early 13th century when it boasted some 11 monasteries and numerous caves for hermits. Paul of Latros, the famous 10th-century saint, lived in solitude in a cave at Latros.

LAUSIAKOS. *See* **GREAT PALACE.**

LAVRA. Monastery that allowed monks to practice semi-independent asceticism (q.v.). Monks lived in individual dwellings (cells [q.v.]), leading solitary lives of work and prayer. However, they remained under the supervision of an *archimandrite* (q.v.). He gathered them together on weekends for prayer and fellowship within a group of buildings that included a common church, refectory, kitchen, bakery, stables, storerooms, and sickbay. Thus, the *lavra* was a form of monasticism (q.v.) somewhere in-between that of the isolated anchorite (q.v.) and the *koinobion* (q.v.). Nevertheless, the term *lavra* came to refer to important *koinobitic* monasteries on Mount Athos (q.v.), most notably the Great Lavra (q.v.).

LAVRA, GREAT. Earliest, largest, and finest of the monasteries on Mount Athos (q.v.), founded in 963 as a *koinobion* by Athanasios of Athos (qq.v.). His friend and admirer Nikephoros II Phokas (q.v.) provided funds for its construction as an imperial monastery. Its *katholikon* (q.v.), contemporary with that of nearby Iviron (q.v.), is among the oldest churches still standing on Mount Athos. In the 14th century Gregory Palamas (q.v.) was an *hegoumenos* (q.v.) at the Great Lavra, as was Philotheos Kokkinos (q.v.).

LAW. Civil law was founded on the *Corpus Juris Civilis* of Justinian I (qq.v.), a work whose significance for western civilization is exceeded only by that of the Bible. The *Corpus* incorporated and superseded previous Roman laws, including those in the law code of Theodosios II (q.v.). The process of supplementing the *Corpus* began almost immediately with the Novels (q.v.) of Justinian I, issued in Greek, not Latin. The *Ecloga, Nomos stratiotikos,* Farmers's Law, and Rhodian Sea Law (qq.v.) continued this process.

In the ninth and 10th centuries interest in the *Corpus* itself revived, as illustrated by the *Epanagogue, Prochiron,* and *Basilika* (q.v.). There were law schools at Berytus and Constantinople (qq.v.), though both had fallen into decline by the seventh century. In the 11th century a new law school was organized by Constantine IX (q.v.), presided over by John (VIII) Xiphilinos (q.v.). Canon law (q.v.), which governed the church, overlapped with civil law.

LAZAROS. *See* **PHOBEROU MONASTERY; THEOPHILOS.**

LAZIKA. Region at the eastern end of the Black Sea (q.v.). From the fourth century it comprised a kingdom that included Abchasia (q.v.), which guarded some of the passes through the Caucasus Mountains (q.v.). Its importance to Byzantium (q.v.) was as a buffer against barbarian tribes north of the Caucasus. That it was also a buffer against any Persian advance to the Black Sea (q.v.) explains why it was one of the main theaters of war with the Persians during the reign of Justinian I (q.v.). The great Byzantine stronghold Petra was taken by the Persians in 542 and not recovered until 551. Peace with Persia (q.v.) in 562 confirmed Byzantine control over Lazika. Maximos the Confessor (q.v.) was exiled to Lazika, where he died on 13 August 662. Within a half century Lazika was under Arab (q.v.) domination.

LEBOUNION, BATTLE OF MOUNT. *See* **ALEXIOS I KOMNENOS; CUMANS; PECHENEGS.**

LEMNOS. *See* **GATTILUSIO.**

LEO I. Emperor (q.v.) from 457–474, chosen by Aspar (q.v.) after the death of Marcian (q.v.). He was the first emperor to be crowned by a patriarch (Anatolios) of Constantinople (qq.v.). The turbulent situation in the West, which produced the rebellions of Ricimer and Majorian (qq.v.), was made worse by the failure of the expedition of Basiliskos against the Vandals (qq.v.) in 468. Leo I (q.v.) gained his independence by promoting Zeno (q.v.), who Leo I married to his daughter Ariadne (q.v.). Zeno and his Isaurians (q.v.) conspired with Leo to assassinate Aspar and his son Ardabourios in 471. For this, Leo's contemporaries called him *Makelles* ("Butcher").

LEO I THE GREAT. Pope (q.v.) from 440–461; greatest pope of the fifth century. He championed Orthodox (q.v.) opposition to Nestorianism (q.v.) and defended papal primacy (q.v.). The force of his personality and diplomatic skills were evident at the Council of Chalcedon (q.v.), also in his negotiations with Attila (q.v.) in 452, and with Petronius Maximus (q.v.) in 455.

LEO II. Emperor from 473–474; grandson of Leo I (q.v.). The son of Ariadne and Zeno (qq.v.), he was only six when he came to the throne. He died shortly after crowning Zeno emperor (474).

LEO III. Emperor (q.v.) from 717–741 who founded the Isaurian dynasty (q.v.). His reign began with the unsuccessful siege (717–718) of Constantinople (q.v.) by the Arab general Maslama (qq.v.), one of several important events of his reign. In 726 Leo issued an edict supporting Iconoclasm (q.v.), subsequently confirmed by a *silentium* (q.v.) in 730. Patriarch Germanos I (qq.v.) was removed. Popes Gregory II and Gregory III (qq.v.) objected in vain. Leo III's response may have been to transfer from the papacy (q.v.) to the patriarch of Constantinople the ecclesiastical administration of Sicily, Calabria, and Illyricum (qq.v.). Leo III's energetic defense of Asia Minor (q.v.) resulted in a string of victories against the Arabs (q.v.), culminating in the great victory at Akroinon (q.v.) in 740. Leo further defended Asia Minor by creating the themes of Thrakesion and Kibyrrhaiotai (qq.v.). His new manual of law, the *Ecloga* (q.v.), was not superceded until the *Basilika* of Leo VI (qq.v.) in the late ninth century. In sum, Leo III's reign was packed with events, the consequences of which reverberated throughout the eighth century. This was particularly true of his pursuit of Iconoclasm.

LEO III. Pope (795–816) who crowned Charlemagne (q.v.) as Emperor of the Romans on Christmas Day 800, one of the chief events of the Middle Ages. The coronation was seen by Byzantium (q.v.) as an act of rebellion, but Pope Leo may have been persuaded that in no way could any woman, including the reigning Irene (q.v.), though she called herself *basileus* (q.v.), be construed as emperor (q.v.). Thus, the throne could be viewed as vacant when Charlemagne was crowned.

LEO IV THE KHAZAR. Emperor (q.v.) from 775–780; son of Constantine V (q.v.) and a Khazar princess, hence the epithet following his name. He was a moderate Iconoclast whose death brought to an end the first period of Iconoclasm (q.v.). The administration of the empire was left in the hands of his wife Irene (q.v.), who served as regent for their infant son Constantine VI (q.v.). Leo IV's reign served as a transition from the aggressive Iconoclasm of his father to the restoration of icon (q.v.) veneration by Irene in 787. He sent expeditions against the Arabs (q.v.) led by Michael Lachanodrakon (q.v.), but Arab expeditions into Asia Minor (q.v.), one of which in 780 was led by Harun al-Rashid (q.v.), were destructive.

LEO V THE ARMENIAN. Emperor (q.v.) (813–820) of Armenian descent who inaugurated the second period of Iconoclasm (q.v.) in 815. John (VII) Grammatikos (q.v.) laid the groundwork for a local council in Constantinople (q.v.) that reinstated Iconoclasm in 815, leading to the persecution of prominent Iconophile (q.v.) monks such as Theodore Graptos (q.v.). The patriarch Nikephoros I (qq.v.) refused to sign the decrees of the council and was deposed; Theodotos I Kassiteras (qq.v.) was put in his place. Leo V's previous experience as *strategos* of the theme of Anatolikon (qq.v.) must have guided his appointment of Thomas the Slav, Manuel, and Michael (II) (qq.v.) to top military commands. Michael assassinated Leo on Christmas Day 820 in the chapel of the Great Palace (q.v.), a deed that tarnished the reputation of the new Amorion dynasty (q.v.).

LEO VI. Emperor (q.v.) from 886–912 whose *Prochiron, Basilika,* and Novels (qq.v.) together constituted an important revision of Justinianic law. Decidedly unpopular, and illegal in the eyes of the church, was his fourth marriage (*tetragamy* [q.v.]) to his mistress Zoe Karbonopsina (q.v.) in 906, the year after she had given birth to Leo's sole male heir to the throne, the future Constantine VII (q.v.). When Patriarch Nicholas I Mystikos (qq.v.) disapproved of the marriage Leo VI removed him, causing a schism within the church. Leo's foreign policy was marred by military failure. His generals suffered defeats at the hands of Symeon of Bulgaria and the Arabs in Sicily (qq.v.). Leo of Tripoli pillaged Thessalonike (qq.v.) in 904, Oleg attacked Constantinople (qq.v.) in 907, and admiral Himerios (q.v.) lost a fleet to the Arabs (q.v.) in 911. Nevertheless, Leo was remembered for his revision of the law as well as for his erudition, for he was a prolific writer of homilies, orations, hymns, and poems. Moreover, he initiated the *Kletorologion* of Philotheos, the Book of the Eparch, and a military manual called the *Taktika of Leo* VI (qq.v.). All of this earned him the epithet "the Wise."

LEO IX. Pope (q.v.) from 1049–1054 whose emissary Humbert (q.v.) initiated the church schism of 1054. Leo was a church reformer, like others in his circle, including Humbert (and Hildebrand, the future Gregory VII [q.v.]). The background of the schism lay in Leo IX's (q.v.) approval of the suppression of Byzantine religious practices in southern Italy by the Normans (qq.v.). The patriarch Keroularios (qq.v.) countered in 1052 by closing down Latin churches in Constantinople (q.v.) for using *azyma* (q.v.). The following year Leo IX was imprisoned by the Normans after the pope and Argyros (q.v.) were defeated at the battle of Civitate seeking further help against the Normans from the Byzantines, Leo sent Humbert to Constantinople to try to resolve outstanding issues between the churches. By the time Humbert initiated the chain of events that produced the schism of 1054 (q.v.), Leo IX had already died, making Humbert's actions technically invalid.

LEO GRAMMATIKOS (LEO THE GRAMMARIAN). *See* **SYMEON LOGOTHETE.**

LEONARD OF CHIOS. Genoese archbishop of Lesbos (q.v.) who wrote an eyewitness account of the Ottoman conquest of Constantinople (qq.v.) in 1453. He arrived in Constantinople in 1452, along with the papal legate Isidore of Kiev (q.v.). Despite being captured by the Ottomans, he escaped to Chios (q.v.) where he sent Pope Nicholas V (qq.v.) a report about the Ottoman siege in August of 1453. After the diary of Nicolo Barbaro (q.v.), Leonard's report is the most important western eyewitness account of the 1453 siege.

LEONTIOS. *Magister militum* of Zeno (qq.v.) who was proclaimed emperor (q.v.) in 484. He was sent by Zeno to suppress the rebellion of Illos, which was supported by Verina (q.v.). Instead, he joined forces with them and was declared emperor by Verina's alleged authority. Leontios was received as emperor at Antioch (q.v.), but he was soon defeated by Zeno's commander Ermenric. He fled to a fortress in the mountains of Isauria (q.v.), which held out for four years (until 488). Once it fell, Leontios and Illos were beheaded.

LEONTIOS. Emperor (q.v.) from 695–698, succeeding Justinian II (q.v.). He was *strategos* (q.v.) of the theme of Anatolikon (qq.v.) when Justinian II imprisoned him in 692. Released in 695 and made *strategos* of the theme of Hellas (q.v.) he plotted Justinian II's overthrow. The chief event of his reign was the capture of Carthage by the Arabs (qq.v.) in 697. The failure to regain the city prompted the rebellion of Apsimar, who overthrew Leontios and ascended the throne as Tiberios II (q.v.).

LEONTIOS OF BYZANTIUM. *See* **SEVEROS.**

LEONTIOS OF NEAPOLIS. *See* **JOHN "THE ALMSGIVER."**

LEONTIUS PILATUS. *See* **BARLAAM OF CALABRIA.**

LEO OF OHRID. *See* **OHRID.**

LEO OF SYNADA. Metropolitan of Synada in Phrygia (qq.v.); writer and diplomat. His letters, some of them to Basil II (q.v.), describe his embassies to the West, including one to Rome (q.v.) in 996–998.

LEO OF TRIPOLI. Admiral of an Arab fleet that in 904 attacked and captured Abydos (q.v.), then pillaged Thessalonike (q.v.). The sack of Thessalonike is described by John Kameniates (q.v.). In 912, off Chios (q.v.), he defeated a Byzantine fleet under Himerios (q.v.). Leo was a Greek who converted to Islam after being taken captive by the Arabs (q.v.).

LEO THE DEACON. Historian whose *History* covers the years 959 –976. It concentrates on the military victories of Nikephoros II Phokas (q.v.), who emerges as a great hero, comparable to Herakles. This and other allusions to Greek mythology, as well as the overall format of the work, which is modeled on the work of Agathias (q.v.), typifies the renewed interest in classical antiquity that characterizes much Byzantine literature and art of the 10th century.

LEO THE MATHEMATICIAN. Teacher and scholar; also called Leo the Philosopher. He was a nephew (or cousin) of John VII Grammatikos and metropolitan of Thessalonike (qq.v.) from 840–843. However, his fame rested on his knowledge of philosophy (q.v.) and mathematics, which attracted the attention of even the caliph Mamun (qq.v.). The caliph invited him to Baghdad (q.v.), but when Theophilos (q.v.) heard of the invitation he employed him to teach in the Magnaura (q.v.) palace. For Theophilos he built some remarkable *automata* (q.v.), as well as a beacon system (q.v.) that warned of Arab raids.

LESBOS (MYTILENE). Island in the eastern Aegean (q.v.), the largest Aegean island after Crete and Euboea (qq.v.). Its strategic importance derived from its close proximity to Asia Minor (q.v.), also from its size. It played an important role in the revolt of Thomas the

Slav (q.v.), and in the maritime principality of Tzachas (q.v.).
Baldwin of Flanders (q.v.) received it in 1204 as part of the *Partitio
Romaniae* (q.v.). It returned to Byzantine possession when John III
Vatatzes (q.v.) conquered it about two decades later. The Gattilusio
(q.v.) family governed it from 1355–1462. Among its famous native
sons are Leonard of Chios and Zacharias of Mytilene (qq.v.). The
historian Doukas (q.v.) describes the siege of Mytilene by the Ottomans (q.v.) in 1462.

LIBANIOS. Rhetorician and teacher (died ca. 393) from Antioch (q.v.).
Eloquent defender of paganism and of classical literature, he taught
at Nikomedia (q.v.), where he met Basil the Great (q.v.), and had
an indirect acquaintance with Julian (q.v.). Julian's reign (361–363)
was the highpoint of his career, though marred by Julian's unpopu-
larity in Antioch. After Julian's death he lived in obscurity until the
death of Valens (q.v.) in 378 when he emerged once more as a
spokesman for the last pagan revival, which was suppressed by 392,
the date of his last known oration.

LIBRI CAROLINI. *See* **CHARLEMAGNE.**

LICINIUS. Emperor (q.v.) in the East from 308–324. His appointment
by Galerius (q.v.) in 308 was challenged by Maximinus Daia (q.v.),
but Licinius defeated him in 313. Relations with Constantine I (q.v.)
were cordial at first. In 313 Licinius married Constantine's half-
sister Constantia, and in the same year he may have issued (with
Constantine) the so-called Edict of Milan (q.v.). However, their relations deteriorated into war in 324. Constantine defeated him in
battle in the region of Adrianople (q.v.). Licinius fled to Byzantion
(q.v.), which Constantine laid siege to with the aid of a fleet commanded by Crispus (q.v.). Licinius then fled to Chalcedon (q.v.),
near which Constantine defeated him (at Chrysopolis, on 18 September 324). Licinius submitted, and he was exiled to Thessalonike
(q.v.), where he was executed the following year. In the *Vita Constantini,* Eusebios of Caesarea (qq.v.) presents the war between
Licinius and Constantine as a struggle between paganism and Christianity.

LIMES. *See* **LIMITANEI; LONG WALL.**

LIMITANEI. The various fortified regions along the empire's frontiers
were called *limes* (q.v.), which is Latin for "border." This explains

the term *limitanei* for the garrison troops who defended the *limes* from the fourth century to the late sixth century. *Limitanei* included both cavalry and infantry units, also auxiliary troops, commanded by a *doux* (q.v.). As garrison troops (as distinct from the *comitatenses* [q.v.], the mobile forces) they became, in effect, farmer-soldiers whose military obligations were passed down from father to son.

LITURGY. The rite of the Eucharist, called the Divine Liturgy, of which there are two versions, one attributed to John Chrysostom (q.v.) and the other to Basil the Great (q.v.). In the eighth century the public nature of the liturgy was curtailed by reducing public processions and preparing the Eucharist behind closed doors. During Iconoclasm, Constantine V (qq.v.) considered the Eucharist the only true representation of Christ.

LIUTPRAND OF CREMONA. Bishop (q.v.) of Cremona; ambassador from Otto I of Germany (q.v.) to the courts of Constantine VII and Nikephoros II (qq.v.). His *Antapodosis* (Tit for Tat) is a general history from 888–949 that includes information about German-Byzantine relations. Another work, the *Relatio de legatione Constantinopolitana* (Narrative of an Embassy to Constantinople) offers a fascinating, though biased, narrative of Liutprand's second embassy to Nikephoros II in 968.

LIZIOS. *See* **FEUDALISM.**

LOGOTHETES. The minister of a financial department, from the seventh century onward. Thus, the *logothetes tou genikou* was the chief finance minister in charge of the genikon, the department that assessed and collected taxes, in addition to keeping lists of current taxpayers. The *logothetes tou stratiotikou* (logothete of the soldiers) had certain fiscal duties relating to the army, and the *logothetes ton agelon* (logothete of the herds) supervised the herds of state mules and horses. The *logothetes tou praitoriou* (logothete of the praitorion) was an assistant to the eparch (q.v.) of the city of Constantinople (q.v.). The *logothetes tou dromou* (q.v.) evolved from a minister of the post to the emperor's (q.v.) chief minister, with wide-ranging responsibilities. From the end of the 12th century, the *megas* (q.v.) *logothetes* coordinated the entire civil service.

LOGOTHETES TOU DROMOU. Chief minister of the empire and director of imperial policy from the ninth century onward. The office, which goes back at least to the eighth century, developed out of the minister of the public post under the former *magister officiorum* (q.v.). He was responsible for such diverse duties as supervision of the imperial post and roads, internal security, court ceremonial, foreigners in Constantinople (q.v.), and making sure that field armies were adequately provisioned. Theoktistos held his position under Theophilos, and under the regent Theodora (qq.v.).

LOMBARDS. Germanic people who conquered much of Italy (q.v.), beginning in 568. They had previously served under Narses (q.v.) as mercenaries of Justinian I (q.v.) in the war against the Ostrogoths (q.v.). The Lombards moved into Italy in 568, led by their king Alboin (died 572). They rapidly conquered most of it, establishing the kingdom of Longobardia (q.v.). Maurice (q.v.) reassembled such Byzantine territory that remained into the Exarchate of Ravenna (q.v.). Constans II (q.v.) attacked the Lombards with some success in 663, but he failed in his siege of Benevento (q.v.). An eighth-century Lombard offensive ended with the fall of Ravenna in 751, leaving Byzantium (q.v.) without territory in northern and central Italy. Nevertheless, in 774 Charlemagne (q.v.) wrested northern Italy from the Lombards. The ninth and 10th centuries saw further Lombard decline, which helps to explain the rapid Norman (q.v.) expansion in southern Italy in the 11th century.

LONGOBARDIA. The term refers loosely to parts of Italy that the Lombards (qq.v.) ruled. More specifically, it refers to the Byzantine theme (q.v.) of the same name that was organized by the late ninth century. It extended along the coast of southeast Italy and included the Lombard principalities of Benevento, Capua, and Salerno (qq.v.) and the non-Lombard city-states of Amalfi, Naples, and Gaeta (qq.v.).

LONG WALL. A wall of considerable length erected (or rebuilt) by Anastasios I (q.v.) to the west of Constantinople (q.v.) for the purpose of protecting the city from invasion. It extended some 45 kilometers from Selymbria (q.v.), on the north shore of the Sea of Marmara (q.v.), to the shore of the Black Sea (qq.v.). Unfortunately, the garrison defending the wall proved inadequate and occasional earthquakes damaged the wall. Zabergan and his Cotrigurs (qq.v.) penetrated the wall and threatened Constantinople in 559. In effect, the Long Wall was an admission that the empire's northern boundary (*limes* [q.v.]) was, in effect, at Constantinople's doorstep.

LOROS. Long jeweled stole worn by the emperor (e.g., as mandatory dress on Easter Sunday) and empress, and by high officials.

LOUIS II. Emperor of the Franks (q.v.) from 854–875. He was much preoccupied with affairs in Italy (q.v.) during his reign, especially with attacks by the Arabs of Sicily (qq.v.). His alliance with Basil I (q.v.) in 869 aided Louis in his capture of Bari (q.v.) in 871. However, Byzantine-Frankish relations deteriorated that same year when Louis II began calling himself Emperor of the Romans, a title which the Byzantine emperor (q.v.) reserved for himself alone.

LOUIS VII. King of France (q.v.) from 1137–1180; leader of one of the main contingents of the Second Crusade (q.v.). The French army passed through Constantinople (q.v.) in 1147, forcing Manuel I Komnenos (q.v.) to remain in the city for fear that French troops might storm its walls. Roger II of Sicily (qq.v.) used the opportunity to capture Kerkyra (q.v.), and to pillage Corinth and Thebes (qq.v.). An account of this Crusade by Louis VII's chaplain, Odo of Deuil (q.v.), confirms the religious hostility toward Byzantium (q.v.) within the ranks of Louis VII's army.

LOUKAS THE YOUNGER. Saint (died 953) born in Stiri, in Greece, not far from Delphi. The *katholikon* (q.v.) of Hosios Loukas (q.v.) is dedicated to him; his stylized portrait is in the narthex (q.v.) of the *katholikon*. His *vita* (q.v.) is of some importance for its description of conditions in central Greece and the Peloponnesos (qq.v.) during the first half of the 10th century.

LUSIGNANS. *See* **CYPRUS.**

LYCIA. Region in southwestern Asia Minor (q.v.); part of the theme of Kibyrrhaiotai (qq.v.). Its metropolis (q.v.) was the city of Myra, on the main maritime Aegean (q.v.) route from Egypt to Italy (qq.v.). Among Lycia's most impressive ruined monuments is the church at Dereağzi (q.v.), dated to ca. 900.

LYDIA. Region in western Asia Minor (q.v.). Its most important cities included Smyrna, Ephesus, Sardis, and Magnesia (qq.v.). The region was lost to the Turks (q.v.) after the battle of Mantzikert (q.v.), but reoccupied by Alexios I Komnenos after the First Crusade (qq.v.). A long period of peace ensued until early in the reign of Manuel I (q.v.) when Turks wreaked destruction through the region. In 1148 forces of the Second Crusade (q.v.) had to fight Turks while making their way through Lydia. After the battle of Myriokephalon in 1176 there were further Turkish inroads. The conquest of Constantinople by the Fourth Crusade (qq.v.) shifted responsibility for Lydia's defense to the Laskarids (q.v.), whose program of fortification brought peace and prosperity to the region until 1261. Thereafter, Palaiologan emperors (qq.v.) failed to protect the region in the face of relentless Ottoman (q.v.) expansion. The important town of Tripolis, which was essential to the defense of the region, was lost ca. 1300. In 1313 Turks from the emirate of Saruhan (qq.v.) captured Lydia's last Byzantine city, Magnesia (q.v.).

LYONS, COUNCIL OF. The council held in 1274 created a union of the churches (q.v.) on paper. This union was extorted from Michael VIII by Pope Gregory X (qq.v.), who threatened to support Charles I of Anjou's (q.v.) planned invasion of Byzantium (q.v.). The church union was a great victory for the papacy (q.v.), and for Michael it had the desired effect of preventing Charles's invasion. Nevertheless, Michael VIII paid a price at home, since the union was repudiated by ordinary citizens and clergy alike. They rejected John XI Bekkos as patriarch (qq.v.), remaining loyal to Arsenios (q.v.). Michael's jailing of opponents only deepened the internal crisis resulting from the union. In 1285, after Michael VIII's death, a church council rejected the union.

LYTHRANKOMI. *See* **CYPRUS.**

– M –

MACEDONIA. Region between Thrace and Epiros (qq.v.) that includes the valleys of the Nestos, Strymon (q.v.), Vardar, and Haliakmon rivers. Though mostly mountainous, with parts of the Pindos Mountain range in the west and the Rhodope Mountains (q.v.) in the east, it includes a large central plain that was traversed by the Via Egnatia (q.v.) and which contained the important cities of Thessalonike, Serres, Kastoria, Berroia, Ohrid (qq.v.), and Prespa. Slavs (q.v.) settled in great numbers in the countryside in the late sixth and early seventh centuries, besieging Thessalonike on occasion. The theme (q.v.) of Macedonia, created in the early ninth century to extend Byzantine authority in the region, was soon challenged by the expansion of Bulgaria (q.v.). Basil II (q.v.) restored Byzantine authority, but that changed with the conquest of Constantinople by the Fourth Crusade (qq.v.). Boniface of Montferrat (q.v.) was awarded Macedonia. After Boniface's death in 1207 the region was contested among the Bulgarians, the Despotate of Epiros (qq.v.), the restored Byzantine Empire, and the Serbs (q.v.), before finally succumbing to the Ottomans (q.v.) in the late 14th century.

MACEDONIAN DYNASTY. Greatest of Byzantine imperial dynasties. It was founded by Basil I (q.v.) in 867 and ended in 1056 with the death of Theodora (q.v.). Under a series of soldier-emperors, the most famous of whom was Basil II (q.v.), medieval Byzantium (q.v.) reached its largest territorial extent. The so-called "Macedonian Renaissance" is a convenient term for the revival of scholarship and the arts that occurred, especially under Constantine VII (q.v.).

MAGIC. *See* **MEDICINE; SCIENCE.**

MAGISTER MILITUM. Title (Master of Soldiers) of a supreme army commander. It was held simultaneously by several generals in both the East and the West in the late fourth and fifth centuries. Under Theodosios I (q.v.) there were five such generals in the East and two in the West. They were frequently German generals such as Stilicho and Aspar (qq.v.), whose loyalty was suspect. No subsequent *magister militum* was allowed to amass the kind of power Aspar had possessed.

MAGISTER OFFICIORUM. Master of the Offices, who headed the entire civil administration of the empire from the fourth century until the seventh century, when his functions were largely taken over by the *logothetes tou dromou* (q.v.).

MAGISTROS. A high-ranking honorary title. First mentioned in the *Kletorologion* of Philotheos (q.v.) in the late ninth century, where it is placed above the titles of *anthypatos* and *patrikios* (qq.v.).

MAGNAURA. A reception hall adjacent to the Great Palace in Constantinople (qq.v.), to the east of the Augustaion (q.v.). It was a basilica (q.v.) of three aisles and galleries. The central aisle terminated in a flight of six stairs that led to an apse (q.v.) where the famous throne of Solomon was placed. It was here that the emperor (q.v.) presided at state receptions and where he greeted foreign ambassadors. Theophilos (q.v.) is said to have had Leo the Mathematician (q.v.) construct *automata* to impress foreign visitors, including a mechanism that could suddenly raise the enthroned emperor nearly to the ceiling. Liutprand of Cremona (q.v.) reports that when this happened, bronze lions beside the throne opened their jaws and roared, beating their tails upon the ground, while mechanical birds fluttered and sang from a golden plane tree, each singing a different tune. Two gold organs played while visitors entered and exited. During the reign of Michael III, Caesar Bardas (qq.v.) organized a school in the Magnaura, where Leo the Mathematician taught.

MAGNENTIUS. Usurper (350–353) who killed Constans I (q.v.) in battle in 350, and took over the western empire after defeating rival Nepotianus. Constantius II (q.v.) defeated him at Mursa in 351, after which Magnentius lost Italy (q.v.) in 352. Constantius II pursued him to Gaul (q.v.), where Magnentius committed suicide in 353.

MAGNESIA. Chief city of the Empire of Nicaea under John III Vatatzes (qq.v.). Located in Lydia in western Asia Minor (qq.v.), its prosperity was based on the secure foundations of abundant agriculture and trade. In 1302 Michael IX (q.v.) tried to save Magnesia from Turkish capture but they besieged him and his Alan (q.v.) mercenaries within its walls. He narrowly escaped death by fleeing the city at night. Roger de Flor arrived with the Catalan Grand Company (qq.v.) in 1304, but the city's inhabitants locked their gates and resisted his siege machines. The emirate of Saruhan (qq.v.) conquered the city in 1313.

MAGNIFICI. *See* **CLARISSIMUS.**

MAGYARS. *See* **HUNGARY.**

MAINA. *See* **MOREA; PELAGONIA, BATTLE OF; WILLIAM II VILLEHARDOUIN.**

MAJORIAN. Western emperor (q.v.) from 457–461, elevated to the throne by the powerful *magister militum* Ricimer (qq.v.). The Latin poet Sidonius acclaimed his accession in uplifting verse. Despite his success against the Goths in Gaul (qq.v.) in 458–459, two failed naval expeditions (in 460 and 461) against Gaiseric left the Vandals (qq.v.) unscathed, but they left Majorian weaker politically. In 461 Ricimir (q.v.) executed him.

MAKARIOS THE GREAT. Egyptian desert saint (ca. 300–ca. 390) who helped to establish Egyptian monasticism (q.v.). Sketis, a monastery he founded around 330, was one of the chief centers of monasticism in Egypt (q.v.). Makarios opposed Arianism (q.v.), and he professed never to have spat since his baptism (a feat of asceticism [q.v.], presumably).

MALALAS, JOHN. Author of the first Byzantine world chronicle (q.v.). He was a native of Antioch (q.v.), which explains the attention he devotes to the city in his chronicle. The work goes from the Creation to 565, and it is distinguished by its use of the common vernacular, his inclusion of gossip and tall tales, and his credulous religiosity. It was meant to entertain ordinary readers and seems to have been popular. Once translated into Church Slavonic (q.v.), its influence spread well beyond Byzantium (q.v.).

MALIKSHAH. *See* **SULTANATE OF RUM.**

MALTA. Island in the Mediterranean Sea south of Sicily (qq.v.). It was conquered from the Ostrogoths by Justinian I (qq.v.) around 535, and it remained in Byzantine hands until the Aghlabids (q.v.) conquered it in 870. It fell to the Normans (q.v.) around 1090. Its connection with the Knights Hospitallers (q.v.) began in 1531 when it was ceded to them by Holy Roman Emperor Charles V.

MAMAS. Saint of obscure origins, whose cult was popular in Byzantium (q.v.). According to legend Mamas was a shepherd from Gangra in Asia Minor (qq.v.) who was martyred by the emperor Aurelian (270–275). There was an area at the south end of the European side of the Bosporos (q.v.) that was called St. Mamas. Near its harbor Rus (q.v.) merchants were assigned to live. A famous monastery in Constantinople (q.v.) dedicated to St. Mamas contained the tombs of the emperor Maurice (q.v.) and his family.

MAMLUKS. Dynasty of sultans that ruled Egypt (qq.v.) from 1250 until the Ottoman (q.v.) conquest in 1517. The dynastic name derives from the Turkish slave (*mamluk* in Arabic) bodyguard of the last Ayyubid sultan (qq.v.) of Cairo. The overthrow of the Ayyubids in 1250 is described in gripping detail in Joinville's *Life of Saint Louis*. Mamluk sultan Baybars (1260–1277) defeated the Mongol (q.v.) army of Hulagu at Ayn Jalut in 1260, becoming master of Syria (q.v.) in the process. The Mamluks next concentrated on ejecting the Crusaders from the Holy Land, which they did with the conquest of Acre in 1291.

MAMUN. Abbasid caliph (qq.v.) from 813–833; son of Harun al-Rashid (q.v.). He supported the revolt of Thomas the Slav (q.v.) and invaded Asia Minor (q.v.) three times during the reign of Theophilos (q.v.): in 830 in response to Theophilos's (q.v.) support of the Khurramites (q.v.), in 831, and in 833. He collected and translated into Arabic many ancient Greek scientific texts, but his effort to persuade Leo the Mathematician (q.v.) to come to Baghdad (qq.v.) on a cultural mission was unsuccessful. He died in 833 while invading Asia Minor. Mutasim (q.v.) succeeded him.

MANASSES, CONSTANTINE. Author of a world chronicle (q.v.) in verse from Adam to 1081, in addition to other works that included a romance (q.v.) entitled *Aristandros and Kallithea*. His close association with the court of Manuel I Komnenos (q.v.) explains his panegyrics to the emperor (q.v.), as well as his more personal and descriptive *Hodoiporikon* (Guidebook), based on his first-hand experience of traveling with a diplomatic embassy to Palestine (q.v.) in 1160. It is unfortunate that he did not choose to continue his chronicle into the 12th century, the period for which he was a contemporary.

MANDYLION. *See* **EDESSA.**

MANFRED. King of Sicily (1258–1266) who opposed Michael VIII Palaiologos (q.v.), restorer of the Byzantine state (reigned 1261–1282). Manfred's opposition, which appeared like a revival of the kind of anti-Byzantine policy that went back to Henry VI (q.v.) and the Norman rulers of Sicily (qq.v.), aimed at expanding his kingdom into the Balkan Peninsula (q.v.). First Manfred occupied Kerkyra (q.v.) and the important cities along the coast of Epiros, including Dyrrachion (qq.v.). Then he made an alliance with Michael II Komnenos Doukas of the Despotate of Epiros (qq.v.), and he added to it the duke of Achaia, William II Villehardouin, the Latin rulers of Euboea, and those of the duchy of Athens (qq.v.). Michael VIII Palaiologos defeated the coalition at the battle of Pelagonia (q.v.) in 1259, which dashed Manfred's Balkan dreams. In 1266 Manfred was killed in battle vainly attempting to defend Sicily against Charles I of Anjou (qq.v.).

MANI. *See* **MANICHAEANISM.**

MANIAKES, GEORGE. One of the great generals of the 11th century. Of humble origins he rose through the ranks due to his exceptional military capabilities. His victories along the Arab frontier in the early 1030s made him famous, especially his capture of Edessa (q.v.) where he seized the alleged letter that Jesus sent to Abgar. He attacked eastern Sicily (q.v.) in 1038, accompanied by Harold Hardrada and a company of Varangians (qq.v.). He quickly won Messina and Syracuse (qq.v.), but enemies at court persuaded Michael IV (q.v.) to recall and imprison him in 1040. When Michael V (q.v.) released him in 1042, he returned to Italy with the authority of *katepano* (q.v.), this time to fight the Normans (q.v.). However, his recall the same year by Constantine IX (q.v.) forced him into rebellion in 1043, just as the Rus under Jaroslav (qq.v.) were preparing to attack the capital. He landed at Dyrrachion (q.v.) and was marching on Constantinople (q.v.) when he was killed in battle near Thessalonike (q.v.). Thus perished a true warrior; there were precious few like him to defend Byzantium (q.v.) in the period from 1025–1081.

MANICHAEANISM. The religion founded in the third century by the Persian Mani. A central doctrine was the conflict between two opposing forces, Good (Light) and Evil (Darkness). The material world was considered evil, and Manichaeans were urged to practice asceticism (q.v.). Though sharing the same basic worldview, adherents of Zoroastrianism, the state religion of the Sassanians (qq.v.), persecuted Manichaeanism. Augustine (q.v.) was a follower of Manicheanism for a while; in his time, it was a major world religion.

MANTZIKERT, BATTLE OF. One of Byzantium's (q.v.) greatest defeats (19 [or 26] August 1071). It resulted in the capture of Romanos IV Diogenes (q.v.) and opened up Asia Minor (q.v.) to Seljuk (q.v.) conquest. The army that Romanos IV led was attempting to provide security to Asia Minor from marauding Seljuks by garrisoning the fortresses around Lake Van that controlled the invasion routes from Armenia (q.v.). Included among Romanos's army were numerous foreign mercenaries, e.g., Pechenegs, Uzes, and Normans under the infamous Roussel de Bailleul (qq.v.). The emperor (q.v.) was confronted by a large Seljuk (q.v.) force under Seljuk sultan Alp Arslan (qq.v.) near the fortress of Mantzikert. The Byzantine defeat can be attributed to several factors that include encirclement by mounted Seljuk archers, a false rumor that the emperor had been killed, and the defection to the Seljuks of some of the Uzes. Asia Minor now lay defenseless to further conquest by the Seljuks. The defeat was doubly felt for it occurred the same year that Bari (q.v.), the last Byzantine stronghold in southern Italy (q.v.), fell to Robert Guiscard's Normans.

MANUEL. Famous general who served under Michael I (q.v.) and three successive emperors (q.v.). When Theophilos (q.v.) came to power in 829 Manuel was falsely accused of plotting Theophilos's overthrow. He fled to the caliph Mamun (qq.v.), but Theophilos sent John (VII) Grammatikos (q.v.) to recall him in 830. As *domestikos ton scholon* (q.v.) he served Theophilos faithfully, dying in 838 of wounds received at the battle of Dazimon (q.v.).

MANUEL I KOMNENOS. Emperor (q.v.) from 1143–1180. Manuel was a great admirer of the West. He married two western princesses (Bertha of Sulzbach [q.v.] and Maria of Antioch), awarded civil and military posts to Latins, and even participated in knightly tournaments. Despite this, the Second Crusade posed a threat to Constantinople (q.v.) in 1147, the same year Roger II of Sicily attacked Corinth and Thebes (qq.v.). His foreign policy was far-reaching, and ultimately overreaching. In alliance with Conrad III (q.v.) he invaded Italy (q.v.) in 1155–1157. The invasion not only failed, but Conrad III's successor, Frederick I Barbarossa (q.v.), broke the alliance when Manuel's support of the Lombard League stymied Frederick's own interests in Italy. Frederick and Manuel also competed for influence in Hungary (q.v.), with Manuel gaining ascendancy by putting Bela III (q.v.) on the throne. His solution to Venetian commercial dominance was to arrest the Venetians within the empire and confiscate their property (1171). Venice (q.v.) nursed a grudge that was repaid in 1204 when the Venetian-led Fourth Crusade conquered Constantinople (qq.v.). Until 1176 Manuel maintained a potent Byzantine threat against Armenian Cilicia, the Seljuks in Asia Minor, and Crusader Antioch (qq.v.). After 1176 when he was defeated by the Seljuks at the battle of Myriokephalon (q.v.), Manuel's foreign policy was too ambitious to be sustained by Byzantium's limited resources.

MANUEL II PALAIOLOGOS. Emperor (q.v.) from 1391–1425. Prior to his accession, from 1382–1387, he vainly attempted to defend Thessalonike against the Ottomans (qq.v.). Other humiliations followed. The year John V (q.v.) died, the first year of Manuel's reign (1391), he was forced to join Bayezid I (q.v.) on an Ottoman campaign along the coast of the Black Sea to Sinope (qq.v.). From 1399–1403 he journeyed to Venice (q.v.), Paris, and London, seeking help against the Ottomans. Ironically, it was Timur (q.v.) who inadvertently aided Byzantium (q.v.) by defeating Bayezid I at the battle of Ankara (q.v.) in 1402. The respite allowed Manuel to refortify the Hexamilion (q.v.) in 1415. However, with the accession of Murad II (q.v.) in 1421, the lull since 1402 (which had extended through the reigns of Musa and Mehmed I [qq.v.]) ended. Murad II unsuccessfully attacked Thessalonike and Constantinople (q.v.), then brushed past the Hexamilion (1423) to ravage the Morea (q.v.). Manuel II made peace with the sultan (q.v.) in 1424, and he died the following year.

MANUEL III KOMNENOS. Emperor of Trebizond (qq.v.) from 1390 –1416. Threatened by Ottoman sultan Bayezid I (qq.v.), Manuel joined forces with Bayezid's foe Timur (q.v.), thereby saving Trebizond from both the Mongols and the Ottomans (qq.v.). Bayezid's defeat and capture by Timur at the battle of Ankara (q.v.) in 1402 was as beneficial to Manuel III as it was to Manuel II Palaiologos (q.v.). For the remainder of his reign, Manuel III was caught up in the commercial rivalry between Venice (q.v.), an ally of Trebizond, and Genoa (q.v.).

MANUEL ANGELOS. See **THEODORE KOMNENOS DOUKAS.**

MANUEL KANTAKOUZENOS. See **MOREA.**

MARCELLINUS COMES. Sixth-century Latin chronicler who served on the official staff of Justinian I (q.v.), earning the title of *comes* (q.v.). His chronicle (q.v.) continues the work of Jerome (q.v.), covering the years 379–518; it was later extended to 534. It concentrates on affairs in the East. His account of the Nika Revolt (q.v.) may reflect the way it was viewed by Justinian's court, e.g., ignoring popular dissatisfaction in favor of the idea that it was a result of a conspiracy by the nephews of Anastasios I (q.v.).

MARCIAN. Emperor (q.v.) from 450–457. A capable soldier promoted by the barbarian general Aspar (q.v.), his reign was a reaction to the pro-Monophysite policy of Theodosios II (qq.v.), whose sister Pulcheria (q.v.) he married. Marcian called the Council of Chalcedon (q.v.) in 451, which overturned the decrees of the "Robber" Council of Ephesus (q.v.). Marcian's refusal to pay Attila (q.v.) provoked the Huns to invade Italy (qq.v.); Attila withdrew in 452 after negotiating with Pope Leo I (q.v.). When Marcian died, Aspar (q.v.) chose Leo (I) as emperor.

MARDAITES. Independent Christian (most likely Monophysite or Monothelite [qq.v.]) tribe living in eastern Asia Minor (q.v.) along the border between Byzantium and Arab Syria (qq.v.). In 677 Byzantium hired them to attack Syria (q.v.), forcing Muawiya (q.v.) to abandon the siege of Constantinople (q.v.). By treaty with Abd al-Malik, Justinian II (qq.v.) resettled many of them in the theme of Kibyrrhaiotai (qq.v.) and elsewhere in the empire. Maslama (q.v.) resettled the remainder in Syria in 707.

MARGARITONE. See **ISAAC KOMNENOS; WILLIAM II.**

MARIA OF ALANIA. Daughter of Bagrat IV of Georgia (q.v.), called "Alania" by the Byzantines. She married Michael VII Doukas (q.v.) ca. 1071, an example of the close political and cultural ties between Byzantium and Georgia (qq.v.) in the 10th century. Her beauty was famous, as was her usefulness to Nikephoros III (q.v.) whose offer of marriage, after Michael VII's downfall, she could hardly refuse. In 1081 she aided Alexios (I) Komnenos (q.v.), warning him in time of the discovery of their plot to revolt. However, her efforts to use the Komneni to advance the rights of her son, Constantine Doukas (q.v.), who was betrothed to Anna Komnene (q.v.), failed.

MARIA OF ANTIOCH. See **MANUEL I KOMNENOS.**

MARICA, BATTLE OF. See **MURAD I.**

MARKELLOS THE AKOIMETOS. See **AKOIMETOI.**

MARK THE DEACON. See **PORPHYRIOS OF GAZA.**

MARMARA, SEA OF. The sea's ancient name was *Propontis,* Greek for "fore-sea," referring to the fact that the Sea of Marmara precedes the Black Sea (q.v.). The island of Marmara (ancient *Prokonnesos*) is the source of its more recent name. Constantinople (q.v.) extends into the Sea of Marmara at a point where the sea meets the Bosporos (q.v.). To the south, the Sea of Marmara connects to the Aegean Sea via the Hellespont (qq.v.).

MARONITES. Christian Arabs (q.v.) of Lebanon whose church goes back at least to John Maron, a bishop of the seventh century. The Maronites may have separated over their support of Monotheletism (q.v.), despite its condemnation at the Sixth Ecumenical Council (680–681). In any case, by the 12th century they returned to Orthodoxy (q.v.), accepting the authority of the papacy (q.v.), and supporting the Crusader conquest of the Holy Land.

MARTIN I. Pope (q.v.) from 649–653 who in 649 condemned Constans II's (q.v.) edict (*Typos*) that forbade any discussion about Monotheletism (q.v.), indeed any discussion about Christ's divine energies and wills. As a result of the pope's action, Constans II sought to depose and arrest him. Constans was able to do so in 653, when the pope was charged with supporting Olympios, the rebel exarch of Ravenna (qq.v.). The senate in Constantinople (qq.v.) found Martin guilty of high treason, and Constans II exiled him to Cherson (q.v.) in 654. He died there a year later.

MARTIN IV. *See* **CHARLES OF ANJOU.**

MARTINA. Empress, niece, and second wife of Herakleios (q.v.). The marriage was widely regarded as incestuous. Popular opinion was incensed to discover, after Herakleios's death in February 641, that his will made her co-ruler with both her son Heraklonas and stepson Constantine III (qq.v.). When Constantine III died an untimely death in May of 641, after a reign of barely three months, Martina became the real power behind the throne. This provoked opposition from the senate and army (qq.v.), resulting in the revolt of Valentinos Arsakuni (q.v.), an event that produced Martina's downfall in September 641. Martina and Heraklonas were deposed; his nose was cut off, and her tongue was slit. Then they were banished to Rhodes (q.v.). This was the first instance of mutilation being used as a sign that the victim was unfit to hold office.

MARTYRION (MARTYRIUM). A shrine that shelters the grave of a martyr, or which marks a holy site connected to the life of Christ, or to the life of a saint. *Martyria* built by Constantine I (q.v.) in the Holy Land were in the form of great sanctuaries, each typically consisting of a basilica (q.v.) attached to a separate structure covering the holy site. Constantine's Church of St. Peter, erected ca. 319–322 in Rome (q.v.), had the *martyrion* within the basilica itself.

MARTYROPOLIS. Like Amida and Edessa (qq.v.), in the fifth and sixth centuries Martyropolis was one of the great frontier fortresses beyond the Euphrates River (q.v.). The Persian king Kavad (qq.v.) captured it in 502 and held it for several years. Justinian I's (q.v.) rebuilding of its fortifications was of little help, for in 589 the city was betrayed to Chosroes II (q.v.). It changed hands again, before the Persians seized it from 602–622. After the Arabs (q.v.) captured it in 640, Martyropolis no longer played much of a role in Byzantine affairs, despite brief occupations by John Kourkouas (q.v.) in 942, and by George Maniakes (q.v.) in 1032.

MARY OF EGYPT. Fifth-century desert saint whose *vita* (q.v.) was written by Sophronios, patriarch of Jerusalem (qq.v.). After living a dissolute life in Alexandria (q.v.), she is said to have been converted in Jerusalem by an icon (qq.v.) of the *theotokos* (q.v.). She spent 17 grueling years in the desert as a hermit (q.v.), for which she is depicted in art in tattered clothes, proudly emaciated, and covered with sores.

MASLAMA. Brilliant Arab general who launched the second great onslaught on Constantinople (the first was by Muawiya [q.v.]). He invaded Asia Minor (q.v.) in 715–717, besieging Constantinople (q.v.) in 717–718. This bold stroke, which occurred at the peak of Umayyad (q.v.) aggression against Byzantium (q.v.), was aided by the anarchy in Byzantium on the eve of Leo III's (q.v.) accession. With the aid of Greek fire (q.v.) and the timely intervention of Bulgar khan Tervel (qq.v.), Maslama was forced to lift the siege on 15 August 718.

MASTER OF THE OFFICES. *See* **MAGISTER OFFICIORUM.**

MASUD I. *See* **SULTANATE OF RUM.**

MASUDI, AL. Arab historian and geographer (died 956). His *Meadows of Gold and Mines of Gems* is a world history from the Creation to 947. It is also filled with information about the culture of the peoples he visited in a lifetime of travel in Africa and the Near East to India (qq.v.). He shows great familiarity with the history, geography, and institutions of Byzantium (qq.v.), and great interest in Byzantine-Arab relations. He is also familiar with Byzantium's relations with other neighboring peoples, e.g., the Khazars and Paulicians (qq.v.).

MATASUNTHA. *See* **GERMANOS; VITIGES.**

MATHEMATICS. *See* **SCIENCE.**

MATTHEW I KANTAKOUZENOS. Co-emperor with John V (q.v.) from 1353–1357; eldest son of John VI Kantakouzenos (q.v.). His career illustrates the internal strife that weakened the Byzantine state during the mid-14th century. Matthew emerged from the civil war of 1341–1347 with some territory to rule in Thrace (q.v.), which included Adrianople (q.v.). When John V besieged Adrianople in 1352, Matthew appealed to his father, who obtained help from Ottoman sultan Orhan (qq.v.). John VI then pressured John V to make Matthew co-emperor (1353). However, the following year John VI Kantakouzenos was forced to abdicate and Matthew's relations with John V turned into open warfare With his father gone, Matthew found his position weakened. In 1357 he was captured by the Serbs (q.v.) and turned over to John V, who forced him to renounce the title of co-emperor. After this Matthew went to the Morea (q.v.), which he ruled until 1380, despite John V's attempts to depose him.

MATTHEW OF EDESSA. His *Chronicle* (q.v.) is the most important Armenian source for the First Crusade (q.v.), covering the years 952–1136. The focus is on events in northern Syria and Cilicia (qq.v.), including Crusader relations with Byzantium (q.v.).

MAURICE. Emperor (q.v.) from 582–602 whose reign was both a transition and retrenchment from the era of Justinian I (q.v.). Justinian I's conquests in the West, reduced by 582, were reorganized into the exarchates of Ravenna and Carthage (qq.v.). His military efforts against the Chosroes II (q.v.) were halted by the rebellion that erupted when Maurice replaced Philippikos with Priskos (qq.v.) in 588. This produced a mutiny not quelled until 590. The situation was saved in 590 when a civil war erupted in Persia (q.v.), and Chosroes II was forced to flee to Byzantine territory. Maurice intervened to help Chosroes II regain his throne in 591. Peace with Persia in that year allowed Maurice to concentrate on the Avar (q.v.) threat to the Balkan Peninsula (q.v.) for the remainder of his reign. Despite the defeat of his general Komentiolos by the Avars in 598, Maurice was making progress against them when he was violently overthrown in 602.

MAUROPOUS, JOHN. Writer; teacher; metropolitan of Euchaita (qq.v.); courtier during the reign of Constantine IX (q.v.). He was part of a circle of intellectuals that included Michael Psellos, John VIII Xiphilinos, and Constantine III Leichoudes (qq.v.). His letters, sermons, and poetry offer numerous insights into the religious and political events of the 11th century. His speeches are particularly important, e.g., the one he gave in 1047 to trumpet the reforms of Constantine IX. As someone who perfected the art of surviving at court by mellifluous speeches, he was perfectly suited to teach that other great master of rhetoric, Michael Psellos.

MAXENTIUS. Son of Maximian (q.v.), proclaimed emperor (q.v.) in 306 (augustus [q.v.] only in 307), the same year Constantine I (q.v.) was proclaimed by his troops, ending the tetrarchy (q.v.). Eventually Maxentius controlled Italy and Africa (qq.v.), until defeated by Constantine I in 312 at the Battle of the Milvian Bridge (q.v.). Eusebios of Caesarea (q.v.) describes Maxentius as a pagan enemy of God who terrorized Rome (q.v.).

MAXIMIAN. Augustus (q.v.) of the West (286–305) and member of the tetrarchy (q.v.), governing from Milan (qq.v.). A fellow soldier and friend of Diocletian (q.v.), who chose him to be augustus, his victories along the Rhine (q.v.) were overshadowed by the loss of Britain (q.v.) to Carausius (286–293). His caesar Constantius Chlorus (qq.v.), father of Constantine I the Great, recovered the province. Forced into retirement in 305 by Diocletian, he was succeeded as augustus of the West by Constantius Chlorus. When Constantius died in 306 Constantine was recognized as augustus in Britain by his father's troops, while in Italy (q.v.) Maximian came out of retirement in 306 to promote his son Maxentius (q.v.) as a rival to Severus (q.v.). Maximian switched his support to Constantine, and he was forced into retirement again (308), only to revolt unsuccessfully against Constantine in 310. Constantine apparently put him to death in the same year.

MAXIMIAN. *See* RAVENNA.

MAXIMINUS DAIA. Licinius's (q.v.) major opponent in the East during the civil wars that erupted after Diocletian (q.v.) retired from the tetrarchy (q.v.) in 305. Diocletian appointed Maximinus caesar (q.v.), but Maximinus's troops illegally declared him augustus (q.v.) in 310. He was a fanatical pagan who continued the Great Persecution (q.v.) after Galerius's edict of toleration in 311. Licinius vanquished Maximinus in 313.

MAXIMOS OF EPHESUS. Fourth-century Neoplatonist (q.v.) philosopher who followed the teaching of Iamblichos (q.v.). He became a mentor to Julian (q.v.), despite his many critics who claimed he was a charlatan who faked miraculous-looking tricks. Mazimos's access to Julian allowed him to amass a personal fortune, much of which he lost after Julian's death in 363.

MAXIMOS THE CONFESSOR. Theologian who led the struggle against Monotheletism (q.v.), whose works had a great influence on Byzantine mystics, and on western theologians. His opposition to Monotheletism took the form of organizing church synods in North Africa (q.v.) in 646, and supporting Pope Martin I (q.v.) in 649, for which Maximos was imprisoned, tortured, and exiled. He died in exile in Lazika (q.v.) in 662. His theological works, which were themselves influenced by the mysticism of pseudo-Dionysios the Areopagite (q.v.), had an influence on the ninth-century western philosopher Johannes Scotus Erigena, as well as on many western theologians, including Bernard of Clairvaux, Thomas Aquinas (q.v.), Robert Grosseteste, Meister Eckhart, and Nicolas of Cusa.

MAXIMUS. Spanish general under Gratian (q.v.) who was proclaimed emperor in Gaul (qq.v.) in 383. From 383–388 he ruled Gaul, Spain, and Britain (qq.v.). The weakness of the young emperor Valentinian II (q.v.) prompted Maximus to invade Italy (q.v.) in 387, forcing the emperor to flee to Thessalonike (q.v.). With the help of Arbogast, Theodosios I (qq.v.) intervened to suppress the revolt, after which Maximus was executed.

MAZDAK. Founder of Mazdakism, a communistic movement among the peasantry of Persia (q.v.) that originated in the late fifth century. It threatened the power of the Persian nobility and of the Zoroastrian (q.v.) clergy. Mazdak preached that all men were equal, and that all property should be held equally. Until he consolidated his power, the Persian king Kavad (q.v.) supported Mazdak as a counterweight to the power of the nobles and Zoroastrian priests. Later Kavad suppressed the movement, killing Mazdak and his compatriots (ca. 528).

MEDICINE. Byzantine medicine was built on the foundation of ancient medicine, including Galen (q.v.) and Hippocrates, so much so that many early Byzantine texts are little more than edited encyclopedias of ancient knowledge (e.g., the work of Julian's physician Oribasios [qq.v.] summarizes Galen). Nevertheless, even the encyclopedists were hardly mere copyists. For example, the work of Alexander of Tralles (q.v.) includes some original ideas on pharmacology, and Aetius of Amida's sixth-century encyclopedia of medicine interprets Galen's theory of drug therapy by degrees. Such works transmitted ancient medicine far beyond the borders of Byzantium (q.v.). Arab doctors used the works of Paul of Aegina, especially the section on surgery in his *Epitome.* The work of Nicholas Myrepsos, court physician to John III Vatatzes (q.v.), was used as a textbook on pharmacology at the University of Paris until 1651. Byzantine hospitals in the major cities of the empire included a variety of specialists (some of whom were women doctors), e.g., in surgery, anesthesiology, orthopedics, gynecology and obstetrics, and epidemiology. Educated persons took an interest in medicine and disease, as seen in Prokopios of Caesarea's (q.v.) description of the plague. Medicine was especially fashionable among 12th-century intellectuals, including Anna Komnene (q.v.), who writes respectfully of the doctors who administered to her dying father. Having said this, Byzantine literature is not without its portrayal of doctors as unscrupulous quacks. Moreover, amulets and other forms of magic, as well as healing icons and holy men, were patronized as forms of alternative medicine.

MEDIKION, MONASTERY OF. *See* **OLYMPOS, MOUNT.**

MEDITERRANEAN SEA. World's largest inland sea, around which the Roman Empire was constructed. Byzantium (q.v.) inherited this geographical focus, maintaining it until the naval expansion of the Vandals and Arabs (qq.v.). During the period of the Crusades (q.v.), Byzantine economic control over the eastern Mediterranean was challenged by the Italian maritime states, especially by rivals Genoa and Venice (qq.v.). Venetian spoils resulting from the Fourth Crusade's conquest of Constantinople (qq.v.) in 1204 consisted largely of islands and ports that gave Venice commercial hegemony in the eastern Mediterranean until the Treaty of Nymphaion (q.v.).

MEGAS. In the first part of a title it means "supreme," or "grand." Alexios I Komnenos (q.v.) introduced its use for the important office of *megas doux* who commanded the navy (q.v.). Loukas Notaras and Alexios Apokaukos (qq.v.) held this post. The 11th century also saw the office of *megas domestikos* (supreme military commander) replace that of *domestikos ton scholon* (q.v.). The *megas logothetes* (grand logothete) administered the entire civil administration.

MEHMED I. Ottoman sultan (qq.v.) from 1413–1421. He emerged victorious in the civil war that erupted after the capture of Bayezid I (q.v.) in 1402 at the battle of Ankyra (q.v.). Manuel II (q.v.) provided Mehmed with aid against Musa (q.v.) in 1411–1413, which insured good relations with Byzantium (q.v.) while Mehmet consolidated his power. Manuel II was even able to rebuild the Hexamilion (q.v.) that guarded the Morea (q.v.). However, the respite came to an abrupt end with the accession of Murad II (q.v.).

MEHMED II. Ottoman sultan (qq.v.) from 1451–1481, known as "the Conqueror" for his conquest of Constantinople (q.v.) on 29 May 1453. The preparation for this began in the reign of his father Murad II (q.v.), but his own preparations were extensive, beginning in 1452 with the construction of the fortresses Rumeli Hisar and Anadolu Hisar to control maritime traffic on the Bosporos (q.v.). After the conquest of Constantinople he chose Gennadios (II) as patriarch (qq.v.), giving him authority over the self-governing community (*millet,* in Turkish) of Christians. His conquest of Mistra (q.v.) in 1460 and Trebizond (q.v.) in 1461 snuffed out the last remnants of Byzantium (q.v.).

MELANIA THE YOUNGER. Saint who was born in Rome (q.v.) in 383 and died in 439 in the monastery she built on the Mount of Olives in Jerusalem (q.v.). A wealthy aristocrat by birth, she and her husband sold their vast estates in 406 and embraced the monastic life. Her *vita* (q.v.) illustrates how attractive were the ideals of asceticism (q.v.) in the West. Even Augustine (q.v.) considered leaving all for the monastic life (*Confessions, Book* Six, Chapter 14). Also see **ATHENAIS-EUDOKIA.**

MELETIAN SCHISMS. The schisms involved two different persons named Meletios. The first was Meletios, bishop of Lycopolis in Egypt (q.v.), who was excommunicated by the archbishop Peter of Alexandria (qq.v.) for being too lenient on Christians who had compromised the faith in 306 during the Great Persecution of Diocletian (qq.v.). Twenty years later Athanasios (q.v.) was a staunch opponent of any compromise with the Meletians. The second Meletian schism involved Meletios, Orthodox bishop of Antioch (qq.v.), who was deposed in 360 in favor of Paulinus, favored by an Orthodox splinter party that followed the teachings of Eusthathios of Antioch (q.v.). Meletios was finally rehabilitated after the death of Valens (q.v.) and presided over the Second Ecumenical Council at Constantinople (qq.v.) in 381.

MELINGOI. *See* **EZERITAI; PELOPONNESOS; SLAVS.**

MELITENE. City in eastern Cappadocia (q.v.); important fortress along the Taurus (q.v.) range bordering northern Mesopotamia (q.v.). From Melitene the great roads to Sebasteia and Caesarea (qq.v.) gave access to Asia Minor (q.v.) for foreign invaders, which explains why Melitene was captured by the Persians (q.v.) in 575 and by the Arabs (q.v.) in 656. Fought over thereafter, it returned to Arab hands from 757–934. Among the famous emirs (q.v.) of Melitene was Umar (q.v.), who died fighting in Asia Minor in 863. In 934 the city fell to John Kourkouas (q.v.). It was sacked by the Seljuks (q.v.) in 1058 and occupied by the Seljuks after the battle of Mantzikert (q.v.) in 1071.

MELKITES. The term means "royalists," referring to those Christians in Arab-dominated Syria and Egypt (qq.v.) who followed Orthodox doctrine as defined by the Council of Chalcedon (q.v.). They were called royalists as a term of scorn by their Monophysite (q.v.) neighbors because their Orthodoxy (q.v.) was that of the imperial capital in Constantinople (q.v.). One of the more famous Melkites was Eutychios, a 10th-century Melkite patriarch of Alexandria (qq.v.) who authored a chronicle (q.v.) from Adam to 938.

MELO. *See* **ARGYROS; ITALY.**

MENANDER PROTECTOR. Historian of the reigns of Justin II and Tiberios I (qq.v.). His *History* covered the years 558–582, continuing the work of Agathias (q.v.). The work survives in numerous fragments, many of them in *Souda* (q.v.).

MENAS. Saint martyred by Diocletian (q.v.) in 296 and national hero of Christians in Egypt (q.v.). His cult center was at Abu Mina (q.v.), where pilgrims could obtain small clay "Menas flasks." Mass-produced beginning in the sixth century, they were used by pilgrims to transport holy water from his shrine, as well as oil from the lamps that burned over Menas's grave.

MENAS. Patriarch of Constantinople (qq.v.) from 536 to 552, perhaps best remembered for his support of Justinian I's edict condemning the Three Chapters (q.v.). For this he was excommunicated twice by Pope Vigilius (q.v.)

MENOLOGION. A *codex* (q.v.) comprising a catalog *(logos)* of brief biographies of saints, arranged in the order that they appear in the church calendar of fixed feasts, the *synaxarion* (q.v.). The earliest *menologia* date from the ninth century. By the 11th century, the standard collection of lives was that of Symeon Metaphrastes (q.v.). Each saint's biography, or life (*vita* [q.v.]), is placed into one of 12 sections for each of the 12 months, in chronological order according to the annual festival day of the saint. *Menologia* were illustrated with scenes from the saintly *vitae,* and none more beautifully than the *Menologion* of Basil II (q.v.), which has 430 miniatures, among them some of the finest examples of miniature painting at its zenith.

MERIAMLIK. *See* **DOMED BASILICA; SELEUKEIA; THEKLA.**

MESARITES, NICHOLAS. Writer; bishop of Ephesus (qq.v.) in the early 13th century. His writings are of particular importance with regard to the political and ecclesiastical situation in the decades after the Fourth Crusade's conquest of Constantinople (qq.v.) in 1204. He describes conditions in Nicaea (q.v.) as well as in Constantinople, both of which he visited.

MESAZON. The term appears in the 11th–12th centuries to designate a high official (e.g., a *megas logothetes* [q.v.]) who was the chief administrator of the empire. Constantine III Leichoudes (q.v.) was the first person to hold this position. Demetrios Kydones (q.v.) also held it, as did Loukas Notaras (q.v).

MESE. The magnificent central (*mese* means "middle") boulevard of Constantinople (q.v.), running through the center of the city, lined on each side with porticoes. It began at the Milion, the milestone from which all distances in the empire were measured, situated in front of

Hagia Sophia (q.v.). It traversed the major forums of the capital, including the Forum of Constantine and the Forum of Theodosios (I). Just past the Forum of Theodosios, the *mese* forked into two main branches. One branch continued on in the same direction to the Gate of Pege, while the other turned southwest to the Golden Gate. When the emperor returned from campaign, his *adventus* (q.v.) began at the Golden Gate and traversed the *mese*.

MESEMBRIA. City and trading center on the east coast of the Black Sea (q.v.) that included an important commercial port and naval base. Krum (q.v.) captured it in 812, seizing a considerable amount of Greek fire (q.v.). Recovered around the mid-ninth century, it remained in Byzantine hands until it was annexed by the Second Bulgarian Empire. Amadeo of Savoy (q.v.) recaptured it in 1367, along with Sozopolis (q.v.), returning both to John V Palaiologos (q.v.). It remained in Byzantine possession until 1452, when Constantine XI (q.v.), unable to defend it properly, gave it to Janos Hunyadi (q.v.). The Ottomans (q.v.) took it in February of the following year, on the eve of their great siege of Constantinople (q.v.).

MESOPOTAMIA. The term in Greek means "land between the rivers," referring to the frontier region between the Tigris and Euphrates (q.v.) rivers. Persia and Byzantium (qq.v.) battled each other from the third to the early seventh centuries, mostly besieging and ceding fortified places like Daras and Nisibis (qq.v.). The futility of centuries of Mesopotamian warfare is illustrated by Julian's (q.v.) fruitless campaign in 363.

MESSALIANISM. Heretical movement that appeared in Asia Minor (q.v.) in the fourth century, and which was condemned at the Council of Ephesus (q.v.) in 431. Messalians were charismatics who challenged the hierarchical church with its priesthood and sacraments, believing instead in a salvation based on individual purification, charismatic experience, and prayer. After the seventh century, the term became one of general reproach, meant to tarnish any charismatic sect that denied the church and its sacraments. The term could also be used to attack forms of charismatic monasticism (q.v.) within the church. For example, Barlaam attacked Palamas (qq.v.) in a work entitled *Against the Messalians,* in which he asserts that Hesychasm (q.v.) is a form of Messalianism.

MESSINA. City on the coast of northeast Sicily (q.v.), strategically situated opposite the mainland of Italy (q.v.) to control the Strait of Messina. Conquered by the Arabs (q.v.) in 843, no Byzantine attempt to retake it was fully rewarded until 1038 when George Maniakes (q.v.) recaptured Messina and Syracuse (q.v.). However, in 1060 the Normans under future Roger I (qq.v.) began their invasion of Sicily, conquering Messina the following year. Messina also played a role in the Sicilian Vespers (q.v.), for it was at Messina that Charles I Anjou's (q.v.) fleet was destroyed in 1282, dashing his hopes of conquering Constantinople (q.v.).

METEORA. Group of monasteries in Thessaly (q.v.), situated "in air" *(meteora),* so to speak, high atop isolated pillars of rock. The oldest monastery, the Great Meteoron, was founded by Athanasios of Meteora (q.v.) in the late 14th century. After Symeon Urosh, son of Stefan Urosh III Dechanski (q.v.) conquered Epiros (q.v.) and Thessaly in 1359, he became a major patron of the monasteries. In the 16th century they numbered as many as 13, in addition to numerous other smaller settlements.

METHODIOS. *See* **CYRIL AND METHODIOS.**

METHODIOS I. Patriarch of Constantinople (qq.v.) from 843–847. He worked with Theodora and Theoktistos (qq.v.) to restore the veneration of icons (q.v.) in 843. His moderation toward former Iconoclasts (q.v.) infuriated the monks of the Stoudios Monastery (q.v.), some of whom Methodios excommunicated. His successor as patriarch, Ignatios (q.v.), was more conciliatory toward the Stoudites.

METOCHITES, THEODORE. Scholar and statesman during the reign of Andronikos II (q.v.). When he came to the attention of the emperor (q.v.) he had already authored a number of philosophical, scientific, and literary works. In 1298 he negotiated arrangements for the marriage of Simonis to Stefan Urosh II Milutin (qq.v.), and the accompanying peace treaty with Serbia (q.v.). The abdication of Andronikos II ended the career of Metochites. He spent his remaining years in the Chora monastery in Constantinople (qq.v.), which he restored magnificently and which contains the donor-portrait of him in mosaic (q.v.); he is portrayed in an elaborate gold and white turban, kneeling before Christ, to whom he offers a model of the restored church.

METROPOLITAN. The church office of metropolitan-bishop illustrates how church organization paralleled that of the state. Every city had its bishop (q.v.), every province its metropolitan (q.v.) who resided in the capital *(metropolis)* of the province. Thus, the metropolitan-bishop had a rank below a patriarch (q.v.), but above an ordinary bishop. The metropolitan-bishop presided over the annual provincial synod (q.v.), and had the power to appoint new bishops within the province.

MICHAEL I KEROULARIOS. Patriarch of Constantinople (qq.v.) from 1043–1058 who was a chief participant in the church schism of 1054 (q.v.). In 1052 Keroularios closed down Latin churches in Constantinople because they used *azyma* (q.v.), i.e., unleavened bread, in the Eucharist (q.v.). This was in response to the Norman (q.v.) closure of Byzantine churches in southern Italy (q.v.), with papal approval. When Pope Leo IX (qq.v.) complained about Keroularios's use of the title "ecumenical," the stage was set. The pope sent an embassy to Constantinople (q.v.) led by his secretary Humbert (q.v.). Humbert's impetuosity led to mutual excommunications that inaugurated the church schism of 1054 (q.v.). As a result, Constantine IX's (q.v.) pro-papal policy, directed by Argyros (q.v.) against the Normans of southern Italy (qq.v.), lay in shambles. In one sense, it proved to be a personal victory for Keroularios, who was pleased to see imperial support of the papacy destroyed. Moreover, Keroularios now knew about the Donation of Constantine (q.v.), and he redefined patriarchal authority in terms comparable to the authority claimed by the papacy (q.v.). When Constantine IX died the following year (1055), Keroularios's victory seemed complete. The patriarch emerged from these events as the most powerful personality in Constantinople, who attracted enormous popular support.

MICHAEL I KOMNENOS DOUKAS. *See* **EPIROS, DESPOTATE OF.**

MICHAEL I RANGABE. Emperor (811–813) who succeeded Staurakios (q.v.). Michael I came under the influence of patriarch Nikephoros I (qq.v.) and, after the end of the Moechian controversy in 809, of Theodore of Stoudios (q.v.). Emperor Nikephoros I's (q.v.) former fiscal management became a thing of the past as Michael increased state donations to monasteries and churches. Most important was the change in Byzantine diplomacy with respect to Charlemagne (q.v.). Replacing hostility with accommodation, Michael I recognized Charlemagne's imperial title (*basileus* [q.v.]) in 812; in return he received back Byzantine territory along the coast of the Adriatic (q.v.) that Charlemagne had seized. Defeated by the Bulgars (q.v.) in 813, Michael was forced to abdicate in favor of Leo V (q.v.).

MICHAEL I THE SYRIAN. Author (died 1199) of the most important Syriac world chronicle (q.v.), which describes events from the Creation to 1195; Jacobite patriarch of Antioch (qq.v.). The chronicle preserves lost Syriac sources, in addition to extant ones, e.g., John of Ephesus and (pseudo-) Dionysios of Tell Mahre (qq.v.). For the 12th century the *Chronicle* is particularly important for Byzantine relations with the Crusader states.

MICHAEL II THE AMORION. Emperor (q.v.) from 820–829 who founded the Amorion (q.v.) dynasty (820–867). His reign began with the stain of Michael's assassination of Leo V (q.v.) in front of the high altar of Hagia Sophia (q.v.). Almost immediately the revolt (820–823) of Thomas the Slav (q.v.) occurred, which Michael suppressed with the aid of Omurtag (q.v.). The Arab invasion of Sicily (qq.v.) began in 827, about the same time as another Arab force invaded Crete (q.v.). Michael II was a moderate Iconoclast (q.v.), but his son Theophilos (q.v.) proved quite the opposite.

MICHAEL II KOMNENOS DOUKAS. *See* **EPIROS, DESPOTATE OF; JOHN I DOUKAS.**

MICHAEL III. Emperor (q.v.) from 842–867. He was not the incompetent drunkard portrayed in historical sources loyal to the memory of Basil I (q.v.), the man who assassinated and succeeded him. However, he spent his reign under the influence of powerful ministers. His mother Theodora and the eunuch Theoktistos (qq.v.) restored veneration of icons (q.v.), governing as regents until 856, when he overthrew them. Thereafter, until 866, his uncle Bardas (q.v.) was the power behind the throne. It was Bardas who organized the university at the Magnaura (q.v.) and who worked with the Patriarch Photios (q.v.) to facilitate the Moravian mission of Cyril and Methodius (qq.v.), as well as the baptism of Bulgarian khan Boris I (qq.v.). Byzantine military forces under Petronas (q.v.) won notable successes against the Arabs (q.v.), including a victory in 863 over Umar, emir of Melitene (qq.v.), that avenged Arab victories over

Michael's father Theophilos, and he inaugurated a new period of Byzantine military supremacy along the eastern frontier. Ankyra (q.v.), destroyed under Mutasim (q.v.), was rebuilt, the fortifications of Nicaea (q.v.) were restored, and in 860 the first Rus attack on Constantinople (qq.v.) was fended off. Such were the important accomplishments of the once reviled emperor.

MICHAEL IV AUTOREANOS. Patriarch of Constantinople at Nicaea (qq.v.) from 1208–1212. The death of John X Kamateros (q.v.) in 1206 left the post vacant, providing the opportunity for Michael's appointment. Almost immediately Michael crowned and anointed Theodore I Lascaris (q.v.) at Nicaea as sole emperor of Byzantium (qq.v.). These actions, four years after the conquest of Constantinople by the Fourth Crusade (q.v.), gave further legitimacy to Nicaea's claim to be the only true Byzantium, though in exile.

MICHAEL IV PAPHLAGON. Emperor (q.v.) from 1034–1041. He gained access to the court through the influence of his brother John the Orphanotrophos and the empress Zoe (qq.v.), Michael's lover and murderer of Romanos III (q.v.). The influence of John the Orphanotrophos at court was opposed by the aristocracy (q.v.), and harsh taxation sparked the revolt of Peter Deljan (q.v.). Stefan Voislav's (q.v.) revolt and the reversal of George Maniakes's (q.v.) conquests (in 1040) in Sicily (q.v.) also contributed to a sense of discontent. Michael IV's epilepsy made it increasingly difficult for him to govern. He retired to a monastery in 1041 and was succeeded by his nephew Michael V (q.v.).

MICHAEL V KALAPHATES. Emperor (q.v.) from 1041–1042. His father was a caulker (*Kalaphates* [q.v.]), hence the popular epithet he acquired. His mother was the sister of Michael IV (q.v.). Zoe (q.v.) was forced to adopt him and make him caesar (q.v.) and heir-apparent prior to Michael IV's death in 1041. Once emperor he banished John the Orphanotrophos (q.v.) and Zoe. Having banished his family, Michael tried to find a base of support in the citizens of Constantinople (q.v.). Instead, their loyalty to Zoe produced a popular revolt in the capital that dethroned Michael V. Psellos (q.v.) provides a chilling, almost surreal, description of the vicious mob that took control of the capital and executed Michael V.

MICHAEL VI STRATIOTIKOS. Emperor (q.v.) from 1056–1057 who was chosen by the advisors of the dying empress Theodora (qq.v.) to succeed her. He was a former palace functionary who conferred honors and gifts upon civil officials, while alienating the army (q.v.), as well as patriarch Michael Keroularios (qq.v.). His disdainful treatment of a delegation of generals led by Isaac (I) Komnenos (q.v.) encouraged Isaac into revolt, forcing Michael VI to abdicate.

MICHAEL VII DOUKAS. Emperor (q.v.) from 1071–1078. He was the son of Constantine X and Eudokia Makrembolitissa (qq.v.), and a pupil of Michael Psellos (q.v.). His reign began in the immediate aftermath of the disastrous battle of Mantzikert (q.v.). Devaluation of the coinage (q.v.) and resulting inflation meant a rise in the price of bread, not helped by Michael's attempt to control the corn trade by making it a state monopoly. Economic unrest, coupled with Turkish raiding in Asia Minor (q.v.), created military revolts, including those of Roussel de Bailleul, Nikephoros Botaneiates, and Nikephoros Bryennios (qq.v.). The revolt of Bryennios succeeded in forcing Michael VII into monastic retirement. Nikephoros III Botaneiates legitimized his usurpation by marrying the wife of Michael VII, Maria of Alania (q.v.).

MICHAEL VIII PALAIOLOGOS. Emperor (q.v.) from 1259–1282, and founder of the Palaiologan dynasty (q.v.). Michael's career had notable triumphs and failures. He began his career as a successful general for John III Vatatzes and Theodore II Laskaris of the Empire of Nicaea (qq.v.), winning an important victory at the battle of Pelagonia (q.v.) in 1259. He reclaimed Constantinople (q.v.) in 1261, bringing to an end the Latin Empire (q.v.). His blinding of co-emperor John IV Laskaris (q.v.) in that same year made him sole emperor, but at the expense of excommunication by Patriarch Arsenios (qq.v.). This produced a schism within the church between the loyal supporters of Arsenios and those who recognized his successor, Joseph I (q.v.). Michael's union of the churches at the Council of Lyons (qq.v.) in 1274 achieved its goal of preventing the planned invasion by Charles I of Anjou (q.v.), who Michael further stymied in the Sicilian Vespers (q.v.). However, his lasting legacy was the spectre of a church and populace disaffected from their emperor over the union of the churches. Church union was repudiated by Michael's immediate successor Andronikos II Palaiologos (q.v.). Nevertheless, the prospect of another church union continued to haunt imperial policy toward the West, and the subsequent union of the churches in 1438–1439 at the Council of Ferrara-Florence (q.v.)

proved just as divisive and fleeting as the church union Michael VIII achieved at Lyons.

MICHAEL IX PALAIOLOGOS. Co-emperor with his father Andronikos II (q.v.) from 1294 until his death in 1320. Had he married Catherine of Courtenay, titular empress (q.v.) of the defunct Latin Empire (q.v.), the western claim to the Byzantine throne would have been solved. However, negotiations for this failed. His subsequent marriage to Rita-Maria of Armenian Cilicia (q.v.) produced the future Andronikos III (q.v.). His military career was checkered. He failed to halt the Turkish advance in Asia Minor (q.v.), ignominiously abandoning Magnesia (q.v.) in 1302. Despite some successes against the Bulgars (q.v.) in 1304, the assassination of Roger de Flor in 1305 by Michael IX's Alan (qq.v.) mercenaries unleashed a rampage by the Catalan Grand Company (q.v.). By 1311 his failed attempts to defend Thrace (q.v.) against the Turks led to his forced retirement in Thessalonike (q.v.).

MICHAEL ITALIKOS. Popular teacher and writer at the Patriarchal School in Constantinople (qq.v.) in the second quarter of the 12th century. The Patriarchal School trained the clergy in theology (q.v.) and related subjects. Michael taught a wide variety of subjects, including the Holy Scriptures, rhetoric, philosophy (qq.v), and mathematics. His patroness at court was Irene Doukaina (q.v.), to whom he wrote a glowing eulogy. In a eulogy to Manuel I (q.v.) he compares the emperor to the sun in a way that suggests a heliocentric conception of the universe (not the typical three-layered scheme of heaven, earth, and hell). Later in his life he became metropolitan of Philippopolis (qq.v.), where he negotiated the passage of the Second Crusade (q.v.) through the city in 1147. He died ca. 1157.

MICHAEL OF EPHESUS. Commentator on Aristotle and Proklos (qq.v.) who lived during the reign of Alexios I Komnenos (q.v.). He was one of the first of a series of commentators on these authors that included Michael Psellos, John Italos, and Eustratios of Nicaea (qq.v.).

MICHAEL SYNKELLOS. Writer (died 846) of hagiography, hymns (qq.v.), homilies, and a treatise on grammar. He was *synkellos* (q.v.) of the patriarch of Jerusalem (qq.v.) and while in Constantinople (q.v.) he was imprisoned by Leo V (q.v.) for being an Iconodule (q.v.). He was imprisoned again by Theophilos (q.v.), who also punished Michael's friends, the brothers Theodore and Theophanes Graptos (qq.v.).

MILAN. Chief city in northern Italy (q.v.), especially in the fourth century when the imperial court resided there. Fourth-century Milan is also known for the so-called Edict of Milan, and for Ambrose (qq.v.), whose tenure as bishop made Milan the spiritual center of the West. Milan declined in importance after 402 when the western emperor Honorios (q.v.) moved the court to Ravenna, in response to Alaric's (qq.v.) invasion of Italy in 401–402. The Huns (q.v.) pillaged Milan in 452, and in 539 during Justinian I's (q.v.) war in Italy it was seriously damaged by the Ostrogoths (q.v.). The Lombards (q.v.) captured it in 569.

MILAN, EDICT OF. *See* **EDICT OF MILAN.**

MILIARESION. *See* **COINAGE.**

MILION. *See* **AUGUSTAION; MESE.**

MILUTIN. *See* **STEPHEN UROSH II MILUTIN.**

MILVIAN BRIDGE, BATTLE OF. Famous battle in Rome (q.v.), where Constantine I the Great (q.v.) defeated his rival Maxentius (q.v.) for control of the West. At the same time he became the imperial protector and promoter of Christianity. According to the Christian writers Eusebios of Caesarea and Lactantius (qq.v.), prior to the battle the Christian God communicated to Constantine (q.v.), prompting him to devise a special battle standard called the *labarum* (q.v.), which Constantine believed won him this victory.

MINISCULE. A Greek script, originating from cursive writing, used to copy manuscripts from the ninth century onward. Its developed form did not separate words and used abbreviations, which allowed more words on a single page, and which essentially made book production (before the age of printing) easier.

MISTRA. Capital of the despotate of the Morea (q.v.) from 1349–1460, comprising a hill below Mount Tayegetos overlooking the plain of Sparta in the Peloponnesos (q.v.). The fortress atop the hill was built by William II Villehardouin (q.v.), who surrendered it to the Byzantines after the battle of Pelagonia (q.v.) in 1259. Thereafter, a city developed within the fortified slopes of the hill below the castle. By the early 15th century Mistra was a center of learning that attracted famous scholars and teachers like Plethon and Chalkokondyles (qq.v.). It surrendered to Mehmet II (q.v.) only in 1460, seven years after the Ottomans conquered Constantinople (qq.v.). Today, its ruined churches, fortress, and palace provide a glimpse into the fading glory of Byzantium's final century.

MOECHIAN CONTROVERSY. The church controversy over the second marriage of Constantine VI (q.v.) that pitted the independent Stoudios monastery against both church and state. The controversy was created when Constantine divorced his wife to marry his mistress Theodote in 795. This was considered adultery *(moechia)* by many in the church, especially by Theodore of Stoudios, Plato of Sakkoudion (qq.v.), and their followers, who were persecuted for opposing the marriage. Patriarch Tarasios (qq.v.), who had reluctantly agreed to the marriage, only reversed his support when Constantine VI was deposed and blinded in 797. The priest (Joseph) who had performed the second marriage was deposed, and Theodore and Plato reconciled with Tarasios. This would have ended the matter had not Nikephoros I (q.v.) called a synod of laymen and clerics in 806 to recognize the marriage. Priest Joseph was received back into the church, and the controversy resumed, with the monks of the Stoudios monastery again leading the opposition. Michael I (q.v.) reversed all this when he came to the throne in 811 by excommunicating Joseph and recalling the Stoudites from exile. This was a triumph for Theodore of Stoudios, who had long struggled to maintain both the independence and influence of the Stoudios monastery.

MOESIA. Roman province (from 29 B.C.) on the lower Danube (q.v.), extending to the Black Sea (q.v.) in what is today Serbia and Bulgaria (qq.v.). It was overrun by the Huns (q.v.) in the fifth century, and lost to the Slavs and Avars (qq.v.) in the seventh century.

MOLDAVIA. Region north of the Danube between the eastern Carpathian Mountains and the Black Sea (q.v.), in what is today eastern Romania. Once part of the Roman province of Dacia, it was overrun successively by the Germans, Huns, and Avars (qq.v.). In the late sixth century it was settled by the Slavs (q.v.). Relations with Byzantium (q.v.) were chiefly in the trade of raw commodities like wax, honey, and wine.

MONASTERY. *See* **KOINOBION; MONASTICISM.**

MONASTICISM. Monasticism began in Egypt (q.v.) with the asceticism (q.v.) of third-century eremites, also called anchorites (qq.v.), as well as monks (from *monachos,* a man who has forsaken society to devote himself to God), who lived in cells (q.v.) in the desert. In the fifth century eremites like Symeon the Stylite the Elder and Daniel the Stylite (qq.v.) became famous in Syria (q.v.). John Moschos (q.v.) collected stories about many of them. In the fourth century Pachomios (q.v.) created the prototype of communal monasticism, the *koinobion* (q.v.), a more developed form of the *lavra* (q.v.). In the same century, Basil the Great (q.v.) created the Long Rules, the enduring organizing principles for Byzantine monasticism, centered around a daily routine of work and prayer. By the fifth century these two chief forms of monasticism, that of the individual ascetic, and of communal *koinobion,* were established. Sometimes these two forms existed together; sometimes they were practiced separately. During the period of Iconoclasm (q.v.), monks proved the greatest defenders of icons (q.v.). After Iconoclasm ended in 843, monasticism experienced a remarkable expansion, fueled by grants of land and the promotion of monks to positions in church and state. Imperial patronage included direct subsidies and exemptions from taxation (such as *exkousseia* [q.v.]). Some emperors (q.v.) became renowned for their support of monasticism. Nikephoros II Phokas (q.v.), for example, supported Athanasios of Athos (q.v.) in founding the Great Lavra on Mount Athos (qq.v). However, monastic estates became so extensive by the 10th century that Nikephoros II tried, unsuccessfully, to limit them. Nowhere did orders develop, as in the West. Monasticism remained administratively fragmented, as compared to the West, and individual monasteries often bore the imprint of the individuals who founded them. Thus, monastic republics like Mount Athos bore no resemblance to the greater size and more centralized administration of Cluny (founded in 910), in French Burgundy. Another difference was how much the inequality of the world was reflected inside Byzantine monasteries, with former aristocrats treated better than poorer monks. The pervasive philanthropy (q.v.) of monastic charitable institutions included hospitals, orphanages, and homes for the aged, even as places of retirement for the aristocracy (q.v.) and for failed political figures. Monasteries were also battlegrounds for important religious movements, e.g., Iconoclasm and Hesychasm (q.v.). Monks wrote hymns, and the *vitae* (q.v.) of saints. Much of Byzantine art and architecture, e.g., manuscript illustration, wall frescoes, and mosaics (qq.v.), were tied to monastic patronage. The golden age of monasticism was actually in the Palaiologan (q.v.) period, as the political and military fortunes of the empire declined. Today, Byzantium continues to live in numerous Byzantine monasteries that still flourish, many of them spectacular in their setting and architecture (e.g., Mount Athos and Meteora [q.v.]).

MONEMVASIA. Fortified island situated close to the southeastern coast of the Peloponnesos (q.v.), accessible from the mainland by a narrow causeway, hence *monemvasia,* meaning "single entrance" in Greek. This Gibralter-like fortress, according to the Chronicle of Monemvasia and pseudo-Sphrantzes (q.v.), claims a date of ca. 582 for its foundation. Presumably the settlement there began as a refuge site for those fleeing from the Slavs (q.v.). Ruins of the small city can still be seen high atop the wall-encircled plateau; it includes the mid-12th century domed octagon Church of Hagia Sophia. Monemvasia was captured by William II Villehardouin (q.v.) in 1248, recovered by Byzantium (q.v.) in 1262, and ceded to Venice (q.v.) in 1462. The Ottomans (q.v.) did not capture it until 1540.

MONEMVASIA, CHRONICLE OF. *See* **MONEMVASIA.**

MONGOLS. By 1240, when the Mongols (also called Tartars) conquered Kiev (q.v.), the Mongol empire extended across the Eurasian steppe (q.v.). They indirectly aided the Empire of Nicaea (q.v.) by defeating the Seljuks of Asia Minor (qq.v.) in 1243. Their southward expansion was halted by the Mamluks (q.v.) in 1260 at the battle of Ayn Jalut. Michael VIII (q.v.) married his daughter Maria to the Mongol khan Hülugü, and in Constantinople the monastery church of Theotokos (qq.v.) Panagiotissa, which Maria patronized, became known as St. Mary of the Mongols. Timur (q.v.), the last great ruler of the Mongols, defeated Ottoman sultan Bayezid I (qq.v.) in 1402 at the battle of Ankyra (q.v.), which halted Ottoman aggression against Byzantium (q.v.) for a generation.

MONOENERGISM. The doctrine of Christ's single energy *(energeia),* i.e., active force, proposed by Patriarch Sergios of Constantinople (qq.v.) as an attempt to reconcile the Monophysites (q.v.) of the eastern provinces (newly conquered from the Persians by Herakleios [qq.v.]) with those who adhered to the Orthodoxy of the Council of Chalcedon (qq.v.). Patriarch Kyros of Alexandria (qq.v.)

was supportive, but the monk Sophronios (q.v.), who became Patriarch of Jerusalem (q.v.) in 634, argued against the compromise doctrine. Sergios agreed to drop all discussion of one or two energies in favor of a compromise doctrine that Pope Honorius I (625–638) proposed, namely, that Christ had a single will *(thelema)*. Thus, Monotheletism (q.v.) was born, supported by Herakleios's edict of 838, the *Ekthesis* (q.v.). Monoenergism and Monotheletism were condemned at the Sixth Ecumenical Council of Constantinople (q.v.), which met in 680–681 to affirm that Christ had two natures (divine and human), with two corresponding wills and energies.

MONOPHYSITISM. The theological doctrine that the Incarnate Christ had one *(mono)* nature *(physis)*, a divine one. This was condemned at the Council of Chalcedon (q.v.) in 451, where the *diophysite* doctrine of two natures, one fully human and one fully divine, perfectly united in Christ, was proclaimed as Orthodoxy. Monophysitism can be seen as a reaction to Nestorianism (q.v.), developed by Eutyches and Dioskoros (qq.v.), followers of Cyril of Alexandria (q.v.). It was a reaction that expressed the rivalry between the bishoprics of Alexandria and Constantinople (qq.v.), as well as the genuine difficulty of understanding the relationship of the human to the divine in Christ. The decision at Chalcedon did not persuade either the Monophysites of Syria (q.v.) (later called Jacobites [q.v.]), or those of Egypt (q.v.), where a Coptic (q.v.) church developed.

MONOTHELETISM. The doctrine of Christ's single will *(thelema)* proposed by Pope Honorius I (625–638) as an alternative to Monoenergism (q.v.). Patriarch Sergios of Constantinople (qq.v.) supported it, as did Herakleios (q.v.), who enshrined it in an imperial edict, the *Ekthesis* (q.v.). Behind this doctrinal compromise was an effort to unite Monophysites (q.v.), particularly in eastern provinces newly conquered from the Persians (q.v.), and adherents of the Council of Chalcedon (q.v.). The compromise formula failed to do this, and, in any case, by the time the *Ekthesis* was issued in 838, the Monophysite provinces were mostly wrested from Byzantium (q.v.), for the Arabs (q.v.) had conquered Syria and Palestine (qq.v.) and were poised to conquer Egypt (q.v.). In an effort to mollify Christians in North Africa (q.v.), Constans II (q.v.) issued an edict *(Typos)* in 648 that ordered the *Ekthesis* removed from Hagia Sophia (q.v.) and forbade any discussion of divine wills and divine energies. Pope Martin I (q.v.) condemned both the *Ekthesis* and the *Typos,* and was himself removed by Constans II. Monotheletism and Monoenergism were subsequently condemned at the Sixth Ecumenical Council at Constantinople (q.v.) in 680–681. The council affirmed that just as Christ had two natures, Christ also had two wills and two energies.

MONREALE. *See* **SICILY; WILLIAM II.**

MONS LACTARIUS. *See* **NARSES.**

MONTANISM. The heresy of Montanus, who began preaching in Phrygia (q.v.) around 172, along with two women, Prisca and Maximilla, whose utterances were considered divine prophecies of the Holy Spirit, and, thus, more authoritative than any bishop (q.v.) of the church. Montanists had an immediate expectation of Judgment Day and practiced an asceticism (q.v.) that excluded marriage. They said that a Christian who sinned after baptism must be rejected by the church. They were persecuted for their beliefs, and, despite Leo III's (q.v.) attempt to forcibly baptize them, they survived into the ninth century.

MONTECASSINO. The chief monastery of the Benedictine Order, located about halfway between Rome and Naples (qq.v.). It was founded by St. Benedict of Nursia, the father of western monasticism (q.v.), in 529. The monastery had close ties with Byzantium (q.v.), both with certain emperors (q.v.) who supported it with gifts, and with Byzantine officialdom in Italy (q.v.). Close ties were also maintained with major eastern monastic centers like Mount Athos (q.v.). Neilos of Rossano (q.v.) lived near the monastery for about 15 years, and from 1036–1038 a Greek monk named Basil was abbot of Montecassino. The monastery's basilican (q.v.) church was decorated with the finest Byzantine liturgical furniture and other objects, including two bronze doors.

MOORS. The native peoples of western North Africa, also called the Mauri or (in Arabic) Berbers. They resisted attempts by the Romans and (after 429) the Vandals (q.v.) to subdue them. Belisarios (q.v.) conquered the Vandals (q.v.) in a matter of months in 533, but the war with the Moors dragged on for years until John Troglita (q.v.), another great general of Justinian I (q.v.), subdued them in 548.

MOPSUESTIA. City in Cilicia (q.v.) whose bishop Theodore of Mopsuestia (qq.v.) figured prominently in Justinian I's Three Chapters (qq.v.). When the Arabs (q.v.) took the city in 703, it became their chief stronghold in Cilicia until John Tzimiskes (q.v.) reconquered it in 965. After the battle of Mantzikert (q.v.) the city was basically lost to Byzantium (q.v.). It came under the jurisdiction of an Armenian named Philaretos Brachamios, who ruled it until 1133. The Byzantine reconquests of the city from the Rubenids (q.v.) in 1137, and again in 1159, were each of brief duration. The Mamluks (q.v.) pillaged and burned Mopsuestia in 1266.

MORAVIA. Ninth-century Slavic kingdom in central Europe where the conversion of the Slavs (q.v.) to Byzantine Orthodoxy (q.v.) began. It was the second state founded by western Slavs, the first being that of Samo in the seventh century. At the invitation of the Moravian ruler Rastislav (846–870) to organize an independent church using the Slavic language, Cyril and Methodios (qq.v.) journeyed to Moravia in 863. There, they briefly established a missionary church using religious texts in Church Slavonic (q.v.). The new church did not long survive, nor did Moravia itself. Within a decade after the death (in 894) of Rastislav's successor Svatopluk, Moravia fell to the Magyars (q.v.).

MOREA. Name for the Peloponnesos (q.v.) from the time of the 13th-century Latin occupation. The etymology of the word is obscure; it may derive from *morea,* the Greek word for the mulberry tree, whose leaf has an outline not unlike that of the Peloponnesos. In 1205 after the Fourth Crusade (q.v.) much of it became the Latin principality of Achaia (q.v.), as described (to 1292) in the anonymous *Chronicle of the Morea.* Despite the battle of Pelagonia (q.v.), which forced William II Villehardouin to cede to Michael VIII (qq.v.) in 1262 the important castles of Mistra, Monemvasia (qq.v.), and Maina, the principality endured to 1430. The renewed Byzantine presence was organized into the despotate of Morea in 1349 by despot (q.v.) Manuel Kantakouzenos (son of John VI Kantakouzenos [q.v.]), its first ruler. Thereafter, it was an appanage (q.v.) of the reigning emperor in Constantinople (qq.v.). After 1428, rivalry among the sons of Manuel II (q.v.), the brothers Theodore II (despot from 1407–1443), Constantine (XI), and Thomas (who ruled from the castle of Chlemoutsi) weakened the despotate. Theodore II exchanged Constantine's appanage of Selymbria (q.v.) for the despotate of Morea in 1443. This solved the political problem, but not the Ottoman (q.v.) military threat. In 1446 the forces of Murad II (q.v.) breached the Hexamilion (q.v.) and entered the Morea, making a tributary out of Constantine. After being proclaimed emperor at Mistra on 6 January 1449 Constantine XI left for Constantinople (q.v.). Thomas and Demetrios Palaiologos (q.v.) governed Mistra jointly until 1460, when it surrendered to Mehmed II (q.v.).

MOREA, CHRONICLE OF. *See* **MOREA.**

MOREA, DESPOTATE OF. *See* **MOREA.**

MOSAIC. Small cubes called *tesserae*, made of glass, marble, brick, and various colored stones, set into floors and walls. Floor mosaics, often geometrical in pattern, and pictorial, are common in early Byzantine churches. Some floor mosaics have been excavated from the remains of the Great Palace in Constantinople (qq.v.). Mosaic was also a medium used to decorate church and palace walls. The wall mosaics of churches (and the mausoleum of Galla Placidia) in Ravenna (qq.v.) are renowned. Wall mosaics over the entire interiors of churches became common in the 11th century, e.g., in the domed-octagon *katholikon* at Hosios Loukas (qq.v.) and the Greek cross-domed octagon (q.v.) church at Daphni, near Athens (q.v.). Mosaic decoration was arguably the greatest medium for Byzantine artistic expression. However, wall mosaics were expensive, and by late-Byzantine times the decoration of walls in fresco (q.v.), always cheaper, became more common.

MOSCHOS, JOHN. Monk, saint, and author of *The Spiritual Meadow,* a popular account of encounters with monks in Palestine, Syria, and Egypt (qq.v.) during the late sixth century. Among those John and his spiritual son Sophronios (q.v.) met were John Klimachos and John "The Almsgiver" (qq.v.). John and Sophronios (who later became patriarch of Jerusalem [qq.v.]) were among the last generation of wandering eastern ascetics (q.v.). John probably died in Constantinople (q.v.) in 634.

MOSCOW. City on the Moscow river that achieved its independence from the Mongols (q.v.) in the late 15th century. Like Kievan Rus (qq.v.) it was deeply influenced by Byzantine religious literature, art, and architecture. Ivan III (q.v.), grand duke of Moscow from 1462–1505, married Sophia Palaiologina, and he took on the trappings of Byzantine imperial symbolism, referring to Moscow as a new Constantinople (q.v.), and himself as the "Tsar of all Orthodoxy" (qq.v.). However, Moscow rejected the Council of Ferrara-Florence (q.v.) and after the fall of Constantinople it came to see itself as the heir to Byzantine Orthodoxy, and thus the new Byzantium (q.v.), the "Third Rome."

MOSUL. See **ZANGI.**

MOUSELE, ALEXIOS. See **CONSTANTINE VI.**

MOUSELE, ALEXIOS. Caesar (q.v.) and heir-apparent to Theophilos (q.v.) by his betrothal to Theophilos's daughter Maria in 836. He came from a distinguished Armenian family. As heir-apparent he was entrusted with the command of a relief army that Theophilos sent to Sicily (q.v.) in 838. Despite his success there, Theophilos recalled him in 839, and, in a fit of misplaced suspicion, he had Alexios beaten and briefly imprisoned. However, he quickly repented and released him from prison, restoring to him his rank and property. Nevertheless, by 840 Maria had died, and Theophilos had a male heir, the future Michael III (q.v.), so Alexios prudently retired to a monastery.

MOUZALON, GEORGE. See **JOHN IV LASKARIS; THEODORE II LASCARIS.**

MUAWIYA. Founder of the Umayyad caliphate in 661. Its capital was Damascus (q.v.). A former Muslim governor of Syria and Palestine (qq.v.), he was a man of great military and administrative skills. Muawiya gave the new Islamic state a stable bureaucracy and built a fleet to contest Byzantine control of the eastern Mediterranean. He attacked Cappadocia (q.v.) in 646, capturing Caesarea (q.v.), Cyprus in 649, Rhodes (qq.v.) and Kos in 654; he defeated Constans II (q.v.) at sea in 655. As caliph (q.v.) from 661–680, the Muslim fleet moved into the northern Aegean (q.v.), attacking Kyzikos (q.v.) in 670 and besieging Constantinople (q.v.) from 674–678. The city was saved by its impregnable walls and by the timely use of Greek fire (q.v.).

MUHAMMAD THE PROPHET. See **ISLAM; PERSIA.**

MUNDUS. General of Justinian I (q.v.). He was a Gepid (q.v.), recruited into the army, who rose to be one of Justinian's trusted commanders and *magister militum* in Illyricum (qq.v.). He checked an invasion of Huns into the Balkan Peninsula (qq.v.) in 530. The following year he replaced Belisarios (q.v.) as commander of the eastern armies in the war against Persia (q.v.). He is perhaps best remembered for helping Belisarios suppress the Nika Revolt (q.v.) in 532. In 535 he seized parts of Ostrogothic-occupied Dalmatia, including Salona (qq.v.), while Belisarios attacked Sicily (q.v.). However, in 536 Ostrogoths under Theodahad (qq.v.) recovered Dalmatia, which Mundus died trying to defend.

MURAD I. Ottoman sultan (q.v.) from 1362–1389. Under Murad the Ottomans (q.v.) continued their expansion into the Balkan Peninsula (q.v.), conquering Adrianople (q.v.) in 1369, and making John V Palaiologos (q.v.) his vassal following the battle of Marica (1371). Gallipolis (q.v.) was returned to the Ottomans in 1377 for Murad I's support of the rebellion of Andronikos IV (q.v.). Manuel II (q.v.), co-emperor from 1373, and his brother Theodore I Palaiologos of Mistra (qq.v.), were forced to make their submission to Murad I in 1387. Murad was assassinated at the moment of his great victory at the battle of Kosovo Polje on 15 June 1389, a victory that made Serbia (q.v.) an Ottoman vassal state. He was succeeded by Bayezid I (q.v.).

MURAD II. Ottoman sultan (qq.v.) from 1421–1451. Murad II renewed the Ottoman offensive, following a lull during the reign of Mehmed I (q.v.). In 1422 Murad besieged Constantinople (q.v.), and the following year he broke through the Hexamilion (q.v.) to invade the Morea (qq.v.), forcing Manuel II (q.v.) to conclude a treaty of peace favorable to Murad. In 1430 Murad conquered Thessalonike (q.v.) and pushed farther north into the Balkan Peninsula (q.v.), defeating the Crusaders at Varna (q.v.) in 1444. In 1448 he invaded the Morea again, forced Constantine (XI) into submission as his vassal, and he conquered Naupaktos (q.v.). Murad II bequeathed to his successor Mehmed II (q.v.) a state that was poised to conquer what few possessions Byzantium (q.v.) still retained, including Constantinople (qq.v.).

MUSA. Son of Ottoman sultan Bayezid I (qq.v.), whose death ended a civil war (1410–1413) with Bayezid's other two sons, Suleyman Celebi and Mehmed. Musa first attacked his brother Suleyman Celebi, defeating and killing him in 1411. He then attacked Manuel II (q.v.) to punish him for his support of Suleyman, besieging Constantinople (q.v.) for almost a year (1411–1412). However, Musa was defeated and executed in 1413, which allowed Mehmed (I) (q.v.) to become undisputed Ottoman sultan (q.v.). This united the Ottomans (q.v.) for the first time since Bayezid's capture by Timur in 1402 at the battle of Ankyra (qq.v.).

MUSIC. Secular music existed, but has not survived. However, it is known that pneumatic organs were used in state ceremonials in Constantinople (q.v.), e.g., at banquets, weddings, receptions, and processionals. It is also known that various other secular musical instruments existed, including the cymbal, flute, drum, harp, and trumpet. They were used for musical performances to accompany theatrical performances, and doubtless in folk music, although no details have survived. What has survived are church hymns, which formed a central feature of church services. The earliest type of hymn was the *kontakion,* chanted by the priest, with the choir providing the refrain. Among the most famous *kontakia* is the Akathistos Hymn by Romanos the Melode. A more elaborate type of hymn called the *kanon* (q.v.) replaced the *kontakion* in the eighth century. Allegedly created by Andrew of Crete, it attracted such famous hymnographers as John of Damascus, Joseph the Hymnographer, and Kosmas the Hymnographer. Byzantine music influenced the medieval West. Byzantine hymns and Latin church hymns, especially the Gregorian chant, show certain similarities that are probably explained by Byzantine cultural influence in Italy and southern Gaul (qq.v.). The first organ to appear in the West was sent in 757 from Constantine V to Pippin, king of the Franks (qq.v.). Pope Leo III's coronation of Charlemagne in Rome (qq.v.) on Christmas Day 800, was accompanied by the Byzantine acclamation *(polychronion)* "May you rule many years!"

MUSLIM. *See* **ISLAM.**

MUTASIM. Abbasid caliph (qq.v.) from 833–842. Mutasim's war against the Khurramites resulted in the flight of Khurramites under Theophobos to Theophilos (qq.v.). Theophilos seemed to further strengthen his position against the caliph when, in 837, he sacked Zapetra, reportedly the birthplace of Mutasim's father, Harun al-Rashid (q.v.). But the following year Mustasim entered Asia Minor (q.v.) with a huge expeditionary force that captured Ankyra and Amorion (qq.v.). Among the captives he executed were the Forty-two Martyrs of Amorion (q.v.).

MYRA. *See* **LYCIA.**

MYREPSOS, NICHOLAS. *See* **MEDICINE.**

MYRIOKEPHALON, BATTLE OF. On 17 September 1176 the army of Manuel I Komnenos (q.v.) found itself trapped in a narrow pass by the forces of Kilij Arslan I (q.v.). When the day was over Manuel's army was in tatters, though not destroyed. However, what was destroyed were any subsequent plans to reconquer Asia Minor from the Seljuks (qq.v.). In retrospect, the battle was the most decisive for Byzantium since Mantzikert (qq.v.) in 1071.

MYTILENE. *See* **LESBOS.**

– N –

NAISSUS. Birthplace of Constantine I (q.v.), and strategic road junction in the Balkan Peninsula (q.v.) where the Naissus to Thessalonike road intersected with the Belgrade to Constantinople (qq.v.) highway, and with other roads. Its strategic location made it a target of invaders. It was destroyed by the Huns (q.v.) in 441, rebuilt by Justinian I (q.v.), then ravaged by the Avars (qq.v.). The medieval city (called Nish) changed hands several times between Byzantium, Bulgaria, and Serbia (qq.v.). The Ottomans (q.v.) sacked it twice (1386, 1428), but they were ejected by John Hunyadi (q.v.) in 1444. The Ottomans reconquered it in 1456.

NAOS. ("Temple," or "church," in Greek.) The term can refer to a church in its entirety, or to the sanctuary of the church. In Christian basilicas (q.v.) through the sixth century it is the nave (q.v.) where the congregation assembled, separated from the *bema* by a *templon* (qq.v.). In later, centrally planned churches, the term refers to the domed, inner sanctuary of the church, reserved for the performance of the liturgy (q.v.) by the clergy, separated from the congregation by an *iconostasis* (q.v.).

NAPLES. Italian city on the Bay of Naples, near Pompeii. It was captured by Belisarios (q.v.) from the Ostrogoths (q.v.) in 536, only to surrender to Ostrogoths under Totila (qq.v.) in 543. In 552 it returned to Byzantine hands, and thereafter the city maintained its independence from the Lombards (q.v.). When Constans II (q.v.) visited the city in 663 the city still owed its allegiance to Byzantium (q.v.), an allegiance it nominally maintained until 838, when Naples joined forces with the Arabs (q.v.), resulting in the conquest of Messina (q.v.) in 843. Naples became an active threat to Byzantium after 1139, the year it fell to the Normans (q.v.), and even more of a threat in 1194 when German emperor Henry VI (q.v.) acquired Naples and Sicily (q.v.). That threat continued with Manfred and Charles of Anjou (qq.v.), who lost Sicily (1282), but retained the Kingdom of Naples. Much later, Alfonso V (q.v.) reunited Sicily and Naples (1443), but his scheme to conquer the Ottomans (q.v.) and reestablish the Latin Empire of Constantinople (qq.v.) never materialized.

NARSES. General of Justinian I (q.v.) who succeeded Belisarios in Italy (qq.v.) in the war against the Ostrogoths (q.v.). He won a decisive blow against the Ostrogothic king Totila (q.v.) at the battle of Busta Gallorum (q.v.) in 552. In the same year he pursued Totila's successor, king Teia, defeating him at the battle of Mons Lactarius. In 553–554 the Franks (q.v.) and Alemanni, a confederation of German tribes, invaded Italy; Narses annihilated them in a battle near Capua (q.v.). He left Italy in 567, having spent over a decade reorganizing its defenses and administration. Despite this, the following year the Lombards (q.v.) invaded Italy, annexing much of it.

NARTHEX. An antechamber to the *naos* (q.v.) situated at its west end, extending the width of the church. Where there is a second narthex, the first is called the *exonarthex* and the innermost one the *esonarthex*. Essentially it is a vestibule that gradually acquired various functions, e.g., as a place where processions into the *naos* assembled, also where baptisms and commemorations of the dead took place.

NAUM OF OHRID. Missionary to the Slavs, Bulgarian priest, translator, saint. He accompanied Cyril and Methodios to Moravia (qq.v.) in 863, as did Kliment of Ohrid (q.v.). After Methodios's death in 885, he went with Kliment to Bulgaria (q.v.) where he created centers at Preslav and Pliska (qq.v.) for the translation of holy texts into Church Slavonic (q.v.). In 893 he took up the work that Kliment had begun in Macedonia (q.v.). He died in 910 at Sveti Naum, the monastery he founded on the shore of Lake Ohrid.

NAUPAKTOS. City at the entrance to the Gulf of Corinth, called Lepanto by the Venetians. Naupaktos was strongly fortified. It was a powerful maritime base and, along with Negroponte and Nauplia, it guarded the northern approaches to the Morea (q.v.). It was part of the Despotate of Epiros (qq.v.) from 1204–1294, when it came under the domination of Philip of Taranto, the prince of Achaia (q.v.). The Catalans (q.v.) conquered it in 1361 and the Venetians (q.v.) seized it in 1407. In 1446, when Murad II (q.v.) invaded the Morea (q.v.), the inhabitants of Patras (q.v.) crossed the Gulf of Corinth to take refuge in Naupaktos. The Venetians continued to control the city until 1499, when it surrendered to the Ottomans (q.v.).

NAUPLIA. *See* **NAUPAKTOS; SGOUROS, LEO.**

NAVARRESE COMPANY. Spanish mercenary band, like the Catalan Grand Company (q.v.) before them, that migrated east in the late 14th century. The name derives from Navarre, where many of them originated. Once in Greece (q.v.), the Navarrese hired themselves out to whoever would pay them. Employed by the Hospitallers (q.v.), they helped conquer Thebes (q.v.) from the Catalans in 1379. This proved to be the beginning of the end of the Catalan domination in Greece. So weakened were the Catalans that the Acciajuoli (q.v.) wrested Athens (q.v.) from them in 1388. The Navarrese then fought for control of Frankish Achaia (q.v.), and subsequently for the Peloponnesos (q.v.) against Theodore I Palaiologos (q.v.) and the Acciajuoli (q.v.). Their meteoric expansion ended in 1402, by which time they had joined forces with an ally more powerful than themselves, the Ottomans (q.v.). In effect, their military intervention served to erode resistance to Ottoman expansion in Greece.

NAVE. *See* **NAOS.**

NAVY. Byzantium (q.v.), despite the geographical centrality of the Mediterranean (q.v.) and an enormous coastline, was never a maritime power. Indeed, fear of the sea was apparently common, judging from Byzantine literature. This may help to explain why the Byzantine navy was relatively small, even after Byzantine hegemony of the western Mediterranean was challenged by the Vandals (q.v.) in the fifth century. However, the Arab (q.v.) naval threat of the seventh century in the eastern Mediterranean produced dramatic changes. The naval theme of Kibyrrhaiotai (qq.v.) was created to help defend the eastern Mediterranean. Its warships (called *dromones*), driven by single or double banks of rowers, were equipped with rams, catapults, and Greek Fire (q.v.). Naval decline began in the 11th century, something clearly illustrated by the dependence of Alexios I (q.v.) on the Venetian fleet while fighting Robert Guiscard (q.v.) in 1081. Alexios I created the title *megas doux* (supreme naval commander), and his immediate successors attempted to create a Byzantine fleet. Nevertheless, the results were modest. After the reconquest of Constantinople (q.v.) in 1261, Michael VIII (q.v.) tried to restore the navy by creating a small fleet. Andronikos II (q.v.) reduced its size considerably, forcing him to depend on the Genoese for naval support when necessary. Andronikos III's (q.v.) small fleet was commanded by *megas doux* Alexios Apokaukos (q.v.). In 1349 the citizenry of Constantinople contributed funds to build nine warships and 100 other vessels to do battle with the Genoese (who won). John VI Kantakouzenos (q.v.) launched another small fleet that was again defeated. From then on Byzantium (q.v.) assembled ships as it could, sometimes making requests to the Venetians. For example, in 1410 Manuel II (q.v.) requested armed galleys from Venice (q.v.) to use against the Ottomans (q.v.), but Venice refused. When Musa (q.v.) besieged Constantinople in 1411 Manuel II managed to find enough ships to repulse him. However, Constantine XI (q.v.) could collect only about a few dozen (mostly Genoese and Venetian) ships to defend the Golden Horn (q.v.) at the beginning of the Ottoman siege of 1453. Of these only nine were proper warships, only three of which belonged to Constantine XI.

NAXOS. *See* **PARTITIO ROMANIAE; SANUDO TORSELLO, MARINO.**

NEA ANCHIALOS. *See* **THESSALY.**

NEA EKKLESIA. *See* **BASIL I.**

NEA MONE. Of the monasteries with this name ("New Monastery"), the most famous is on Chios (qq.v.), where there is a domed octagon church (q.v.) built during the reign of Constantine IX (q.v.). Its basic architectural plan is like the *katholikon* of Hosios Loukas (qq.v.), but unlike the latter it has no aisles or galleries. Its mosaics (q.v.) and marble veneering are of exquisite Constantinopolitan workmanship, offering a glimpse of what church and palace interiors in the capital must have been like.

NEAPOLIS. *See* **PALESTINE.**

NEGEV. *See* **PALESTINE.**

NEGROPONTE. *See* **EUBOEA.**

NEILOS OF ROSSANO. Saint (died 1004) and monk; writer of hymns. He was an exemplar of Italo-Greek monasticism (q.v.), founding the monastery of St. Adrian and subsequently living with a band of followers near Montecassino (q.v.) for 15 years. His life and career demonstrate how powerful was the influence of Byzantine culture and spirituality on Italy (q.v.) during the Middle Ages.

NEKTARIOS. Patriarch of Constantinople (qq.v.) from 381–397, chosen by Theodosios I (q.v.) for political skills previously demonstrated in the senate (q.v.). Those skills were put to good use at the Council of Constantinople (q.v.) in 381, which Nektarios convened, and were further demonstrated in his ability to avoid direct conflict with the other patriarchs, including the bishop of Rome (qq.v.).

NEMANJIDS. Serbian royal dynasty founded by Stefan Nemanja (q.v.) ca. 1167 and lasting until 1371. It included such famous Serbian rulers as Stefan Urosh I, Stefan Urosh II Milutin, Stefan Urosh III Dechanski, and Stefan Urosh Dushan (qq.v.). Under the Namanjids medieval Serbia (q.v.) extended its borders for a while into central Greece (q.v.). An impressive number of churches were endowed by Nemanjid rulers, including Gračaniča, Studenica, and the *katholikon* of Hilandar Monastery (qq.v.).

NEOPATRAS. *See* **THESSALY.**

NEOPHYTOS. *See* **CYPRUS.**

NEOPLATONISM. The philosophy of Plotinos (q.v.), who sought to transform the dialogues of Plato (ca. 427–347 B.C.) into a philosophy of mysticism. His commentators included Porphyry (q.v.) and Porphyry's pupil Iamblichos (died ca. 325), who was accused of corrupting Plotinos's thought into magic and theatrically staged tricks, such as were also popular with Maximos of Ephesus (q.v.), the emperor Julian's (q.v.) spiritual mentor. In the fifth century, Proklos (q.v.) used mathematics and prayer to lead the soul to the One. Athens (q.v.) remained a center of study until Justinian I closed the Academy of Athens (qq.v.) in 529. Other early centers included Pergamon and Alexandria (q.v.), where Neoplatonists like John Philoponos (ca. 490–ca. 574) taught. Plato continued to be known chiefly through Neoplatonism; this was the case even for Michael Psellos (q.v.), who probably understood Neoplatonism better than anyone since the sixth century. The final Byzantine commentator on Neoplatonism was Plethon (q.v.), who helped found the Platonic Academy in Florence (q.v.).

NEREZI. *See* **CROSS-IN-SQUARE CHURCH; SKOPJE.**

NESTORIANISM. Heresy (q.v.) that takes its name from Nestorios, patriarch of Constantinople (qq.v.) from 428–431. Nestorios maintained, in opposition to Cyril, patriarch of Alexandria (qq.v.), that the divine and human natures of Christ had less intimate contact; and he labeled as fables, as did Theodore of Mopsuestia (q.v.), the belief that Mary gave birth to God, and should be called *Theotokos* (q.v.), "Mother of God" (literally "Bearer of God"), preferring that she be called *Christotokos,* bearer of the man Christ. He was accused by theological opponents of separating the two natures of Christ, but his attack on the Virgin Mary aroused many ordinary people against him. He was deposed, and his doctrines were condemned, at the Council of Ephesus (q.v.) in 431.

NESTORIOS. *See* **NESTORIANISM.**

NICAEA. Important city in Bithynia (q.v.) that hosted two ecumenical councils (q.v.), the first in 325 and the seventh in 787. Its stout walls resisted Arab attacks in the eighth century only to fall to the Seljuks (q.v.) in 1081. It was reconquered from sultan (q.v.) Kilic Arslan I by the First Crusade (qq.v.) in 1097 and restored to Byzantine administration. Its greatest historical role was as capital of the Empire of Nicaea (q.v.), which was Byzantium-in-exile from 1208–1261. The Ottomans (q.v.) captured Nicaea in 1331.

NICAEA, COUNCILS OF. *See* **ECUMENICAL COUNCILS.**

NICAEA, EMPIRE OF. The center of Byzantium-in-exile from 1208–1261. Theodore I Laskaris (q.v.), its first emperor, was crowned in 1208. The victory of Kalojan over Baldwin of Flanders (qq.v.) in 1205 weakened subsequent Latin military initiatives in Asia Minor by Henry of Hainault (qq.v.). Theodore I's victory over the Seljuks (q.v.) in 1211 further insured the immediate survival of the Empire of Nicaea. John III Vatatzes (q.v.), who reigned from 1222–1254, expanded the empire into Thrace (q.v.), conquering Thessalonike (q.v.) in 1246. Theodore II Laskaris ([q.v.], reigned 1254–1258) turned back a Bulgarian invasion in 1254–1255. The ineffectual John IV Laskaris, a child of seven when he came to the throne, gradually fell sway to his general Michael (VIII) Palaiologos, who was crowned co-emperor in 1259. The Latin Empire (q.v.) ended in 1261 when the forces of Michael VIII captured the city, restoring, in effect, Byzantium (q.v.) to its proper capital.

NICHOLAS I. Pope (q.v.) from 858–867 whose interference in the affairs of the eastern church triggered a crisis between the churches. It began with Nicholas's refusal to agree to Michael III's deposition of Patriarch Ignatios (qq.v.) in favor of Photios (q.v.). In 863 Nicholas declared that Ignatios was restored. The pope also competed for the ecclesiastical allegiance of the Bulgars (q.v.) through correspondence with Boris I of Bulgaria (qq.v.), and entertained Cyril and Methodios in Rome (qq.v.). In 867 a council in Constantinople (q.v.) declared Nicholas I excommunicated and deposed. The council also rejected the Roman church's doctrine of *filioque* (q.v.).

NICHOLAS I MYSTIKOS. Patriarch of Constantinople (qq.v.) from 901–907 and 912–925. He became immersed in controversy because of his refusal to accept Leo VI's (q.v.) fourth marriage, the so-called *tetragamy*. Leo VI deposed and exiled him in 907, appointing Euthymios (q.v.) in his place. This created a schism in the church between the followers of Nicholas and those of Euthymios. Nicholas was recalled in 912, whereupon he energetically deposed the supporters of Euthymios. Only later, after the death of Euthymios in 917, was the Tome of Union (q.v.) able to achieve church reconciliation.

NICHOLAS III. Pope from 1277–1280. He negotiated with Michael VIII about how to implement the church union achieved on paper at the Council of Lyons in 1274 (q.v.). At the same time, Nicholas refused to approve of Charles I's plans to attack Byzantium (q.v.), secretly supporting Michael VIII's alliance with Peter III of Aragon (q.v.) against Charles I of Anjou (q.v.). Nicholas III's death was a blow to Michael VIII, for the new pope, Martin IV (q.v.), proved more cooperative in promoting Charles I's plans to destroy Byzantium.

NICHOLAS III GRAMMATIKOS. Patriarch of Constantinople (qq.v.) from 1084–1111, during the reign of Alexios I Komnenos (q.v.). He supported the emperor's (q.v.) persecution of the Bogomils (q.v.). However, he opposed the attempt by the patriarchal clergy to promote the power of their spokesman, the *chartophylax* of Hagia Sophia (qq.v.), in the patriarchal synod at Constantinople (q.v.). Alexios I sided with the patriarchal clergy and affirmed the *chartophylax* as the patriarchal deputy with the right to preside over the permanent synod in the patriarch's absence.

NICHOLAS V. Pope (q.v.) from 1397–1455. He was pope when Constantinople fell to the Ottomans (qq.v.) in 1453. His sluggish response to the Ottoman threat to the city can be explained first by an unwillingness to send any help unless the Byzantines were serious about the union of the churches (q.v.). That obstacle was solved on 12 December 1452 when the pope's emissary Isidore of Kiev (q.v.) proclaimed church union in Justinian I's Hagia Sophia (qq.v.). Nicholas was preparing a fleet to aid the beleaguered city when the city fell to the Ottomans some five months later. In any case, the pope was providing funds for Alphonso V, King of Naples (q.v.), who had plans to restore the Latin Empire (q.v.) in Constantinople. More profitable results came from Nicholas's foundation of the Vatican library, his collection of Greek manuscripts, and his support of Greek scholars like Bessarion (q.v.).

NICHOLAS OF METHONE. *See* **PANTEUGENOS, SOTERICHOS; THEOLOGY.**

NICHOLAS OF OTRANTO. *See* **OTRANTO.**

NIKA REVOLT. Revolt of 11–19 January 532 that nearly overthrew Justinian I (q.v.). Before it was suppressed, the rioters (whose watchword was *Nika,* meaning "Conquer!") had burned down Hagia Sophia (q.v.), the Church of St. Irene, the baths of Zeuxippus, the Chalke, and part of the Augustaion (qq.v.). Hatred of Justinian I's autocracy, most visible in John of Cappadocia's (q.v.) fiscal oppression of aristocrats and commoners alike, was the underlying cause. The immediate spark was a riot in the Hippodrome (q.v.) over the emperor's (q.v.) refusal to pardon members of the Blues and Greens for a previous disturbance in the Hippodrome. Once these factions joined forces, the violence began. Only the strong will of Theodora (q.v.) and the personal troops of Belisarios and Mundus (qq.v.) saved Justinian's throne. Some 30,000 rioters in the Hippo-drome were slaughtered, after they had crowned Hypatios (q.v.). The suppression of the revolt necessitated a grand rebuilding pro-gram that created the present Hagia Sophia (q.v.).

NIKEPHORITZES. *Logothetes tou droumou* under Michael VII (q.v.). He was a eunuch (q.v.) whose administrative capabilities had been recognized by Constantine X and Romanos IV (qq.v.). Under Michael VII he became the real ruler of the empire. His attempt to create a monopoly over the corn trade in Thrace (q.v.) failed miser-ably, and it produced a revolt in Thrace in 1077. His other attempts at centralization produced opposition from the guilds, provincial landowners, and bishops that resulted in a revolution in 1078 that brought Nikephoros III Botaneiates (q.v.) to power. Nikephoritzes fled to Roussel of Bailleul (q.v.), but to no avail. He was seized and killed.

NIKEPHOROS I. Emperor (q.v.) from 802–811. A former chief fi-nance minister *(logothetes tou genikou)* of Irene (q.v.), he took pru-dent steps to remedy deficiencies in tax collection and low state rev-enues. The tax rolls were reassessed and land taxes raised. The hearth tax *(kapnikon* [q.v.]) was applied to peasant tenants *(paroikoi* [q.v.]) working on church and monastic lands (apparently exempted from payment by Irene). He made villages collectively liable for financing the military equipment of their poorer inhabitants by re-quiring them to pay the latter's *allelengyon* (q.v.). He taxed slaves purchased beyond the customs border at Abydos (q.v.) and enforced inheritance taxation. Theophanes the Confessor (q.v.) condemned these and other taxes as horrid misdeeds. No doubt other ecclesias-tics and monks felt the same hatred for the emperor, enforced partly by the emperor's support of the patriarch Nikephoros I (qq.v) and the revival of the Moechian controversy (q.v.). However, with in-creased revenues Nikephoros replenished the army and navy (qq.v.), and he inaugurated a program of refortification. He repopulated and rehellenized Greece (q.v.) with villagers from Asia Minor (qq.v.), and he reorganized Greece's defenses with the establishment of new themes (q.v.), including the theme of Thessalonike (q.v.). However, the success of his internal administration was not matched by mili-tary success. A revolt by Bardanes Tourkos (q.v.) in 803 weakened the defenses of Asia Minor allowing Harun al-Rashid to capture Tyana (qq.v.) in 806. Nikephoros sued for peace, which was achieved in 807 only at the expense of a humiliating tribute.

Nikephoros himself was killed in battle against the Bulgar khan Krum (qq.v.) in July 811, the first emperor to be killed in battle by barbarians since the battle of Adrianople (q.v.) in 378.

NIKEPHOROS I. Patriarch of Constantinople (qq.v.) from 806–815, appointed after the death of Tarasios (q.v.). He was a respected scholar and theologian, also an historian, but still a layman when he was made patriarch. This infuriated the supporters of Theodore of Studion (q.v.), as did the emperor Nikephoros I's (q.v.) reopening of the Moechian controversy (q.v.). Ironically, in 815, Nikephoros found himself aligned with his old opponent Theodore of Studion against the Iconoclasm of Leo V (qq.v.), who deposed the patriarch. His legacy to modern historians is his *Historia Syntomos* (Brief History), covering the years 602–769, an important historical source for a period nearly destitute of historical sources except for the chronicle of Theophanes the Confessor (qq.v.).

NIKEPHOROS II PHOKAS. Emperor (q.v.) from 963–969. His greatest triumph as general *(domestikos* [q.v.] *ton scholon)* for Romanos II (q.v.) was the conquest of Crete (q.v.) in 961. As emperor, his victories against the Arabs (q.v.) continued with the capture of Cyprus, Tarsos, and Mopsuestia in 965. His generals Peter Phokas and Michael Bourtzes (qq.v) captured Antioch (qq.v.) in 969. He called upon Svjatoslav (q.v.) to defeat the Bulgars (q.v.) in 968, the same year of the unsuccessful embassy of Liutprand of Cremona on behalf of Otto I (qq.v.). He increased the minimum size of land held by soldiers (the *stratiotika ktemata* [q.v.]) in order to support his new armored troops, the *kataphraktoi* (q.v.). He forbade new bequests of land to the church (something the patriarch Polyeuktos [q.v.] opposed), but he supported the work of Athanasios of Athos on Mount Athos (qq.v.), where the Great Lavra (q.v.) was founded in 963. He was murdered in 969 in a plot that included his wife Theophano and his general John Tzimiskes (qq.v.).

NIKEPHOROS III BOTANEIATES. Emperor (q.v.) from 1078–1081. He was a general and member of the landed aristocracy of Asia Minor (qq.v.) who rebelled against Michael VII Doukas (q.v.), forcing him to abdicate. He proved to be ineffectual against the Seljuk (q.v.) onslaught in Asia Minor. By 1080 most of Asia Minor was in their hands, the Sultanate of Rum (q.v.) was founded, and Seljuks were raiding the Asiatic suburbs of Constantinople (q.v.). The failure to provide any effective resistance to the Seljuks, in addition to the debasement of the *nomisma* (q.v.), prompted several revolts, including the successful one of Alexios (I) Komnenos (q.v.). His good fortune was to have Michael Attaleiates (q.v.) as one of his chief historians (among whom was also Michael Psellos [q.v.]). Attaleiates dedicated his work to Nikephoros, and he showers him with praise.

NIKETAS. *See* **PHOKAS.**

NIKOMEDEIA. City in Bithynia where Diocletian (qq.v.) resided, and where Libanios (q.v.) taught. It declined in importance after an earthquake in 358, but it never lost its importance as a military camp on the main road to Constantinople (q.v.). Alexios I Komnenos (q.v.) used it as a base of operations against the Seljuks (q.v.), and John II Komnenos settled Serbs (qq.v.) in the vicinity. After the battle of Bapheus (q.v.) in 1302 the Ottomans (q.v.) threatened the city on several occasions. It finally fell to Orhan (q.v.) in 1337.

NIKOPOLIS, CRUSADE OF. Crusade in 1396 led by King Sigismund of Hungary (1387–1437) to halt the Ottoman (q.v.) advance in the Balkan Peninsula (q.v.). Many French knights took a break from the Hundred Years War to aid the Hungarians, as did knights from all over Europe. This western European coalition confronted an Ottoman army outside the walls of Nikopolis, a fortress on the Danube (q.v.) (not to be confused with the city of Nikopolis in Epiros [q.v.]). The result was a stunning victory (25 September 1396) for sultan Bayezid I (qq.v.). Not only did this attempt to defend Hungary (q.v.) against Ottoman encroachment fail, but Manuel II (q.v.), who was allied with Sigismund, could expect no help against the Ottoman siege of Constantinople (q.v.), begun by Bayezid I in 1394.

NINEVAH, BATTLE OF. *See* **CHOSROES II.**

NISH. *See* **NAISSUS.**

NISIBIS. Frontier fortress in Mesopotamia (q.v.) that became a focal point in the struggle between Byzantium and Persia (qq.v.) during the fourth century. After the death of Julian (q.v.) in 363 it was surrendered to Persia, and it remained in Persian hands until the Arabs (q.v.) conquered it in 639. Under Persian rule (after 489), it offered protection to a thriving Nestorian (q.v.) community. Only much later did Byzantine general John Kourkouas (q.v.) reoccupy it briefly (942–944), along with Amida, Dara, and Martyropolis (qq.v.).

NITRIAN DESERT. Located in Upper Egypt south of Alexandria (qq.v.), where the celebrated hermit Ammon (died ca. 350) established a loose association of hermits (q.v.) who practiced individual asceticism (q.v.). It was left to Ammon's contemporary, Pachomios (q.v.), to establish the first *koinobion* (q.v.) for monks.

NOMISMA. *See* **COINAGE.**

NOMOKANONES. *See* **CANON LAW.**

NOMOPHYLAX. *See* **EDUCATION.**

NOMOS STRATIOTIKOS. A collection of about 55 penal and disciplinary laws for soldiers. Although of uncertain date, they must have been compiled between the sixth and mid-eighth centuries for some laws derive from the *Corpus Juris Civilis* (q.v.), some apparently from the *Strategikon* of Maurice (q.v.), still others from later texts. The *Nomos Stratiotikos* (Soldier's Law) is found appended to the *Ecloga*, the *Farmer's Law*, and Rhodian Sea Law (qq.v.).

NORICUM. Roman province located between the provinces of Raetia and Pannonia (q.v.), in what is now Austria (south of the Danube [q.v.]). It was overrun by German barbarians in the fifth century, and by Avars and Slavs (qq.v.) in the early seventh century.

NORMANS. Byzantium's (q.v.) chief western foes in the 11th and 12th centuries. The Normans ("Northmen") were Vikings who emigrated to southern Italy (qq.v.) in the late 10th century; by 1071 the last Byzantine stronghold there, Bari (q.v.), had fallen into their hands. They essentially conquered Sicily from the Arabs (qq.v.) between 1060–1072, with the final conquest in 1091. Robert Guiscard and his son Bohemund (qq.v.) attacked Dyrrachion and other cities along the Via Egnatia (qq.v.) from 1081 until Robert's death in 1085. At the same time, Normans entered Byzantine service as mercenaries, some of them, e.g., Hervé Frankopoulos and Roussel de Bailleul (qq.v.), rising to high military commands. The Treaty of Devol (q.v.) in 1108 with Bohemund temporarily halted Norman aggression, but it revived later in the 12th century with Roger II's attack on Greece (qq.v.) in 1147–1148, and with the brief Norman occupation of Thessalonike (q.v.) in 1185.

NOTARAS, LOUKAS. Diplomat, high officeholder under Manuel II, John VIII, and Constantine XI (qq.v.). He was grand duke *(megas* *doux),* i.e., high admiral and *mesazon* (q.v.) under Constantine XI. He opposed the union of the churches (q.v.), and he is reported (by Michael Doukas [q.v.]) to have said that he preferred the Turkish turban reigning over Constantinople (q.v.) than the Latin (i.e., papal) tiara. Nevertheless, in 1453 he took responsibility for defending the walls along the Golden Horn (q.v.) during the siege of Constantinople by the Ottomans (q.v.). After the conquest of the city, he and his sons were executed by Mehmed II (q.v.).

NOTITIA DIGNATUM. A list of imperial officials, both civil and military, as they existed in the eastern and western parts of the empire in the late fourth and early fifth centuries (ca. 395–429). After each office, e.g., praetorian prefect (q.v.), there is a brief description of function and mention of subordinate officials and military units.

NOTITIA EPISCOPATUUM. List of church dioceses (q.v.). Various lists survive, the earliest dating from the seventh century. Often lists do not coincide with those dioceses represented at contemporary church councils, making one wonder how rigorously they were kept up-to-date. As a result, for example, they may not reflect the decline of cities in the East as a result of invasions by Arabs, and, later, by Seljuks and Ottomans (qq.v.).

NOVATIANISM. A separatist sect founded by Novatian (died 257/258), a Roman priest who refused to readmit Christians who had compromised the faith during the persecution of the emperor Decius in 250–251. Though Orthodox (q.v.) in doctrine, the Novatians continued in their belief that they were a purer church, for which they were excommunicated. Nevertheless, the church persisted into the fifth century, after which it declined.

NOVELS. Novels (*Novellae* in Latin) is a term that from the fourth century referred to imperial edicts. The most famous are those issued during Justinian I's (q.v.) reign after publication of the *Codex Justinianus* (q.v.) in 534. The *Novellae Constituiones* (New Laws) include laws that ameliorate the condition of slaves, freeborn women, and children. Justinian had intended to make the collection, but never did, perhaps because Tribonian (q.v.) died unexpectedly. It was left to private jurists to do so. Another famous collection of Novels is that of Leo VI (q.v.).

NOVGOROD. Rus (q.v.) city along the Volkhov River. The *Russian Primary Chronicle* describes Novgorod as an important trading center on the water route that the Varangians (q.v.) used to get to Constantinople (q.v.). There was an important Scandinavian colony in Novgorod, established by Rurik ca. 862, that traded with Byzantium (q.v.) for furs, wax, and honey. It was one of the chief artistic centers of Kievan Rus in the 11th and 12th centuries, with churches whose architecture and decoration are essentially Byzantine, including Novgorod's famous church of Hagia Sophia whose very name was inspired by Justinian I's (q.v.) great church. Novgorod travelers (e.g., Antony of Novgorod) describe Justinian I's Hagia Sophia (q.v.) as well as other churches in Constantinople. Novgorod's independence came to an end in 1475 when Ivan III (q.v.), grand duke of Moscow, revoked its charter. Ivan IV "the Terrible" captured it in 1570.

NUBIA. Region of northeast Africa (q.v.) that extended from the first cataract of the Nile, near Aswan, to Khartoum in the Sudan. Byzantine interest in Nubia in the sixth century lay in the desire to secure an overland route to Axum (q.v.). Merchants and missionaries visited Nubia's three tribal kingdoms of Nobatia, Makuria, and Alodia. During the reign of Justinian I, both Orthodox and Monophysite (qq.v.) missionaries competed in Nubia for converts. Byzantine influence on the region was dramatically curtailed when the Arabs conquered Egypt (qq.v.) in the seventh century.

NUMIDIA. Province in northwest Africa (q.v.), roughly the equivalent of modern Algeria, that included the city of Thamugadi (q.v.), modern Timgad. In the fourth century, the province became a bastion of Donatism (q.v.); in the fifth century the Vandals (q.v.) occupied a portion of it. Conquest of the entire province by Justinian I (q.v.) took from 534–541. Justinian built a number of forts to protect it against attacks by the indigenous Moors (q.v.). The province was conquered by the Arabs (q.v.) in the late seventh century.

NUR AL-DIN. Successor to Zangi as *atabeg* (independent governor) of Aleppo and Edessa (qq.v.) from 1146–1174. He succeeded to Zangi's determination to unite Muslim Syria (q.v.), which he did by taking advantage of the failure of the Second Crusade (q.v.) to conquer Damascus (q.v.) in 1154. This united Muslim Syria (qq.v.) against the Crusaders. The intervention of Manuel I Komnenos (q.v.) in Syria from 1158–1176 neutralized this threat, but it reappeared in 1168, when Nur al-Din's Kurdish general Shirkuh conquered Egypt (q.v.), drawing the noose around the Crusader states even tighter. Shirkuh's nephew Saladin (q.v.) tightened that noose in 1187 at the battle of Hattin (q.v.).

NYMPHAION, TREATY OF. City in western Asia Minor (q.v.), where Michael VIII Palaiologos (q.v.) signed a commercial treaty with Genoa (q.v.) on 13 March 1261, directed against Venice (q.v.). Genoa was to make 50 ships available to Michael to help wrest Constantinople (q.v.), defended by a Venetian fleet, from the Latin Empire (q.v.). Once Constantinople had been reconquered, Byzantium (q.v.) was obliged to give to Genoa all the commercial privileges formerly enjoyed by Venice. As it turned out, no Genoese help was needed to recapture Constantinople. What the treaty did produce was nearly two centuries of conflict in the eastern Mediterranean between Genoa and Venice. It also laid the foundation of a Genoese trading empire that stretched into the Black Sea (q.v.).

NYSSA. There were two cities in Asia Minor (q.v.) with this name. The Nyssa in Cappadocia (q.v.), located northwest of Caesarea (q.v.), was the bishopric of Gregory of Nyssa (q.v.). The other Nyssa was located in Lycia (q.v.), on the north bank of the Meander River.

– O –

OCHRID. *See* **OHRID.**

ODOACER. Ruler of Italy (q.v.) from 476–493. He was a barbarian (Skirian or Hunnic) military officer who deposed Romulus Augustulus (q.v.) in 476, a date traditionally seen as the fall of the Roman Empire in the West. Since he acknowledged the overlordship of Zeno (q.v.), whose recognition he sought, Zeno conferred on him the title of *patrikios* (q.v.) and allowed him to administer Italy (q.v.). The death of Julius Nepos (q.v.) in 480 removed the only possible rival claimant to Odoacer's power. However, Zeno's desire to rid Thrace (q.v.) of the Ostrogothic chieftain Theodoric (qq.v.) proved to be Odoacer's undoing. To entice Theodoric to move westward, Zeno offered Theodoric Italy if he could wrest it from Odoacer. This he did from 489–493, after besieging Ravenna (q.v.) for over two years. After Odoacer surrendered Ravenna, Theodoric killed him with his own hand.

ODO OF DEUIL. Latin historian of the Second Crusade (q.v.), who was secretary and chaplain to Louis VIII of France (q.v.), a leader of the Second Crusade (q.v.). His position gave him access to the inner leadership circle of of the Crusade. The religious hostility toward Byzantium (q.v.) that he reports fully justified the fear with which Manuel I Komnenos (q.v.) viewed the approach of the French army. Odo's account is rich in descriptive details about the city of Constantinople (q.v.) and the court of Manuel I.

OHRID. City in southwestern Macedonia, key position on the Via Egnatia (qq.v.); archbishopric; capital of Bulgaria under Samuel of Bulgaria (qq.v.). Perhaps most importantly, it became a center for the diffusion of Byzantine culture throughout the region. Kliment of Ohrid (q.v.) laid the foundations for this by training a Slavonic-speaking clergy and helping to create a Slavonic literature. The city had several learned archbishops (q.v.), including Theophylaktos (patriarch from ca. 1090–ca. 1108), and Demetrios Chomatenos (qq.v.). Theophylaktos was a student of Michael Psellos (q.v.), and a theologian whose correspondence is an important source of information about the region during the reign of Alexios I Komnenos (q.v.). The extant literary works of Demetrios Chomatenos are the chief source for the internal history of the Despotate of Epiros (to which Ohrid belonged) during the first half of the 13th century.

OLEG. Prince of Kiev (q.v.) from 879–ca. 912; successor of Rurik (q.v.). He founded Kievan Rus (q.v.), according to the *Russian Primary Chronicle* (q.v.), which mentions a Rus attack on Constantinople (q.v.) in 907. The treaty that resulted in 911 inaugurated regular trade relations with Byzantium (q.v.). He was succeeded by Igor (q.v.).

OLGA. Princess of Kiev (q.v.), wife of Igor (q.v.), who visited Constantinople (q.v.) in 957 (or 946?), where she was received with great honor by Constantine VII (q.v.), as described in the *De ceremoniis* (q.v.) and in the *Russian Primary Chronicle* (q.v.). It is not clear when she was actually baptized, though it may have been in Constantinople. In 959, for reasons unclear, she turned her back on Byzantium (q.v.) and requested a German bishop (q.v.) from Otto I (q.v.). The bishop who was sent quickly returned home when he found a pagan resurgence among the Rus (q.v.). Not until the reign of Vladimir I (q.v.) was this religious instability resolved (in favor of Byzantium [q.v.]).

OLYMPIODOROS OF THEBES. Historian, traveler, and poet. He was the first traveler to have written an account of a personal visit to the Huns (q.v.), which occurred through an embassy he undertook to the Hunnic king Donatus in 412. Indeed, his account is all that is known about Donatus. Unfortunately, his general history (originally covering the years 407–425) survives only in fragments. Fortunately, Philostorgios, Sozomenos, and Zosimos (qq.v.) all used his work. It is Olympiodoros who, in one of the surviving fragments of his work, relates the legend that in 410 Alaric (q.v.) received a miraculous warning by a statue that impeded his attempt to cross from Italy to North Africa (qq.v).

OLYMPIOS. *See* **MARTIN I.**

OLYMPOS, MOUNT. One of the great monastic holy mountains of Byzantium (q.v.), along with Mount Athos, Latros, Meteora, the Monastery of St. Catherine at Mount Sinai, and Wondrous Mountain (qq.v.). Located in Bithynia (q.v.), its numerous monasteries included those on Mount Olympos itself, and those within the mountain's larger environs, extending from Prousa to the Sea of Marmara (qq.v.). Some of the monasteries of the region (e.g., at Atroa, Medikion, and Pelekete) were renowned for their resistance to Iconoclasm (q.v.). Around 764, for example, Michael Lachanodrakon (q.v.) burned down the monastery of Pelekete, torturing and killing some of the monks who were noted for their resistance to Iconoclasm. The region produced numerous saints, including Euthymios the Younger, patriarch Methodios (qq.v.), Peter of Atroa, Plato of Sakkoudion, and Theodore of Stoudios (q.v.). It was also a place that received high officials forced out of office, such as Michael Psellos (q.v.), who became a monk there at the end of his career.

OMURTAG. Khan of Bulgaria (qq.v.) from 814–831. His relations with Byzantium (q.v.) were peaceful, in marked contrast to those of his father, Krum (q.v.). He concluded with Leo V (q.v.) a 30-year peace treaty, preserved in a proto-Bulgarian inscription (i.e., in an inscription in Turkic runes such as usually predate the mass introduction of Christianity in 864). Omurtag's aid to Michael II (q.v.) in 823, when the khan forced Thomas the Slav (q.v.) to lift his siege of Constantinople (q.v.), was decisive in ending Thomas's rebellion. Peaceful relations served to increase Byzantine cultural influence in Bulgaria during his reign. At Pliska (q.v.), his capital, he created a palace with a throne room that must have rivaled the audience halls of emperors in Constantinople (q.v.).

ON THE THEMES. *See* **DE THEMATIBUS.**

OPSIKION. One of the chief themes of Asia Minor (qq.v.), created in the seventh century, perhaps as early as 626 in order to provide Herakleios (q.v.) with an elite army to support his war against Persia (q.v.). In 715 it revolted against Anastasios II (q.v.), and placed Theodosios III (q.v.) on the throne. It supported the revolt of Artabasdos (q.v.) in 742. In the eighth century two new themes, the Optimatoi and Boukellarion (qq.v.) were carved out of Opsikion, whose command center was shifted from Ankyra to Nicaea (qq.v.). Part of the reason for this may have been to make revolts by thematic commanders more difficult.

OPTIMATOI. Theme in northwest Asia Minor (qq.v.) carved out of Opsikion (q.v.) in the eighth century, with its command center at Nikomedeia (q.v.). The soldiers of this theme supplied and looked after the pack animals that carried the baggage of imperial *tagmata* from Constantinople (qq.v.), when the latter went out on campaign.

ORANT. Also *orans* (Latin for "praying"), referring to the manner in which early Christians prayed: standing with upright, open palms at shoulder height. This is illustrated frequently in pre-Iconoclastic (q.v.) art. After the eighth century the position of *proskynesis* (q.v.) becomes the normative form of prayer depicted in art.

ORHAN. Ottoman sultan (qq.v.) from 1326–1362; son of Osman (q.v.), the sultan who first established the Ottomans on European soil. Orhan's conquest of Prousa in 1328, Nicaea in 1331, and Nikomedeia (qq.v.) in 1337 helped the Ottomans to consolidate their domain in northwest Asia Minor (q.v.). It also entangled them, in the process, in the internal affairs of Byzantium (q.v.). In 1346 Orhan married Theodora Kantakouzene, daughter of John VI Kantakouzenos (q.v.), who called on Orhan's help several times in the civil war that punctuated John VI's reign. As a result, Orhan and his son Suleyman Pasha were able to establish an Ottoman base in Europe at Gallipoli (q.v.) in 1354, which Orhan then used to expand into Thrace (q.v.).

ORIBASIOS. Physician and friend of Julian "the Apostate" (q.v.). He followed Julian to Gaul (q.v.) in 355 and was with him when he was killed in Persia (q.v.) in 363. Oribasios's personal memoir of Julian has not survived, but it was used in the *History* of Eunapios of

Sardis (q.v.), who also wrote a brief biography of Orobasios. A summary of Galen (q.v.) by Oribasios was much relied on by subsequent Byzantine and Arab physicians.

ORIGEN. Controversial Alexandrian theologian. His ideas, some of them as basic to Christian theology (q.v.) as that of *homoousios* (q.v.), continued to have a powerful impact on Christian thinkers for centuries after his death in 254. Among those ideas for which he was attacked was his belief in the preexistence of souls. Origin wrote some 2,000 works, most of which have not survived. His *Contra Celsus* (Against Celsus) is the chief source for the writing of Celsus, early Christianity's greatest critic. Nevertheless, his work was deemed suspected of heresy (q.v.). As late as 543 Justinian I (q.v.) issued an edict, supported by the patriarch Menas (qq.v.), condemning Origen.

OROSIUS, PAUL. Fifth-century Latin historian who wrote *History against the Pagans,* a work that begins with the Creation and ends in 417. It was much influenced by Augustine's (q.v.) view (in his *City of God)* that the decline of Rome (q.v.) did not result from neglecting the traditional Roman gods. In the medieval West the work achieved considerable popularity as a world history.

ORPHANOTROPHOS. *See* **JOHN THE ORPHANOTROPHOS; PHILANTHROPY.**

ORTHODOXY. Greek for "right belief," referring to matters of Christian faith and doctrine, the core of which is defined in the ecumenical councils (q.v.) of the church. Beliefs and practices condemned by accepted church councils are considered heresy (q.v.). The Byzantine and western churches were frequently suspicious of each other's Orthodoxy, indeed were intermittently schismatic down to the final church schism of 1054 (q.v.), so that today the term is used to refer to the doctrines and liturgy of the eastern churches whose roots lie in the Byzantine church. Orthodoxy survived the fall of Constantinople (q.v.) in 1453 to become Byzantium's living legacy. It is an active force in lands that formerly comprised Byzantium (q.v.), as well as in Slavic (q.v.) lands proselytized by Byzantium. Byzantine art and church architecture cannot be understood without a basic understanding of Orthodoxy.

OSMAN. Founder of the Turkish dynasty of the Ottomans (q.v.) and its first sultan (q.v.) from 1288–1326. It was Osman whose victory over Byzantine forces in 1302 at the battle of Bapheus (q.v.) established his small emirate in western Asia Minor (q.v.) as the nucleus of the future Ottoman Empire. His son Orhan (q.v.) greatly expanded the emirate.

OSTROGOTHS. Major division of the Goths (q.v.) who settled north of the Black Sea (q.v.) until the Huns (q.v.) drove them westward (ca. 375) and subjugated them in Pannonia (q.v.). Only the death of Attila in 453 loosened the Hun's hold over the Ostrogoths, who found employment as Byzantine *foederati* (q.v.). In 488 Zeno (q.v.) persuaded the Ostrogothic king Theodoric (q.v.) to invade Italy (q.v.) and depose Odoacer (q.v.). After Odoacer's death (493) an Ostrogothic kingdom was established in Italy with its capital at Ravenna (q.v.). Though an untutored Arian (q.v.), Theodoric respected Roman civilization, tolerated Orthodoxy (q.v.), and allowed the bureaucracy to function without interference. After Theodoric's death in 526 his daughter Amalasuntha (q.v.) put herself under the protection of Justinian I (q.v.). Amalasuntha's murder in 535 was the excuse Justinian I used to invade Italy that same year. The war dragged on until 552 when Narses (q.v.) defeated Totila (q.v.). However, the Byzantine victory over the Ostrogoths proved hollow. Three years after Justinian's death (565), another Germanic tribe, the Lombards (q.v.), entered Italy and quickly subdued much of it.

OTHON DE LA ROCHE. French duke of Athens and Thebes (qq.v.) from 1205–1225. He was a young Burgundian knight who was granted Athens and Thebes by Boniface of Montferrat (q.v.). When he retired to his native Burgundy in 1225, he left his domain to his nephew Guy I de la Roche. Under Guy I and his successors the duchy of Athens and Thebes became prosperous and increasingly French in its institutions. It was conquered by the Catalan Grand Company (q.v.) in 1311.

OTRANTO. Coastal city in southernmost Apulia (q.v.), located on the strait of Otranto where the Ionian Sea meets the Adriatic Sea (qq.v.). It served as an entrance to Italy (q.v.), and a place to cross to Avlon in Epiros (q.v.). Belisarios (q.v.) landed troops there in 544 during the war with the Ostrogoths (q.v.). The Lombards (q.v.) seized it in the early eighth century, but it was recaptured by Byzantine forces in 758. The Normans under Robert Guiscard (qq.v.) conquered it in

1068. The city's most famous medieval citizen was writer and diplomat Nicholas of Otranto. The cross-in-square church (q.v.) of St. Pietro stands today as a reminder of Otranto's long Byzantine occupation.

OTTO I THE GREAT. King of Germany (q.v.) from 936 until 962, the year he was crowned western emperor by Pope (qq.v.) John XII. By that time Otto's troops had control of much of Italy (q.v.), and had attacked Byzantine Bari (q.v.). Several centuries later, the coronation would be seen as the foundation of the Holy Roman Empire (962–1806), but to contemporaries it appeared as a revival of Charlemagne's (q.v.) empire and title. Nikephoros II Phokas (q.v.) demanded that Otto I renounce the title. Otto responded by sending Liutprand of Cremona to Constantinople (qq.v.) in 968 to negotiate. The embassy failed, and the problem was left for John I Tziemiskes (q.v.) to resolve in 972, with the betrothal of princess Theophano to Otto II (qq.v.).

OTTO II. *See* **THEOPHANO.**

OTTO III. German king from 983, and western emperor (q.v.) from 996–1002; son of Otto II and Theophano (qq.v.). His mother insured that he was instilled with a profound respect for Byzantine civilization. His dream was to create a revival of the ancient Roman Empire *(Renovatio Imperii Romanorum),* to which end he sought to make Rome (q.v.), where he was crowned western emperor, his capital. He adopted Byzantine court ceremonial and titles, and he called himself *Imperator Romanorum.* He continued his predecessors policy of asserting his supremacy over the papacy (q.v.) by rejecting the Donation of Constantine (q.v.). During the last years of his reign he had the support of his tutor Gerbert, whose installation as Pope Sylvester II (999–1003) he arranged. Amid dreaming of *renovatio* the reality of death intervened. At age 22 he died suddenly, while negotiating for a Byzantine bride.

OTTOMANS. Turkish dynasty founded by Osman (q.v.), son of Ertoghrul. Osman established a small emirate ca. 1282 around Eskishehir (Byzantine Dorylaion [q.v.]), amid the crumbling Seljuk (q.v.) state. From there he raided into Bithynia (q.v.), defeating a Byzantine army at the battle of Bapheus (q.v.) in 1302. Orhan (q.v.) captured Prousa in 1326, Nicaea in 1331, and Nikomedeia (qq.v.) in 1337. It was Orhan, responding to requests from John VI Kantakouzenos (q.v.), who introduced Ottoman troops to European soil during the civil war of 1341–1347. In 1354 Orhan made Gallipoli (q.v.) a base of operations for expansion into Thrace (q.v.). Their subsequent ejection from Gallipoli in 1366 by Amadeo VI of Savoy (q.v.) proved only temporary. A decade later, Murad I (q.v.) possessed it again, this time for good. Adrianople (q.v.) fell in 1369 and became the Ottoman capital in 1377. Thessalonike (q.v.) surrendered in 1387, and after the battle of Kosovo Polje (q.v.) in 1389 the Ottomans made Serbia (q.v.) a vassal state. The defeat of the Crusader army by Bayezid I at Nikopolis (qq.v.) in 1396 further demonstrated the weakness of western arms against Ottoman armies strengthened with janissaries (q.v.). In Asia Minor (q.v.) Bayezid's attack on Saruhan and other Turkish emirates (qq.v.) was reversed by his capture by Timur at the battle of Ankara (qq.v.) in 1402. From 1402–1413 the Ottoman state collapsed into civil war between the sons of Bayezid, Musa and Suleyman Celebi (qq.v.). Not until the reign of Murad II, son of Mehmed I (qq.v.), did Ottoman expansion resume. Thessalonike was captured for the second time in 1430, much of Serbia was annexed by 1439, and at Varna (q.v.) in 1444 another Crusader army was annihilated. It was left to Mehmed II to conquer Constantinople (qq.v.) in 1453 and transfer the Ottoman capital there from Adrianople. Mehmed II conquered the last Byzantine outposts of Mistra in 1460 and Trebizond (qq.v.) in 1461, by which time the Ottomans had established themselves as a powerful empire extending into eastern Europe.

OTTO OF FREISING. Latin chronicler of the Second Crusade (q.v.). Bishop of Freising in Germany and half-brother of Conrad III (qq.v.). Otto led a main contingent of the Crusader army that marched south through Asia Minor to Attaleia on the Aegean (qq.v.) coast. His *Gesta Frederici* (The Deeds of Frederick), commissioned by Frederick I Barbarossa (q.v.), Otto's uncle, is an important eyewitness account of the Second Crusade, in addition to the comments it provides on Byzantine affairs during the reigns of John II Komnenos and Manuel I Komnenos (qq.v.), e.g., the marriage of Bertha of Sulzbach (q.v.) and Manuel I.

OURANOS, NIKEPHOROS. *See* **SAMUEL OF BULGARIA.**

– P –

PACHOMIOS. Founder of cenobitic (communal) monasticism (q.v.); Egyptian saint (ca. 290–346). He was the first to organize monks into a communal life with a written rule. Around 320 this former soldier founded his first *koinobion* (q.v.) at Tabennisi in the upper part of the Nile River valley; there he organized his small group of disciples, devising for them the first monastic rule. Jerome (q.v.) subsequently translated his *Rules,* as well as his letters. Eight more such monasteries were organized at Tabennisi. In 330 Pachomios founded a *koinobion* at Pbow that subsequently administered the entire group of monasteries.

PACHYMERES, GEORGE. Historian (died ca. 1310) whose history, covering the years 1260–1308, is the chief source for the reign of Michael VIII (q.v.) and for part of the reign of Andronikos II (q.v.). Pachymeres describes, for example, the extensive frontier defenses erected in Thrace, Macedonia, and Asia Minor by the Empire of Nicaea (qq.v.). A student of George Akropolites (q.v.), he became perhaps the greatest Byzantine scholar of the 13th century, with a legacy of writings on topics as diverse as mathematics, law, and rhetoric.

PĂCUIUL LUI SOARE. *See* **DOBRUDJA.**

PALAIOLOGAN DYNASTY. Longest-lived of Byzantine imperial dynasties, founded by Michael VIII Palaiologos (q.v.), who recovered Constantinople from the Latin Empire (qq.v.) in 1261. The dynasty included Michael VIII (1261–1282), Andronikos II (1282–1328), Andronikos III (1328–1341), John V (1341–1391; and during his turbulent reign these rulers: John VI Kantakouzenos [1347–1354], Andronikos VI [1376–1379]), and John VII [1390]), Manuel II (1391–1425), John VIII (1425–1448), and Constantine IX (1448–1453). The dynasty ended with the death of Constantine XI (q.v.) during the final Ottoman assault on Constantinople (qq.v.) in 1453. Ultimately, the destruction wrought by the Fourth Crusade and the Latin Empire (qq.v.) was something Palaiologan dynasts were not able to surmount. Palaiologan emperors (q.v.) sought vainly to stem the decline of restored Byzantium (q.v.), but this proved virtually impossible in the face of unrelenting Ottoman expansion and threats from the West (e.g., from Charles I Anjou and the Catalan Grand

Company [q.v.]). Help sought from the West proved to be a chimera. Despite this decline, Byzantine art and architecture, as well as Byzantine literature and cultural interactions with the West, flourished. Moreover, the Palaiologan period produced some of Byzantium's finest scholars, including Bessarion, George Gemistos Plethon, and Demetrios Kydones (qq.v.).

PALAMAS, GREGORY. Theologian and chief defender of Hesychasm (q.v.) who became archbishop of Thessalonike (qq.v). from 1347–1359. He was subsequently elevated to sainthood in 1368. His writings form a core of apologetic literature called Palamism, which defended the meditative prayer developed by the monks of Mount Athos (q.v.) as a way for direct, mystical experience of God in the form of the divine light seen by Jesus' disciples on Mount Tabor. In this way the inaccessibility of God was bridged by divine energy, as opposed to the bridge of cosmic hierarchy espoused by Pseudo-Dionysios (q.v.). Barlaam of Calabria (q.v.) ridiculed Hesychasm as superstition, denying the possibility of seeing the Light of Tabor. Palamas, who was himself a former Athonian monk, defended Hesychasm against Barlaam with vigor, arguing that the Light of Tabor was one of God's uncreated energies that manifest God's power in the world. He gained a wide circle of supporters for his views, among whom were the patriarchs Isidore I, Kallistos I, and Philotheos Kokkinos, and Emperor John VI Kantakouzenos (qq.v.). Among his opponents were the Zealots (q.v.), who until 1350 prohibited him from assuming his duties as archbishop of Thessalonike.

PALAMISM. *See* **PALAMAS, GREGORY.**

PALERMO. City in northwest Sicily (q.v.). Taken by the Vandals (q.v.) in 440, it was recaptured in 536 by Belisarios (q.v.) when he invaded Sicily. The Arabs (q.v.) captured Palermo in 831, making it their capital. After 1072 it was the capital of Norman Sicily (qq.v.), and the site of a flourishing silk (q.v.) industry. Roger II (q.v.) was crowned in Palermo in 1130, as was Henry VI (q.v.) in 1194. It was in Palermo that the Sicilian Vespers (q.v.) erupted in 1282.

PALESTINE. Region called the Holy Land situated between the Mediterranean (q.v.) and the Jordan River valley, including the Dead Sea and Sea of Galilee, and the Golan Heights in the north. Its southern extent was the Negev desert. Its major cities included Caesarea Maritima, Jerusalem (qq.v.), Skythopolis, Neapolis, and Gaza (q.v.). The impact of state-supported Christianity on the region was great. Palestine became a focus for pilgrimage after Constantine I's mother Helena (qq.v.) made her own journey there, where she allegedly discovered the True Cross (q.v.). Monasticism (q.v.) spread quickly; among its many famous monks were Euthymios the Great and Sabas (qq.v.). Palestine also produced the famous historians Eusebios of Caesarea, Sozomenos, and Prokopios of Caesarea (qq.v.). Chorikos of Gaza and Prokopios of Gaza (qq.v.) were among the notable rhetoricians from the school of rhetoric at Gaza. Up to the Muslim conquest, Palestine continued to be home to Jews, Orthodox Christians, Monophysites, and Samaritans (qq.v.). In 614 the Persians (q.v.) captured Jerusalem and carried off the True Cross. Herakleios (q.v.) restored the True Cross to Jerusalem ca. 629, but Byzantine rule over the region proved to be ephemeral. Muslim (q.v.) domination of the region was completed by 638, the year bishop Sophronios (q.v.) was forced to surrender Jerusalem to the Arabs (q.v.).

PALMYRA (Tadmor in Syriac). Oasis capital of the kingdom of Palmyra, in the Syrian desert. After it fell to the Roman emperor Aurelian in 273, Diocletian (q.v.) made it into a military bastion that helped to protect the eastern frontier. Justinian I (q.v.) restored its fortifications. However, those fortifications could not resist the Arabs (q.v.), who conquered it in 633.

PAMMAKARISTOS, CHURCH OF HAGIA MARIA.
See **GLABAS, MICHAEL TARCHANEIOTES.**

PAMPHYLIA. The coastal plain of south Asia Minor (q.v.) between Lycia and Cilicia (qq.v.). The region was difficult to defend against Arab naval attack from Syria (q.v.). The only havens of safety were its fortified cities, including Side, Syllaion, and above all the major port of Attaleia (q.v.), seat of the theme of Kibyrrhaiotai (qq.v.). A section of the army of the Second Crusade commanded by Otto of Freising (qq.v.) reached Attaleia (q.v.) in 1148, and they found it almost isolated amid a countryside much ravaged by the Seljuks (q.v.).

PANAGHIA TON CHALKEON. *See* **THESSALONIKE.**

PANARETOS, MICHAEL. His chronicle (q.v.), covering the years 1204–1390, is the principal source for the history of the Empire of Trebizond (q.v.). His long service to Alexios III Komnenos included participation in the emperor's (q.v.) military expeditions and acquisition of direct knowledge of the major political and ecclesiastical events at court for the years after 1340, the period for which the chronicle is most useful.

PANDECTS. *See* **DIGEST.**

PANHYPERSEBASTOS. *See* **SEBASTOS.**

PANNONIA. Roman province in central Europe that bordered the Danube (q.v.) to the north and east, and the province of Noricum (q.v.) to the west. Diocletian (q.v.) divided it into four provinces (Pannonia I, Pannonia II, Savia, and Valeria) ca. 295. It was overrun by barbarians in the late fourth century and settled by Avars (q.v.) in the sixth century.

PANTELEEMON MONASTERY. *See* **ATHOS, MOUNT.**

PANTEUGENOS, SOTERICHOS. Theologian who was condemned in 1157 for his views on the Eucharist; patriarch-designate of Antioch (q.v.) and a deacon of Hagia Sophia in Constantinople (qq.v.). He was attacked in 1156 by Nicholas of Methone, theologian and supporter of Manuel I Komnenos (q.v.), for supporting the view that it was to the Father alone (not to the entire Trinity) that the Eucharist was offered. This view had been condemned at a synod in Constantinople earlier that same year. Manuel I called a new council in 1157 that condemned Panteugenos and cast Manuel in the role of defender of Orthodoxy (q.v.).

PANTOKRATOR. Greek for "all-sovereign" (or "Ruler of All"), a term applied to God in Revelation 19:6. In art, the Pantokrator refers to a way of representing Christ in a bust-length, frontal portrait, holding a Gospel book in his left hand and blessing with his right hand. This image was frequently painted in the central dome (q.v.) of churches, as in the church at Daphni, near Athens (q.v.). The Pantokrator Monastery in Constantinople (qq.v.) was renowned.

PANTOKRATOR MONASTERY. *See* **PANTOKRATOR; PHILANTHROPY.**

PAPACY. Office and administrative jurisdiction of the pope of Rome (qq.v.). The term comes from the Greek "papas," which means father, from which "pope" is also derived. Eastern influence on the papacy is also seen in the many Greek and Syrian popes during the seventh and eighth centuries. The claim of the pope to be father over the entire church is at the heart of papal primacy (q.v.), the most intractable issue between the eastern and western churches.

PAPAL PRIMACY. The eastern and western churches defined this differently, which became a central issue in the separation of the eastern and western churches. The Byzantine church gave the bishop of Rome (qq.v.) honorary primacy, but it never accepted the papacy's (q.v.) view that the bishop of Rome was a primate over the entire church. This the papacy (q.v.) demanded, claiming inherited apostolic power from the first apostle St. Peter, using Matthew 10:2 and 16:18 as supporting texts, along with the forged *Donation of Constantine* (q.v.). In any case, the Byzantine church took a more collegial view toward the power of bishops, seeing ultimate primacy as residing in the consensus of bishops at an ecumenical council (q.v.).

PAPHLAGONIA. Region of north Asia Minor (q.v.) situated between Bithynia and Pontos (qq.v.), consisting of the south shore of the Black Sea (q.v.) and inland territory. The chief cities included Amastris and its metropolis Gangra (qq.v.). It belonged to the theme of Opsikion (qq.v.) before becoming its own theme (q.v.) in the early ninth century. Theophilos's wife Theodora (qq.v.) came from Paphlagonia, as did Michael IV Paphlagon (q.v.). After the battle of Mantzikert in 1071 the Turks (qq.v.) overran the interior. However, the coast remained in Byzantine possession until the late 14th century.

PARAKOIMOMENOS. The imperial chamberlain who guarded the emperor's (q.v.) bedchamber. Usually *parakoimomenoi* were eunuchs (q.v.), but sometimes not, as in the case of the future emperor Basil I (q.v.), appointed to the post by Michael III (q.v.). In the 10th century it became an extremely powerful office. For example, Joseph Bringas (q.v.) administered the empire as *parakoimomenos* of Romanos II (q.v.).

PAREKKLESION. A chapel, free-standing or attached, along the side of a church, or located within a church's upper story. Perhaps the most famous *parekklesion* is the one built alongside the Church of the Chora Monastery in Constantinople (qq.v.) which contains frescoes (q.v.) important for the study of 14th-century monumental painting.

PARIS PSALTER. *See* **PSALTER.**

PAROIKOS. A peasant dependent on a large landowner (including monasteries, churches, even charitable institutions). The *colonus* (q.v.) of earlier centuries may provide a link to the *paroikos,* but this has been impossible to demonstrate. The numbers of *paroikoi* seem to have increased during the 10th century. In the 11th century their status became hereditary, with the recipient assuming all obligations to the landowner. From Romanos I through Basil II (qq.v.) legislation against the *dynatoi* (q.v.) attempted to deal with the replacement of independent farmers by the growing number of *paroikoi.* However, by the 13th century *paroikoi* on large estates increased so much that they replaced independent village communities almost entirely. *Pronoia* (q.v.) grants could involve the tax revenues and services of *paroikoi.*

PARTITIO ROMANIAE. Literally, "the sharing of Romania," the title of the treaty of 1204 that ruthlessly divided up Byzantium (q.v.) among the major participants of the Fourth Crusade (q.v.). Latin emperor Baldwin of Flanders (q.v.) received five-eighths of Constantinople (q.v.), in addition to a quarter of imperial territory that included Thrace, a portion of northwest Asia Minor, and several islands in the Aegean Sea (qq.v), notably Lesbos, Chios, and Samos (qq.v.). Boniface of Montferrat seized Thessalonike (qq.v.) and its surrounding territory to form the Kingdom of Thessalonike. Subsequent to the treaty, in 1205 a Latin principality was founded in the Peloponnesos by William (I) Champlitte and Geoffrey (I) Villehardouin (qq.v.). In that same year, Othon de la Roche (q.v.) was granted Athens and Thebes (q.v.). The Venetians got the lion's share, including three-eighths of Constantinople (q.v.), the Ionian islands, the islands of Crete, Euboea (qq.v.), Andros, and Naxos (q.v.), as well as the most important ports of the Hellespont and the Sea of Marmara (qq.v.). This allowed them, in effect, to dominate the sea route from Venice (q.v.) to Constantinople. Long after the Latin Empire had collapsed the Venetians could look back on this treaty as providing them with the foundation for their colonial empire in the eastern Mediterranean (q.v.).

PASTOPHORIA. *See* **DIAKONIKON; PROTHESIS.**

PATMOS. Island off the southwest coast of Asia Minor in the Aegean Sea (qq.v.), where tradition has it St. John the Divine wrote the New Testament's Book of Revelation. Its great Byzantine monument is the monastery of St. John the Theologian, founded by Christodoulos of Patmos, who was given the island by Alexios I Komnenos (q.v.) in 1088. Thereafter, Patmos was attacked by pirates and Arabs, including Tzachas (qq.v.) ca. 1090. It fell into Venetian hands in 1207. In 1461, as a consequence of the fall of Constantinople (q.v.), Pope Pius II placed the island under papal protection. The Ottomans (q.v.) occupied it in 1537.

PATRAS. *See* **DANELIS; SPHRANTZES, GEORGE.**

PATRIARCH. Title of the bishop (q.v.) of one of the five patriarchal sees (q.v.): Rome, Constantinople, Alexandria, Antioch, and Jerusalem (qq.v.). From the perspective of the Byzantine church, authority over Christendom was shared collectively by the five bishops as a *pentarchy* ("the power of five," in Greek), with the bishop of Rome given honorary primacy only, not papal primacy (q.v.). Likewise, the title "Ecumenical Patriarch," used by the bishops of Constantinople (q.v.) from the time of Patriarch John IV "Faster" (q.v.) onward, did not signify universal overlordship over the entire church, but rather the preeminence of the bishop of Constantinople over those bishops under the political dominion of Byzantium (q.v.).

PATRIARCHAL SCHOOL. Established by Alexios I (q.v.), if not earlier, the school provided higher education for clergy and monks. Core subjects included theology (q.v.) and related subjects, but other topics could be introduced, depending on the teacher. Michael Italikos (q.v.), for example, taught a broad range of topics that included the Holy Scriptures, rhetoric, philosophy, and mathematics. Other famous 12th-century scholars who taught in the school included Eustathios of Thessalonike (q.v.) and the rhetorician Nikephoros Chrysoberges.

PATRIARCHATE. *See* **PATRIARCH.**

PATRIKIOS. A long-lived honorary title, created by Constantine I (q.v.), granted to important military and civil officials. Its importance gradually diminished after the 10th century; it disappeared entirely after the beginning of the 12th century.

PATZINAKS. *See* **PECHENEGS.**

PAULICIANS. Armenian sect whose state was centered at Tephrike in northeastern Cappadocia (q.v.). It flourished briefly from ca. 843, until Byzantine forces stormed it in 878, establishing on its ruins first a *kleisoura*, then a theme (qq.v.). What is known about Paulician doctrine is that it embraced Iconoclasm (q.v.). Paulician beliefs may have had roots in ancient Manichaeanism (q.v.). It seems likely that the Paulicians influenced the Bogomils of Bulgaria (qq.v), who subsequently influenced the Cathars of western Europe, who were known by various names, e.g., the Albigensians.

PAUL OF AEGINA. Physician whose seventh-century *Epitome of Medicine,* based on Hippocrates, Galen, and Oribasios (qq.v.), remained the chief medical text in Byzantium (q.v.). It exerted considerable influence on Islamic and European medicine through translations into Arabic and Latin. The sections on pharmacology and on surgery were particularly influential.

PAUL OF LATROS. *See* **LATROS.**

PAUL SILENTIARIOS. *See* **GREEK ANTHOLOGY; HAGIA SOPHIA.**

PAUSANIUS. *See* **GEOGRAPHY.**

PBOW. *See* **PACHOMIOS.**

PEC. Serbian cultural and religious center. In 1346 Stefan Urosh IV Dushan (q.v.) proclaimed an independent Serbian patriarchate át Pec, something never acknowledged by the Byzantine church. The estrangement caused by this proclamation was resolved in 1375 when the head of the Serbian church was accorded the title of patriarch (q.v.).

PECHENEGS (Patzinaks). Warlike, nomadic people from the Eurasian steppe (q.v.) who appeared on Byzantium's (q.v.) northern frontier in the late ninth century. They moved westward from the Volga, perhaps under pressure from the Uzes (q.v.), driving the Magyars (q.v.) beyond the Dnieper, then settling between the Don and lower Danube (q.v.). They were organized into eight tribes, and they had no king. They were often enemies of Bulgaria and the Rus (qq.v.), which usually suited Byzantine interests; for example, they killed Svjatoslav (q.v.), Byzantium's Rus adversary, in 972. They also served as mercenaries in Byzantine armies. Thus, the Pechenegs helped to stabilize Byzantium's northern frontier. However, in 1047 they became a direct threat when a new horde of Pechenegs crossed the Danube to plunder Thrace (q.v.). In 1053, a 30-year truce was arranged that accepted Pecheneg settlement south of the Danube. Nevertheless, raids into Thrace followed in 1078 and 1087; the 1087 raid included Uzes and Cumans (q.v.). The Pecheneg problem was solved temporarily by Alexios I Komnenos (q.v.), who nearly wiped them out at the battle of Mount Lebounion in 1091. The remnants were resettled and found work as mercenaries in Alexios I's armies. A final wave of Pechenegs met the same end in 1122. Crossing the Danube, they pillaged Macedonia (q.v.) and Thrace before being defeated by John II (q.v.), who instituted an annual day of celebration to commemorate his victory.

PELAGIA THE HARLOT. Famous and beautiful fourth-century (or fifth-century?) dancer of Antioch (q.v.) who became a saint. She experienced a sudden conversion to Christianity due to the influence of Bishop (q.v.) Nonnos. Disguised as a eunuch (q.v.), she retired to an obscure grotto on the Mount of Olives in Jerusalem (q.v.) where she lived out her days. Only upon her death was the truth discovered. The Menologion of Basil II (qq.v.) refers to her as a harlot, hence the epithet.

PELAGONIA, BATTLE OF. Decisive battle fought in 1259 on the plain of Pelagonia, near Kastoria (qq.v.). The army of the Empire of Nicaea (q.v.), led by John, the brother of Michael VIII Palaiologos (q.v.) won a decisive victory over coalition forces from Michael II Komnenos Doukas of the Despotate of Epiros (qq.v.), Manfred of Sicily (qq.v.), and William II Villehardouin of the principality of Achaia (qq.v.). As soon as the battle began the coalition forces began to desert. John's Cuman (q.v.) archers carried the day. William II Villehardouin was captured and all of Manfred's 400 knights surrendered. Michael VIII Palaiologos (q.v.) was now able to concentrate on the recovery of Constantinople (q.v.) without fear of attack from the West. In addition, William II's ransom included handing over to Michael VIII three key fortresses of Frankish Achaia (q.v.): Mistra, Monemvasia (qq.v.), and Maina.

PELEKETE MONASTERY. *See* **LACHANODRAKON, MICHAEL; OLYMPOS, MOUNT.**

PELLA. *See* **VIA EGNATIA.**

PELOPONNESOS. The peninsula of southern Greece (q.v.), whose name means "Island of Pelops," joined to the Greek mainland by the narrow Isthmus of Corinth (q.v.). It was part of the Roman province of Achaia (q.v.), whose capital was Corinth (q.v.), in Roman and Early Byzantine times. The devastation wrought by Alaric's (q.v.) invasion of 396–397 resulted in a barrier wall called the Hexamilion (q.v.) across the Isthmus of Corinth. Nevertheless, in the late sixth century the Peloponnesos was invaded by Slavs (q.v.) who settled chiefly in mountainous regions, like the Melingoi and Ezeritai who lived in the Taygetos Mountains. Byzantine power was reestablished during the reign of Nikephoros I (q.v.). In 1205, in the aftermath of the Fourth Crusade (q.v.), William I Champlitte and Geoffrey I Villehardouin (qq.v.) began their conquest of the Peloponnesos, creating the Frankish principality of Achaia (q.v.), with strongholds at Mistra, Monemvasia (qq.v.), and Maina. The Franks referred to the Peloponnesos more generally by the enigmatic name Morea (q.v.). In 1262 much of Frankish Achaia, including Mistra (q.v.), was returned to Byzantine hands following the battle of Pelagonia (1259). The Byzantine despotate of Mistra (1348–1460) was intermittently threatened by the Ottomans (q.v.). Manuel II Palaiologos (q.v.) rebuilt the Hexamilion in 1415, but the Ottomans overran it in 1423 and 1446. The last vestige of Byzantium (q.v.) in the Peloponnesos fell in 1460, when Mistra surrendered to Mehmed II (q.v.).

PENDENTIVE. Spherical triangles of brick or stone that fill in the corners of four arches to create a continuous surface for the base for a dome (q.v.) to rest on. It solves the problem, as does the squinch (q.v.), of how to put a round dome over a square space defined by four arches. Invented in the sixth century, the pendentive was used most impressively at Constantinople (q.v.) in the great church of Hagia Sophia built by Justinian I (qq.v.).

PENTAPOLIS. *See* **CYRENAICA.**

PENTARCHY. Greek term for "the rule of five," referring to the Byzantine theory, which evolved in the fifth and sixth centuries (formally sanctioned by Justinian I [q.v.]), that church authority is collective, residing in the five patriarchates (q.v.) of Rome, Constantinople, Alexandria, Antioch, and Jerusalem (qq.v.). It followed that no church council could be called unless all five were present. This theory was contested by the papacy (q.v.), which subsequently claimed exclusive papal primacy (q.v.) over the church, not just honorary primacy among equal partners. The theory was also weakened by the conquest of the Near East by the Arabs (q.v.), since the sees (q.v.) of Alexandria, Antioch, and Jerusalem were no longer a part of Byzantium (q.v.).

PERA. See **GALATA.**

PERGAMON. See **MAXIMOS OF EPHESUS; NEOPLATONISM.**

PERIBLEPTOS MONASTERY. See **CONSTANTINOPLE; ROMANOS III ARGYROS.**

PERI STRATEGIKES. See **STRATEGIKA.**

PERSIA. The Persia known to Byzantium (q.v.) was created in 226 when the Sassanians (q.v.) overthrew the Parthians. This new and highly nationalistic state made Zoroastrianism (q.v.) the state religion and revived the imperialistic aspirations of ancient Persia. This resulted in centuries of intermittent struggle with Byzantium. However, interaction with Persia went beyond warfare. Active diplomatic relations acquainted Byzantium with Persian court ceremonial, which was adopted in the Byzantine court. Herakleios (q.v.), after defeating Persia, expropriated the title of the Persian king, *basileus* (q.v.), making it the chief title of the Byzantine emperor (q.v.). Until Justinian I (q.v.) developed domestic silk production, the Persians acted as intermediaries in the silk trade. Manichaeanism (q.v.), which the Persians persecuted, had an impact on Byzantium, notably on Augustine (q.v.). Nestorians (q.v.), persecuted in Byzantium, found refuge in Persia. Nevertheless, it is the centuries of intermittent warfare, chiefly in Mesopotamia, that characterized Byzantine-Persian relations (e.g., in the sixth century Byzantium was at war with Persia from 505–507, 527–532, 540–545, and 572–591). The Persians even sacked Antioch in 540, but it was in the early seventh century that Persian armies made extraordinary advances. From 609–619 they conquered Syria, Palestine, and Egypt (qq.v.). The long counteroffensive from 622–628 by Herakleios (q.v.), among the greatest military exploits in Byzantine history, culminated in the utter defeat of Persia. In 631 the True Cross (q.v.) was restored to Jerusalem (q.v.) with great celebration. This final victory in Persia marked the utter triumph of Byzantium after centuries of intermittent warfare with Persia. It also came a year before the death of Muhammad the Prophet. Soon after Muhammad's death in 632 Persia was attacked by the Arabs (q.v.); by the middle of the seventh century the Arab conquest of Persia was complete. In effect, the Byzantine defeat of Persia only paved the way for Arab expansion.

PETER III OF ARAGON. *See* **SICILIAN VESPERS.**

PETER MONGOS. *See* **TIMOTHEOS AILOUROS.**

PETER OF ATROA. *See* **OLYMPOS, MOUNT.**

PETER OF BULGARIA. Tsar of Bulgaria (qq.v.) from 927–969; son of Symeon (q.v.). Unlike his bellicose father, Peter sought peace with Byzantium (q.v.), concluding a treaty (927) that lasted almost 40 years. This policy produced important concessions from Byzantium. Peter's title *basileus* (q.v.) of Bulgaria was recognized, as was the independence of the Bulgarian church. His marriage to Maria, daughter of the brother of Romanos I Lekapenos (q.v.), made Peter a subservient member of the imperial family. The remainder of his reign saw Bulgaria weakened by internal dissension with the Bogomils (q.v.) and by the plotting of his nobility. The weakness of Bulgaria toward the end of Peter's reign prompted Nikephoros II Phokas (q.v.) to rescind tribute in 966, and to encourage Svjatoslav (q.v.) to invade Bulgaria. This Svjatoslav did in 968, shortly before Peter died.

PETER OF BULGARIA. Founder with his brother Asen I (q.v.) of the Second Bulgarian Empire in 1185; its capital was at Turnovo (q.v.). The brothers may have been Vlachs (q.v.), as suggested by Niketas Choniates (q.v.). By 1190 Peter and Asen had defeated every attempt of Isaac II Angelos (q.v.) to gain control of Bulgaria (q.v.). Peter's alliance with Isaac II in 1193 produced a split between the brothers. Peter died in Turnovo in 1197, a year after Asen was murdered by Ivanko (q.v.).

PETER OF COURTENAY. *See* **LATIN EMPIRE.**

PETER THE FULLER. Patriarch of Antioch (qq.v.) three times; he was ejected twice for his Monophysitism (q.v.). The second of his two terms (476–477; the first was 469–471) occurred during the brief reign of the usurper Basiliskos (q.v.). Zeno (q.v.) allowed him back for a third term in 482 after he accepted the Henotikon (q.v.). He remained at his post until his death in 488. His career is an example of how, after the Council of Chalcedon (q.v.), Monophysitism continued to provoke serious discord within the eastern church. An uncertain tradition claims he was a fuller, hence the epithet.

PETER THE HERMIT. Popular preacher of the First Crusade (q.v.), who led a multitude of poor people and petty knights to Constantinople (q.v.) in 1096. Alexios I Komnenos (qq.v.) helped transport them to Asia Minor (q.v.), where they were ambushed and defeated by Kilij Arslan I near Nicaea (qq.v.) on 21 October 1096. Peter's failure left an unfavorable impression of the crusader movement on Byzantium (q.v.), and the Seljuks of Asia Minor (qq.v.) expected further easy victories over subsequent crusader forces. In the *Alexiad* of Anna Komnene (q.v.) there is an unflattering portrait of Peter and his followers, who are rightly condemned for their lack of discipline.

PETER THE PATRICIAN. *Magister officiorum* under Justinian I (qq.v.) from 539–565; lawyer, diplomat, and historian. His diplomatic embassies included negotiations with Persia (q.v.) in 562, and with the king of the Ostrogoths (q.v.), Theodahad (q.v.). In his *Secret History,* Prokopios (q.v.) claims that Peter, acting on orders from Theodora, persuaded Theodahad to kill Amalasuntha (qq.v.). Peter's own historical work, judging from the fragments that survive, went from Augustus to the time of Julian (q.v.). He also wrote a work on state ceremonial that Constantine VII included in his *De ceremoniis* (qq.v.).

PETRA. Capital of the ancient desert kingdom of the Nabataeans (an Arab [q.v.] tribe), located in modern Jordan. Conquered by the Romans in 106, it continued to be the center of a vast caravan trade until the rise of Palmyra (q.v.).

PETRONAS. Highly decorated general under Theophilos and Michael III (qq.v.) who was a brother of Theophilos's wife Theodora and Bardas (qq.v.). Theophilos made him *patrikios* (q.v.), and *droungarios tis viglas*. During the reign of Michael III he was made *strat-*

egos of the theme of Thrakesion (qq.v.). In 856 he led an army deep into Mesopotamia as far as Amida (qq.v), then attacked Tephrike (q.v.). In 863 at the battle of Poson he won a brilliant victory over Umar, the emir of Melitene (qq.v.), who was killed in this battle and whose army was destroyed.

PETRONIUS MAXIMUS. Roman emperor (q.v.) in the West (455). Consul in 433 and 443, he plotted the murder of Aetius (q.v.) in 454, and he may have plotted the murder of Valentinian III (q.v.), who he succeeded in 455. He forced Valentinian's widow Eudoxia to marry him and gave her daughter Eudokia to his son Palladius. Eudokia had been promised to Gaiseric, leader of the Vandals (qq.v.). Aggrieved, Gaiseric besieged Rome (q.v.), and Petronius tried to flee, only to be recognized and killed by angry citizens.

PHILADELPHIA. Despite its rescue in 1304 by the Catalan Grand Company (q.v.), this heavily fortified city, the key to the defense of western Asia Minor against the Turks (qq.v.), remained in a precarious position throughout the 14th century. When Bayezid I (q.v.) finally conquered it in 1390, it was the last Byzantine city in Asia Minor (q.v.). Tragically, Manuel (II) Palaiologos (q.v.), as a vassal of Bayezid I, was forced to participate in the reduction of this proud city.

PHILANTHROPY. Philanthropy was important in Byzantium (q.v.) both in theory and in practice. In theory, the emperor (q.v.), as God's viceroy on earth, was expected to set an example of Christian philanthropy. To this end, in major cities the state funded public hospitals, poor houses, inns for travelers, homes for the aged, and orphanages (the imperial supervisor of state orphanages was called the *orphanotrophos* [q.v.]). Monasteries (q.v.) had parallel philanthropic institutions. The monastic *xenon* provided lodging for travelers. Some *xenones* were homes for the aged, even medical facilities. The most famous *xenon* in Byzantium (q.v.) was located in the Pantokrator Monastery in Constantinople (qq.v.). Endowed by Emperor John II Komnenos (q.v.), it included a hospital with 50 beds, a home for older men, and psychiatric services as well.

PHILARETOS THE ALMSGIVER. The *vita* (q.v.) of this saint, who died in 792, is important for what it reveals about conditions in northeastern Asia Minor (q.v.) in the eighth century, particularly about the destructive effects of Arab raids and the encroachments of powerful magnates (the *dynatoi* [q.v.]). Philaretos came from a wealthy Armenian family, whose landholdings were impoverished by Arab raids. The saint gave away much of his property, and his neighbors, some of whom were powerful magnates, took the rest. The family fortunes were restored only when his granddaughter Maria was chosen as wife for Constantine VI in a bride show (qq.v.) in 788.

PHILES, MANUEL. *See* **GLABAS, MICHAEL TARCHANEIOTES.**

PHILIP OF SWABIA. Son of Frederick I Barbarossa (q.v.) and king of Germany (1198–1208). Philip apparently conspired with Boniface of Montferrat (q.v.) to restore Alexios IV and Isaac II (qq.v.) to the throne of Byzantium (q.v.). Philip's motives had to do with the fact that his wife Irene was Alexios IV's sister, making deposed emperor Isaac II his father-in-law. Philip saw himself as helping to reclaim Byzantium for his in-laws, and, thus, by extension, for himself as well.

PHILIP OF TARANTO. *See* **NAUPAKTOS.**

PHILIPPI. City in western Macedonia on the Via Egnatia (qq.v.) midway between Thessalonike and Constantinople (qq.v.). The city's former wealth derived from its location on the major east-west highway across the Balkan Peninsula, the Via Egnatia (qq.v.), and the maritime trade of its port, Christoupolis. After the sixth century the city continued as a Byzantine *kastron* (q.v.), interrupted by occasional periods of foreign occupation; the Ottomans (q.v.) captured it ca. 1387.

PHILIPPIKOS. Emperor (q.v.) from 711–713; general under Justinian II (q.v.). When he usurped power, he executed not only Justinian II but also the emperor's son and advisors. In support of Monotheletism (q.v.) he deposed Patriarch Kyros and convened a council in 712 that condemned the Sixth Ecumenical Council (q.v.). It was his failure to stem the victories of Maslamah (q.v.) in the East and Tervel in Thrace (qq.v.) that led to his downfall. Soldiers from the theme of Opsikion (qq.v.) deposed and blinded him in 713.

PHILIPPIKOS. *Magister militum* (q.v.) of the East under Maurice (q.v.); he was also Maurice's son-in-law. His successes against the

Persians from 584–587 failed to deliver a knockout punch so Maurice replaced him with Priskos (q.v.) in 587. Philippikos's soldiers mutinied in protest and he was reappointed in 589, only to lose his command to Komentiolos (q.v.) that same year. Phokas (q.v.) forcibly retired him to a monastery in 603. In 613, shortly before Philippikos's death, Herakleios (q.v.) recalled him to active service. The vagaries of Philippikos's career reflect the vagaries of warfare with Persia (q.v.) in this period.

PHILIPPOPOLIS. City in northern Thrace (q.v.) situated on the highway from Belgrade to Constantinople (qq.v.). Its strategic location meant that it was occasionally subject to hostile attack by Pechenegs, Crusaders, and especially Bulgarians (qq.v.), whose border with Byzantium (q.v.) was near Philippopolis. Basil II (q.v.) stopped at the city on his way back to Constantinople after campaigning against Samuel (qq.v.) in 1004. During the Third Crusade (q.v.) it was occupied briefly by Frederick I (q.v.). The Ottomans (q.v.) captured it in 1363, making it their capital of Rumeli (q.v.), before moving the capital to Adrianople (q.v.).

PHILOKALIA. An 18th-century collection of Byzantine texts written by the great mystics and ascetics of Byzantium (qq.v.). The collection includes Antony the Great, Gregory Palamas, John of Damascus, Symeon the New Theologian (qq.v.) and many others. It was translated into Church Slavonic (q.v.) in 1793.

PHILOPONOS, JOHN. *See* **NEOPLATONISM; PHILOSOPHY; SCIENCE.**

PHILOSOPHY. In early Byzantine times the Academy of Athens (q.v.) was the center of philosophical inquiry, especially of Neoplatonism (q.v.) as taught by Proklos and his student Ammonios of Alexandria (q.v.). Ammonios's students included Damaskios and John Philoponos (q.v.), whose attacks on Aristotle's (q.v.) cosmology prefigured later attacks by Galileo. When Justinian I (q.v.) closed the Academy of Athens in 529, Damaskios and six other philosophers sought refuge in Persia (q.v.). Justinian allowed them to return to the empire in 532 with the promise that they would not be harassed. Despite the church's suspicion of Neoplatonism, its impact on theology can be seen in the writings of the so-called Pseudo-Dionysios the Areopagite, also in those of John of Damascus (qq.v.). Prior to the revival of education in the 11th century, Leo the Mathematician,

Photios, and Arethas of Caesarea (qq.v.) kept philosophical studies alive. The University of Constantinople, revived by Constantine XI (q.v.), included a school of philosophy led by Psellos (q.v.), whose interests lay chiefly in Neoplatonism. However, Psellos's pupil John Italos (q.v.) focused on Aristotle, as did Italos's students Eustratios of Nicaea and Michael of Ephesus (qq.v.). In the Palaiologan (q.v.) period, philosophical studies flourished under George Akropolites (a student of Nikephoros Blemmydes), George Pachymeres, Theodore Metochites, Nikephoros Choumnos, and Nikephoros Gregoras (qq.v.). Even on the eve of Byzantium's (q.v.) extinction, Neoplatonic studies continued under Bessarion and George Gemistos Plethon (q.v.). Plethon so impressed Cosimo de'Medici at the Council of Ferrara-Florence (q.v.) that Cosimo founded the Platonic Academy. Gennadios II Scholarios (q.v.) defended Aristotle against Plethon's criticism, in addition to defending Thomas Aquinas (q.v.).

PHILOSTORGIOS. Ecclesiastical historian who wrote a continuation of the *Church History* of Eusebios of Caesarea (q.v.) that spans the years 300–435. That his work survives only in fragments (in the *Epitome* of Photios [q.v.]) is perhaps explained by his espousal of Arianism, and of its proponent Eunomios (qq.v.). Much better preserved are the works of Socrates, Sozomen, and Theodoret of Cyrrhus (qq.v.), who also continued Eusebios's work but who embraced Orthodoxy (q.v.).

PHILOTHEOS, KLETOROLOGION OF. The most important and exhaustive of official lists (called *taktika* [q.v.]) of offices and dignities of the Byzantine state. It was composed in 899 by a certain Philotheos, who was both a *protospatharios* as well as an *atriklines* (qq.v.), i.e., an official in charge of official banquets. The term *kletorologion* means roughly an invitation list to a banquet, the immediate use of which would have been to offer instruction on the order of seating at state banquets. The significance to modern scholars is that it provides the most complete list of its kind, with definitions of each title and its importance. Essentially, the *kletorologion* provides a detailed glimpse of the Byzantine bureaucracy in the late ninth century.

PHILOTHEOS KOKKINOS. Patriarch of Constantinople (qq.v.) from 1353–1354, and again from 1364–1376; writer; monk. He was a disciple and admirer of Gregory Palamas, also a friend of John VI Kantakouzenos (qq.v.). He was made patriarch when the previous patriarch Kallistos I refused to crown Matthew I Kantakouzenos (qq.v.). In a larger sense, his elevation as patriarch demonstrated the victory of Hesychasm (q.v.); indeed, he was one of a series of Hesychast patriarchs of the 14th century who included Isidore I Boucheiros and Kallistos I (qq.v.). Deposed when John V (q.v.) regained the throne in 1354, he engineered in his second term the canonization of Gregory Palamas (1368) and led opposition to John V's conversion to Roman Catholicism. He also made claims for his authority over the entire church that proved quite unrealistic in the face of growing ecclesiastical regionalism. His numerous writings include hagiography, hymns (qq.v.), polemics, and dogmatic works.

PHOBEROU MONASTERY. The Monastery of St. John the Baptist in Phoberon, at the north end of the Bosporos (q.v.). The famous icon painter Lazaros was allowed to take refuge there after the emperor Theophilos (qq.v.) flogged him and burned his palms with red-hot nails.

PHOKAIA. City situated at the entrance to the Gulf of Smyrna in Asia Minor (qq.v.). From 1088–1092 Tzachas (q.v.) made it notorious as the home base for his marauding fleet. From 1275 when it was ceded by Michael VII Palaiologos (q.v.), the Zaccaria family of Genoa (qq.v.) made it their key to good fortune, exploiting its harbor to export alum (derived from the mineral kalunite, used in leather tanning and dyeing). Prosperity attracted envy in the form of the Catalan Grand Company (q.v.), which sacked Phokaia and the Zaccaria stronghold of "New Phokaia" (north of the city) in 1307 or 1308. In 1402 the Gattilusio (q.v.) family of Genoa (q.v.) seized old Phokaia. Genoese rule came to an end in 1455 when the Ottomans (q.v.) conquered the region.

PHOKAS. Emperor (q.v.) from 602–610. His tyranny and military failures mark him as perhaps the worst of Byzantine emperors. A junior military officer raised to the throne by rebellious soldiers who overthrew Maurice, he proved utterly incapable of resisting Chosroes II (q.v.), who captured the frontier fortress of Dara (q.v.) in 604 and invaded Asia Minor (q.v.) allegedly to avenge Maurice. Avars and Slavs (qq.v.) flooded the Balkan Peninsula into Thrace (qq.v.), all of which produced army rebellions and internal dissension that Phokas responded to with a reign of terror. The revolt that succeeded in toppling him was engendered by the exarch of Carthage (qq.v.), who sent a fleet commanded by his son Herakleios (q.v.) against Phokas and that was supported by his cousin Niketas, whose troops wrested Egypt (q.v.) from Phokas in 610. When Herakleios's fleet appeared before Constantinople (q.v.) on 3 October 610 Phokas was overthrown.

PHOKAS, BARDAS. *See* **BASIL II; VLADIMIR I.**

PHOKAS, PETER. *See* **BOURTZES, MICHAEL; NIKEPHOROS II PHOKAS.**

PHOTIOS. Controversial patriarch of Constantinople (qq.v.) from 858–867, and again from 877–886. The controversy began when he was made patriarch in 858 while still a layman. The deposed Ignatios (q.v.) garnered much sympathy, including the support of Pope Nicholas I (q.v.), especially after Photios condemned the *filioque* (q.v.) in the Latin creed. Basil I's (q.v.) need of papal support in Italy (q.v.) lay behind the formal deposition of Photios at a council held in Constantinople in 869–870, which restored Ignatios as patriarch. Only after Ignatios's death was Photios returned to the patriarchal throne, through the action of yet another council in Constantinople, held in 879–880, which revoked the decision of the previous council. Photios was a noted teacher like Leo the Mathematician (q.v.), also a writer of homilies and letters. In one of his homilies he describes a Rus (q.v.) attack on Constantinople in 860. He compiled a *Lexicon* of words and expressions, and he wrote a commentary on Aristotle's (q.v.) *Physics*. His *Bibliotheca* is a priceless legacy. It summaries 386 books by pagan and Christian authors that he read. Many of these works, such as those of Philostorgios (q.v.), are known chiefly, or only, through the *Bibliotheca*.

PHRANTZES, GEORGE. *See* **SPHRANTZES, GEORGE.**

PHRYGIA. Landlocked region of rugged topography in west-central Asia Minor (q.v.), traversed by major military roads, along which the strategic military station of Dorylaion (q.v.) was situated. Other important cities included Kotyaion, Synada, Akroinon, and Amorion (qq.v.). The region was the original home of an assortment of Christian heretics, including Montanists, Novatians (qq.v.), and the sect of Athinganoi who observed the Jewish Sabbath and kept the Mosaic law (though not circumcision). Phrygia was defended from Arab raids by the themes of Opsikion and Thrakesion (qq.v.), but in the late 11th century it succumbed to the Seljuks (q.v.). Indeed, victories over the Seljuks by the armies of the First Crusade (q.v.) had the effect of pushing the Seljuks back from the Aegean (q.v.) coast and concentrating them in Phrygia, making the region a barrier to Byzantine and Crusader armies. By 1098 Alexios I Komnenos (q.v.) was resettling some of the Greek population farther to the west. By the early 13th century the region was lost to the Seljuks (q.v.).

PHYSIOLOGOS. *See* **GLYKAS, MICHAEL.**

PIAZZA ARMERIA. Site in Sicily (q.v.) of a vast imperial villa, construction of which began in the early fourth century. It is among the most elaborate villas of its kind, incorporating approximately 3,500 square meters of floor mosaics, many of them hunting scenes. It may have been a country villa for one of the tetrarchs, perhaps Maximian (qq.v.).

PILGRIM FLASK. Pilgrim flasks *(ampullae)* of various materials contained oil, water, or earth from a holy site for use as amulets (q.v.), or for supposed medicinal purposes. Well-known types include Menas flasks from Abu Mina (qq.v.), and small pottery flasks called *ungentaria*. Pilgrim tokens and medallions, made of sanctified earth and stamped with a blessing or with an image of a saint, were valued for the same reasons.

PILGRIMAGE. *See* **HELENA; JERUSALEM; PALESTINE.**

PINDAR. Perhaps the greatest lyric poet of ancient Greece (died ca. 438 B.C.), whose work was much read in Byzantium (q.v.). Those who wrote commentaries on Pindar included Eustathios of Thessalonike (q.v.).

PINDOS. The great mountain range of northwest Greece (q.v.) that extends south from Albania, east of Epiros, and west of Macedonia (qq.v.). Kekaumenos (q.v.) mentions the Vlachs (q.v.) inhabiting Pindos in the 11th century.

PIPPIN III. *See* **CONSTANTINE V.**

PISA. Italian maritime republic in Tuscany on the Arno River. Byzantium (q.v.) used Pisa, like Genoa (q.v.), as a counterweight to the rising commercial power of Venice (q.v.). In 1111 Alexios I Komnenos (q.v.) extended Pisa trading privileges that included trading quarters along the Golden Horn (q.v.). Privileges were renewed in 1136 by John II (q.v.), lost in 1163, and restored in 1170 by Manuel I. The Pisans suffered in the general slaughter of Latins in Constantinople (q.v.) in 1182. Nevertheless, their privileges were again renewed in 1192 by Isaac II (q.v.), partly because some Genoese had taken to piracy in Byzantine waters. The conquest of Constantinople by the Fourth Crusade (qq.v.) in 1204 was a triumph for Venice and a setback for Pisa and Genoa. Pisa never fully recovered its commercial position in Byzantium, and in 1439 its privileges were given to Florence (q.v.).

PISIDIA. Region in southwestern Asia Minor north of Pamphylia, northeast of Lycia, and south of Phrygia (qq.v.). A mountainous region, parts of it were almost inaccessible. Antioch, its metropolis (qq.v.), never fully recovered from its destruction by the Arabs (q.v.) in 717. The Seljuks (q.v.), who penetrated the region after the battle of Mantzikert (1071), were forced to retreat in 1097 when the First Crusade (q.v.) entered Pisidia, but they returned after the army's passage. John II retook Sozopolis (qq.v.) in 1120, but it fell again to the Seljuks in 1180, after which the region was effectively lost to Byzantium (q.v.).

PLAGUE. Two major plagues are described in Byzantine historical sources. The first occurred from 541–544, a graphic account of which is given by Prokopios of Caesarea (q.v.) in his *Wars*. The second was the Black Death of 1348–1349, described by John VI Kantakouzenos (q.v.) in his personal memoir, the *Histories*.

PLANOUDES, MAXIMOS. Scholar, teacher, and philologist, noted for his translations of Latin authors, e.g., Cato the Elder, Cicero, Caesar, Boethius, and Augustine (q.v.), for his collection of epigrams included in the Greek Anthology (q.v.), as well as for his letters and other writings.

PLATO. *See* **NEOPLATONISM.**

PLATO OF SAKKOUDION. *See* **MOECHIAN CONTROVERSY; OLYMPOS, MOUNT.**

PLETHON, GEORGE GEMISTOS. Philosopher from Mistra (q.v.) whose deep understanding of Plato (q.v.) inspired the Medici foundation of the Platonic Academy in Florence. His trip to Italy (q.v.) to attend the Council of Ferrara-Florence (q.v.) in 1438–1439 brought him in contact with scholars in Florence, providing an important opportunity for the transmission of Greek classical learning to the Renaissance. At Mistra he continued to teach (Laonikos Chalkonkondyles [q.v.] was one of his students) and to write. Among his works is the controversial *A Treatise on the Laws,* which espouses Neoplatonism (q.v.), including a belief in the Olympian gods.

PLISKA. First capital of Bulgaria (q.v.). According to tradition, it was founded by Asparuch (q.v.). Nikephoros I (q.v.) sacked it in 811. Despite Omurtag's (q.v.) reconstruction, it declined after Symeon of Bulgaria founded Preslav (qq.v.) in 893. Basil II's (q.v.) forces captured it ca. 1000, along with Preslav, as part of the Byzantine conquest of northern Bulgaria.

PLOTINOS. The great philosopher of Neoplatonism (q.v.), born in Egypt (q.v.) in 205. His essays, which were arranged by his pupil Porphyry (q.v.) into groups of nines (the *Enneads*), and Porphyry's *Life of Plotinos,* exerted an enormous impact on subsequent philosophy, especially the study of Plato, theology (qq.v.), even art. For Plotinos, the reality of the universe consists of a hierarchical ascendancy, toward the One (the Good, Divine Intellect, God), upward through the stages of Body (the lowest stage), Soul, and Mind. Thus, the ascendant reality of the cosmos is mirrored in the microcosm of each individual, in whom is embedded the desire to be united with the One. An individual's ascent begins with a recognition of this innate desire, and is accomplished through contemplation. Maximos of Ephesus and Proklos (qq.v.) identified contemplation with theurgy, i.e., a magic (q.v.) that relied on rites and prayers to invoke the aid of the gods. Plotinos was still read with great interest by later Byzantine intellectuals, including Michael Psellos, Theodore Metochites, and Plethon (qq.v.). Except for works of Aristotle (q.v.), Plotinos's works form the most intact body of philosophy preserved from antiquity.

PNEUMATOMACHOI. *See* **ECUMENICAL COUNCILS.**

POLYEUKTOS. Patriarch of Constantinople (qq.v.) from 956–970. Polyeuktos's intervention in political affairs contradicts the popular image of the Byzantine church as utterly subservient to the state. He came into conflict with Nikephoros II Phokas (q.v.) over the emperor's (q.v.) edicts curtailing monastic properties. He continued to oppose the emperor on one policy after another. When John I Tz-imiskes and Nikephoros II's wife Theophano (qq.v.) conspired to-gether to murder Nikephoros II, Polyeuktos demanded that John expel his mistress Theophano from the palace and abolish Nike-phoros's hated edicts. Only when he did these things did Polyeuktos permit John's coronation to take place.

POLYEUKTOS, CHURCH OF SAINT. *See* **HAGIA SOPHIA.**

PONTOS. Region in northern Asia Minor (q.v.) that borders the south coast of the Black Sea (q.v.), situated east of Bithynia and Paphlag-onia and north of Cappadocia (qq.v.). Its fertile coastline is sheltered by the natural protection of a dense, mountainous interior, rich in mineral deposits. Its chief city was the strongly fortified Trebizond, capital of the Empire of Trebizond (q.v.).

POPE. *See* **PAPACY.**

PORPHYRIOS OF GAZA. Saint and bishop of Gaza (qq.v.) who in 401 journeyed to Constantinople (q.v.) to appeal to Emperor Arka-dios (qq.v.) to help him stamp out paganism in Gaza. Arkadios, his wife Eudoxia, and the patriarch John Chrysostom (qq.v.) all agreed that the famous temple in Gaza called the Marneion, dedicated to the local god Marnas, must be destroyed. Arkadios (q.v.) ordered its de-struction, and Eudoxia (q.v.) provided the money to build a church basilica (q.v.) in its place. The *vita* (q.v.) of Porphyrios is tradition-ally attributed to his disciple Mark the Deacon.

PORPHYROGENNETOS. The term, which means "born in the purple," appeared in the sixth century. The epithet was given to any child born to a reigning emperor (q.v.). A *porphyrogennetos* was typically born in the Porphyra, part of the Great Palace (q.v.) where there was a bedchamber of porphyry stone of deep reddish purple, the color associated with emperors.

PORPHYRY. Neoplatonist philosopher (ca. 233–ca. 306), and student of Plotinos (q.v.) who was born in Tyre (q.v.). He was Plotinos's bi-ographer and editor of his *Ennead,* and a severe critic of Chris-tianity. He wrote an enormous number of works, some of them having little or nothing to do with Neoplatonism (q.v.), including his *Against the Christians,* surviving only in fragments. It was a work that Christian intellectuals such as Eusebios of Caesarea, Jerome, and even the great Augustine (qq.v.) wrestled with. Theodosios II (q.v.) read it and found it so dangerous that he ordered it burned in 448.

PRAECEPTA MILITARIA. (Military maxims). Traditional title for a work written by Nikephoros II Phokas (q.v.); the title in Greek is *Strategike ekthesis kai syndaxis Nikephorou despotou* (Exposition and Treatise on Warfare by the Emperor Nikephoros). It was intended as a practical manual for field commanders; such practical handbooks on military affairs (called *strategika* [q.v.]) were not uncommon in Byzantium (q.v.). Interestingly, Nikephoros II, whose expertise lay with offensive warfare, and whose favorite part of the army was his *kataphraktoi* (qq.v.), devotes the first two of six chapters to the use of infantry. Chapters three and four deal with the *kataphraktoi,* and they conclude with advice on diverse topics, including how to lay out camps and fortify them.

PRAEPOSITUS SACRI CUBICULI. The grand chamberlain, invariably a eunuch (q.v.), and one of the most powerful civil officials. He administered the emperor's private chambers, imperial receptions, even the imperial estates in Cappadocia (q.v.), using a large staff of eunuchs called *koubikoularioi*. In the case of weak emperors, his influence could be enormous, as seen in the career of Eutropios (q.v.).

PRAETORIAN PREFECT. Civil official who governed one of the four great praetorian prefectures (the Gauls, Italy, Illyricum [qq.v.], and the East) from the fourth to seventh centuries. A praetorian prefect supervised all aspects of civil administration, from the grain supply to judicial and financial matters. Under praetorian prefect were the *vicarii* of dioceses (qq.v.) and the governors of provinces (q.v.). Constantinople and Rome (qq.v.) each fell under the separate administration of an urban prefect, the Eparch of the City (q.v.).

PRAITOR. Provincial civil administrator in the 11th–12th centuries who was responsible for fiscal and judicial matters. After the conquest of Constantinople (q.v.) in 1204 the office fell into disuse. Provincial military administration during the 11th–12th centuries shifted (with the decline of *stratiotika ktemata* and themes [qq.v.]) from the *strategos* (q.v.) to a military governor called the *doux* (or *katepano* [qq.v.]).

PRAKTIKA. *See* **TAXATION.**

PREFECT. *See* **EPARCH OF THE CITY; PRAETORIAN PREFECT; PREFECTURE.**

PREFECTURE. Any administrative unit governed by a prefect. The largest were the four great prefectures organized by Constantine I (q.v.) that comprised the empire from the fourth to the seventh centuries: the Gauls, Italy, Illyricum (qq.v.), and the East. Each of these great administrative units (governed by a praetorian prefect [q.v.]) was further divided into dioceses (q.v.); each diocese was divided into provinces (q.v.). In the seventh century this system collapsed and was replaced by administrative units called themes (q.v.).

PRESLAV. Great Preslav (not to be confused with Little Preslav, the Bulgarian port at the mouth of the Danube River [q.v.]). Symeon of Bulgaria (q.v.) transferred the capital of Bulgaria from Pliska (qq.v.) to Great Preslav in 893. Svjatoslav (q.v.) conquered it in 969, but John I Tzimiskes (q.v.) took it from him in 971, forcing Svjatoslav to withdraw from Bulgaria entirely. Byzantium (q.v.) then annexed Bulgaria and abolished its patriarchate (q.v.). Another dramatic reversal occurred in 986 when Tsar Samuel (qq.v.) reoccupied it. However, Basil II (q.v.) recaptured Preslav in his campaign of 1000–1004 in northern Bulgaria. By the middle of the 11th century it was in Pecheneg (q.v.) hands.

PRESLAV, LITTLE. *See* **PRESLAV.**

PRESPA. *See* **MACEDONIA.**

PRICE EDICT. *See* **EDICT ON PRICES.**

PRIMARY CHRONICLE. *See* **RUSSIAN PRIMARY CHRONICLE.**

PRIMIKERIOS. Honorary title used for the senior person holding any of a number of civil, military, or church offices. For example, each of the palatine guards had a *primikerios,* as did each of the civil services. The *primikerios sacri cubiculi* was chief of staff of the imperial bedchamber, and the *megas primikerios* was the master of ceremonies in the palace. Both of these palace officials were eunuchs (q.v.).

PRINCES'S ISLANDS. Group of nine islands in the Sea of Marmara (q.v.). They contained numerous monasteries, and they were used as places of exile, especially the island of Prote.

PRISCIAN. Distinguished Latin grammarian and poet who left Vandalic North Africa to settle in Constantinople, where he wrote a panegyric to the emperor Anastasios I (qq.v.) ca. 503. His chief work was a voluminous work on Latin grammar that became a standard textbook in the medieval West.

PRISKOS. Author of an eyewitness account of an embassy to Attila (q.v.) in 448. Priskos accompanied his friend Maximin, who was ambassador to the Huns (q.v.), across the Danube (q.v.) to the court of Attila. He describes Naissus (q.v.) as deserted. The court of Attila is described in detail, including the food and entertainment at a banquet hosted by Attila for his guests. Priskos wrote a longer work known as *Byzantine History*. It survives only in fragments and may be the source of the account of the embassy.

PRISKOS. General who was briefly *Magister militum* under Maurice (qq.v.) in 588 until a mutiny against him forced the emperor to reappoint Philippikos (q.v.). In 592 Maurice made him commander of the army along the Danube (q.v.), where he won some victories against the Avars (q.v.). He weathered a series of revolts among his troops in 593, was briefly replaced by Maurice's brother Peter in 594, and reappointed to his command the following year. He survived the reign of Phokas, but Herakleios (qq.v.) forced him into retirement (as a monk) in 612 when he failed to entrap a Persian army.

PRIZREN. *See* **CONSTANTINE BODIN.**

PROCHIRON. A handbook of law published in 907 by Leo VI (q.v.) that revised the *Epanagoge* (q.v.). Its purpose was to provide a brief overview of the laws that governed Byzantium (q.v.). It proved popular until the end of the empire, and its translation into Slavonic was treated with great authority by the Bulgarians, Serbs, and Rus (qq.v.).

PROCOPIUS. *See* **PROKOPIOS.**

PRODROMOS, THEODORE. Twelfth-century panegyrist, poet, and writer of romance (q.v.). He worked at the court of John II Komnenos and Irene Doukaina (qq.v.), becoming immensely popular. His romance *Rodanthe and Dosikles* is derivative in its plot, harkening back to a novel of the third century by Heliodoros of Emesa entitled the *Aithiopica*.

PROKLOS. Neoplatonist (q.v.) philosopher, mathematician, and astronomer, who taught at the Academy of Athens (q.v.). For Proklos (unlike Porphyry [q.v.]), Plotinos's (q.v.) philosophy became a way of self-knowledge that used theurgy and mathematics to unite the soul with the divine. He died in 485, but his subsequent influence was enormous. Despite the hostility of John Philoponos, Pseudo-Dionysios the Areopagite (qq.v.) incorporated his ideas into Christian theology (q.v.). In the 11th century, interest in him was revived by Michael Psellos, John Italos, Eustratios of Nicaea, and Michael of Ephesus (qq.v.). Thereafter, interest in his work, if only for the purpose of refutation, never flagged in Byzantium (q.v.).

PROKONNESOS. *See* **MARMARA, SEA OF.**

PROKOPIOS. Usurper (365–366) and relative of the emperor Julian (q.v.). His revolt expressed army discontent with Valens (q.v.) over changes in some of Julian's policies and the removal of officials appointed by Julian. Prokopios presented himself as Julian's legitimate successor, but the revolt found little support in the army (q.v.) as a whole. He was arrested and executed.

PROKOPIOS OF CAESAREA. The historian of Justinian I's (q.v.) reign. His works include the *Wars,* which, though concentrating primarily on Justinian's wars against the Vandals, Persians, and Ostrogoths (qq.v.), also provide something of an internal history of the emperor's (q.v.) reign. The *Buildings* (De aedificiis) is even more laudatory of Justinian than is the *Wars,* as one might expect of works written on commission. Prokopios's true feelings about Justinian and Theodora (q.v.) are expressed in his *Anekdota* (Secret History) (q.v.), which is a mix of scurrilous gossip and fact. Belisarios (q.v.), whose secretary Prokopios had been, is portrayed in this work as a weakling, completely under the control of his wife Antonina. Antonina is herself accused of political intrigues with Theodora and of a scandalous relationship with her adopted son Theodosios. Justinian and Theodora are viewed as demons intent on destroying Byzantium (q.v.).

PROKOPIOS OF GAZA. Rhetorician from Gaza (q.v.) whose varied works include polemics against the Neoplatonism of Proklos (qq.v.), commentaries on the Old Testament, a description of a mechanical clock *(horologion* [q.v.]), and numerous letters. His panegyric on Anastasios I (q.v.) makes mention of the so-called Long Wall (q.v.) that Anastasios I built.

PRONOIA. Fiscal institution consisting of a grant of revenues (in the form of taxes, rents, labor services) from dependent peasants *(paroikoi* [q.v.]) on an estate. The grantee is referred to by the conventional term "pronoiar." Military *pronoia* seems to have begun with Manuel I Komnenos (q.v.) in response to the decline of *stratiotika ktemata* (q.v.). No class of feudal (q.v.) knights resulted, since soldier-pronoiars derived money from their granted lands, but they did not live on the land, nor could their sons inherit *pronoia* grants (until Michael VIII Palaiologos [q.v.] allowed this for the sons of soldiers). Soldier-pronoiars, along with paid mercenary troops, undergirded the military revival of the Komnenian period, and they continued to be the basic components of late Byzantine armies.

PROPONTIS. *See* **MARMARA, SEA OF.**

PROSKYNESIS. (Greek for "prostration," "obeisance.") The act of full prostration before a Byzantine emperor (q.v.), required as a sign of servility. It was commonly performed by foreign diplomats during interviews with the emperor. For example, when Liutprand of Cremona (q.v.) had an audience with Constantine VII (q.v.) in 949 he did the required *proskynesis* three times. When he looked up he found that the emperor had been mechanically elevated on his throne to ceiling height. In art after the eighth century the *proskynesis* replaced the *orant* (q.v.) as an indication of prayer.

PROTHESIS. The term means "offering" in Greek, referring to the preparation of the bread and wine during the Eucharist (q.v.). It has other related meanings, including the Eucharist itself, and in Byzantine churches it refers to the northern of two storage chambers (collectively referred to as *pastophoria*) flanking the central apse (q.v.). The *prothesis* is the chamber where the sacred bread and other elements of the Eucharist were stored and prepared. The other storage chamber, the *diakonikon* (q.v.), is located on the south side of the church's central apse.

PROTO-BULGARIAN INSCRIPTION. *See* **OMURTAG.**

PROTONOTARIOS. *See* **PROTOS (PROTO-).**

PROTOS (PROTO-). Literally "the first." A *protos* was the chief administrator of a group of monasteries, e.g., Mount Athos and Meteora (qq.v.). However, "proto-" as the first part of a title could mean simply the highest-ranked member of a category of officials or dignitaries. For example, the *protosebastos* was the highest-ranked *sebastos* (q.v.). The *protonotarios* was the chief of a group of notaries, e.g., of the emperor's (q.v.) personal notaries. It can also indicate a high-ranking palace official or dignitary with various specialized duties, such as the *protovestarios* (q.v.).

PROTOSEBASTOS. *See* **PROTOS (PROTO-).**

PROTOSPATHARIOS. An honorific title that ordinarily gave its recipient a member of the senate (q.v.). Prior to the 10th century it was usually awarded to commanders of the themes (q.v.). In the 10th century two categories were created, the eunuchs (q.v.) and the "bearded," each with a different distinguishing garb. The title was further expanded to include civil officials, some with special court functions, including judicial duties.

PROTOSTRATOR. Keeper of the imperial stables, according to the *Kletorologion* of Philotheos (q.v.). He supervised a large staff of grooms and stable managers, as well as officials in charge of chariots and weapons. During the Palaiologan (q.v.) period, the *protostrator* was a high military commander responsible for certain ceremonial functions.

PROTOVESTIARIOS. Technically speaking, keeper of the emperor's *vestiaron* (qq.v.), the imperial wardrobe. However, from the ninth to 11th centuries the *protovestiarios* commanded armies, conducted peace negotiations, and performed other significant public tasks. From the 12th century onward the office became a highly honorary title, without specific responsibilities, conferred upon a trusted relative of the emperor's family.

PROUSA. City (modern Bursa) situated in Bithynia near Mount Olympos (qq.v.). In the early 14th century relatively few cities in Asia Minor (q.v.) remained in Byzantine hands as the Ottomans (q.v.) rapidly expanded. Prousa resisted Sultan Osman's (qq.v.) sieges of 1302, 1304, and 1315. The city finally fell in 1326 to Orhan (q.v.), who made it his capital. Osman was buried there. Prousa was one of the casualties of Timur's invasion of Asia Minor (qq.v.) in 1402. Timur's Mongols captured and pillaged the city.

PROVINCES. The Roman Empire was administered through its provinces. This provincial administration was dramatically reorganized by Diocletian (q.v.), who divided larger provinces into smaller ones (thereby increasing their number to nearly 100) and organized them into 12 dioceses (q.v.). Constantine I (q.v.) subsequently created still larger administrative units called prefectures (q.v.).

PRUDENTIUS. Christian Latin poet (348–ca. 410) born in Spain; high official under Honorius (q.v.). He was a writer of Christian hymns (q.v.), and of instructive poems on the Trinity and on the derivation of sins and vices. His poems, e.g., *Pschomachia* (The Battle for the Soul of Man) were the first to combine Christian themes within the stylistic format of classical Roman poetry. In his poetry old pagan modes were renewed. Prudentius became noted for using allegory for Christian purposes. In effect, he placed Christian themes for the first time squarely within the great cultural tradition of classical Latin poetry. He died ca. 410.

PSALTER. Christian prayer book containing the Old Testament Book of Psalms and other devotional works. It was used in the liturgy, as well as for private reading. Like Gospel Books, psalters were often richly illustrated, especially aristocratic psalters (q.v.), a chief example of which is the 10th-century Paris Psalter.

PSELLOS, MICHAEL. Historian, premier intellectual and writer of his time, courtier and advisor to several 11th-century emperors (q.v.). Michael VII (q.v.) was his pupil. Whatever one thinks of his character (which was necessarily chameleon-like to have survived so long as a courtier) his active participation from 1042–1078 in the affairs of state gave him an extraordinary understanding of court life. His *Chronographia,* covering the years 976–1078, is a work, which, like the *Alexiad* of Anna Komnene (q.v.), has profoundly shaped modern understanding of 11th-century Byzantium (q.v.). The understanding of human behavior displayed in the *Chronographia* is profound. Indeed, some of the portraits he draws, e.g., of imperial personalities like Zoe and Constantine IX (qq.v.), are unforgettable. Together these portraits form an explanation of the 11th-century decline that focuses on the failure of imperial leadership after Basil II's (q.v.) death in 1025. Psellos's letters contain vivid description and exploration of psychological motivation (e.g., regarding the nature of friendship). The impact of his learning on contemporaries was great, combining as it did theology and philosophy (qq.v.), including Neoplatonism (q.v.), the study of which he revived. He was enormously curious about everything, including things occult. He and his circle of friends, who included patriarch John VIII Xiphilinos (qq.v.) and Constantine Leichoudes, created a vibrant intellectual atmosphere in mid-11th century Constantinople (q.v.). Psellos may have died around 1082, the year John Italos (q.v.) was tried for heresy (q.v.).

PSEUDO-SYMEON, CHRONICLE OF. *See* **SYMEON LOGOTHETE.**

PTOLEMY. *See* **ASTRONOMY; GEOGRAPHY; KOSMAS INDIKOPLEUSTES.**

PULCHERIA. Empress (q.v.); sister of Theodosios II (q.v.). She exemplifies how a woman could exercise power due to her proximity to the throne; other prominent fifth and sixth century examples include Eudoxia, Athenais-Eludoxia, Verina, Ariadne, Theodora, and Sophia (qq.v.). When Pulcheria's father Arkadios (q.v.) died in 408, she became head of the regency for her brother Theodosios II, then only seven. Her influence over the young, kindly, and weak-willed brother was great, despite disputes with Theodosios's wife Athenais-Eudokia and with the patriarch Nestorios (q.v.). When Theodosios II died in 450, Pulcheria, who had taken a vow of virginity, agreed to a nominal marriage to the aged general Marcian (q.v.) in order to support his accession to power.

– Q –

QALAT SEMAN. *See* **SYMEON THE STYLITE THE ELDER.**

QUAESTOR. The Quaestor of the Sacred Palace *(quaestor sacri palatii)* was the supreme legal minister whose duty it was to draft imperial laws, in addition to being the emperor's (q.v.) chief legal advisor. The famous Tribonian (q.v.) occupied this post during the reign of Justinian I (qv.).

QUINCUNX. *See* **CROSS-IN-THE-SQUARE CHURCH.**

– R –

RADAGAISUS. *See* **RAETIA.**

RAETIA. Roman alpine province that included parts of modern Switzerland, Bavaria, and the Tyrol. It provided a buffer for Italy (q.v.) until the northern part was abandoned to the Alemanni after 389. In 401 the German chieftain Radagaisus invaded Raetia. It was recovered around 430 by Aetius (q.v.), then lost again around 450, after Aetius's (q.v.) death.

RASAFAH. *See* **SERGIOPOLIS.**

RAŠKA. *See* **SERBIA; ZETA.**

RASTISLAV. *See* **CYRIL AND METHODIOS; MORAVIA.**

RAVENNA. City in northeastern Italy near the Adriatic (qq.v.) coast. Honorios (q.v.) transferred his court from Milan (q.v.) to Ravenna in 402, making it the capital of the West. It was the capital of Odoacer's (q.v.) regime, as well as that of the Ostrogoths (q.v.). The Exarchate of Ravenna (q.v.) was itself created in response to the Lombard invasion of Italy (568); Ravenna fell to the Lombards (q.v.) in 751. Perhaps the city's most famous monument is the church of St. Vitale, with its mosaic (q.v.) wall panels depicting Justinian I, Theodora (qq.v.), and Maximian, archbishop of Ravenna from 546–556. Other monuments include the Mausoleum of Galla Placidia (q.v.) and the churches of St. Apollinare Nuovo and St. Apollinare in Classe.

RAYMOND OF AGUILERS. Historian of the First Crusade (q.v.) who participated in the First Crusade as chaplain of Raymond of Toulouse (q.v.). His work, entitled *Historia Francorum qui ceperunt Iherusalem* (History of the Franks Who Captured Jerusalem), covers the years 1095–1099, is one of the best sources for the later part of the Crusade, from the capture of Antioch (q.v.) onward. He is clearly antagonistic toward the Byzantines.

RAYMOND OF POITIERS. Prince of Antioch (1136–1149). When John II Komnenos (q.v.) besieged Antioch (q.v.) in 1137, Raymond capitulated and accepted the Treaty of Devol (q.v.). He swore homage to John, gave John free entry into Antioch, and promised to return it to Byzantine hands. However, he reneged on his promise, which prompted John II to invade the region again in 1142. The problem resolved itself after the fall of Edessa (q.v.) in 1144. With Antioch more directly endangered Raymond was forced to swear homage to Manuel I (q.v.). The alliance with Antioch was sealed in 1161 when Maria of Antioch (q.v.), the daughter of Raymond of Poitiers, married Manuel I.

RAYMOND OF TOULOUSE. Military chief of the First Crusade (q.v.); count of Toulouse in France (qq.v.). His relationship with Alexios I Komnenos (q.v.) was a model of cooperation and trust. He accepted Byzantine overlordship of his County of Tripoli (q.v.), in return for material aid from Alexios I Komnenos (q.v.), sent to him from Cyprus (q.v.). He also worked with Alexios I to ease passage of the Crusade of 1100–1101 through Constantinople (q.v.). Raymond died in 1105 outside the walls of Tripolis (q.v.) while still besieging the city (it did not fall until 1109). Anna Komnene (q.v.) in her *Alexiad* has only praise for Raymond, who appears to have personified the Byzantine vision of a Crusader: noble, courageous, and a willing client of Byzantium (q.v.).

REFECTORY. (*Trapeza,* in Greek.) Dining hall in a monastery of the *koinobion* (qq.v.) type.

RELICS. *See* **RELIQUARY.**

RELIQUARY. A container for relics, i.e., typically for the bodily remains (perhaps a fragment) of a saint after his death, as well as for objects that the saint may have worn or used. Reliquaries were also used for alleged pieces of the True Cross (q.v.). Such containers could be placed under altars, hidden from view, or could be elaborate gem-studded receptacles meant for viewing. An *enkolpion* (Greek for "on the chest"), which was worn around the neck, was a type of jewelry that could contain a fragmentary relic (amulet or inscription) to protect the wearer.

RHETORIC. *See* **EDUCATION.**

RHINE. The Rhine River (1,320 kilometers long) comprised the northern frontier of the Roman Empire, along with the Danube River (q.v.) farther to the east. The Rhine's defenses *(limes* [q.v.]) were abandoned in 406 in the face of massive numbers of invading Germans who included Vandals and Alans (qq.v.).

RHODES. Island in the Aegean Sea (q.v.) off the southwest coast of Asia Minor (q.v.). In 654 Muawiya (q.v.) briefly occupied the island, destroying the famous Colossus of Rhodes. Despite this and subsequent attacks, the island remained in Byzantine hands. Its strategic importance increased during the period of the Crusades (q.v.) when it was one of the chief points of call for ships going between Italy and Syria (qq.v.). After the capture of Constantinople (q.v.) in 1204 it came under the control of the Gabalas family, who had a long history of service with the Byzantine fleet. Leo Gabalas was succeeded by John Gabalas in 1240, and not until 1249 was the Empire of Nicaea (q.v.), under John III Vatatzes (qq.v.), able to retake the island. Thereafter, it was ruled by Genoa, and, after 1309, by the Hospitallers (q.v.), who held it until it was conquered by the Ottomans (q.v.) in 1522.

RHODIAN SEA LAW. The *Nomos Nautikos* (Maritime Law), or, as it is sometimes called, the *Nomos Rhodios* (Rhodian Law), is a collection of maritime law dating from the seventh or eighth century, and appended to the *Ecloga* (q.v.). It deals with diverse aspects of commercial navigation, including liability for losses in case of piracy or storm, and punishable offenses.

RHODOPE MOUNTAINS. The most impenetrable mountain range of the Balkan Peninsula (q.v.), densely wooded and rugged, whose few passes impede communications between the coastal plain of Thrace (q.v.) and the upper Hebros River valley. The theme of Strymon (qq.v.) was created partly to defend those passes.

RHOMAIOI. Greek term meaning "Romans," which is how the Byzantine state referred to its citizens. The imperial title *Basileus* (q.v.) *ton Romaion* ("Emperor of the Romans") was jealously guarded from the time of Charlemagne (q.v.) onward. "Rum" is how Muslim writers referred to the empire, and, thus, the sultanate of Rum (qq.v.) was what the Seljuks (q.v.) called their conquests in Asia Minor (q.v.). After 1265, as Byzantium (q.v.) contracted to something approaching the confines of ancient Greece (q.v.) and as Palaiologan (q.v.) scholars became seriously interested in ancient Greek civilization, the term *hellenes* ("Greeks") was also used to designate the inhabitants of Byzantium.

RICHARD I LIONHEART. *See* **CYPRUS; ISAAC KOMNENOS; THIRD CRUSADE.**

RICIMER. *Magister militum* (q.v.) who made and unmade western emperors (q.v.) from 456–472. He was a barbarian (grandson of Wallia, king of the Visigoths [q.v.]) who defeated the Vandals (q.v.) at sea, off Corsica (456), and fought the Ostrogoths (q.v.) and Alemanni in defense of Italy (q.v.). In 456 he deposed Avitus (q.v.), made Majorian (q.v.) emperor in 457, then deposed Majorian in 461. He accepted Leo I's nominee Anthemios (qq.v.) as emperor (467–472), but he replaced him with Olybrius in 472.

RILA MONASTERY. *See* **JOHN OF RILA.**

ROBERT CRESPIN. *See* **HERVÉ FRANKOPOULOS; ROUSSEL DE BAILLEUL.**

ROBERT DE CLARI. Author of an eyewitness account of the Fourth Crusade (q.v.). Robert's viewpoint as a lowly knight stands in contrast to that of Geoffrey de Villehardouin (q.v.), whose work more closely reflects the Fourth Crusade's leadership. Robert's account supports the view that the Crusade's diversion to Constantinople (q.v.) had more to do with accident than conspiracy. Nevertheless, Doge Enrico Dandalo and Conrad of Montferrat (qq.v.) are viewed as playing decisive roles in the decision to divert the Crusade. Also valuable in his work is the description he provides of monuments and relics in Constantinople (qq.v.).

ROBERT GUISCARD. Robert the "Crafty" (Guiscard), the Norman (q.v.) adventurer who conquered Byzantine southern Italy (q.v.) from 1057–1071. In 1059 Pope Nicholas II (q.v.) legitimized his rule in return for an alliance, recognizing him as duke of Apulia and Calabria (qq.v.). In 1071 his forces conquered Byzantium's (q.v.) last stronghold, Bari (q.v.), in 1071. Palermo in Sicily (qq.v.) fell in 1072 to the Normans. Robert and his son Bohemund (q.v.) invaded Byzantine possessions in northern Greece (q.v.) in 1081–1082, hoping to march eastward on the Via Egnatia (q.v.). Alexios I (q.v.) eventually succeeded in stemming their assault, reconquering Dyrrachion (q.v.) after the death of Guiscard in 1085.

ROBERT OF COURTENAY. See **LATIN EMPIRE.**

ROBERT OF FLANDERS. See **FIRST CRUSADE.**

ROBERT OF NORMANDY. See **FIRST CRUSADE.**

ROBERT THE MONK. See **GESTA FRANCORUM ET ALIORUM HIEROSOLIMITANORUM.**

ROGER II. Norman king of Sicily (qq.v.) from 1130–1154 who attacked Byzantium (q.v.) in 1147 while Manuel I (q.v.) was preoccupied with the Second Crusade (q.v.). Roger's fleet captured Kerkyra, and pillaged Euboea, Thebes, and Corinth (qq.v.), carrying off silk weavers to Palermo (q.v.) to support the fledgling silk industry there. Hostilities continued into 1149, when Byzantium recaptured Kerkyra, and Roger's fleet made a vain attack on Constantinople. Modern visitors to Sicily connect his name to two great monuments that he constructed, the Capella Paltina in Palermo and Cefalù, the mosaics of which were executed by Byzantine craftsmen. Cefalù has one of the great images of Christ Pantokrator (q.v.) in the semidome of its apse (q.v.).

ROGER DE FLOR. See **CATALAN GRAND COMPANY.**

ROMAIOI. See **RUM.**

ROMANCE. This popular type of novel, inherited from the ancient world, was revived in the 12th century. For example, the *Achilleis* (q.v.), probably composed around the beginning of the 15th century, recalls Homer's (q.v.) Trojan war, as do the main characters, a hero of chivalry named Achilles and his companion Patroklos. However, the setting, with its jousts and tournaments, is more that of Frankish feudalism (q.v.). Certain features remind one of the Byzantine epic poem *Digenes Akritas* (q.v.). Another example is *Rodanthe and Dosikles* by Theodore Prodromos (q.v.).

ROMANOS I LEKAPENOS. Emperor (q.v.) from 920–944. He was the first of a series of emperors, the last being Basil II (q.v.), who legislated against powerful landed magnates, the *dynatoi* (q.v.), by making it difficult for them to purchase peasant landholdings. His first edict, the novel (q.v.) of 922, made it difficult for the *dynatoi* to purchase peasant land except when they already owned property in the village. A subsequent edict in 934 expresses frustration that the *dynatoi* were circumventing the law and decreed the restoration of peasants' properties. At the beginning of his reign, the Tome of Union (q.v.) ended the long controversy over the tetragamy (q.v.). Externally, the war with Symeon of Bulgaria (q.v.) ended in 927, after which general John Kourkouas (q.v.) began offensive operations in Armenia and northern Mesopotamia (qq.v.), having mixed results against Sayf al-Dawla (q.v.) until he captured Melitene (q.v.) in 934. Nisibis, Dara, Amida, and Martyropolis (qq.v.) were captured in 943. In 944 he besieged Edessa (q.v.), which was forced to relinquish its famous *mandylion* (q.v.). Also worthy of mention is the failed attack on Constantinople by the Rus (qq.v.) in 941.

ROMANOS II. Emperor (q.v.) from 959–963, succeeding his father Constantine VII (q.v.). His second wife was the infamous Theophano (q.v.). Like Romanos I (q.v.) he legislated against the *dynatoi* (q.v.), attempting to protect the *stratiotika ktemata* (q.v.) against their encroachments. Externally, his great general Nikephoros (II) Phokas reconquered Crete (qq.v.) in 961, and he had great success against Sayf al-Dawla (q.v.), capturing Anazarbos in Cilicia and Germanikeia (qq.v.). In 962 Aleppo (q.v.), Sayf al-Dawla's capital, fell after a determined siege. It was Nikephoros (II) Phokas who succeeded in gaining the throne after Romanos died, despite opposition from Romanos's *parakoimomenos,* Joseph Bringas (qq.v.).

ROMANOS III ARGYROS. Emperor (q.v.) from 1028–1034, succeeding Constantine VIII (q.v.). He held the prestigious office of eparch of the city (q.v.), and by marrying Constantine VIII's daughter Zoe (q.v.) he established a connection with the Macedonian dynasty (q.v.). His reign is generally counted a disaster. He abandoned Basil II's (q.v.) policy of requiring the *dynatoi* (q.v.) to pay additional taxes for peasant holdings by rescinding the *allelengyon* (q.v.). He lavished money on church construction, including the Peribleptos Monastery and the church at Blachernai in Constantinople (qq.v.), both of which he paid for out of state funds. His humiliating defeat before Aleppo (q.v.) in 1030 only added to the general feeling of dissolution about his reign. Zoe and others conspired to drown him in 1034.

ROMANOS IV DIOGENES. Emperor (q.v.) from 1068–1071. He is remembered for losing the battle of Mantzikert to Alp Arslan (qq.v.) in 1071, one of the most famous of Byzantine defeats, one that opened up Asia Minor to Seljuk (qq.v.) expansion. Romanos also failed to properly defend Bari (q.v.), which fell to the Norman Robert Guiscard (qq.v.) in 1071, completing the Norman conquest of Byzantine Italy (q.v.). Taken captive at the battle of Mantzikert, Romanos was released only after making a treaty with Alp Arslan that promised an annual tribute and a personal ransom. However, upon reaching Byzantine territory he was deposed and blinded by palace conspirators. Mantzikert exposed the failure of Byzantium to defend its borders after the death of Basil II (q.v.) in 1025. Basil II's aggressive expansionism had to be discarded as impractical, but his professionalization of the army might have been continued. In any case, undisciplined rag-tag armies that mixed conscripts from the themes (q.v.) with unreliable mercenaries were not the answer.

ROMANOS THE MELODE. Creator of the Byzantine hymn (q.v.). He was a church deacon from Syria (q.v.), possibly of Jewish heritage, who settled in Constantinople during the reign of Anastasios I (q.v.). He composed a thousand hymns, only a fraction of which survive under his name. He developed and promoted the *kontakion* (q.v.), a sermon in verse, chanted by preacher and choir, that was the most popular form of hymn in the late fifth and sixth centuries. Much modern discussion has focused on the authorship of particular hymns, e.g., the Akathistos Hymn (q.v.), as well as how much Romanos was influenced by Syriac religious poetry and Jewish psalmody. Subsequent hymnographers, including Kosmas the Hymnographer (q.v.), were much influenced by Romanos, although his beloved *kontakion* was gradually replaced by another kind of church hymn, the *kanon* (q.v.).

ROME. Rome's political decline began with the establishment of Constantinople (q.v.), referred to as New Rome, in 324. The Visigoths (q.v.) pillaged Rome in 410, as did the Vandals (q.v.) in 455. It changed hands during Justinian I's war against the Ostrogoths (qq.v.). As Byzantine influence in Italy (q.v.) declined, beginning in 568 with the Lombard (q.v.) invasion, popes such as Gregory I (qq.v.) were able to carve out an independent role for the papacy (q.v.). This increased Rome's political importance in the West, but not until the Italian Renaissance did the city regain its former glory.

ROMULUS AUGUSTULUS. Last western emperor (q.v.), who reigned from 475–476. He came to power after the overthrow of Julius Nepos (q.v.). His own overthrow by Odoacer (q.v.) in 476 long provided the traditional date for the end of the Roman Empire. In reality, the medieval Roman Empire (what modern scholars called Byzantium [q.v.]) survived in Italy (q.v.) until the Normans conquered Bari (qq.v.) in 1071. In the East, of course, Byzantium survived until 1453.

ROSSANO. City in southern Italy that Byzantium (qq.v.) controlled until the Normans (q.v.) conquered it ca. 1059. Rossano and its environs were a center of monasticism (q.v.). Neilos of Rossano founded the monastery of St. Adrian near Rossano. Rossano is also known for the famous Rossano Gospels *(Codex Rossanensis),* the earliest known illustrated Greek Gospel texts.

ROSSANO GOSPELS. *See* **ROSSANO.**

ROUSSEL DE BAILLEUL. Commander of the Norman (q.v.) mercenaries at the battle of Mantzikert (q.v.) in 1071. Previous Norman commanders Robert Crespin and Hervé Frankopoulos (q.v.) proved unreliable, as did Roussel, who sought to use the turmoil in Asia Minor (q.v.) as an opportunity to carve out a kingdom for himself, much the same as other Normans had in southern Italy (q.v.). His rebellion of 1073 was successful in this regard, creating a brief Norman mini-state in the Armeniakon (q.v.). Roussel was suppressed in 1075 by general and future emperor Alexios (I) Komnenos (qq.v.).

RUBENIDS. Fleeing from the Seljuks in the aftermath of Mantzikert (q.v.), this Armenian dynasty established itself in Cilicia (q.v.) from ca. 1073–1226. There, in Cilicia's eastern coastal plain and mountains to the north, the Rubenids created a prosperous kingdom. In 1085 Thoros I captured Anazarbos and made it his capital. John II Komnenos (q.v.) recaptured Anazarbos in 1137, forcing the Rubenids back into the mountains for a while. Manuel I Komnenos (q.v.) recaptured Anazarbos again in 1158, forcing the submission of Thoros II. The battle of Myriokephalon (1176) ended Byzantine influence in Cilicia, but the Rubenids continued to struggle with the principality of Antioch (q.v.) until the end of the dynasty in 1226.

RUFINUS. The individual who served as the power behind the throne in the East from the death of Theodosios I (q.v.) on 17 January 395 until Rufinus's own death on 27 November 395. He was *magister officiorum* from 388–392 and Praetorian prefect (qq.v.) from 394. After Theodosios's death, Rufinus held sway over the mind of the child-emperor Honorios (q.v.), becoming his trusted advisor. However, nothing could save him from his western rival Stilicho (q.v.), who had the Gothic general Gainas (qq.v.) arrange for Rufinus's murder (a description of which is preserved in a poem by Claudian [q.v.]).

RUM. Arabic term for Byzantium (q.v.), derived from the fact that the Byzantines, as they are called by modern scholars, referred to themselves as *romaioi,* meaning Romans, and, until 1204 (when the Latin Empire appropriated the term) to their empire as *Romania.* The Seljuks of Anatolia (qq.v.) used the term for their Sultanate of Rum, and the Ottomans (qq.v.) later used *Rumeli* (q.v.) to designate their Byzantine territorial conquests in the Balkan Peninsula (q.v.). Rumeli Hisar, for example, is the famous fortress built in 1451 by Mehmed II (q.v.) on the European side of the Bosporos (q.v.).

RUM, SULTANATE OF. Seljuk (q.v.) state established in Anatolia (q.v.) after the battle of Mantzikert (q.v.), organized by its first ruler, Suleyman Ibn Kutlumush ca. 1078. Nicaea (q.v.), its first capital, surrendered to the forces of Alexios I Komnenos (q.v.) in 1097, after it was besieged by the army of the First Crusade (q.v.). After this, the capital was moved to Ikonion (q.v.). The sultanate declined in the 13th century, following the appearance of the Mongols in Asia Minor (qq.v.), and it disintegrated in the early 14th century.

RUMELI. *See* **RUM.**

RUMELI HISAR. *See* **BOSPOROS.**

RUS. Name given to the Vikings (also called Varangians [qq.v.]), who organized the first Russian state at Kiev (qq.v.), and who traversed the Dnieper (q.v.) to attack and trade with Constantinople (q.v.). The first Rus attack on the city was in 860, according to a homily of Photios (q.v.). An attack by Oleg (q.v.) in 907 was followed by a trading agreement in 911. Igor (q.v.) launched more raids in 941 and 943 (or 944), resulting in a renewal of trading privileges; the last Rus attack on Constantinople was in 1043. The growing power of the Rus is seen in Nikephoros II Phokas's (q.v.) request for the Rus to invade Bulgaria (q.v.). Svjatoslav did so in 968. The highpoint in this trajectory of Byzantine-Rus relations was Vladimir I's (q.v.) marriage in 988 to Anna, sister of Basil II (q.v.), followed by Vladimir's conversion to Christianity. Vladimir's loan of 6,000 Varangians to help Basil II (q.v.) fight against Bardas Phokas (q.v.) inaugurated a policy of using Varangians as mercenaries, most prominently in the elite Varangian Guard. Byzantine civilization had a profound impact on the converted Rus. For example, Jaroslav the Wise (q.v.) remade Kiev in the image of Constantinople, with a Cathedral of St. Sophia and its own Golden Gate (q.v.). After the demise of Byzantium (q.v.) the influence of Byzantine civilization continued in Moscow (q.v.), the self-proclaimed "Third Rome."

RUSSIAN PRIMARY CHRONICLE. Conventional title for a compilation (dated to the second decade of the 12th century), that has been variously referred to as the *Chronicle of Nestor,* or *The Tale of Bygone Years* (this last derived from a phrase in the first sentence of the text). The work's importance is that it is the chief historical source for the early history of Rus (q.v.) and for early Rus-Byzantine relations, including treaties resulting from Rus attacks on Constantinople (q.v.). Its authorship has been attributed to Nestor, a monk from Caves monastery in Kiev (q.v.).

– S –

SABAS. Saint from Caesarea in Cappadocia (qq.v.) who founded a *lavra* near Jerusalem (qq.v.) in 483. Today it is called Mar Saba, and it is one of the oldest functioning monasteries. He continued the work of his mentor, Euthymios the Great (q.v.), who also exerted a great influence on the development of monasticism in Palestine (qq.v.). Sabas twice went to Constantinople (q.v.) on missions from the patriarch (q.v.) of Jerusalem, where he defended the decrees of the Council of Chalcedon (q.v.). His *vita* (q.v.) was written by Cyril of Skythopolis.

SABELLIANISM. *See* **EUSTATHIOS OF ANTIOCH.**

SAGION. Short cloak, i.e., *chlamys* (q.v.) that was commonly worn in the imperial court. Emperors wore a purple, jeweled *sagion* over the *skaramangion* (q.v.).

SAINT HILARION CASTLE. *See* **CYPRUS.**

SAKELLARIOS. (Greek for "treasurer.") Title of a high-ranking civil or ecclesiastical official whose duties were mostly financial. The emperor's (q.v.) *sakellarios* supervised the *sakellion* (the imperial treasury), but by the mid-ninth century the office had evolved to that of a general controller.

SAKELLION. The imperial treasury where coined money was stored, supervised by the *sakellarios* (q.v.). Other duties were gradually added to the staff of the *sakellion,* including the control of weights and measures, the keeping of an inventory of imperial monastic properties, and the financial responsibility for public amusements. It is not to be confused with the *vestiarion* (q.v.).

SALADIN. Sultan of Egypt (q.v.) from 1169–1193, and scourge of the Crusaders. He founded the Muslim dynasty of the Ayyubids (q.v.). With Egypt (q.v.) firmly in his possession in 1169, he reunited the conquests of Nur al-Din in Syria (qq.v.), taking Damascus in 1174 and Aleppo (qq.v.) in 1183. For the first time, the Crusaders faced a united Muslim world. This helps to explain Saladin's stunning defeat of a Crusader army at the battle of Hattin in 1187. After Hattin, Byzantine policy became pro-Saladin, which inflamed Crusader sentiments. It was Saladin who urged Isaac II (q.v.) to resist the army of Frederick I Barbarossa (q.v.) as it traversed Byzantine territory in 1189–1190 during the Third Crusade (q.v.).

SALAMIS (CONSTANTIA). *See* **CYPRUS; EPIPHANIOS.**

SALERNO. City on the Gulf of Salerno in southwest Italy (q.v.), conquered by the Lombards from Byzantium (qq.v.). It was part of the duchy of Benevento (q.v.), despite Byzantine technical sovereignty. After the Arab victory at Garigliano (q.v.) in 915, Salerno switched allegiance to Otto I of Germany (qq.v.). Despite the waning of Byzantine political influence, Byzantium's cultural influence on Salerno continued, as seen in the huge bronze doors (dated 1100) of its cathedral.

SALONA. Birthplace of Diocletian (q.v.), located on the coast of Dalmatia near Split (qq.v.) and the site of Diocletian's retirement palace. Ruled by the Ostrogoths (q.v.) in the fifth century, Justinian I's general Mundus (qq.v.) reconquered it in 535. In the 630s, in order to escape the attacks of Slavs and Avars (qq.v.), the inhabitants moved to Split.

SAMARITANS. Jewish separatists who were never tolerated by the state, and who were persecuted repeatedly for their insurrections in Palestine (q.v.) during the fifth and sixth centuries. After the revolt of 529, in which they crowned one of their leaders, Justinian I (q.v.) killed tens of thousands of them, destroyed their synagogues, and deprived them of their sacred Mount Gerizim.

SAMO. *See* **MORAVIA; SLAVS.**

SAMOS. Island in the Aegean Sea (q.v.) off the coast of Asia Minor (q.v.). The Arabs (q.v.) attacked it repeatedly in the seventh and eighth centuries. In the ninth century it became part of the theme (q.v.) of Samos with its capital at Smyrna (q.v.). Around 1088 Tzachas (q.v.) captured it, making it part of his maritime principality, but it was in Byzantine hands again several years later. In 1204 Baldwin of Flanders (q.v.) was given Samos, along with Lesbos and Chios (qq.v.). A fleet of John III Vatatzes (q.v.) seized it around 1225, but in 1304 it fell to the Genoese, who held it (despite a Byzantine reconquest of 1329–1346) until 1475, when it was captured by the Ottomans (q.v.).

SAMOSATA. City located at a strategic crossing of the upper Euphrates River (q.v.). It is mentioned in the wars with Persia (q.v.). Julian (q.v.), for example, used it as a naval station in his Persian campaign of 363. Once occupied by the Arabs (q.v.) in 639, it was often attacked by Byzantine expeditions. In 873 Basil I (q.v.) seized it temporarily. It was reconquered by John I Tzimiskes (q.v.) in 958. By the late 11th century it was in the hands of the Turks (q.v.).

SAMOTHRACE. *See* **GATTILUSIO.**

SAMUEL OF BULGARIA. Ruled Bulgaria (q.v.) from 976–1014; first Bulgarian ruler to adopt the title tsar (q.v.). Samuel's invasions of Greece (q.v.) from 981–986, which reached as far as the Peloponnesos (qq.v.), culminated in a great victory over Basil II at the pass called Trajan's Gate (q.v.). However, from 991–1014 Basil II (q.v.) struck back in a series of expeditions that reclaimed Greece and took the war into Bulgaria. In 997 Basil's general Nikephoros Ouranos won a decisive victory over Samuel in central Greece at the

Spercheios River. In 1004 he captured Skopje, and Dyrrachion (qq.v.) fell in 1005. In 1014 Basil surrounded Samuel's army in the mountain passes of Kleidion and captured 14,000 prisoners, whom he blinded, sending them back to Samuel in groups of a hundred, each group led by a single soldier with one eye. Samuel is said to have died, presumably from a stroke, when he saw his blinded troops.

SANUDO TORSELLO, MARINO. Venetian nobleman related to the Venetian dukes of Naxos; historian; anti-Ottoman propagandist. His failed efforts to arouse the West to a Crusade against the Ottomans (q.v.) left a rich legacy of letters (from 1323–1337), including some to Andronikos II Palaiologos (q.v.). His historical essays include a valuable account of Frankish Greece (q.v.) and of the Venetian colonies, which continues (to 1310) the work of Geoffrey Villehardouin (q.v.).

SARDINIA. Island in the western Mediterranean Sea (q.v.), separated from Corsica (qq.v.) to its north by the Strait of Bonifacio. The Vandals (q.v.) seized it around 455 and held it until Justinian I (q.v.) reconquered it in 534. Despite its brief occupation in 551–552 by Totila (q.v.), and subsequent attacks by the Lombards (q.v.), it remained in Byzantine hands until Arabs (q.v.) from Spain (q.v.) conquered it in 1003.

SARDIS. Metropolis of Lydia in Asia Minor (qq.v.). The city flourished until the early seventh century. The historian Eunapios (q.v.), who wrote from Sardis, describes a philosophical school there. Recent excavations have revealed the extent of its civic monuments and churches, many of which were destroyed ca. 616, perhaps by a Persian raid. The seventh-century Byzantine fortress survived for centuries, despite a brief occupation by the Arabs in 716 and by Tzachas (qq.v.) from 1092–1098. Sardis flourished again under the Lascarids (q.v.), as did the entire region. However, after 1261 the Turkish advance in Lydia was relentless. The emirate of Saruhan (qq.v.) conquered Sardis ca. 1315.

SARKEL. The name, which means "White House," refers to a fortress on the mouth of the Don River constructed by Theophilos (q.v.) ca. 833 at the request of the Khazars (q.v.). Its purpose was to protect against the Rus (q.v.), who threatened the Khazars on the lower Don and the Byzantine theme of Cherson (qq.v.). Nevertheless, Rus forces under Svjatoslav (q.v.) destroyed Sarkel in 965.

SARMATIANS. Nomadic people, related to the Scythians (q.v.), who settled in a broad swath along the northern periphery of the Black Sea (q.v.), and north of the lower Danube River (q.v.). During the reign of Constantine I (q.v.) they crossed the Danube in 323, and pillaged Thrace (q.v.) before the emperor (q.v.) chased them back across the Danube. Constantine I conquered them in 334, after which they were settled within the empire as farmers and soldiers.

SARUHAN. One of the early 14th-century emirates (q.v.) founded in western Asia Minor (q.v.) on the ruins of the Sultanate of Rum (q.v.). Its capital was Magnesia (q.v.), which Saruhan conquered in 1313; Sardis fell soon thereafter (q.v.). Andronikos III Palaiologos (q.v.) concluded treaties with Saruhan in 1329 and 1335, and, for a time, the Saruhan emirate seemed of more importance than the emirate of Osman (q.v.). However, in 1410 the Ottomans (q.v.) occupied it.

SASSANIANS. Dynasty that ruled Persia (q.v.) from 226–651, with its capital at Ctesiphon; Byzantium's (q.v.) long-time eastern foe until Herakleios (q.v.) conquered the Sassanian state in 628. Ardashir I made its official religion Zoroastrianism (q.v.). His successor Shapur I (240–270) was one of Rome's (q.v.) most dangerous enemies, and subsequent kings Chosroes I and Chosroes II (qq.v.) posed grave threats to Byzantium. Under Yazdgird III, the last Sassanian king, the Arabs (q.v.) advanced into Persia, destroying Persian resistance in 642. Yazdgird III remained a fugitive at large for another 10 years before he was killed, bringing to an end a dynasty that ruled Persia for more than four centuries.

SAVA OF SERBIA. Serbian saint and monk who organized the Serbian church. At the request of his father, Stefan Nemanja (q.v.), he founded the Serbian monastery of Hilandar on Mount Athos (qq.v.), where he lived as a monk before being consecrated in 1219 as the first archbishop (q.v.) of the church of Serbia (q.v.). He traveled widely, endowing other churches and monasteries in the Holy Land, Thessalonike, and Constantinople (qq.v.).

SAYF AL-DAWLA. Hamdanid emir (qq.v.) of Mosul and Aleppo (qq.v.), who was Byzantium's (q.v.) chief Arab opponent in Syria and Mesopotamia (qq.v.) from 936–962. He defeated John Kourkouas (q.v.) in 938 on the upper Euphrates (q.v.), and he won a victory near Aleppo in 944 and another major victory in 953. However, the tide began to turn in Byzantium's favor. In 958 John (I) Tzimiskes (q.v.) defeated him, capturing Samosata (q.v.) in northern Mesopotamia. In 962 Nikephoros (II) Phokas (q.v.) captured Aleppo and plundered it. Still, only after Sayf al-Dawla's death in 967 was Byzantium able to make significant territorial gains in Syria and Mesopotamia.

SAYINGS OF THE DESERT FATHERS.
See **APOPHTHEGMATA PATRUM.**

SCHISM OF 1054. *See* **CHURCH SCHISM OF 1054.**

SCHOLAE PALATINAE. Senior imperial guard unit, originally five regiments of 500 cavalrymen each, perhaps created by Constantine I (q.v.). Justin I (q.v.) added four additional regiments. They had a long and distinguished history, especially from the time of Constantine V (q.v.), when it became the most important *tagma* (q.v.), under the command of the *domestikos* (q.v.) *ton scholon,* who, on occasion, commanded the entire field army. Together, the *scholae palatinae,* the *exkoubitores* (q.v.), and (from the early ninth century) the *hikanatoi* (q.v.) formed an elite strike force.

SCHOLARES. *See* **SCHOLAE PALATINAE.**

SCHOLASTICISM. *See* **AQUINAS, THOMAS; GENNADIOS II SCHOLARIOS; THEOLOGY.**

SCIENCE. Byzantine science was, for the most part, unoriginal. It depended heavily on ancient science, which was revered, copied, and commented on. Commentators could be critical in their appraisals. For example, John Philoponos (q.v.) attacked Aristotle's law of falling bodies and demonstrated, contrary to Aristotle, that a vacuum can exist. Such original achievements as there were tended to be in areas of applied science, e.g., in medicine (q.v.) and in engineering (e.g., the dome of Justinian I's Hagia Sophia [qq.v.]). Kallinikos invented Greek fire (q.v.), and Leo the Mathematician invented a beacon system (qq.v.) to warn of Arab attacks in Asia Minor (qq.v.). Both theoretical and applied science overlapped with superstition and magic (q.v.). For example, the study of astronomy (q.v.) could easily degenerate into astrology (q.v.). Chemistry was synonymous with alchemy. The boundary between mathematics and numerology was hardly clear, and number symbolism overlapped with Neoplatonic philosophy and theology (qq.v.). Byzantium's chief scientific contribution was to transmit ancient Greek science to the Islamic world.

SCRIPTOR INCERTUS. Anonymous Greek historical source (the Latin title means "writer unknown") for the years 811–816. It contains two fragments, one describing Nikephoros I's (q.v.) disastrous expedition against the Bulgars (qq.v.) in 811, the other the reigns of Michael I and Leo V (qq.v.). The second fragment seems definitely part of a longer (lost) work, perhaps of a contemporary historian like Sergios the Confessor. He died ca. 829 and is known to have authored an historical work covering the years 741–828.

SCYTHIA MINOR. *See* **DINOGETIA; DOBRUDJA; SCYTHIANS.**

SCYTHIANS. Nomadic steppe (q.v.) tribe settled north of the Black Sea (q.v.) until it was displaced by the Sarmatians (q.v.) in the second or first century B.C. However, the name survived in Scythia Minor, a province south of the Danube (q.v.), that flourished from the fourth through sixth centuries and included such prosperous cities as Histria (q.v.).

SEBASTEIA. City in Cappadocia (q.v.) whose location on a major road across Asia Minor (q.v.) explains why the Persians (q.v.) burned it in 575, and why the Arabs (q.v.) repeatedly attacked it. In 1021 it was ceded to King Senacherim Arcruni in return for Vaspurakan (q.v.). In 1059 it became the first important city in Asia Minor to be plundered by Turks (q.v.), who occupied it permanently toward the end of the 11th century. Legendary martyrs include the Five Martyrs of Sebasteia and the 40 Martyrs of Sebasteia (qq.v.).

SEBASTOKRATOR. Alexios I Komnenos (q.v.) created the title of "sebastos" (q.v.) and its variations, this title being one of them. It was awarded to imperial relatives, the first being Alexios I's brother Isaac Komnenos (q.v.). Only the title of *basileus* (q.v.) and, beginning with Manuel I Komnenos (q.v.), despot (q.v.) were of higher rank.

SEBASTOS. "Revered," in Greek, and the basis of Alexios I Komnenos's (q.v.) new array of titles, e.g., *sebastokrator* (q.v.), *protosebastos* (the highest-ranked *sebastos*), and *panhypersebastos* (an even higher-ranking title than *protosebastos*). Alexios I conferred it on his own relatives and on members of the nobility. By the end of the 12th century it was dispensed so frequently as to become debased. In the 13th century it was awarded to important foreigners as a tool of diplomacy.

SECOND CRUSADE. The Second Crusade (1147–1149) was launched in response to the fall of Edessa (q.v.) to Zangi in 1146. The threat to Constantinople (q.v.) posed by the First Crusade (q.v.) was renewed during this Crusade, as the armies of Conrad III and Louis VII (qq.v.) passed through the city in 1147. Manuel I viewed the approaching armies with justifiable apprehension. Conrad's army committed acts of violence at Adrianople (q.v.) and outside the walls of Constantinople. Odo of Deuil (q.v.) reports that some in Louis VII's army called for an attack on Constantinople. Manuel I (q.v.) was forced to remain in Constantinople in order to protect the city. He tried to persuade Louis VII to join him in an alliance against Roger II of Sicily (q.v.). This attempt not only failed but Roger II used Manuel I's preoccupation with the Crusade to occupy Kerkyra (q.v.) and to attack Corinth and Thebes (qq.v.) in 1147. As soon as the Second Crusade was on its way, Manuel I opened hostilities against Roger II, regaining Kerkyra (q.v.) in 1149. Thus, the Second Crusade was as fraught with danger for Byzantium (q.v.) as the First Crusade had been.

SECRET HISTORY. *See* **ANEKDOTA.**

SEE. The administrative jurisdiction of a bishop (q.v.), which invariably included the bishop's city and surrounding territory. Metropolitan-bishops (q.v.), including archbishops (q.v.), exercised ecclesiastical jurisdiction over provinces (q.v.). The sees of patriarchs (q.v.) were dioceses (q.v.).

SEKRETON. Generally speaking, a governmental bureau. For example, the fiscal administration was comprised of a number of *sekreta,* including the *genikon* and *sakellion* (qq.v.), which handled both expenditure and revenue. From the seventh century onward it could also refer to a patriarchal court, council, or bureau of the *chartophylax* (q.v.). From the 14th century the term also included imperial supreme courts.

SELEUKEIA. Coastal city in Isauria (q.v.) in southeastern Asia Minor (q.v.). Its importance lay chiefly in its role as defender of the Isaurian coast from Arab (q.v.) raids. To this end, it became capital of the theme of Kibyrrhaiotai (qq.v.), then of a *kleisoura* (q.v.), and finally, in the 10th century, of the theme of Seleukia (q.v.). A local synod of 359 achieved prominence in 370 when Valens (q.v.) demanded that all eastern bishops (q.v.) follow its support of Arianism (q.v.). The city was also noted for Saint Thekla (q.v.), whose shrine was at nearby Meriamlik.

SELJUKS. Turkish dynasty of steppe (q.v.) nomads founded by Seljuk. His grandson Tughrul Beg conquered Baghdad (q.v.) in 1055, bringing the Islamic caliphate (q.v.) under his possession. Superior mobility allowed Seljuk horsemen to penetrate the border defenses of Asia Minor (q.v.) and sack Melitene (q.v.) in 1058. In 1067 they pillaged Caesarea (q.v.). But it was the victory of Tughrul Beg's son and successor, sultan Alp Arslan (q.v.), at the battle of Mantzikert (q.v.) in 1071 that opened up Asia Minor to Seljuk expansion. The sultanate of Rum (q.v.) was quickly established with its capital at Nicaea (q.v.), until 1097, when they were forced to surrender the city to Alexios I and the army of the First Crusade (qq.v.). Their new capital was established at Ikonion (q.v.), from where (after the defeat of Manuel I in 1176 at the battle of Myriokephalon [qq.v.]), they extended their control over most of Asia Minor. Their decline began with their defeat by the Mongols (q.v.) in 1243 and continued until the early 14th century when the emirate of Osman (qq.v.) began its phenomenal expansion in Asia Minor.

SELYMBRIA. Port-city located west of Constantinople (q.v.) along the northern shore of the Sea of Marmara (q.v.) at the end of the Via Egnatia (q.v.). The southern end of the Long Wall of Anastasios I (qq.v.) extended to the west of Selymbria. The city was strongly fortified, as attested by the fact that in 1385 when future John VII received Selymbria to administer, it was one of the few places independent of Ottoman rule in the vicinity of Constantinople (q.v.). It surrendered to the Ottomans (q.v.) after Constantinople was captured in 1453.

SEMISSIS. *See* **COINAGE.**

SENATE. Advisory and ceremonial body in Rome (q.v.) that Constantine I duplicated in Constantinople (qq.v.) and which continued to exist until the end of Byzantium (q.v.). Occasionally its actions were significant, as in the accession of Anastasios I (q.v.), in the support of many senators of the Nika Revolt (q.v.), and when the senate deposed Martina and Heraklonas (qq.v.). It might also act as a tribunal, as in 653 when Pope Martin I (q.v.) was accused of supporting the rebellion of Olympios (q.v.) and tried for high treason. Revocation of its authority by Leo VI (q.v.) accelerated its decline. However, despite its loss of any real power, it remained an advisory body to the emperor (q.v.) until the end of the empire.

SERBIA. The first organized Serbian state was called Raška (q.v.). It was established in the ninth century by Serbs, namely, Slavs (q.v.) who settled in the Balkan Peninsula (q.v.) during the reign of Herakleios (q.v.), who converted to Orthodoxy (q.v.) and recognized Byzantine authority. Until ca. 930 it was dominated by neighboring Bulgaria (q.v.). In ca. 1170 Stefan Nemanja (q.v.) proclaimed an independent Serbia, but he was forced to acknowledge Byzantine overlordship when Manuel I Komnenos (q.v.) led an army into Serbia. Nevertheless, the successors of Stefan Nemanja expanded Serbia over the next two centuries (from ca. 1168–1371) into a powerful state under such famous rulers as Stefan Urosh I, Stefan Urosh II Milutin, Stefan Urosh III Dechanski, and Stefan Urosh IV Dushan (qq.v.). The location of Serbia was such that it threatened the two main roads through the Balkan Peninsula: the Via Egnatia (qq.v.) and the military road from Belgrade through Nish and Serdica to Adrianople and Constantinople (qq.v.). Serbia resisted the Ottomans (q.v.), even after the defeat in 1389 at Kosovo Polje (q.v.). Despite the leadership of Stefan Lazarevich and George Brankovich (qq.v.), Serbia in its entirety was occupied by the Ottomans by 1459.

SERBS. *See* **SERBIA.**

SERDICA. Modern Sophia, Bulgaria (q.v.). Serdica's importance lay in its strategic location along major road systems, the most important of which was the Belgrade-Naissus-Serdica-Philippopolis (qq.v.) road to Constantinople (q.v.). The Council of Serdica (ca. 343) attempted to settle the question of Athanasios's Orthodoxy (qq.v.), but it failed. The western bishops (q.v.) confirmed it, but the eastern bishops did not. The city suffered from the attacks of Visigoths (q.v.) in the late fourth century and Huns (q.v.) during the time of Attila (q.v.), but it remained in Byzantine hands until Krum (q.v.) conquered it and massacred its garrison in 809. With the victory of

Basil II (q.v.) over Bulgaria, it became a Byzantine city again, until it was captured by Asen I (q.v.) in 1194. The Ottomans (q.v.) conquered it in 1382.

SERFDOM. *See* **COLONUS.**

SERGIOPOLIS (Arabic Rasafah). Major sixth-century garrison city on the Euphrates (q.v.) frontier, north of Palmyra (q.v.). Anastasios I (q.v.) named the town after a saint named Sergios (q.v.), who was martyred during the reign of Diocletian (q.v.) with a saint named Bakchos (the church of Sts. Sergios and Bakchos in Constantinople [q.v.] is named after them). Justinian I (q.v.) rebuilt the city, refortifying its walls, but it fell to Chosroes I (q.v.) in 540, and to the Arabs (q.v.) in the seventh century. Today its ruins, including the monumental Basilica A, form (along with the Monastery of Symeon Stylites [q.v.]) an impressive example of the architectural richness of late antique Syria (q.v.).

SERGIOS I. Patriarch of Constantinople (qq.v.) from 610–638. He allowed Herakleios (q.v.) to expropriate church valuables in 621 to finance the war against the Persians (q.v.). He led the defense of Constantinople in 626 during its siege by Avars (q.v.) and Persians. His Monoenergism and support of the *Ekthesis* (qq.v.) were subsequently condemned (in 680).

SERGIOS AND BAKCHOS, CHURCH OF. *See* **BOUKOLEON; CONSTANTINOPLE.**

SERGIOS THE CONFESSOR. *See* **SCRIPTOR INCERTUS.**

SERGIUS I. *See* **JUSTINIAN II; TRULLO, COUNCIL IN.**

SERRES. City in Macedonia (q.v.) northeast of Thessalonike (q.v.), strategically situated on the broad, fertile plain through which the Strymon ([q.v.] modern Struma) River passes before exiting into the Aegean Sea (q.v.). It changed hands between Normans and Bulgars (qq.v.) in the late 12th century. It was recaptured by John III Vatatzes (q.v.) in 1246 and fell to Stefan IV Dushan (q.v.) in 1345. The Ottomans (q.v.) captured it in 1383.

SERVIA. City in Greece south of Berroia (qq.v.) that guarded the road to Larissa (q.v.), where the middle course of the Haliakmon River runs through a broad plain. Its name may derive from its settlement by Serbs (q.v.) under the protection of Heraklios (q.v.). The city's strategic location explains its capture and recapture, beginning with Basil II's war with Bulgaria (qq.v.). It fell to the Ottomans (q.v.) in the late 14th century.

SEVERIANOS. Bishop of Gabala in Syria (q.v.) who became embroiled in a power struggle with John Chrysostom in 401. He was a trusted deputy of Chrysostom until the latter tried to send him back to Gabala. Gabala resisted this, turned to Chrysostom's opponents for support, and they rallied behind him. Chrysostom was forced to reconcile with him, and he had to abandon his attempt to force Severianos's removal to Gabala.

SEVEROS. Bishop of Antioch (qq.v) from 512–518 and untiring promoter of Monophysitism (q.v.). He gained great prominence during the reign of Anastasios I (q.v.), who favored him. However, in 518 Justin I (q.v.) sent Severos into exile and launched a persecution of Monophysites. Justinian I (q.v.) invited him to Constantinople (q.v.) for negotiations, where Theodora (q.v.) arranged for him to stay at the Great Palace (q.v.). Nevertheless, he was condemned at a synod in Constantinople in 536 and spent the last years of his life in the Egyptian desert. The theologian Leontios of Byzantium (died ca. 543) wrote a work attacking him. Zacharias of Mytilene (q.v.) wrote his *vita* (q.v.).

SEVERUS. Emperor and augustus (qq.v.) in the West from 306–307. Made caesar to Constantius Chlorus (qq.v.) in 305, he became augustus upon the death of Constantius in 306. Galerius (q.v.) sent him against the usurper Maxentius, son of Maximian (qq.v.). However, Maximian's troops revolted and Severus soon found himself a prisoner of Maxentius, who executed him in 307.

SGOUROS, LEO. Byzantine administrator of Nauplia who carved out an independent state for himself in the northeast Peloponnesos (q.v.) from 1201 until his death in 1207. His was one of several revolutions (like that of Ivanko [q.v.]) that occurred as Alexios III's (q.v.) regime disintegrated. Sgouros first seized Nauplia, then Argos and Corinth (q.v.). The Fourth Crusade's (q.v.) conquest of Constantinople (q.v.) produced a brief power vacuum in the Peloponnesos that allowed Sgouros to attack Athens (q.v.), where Michael Choniates (q.v.) defended the Acropolis. Thebes (q.v.) was captured and Thessaly (q.v.) fell under his sway. However, with the arrival of Boniface Montferrat (q.v.) Sgouros was forced to flee to the Acrocorinth, where he died under siege in 1207.

SHAPUR I. *See* **SASSANIANS.**

SHIITES. *See* **FATAMIDS.**

SHIRKUH. *See* **NUR AL-DIN.**

SICILIAN VESPERS. The uprising in Sicily (q.v.) in March 1282 that thwarted Charles I of Anjou's (q.v.) planned attack on Constantinople (q.v.). Charles's fleet at Messina (q.v.) was destroyed, and with the arrival of Peter III of Aragon (son-in-law of Manfred [q.v.]) in August of that year the French were driven from the island. Michael VIII (q.v.) seems to have promoted and subsidized the Aragonese invasion. In any case, it was a stunning humiliation of Charles I of Anjou, and of the papacy (q.v.) that had supported him.

SICILY. Largest island in the Mediterranean (q.v.), separated from the Italian mainland by the Strait of Messina (q.v.). While Sicily linked Italy to Africa (qq.v.), it also divided the Mediterranean (q.v.) into eastern and western parts. Conquered by Gaiseric (q.v.) in 475, it remained in Vandal (q.v.) hands until the Ostrogoths (q.v.) captured it in 491. Belisarios (q.v.) took the island for Justinian I (q.v.) in 535–536, after defeating the Vandals in North Africa (q.v.). Arab raids on the island began in 652, and when Constans II (q.v.) took up residence in Syracuse (q.v.) from 663–668, it was ostensibly to defend Sicily against the Arabs (q.v.). Despite Sicily's elevation to the status of a theme (q.v.) by ca. 700, Arab raids continued throughout the eighth century. In 826 the Aghlabids (q.v.) invaded the island, capturing Palermo (q.v.) in 831. Syracuse (q.v.) fell in 878 and by 902, when Taormina (q.v.) fell, the Aghlabids had effective control of the island. Byzantine expeditions to recover Sicily, most notably under George Maniakes (q.v.) from 1038–1042, failed. What Byzantium (q.v.) was unable to do the Normans (q.v.) succeeded at. Their conquest began in 1060 and was completed by 1091. Norman rule, which produced such architectural gems as the Capella Palatina and Cefalù (built by Roger II [q.v.]), and Monreale (built by William II [q.v.]), were decorated in the Byzantine style, perhaps using Byzantine artisans. Henry VI of Germany (qq.v.), married to Constance, daughter of Roger II, inherited Sicily after the death of William II in 1189. The death of Frederick II's son Manfred (qq.v.) in 1266 allowed Charles I of Anjou (q.v.), with papal support, to claim Sicily as his own. However, the Sicilian Vespers (q.v.), conspired for by Michael VIII Palaiologos (q.v.), ejected Charles from Sicily in 1282.

SIDE. *See* **PAMPHYLIA.**

SIDON. *See* **BERYTUS; TYRE.**

SIDONIUS. *See* **AVITUS; EPARCHIUS; MAJORIAN.**

SIGISMUND OF HUNGARY. *See* **NIKOPOLIS, CRUSADE OF.**

SILENTARIOS. *See* **ANASTASIOS.**

SILENTIUM. By the sixth century this was an imperial council consisting of the *consistorium* and senate (qq.v.). However, the *silentium* subsequently evolved toward a less permanent body that met at the command of the emperor (q.v.) to discuss important affairs or state, or even of the church. The term might even refer to ceremonial occasions over which the emperor presided.

SILK. Silk production was a privatized state industry, centered in Constantinople (q.v.) and also, from the 11th century, in Athens, Corinth, Thebes, and Thessalonike (qq.v.). Justinian I (q.v.) established the industry by first smuggling silkworm eggs from China (q.v.). He then created the mulberry-tree plantations necessary to support silkworms, and he set up the factories necessary for weaving. The industry's importance was twofold: as a supplier of rich court and church vestments and furnishings (e.g., for curtains and tapestries) and as a controlled luxury item for foreign trade. The *Book of the Eparch* (q.v.) describes the guild (q.v.) that controlled all aspects of its production. Exported silk, which was as highly coveted as gold by foreign rulers, was rigorously monitored. Much of it was exported as imperial gifts or tribute. Byzantine officials, themselves dressed in the finest silks, reminded ambassador Liutprand of Cremona (q.v.) that in his native Saxony people wore the skins of animals, a remark that infuriated Liutprand. Liutprand's attempt in 968 to smuggle five pieces of purple silk out of Constantinople for Otto I (q.v.) met with failure; they were confiscated. Byzantium's monopoly of silk began to erode in the 12th century. In 1147 Roger II (q.v.) of Sicily (q.v.) attacked Corinth and Thebes (qq.v.), carrying off their silk weavers. Despite this the silk industry survived. According to Benjamin of Tudela (q.v.), in the 1160s the silk industry in Thebes (q.v.) was flourishing.

SILVESTER I. *See* **DONATION OF CONSTANTINE.**

SIMOKATTES, THEOPHYLAKTOS. The last of the Roman imperial historians. He wrote a history of the reign of Maurice (q.v.), who ruled 582–602, continuing the work of Menander Protector (q.v.). He was a contemporary of the emperor Maurice, probably a judge, who was born in Egypt (q.v.). Incidental to his main theme, but of unusual interest is information about Asia, including the Turks (q.v.) of central Asia and the Chinese empire.

SIMONIS. The daughter of Andronikos II and Irene-Yolanda of Montferrat (qq.v.) who was married in 1299 at age five to Serbian king Stefan Urosh II Milutin (q.v.). He was then about 40, and Simonis was his fourth wife, all of which meant that the marriage was considered scandalous. Milutin agreed to raise her as a child in the royal family until she was of suitable age to become a real wife to him. Theodore Metochites (q.v.) negotiated the arrangements that secured peace with Serbia (q.v.), which was the whole point of the marriage to begin with. After Milutin's death in 1321, she returned to Constantinople (q.v.), where she lived out her life as a nun.

SINAI. *See* **CATHERINE, MONASTERY OF SAINT.**

SINGIDUNUM. *See* **BELGRADE.**

SINOPE. Port-city in Pontos (q.v.) on the south shore of the Black Sea (q.v.). After the revolt of the Armeniakon (q.v.) in 793, Constantine VI (q.v.) executed the bishop (q.v.) of Sinope for supporting the rebellion. In 834 Sinope was at the center of the rebellion of Theophobos (q.v.) and his followers. Captured by the Seljuks (q.v.) in 1081, it was recaptured by Alexios I (q.v.). Annexed by the Empire of Trebizond (q.v.) in 1204, it was lost to the Turks (q.v.) soon after 1214.

SIRMIUM. City and border fortress on the Middle Danube (q.v.), in the diocese of Pannonia (qq.v.). It surrendered to the Avars (q.v.) in 582 after a siege of two years. Belgrade (q.v.) fell two years after

Sirmium was conquered. From these two cities both the Avars and Slavs (q.v.) were positioned to menace northern and central Greece (q.v.).

SKANDERBEG. George Kastriota of Albania (q.v.), the last Christian leader to successfully oppose the Ottomans in the Balkan Peninsula (qq.v.). Son of a prince in northern Albania, he was taken hostage to the court of Murad II (q.v.) where he converted to Islam (q.v.), and he became an officer in the Ottoman army. He deserted in 1443, renounced Islam, and successfully organized Albanian resistance to the Ottomans until his death in 1468. The Ottomans called him *Iskender Beg* (meaning Alexander *beg,* or Lord Alexander), which translated into Albanian as Skanderbeg.

SKARAMANGION. A kind of chaftan in the form of a long silk undertunic (*chiton* [q.v.]) with a belt, worn under a *sagion* (q.v.). Only the emperor could wear a purple *skaramangion*.

SKLAVENIA. See **CONSTANS II; DROUGOUBITAI; SLAVS.**

SKLAVENOI. See **SLAVS.**

SKLEROS, BARDAS. See **BASIL II; BOURTZES, MICHAEL.**

SKLEROS, ROMANOS. See **MANIAKES, GEORGE.**

SKOPJE. City in northern Macedonia (q.v.). It was destroyed by earthquake in the early sixth century. Thereafter the city's history is obscure until Basil II (q.v.) seized it in the early 11th century. In 1282 the Serbs (q.v.) occupied it; Stefan Urosh IV Dushan (q.v.) was crowned there in 1346. The Ottomans (q.v.) captured it in 1391. The lovely church of St. Panteleemon at Nerezi (dated ca. 1164) is located near Skopje.

SKRIPOU, CHURCH OF THE PANAGHIA. See **BOEOTIA.**

SKYLITZES, JOHN. Historian who wrote a chronicle (q.v.) from 811–1057, continuing the chronicle of Theophanes the Confessor (q.v.). Its value as an independent source increases dramatically with the reign of Basil II (q.v.). The later historian George Kedrenos (q.v.) copied Skylitzes almost word for word in his own work.

SKYTHOPOLIS. *See* **PALESTINE.**

SLAVERY. Slavery existed throughout the history of Byzantium (q.v.) as an inheritance from Roman times that the church tolerated. Prisoners of war were a common source of slaves. From the 10th century onward campaigns in the Balkan Peninsula (q.v.) were a major source of slaves, as were lands north of the Black Sea (q.v.). Slaves were used in imperial workshops and for a variety of other urban tasks. However, their use in the countryside never eclipsed free villages and a free peasantry, which remained the norm. Slavery was accepted in the West as well. The eastern shore of the Adriatic (q.v.) became Europe's "slave coast," so to speak, where Slavs (q.v.) were obtained. In west European languages "slave" became synonymous with Slavs; the term in Greek was *doulos,* which could also be used in reference to holy men, in the sense of being a servant of God.

SLAVS. Indo-European peoples from central and eastern Europe, called *sklavenoi* in Byzantine historical sources. Their raids across the Danube (q.v.) in the sixth century posed a serious threat from ca. 579 onward, when the Avars (q.v.) led them into Byzantine territory in great numbers. The Slavs settled as far south as the Peloponnesos (q.v.), and in 626 they combined with the Avars and Persians (qq.v.) to attack Constantinople (q.v.). With the Avars, they attacked Thessalonike in the late sixth and early seventh centuries; their first attack came in 586. In Greece (q.v.) the Slavs usually settled in more remote areas, which Byzantine historians referred to as *sklaviniai.* Each *sklavinia* had its own leader *(archon).* From the ninth century onward they were gradually brought under Byzantine administrative control and Hellenized, becoming, in effect, Byzantines. However, pockets of independent *sklavenoi,* notably the *Melingoi* and *Ezeritai,* survived into the 15th century in the Peloponnesos (q.v.). North of Greece, Christianization of the Slavs was aided by Church Slavonic (q.v.) and missionary efforts that began with the work of Cyril and Methodios in Moravia (qq.v.). The creation of a Bulgar state by Asparuch (qq.v.) ca. 680, as well as the appearance of the Serbs and Rus (qq.v.), provided new threats on Byzantium's (q.v.) northern borders. These events had the effect of changing the ethnic composition of much of the Balkan Peninsula (q.v.). One of the great triumphs of Byzantium (q.v.) was that it evangelized these peoples, in the process giving them an alphabet and, thus, a literature. In effect, it civilized them.

SMEDEREVO. *See* **GEORGE BRANKOVICH.**

SMYRNA. Port-city (modern Izmir) on the Aegean coast of Asia Minor (qq.v.). Tzachas (q.v.) operated his fleet from Phokaia (q.v.), at the northern entrance of the bay of Smyrna, until Alexios I Komnenos (q.v.) captured Smyrna. During the period of the Laskarids (1208–1258) of the Empire of Nicaea (q.v.) it was a thriving commercial center. However, in 1317 Turks (q.v.) from the adjacent emirate of Aydin (qq.v.) took the city from the Byzantines when they stormed the city's great upper fortress.

SOKRATES. Church historian whose *History of the Church,* covering the years 305–439, provides a reliable continuation of Eusebios of Caesarea's (q.v.) ecclesiastical history. Sokrates includes some information on secular affairs, unlike Theodoret (q.v.), and the work was mined by Sozomenos (q.v.) for the latter's own ecclesiastical history.

SOLIDUS. *See* **COINAGE.**

SOL INVICTUS. *See* **CONSTANTIUS CHLORUS.**

SOLOMON. General of Justinian I (q.v.) who fought under Belisarios (q.v.) against the Vandals of North Africa (qq.v.) in 533–534. He was a eunuch like Narses (qq.v.), another great general of Justinian I. Remaining in North Africa to battle the Moors (q.v.), in 536 Solomon faced a serious revolt of two-thirds of the army that forced him to flee to Sicily (q.v.). He was replaced by Germanos (q.v.), who defeated the rebel leader Stotzas in 537. Reinstated to his command in 539, Solomon was killed fighting the Moors (q.v.) in 544, a year before Stotzas himself was killed in battle.

SOPHIA. Empress (q.v.) and wife of Justin II (q.v.). Like her aunt Theodora (q.v.), she was ambitious and quite capable. As Justin II's mental health declined, she turned to Tiberios (I) (q.v.) for support, promoting him as heir-apparent and making him caesar (q.v.) in 574. She may have hoped to become Tiberios's queen after Justin II's death in 578, but Tiberios I kept her at arm's length. She died toward the end of Maurice's (q.v.) reign.

SOPHIA PALAIOLOGINA. *See* **IVAN III.**

SOPHOCLES. *See* **EURIPIDES; THOMAS MAGISTROS.**

SOPHRONIOS. Patriarch of Jerusalem (qq.v.) from 634–638, and pupil of John Moschos (q.v.). His staunch resistance to Herakleios's Monoenergism (qq.v.) brought him into opposition with the patriarchs Kyros of Alexandria and Sergios I of Constantinople (qq.v.). He was forced to surrender Jerusalem (q.v.) to the caliph Umar (qq.v.) in 638, but he did so only after Umar agreed to guarantee certain religious and social rights of the Christian citizenry.

SOUDA. Popular lexicon of classical and biblical words, phrases, and personages, probably composed during the reign of Basil II (q.v.). The enigmatic title means "palisade," or, more loosely, "stronghold." Its value lies partly in its occasional mention of Byzantine writers (e.g., Menander Protector [q.v.]) and partly in the insight it provides into matters about which educated Byzantines of the late 10th century wanted to know. It is also a good example of how ninth- and 10th-century scholars attempted to organize the legacy of literature that Byzantium (q.v.) inherited from the ancient world.

SOZOMENOS. Church historian whose *History of the Church* continues the ecclesiastical history of Eusebios of Caesarea (q.v.), covering the years 324–425. Much of his information he derived from the church historian Sokrates (q.v.), and also other sources, including Olympiodoros of Thebes (q.v.).

SOZOPOLIS. Two cities shared this name. One of them was ancient Apollonia on the Black Sea (q.v.), which in the early 14th century was a prosperous port occupied by the Bulgars (q.v.). It was liberated from the Bulgars in 1366 by Amadeo VI of Savoy (q.v.), who turned it and Mesembria over to John V (qq.v.). For a time the west coast of the Black Sea was again in Byzantine hands. The second Sozopolis was in Pisidia in Asia Minor (qq.v.). It was particularly important in the defense of Asia Minor against the Seljuks (q.v.) in the 12th century, since it protected the land route from the Meander valley to Attaleia (q.v.). It fell to the Seljuks sometime after 1070, was retaken by John II Komnenos (q.v.) in 1120, and held out until 1180, when captured by the forces of Kilij Arslan II (q.v.).

SPAIN. The Iberian Peninsula, which became a diocese (q.v.) within the administrative reforms of Diocletian (q.v.). In 409 it was overrun by various barbarian peoples, most notably the Vandals (q.v.), who crossed over into North Africa (q.v.) in 429. In 456, the Visigoths (q.v.) established a state in Spain that effectively ended Byzantine control, except for the brief reconquest ca. 550 of the southeastern corner of the peninsula by Justinian I (q.v.). The Visgothic state fell to the Arabs (q.v.) in 711, but Christian states formed in the northern part of the peninsula. Aragon played an important role in the Sicilian Vespers (q.v.), and the Catalan Grand Company (qq.v.) played a significant role in Byzantine affairs in the 14th century.

SPATHARIOS. The term means "sword-bearer" and refers to a body-guard. Imperial *spatharioi* were eunuchs (q.v.). However, by the eighth century the term was simply a dignity, one which declined in importance until it disappeared in the late 11th century.

SPECTABILIS. The middle-rank title for members of the senate (q.v.) from the fourth century. It was below the rank of *illustris* (q.v.) and above the rank of *clarissimus* (qq.v.). In the sixth century those who held the rank of *spectabilis* were raised to the rank of *illustris*. Those with the rank of *illustris* were raised to a new rank, that of *gloriosus* (q.v.).

SPHRANTZES, GEORGE. Historian, diplomat, close friend of Constantine XI (q.v.). He undertook the most sensitive diplomatic missions for Constantine XI, held important administrative posts, including governor of Patras and governor of the Morea (q.v.), and was an eyewitness to the fall of Constantinople (q.v.) in 1453. His historical work, the *Chronicon Minus,* which covers the years 1413–1477, is one of the chief sources for the final decades of Byzantium (q.v.). An expanded version of his work, the *Chronicon Maius,* is primarily a 16th-century compilation.

SPLIT. Modern city on the coast of Dalmatia (q.v.), and site of the palace (more a fortified country residence) to which Diocletian (q.v.) retired in 305. The overall plan of the palace resembles that of a traditional Roman military camp; but, unlike an army camp, the interior contains public and private structures, including a large audience hall and Diocletian's intended mausoleum. The residents of nearby Salona (q.v.), Diocletian's birthplace, fled to Split in the early seventh century to escape the attacks of Slavs and Avars (qq.v.).

SQUINCH. An architectural device used, like the pendentive (q.v.), to place a dome (q.v.) on a square bay. It consists of a small arch, or a corbeled, half-conical niche, placed across the corners of a square bay. The result is an octagonal base, suitable for resting a dome upon.

STAGOI. *See* **THESSALY.**

STAURAKIOS. *See* **IRENE.**

STAURAKIOS. Emperor (q.v.) briefly in 811. Crowned in 803, he was the son and heir of Nikeophoros I (q.v.) who died in 811 at the hands of Krum (q.v.). He was married in a bride show (q.v.) in 807 to a relative of the former empress Irene (q.v.) named Theophano. In the same battle that killed his father he suffered grave wounds from which he never recovered. He reigned, if one can call it that, for little more than two months before he died.

STEFAN LAZAREVICH. *See* **GEORGE BRANKOVICH.**

STEFAN NEMANJA. Ruler of Serbia (q.v.) from ca. 1168–1196; founder of the Nemanja (q.v.) dynasty of Serbia, which ruled Serbia to 1371. His declaration of independence faltered before an invasion of Raška by Manuel I Komnenos (qq.v.) in 1172. Nevertheless, after Manuel I's death he was able to extend his territory, uniting Zeta (q.v.) with Raška. In 1168 he founded Hilandar monastery on Mount Athos (qq.v.) with the aid of Sava of Serbia (q.v.). In 1196 he retired to a monastery he founded at Studenica, taking the monastic name of Symeon.

STEFAN UROSH I. King of Serbia (q.v.) from 1243–1276. In 1258 he joined with Manfred of Sicily (qq.v.) and Michael II Komnenos Doukas of the Despotate of Epiros (qq.v.) to oppose the expansion of the Empire of Nicaea (q.v.). He was defeated in 1259 by Michael VIII Palaiologos at the battle of Pelagonia (qq.v). Subsequent negotiations to marry his son Stefan Urosh (II) Milutin (q.v.) to Anna, daughter of Michael VIII, failed in 1272.

STEFAN UROSH II MILUTIN. King of Serbia (q.v.) from 1282–1321, during whose reign Serbia became a major power in the Balkans. Expansion into Byzantine Macedonia (q.v.) characterized the first part of his reign. In 1282 he launched a great offensive against Byzantine Macedonia, having allied Serbia with Byzantine foes Charles I of Anjou (q.v.) and John I Doukas of Thessaly (qq.v.). Skopje (q.v.) was conquered (1282), as was Dyrrachion (q.v.). By 1298 his conquests reached just to the north of a line running from Ohrid east to Prilep (qq.v.) and Stip. At this point, Andronikos II (q.v.), on the advice of his general Michael Tarchaneiotes Glabas (q.v.), made peace (1299). Milutin accepted Andronikos's five-year-old daughter Simonis (q.v.) as his bride, along with acceptance of his conquests. Thereafter, Byzantine ceremonial and dress conquered the Serbian court, and Milutin constructed churches, using Byzantine artisans, in Serbia and throughout eastern Christendom, even in remote Jerusalem and on Mount Sinai (qq.v.). Included among them are those at Studenica, Hilandar monastery on Mount Athos (qq.v.), and, what is perhaps the most magnificent of all late Byzantine churches, Gračaniča (q.v.).

STEFAN UROSH III DECHANSKI. Serbian king (1321–1331); son of Stefan Urosh II Milutin (q.v.). He supported Andronikos II against Andronikos III (qq.v.) during the civil war of the 1320s. After Andronikos II died in 1328, the expansion of Serbia into Byzantine Macedonia (qq.v.) prompted Andronikos III to form an alliance with Bulgaria (q.v.). Stefan promptly defeated the Bulgarians in 1330 at the historic battle of Velbuzd (q.v.). The next year the nobles of Serbia ousted Stefan and gave the throne to his son.

STEFAN UROSH IV DUSHAN. Serbian king (1331–1355); son of Stefan Urosh III Dechanski (q.v.). The battle of Velvuzd (q.v.) in 1330 laid the foundation for Serbian expansion into Byzantine Macedonia (q.v.), but it was the Byzantine civil war of 1341–1347 that allowed Dushan to conquer half of the remaining Byzantine territory. He first supported John VI Kantakouzenos, then John V Palaiologos (qq.v.), all the while extending his conquests into Epiros and Thessaly (qq.v.). In 1345 he conquered Serres (q.v.) and began to style himself "Emperor of the Serbs and Romans." In truth his kingdom stretched from the Danube south to the Gulf of Corinth (qq.v.) and from the Adriatic to the Aegean (qq.v.).

STEPHEN II, POPE. *See* **CONSTANTINE V.**

STEPHEN OF BYZANTIUM. Sixth-century author of the *Ethnika,* a list of geographical names with etymologies and other bits of information attached to the names. The identity of Stephen is unknown, and his information is unoriginal, being drawn primarily from ancient sources such as Ptolemy, Strabo, and Pausanius.

STEPHEN THE YOUNGER. Iconodule (q.v.) saint martyred in 764 during the reign of Constantine V (q.v.). Stephen was a leader of monastic opposition to the emperor's Iconoclastic (qq.v.) policy, and his refusal to accept the decrees of the synod of Hiera (754) resulted in his imprisonment and torture, finally in his execution. Stephen's *vita* (q.v.), written some years later (ca. 806) by Stephen the Deacon, is replete with interesting details, including the comment that the famous Church of the Virgin at Blachernai (q.v.) was covered with new paintings, making it resemble a fruit store and aviary.

STEPPE. The great expanse of grassland that extends across Eurasia from Ukraine to the Altai Mountains of western Mongolia. Its historical impact on Byzantium (q.v.) was as a kind of conveyor belt that allowed groups of pastoralists (e.g., Huns, Avars, Pechenegs, Seljuks, and Uzes [qq.v.]) westward movement to the borders of Byzantium, where either by a desire for booty and tribute (and employment as mercenaries), or impelled by pressure from other steppe peoples, they invaded Byzantium.

STILICHO. *Magister militum* (q.v.), regent for Honorios (q.v.); and son-in-law of Theodosios I (qq.v.). Son of a Vandal (q.v.) father and Roman mother, Stilicho was the most powerful general in the West from 395 until Honorios assassinated him on suspicion of treason in 408. Despite his faithful service in suppressing Gildo (q.v.), and the praise of Claudian (q.v.), he failed to stop Alaric's invasion of Italy (qq.v.) in 401. Radagaisus and his Ostrogoths (qq.v.) ravaged Italy in 405, and hordes of other Germans crossed the Rhine (q.v.) in 406. In 408, after Alaric had extorted 4,000 pounds of gold from the senate in Rome (qq.v.), Honorios had Stilicho assassinated.

STOBI. City in northern Macedonia (q.v.) that flourished in the fifth century, before being abandoned in the late sixth century. Its importance lay in its location, at the juncture of the Vardar and Crna rivers, along the great highway that traversed the Balkan Peninsula from Thessalonike to Belgrade (qq.v.), and from there to the middle Danube (q.v.).

STOTZAS. *See* **GERMANOS; SOLOMON.**

STOUDIOS MONASTERY (MONASTERY OF ST. JOHN OF STOUDIOS). *See* **CONSTANTINOPLE.**

STRABO. *See* **GEOGRAPHY.**

STRATEGIKA. Military manuals; also called *taktika* (q.v.). The *Strategikon* of Maurice (q.v.) is among the earlier of these handbooks of military tactics and maxims, as is the *Peri Strategikes* (written during the reign of Justinian I [q.v.]). The 10th century saw a renewal of interest in military science, exemplified by other *strategika,* including the *Taktika* of Leo VI (q.v.), the *Sylloge Tacticorum,* the *Naumachika,* the *Taktika* of Nikphoros Ouranos, the *Praecepta Militaria* (q.v.), the *De Velitatione,* and the *De Re Militari* (qq.v.).

STRATEGIKON OF MAURICE. The first of several Byzantine military manuals *(taktika, strategika* [qq.v.]), attributed to the emperor Maurice (q.v.). The emphasis is on cavalry, not infantry, warfare. As with later military manuals it summarizes the tactics of foreign enemies, including northern ones like the Avars and Huns (qq.v.).

STRATEGOS. Governor of a theme (q.v.), whose duties, like those of the *exarchs* of Carthage and Ravenna (qq.v.), were primarily military. The *strategoi* of major themes (q.v.), e.g., Opsikion and Anatolikon (qq.v.), were frequent contenders for imperial power in the eighth century, resulting in the division of themes into smaller units in the ninth century. Bardanes Tourkos (q.v.) was *monostrategos* of five themes in Asia Minor (q.v.) when he rebelled against Nikephoros I (q.v.). In the 11th century, as themes declined, the power of the *strategos* declined in favor of the *praitor, doux,* and *katepano* (qq.v.).

STRATIOTIKA KTEMATA. *See* **ARMY; NIKEPHOROS II PHOKAS; PRAITOR; THEMES.**

STRYMON, THEME OF. The theme (q.v.) of Strymon took its name from the Strymon (modern Struma) River, which rises in western Bulgaria (q.v.) and flows south, exiting into the Aegean Sea (q.v.) near Amphipolis. The theme was situated to the east of the theme of Thessalonike (q.v.) between the Strymon and Mesta rivers. It protected the passes across the Rhodope Mountains (q.v.) and provided more administrative control over the Slavs (q.v.) of the region.

STUDENICA. *See* **STEFAN NEMANJA; STEFAN UROSH II MILUTIN.**

STYLITE. Monk who lived atop a pillar *(stylos)*. Symeon the Stylite the Elder (q.v.) was the first to practice this type of asceticism (q.v.). From a platform secured to the top of a high (ca. 16 meters) pillar he preached and responded to the queries of visitors for some 30 years. He was followed by others in the fifth and sixth centuries, including Symeon the Stylite the Younger, and Daniel the Stylite (q.v.). Michael Psellos (q.v.) mentions in his *Chronographia* that in 1057 stylites in Constantinople (q.v.) dismounted from their pillars to see the new emperor Isaac I Komnenos (qq.v.) enter the city.

SULEYMAN CELEBI. *See* **MUSA.**

SULEYMAN IBN KUTULMUSH. *See* **RUM, SULTANATE OF.**

SULEYMAN PASHA. *See* **JOHN VI KANTAKOUZENOS; ORHAN.**

SULTAN. Arabic title used by independent Seljuk (q.v.) rulers, though technically still under the authority of the caliph (q.v.). The title was used subsequently by Mamluk and Ottoman (qq.v.) rulers.

SUTTON HOO TREASURE. *See* **BRITAIN.**

SVATOPLUK. *See* **MORAVIA.**

SVJATOSLAV. Prince of Kiev (ca. 945–972), son of Igor and Olga (qq.v.). After defeating the Khazars and destroying Sarkel (qq.v.) in 965, he was encouraged by Byzantium to invade Bulgaria (qq.v.), which he did in 968. Svjatoslav's plans to make Little Preslav (q.v.) his new capital alarmed the Byzantines, who invaded Bulgaria in 971, and forced Svjatoslav to return to Kiev (q.v.). Along the way he was killed by Pechenegs (q.v.).

SYLLAION. *See* **PAMPHYLIA.**

SYLLOGE TACTICORUM. *See* **STRATEGIKA.**

SYMEON LOGOTHETE. Author of a chronicle (q.v.) that begins where Theophanes (q.v.) ends in 842 and continues to 948. It exists in several versions made by copyists and revisers of Symeon's chronicle, including Theodosios of Melitene, George Hamartolos (q.v.), Leo Grammatikos (Leo the Grammarian), and the so-called Pseudo-Symeon (also 10th century in date) that relies on Symeon's chronicle and some additional sources. For the period 848–948, Symeon Logothete's chronicle is the most important of narrative sources; even Theophanes Continuatus (q.v.) relies on it for the period after 886. Just who Symeon Logothete was is a mystery; it is doubtful that he was Symeon Metaphrastes (q.v.).

SYMEON METAPHRASTES. Author of a late 10th-century *menologion* (q.v.) of 150 texts of saints's lives *(vitae* [q.v.]) arranged in 10 volumes, which became the *menologion* most used in Byzantine monasteries. Symeon was a high official who died ca. 1000, and not to be identified with the chronicler Symeon Logothete (q.v.).

SYMEON OF BULGARIA. Tsar of Bulgaria (qq.v.) from 893–927; son of Boris (q.v.). He was, like Krum and Samuel (qq.v.), among the great Bulgarian adversaries of Byzantium (q.v.). Educated in Constantinople (q.v.), he strove repeatedly for supremacy in the Balkan Peninsula (q.v.), winning victories on several occasions, including the battle of Achelous, near Anchialos in Thrace (qq.v.), where he annihilated a Byzantine army on 20 August 917. His goal was to capture Constantinople and unite the two states. Romanos I (q.v.) was as unsuccessful in dealing with Symeon as was the previous regency headed by Nicholas I Mystikos (q.v.). However, only the sudden death of Symeon in 927 produced peace, negotiated by Symeon's son Peter of Bulgaria (q.v.).

SYMEON THE NEW THEOLOGIAN. The greatest medieval Byzantine mystic (949–1022). Born into wealth, he rejected it all for the life of a monk, first at the monastery of St. John Stoudios (q.v.). He challenged his contemporaries with provocative ideas, e.g., that formal church ordination is from men (not necessarily connected with divine ordination), and that personal experience of God is sufficient for the Christian, and without it there is no genuine Christianity. Above all, he rejected the idea that the Christian life was something formalized and ritualistic. For him, the Christian life was the personal experience of God, the gift of the Holy Spirit, the vision of divine light. Ultimately, his ideas provoked the resistance of the church, which, for a while, forced him into exile. His career revived a tension between individual holy men and the church seen centuries earlier (e.g., in the *vita* of Daniel the Stylite [qq.v.]) while his writings laid the foundation for the future teaching and practices of Hesychasm (q.v.).

SYMEON THE STYLITE THE ELDER. The first pillar saint (stylite [q.v.]). He was born (ca. 389) the son of a shepherd on the borders of Syria and Cilicia (qq.v.). He tried and rejected other forms of eremitical (q.v.) practice before stepping onto a low pillar about three meters high. On this pillar in the Syrian desert near Antioch (q.v.) he stood for some 30 years without shelter from the elements. As the height of the pillar increased to about 16 meters, so did his fame. He was hardly inactive. One visitor counted 1,244 prostrations for prayer in a single day, and he was besieged by petitioners who needed advice, cures, and legal judgments. By the time he died in 459 he was internationally famous. A monastery (Qalat Seman) of exquisite architecture sprang up to deal with the many pilgrims who came to see his pillar. His successors included the sixth-century ascetics (q.v.) Symeon the Stylite the Younger, whose pillar was located southwest of Antioch (q.v.) at a place called Wondrous Mountain, and also Daniel the Stylite (q.v.).

SYMEON THE STYLITE THE YOUNGER. *See* **STYLITE; SYMEON THE STYLITE THE ELDER.**

SYMEON UROSH. *See* **EPIROS, DESPOTATE OF; METEORA.**

SYMMACHUS. Quintus Aurelius Symmachus, Roman orator and statesman (ca. 340–402). He is remembered for his appeal to Valentinian II (q.v.) to restore the Altar of Victory, a statue of Victory *(Nike),* and a small altar that Gratian (q.v.) had removed from near the senate house in Rome (q.v.). Ambrose's (q.v.) threat of excommunication insured that the statue, and its altar, were not restored.

SYNADA. *See* **LEO OF SYNADA.**

SYNAXARION. The Byzantine church calendar of fixed feasts, each with a short account, often no more than a paragraph, of each saint's life. Such accounts *(synaxaria)* emphasize the details of each saint's martyrdom, to be read during the early morning service on the appropriate feastdays. A *menologion* (q.v.) is similar in format, but the notices are longer, constituting a collection of saintly biographies *(vitae* [q.v.]).

SYNESIOS OF CYRENE. Neoplatonist (q.v.) philosopher (a former student of Hypatia [q.v.]), who adopted Christianity and became bishop of Ptolemais, in North Africa (q.v.). He was a native of Cyrene, on whose behalf he went to Constantinople (q.v.) from 399–402 to seek tax relief. While there he wrote a work called *On Kingship,* in which he urged Arkadios (q.v.) to expel the Goths (q.v.) from the army (q.v.) and drive them back across the Danube (q.v.).

SYNKELLOS. Chief advisor and assistant to a patriarch (q.v.) Typically, he was a priest or deacon who actually shared the patriarch's residence. The *synkellos* of the patriarch of Constantinople (q.v.) was nominated by the emperor (q.v.), and frequently succeeded to the patriarchal throne of Constantinople.

SYNOD. Council of a patriarch (q.v.). Patriarchal synods were, in effect, regional church councils whose doctrinal decrees were authoritative, especially after the schism of 1054 (q.v.). The patriarch of Constantinople (q.v.) presided over a permanent resident synod of patriarchal clergy and metropolitan bishops (qq.v.) that was the means through which patriarchal power was exercised. Patriarch Nicholas III Grammatikos (q.v.) opposed any interference to his own power over the synod, since it was chiefly through the permanent synod that the power of the patriarch of Constantinople emanated.

SYNODICON VETUS. *See* **SYNODIKON.**

SYNODIKON. Most commonly, a liturgical document. The most famous was the *Synodikon of Orthodoxy* (q.v.), read every year at the Feast of Orthodoxy to commemorate the restoration of icon (q.v.) veneration. The term can also refer to a letter from a patriarch (q.v.) written to another patriarch, e.g., in order to circulate the decrees of a patriarchal synod (q.v.). The *Synodikon Vetus,* written between 887–920, is a brief history of church councils that ends at the deposition of Photios (q.v.) in 886.

SYNODIKON OF ORTHODOXY. Liturgical document (*synodikon*) read every year at the Feast of Orthodoxy to commemorate the restoration of icon (q.v.) veneration in 843. Condemnation of Iconoclasts (q.v.) and praise for those who defended icons is at the core of the document. Subsequent additions (the last made in 1439) created an even longer list of church heroes (e.g., martyrs, patriarchs, emperors [qq.v.]) as well as condemnations (anathemas) of a variety of heretics.

SYNTHRONON. *See* **APSE.**

SYRACUSE. Center of Byzantine administration in Sicily (q.v.), captured in 491 by the Ostrogoths (q.v.). In 535 Besilarios (q.v.) recaptured the city from the harbor side by hoisting boats full of soldiers to the top of the masts of his ships, from which they cleared the city walls of defenders. Totila's (q.v.) attempt to regain the city in 550 was turned back. Constans II (q.v.) made it his imperial residence for five years (663–668), consolidating Byzantine control over the island in the face of increasing Arab attacks. Leo III's (q.v.) transfer of its bishopric from Rome (q.v.) to the patriarch of Constantinople (qq.v.) consolidated ecclesiastical control over the city. Nevertheless, Arab attacks were relentless, and in 878 after a ninth-month siege, described in an eyewitness account by Theodosios the Monk, the Arabs (q.v.) took the city. The Arabs held it, despite a brief occupation by George Maniakes (q.v.) in 1040, until 1085, when the Normans (q.v.) seized it.

SYRGIANNES. *See* **ANDRONIKOS III PALAIOLOGOS.**

SYRIA. Region between the Mediterranean and Mesopotamia (qq.v.). To the north is the Taurus (q.v.) mountain range, to the south Palestine (q.v.). Moving east beyond the Hellenized densely settled coastal plain of Syria the geography changes to fertile farmland, then to a desert that continues to the Euphrates River (q.v.), Syria's eastern border. Among its cities Antioch (q.v.) overshadowed the rest in size and sophistication. Other cities, e.g. Apamea, Berroia, Damascus, and Edessa (qq.v.) were considerably smaller by comparison. The region apparently continued to prosper, despite religious instability (notably Nestorianism and Monophysitism [qq.v.]), plague, and damaging Persian raids, both beginning in the 540s, and then by the Arab conquest of the region that followed the battle of the Yarmuk River (q.v.) in 636. Even after the Arab conquest, Syria's large Christian population looked to Byzantium (q.v.), whose armies reconquered the region beginning in 969. Nevertheless, Syria fell to the Seljuks (q.v.) in 1084. Thereafter, Byzantium attempted to retain a presence in Syria by its claim to overlordship of Crusader-dominated Antioch (q.v.). This claim was realized in 1108, but it was shattered after Manuel I's defeat at Myriokephalon (qq.v.) in 1176.

– T –

TABARI. Arab historian (839–923), jurist, commentator on the Koran. He was born in Tabaristan, Persia (q.v.), but it was in Baghdad (q.v.) that he pursued his scholarly career. His chief work is his *History of the Prophets and Kings,* which goes from the Creation to 915. It is particularly important for the history of Islam (q.v.), including most aspects of Byzantine-Arab military affairs, e.g., Arab expeditions into Asia Minor (q.v.) and attacks by Arabs on Constantinople (qq.v.). It is a particularly important source for military and diplomatic affairs during the reign of Leo VI (q.v.).

TAFUR, PERO. Spanish traveler whose travel journal provides rich details of his trip to the Crimea (q.v.) in 1436–1439. He describes Constantinople (q.v.) as sparsely populated, its citizens reduced to poverty, and the Blachernai (q.v.) palace in a ruinous condition. Among the other places he visited were Trebizond (q.v.) and the Aegean islands of Rhodes, Chios, and Tenedos (qq.v.).

TAGMATA. Elite regiments of cavalry and infantry organized by Constantine V (q.v.) into a professional field army (q.v.) stationed at Constantinople (q.v.). The *tagmata* were supported by the Optimatoi (q.v.), a special theme (q.v.) of muleteers for carrying supplies, which together gave the emperor (q.v.) a new mobile strike force. The *tagmata* also served as a counterweight to the occasionally rebellious *strategoi* (q.v.) of the armies of the themes. Initially Constantine V created two *tagmata,* the *scholae palatinae* and the *exkoubitores* (qq.v.), each under the command of a *domestikos* (q.v.). Additional *tagmata* were added subsequently, including the *vigla* and *hikanatoi* (qq.v). At the end of the 10th century, the distinction between *tagmata* and the armies of the themes began to blur, as *tagmata* were stationed in the provinces.

TAKTIKA. Official lists *(taktika, notitiae* in Latin) of imperial dignities and offices. They had a practical use as court manuals for ceremonial occasions, allowing each official to be placed in his appropriate location (seat, in the case of state banquets). For the modern historian the *taktika* reveal the chief offices of the imperial bureaucracy at the time each list was compiled. The *Notitia Dignitatum* (q.v.) is fifth century in date; the latest is the 14th-century list of pseudo-Kodinos. The *Taktikon of Uspenskij* and *Kletorologion* of

Philotheos (q.v.) are both ninth century in date; the Escurial *taktikon* is 10th century. The term can also refer to treatises on military tactics, as in the *Taktika* of Leo VI (q.v.).

TAKTIKA OF LEO VI. Treatise on military tactics written by Leo VI (q.v.) in the early 10th century. It relies heavily on the *Strategikon* of Maurice (qq.v.) among its various sources. Leo's work continued a tradition of imperial military manuals, called *taktika* or *strategika* (qq.v.), that blossomed in the 10th century.

TAMERLANE. *See* **TIMUR.**

TANCRED. Norman (q.v.) adventurer like his uncle Bohemund (q.v.), both of whom participated in the First Crusade (q.v.). Renowned for his bravery, he was among the first to surmount the walls of Jerusalem (q.v.) in the siege of 1099. After the Turks (q.v.) captured Bohemund in 1101, Tancred administered Antioch (q.v.) for him, actively resisting Byzantine encroachments on Laodikeia and in Cilicia (qq.v.). Rejecting the Treaty of Devol (q.v.), Tancred continued to rule Antioch until his death in 1112, a year after Bohemund's death in Apulia (q.v.).

TAORMINA. City on the east coast of Sicily (q.v.), below Mount Etna. After Arabs (q.v.) from North Africa (q.v.) conquered Syracuse (q.v.) in 878, Taormina remained the last important Byzantine stronghold on the island. It was finally captured in 902, and with it Sicily was effectively lost to the Arabs.

TARANTO (TARENTUM). Port-city in southern Italy (q.v.) on the coast of the Ionian Sea (q.v.). In 663 Constans II (q.v.) used it as a base to campaign against the Lombards (q.v.). By the end of the seventh century, it had fallen to the Lombard duke of Benevento (q.v.). It was lost to the Arabs (q.v.) during the reign of Theophilos (q.v.), who pressured Venice (q.v.) to send a fleet to recover it in 840. This attempt failed, and only in 880 was it recovered by Basil I (q.v.). In the 11th century it fell to the Normans under Robert Guiscard (qq.v.).

TARASIOS. Patriarch of Constantinople (qq.v.) from 784–806. He was secretary (*asekretis* [q.v.]) to Irene (q.v.) when she appointed him patriarch. He presided over the Seventh Ecumenical Council at Nicaea (q.v.) in 787, which condemned Iconoclasm (q.v.). From 795 until Constantine VI (q.v.) was deposed in 797 Tarasios was embroiled in the Moechian controversy (q.v.), supporting the emperor's divorce and persecuting Theodore of Stoudios (q.v.) and his supporters.

TARON. Armenian principality situated on the upper Euphrates River (q.v.), important because it commanded access to the relatively open country north of Lake Van. It was annexed by Byzantium (q.v.) in 966.

TARSOS. City in Cilicia in southeast Asia Minor (qq.v.), famous as the birthplace of St. Paul. Its close proximity to the Cilician Gates (q.v.) explains its importance, especially for the Arabs (q.v.), who captured it in 637 and used it as a base of operations for their raids into Asia Minor. In 965 it surrendered to Nikephoros II Phokas (q.v.), who created a new theme (q.v.) of Tarsos, which endured until the advance of the Turks (q.v.) in the late 11th century.

TARTARS. *See* **MONGOLS.**

TAURUS. Mountain range in southwest Asia Minor (q.v.) that forms a rugged natural barrier between Anatolia and northern Syria (qq.v.). Five major passes cross the Taurus, the most famous of which is the Cilician Gates (q.v.), which the Arabs (q.v.) used to raid Asia Minor.

TAXATION. Byzantium (q.v.) was comprised chiefly of landowners. Hence, the bulk of taxation was imposed on rural populations, both on their land (including houses and livestock) and on their persons. Diocletian's *capitatio-jugatio* (qq.v.) system used such a combination assessment for the *annona,* a tax paid in kind with provisions or commodities, often grain. After Constantine I's (q.v.) stabilization of the coinage with the *nomisma* (qq.v.) the land tax (called the *kanon* after the seventh century) was more likely to be paid in cash. The tax base was considerably eroded in the 10th and 11th centuries by the growth of large estates owned by the wealthy (*dynatoi* [q.v.]). Because wealthy landowners, including monasteries, often gained tax exemptions (by *exkousseia* [q.v.]), such burdens fell particularly hard on ordinary peasants. In a series of laws enacted by emperors from Romanos I to Basil II (qq.v.), the state attempted to preserve the tax base of small landowners by requiring the *dynatoi* to make up the deficient tax payments of their neighbors (the *epibole,* later the *allelengyon* [q.v.]). Urban populations paid taxes on their land

and buildings, and special taxes like the *chrysargyron* (q.v.). There were export and import taxes as well. Tax payments flowed to the appropriate *genikon* (q.v.), and to other treasuries (e.g., the *vestiarion* and *sakellion* [qq.v.]). With the growth of the *pronoia* (q.v.) system in the 12th century, general taxation (called *telos*), based on tax inventories *(praktika),* was separated from the taxation on *paroikoi* (q.v.) granted to the holders of *pronoia* grants (called *pronoiars*). The Byzantine tax system, constantly under threat of being eroded by social privilege, was further complicated by variation in tax burdens from region to region, the manner in which taxes were assessed, the variety of taxes, the way they were collected (directly by the state, or by tax farmers), and the extent of Byzantine territory at any given time. Ultimately, this last factor proved to be decisive in the long decline of Byzantium (q.v.), as the empire lost its tax base to the Venetians, Genoese, Seljuks, and Ottomans (qq.v.).

TEDALDI, JACOPO. Florentine eyewitness to the conquest of Constantinople by the Ottomans (qq.v.) in 1453. His record is among the most useful accounts written by westerners present at the siege, partly because of its relative impartiality, but chiefly because it includes details of the siege not found in other accounts.

TEKFUR SARAYI. *See* **CONSTANTINE VII.**

TELERIG. Khan of the Bulgars (qq.v.) from ca. 770–777 who revived Bulgaria (q.v.) as a military power to be reckoned with. Constantine V (q.v.) responded by marching into Bulgaria in 773 and forcing Telerig to sue for peace. However, in the same year Telerig invaded Thessaly (q.v.), creating another confrontation that ended in defeat of the Bulgars. For some reason, Telerig fled to Constantinople (q.v.) in 777, where he was baptized, rewarded with the title of *patrikios* (q.v.), and married to a niece of Leo IV's (q.v.) wife.

TEMPLON. Low screen in-filled with decorated, waist-high marble slabs to form a barrier between the *bema* and the *naos* (qq.v.). of a basilican (q.v.) church. By the mid-fifth century, it was treated architecturally more as an arcade consisting of marble slabs inserted between small columns, surmounted by a beam (called an *epistyle,* or *architrave*). The wooden *iconostasis* (q.v.) of later centuries developed from the *templon.*

TENEDOS. Small island controlling the entrance to the Hellespont (q.v.) that was coveted by the commercial powers of Venice and Genoa (qq.v.) in the mid-14th century. John V (q.v.) promised it to Venice in 1370, but before the Venetians could take possession the Genoese engineered a plot that deposed John and put Andronikos IV (q.v.) on the throne (1376). Andronikos then assigned Tenedos to the Genoese as a reward for their help in the coup. But the Venetians refused to accept this and went to war with Genoa in 1377; the war ended in 1381 when peace was made at Turin, the capital of Savoy. The treaty forced the Venetians to leave the island. Its fortifications were destroyed, and Amadeo VI (q.v.), count of Savoy, who was related to the Palaiologan dynasty (q.v.) through Anna of Savoy (q.v.), administered the island through his representative.

TEPHRIKE. See **PAULICIANS.**

TERVEL. Khan of the Bulgars (qq.v.) from 701–718 who restored Justinian II (q.v.) to the throne in 705 and helped save Constantinople (q.v.) from Arab attack in 718. For the first service Justinian II granted Tervel the title of caesar (q.v.); he may have also given him his daughter in marriage. In 711 Tervel sent Justinian II some 3,000 soldiers to put down the revolt of Philippikos (q.v.). In 718 Tervel assisted Leo III (q.v.) by inflicting numerous casualties on the Arabs (q.v.), who were besieging Constantinople (q.v.). Tervel's military aid produced closer economic ties with Byzantium (q.v.), as seen in a treaty of 716, which provided for regular Byzantine trade relations with Bulgaria (q.v.).

TETARTERON. See **COINAGE.**

TETRACONCH. A building, including a church, with four conches, i.e., four semicircular niches with half-domes (a triconch [q.v.], thus, has three niches). Among the early tetraconch churches is the one at Abu Mina (q.v.). The design persisted as a church type into the Palaiologan (q.v.) period.

TETRAGAMY. See **LEO VI; NICHOLAS I MYSTIKOS.**

TETRARCHY. The term means "the rule of four," referring to the new form of government established by Diocletian (q.v.) in 293. Two augustii, Diocletian in the East and Maximian (q.v.) in the West, ruled each half of the empire. Each augustus (q.v.) had a subordinate, his adopted caesar (q.v.). Diocletian adopted Galerius (q.v.) and Maximian adopted Constantius Chlorus (q.v.). The idea was that when an augustus retired, his caesar would take his place and adopt a new caesar. That was the theory. The reality was a series of civil wars that began with the death of Constantius Chlorus in 306, and which concluded with Constantine I's (q.v.) victory over Licinius (q.v.) in 324.

THAMUGADI. Modern Timgad in Algeria, formerly an important city in the province of Numidia (q.v.) founded by the emperor Trajan (98–117). It became a center of Donatism (q.v.) in the late fourth century, was seized by Vandals and Moors (qq.v.) in the late fifth century, and retaken by Justinian I's (q.v.) general Solomon (q.v.) in 539. Solomon created a long line of fortifications, including previously fortified cities like Thamugadi, as protection against incursions by the Moors into the province. Nevertheless, the city fell to the Arabs (q.v.) in the late seventh century, along with the rest of Numidia.

THASOS. *See* **GATTILUSIO; ZACCARIA.**

THEBES. Metropolis (q.v.) and chief city of Boeotia in central Greece (qq.v.). Its fortifications deterred Alaric's Visigoths (qq.v.) in 396, but greater security was provided by its incorporation into the theme of Hellas (qq.v.) in the late seventh century. Nevertheless, foreign conquest punctuated its later history. The city's flourishing silk (q.v.) industry was a target of Roger II of Sicily (qq.v.), who plundered Thebes (q.v.) in 1147. Leo Sgouros (q.v.) captured it in 1204, and the following year it was taken by Boniface of Montferrat (q.v.), who awarded it to Othon de la Roche (q.v.) and who made it part of the duchy of Athens (q.v.) and Thebes. The Catalan Grand Company (q.v.) captured it in 1311, ruling it until 1378, when the Acciajuoli (q.v.) family acquired it. Thebes fell to the Ottomans (q.v.) around 1456.

THEKLA, SAINT. According to legend, St. Paul converted Thekla in Ikonion (q.v.), after which she preached and gained great fame as a worker of miracles. By the fourth century her shrine at Meriamlik, near Seleukeia, in Isauria (qq.v.), was already a major pilgrim site. When Egeria (q.v.) visited it in 384, it had a church and monasteries, whose considerable wealth was protected from Isaurian raids by fortification walls.

THEMES. Themes (*themata* in Greek) were military zones, each administered by a military governor, the *strategos* (q.v.), much like the exarchates of Carthage and Ravenna (qq.v.). The earliest themes, including the Anatolikon, Armeniakon, Opsikion, and Thrakesion (qq.v.) protected Asia Minor (q.v.) against the attacks of Arabs (q.v.). The backbone of the theme system consisted of soldier-farmers, each of whom pledged personal and hereditary service in return for a grant of land; the system seemed to infer that funds derived from taxation (q.v.) were insufficient (or not the best way) to maintain such widely scattered soldiers. Such soldiers' properties *(stratiotika ktimata)* may have originated as early as 622 under Herakleios (q.v.), in response to the Persian (q.v.) threat. Their preservation of *stratiotika ktimata* demanded the vigilance of 10th-century emperors (q.v.) such as Nikephoros II Phokas (q.v.). Themes appear to have been developed in response to regional needs. The tendency of large thematic armies to revolt led to the division of large themes into smaller themes in the eighth and ninth centuries. In the 11th century the system deteriorated rapidly, beginning with Basil II (q.v.), who relied more on his Varangians (q.v.) and on a paid army. At the battle of Mantzikert in 1071, roughly a half-century later, the thematic levies that faced the Seljuks (q.v.) were utterly ill-disciplined and ill-equipped. The core of Romanos IV's army were mercenaries.

THEODAHAD. King of the Ostrogoths (q.v.) from 534–536 whose downfall resulted from his ineffectual defense of Italy (q.v.) against Justinian I's general Belisarios (qq.v.). Theodahad's brutal overthrow of Amalasuntha (q.v.), an ally of Justinian, provided the emperor (q.v.) with a pretext to invade Italy. Belisarios's capture of Naples (q.v.) in 536, after a siege of only 20 days, prompted the Ostrogoths to replace Theodahad with Vitiges (q.v.). Theodahad fled to Ravenna (q.v.), where an agent of Vitiges killed him.

THEODORA. Empress (q.v.) from 527–548; wife of Justinian I (q.v.). Prokopios (q.v.), in his *Anekdota* (Secret History) (q.v.) claims that before marrying Justinian in 525 she led the life of a stripper and courtesan. Whether true or not, her iron will saved Justinian during the Nika Revolt (q.v.) and she continued to be his partner in the affairs of state. She seemed to have her own religious policy (favoring Monophysitism [q.v.]), and she was a master of intrigue who engineered the downfall of Justinian's powerful minister, John of Cappadocia (q.v.). She also caused the downfall of two popes, Silverius and Vigilius (qq.v.). Some of the behavior that Prokopios maligns a modern reader might call feminism. Her charitable works were many, including the founding of orphanages, hospitals, and even a home to rehabilitate prostitutes. The dazzling portrait of her in the church of San Vitale in Ravenna (qq.v.) is as unforgettable as that which Prokopios paints of her.

THEODORA. Empress (q.v.) and wife of Theophilos (q.v.); regent for Michael III (q.v.); saint. Her brothers were Petronas and Bardas (qq.v.). She is remembered for her bride show (q.v.), but primarily as the Iconodule (q.v.) wife of the last Iconoclast emperor. She venerated icons (q.v.) in secret in the palace, and after Theophilos's death she aided in the restoration of icons in 843, for which she was made a saint. She insured that Theophilos was not condemned by claiming that he had repented on his deathbed. She was deposed in 856 after the murder of Theoktistos (q.v.).

THEODORA. Co-empress with her sister Zoe (q.v.) in 1042, and empress (q.v.) in her own right from 1055–1056, after the death of Constantine IX Monomachos (q.v.). She was the third daughter of Constantine VIII (q.v.) and became the last surviving member of the Macedonian dynasty (q.v.). Her brief sole rule evoked the hostility of patriarch Michael I Keroularios (qv.), who resented a female exercising imperial authority. One of her generals, a certain Bryennios, raised a revolt and was exiled. Before she died in 1056 she consented to the choice of Michael (VI) Stratiotikos (q.v.) as her successor.

THEODORE I LASKARIS. First emperor (q.v.) (1205–1221) and founder of the Empire of Nicaea (q.v.). After the Fourth Crusade conquered Constantinople (qq.v.) Theodore was unable to persuade patriarch (q.v.) John X Kamateros (1198–1206) to come to Nicaea (q.v.). So he was crowned by his own patriarch, Michael IV Autoreianos (q.v.), in 1208. Theodore's chief legacy was in preserving the empire against the Latin Empire and the Seljuks (qq.v.), despite all odds. In 1211 he won a decisive victory over the Seljuks, capturing the former emperor Alexios III (q.v.).

THEODORE I PALAIOLOGOS. *See* **MOREA; NAVARRESE COMPANY.**

THEODORE II LASKARIS. Emperor of Nicaea (1254–1258); son of John III Vatatzes (q.v.). He was a man of great learning and refinement, who was taught by George Akropolites and Nikephoros Blemmydes (qq.v.). His childhood companion George Mouzalon, a man of lowly origins, served as his chief advisor, earning the hostility of the aristocracy (q.v.) and ultimately weakening Theodore II's position. He died leaving Mouzalon as regent for his seven-year-old son John IV Laskaris (q.v.).

THEODORE II PALAIOLOGOS. *See* **MOREA.**

THEODORE GRAPTOS. He and his brother Theophanes Graptos (q.v.) were champions of icons (q.v.) during Theophilos's (q.v.) revival of Iconoclasm (q.v.). They were from Palestine (q.v.) and were pupils of Michael Synkellos (q.v.), whose *vita* (q.v.) is the chief source of information about them. Theodore and Theophanes were each called *graptos,* meaning "branded," because the emperor Theophilos, in the most dramatic instance of persecution during his reign, punished them by tattooing 12 iambic pentameters on their foreheads. The verses advertised the emperor's view that they were evil vessels of superstition and lawlessness, since they venerated icons in violation of imperial law.

THEODORE OF GAZA (Theodore Gazes, in Greek). Byzantine scholar and translator (ca. 1400–1475) who was among the first wave of genuine Byzantine humanists (including Manuel Chrysoloras, Bessarion, and Plethon [qq.v.]) to influence the 15th-century Italian Renaissance. Born in Thessalonike (q.v.), his studies there and in Constantinople (q.v.) benefited from the Palaiologan revival of ancient Greek literature, philosophy, and science, which was much broader than the *studia humanitatis* of rhetoric, history, poetry, and ethics being studied in Italy (q.v.). It was this breadth of knowledge that he brought to Ferrara (q.v.) in 1440, where he translated not only Aristotle's (q.v.) philosophic works, but also his scientific treatises. There, he also wrote a Greek grammar that was recognized as the best of all such manuals; Erasmus, for example, praised it highly. He subsequently taught in Naples (q.v.) and was invited to Rome (q.v.) by Pope Nicholas V (q.v.), where he joined a literary circle of Greek scholars, among whom was Bessarion. His pupils included many Italian humanists who later became famous, such as Lorenzo Valla. Along with a handful of other Byzantine scholars, he helped to establish Greek studies as an important component of Italian humanism.

THEODORE KOMNENOS DOUKAS. Ruler of the Despotate of Epiros (q.v.) from ca. 1215–1230. He was emperor at Thessalonike (qq.v.) from 1224–1230, and he posed the chief threat to the Latin Empire (q.v.) until 1230. He captured Peter of Courtenay in 1217 and occupied Thessalonike in 1224, where he was crowned emperor. After his conquest of Adrianople (q.v.) in 1225, he was poised for an attempt on Latin-occupied Constantinople (q.v.) when he was defeated and captured at the battle of Klokotnitsa (q.v.) in 1230. His younger brother Manuel Angelos (both were members of the Angelos family) escaped capture and gained control of Thessalonike from 1230–ca. 1237, by which time Bulgar Tsar John Asen II (qq.v.) released Theodore. In 1252 John III Vatatzes (q.v.) imprisoned him in Nicaea (q.v.), where he died soon afterward.

THEODORE OF MOPSUESTIA. Bishop of Mopsuestia (qq.v.) whose theological writings, part of the so-called Three Chapters (q.v.), were condemned in 553 at the Fifth Ecumenical Council at Constantinople (qq.v.). Adherents to Monophysitism (q.v.) considered him to be the spiritual father of Nestorianism (q.v.).

THEODORE OF STOUDIOS. Theologian; anti-Iconoclast leader during the reign of Leo V (q.v.); monastic reformer; saint. In 795, when he was a monk in Bithynia, Constantine VI (qq.v.) banished him for a year for his opposition to the emperor's (q.v.) adulterous marriage (the so-called Moechian Controversy [q.v.]). In 799 he refurbished the old Monastery of St. John Stoudios in Constantinople (qq.v.), which became a center of militant opposition to Iconoclasm (q.v.). When Leo V (q.v.) revived Iconoclasm in 815, Theodore was exiled until 821, when Michael II (q.v.) came to the throne. Whereupon he determined to create a monastic center independent from imperial interference. His writings include panegyrics, hymns (q.v.), homilies, a defense of icons (q.v.), and an extensive correspondence. His disciples collected at least 1,124 letters, of which over 550 are preserved.

THEODORE OF SYKEON. Saint, whose *vita* (q.v.) offers the reader the best picture of life in Asia Minor (q.v.) on the eve of the Arab (q.v.) invasions. It contains numerous interesting details, including some about the rebellion of Komentiolos against Herakleios (qq.v.). For a while, this "iron-eater," as he was called, practiced asceticism (q.v.) in an iron cage, wearing a heavy iron corselet, iron collar and iron belt, with added iron rings around his feet and hands. Despite this proclivity, he traveled extensively, and he founded a monastery in the village of Sykeon, where he was born.

THEODORET OF CYRRHUS. Bishop (q.v.) of Cyrrhus in Syria (q.v.) from 423–ca. 466; theologian whose works were condemned in Justinian I's edict of the Three Chapters (qq.v.), and at the Fifth Ecumenical Council at Constantinople (q.v.) in 553. He supported Nestorios against Cyril of Alexandria (qq.v.), was condemned at the "Robber" Council of Ephesus (q.v.) in 449, and was briefly exiled. At the Council of Chalcedon (q.v.) he admitted the error of his ways and was allowed to return to his diocese (q.v.). Despite this, pressure from Monophysites (q.v.) persuaded Justinian I to have his writings condemned. His *History of the Church,* which covers the years 323–428, bears some similarity to Sokrates and Sozomenos (qq.v.), who also wrote continuations of the work of Eusebios of Caesarea (q.v.). Theodoret's other writings include treatises on Christian faith and dogma that were later used by John of Damascus (q.v.), as well as numerous *vitae* (q.v.) of Syrian monks.

THEODORIC THE GREAT. King of the Ostrogoths (q.v.) who administered Italy (q.v.) from 493–526. He spent 10 years of his youth as a hostage in Constantinople (q.v.), where he cultivated a high regard for classical culture and civilization. Despite this, he remained illiterate, forced to use a gold stencil to sign state documents. Zeno (q.v.) encouraged him to take the Ostrogoths to Italy (qq.v.) and overthrow Odoacer (q.v.), which he did (489–493). In 497 Anastasios I (q.v.) formally recognized Theodoric's status as a kind of imperial deputy. Theodoric left the civil administration of Italy (q.v.) alone, and he even encouraged writers like Boethius and Cassiodorus (q.v.). Boethius wrote his *Consolation of Philosophy* while in prison for alleged treason. Despite the fact that the Ostrogoths embraced Arianism (q.v.), Theodoric left alone the Orthodox population of Italy. In this and in most other respects he was among the most remarkable rulers of his age. His stone mausoleum in Ravenna (q.v.) recalls imperial mausolea of an earlier age. His other monuments in Ravenna include what are thought to be the ruins of his palace, a church (S. Apollinare Nuovo), and a baptistry, the latter two of which were intended for his Arian followers.

THEODOSIOS I. Emperor (q.v.) from 379–395, he succeeded in suppressing civil wars in the West and reuniting the empire under his sole rule. His reign is associated with the triumph of Orthodoxy (q.v.) as defined by the First Ecumenical Council at Nicaea (qq.v.) in 325. By decree in 380 he affirmed Orthodoxy and called the Second Ecumenical Council (381) to condemn Arianism (q.v.) yet again and to condemn the so-called *Pneumatomachoi,* who taught that the Holy Spirit was created. In 391–392 he outlawed pagan rituals and the offering of sacrifices. The year 393 was the last year that the Olympic games were held. These acts insured the decline of public paganism and the triumph of Nicene Orthodoxy, earning him the epithet "the Great." However, his promotion of Nicene Orthodoxy made it less likely that the Arian German soldiery could be integrated into Roman society. His settlement with the Visigoths (q.v.) in 382 did little to change matters, as did his enrollment of Germans as *foederati* (q.v.) in separate units with their own officers, some of whom he promoted to the highest commands. Popular hostility against the Germans erupted in 390 in Thessalonike (q.v.), where numerous soldiers and their commanders were killed for outrages against the populace. Theodosios I massacred 7,000 citizens in response, and he was forced to do penance by Ambrose (q.v.) for this deed.

THEODOSIOS II. Emperor (q.v.) in the East from 408–450. He was the son of Arkadios (q.v.) and only seven years old when he came to the throne. Bookish and retiring, he left much of actual governance to his sister Pulcheria (q.v.), to high officials like the praetorian prefect Anthemios (q.v.), and to his wife Athenais-Eudokia (q.v.). Nevertheless, there were three important accomplishments during his reign: the *Codex Theodosianus* (q.v.); the famous land walls of Constantinople (q.v.), completed by 413; and the foundation of the University of Constantinople (q.v.). His support of Nestorianism (q.v.) was not sufficient to avoid its condemnation at the Third Ecumenical Council at Ephesus (qq.v.) in 431. He also supported the "Robber" Council at Ephesus (q.v.) in 449, overturned two years later by the Fourth Ecumenical Council at Chalcedon (q.v.).

THEODOSIOS III. Emperor (q.v.) from 715–717 during a period of near anarchy that followed the death of Justinian II (q.v.) in 711. He was a tax collector who was proclaimed emperor by troops of the Opsikion theme (qq.v.) in revolt against Anastasios II (q.v.). His brief reign was marked by a treaty with Tervel of Bulgaria (qq.v.) and by an invasion of Asia Minor in 715–716 by Maslama (qq.v.), who besieged Constantinople (q.v.) in 717–718. It was this event that produced Theodosios's overthrow by Leo III (q.v.).

THEODOSIOS OF MELITENE. *See* **SYMEON LOGOTHETE.**

THEODOSIOS THE MONK. *See* **SYRACUSE.**

THEODOSIOUPOLIS. City in Armenia (q.v.) named after Theodosios II (q.v.); modern Ezerum, in Turkey. The *magister militum* for Armenia resided there after Byzantium and Persia (qq.v.) partitioned Armenia in the late fourth century. A synod in Theodosioupolis in 633 won the Armenian church over to Monoenergism (q.v.). The Arabs (q.v.) conquered it in 653; not until 949 was it again firmly under Byzantine control. In the 11th century Basil II (q.v.) made it capital of the theme of Iberia (qq.v.). The Seljuks (q.v.) conquered it in 1201.

THEODOTOS I KASSITERAS. Patriarch (q.v.) from 815–ca. 821 who engineered Leo V's (q.v.) restoration of Iconoclasm (q.v.). Theodotos had impeccable Iconoclast credentials, for he was a relative of Constantine V (q.v.). He presided over a local synod at Hagia Sophia (q.v.) in 815 that forbade the veneration of icons (q.v.) and repudiated the Seventh Ecumenical Council (q.v.) of 787. He supported the persecution of Theodore of Stoudios, Theophanes the Confessor (qq.v.), and others.

THEOKTISTOS. Arguably the most important chief minister of the ninth century. He was a eunuch (q.v.) and perhaps a member of the *exkoubitores* (q.v.) when, in 820, he organized the assassination of Leo V (q.v.). He was rewarded by Michael II (q.v.) with the title of *patrikios* and the office of *chartoularios tou kanikleiou* (qq.v.). Theophilos made him *magistros* and *logothetes tou dromou* (qq.v.). He served as regent to Michael III (q.v.) until he was deposed and killed in 855.

THEOLOGY. Theology (from the Greek *theologia,* which means "the science of God") was much studied in Byzantium (q.v.). Among the topics considered were the nature of God (the Trinity), the relationship of Christ's human and divine natures, and the meaning of salvation. Basic ideas from Neoplatonism (q.v.), in particular from Pseudo-Dionysios the Areopagite (q.v.), were used to express what was considered inexpressible, even unknowable, namely, a full knowledge of God. The influence of Neoplatonism is seen in apophatic theology, which evolved to deal with problems about the knowledge of God. This tendency inclined toward mysticism (e.g., with Symeon the New Theologian [q.v.]), in opposition to the rational discussion about God seen in western Scholasticism (q.v.). Theology was rarely free from controversies, the resolution of which was attempted at ecumenical councils (q.v.), where heresy (q.v.) was condemned. Arianism (q.v.) was condemned at the First Ecumenical Council at Nicaea (qq.v.) in 325 and at the Second Ecumenical Council at Constantinople (q.v.) in 381. Nestorianism (q.v.) was condemned at the Third Ecumenical Council at Ephesus (q.v.) in 431, and Monophysitism (q.v.) at the Fourth Ecumenical Council at Chalcedon in 451 (q.v.). The so-called Three Chapters (q.v.) were condemned at the Fifth Ecumenical Council at Constantinople (qq.v.) in 553. The Sixth Ecumenical Council at Constantinople (qq.v.) in 680/681 condemned Monotheletism (q.v). Iconoclasm (q.v.) was condemned at the Seventh Ecumenical Council at Nicaea (qq.v.) in 787. The 11th century was dominated by the church schism of 1054, with the issues that accompanied the schism (e.g., *filioque* and *azyma* [qq.v.]), and by the less dramatic revival of theological interest in Neoplatonism and Aristotle (q.v.). The belief of the 12th-century theologian Sotericho Panteugenos (q.v.) that only the Father was present at the Eucharist was condemned by Nicholas of Methone and by Manuel I Komnenos (qq.v.). Astrology (q.v.) was also a controversial topic in the 11th and 12th centuries. The union of the churches (q.v.), achieved on paper at the Council of Lyons in 1274 (q.v.) and at the Council of Ferrara-Florence (q.v.) in 1438–1439, remained a center of controversy. The defense of Hesychasm by Gregory Palamas (qq.v.) also aroused great controversy, as did the defense of western scholasticism, which applied the logic of Aristotle to analyze Christian doctrine, among some Byzantine scholars. The works of scholastic theologian Thomas Aquinas (q.v.) were translated by Demetrios Kydones and Prochoros Kydones (qq.v.), and they influenced the writing of Gennadios II Scholarios (q.v.). However, theology was composed of more than its controversies, and those controversies consisted of more than extensions of Greek philosophical thought. Some controversies, like Monophysitism, can be viewed as mass movements. The controversy over papal primacy (q.v.) manifested itself in the Fourth Crusade (q.v.) during the final Latin assault on Constantinople (q.v.). Robert of Clari (q.v.) reports that when western knights expressed concern about killing fellow Christians, they were assured by their Latin clergy that the Byzantines were not Christians at all but enemies of God who had seceded from the papacy (q.v.). Thus, the clergy concluded, attacking Constantinople was not a sin, but a righteous deed.

THEON OF ALEXANDRIA. *See* **HYPATIA.**

THEOPASCHITISM. The core meaning of this term is "the suffering of God," referring to a version of Monophysitism (q.v.) that appeared in Constantinople (q.v.) in 519, namely, that the Godhead (the Word, or *logos*) actually suffered and died on the cross, as expressed by the formula "one of the Trinity suffered in the flesh." Peter the Fuller's (q.v.) addition of a theopaschite phrase to the *Trisagion* (q.v.) produced an uproar that resulted in his exile. The *akoimetoi* (q.v.) monks staunchly opposed this view. Nevertheless, Justinian I (q.v.), in an attempt to pacify the Monophysites, issued a law in 533 supporting the heresy (q.v.), though to no avail.

THEOPHANES CONTINUATUS. Often unreliable 10th-century chronicle (q.v.) written by an anonymous author who was commissioned by Constantine VII (q.v.). It covers the years 813–961, continuing the chronicle of Theophanes the Confessor (q.v.), hence its name. The work is a hodgepodge of material that sometimes draws on a common source used by Genesios (q.v.) and occasionally repeats the chronicle of Symeon Logothetes (q.v.). An added section, devoted to Basil I (q.v.), was written by Constantine VII around 950 and is referred to as the *Vita Basilii*. In this obvious panegyric, Constantine VII attempts to whitewash his grandfather. It has been suggested that Theodore Daphnopates (q.v.) wrote the chronicle's final section.

THEOPHANES GRAPTOS. He and his brother Theodore Graptos (q.v.) were the chief opponents of Iconoclasm (q.v.) during the reign of Theophilos (q.v.). They were each branded *(graptos)* on their foreheads for supporting the veneration of icons (q.v.). After Theophilos's death Theophanes became archbishop of Nicaea (qq.v.), and he wrote hymns and a *kanon* of Romanos the Melode (qq.v.). Theophanes lived to see his own poetry acclaimed more than Theophilos's clumsy iambic pentameters, which Theophanes displayed as a badge of honor on his forehead.

THEOPHANES THE CONFESSOR. Chronicler (died 817/818) and monk whose *Chronographia* covers the years 284–813, forming a continuation of the unfinished world chronicle (q.v.) of his friend George the Synkellos (q.v.). It is particularly important for the seventh and eighth centuries (as is the work of the Patriarch Nikephoros I [q.v.]), in part because its chronology (q.v.) forms the basis for these centuries, also because some of the historical sources that it relies on have not been preserved. The *Chronographia* is a major source for the first period of Iconoclasm (q.v.); its bias is fiercely anti-Iconoclastic.

THEOPHANO. First wife and empress of Leo VI (qq.v.). She was chosen for him in a bride show (q.v.) arranged by Basil I and Eudokia Ingerina (qq.v.). This proved to be an unhappy marriage, and after Theophano's untimely death in 895, at about age 20, Leo VI married his mistress. Leo VI's reputation suffered throughout, more so with the subsequent *tetragamy* (q.v.) controversy. Theophano's reputation, on the other hand, only increased. For her piety and good works she was sanctified soon after her death.

THEOPHANO. Wife and empress of two emperors, Romanos II, and Nikephoros II Phokas (qq.v.). She conspired with her lover, future John I Tzimiskes (q.v.), to murder Nikephoros II. For her role in his murder, the patriarch Polyeuktos (qq.v.) demanded of John I Tzimiskes that Theophano be banished. Tzimiskes reluctantly agreed to this in order to be crowned emperor (q.v.). She was allowed to return from exile in the Prokonnesos (q.v.) in 976, long after John I Tzimiskes had married Theodora, the sister of Romanos II. Theophano's lasting legacy to Byzantium (q.v.) was that she was mother of future emperor Basil II (q.v.).

THEOPHANO. Married western emperor Otto II (qq.v.) (973–983) in 972; regent and mother of Otto III (q.v.). She was a niece of John I Tzimiskes (q.v.). The marriage was accompanied by a peace treaty and alliance between the two empires that halted their hostilities in Italy (q.v.). Thephano and her large Greek entourage were living advertisements for Byzantine culture and refinement in the German court. She shocked Germans by taking baths (considered unhealthy in the West) and by her luxurious silk clothes. (A German nun claimed to have a dream in which she saw Theophano in hell for these sins.) Theophano's true audience was her son, the future Otto III (q.v.), who was taught to love all things Byzantine and who assumed, as western emperor, all the trappings and pretensions of the Byzantine court.

THEOPHILOS. Emperor (q.v.) from 829–842 who revived Iconoclasm (q.v.) for the last time, perhaps due to the influence of John VII Grammatikos (q.v.). Yet despite making examples of prominent

Iconodules (q.v.) like Theodore and Theophanes Graptos and the icon-painter Lazaros (qq.v.), he could not prevent his own wife Theodora (q.v.) from venerating icons (q.v.) within the Great Palace (q.v.). He was diligent in defending the empire, as demonstrated by his construction of Sarkel (q.v.) on the Don River and his new themes (q.v.) of Cherson, Paphlagonia, and Chaldia (qq.v.). He also created the *kleisourai* (q.v.) of Charsianon, Cappadocia, and Seleukeia (qq.v.). However, he neglected the Arab threat in Italy (q.v.) in order to concentrate on the Arab threat in Asia Minor (q.v.). Despite aid from two famous generals, Theophobos and Manuel (qq.v.), in 838 Caliph Mutasim (q.v.) defeated Theophilos at the battle of Dazimon (q.v.), and he sacked Ankyra and Amorion (qq.v.). The loss of Amorion, Theophilos's paternal city, was particularly humiliating. The emperor was a colorful personality whose bride show, new Bryas palace, new copper follis (qq.v.), love of learning, and love for justice seems to have earned him a certain popularity. In the Timarion (q.v.) he is made a judge in hell.

THEOPHILOS OF ALEXANDRIA. *See* **JOHN CHRYSOSTOM.**

THEOPHOBOS. Nasr (in Arabic), the Khurramite (q.v.) general of Persian or Kurdish descent who fled to Byzantine territory in 834 after suffering a defeat at the hands of Mamun (q.v.) the year previous. Theophilos (q.v.) created a Khurramite cavalry *tagma* stationed at Sinope (qq.v.), which Theopobos commanded. He converted to Christianity and married either a sister of Theophilos or of Theodora (q.v.). He campaigned with the emperor (q.v.) in 837, and in 838, where he saved the emperor's life at the battle of Dazimon (q.v.). However, in the aftermath of Theophilos's disastrous defeats of 838, Theophobos was accused by his enemies of plotting to overthrow the emperor. Fearing for his life, Theophobos fled to Amastris (q.v.) where his troops proclaimed him emperor. Faced with a major rebellion, Theophilos negotiated a peaceful solution that pardoned Theophobos and dispersed the Khurramite troops throughout the themes (q.v.), making them much less of a threat. The threat of any future Khurramite rebellion was further dampened by Theophobos's execution, ordered by Petronas and Theoktistos (qq.v.) as Theophilos lay on his death bed.

THEOPHYLAKTOS. Patriarch of Constantinople (qq.v.) from 933–956; son of Romanos I Lekapenos (q.v.). He was a youth of 16 when his father made him patriarch. Clearly his interests were elsewhere, e.g., his stables where he kept 2,000 horses fed on fruits and wine. In 954 a riding accident made him an invalid; he died two years later. Among his few legacies as patriarch is a letter he wrote ca. 940 to Tsar Peter of Bulgaria (qq.v.) that is one of the few sources for early Bogomilism (q.v.).

THEOPHYLAKTOS. *See* OHRID.

THEOTOKOS. "Mother of God" (or, more precisely, "Bearer of God") a common Greek epithet of the Virgin Mary. For the opponents of Nestorianism (q.v.) the central issue was the claim of Nestorios (q.v.) that Mary, as a mortal, should not be considered *Theotokos*, but rather *Christotokos*, which is to say bearer of the man Christ.

THERMOPYLAE. Narrow pass that provides access from northern Greece into central Greece and the Peloponnesos (qq.v.). It is best known for its famous defense against Xerxes in 480 B.C. In the Byzantine period, Justinian I (q.v.) provided it with a garrison (briefly withdrawn in 552 to help in the defense of Crotone [q.v.]). A raiding party of Cotrigurs under Zabergan (qq.v.) got as far as Thermopylae in 558. When historical sources of the sixth through eighth centuries mention Greece (*Hellas*) they are referring to the regions south of Thermopylae.

THESSALONIKE. Second most important city of Byzantium (q.v.), after Constantinople (q.v.). It was also the chief city of Thrace (q.v.) whose port was a major center of trade. The 12th-century *Timarion* (q.v.) describes the annual fair of the city as hosting merchants from as far away as Egypt and Spain (qq.v.). The city's strategic importance derived mainly from its location at the juncture of two main highways: the Via Egnatia (q.v.) and the route that went south from the Danube (q.v.) via Belgade and Skopje (qq.v.). It was the capital of the prefecture of Illyricum (qq.v.) from the fifth century, and capital of the theme (q.v.) of Thessalonike from the ninth century. Its history was punctuated by sieges and conquests, in part because any invasion of the Balkan Peninsula (q.v.) along its major land routes put the city at risk. There were numerous sieges by Avars Slavs (qq.v.), the first in 586; on these occasions, according to *The Miracles of St. Demetrios*, the city's patron saint, Demetrios, aided the city's defense. It was also besieged by the Serbs and by the Catalan Grand Company (qq.v.). The city was captured by Leo of Tripoli in 904, briefly by the Normans (q.v.) in 1185, by Boniface of Montferrat in 1204, by Theodore Komnenos Doukas in 1224, by John III Vatatzes in 1246, and by the Ottomans (qq.v.) in 1387 (and again in 1394). The Zealots (q.v.) held it from 1342–1350. It surrendered to Venice (q.v.) in 1423, but Murad II (q.v.) seized it for the Ottomans in 1430. Thessalonike preserves numerous Byzantine monuments, from its circuit walls (ca. 450) to splendid churches that include the famous fifth-century church of St. Demetrios, also the churches of Acheiropoietos, Hosios David, and Hagios Georgios (all fifth century in date), as well as the later churches of Hagia Sophia (eighth century?), Panaghia ton Chalkeon (1028), Nicholas Orphanos (early 14th century), St. Catherine (late 13th century.), and of the Holy Apostles (ca. 1329).

THESSALY. Region in central Greece (q.v.) distinguished by a large plain that is surrounded by mountains. The famous rock-top monasteries of Meteora (q.v.) are situated on the edge of this plain. Thessaly's chief Byzantine cities included Larissa, Lamia (qq.v.), Neopatras, and Trikkala (q.v.), as well as the port-cities of Demetrias (q.v.), Nea Anchialos, and Halmyros. The region's importance derived from the fertility of its large plain, which also served as an intersection of major road systems. Slavs (q.v.) settled in Thessaly beginning in the later sixth century. Vlachs (q.v.) settled in numbers by the 11th century. The region was subjected to numerous and occasionally devastating invasions (e.g., that of the Catalan Grand Company [q.v.] in 1309), and to successive foreign rulers (e.g., the Gabrielopoulos family).

THIRD CRUSADE. The Third Crusade was called in 1187 in order to reverse the conquests of Saladin (q.v.) that followed the disastrous battle of Hattin. Richard I Lionheart, king of England (1189–1199), and Philip II Augustus, king of France (1180–1223), arrived by sea to besiege Acre, which surrendered on 12 July 1191. In the process, Byzantium was deprived of Cyprus (qq.v.), which was captured by Richard I Lionheart from "emperor" Isaac Komnenos (q.v.). The Third Crusade also threatened Constantinople (q.v.) when the army of Frederick I Barbarossa (q.v.) passed through Thrace (q.v.) in the spring of 1191. Isaac II's (q.v.) alliance with Saladin aroused the ire of Frederick, as did Isaac's attempt to hinder Frederick's army. In such ways did this Crusade contribute to a pattern of distrust that began with the First Crusade (q.v.), and culminated in the Fourth Crusade (q.v.).

THOMAS MAGISTROS. Philologist and teacher (died ca. 1347) from Thessalonike (q.v.) who went on an embassy to Constantinople ca. 1316 to see Andronikos II (qq.v.). The letter describing the embassy contains interesting descriptive details of the trip, quite in contrast to his dry commentaries on ancient authors like Pindar, Euripides (qq.v.), and Aristophanes. He taught Demetrios Triklinios, a teacher of grammar in Thessalonike, and a classical philologist in his own right, who edited the extant works of Sophocles, Euripides (qq.v.), and Aeschylus. Philotheos Kokkinos and Gregory Akindynos (qq.v.) were also his pupils.

THOMAS MOROSINI. First Latin patriarch of Constantinople (qq.v.) from 1204–1211. By terms of the *Partitio Romaniae* (q.v.) the Venetians were able to choose him, which meant that he incurred the hostility of the Greek clergy, the Latin emperor, and the papacy (q.v.). Innocent III (q.v.) protested that his election was uncanonical.

THOMAS PALAIOLOGOS. *See* **MOREA.**

THOMAS THE SLAV. General (called "the Slav") whose rebellion (820–823) against Michael II (q.v.) may have been provoked by Michael II's assassination of Leo V (q.v.). Assuming the guise of the late Constantine VI (q.v.), he attracted support from most of the themes of Asia Minor (qq.v.), including the naval theme of Kibyrrhaiotai (qq.v.), with whose help he besieged Constantinople (q.v.) from 821–823. Thomas's opposition to Iconoclasm (q.v.) and his claim to be the champion of the poor may have won him followers. However, it is not clear if his rebellion is better characterized as the last great uprising of thematic armies, rather than as a civil war supported by a massive social movement. In any case, the intervention of Bulgar khan Omurtag (qq.v.) turned the tide in favor of Michael II, who captured and executed Thomas.

THOROS II. *See* **RUBENIDS.**

THRACE. Region defined by the Aegean Sea and Sea of Marmara (qq.v.) to the south, the Black Sea (q.v.) to the east, the Balkan range to the north, and the Nestos River to the west. The plain of Thrace was of great strategic importance, not only for its fertility (e.g., its production of corn) but because through it ran the great east-west highway, the Via Egnatia (q.v.), as well as the highway from Constantinople to Belgrade (qq.v.), which provided access to the north.

The region suffered from repeated invasions, including that of the Visigoths (q.v.), who defeated Valens at the battle of Adrianople (qq.v.) in 378.

THRAKESION. Important theme in western Asia Minor (qq.v.). Its name derived from its original army corps, which was transferred from Thrace (q.v.), probably in the late seventh century. The theme's importance lay in its location, defending the rich cities of the Aegean coast, including Ephesos (qq.v.), against attacks by the Arabs, and later by the Turks (qq.v.). Its importance is also demonstrated by the quality of its *strategoi* (q.v.), who included Michael Lachanodrakon and Petronas (qq.v.).

THREE CHAPTERS. The writings of three theologians, Theodore of Mopsuestia, Theodoret of Cyrrhus, and Ibas of Edessa (qq.v.), accused of Nestorianism by Monophysites (qq.v.). Justinian I's (q.v.) attempt to appease the Monophysites, including an edict that condemned these theologians, produced a chain of events that brought Pope Vigilius to Constantinople (qq.v.) under duress and concluded with the Fifth Ecumenical Council at Constantinople (qq.v.) in 553.

THUCYDIDES. *See* **HISTORY.**

TIBERIOS I. Emperor from 578–582. He was a young notary when the empress Sophia persuaded Justin II (qq.v.) to appoint him caesar (q.v.) in 574, and co-emperor a week before Justin II's death. In Maurice (q.v.) Tiberios had a competent general, and Tiberios himself was a popular, capable, though not brilliant emperor. He inherited grave military threats on several fronts. There was an invasion of Chosroes I (q.v.), the Lombards (q.v.) continued to expand their domains in Italy (q.v.), while Slavs and Avars launched raids in the Balkan Peninsula (qq.v.). The Avar conquest of Sirmium (q.v.) in 582 was a particularly grievous loss. Ultimately, Tiberios I's decision that Maurice should succeed him was arguably his most important act.

TIBERIOS II. Emperor from 698–705. He was *droungarios* of the theme of Kibyrrhaiotai (qq.v.) when he rebelled against Leontios q.v.). His baptismal name was Apsimar; he assumed the name Tiberios when he came to the throne. He repatriated to Cyprus (q.v.) those inhabitants of the island captured by Abd al-Malik (q.v.), repaired the sea walls of Constantinople (q.v.), and attempted, unsuccessfully, to invade Syria (q.v.). However, he did nothing to check the advance of the Arabs (q.v.) across western North Africa (q.v.). He was overthrown by Justinian II (q.v.).

TIGRIS RIVER. *See* **MESOPOTAMIA; ZANGI.**

TIMARION. Famous anonymous satire (ca. 1150), almost anti-Christian in tone, that illustrates the revival of ancient literary genres (including the romance [q.v.]) in the 12th century. It has been attributed variously to Nicholas Kallikles, Michael Italikos, and Theodore Prodromos (qq.v.). In imitation of a work of Lucian, the second century A.D. Greek satirist, it tells the story of a descent into the underworld. Timarion dies and descends into Hades, where he is judged by the Iconoclast Theophilos (qq.v.), and a group of pagan gods. The work begins with Timarion's description of the fair of Thessalonike (q.v.), which is of serious value for the study of 12th-century Byzantine commerce.

TIMOTHEOS AILOUROS. Monophysite patriarch of Alexandria (qq.v.) from 457–ca. 460 and 476–477. He was called *Ailouros* ("cat" in Greek) by his enemies, who imagined him creeping about at night to stir up mob violence against his Orthodox (q.v.) enemies. He and his successor Peter Mongos (q.v.) led the attack on the decrees of the Fourth Ecumenical Council at Chalcedon (q.v.), which caused Leo I (q.v.) to exile Ailouros to Gangra (q.v.). During the usurpation of Basiliskos (q.v.), he was recalled briefly. He died in 477.

TIMOTHY OF GAZA. Zoologist who, at the beginning of the sixth century, wrote four derivative works on exotic fauna. One of them, entitled *Indian Animals*, exhibits, as does the work of another sixth-century author, Kosmas Indikopleustes (q.v.), the Byzantine fascination with India (q.v.).

TIMOTHY "THE CAT." *See* **TIMOTHEOS AILOUROS.**

TIMUR. (Or Tamerland [Timur the Lame]). Mongol ruler who from 1369–1399 created a vast empire across the Eurasian steppe (q.v.), extending to the borders of Asia Minor (q.v.). Timur's incursion into Asia Minor brought him into direct conflict with Ottoman sultan Bayezid I (qq.v.). At the battle of Ankyra (q.v.), on 28 July 1402, Bayezid himself was taken prisoner. For Byzantium (q.v.) this battle had enormous consequences. Bayezid I's forces abandoned their siege of Constantinople as Timur's army continued to cut a swath through Ottoman possessions in Asia Minor, before withdrawing in 1403. Ottoman power did not even begin to recover until 1413. In effect, Timur helped to extend the life of Byzantium for another half-century.

TOME OF UNION. The ecclesiastical decree *(tome)* that healed the rancorous dispute over the *tetragamy* of Leo VI (qq.v.), by declaring that a fourth marriage was illegal and void. However, it pointedly did not actually condemn Leo VI's fourth marriage. Nevertheless, it provided a political solution acceptable to the followers of the two chief antagonists, the former patriarch Euthymios (qq.v.) and the patriarch Nicholas I Mystikos (qq.v.). The decree was issued in 920, eight years after Leo VI's death, indicating how seriously the church continued to be split over this issue.

TOMIS. *See* **DOBRUDJA.**

TOMISLAV. Prince of Croatia (q.v.) from 910–928. He was a close ally of Byzantium (q.v.) and victor over the Serbs (q.v.) in 926, when he handed Symeon of Bulgaria (q.v.) his worst defeat. After Tomislav's death, Croatia's power declined in the face of increasing threats from Bulgaria and Serbia (qq.v.).

TORCELLO. *See* **VENICE.**

TORNIKOS, LEO. Nephew of Constantine IX (q.v.); governor of Iberia (q.v.) who revolted in 1047. The revolt was put down quickly, as was the previous revolt of George Maniakes (q.v.) in 1043. Tornikos drew supporters from Macedonia and Thrace (qq.v.), especially from the military base in Adrianople (q.v.), where the dissatisfaction of the western military establishment with Constantine IX was particularly intense. Tornikos marched on Constantinople (q.v.), but his army melted away when he failed to gain entrance. He was hunted down and blinded.

TOTILA. King of the Ostrogoths (q.v.) from 541–552 who revived Ostrogothic power in Italy (q.v.) after the capture of Vitiges (q.v.). His occupation of Naples (q.v.) in 543 forced Justinian I to recall Belisarios (qq.v.) to Italy in 544. Still, Totila was able to capture Rome (q.v.) in 546, and again in 550. Then he attacked Sicily (q.v.), almost capturing Syracuse (q.v.). Justinian responded by supporting the occupation of parts of northern Italy by the Franks (q.v.), forcing Totila to return to defend Italy. In 552, at the battle of Busta Gallorum (q.v.), his army was defeated by Narses (q.v.), whose archers and spearmen fended off attacks by Totila's cavalry. Totila fled, was overtaken, and killed.

TRAJAN'S GATE. Famous mountain pass in Bulgaria (q.v.) about three days march from Serdica (q.v.), where Samuel of Bulgaria defeated Basil II (qq.v.) in August of 986. Basil II was retreating from his unsuccessful siege of Serdica when the Bulgars surprised his army in the pass, gaining total victory. Basil II's defeat allowed Samuel to continue to expand into Byzantine territory, and it prompted Bardas Skleros (q.v.) to revolt. Not until the end of the 10th century was Basil II again able to turn his attention to conquering Bulgaria.

TREBIZOND, EMPIRE OF. One of three Byzantine states created in exile after the fall of Constantinople to the Fourth Crusade (qq.v.). From 1204–1461 the dynasty of the "Grand Komnenoi," founded by Alexios I Komnenos and David Komnenos (qq.v.), whose grandfather was Andronikos I Komnenos (q.v.), governed from the city of Trebizond in Pontos (qq.v.), which had an excellent harbor and was well fortified. Trebizond was too remote from Constantinople to be a serious competitor with either the Empire of Nicaea or the Despotate of Epiros (qq.v.). However, its remoteness contributed to it being the last bastion of Byzantine civilization to fall to the Ottomans (q.v.). The empire's history was recorded by the chronicler Michael Panaretos (q.v.).

TREMISSIS. *See* **COINAGE.**

TRIBONIAN. Finest legal mind of the sixth century, to whom must go much of the credit for the legislative work of Justinian I (q.v.). He was first chosen by Justinian I to be Quaestor (q.v.) of the Sacred Palace, which is to say the supreme legal minister of the empire. Justinian I appointed him to head the commission of legal scholars that created the *Corpus Juris Civilis* (q.v.), arguably the most glorious achievement of Justinian I's reign.

TRICONCH. A building, including a church, that has three "conches," i.e., semicircular niches surmounted by halfdomes, on three sides.

Theophilos (q.v.), for example, built a triconch audience hall in the Great Palace (q.v.) that had an imperial throne in the central (eastern) apse. In 1303 Stefan Urosh II Milutin (q.v.) rebuilt the *katholikon* at Hilandar monastery on Mount Athos (q.v.) as a triconch church. A tetraconch (q.v.) has four conches.

TRIKKALA. One of the chief cities of Thessaly (after Larissa [q.v.]) in Greece (qq.v.). Its rich agricultural hinterland, and its strategic location along the major roads running north to Kastoria (q.v.) and west into the Pindos (q.v.), insured its economic prosperity. The Normans seized it briefly in 1083, but otherwise until the 13th century it seems to have remained in Byzantine hands. The Serbs (q.v.) occupied it from 1348 until the Ottomans (q.v.) captured it in 1393.

TRIKLINIOS, DEMETRIOS. *See* **THOMAS MAGISTROS.**

TRIPOLI, COUNTY OF. Crusader principality in what is now Lebanon, founded by Raymond of Toulouse after the First Crusade (qq.v.). Its capital was Tripolis (q.v.), which the Crusaders conquered in 1109 with Byzantine material support. Raymond's oath of loyalty to Alexios I Komnenos (q.v.), reaffirmed by his successors, allowed Alexios I and his immediate successors, John II and Manuel I (qq.v.), to establish a semblance of authority in a region that had once belonged to Byzantium (q.v.).

TRIPOLIS. Ancient Phoenician seaport (modern Tripoli, in Lebanon). It was occupied by the Persians (q.v.) from 612 until 628 when Herakleios (q.v.) regained it. It was starved into submission by Arab (q.v.) forces under a general of Muawiya (q.v.) in 635. Despite attempts to reconquer it, it remained under Muslim (q.v.) control until after the First Crusade, when Raymond of Toulouse (qq.v.) besieged it. It fell to Raymond in 1109, and it became the administrative center of the County of Tripoli (q.v.).

TRIPOLIS. *See* **LYDIA.**

TRISAGION. The term means "thrice-holy," referring to the refrain "Holy God, holy and mighty, holy and immortal, have mercy upon us," which is chanted at the beginning of the Eucharist (q.v.) in the eastern church. Peter the Fuller, Monophysite patriarch of Antioch (qq.v.), added to this important refrain the phrase, "Who was crucified for us." This was obviously Theopaschitism (q.v.), and it resulted in Peter's exile in 471.

TRUE CROSS. The wooden cross on which Christ was crucified, which Helena, mother of Constantine I the Great (qq.v.), allegedly discovered in Jerusalem (q.v.). She sent part of it to Constantinople (q.v.), but already in the fourth century smaller fragments were soon in circulation as relics (q.v.), each encased in a reliquary (q.v.). In 614 the relic of the True Cross in Jerusalem was carried off by the Persians (q.v.), but in 631 Herakleios (q.v.) returned it to the city. In 635 Herakleios transferred it to Constantinople when the Arabs (q.v.) threatened Jerusalem. In 1204 most of these relics were stolen by knights of the Fourth Crusade (q.v.).

TRULLO, COUNCIL IN. Church council called by Justinian II (q.v.) that met in Constantinople (q.v.) in 691–692. The council issued 102 cannons concerning church discipline, which, in the view of the council, completed the work of the Fifth and Sixth Ecumenical Councils (q.v.), hence the name "Fifth-Sixth" (Quinisextum), which the Council in Trullo is sometimes called.

TSAR. Slavic for "emperor" (*basileus* [q.v.] in Greek). The term was long used to refer to the Byzantine *basileus*. Symeon of Bulgaria (q.v.) was the first Slavic ruler to appropriate this imperial title.

TUGHRUL BEG. *See* **SELJUKS.**

TURKOMANS. *See* **TURKS.**

TURKS. Generic term for various peoples from the steppe (q.v.), including the Huns, Avars, Bulgars, Khazars, Seljuks, and Ottomans (qq.v.). The battle of Mantzikert (q.v.) in 1071 opened up Asia Minor to the Seljuks (qq.v.) and to disparate Turkoman nomads searching for plunder and pasturage for their flocks. Besides the Seljuks, who established the sultanate of Rum (q.v.), other competing Turkish emirates appeared, including the emirates of Aydin, Germiyan, Karaman, Karasi, Saruhan, and Osman (qq.v.). The followers of Osman were the famed Osmanli, or Ottomans (q.v.), as Europeans called them.

TURM. *See* **BANDON.**

TURNOVO. *See* **BULGARIA.**

TYANA. *See* **CILICIAN GATE.**

TYPIKON. A document that regulates the liturgical calendar of the Byzantine church, with instructions for the celebration of services. The term is also used for a document that regulates the organization and rules of a monastery. Monastic *typika* are often valuable sources of information about such varied topics as monastic property, food, lighting, and clothing.

TYPOS. *See* **CONSTANS II; EKTHESIS; MARTIN I; MONOTHELETISM.**

TYRE. Seaport on the southwest coast of modern Lebanon, south of Berytus and Sidon (qq.v). It was the birthplace of the pagan philosopher Porphyry (q.v.), who died ca. 306. Within a decade of his death, it was equally famous for its sumptuous Christian basilica (q.v.), consecrated in 316/317, and described in glowing terms by Eusebios of Caesarea (q.v.). Less glowing was the contentious church council of 335 that condemned Athanasios (q.v.). Tyre, like Berytus, flourished as a center of silk (q.v.) production, and as a center of the purple dye industry; the shellfish (the murex), the source of the dye, was found off Tyre's coast.

TZACHAS. Turkish emir (q.v.) whose pirate fleet, based at Phokaia (q.v.), at the northern entrance of the bay of Smyrna (q.v.), menaced the Aegean (q.v.) from ca. 1088–1092, capturing Chios, Lesbos, Rhodes, and Samos (qq.v.). Tzachas aligned himself with Pechenegs (q.v.) and attacked Abydos (q.v.) in 1092, creating the possibility of Turkish raids into mainland Greece (q.v.). Once he rebuilt his navy (q.v.), Alexios I (q.v.) was able to prevent this by going on the offensive, recapturing Chios and Lesbos. He then conspired with Kilij Arslan I (q.v.) to assassinate Tzachas (ca. 1093).

TZETZES, JOHN. Poet and commentator on Homer (q.v.), who died ca. 1180. He was a contemporary of another great commentator on Homer, Eustathios of Thessalonike (q.v.). Tzetzes wrote in didactic verse about classical literature, for the instruction of students. His work entitled *The Histories* contains letters that describe contemporary events during the reign of Manuel I Komnenos (q.v.).

– U –

ULDIN. *See* **GAINAS.**

ULFILAS. Arian missionary to the Goths (q.v.). He was captured by the Goths and spent several years among them before being sent by them on an embassy to Constantinople (q.v.). There, in 341, he allowed Eusebios of Nikomedia (q.v.), who was an Arian, to consecrate him as bishop (q.v.). Subsequent missionary activity among the Goths included his translation of the Bible into Gothic, for which purpose he created a Gothic alphabet. This, the first vernacular Bible, undoubtedly strengthened Arianism (q.v.) among the Goths. Nevertheless, Arianism proved to be an obstacle to their acceptance as citizens of the empire, once Nicene Orthodoxy (q.v.) became the official state religion under Theodosios I (q.v.).

UMAR. Caliph (q.v.) from 634–644, succeeding Abu Bakr (q.v.). It was during his reign that the Arabs conquered Byzantium's (qq.v.) eastern provinces. Syria fell to Khalid (qq.v.) in 636, after the battle of the Yarmuk (q.v.) River. In 638 Jerusalem (q.v.) was surrendered by its patriarch Sophronios (qq.v.) after a lengthy siege. Mesopotamia (q.v.) was in Arab possession by 640. Alexandria (q.v.) was captured in 642, along with the remainder of Egypt (q.v.), and much of Cyrenaica (q.v.) was in Arab possession by 644, when Umar was assassinated.

UMAR, EMIR OF MELITENE. *See* **MELITENE; MICHAEL III; PETRONAS.**

UMAR BEG. *See* **AYDIN.**

UMAYYAD CALIPHATE. Dynasty of caliphs founded by Muawiya (qq.v.) in 661, ending the civil war with Ali (son-in-law of the Prophet Muhammad [q.v.]) that had erupted after the assassination of Uthman (q.v.) in 656. Its capital was Damascus (q.v.). Until the battle of Akroinon (q.v.) in 740 the Umayyads maintained the offensive against Byzantium (q.v.) at sea, and in Asia Minor (q.v.), besieging Constantinople (q.v.) twice (674–678, and in 717–718 under Maslamah [q.v.]). The caliphate was overthrown in 750 by the Abbasids (q.v.), but one member of the Umayyads escaped to Spain (q.v.) to found the Umayyad caliphate at Cordoba (q.v.), which lasted until 1031.

UNION OF THE CHURCHES. The separation of the eastern and western churches had its origins as far back as the foundation of Constantinople (q.v.) in 330, which diminished the importance of Rome (q.v.). It also had its origins in the Council of Chalcedon (q.v.) which seemed to threaten the stature of the bishop (q.v.) of Rome, and in the gradual diminution of Byzantine power in Italy (q.v.) beginning with the Lombard (q.v.) invasion of 568. Differences in ritual and practice were also important, including the western use of *azyma,* the *filioque,* and papal primacy (qq.v.). The intolerance of western church reformers in the 11th century was reflected in the person of Humbert (q.v.), who played a chief role in instigating the schism of 1054 (q.v.). In retrospect, it was the conquest of Constantinople by the Fourth Crusade (q.v.) that made reconciliation with the West impossible. Moreover, efforts to heal the schism were intertwined with the Byzantine state's need of western military aid against the Seljuks and Ottomans (qq.v.); inevitably this meant a Crusade, which only the papacy (q.v.) could proclaim. The union of the churches proclaimed at the Council of Lyons (q.v.) in 1274, and subsequently at the Council of Ferrara-Florence (q.v.) in 1439, failed to gain popular support, much less any realistic military aid, as seen in the failed Crusade of Varna (q.v.).

URBAN II. *See* **FIRST CRUSADE.**

UTHMAN. Caliph (q.v.) from 644–656; he succeeded Umar (q.v.). Under him, the Arabs (q.v.) completed much of their westward march across North Africa (q.v.), defeating the Byzantine exarch Gregory (qq.v.) in 647. In the east Mediterranean (q.v.) equally important Byzantine reverses occurred, the first in 648 when, for the first time, an Arab fleet invaded Cyprus (q.v.). In 655, off the coast of Lycia (q.v.), in the first major naval battle with the Arabs, Constans II (q.v.) lost his fleet and almost his life. Further expansion was stalled for several years by the civil war that broke out upon Uthman's assassination in 656.

UTRIGURS. A Turkic people from the Eurasian steppe (q.v.) who migrated westward, by the late fifth century settling beyond the river Don to the east of the Sea of Azov. Justinian I (q.v.) used them as a check on their neighbors, the Cotrigurs (q.v.). The Avars (q.v.) briefly subjected them in the 560s, and they were subsequently incorporated into Bulgaria (q.v.).

UZES. Confederation of Turks from the Eurasian steppe (q.v.). They fled the advancing Cumans (q.v.) by following the Pechenegs across the Danube (qq.v.) in 1064. After wreaking havoc as far south as Greece (q.v.), plague and starvation forced them to retreat back across the Danube. Most eventually settled among the Pechenegs and Rus (q.v.). Others were accepted into the Byzantine army as mercenaries. At the battle of Mantzikert (q.v.) in 1071, the army of Romanos IV Diogenes (q.v.) included Uzes, whose loyalty was suspect, given their close ethnic affinity to the Seljuks (q.v.). Indeed, some Uzes defected to Alp Arslan (q.v.) during the battle.

– V –

VALENS. Eastern emperor (q.v.) from 364–378, appointed by Valentinian I (q.v.), who was his older brother and western co-emperor. Valens's adherence to Arianism (q.v.) resulted in a persecution of the Orthodox (q.v.) late in his reign, but he was soon consumed with the revolt of the Visigoths (q.v.) in 376. Two years later he died fighting the Visigoths at the battle of Adrianople (q.v.) in 378.

VALENTINIAN I. Emperor of the West from 364–375, chosen by the army (q.v.) after the death of Jovian (q.v.). He appointed his younger brother Valens (q.v.) as emperor in the East, while he ruled the West, including Illyricum, from Milan (qq.v.). Their joint rule reflected the increasing separation of the eastern and western halves of the empire. For example, Arianism (q.v.), which had more support in the East, was embraced by Valens. Valentinian I remained loyal to the Council of Nicaea (q.v.), as did most citizens in the West. Throughout his reign, Valentinian I was preoccupied chiefly with barbarian invasions in Britain (q.v.), and along the Rhine (q.v.).

VALENTINIAN II. Emperor (q.v.) of the West from 375–392, succeeding his father Valentinian I (q.v.) when he was only four years old. He never actually ruled in his own right. His half-brother Gratian (q.v.) exercised actual power until Gratian was murdered in 383. Thereafter, Valentinian II was dominated by Theodosios I (q.v.), and by the western general Arbogast (q.v.), who may have been responsible for the young emperor's death in 392. Valentinian II's reign was punctuated by the revolt of Maximus (q.v.), who ruled Britain, Gaul, and Spain (qq.v.) from 382–388, and who invaded Italy (q.v.) in 387, forcing the young emperor to flee to Thessalonike (q.v.).

VALENTINIAN III. Emperor (q.v.) of the West from 425–455. For the first part of his reign (he was six when he became emperor) his mother Galla Placidia (q.v.) exerted real power, as did the general Aetius (q.v.). His independence came only late in his reign, when he assassinated Aetius (454). However, Valentinian III was himself assassinated in 455 by one of Aetius's followers, the same year the Vandals sacked Rome (qq.v.). These events plunged Italy (q.v.) into political turmoil.

VALENTINOS ARSAKUNI. Usurped the throne briefly in 645 before being lynched in a popular uprising in Constantinople (q.v.). He was a former commander of the theme of Opsikion (qq.v.) who became count of the *exkoubitores* (q.v.) and who engineered the downfall of Martina (q.v.). His death in 645 left Constans II (q.v.) in sole control.

VALLA, LORENZO. *See* **DONATION OF CONSTANTINE; THEODORE OF GAZA.**

VANDALS. Germanic people who crossed the Rhine (q.v.) in 406, moved into Spain (q.v.), and who in 429 crossed into North Africa (q.v.). In 439 they seized Carthage (q.v.), and they soon created a pirate fleet that menaced the coasts of Sicily, Sardinia, and Italy (qq.v.). By treaty in 442, the emperor Valentinian III (q.v.) recognized the existence of a Vandal state, doubtless in the vain hope that formal relations with the Vandal king Gaiseric (q.v.) would curb his ambitions. Instead, Gaiseric's fleet sacked Rome (q.v.) in 455, kidnapping Valentinian III's widow and daughters. Leo I's (q.v.) expedition against the Vandals in 468, led by the incompetent Basiliskos (q.v.), failed. By 475 the Vandals had conquered Sicily, Sardinia (q.v.), and Corsica. Only much later (in 533) did Justinian I's general Belisarios (qq.v.) vanquish the Vandal state, a state that had promoted Arianism (q.v.), persecuted its Orthodox citizens, and menaced the entirety of the western Mediterranean (q.v.) for a century.

VARANGIAN GUARD. *See* **VARANGIANS.**

VARANGIANS. Name of those Vikings, also called Rus (qq.v.), who served as mercenaries in the Byzantine army (q.v.). In 988 a contingent of 6,000 Varangians was sent by Vladimir I of Kiev (qq.v.) to help Basil II (q.v.) suppress the revolt of Bardas Phokas (q.v.). They became the elite shock troops of Basil II's army. Subsequently they formed the famous Varangian Guard, the imperial bodyguard stationed in the Great Palace at Constantinople (qq.v.). The most famous commander *(akolouthos)* of the Varangians was Harold Hardrada (q.v.), who fought under George Maniakes in Sicily (qq.v.) in 1038. Hardrada died fighting Harold of England at Stamford Bridge in 1066 in an attempt to claim the English throne. After 1066, defeated Anglo-Saxons migrated to Byzantium (q.v.) where they found employment in the Varangian Guard. By the 13th century the Varangian Guard was almost entirely English and their acclamations to the emperor were in that language. The Guard was fiercely loyal to the reigning emperor, and fierce to behold with their swords and battle axes. In battle, the "axe-bearers" were sometimes pitted against western troops, though not always successfully. When Alexios I Komnenos (q.v.) attempted to raise the siege at Dyrrachion (q.v.) in October 1081, he placed on the front line a shield wall of Varangians that was almost wiped out by a Norman cavalry charge, reminiscent of the battle of Hastings. In 1204 Varangians vainly defended the walls of Constantinople against knights of the Fourth Crusade (q.v.). In the late Byzantine army (i.e., from 1261–1453) their role changed to that of imperial bodyguards and prison guards. The last historical reference to the Varangians is from the chronicler Adam of Usk, who in Rome (q.v.) in 1404 inquired of Byzantine ambassadors whether any of his countrymen lived in Byzantium. They told him of British axe-bearers who fought there for the emperor.

VARNA, CRUSADE OF. The last effort by western Christendom to save Constantinople (q.v.) and eastern Europe from the Ottomans (q.v.). Preached by Pope Eugenius IV (qq.v.) in 1440, the Crusade included forces under Hunyadi and George Brankovich (qq.v.). After agreeing to a 10-year truce, the Crusaders broke their agreement, which prompted a quick response from Sultan Murad II (qq.v.), who annihilated the western army (10 November 1444) on the coast of the Black Sea (q.v.) near Varna, before the Crusade could relieve Constantinople.

VASPURAKAN. Region of southeast Armenia annexed in 1022 by Basil II (q.v.), as Byzantium (q.v.) expanded eastward. From the opposite direction there was pressure on Armenia from the Turks (q.v.), all of which combined to encourage large-scale Armenian emigration into Byzantine territory. In exchange for ceding Vaspurakan, its last king, Senecherim Arcruni, received Sebasteia (q.v.), along with landed estates in Cappadocia (q.v.).

VELBUZD. A decisive battle (28 July 1330) in the history of the medieval Balkan Peninsula (q.v.) that laid the foundation for the rise of Serbia (q.v.) as a great power. Andronikos III Palaiologos and his Bulgarian (qq.v.) allies were defeated by Stefan Urosh III Dechanski and his son Stefan Urosh IV Dushan (qq.v.). The Serbian victory (q.v.) opened up Byzantine Macedonia (q.v.) to further Serbian expansion.

VENICE. Greatest of the Italian maritime republics. Its traditional foundation date is 421, but more likely is a date after 568 when refugees fled there to escape the Lombards (q.v.). Its location on a lagoon in the Gulf of Venice (part of the Adriatic Sea [q.v.]) provided a safe haven for commercial expansion, and, in the ninth century, independence from Byzantium (q.v.). Basil II (q.v.) extended commercial privileges to Venice, but those it received from Alexios I Komnenos (q.v.) provided the cornerstone of Venetian commercial power in the East. In return for help against the Normans (q.v.) in 1082 Alexios I granted Venice unrestricted trade throughout the empire, exemption from customs duties, in addition to several warehouses and quays in Constantinople (q.v.). These privileges were confirmed in 1126. In retrospect, this proved to be a major blunder, one that slowly increased Venice's role in the Byzantine economy, altering the political equation between Byzantium and Venice in the process. Manuel I Komnenos (q.v.) attempted to reverse Venice's growing stranglehold over eastern trade by confiscating Venetian goods and expelling Venetians from the empire in 1171. Increasingly, support was given to Venice's rivals Pisa and Genoa (qq.v.), in a vain attempt, as the events of 1203–1204 demonstrated, to thwart Venetian expansion. The conquest of Constantinople by the Fourth Crusade (q.v.), led by Doge Enrico Dandalo (q.v.), was the culmination of this process and, indeed, Venice was the greatest single beneficiary, gaining Crete, Euboea (qq.v.), numerous other islands, and mainland ports. A Venetian, Thomas Morosini (q.v.), was the first patriarch of the Latin Empire (qq.v.). The reconquest of Constantinople proved to be a temporary setback for Venetian commercial expansion, despite the favoritism Michael VIII (q.v.) showed to the Genoese. The Venetians fought and intrigued their way through the 14th century, intervening in Byzantine politics in hope of placing an emperor (q.v.) on the throne who would favor their interests against the preferred Genoese. This long and bitter rivalry reached a peak in 1376–1381 when fleets from Venice and Genoa (qq.v.) fought for control of Tenedos (q.v.). Andreas Dandalo (q.v.), writing in the 14th century, could look back with pride on Venetian expansion, especially on the contribution made by his ancestor Enrico Dandalo. However, the 15th century was more mixed for the Venetians. They were given Thessalonike (q.v.) to defend in 1423, but they lost it to the Ottomans (q.v.) in 1430. Further losses seemed inevitable after the Ottomans conquered Constantinople in 1453. However, not until the next century did the Ottomans develop a fleet that could effectively challenge Venetian maritime supremacy, a supremacy founded on the ruthless pursuit of profit in Byzantine waters.

VERINA. Wife of Leo I (q.v.), whose daughter Ariadne married Zeno (qq.v.). She was a remarkable intriguer. She helped her brother Basiliskos (q.v.) gain Zeno's throne. Shunted aside, she intrigued for the return of Zeno, but once that occurred she plotted unsuccessfully to assassinate the real power behind Zeno's throne, Illos (q.v.). For this Zeno banished her to a nunnery in Tarsos (q.v.). In 484 she joined forces with Illos in a revolt against Zeno that ended up supporting the very general, Leontios (q.v.), who was sent by Zeno to suppress the revolt. Verina crowned the usurper with her own hands, but soon thereafter she died while the revolt was being suppressed.

VERROIA. See **BERROIA.**

VESTIARION. The term can refer to any treasury administered by a *vestiarios* (treasurer). It can also refer to the state treasury, which served as an arsenal for the army (q.v.) and fleet, and was the repository for precious objects. It should not be confused with the *sakellion* (q.v.), which was the state treasury for coined money.

VIA EGNATIA. Major road that traversed the Balkan Peninsula (q.v.) laterally from Constantinople to the Adriatic (qq.v.), via Thessalonike, Pella, Edessa (Vodena), Herakleia, Ohrid (qq.v.), and then, finally, to either Dyrrachion (q.v.) or Apollonia (it had two terminal points). Across the Adriatic at Brindisi (q.v.) it connected to the Via Appia, which continued on to Rome, via Capua (qq.v.). Built by the Romans around 130 B.C. as the shortest route to their Asian possessions, the Via Egnatia continued to be used throughout the Byzantine period as one of the main roads to and from western Europe. In the 12th century, for example, Manuel I's bride, Bertha of Sulzbach (qq.v.), used the Via Egnatia to reach Constantinople. The road was particularly important in connection with invasions of Byzantium (q.v.) from the West. When the Normans (q.v.) attacked Dyrrachion in 1081 it was with the object of marching along the Via Egnatia to Constantinople. In 1185 William II of Sicily (q.v.) sacked Dyrrachion and used the Via Egnatia to march to Thessalonike (q.v.), which was captured and pillaged. Charles of Anjou (q.v.) had the same intentions when he besieged Dyrrachion in 1274.

VICTOR OF VITA. Bishop of Vita in North Africa (q.v.) who wrote a history (ca. 489) of the cruel persecution of the Orthodox population by the Vandals (q.v.) during the reigns of Gaiseric (q.v.), Huneric, and Gunthamund. He wrote his work (in Latin, entitled *Historia persecutionis Africanae provinciae*) from exile near Tripoli (q.v.). While dealing chiefly with the Orthodox church, the work is also valuable as a contemporary account of fifth-century North Africa.

VIDIN. Bulgarian fortress, strategically situated on the Danube (q.v.), which Basil II (q.v.) captured in 1003 after a siege of eight months. It was restored to Bulgaria (q.v.) in the early 14th century and was occupied by the forces of Hungary (q.v.) from 1365–1369. For a while in the late 14th century, the Ottomans (q.v.) allowed Vidin to became a semi-independent Bulgarian principality before it was conquered by Bayezid I (q.v.) in 1396.

VIGILIUS. Pope (q.v.) from 537–555. He was installed by Justinian I (q.v.) after Belisarios captured Rome from the Ostrogoths (qq.v.). When Vigilius refused to approve of the Three Chapters (q.v.), Justinian had him arrested (545), and transported him to Constantinople (q.v.). There, after first condemning Patriarch Menas (q.v.), he yielded to Justinian and condemned the Three Chapters in a statement called *Judicatum* (Pronouncement). When Vigilius heard that a council of African bishops excommunicated him for this, he changed his mind once again and condemned his statement. Justinian exiled him to an island in the Sea of Marmara (q.v.) until he consented to sign the decrees of the Fifth Ecumenical Council (q.v.). Only then was he allowed to return to Rome. He died along the way.

VIGLA. The tagma (q.v.) of the Watch, a cavalry corps stationed in Constantinople (q.v.) to guard the Great Palace (q.v.). It was created in the eighth century, probably by Irene (q.v.). Among its commanders was Petronas (q.v.), who served as *droungarios* (q.v.) *tes viglas* under Theophilos (q.v.).

VIKINGS. Northmen from Scandinavia (q.v.) who traversed the waterways of Europe in the eighth and ninth centuries as pirates and merchants. From ca. 835 Viking raids on Britain (q.v.), Ireland, and the Carolingian empire became incessant. The first Rus (q.v.) were Vikings who established a state at Kiev (q.v.), from which they launched an attack on Constantinople (q.v.) in 860. In 988 Vladimir I (q.v.) of Kiev sent 6,000 Rus soldiers to serve with Basil II (q.v.), after which the Varangians (q.v.), as they were called, fought for Byzantium (q.v.). The elite Varangian Guard (q.v.) was stationed in the Great Palace in Constantinople (qq.v.). In the 11th century, adventurers from the Viking state of Normandy, carved out a state in southern Italy (q.v.) by 1071, then conquered Sicily (q.v.). Normans (q.v.) also fought as mercenaries in Byzantine armies throughout the 11th century, including at the battle of Mantzikert (q.v.) in 1071. Among the most famous Viking adventurers was Harold Hardrada (q.v.), whose career included service with George Maniakes in Sicily (qq.v.).

VILLEHARDOUIN, GEOFFREY. *See* **GEOFFREY DE VILLEHARDOUIN.**

VISIGOTHS. Division of the Goths (q.v.) who, along with the Ostrogoths (q.v.), converted to Arianism (q.v.). This probably occurred (in the third century, rather than in the fourth century) through the missionary activity of Ulfilas (q.v.). In 376 the Visigoths requested permission from Valens (q.v.) to seek safety from the Huns by crossing the Danube (qq.v.), which they promised to defend. This first experiment in settling an entire German tribe on Roman soil proved disastrous. Valens died in the battle of Adrianople (378) trying to suppress their rebellion. Not until 382 was peace restored following an agreement to settle the Visigoths as *foederati* in Thrace (qq.v.). Under Alaric (q.v.) in 395 they rebelled again, launching a series of invasions into Greece (396–397) and Italy (401, 408) that culminated in the pillage of Rome (q.v.) in 410. Alaric's successor Athaulf married Galla Placidia (q.v.) and invaded Spain (q.v.), where, as *foederati,* the Visigoths warred against the Vandals (q.v.), creating a kingdom for themselves in the process. Despite attacks by the Franks under Clovis (qq.v.) the Visigothic kingdom survived until 711 when it fell to the Arabs (q.v.).

VITA. Latin for "life," referring to the biography of a saint. Typically, the *vita* of any saint contains visions, miracles, and heroic asceticism (q.v.). Invariably, hagiography (q.v.), which is the study of saints's lives, provides rich information on social conditions in the empire. Eusebios of Caesarea's biography of Constantine I the Great (qq.v.), the *Vita Constantini* (q.v.), can be viewed as having a hagiographic intent, given the saintly qualities Eusebios attributes to this ideal Christian emperor (q.v.).

VITA BASIL II. *See* **THEOPHANES CONTINUATUS.**

VITA CONSTANTINI. Eusebios of Caesarea's (q.v.) *Life of Constantine,* composed between 337–339. It is a panegyric that approaches hagiography (q.v.) whose historical value has been much debated. In it we hear in Constantine's own words the story of his miraculous vision of a cross of light in the sky, accompanied by the words "By this, conquer!" Even Eusebios found the story incredible, and made Constantine swear an oath that it was true. However, there are decrees, including a letter to the king of Persia (q.v.), from Constantine's own hand, that Eusebios seems to quote verbatim. In these the reader may perhaps hear the words of a new convert, even a religious zealot, convinced by the victory-bringing *labarum* (q.v.).

VITALIAN. Army (q.v.) commander in Thrace (q.v.) who revolted against Anastasios I (q.v.) from 513–515, representing himself as a champion of Orthodoxy against Monophysitism (q.v.). After Anastasios's death in 518, Justin I (q.v.) conciliated Vitalian (q.v.) by honoring him with the tiles of *patrikios* and consul (qq.v.). Vitalian was assassinated in 520, apparently at the instigation of the future Justinian I (q.v.), who regarded him as a rival.

VITIGES. King of the Ostrogoths (q.v.) from 536–540, succeeding Theodahad (q.v.). Vitiges besieged Belisarios in Rome (qq.v.) in 537. However, when in 538 Byzantine reinforcements arrived in Italy (q.v.), Vitiges retreated to Ravenna (q.v.), where he attempted vainly to convince Chosroes I (q.v.) to launch a diversionary attack in the East. In 540 Belisarios tricked Vitigis into opening the gates of Ravenna and he was taken prisoner. He died in exile two years later.

VLACHS. Pastoralists of the Balkan Peninsula (q.v.) who speak a Romance language, and whose ancestors probably originated in ancient Dacia (q.v.). For centuries they moved their sheep and goats from winter pastures in the plains to summer pastures in the mountains, as far south as the Pindos and Thessaly (qq.v.), appearing first in Byzantine sources of the 11th century, e.g., in the works of Anna Komnene and Kekaumenos (qq.v.). Niketas Choniates (q.v.) suggests that Peter of Bulgaria and his brother Asen I (qq.v.), founders of the Second Bulgarian Empire (q.v.), were Vlachs.

VLAD IV "THE IMPALER." *See* **WALLACHIA.**

VLADMIR I. Prince of Kiev (q.v.) from 980–1015; saint; son of Svjatoslav (q.v.). In 988 he contributed 6,000 Varangians (q.v.) to help Basil II (q.v.) subdue the rebel Bardas Phokas (q.v.). In return he was rewarded with a Byzantine bride, Basil II's sister Anna (q.v.). Vladimir's marriage to Anna was an opportunity to greatly enhance his prestige, which is why he took the daring step of converting to Christianity (988) in order to marry her. It was more than just a marriage, for it brought Kievan Rus (q.v.) into the orbit of Byzantine civilization. It can be seen as the single greatest historical event in Kievan Rus history, perhaps in the entirety of Russian history.

VODENA. The Slavic name for Edessa, the last major city (heading east) on the Via Egnatia (q.v.) before reaching Thessalonike (q.v.). When southern Macedonia (q.v.) was threatened, Vodena was a likely target. For example, Bohemund (q.v.) captured it briefly in 1083, when he fought Alexios I Komnenos (q.v.) for control of south Macedonia.

VOISLAV, MICHAEL. *See* **CONSTANTINE BODIN.**

VOISLAV, STEFAN. Prince of Zeta (q.v.) who revolted against Byzantine rule around 1034. In 1042 he defeated the *strategos* of Dyrrachion (qq.v.), gaining for Zeta its independence, which Byzantium (q.v.) recognized by awarding him the title of *protospatharios* (q.v.).

VOITECH, GEORGE. *See* **CONSTANTINE BODIN.**

– W –

WALID I. *See* **MASLAMA.**

WALLACHIA. Region north of the Danube (q.v.) in modern Romania. The principality of Wallachia, founded ca. 1290, established close relations with Serbia and Bulgaria (qq.v.) in the 14th century. Wallachia's support of attempts to oppose the Ottomans (q.v.) ended in disastrous defeats at Kosovo in 1389, Nikopolis in 1396, and Varna in 1444 (qq.v.), and Wallachia was forced to pay tribute to the Ottomans. After the demise of Byzantium (q.v.), Vlad IV "the Impaler" (reigned 1448, 1456–1462, 1476), the historical Dracula, briefly restored Wallachia's independence.

WATCH. *See* **VIGLA.**

WHITE HUNS. *See* **EPHTHALITES.**

WILLIAM I. King of Sicily (q.v.) from 1154–1166. In 1156 he defeated the forces that Manuel I Komnenos (q.v.) sent the previous year to reconquer southern Italy (q.v.). The peace settlement of 1158 required Manuel I's recognition of William I as king.

WILLIAM I CHAMPLITTE. Prince of Achaia (i.e., of the Principality of Achaia, or Morea [qq.v.]) from 1205–1208. With the permission of Boniface of Montferrat (q.v.), and with the aid of Geoffrey I Villehardouin (q.v.), he began the conquest of the Morea in 1205. The resulting principality of Achaia survived until 1430.

WILLIAM II. King of Sicily (q.v.) from 1166–1189. In 1167, threatened by Frederick I Barbarossa (q.v.), he obtained protection from Manuel I Komnenos (q.v.) through a marriage alliance; in return, Manuel was recognized overlord of Italy (q.v.). However, these negotiations failed. In August 1185, taking advantage of the Byzantine weakness created by Andronikos I Komnenos's (q.v.) reign of terror, William II attacked Dyrrachion and Thessalonike (qq.v.). Dyrrachion surrendered, but Thessalonike resisted. The Norman forces cruelly sacked it. William II allied himself with Isaac Komnenos of Cyprus (qq.v.), dispatching his admiral (and ex-pirate) Margaritone to defeat a fleet sent by Isaac II (q.v.) to recover the island. The lasting monument of William II's reign is the magnificent cathedral of Monreale, decorated by Byzantine mosaicists. William II was buried there in 1189.

WILLIAM II VILLEHARDOUIN. Prince of Achaia (i.e., of the Principality of Achaia, or Morea [qq.v.]) from 1246–1278. He was the son of Geoffrey I Villehardouin (q.v.), and successor of his brother Geoffrey II Villehardouin (q.v.). He figures prominently in the *Chronicle of the Morea* (q.v.), which describes his success in extending the boundaries of the Frankish Morea to include Monemvasia (q.v.). Today the castles he built at Maina and Mistra (q.v.) remain impressive, though ruinous. However, his good fortune was ruined when he was captured at the battle of Pelagonia (q.v.) in 1259. In return for his freedom he was forced to become a vassal of Michael VIII (q.v.).

WILLIAM OF APULIA. Historian whose *Gesta Roberti Wiscardi* is the most valuable single source for the career of Robert Guiscard (q.v.). His account of the rise of the Normans in Apulia (qq.v.), and of their seizure of the remainder of south Italy (q.v.), is much more detailed than any other historical source. His account overlaps with that of Anna Komnene's (q.v.) *Alexiad* with respect to Robert's war with Alexios I Komnenos (q.v.).

WILLIAM OF TYRE. Greatest of the Crusader historians, and among the greatest historians of the Middle Ages. He was Amalric I's ambassador to Manuel I (qq.v.) in 1168, and subsequently archbishop of Tyre, and chancellor of the Latin Kingdom of Jerusalem. His *History of Deeds Done Beyond the Sea,* in Latin, is important for events of his own lifetime (ca. 1130–1186), especially for the Second Crusade (q.v.), and for relations between the Crusader states and Byzantium (q.v.). For the First Crusade (q.v.) he relied chiefly on Albert of Aachen (q.v.), in addition to other works (e.g., Fulcher of Chartres [q.v.]). His history (q.v.), and continuations of it, are included in the so-called Estoire d'Eracles (q.v.).

– X –

XENON. *See* **PHILANTHROPY.**

XIPHILINOS, JOHN. *See* **JOHN VIII XIPHILINOS.**

– Y –

YAHYA OF ANTIOCH. Christian Arab historian of the 11th century who lived in Egypt under the Fatamids (qq.v.). He authored a continuation of the *History* by Eutychos of Alexandria covering the years 938–1034. His work concentrates on Egypt and on Byzantine Syria (q.v.), about which there is much useful information on the military campaigns of Nikephoros II and John I Tzimiskes (qq.v.), as well as the persecution of the caliph al-Hakim (qq.v.) in 1009.

YARMUK, BATTLE OF. *See* **HERAKLEIOS; KHALID.**

YAZDGIRD III. *See* **SASSANIANS.**

YAZID II. Caliph of the Umayyads (qq.v.) from 720–724, remembered for his edict of 721 that ordered the destruction of all images, which he viewed as a form of idolatry. Despite the fact that this decree was issued several years before a similar one by Leo III (q.v.), there is no evidence that Yazid II's decree inspired Leo III's Iconoclasm (q.v.).

YOLANDE. *See* **LATIN EMPIRE.**

– Z –

ZABERGAN. Khan of the Cotrigurs (qq.v.), who was repulsed by the aged Belisarios (q.v.) in 559. Zabergan crossed the frozen Danube (q.v.) in the winter of 558–559. Reaching Thrace (q.v.), he divided his forces into three units. One unit ravaged Thrace, while another drove into Greece (q.v.) as far as Thermopylae (q.v.). The third unit raced toward Constantinople (q.v.), only to be repulsed by Belisarios (q.v.), called out of retirement to defend the capital with a hastily assembled force of several hundred troops. Zabergan retreated back to Thrace, and finally back across the Danube. Any further thought of renewing the attack was discouraged by Justinian I (q.v.), who persuaded the Utrigurs (q.v.) to attack the Cotrigurs.

ZACCARIA. Family of Genoese entrepreneurs who amassed a fortune from alum mines at Phokaia (q.v.). Michael VIII (q.v.) ceded Phokaia to Benedetto Zaccaria in 1275, and the Zaccaria quickly monopolized much of the alum trade with the West. In 1304 (or 1305) Benedetto seized Chios (q.v.) and monopolized the trade in mastic, until a local rebellion dispossessed them of the island in 1329. What they could not get by seizure, they often got by legal acquisition and marriage, as they did in Achaia (q.v.), where they became firmly entrenched. In the first half of the 15th century their estates were whittled away by the Ottoman (q.v.) expansion.

ZACHARIAS OF MYTILENE. Church historian, bishop of Mytilene (qq.v.) in the early sixth century. His *History of the Church*, biased in favor of Monophysitism (q.v.) (although he later converted to the Chalcedonian creed) covers the years 450–491. It is preserved only in a Syriac epitome. He also wrote a *vita* (q.v.) of Severos, bishop of Antioch (qq.v.).

ZANGI. In 1127 he became Muslim (q.v.) *atabeg* (i.e., independent governor) of Mosul, located in northern Iraq on the Tigris River across from ancient Ninevah. In 1128 he united Mosul and Aleppo (q.v.). In 1144, a year after the death of John II (q.v.), he conquered Edessa (q.v.), which created panic in the Crusader states. The Second Crusade (q.v.) was called as a result of the fall of Edessa. After his death in 1146, the unification of the Muslim Near East continued with Nur-al-Din and Saladin (qq.v.).

ZAOUTZES, STYLIANOS. *See* **ARETHAS OF CAESAREA.**

ZAPETRA. *See* **MUTASIM.**

ZARA. *See* **FOURTH CRUSADE.**

ZEALOTS. Revolutionaries who established an independent regime in Thessalonike (q.v.) from 1342–1350. The Zealots ejected the local aristocracy (q.v.) and expropriated the property of all the landed magnates, including the property of monasteries and churches. The context of the revolution was the civil war of 1341–1347, and the chief enemy of the Zealots was John (VI) Kantakouzenos (q.v.). Their eventual demise is explained by the victory of Kantakouzenos in 1347, and the conclusion of the civil war. Isolated politically, the Zealots threatened to hand the city over to Stefan Urosh IV Dushan (q.v.), a proposal which lost them support within the city. Racked by internal dissension, Zealot rule collapsed. John VI took control of the city in 1350 with the aid of Ottoman (q.v.) troops. Among those now able to enter Thessalonike was the appointed archbishop Gregory Palamas (qq.v.), previously refused entry by the Zealots.

ZENO. Emperor (q.v.) from 474–491. He was an Isaurian (q.v.) chieftain named Tarasis who Leo I (q.v.) called on to free Constantinople (q.v.) from the domination of Aspar (q.v.). Once married to Leo I's daughter Ariadne (q.v.) in 466, Tarasis took the name Zeno and inaugurated a struggle with Aspar that ended in the latter's assassination in 471. When Leo I died in 474, Zeno ruled briefly with his son and child-emperor Leo II (q.v.), but Leo II died that same year. Almost immediately thereafter Zeno was overthrown (in 475–476) by his mother-in-law Verina and her brother Basiliskos (qq.v.). Two chief events mark the remainder of his reign. In 482 he attempted to appease the Monophysites with the *Henotikon* (qq.v.). Not only did the *Henotikon* fail in this regard, but it led to the Akakian Schism (q.v.). In 488 he encouraged Theodoric to overthrow Odoacer (qq.v.) and take control of Italy (q.v.), which Theodoric did, postponing direct Byzantine intervention into Italy until the reign of Justinian I (q.v.).

ZETA. First prominent Serbian principality. It was called Diokleia (q.v.) until Stefan Voislav (q.v.) gained independence from Byzantium (q.v.) in 1042. After the mid-12th century the political center of Serbia (q.v.) was transferred to Raška (q.v.), which was dominated by the dynasty of the Nemanjids (q.v.) until 1371. Zeta resisted the Ottomans (q.v.) until the late 15th century, by which time it was referred to as Montenegro.

ZEUXIPPUS, BATHS OF. *See* **AUGUSTAION; NIKA REVOLT.**

ZIGABENOS, EUTHYMIOS. Theologian. At the request of Alexios I Komnenos (q.v.), he authored a refutation of heresies entitled *Panoplia dogmatike* (The Dogmatic Panoply). In this work, Zigabenos gives particular attention to the Bogomils (q.v.), and to their leader in Constantinople, Basil the Bogomil (qq.v.). Zigabenos provides a description of Basil's execution.

ZOE. Empress (q.v.) from 1028 to her death in 1050; co-ruler in 1042 with her younger sister Theodora (q.v.). She was intimately connected with the succession of five emperors (q.v.) during the final decades of the Macedonian dynasty (q.v.). Her father Constantine VIII (q.v.) had no sons, and on his death bed in 1028 arranged for her to marry the eparch of Constantinople (qq.v.), who became Romanos III (q.v.). She plotted with her lover Michael (IV) Paphlagon (q.v.) the assassination of Romanos III in 1034, but when Michael IV took power he had Zoe put away in a monastery. However, before Michael IV was himself forced to retire in 1041, John the Orphanotrophos (q.v.) was able to persuade Zoe to adopt Michael V (q.v.). After Michael V's death she reigned with her sister Theodora in 1042, and then chose Constantine IX (q.v.) as her third imperial husband. Zoe did not outlive him, dying in 1050. The literary portrait of her in the *Chronographia* of Michael Psellos (q.v.) is unforgettable.

ZOE KARBONOPSINA. Fourth wife and empress of Leo VI (q.v.), mother of Constantine VII (q.v.). She was at the center of the tetragamy (q.v.) controversy, which made her politically vulnerable after Leo VI's death in 912. Alexander (q.v.) forced her into a nunnery, but following his death in 913, and the ineffectual response to the invasion of Symeon of Bulgaria by regent Nicholas I Mystikos (qq.v.), she was able to take power again. However, she proved no better at resisting Symeon, and in 919 she was forced back into a nunnery by Romanos I Lekapenos (q.v.) and his supporters.

ZOGRAPHOU MONASTERY. *See* **ATHOS, MOUNT.**

ZONARAS, JOHN. Author of one of the great world chronicles (q.v.) of the Palaiologan (q.v.) period, on par with that of John Skylitzes (q.v.). The chronicle (entitled *Epitome historion*), which goes from the Creation of the world to 1118, draws on the works of Skylitzes, Psellos, and Attaleiates (qq.v.). Zonaras was an original thinker whose consideration of the rise and fall of the Roman Empire led him to the conclusion that Byzantium (q.v.) in his own day had strayed far from the greatness of republican institutions. As a result, his treatment of Alexios I Komnenos (q.v.), however independent, critical (in places brilliantly original), and a product of his personal experience as chief imperial secretary *(protoasekretis)* and *megas droungarios tis viglas* (qq.v.), nevertheless reflects an antiquarian view of what an emperor (q.v.) should be like. The influence of this chronicle spread beyond Byzantium (q.v.) due to its translation into Church Slavonic (q.v.).

ZOROASTRIANISM. Persian religion founded by the legendary Zoroaster (died ca. 551 B.C.); state religion of the Sassanians (q.v.).

Central to Zoroastrianism is a belief in the ongoing strife between the Ohrmazd (Ahuramazda), the god of light, who represents goodness, and Ahriman, the god of darkness and evil. Ohrmazd's eventual triumph is predicted; when it occurs the dead will be raised for their final reward or punishment. Special veneration was given to fire in religious ceremonies, as seen on the back of Sassanian coins, where a fire-altar is depicted. From the mid-third century Zoroastrianism had a competitor in Manichaeanism (q.v.).

ZOSIMOS. One of the last pagan historians of Rome. His *Historia Nova* (New History) begins with Augustus and ends in 410. He relied heavily on the works of Eunapios and Olympiodoros (qq.v.). His bias is clearly anti-Christian, as can be seen in his treatment of Julian (q.v.). Except for Peter the Patrician (q.v.), whose work survives only in fragments, Zosimos is the only major historian of the fifth and sixth centuries who wrote a history of such chronological breadth.

Hagia Sophia, Constantinople. Facing northeast.
Byzantium's greatest church, whose influence was such that subsequent
Byzantine churches had one or more domes. However, no Byzantine
church was ever again attempted on this scale. Dedicated to Holy
Wisdom (Hagia Sophia), Justinian I's architects created a church without precedent. Never before had a dome of this size been placed on a
square (defined by four massive arches). For western Christians, accus-
tomed to more straightforward basilican church plans, the architecture
may have been difficult to comprehend, even enigmatic. However, there
is much that is traditional in this church (though not the Ottoman
minarets, added after 1453 when Hagia Sophia became a mosque). Its
basic plan is that of a Roman basilica, and centrally planned domed constructions were hardly unknown to Roman architecture (e.g., the
Pantheon). Nevertheless, the resulting architectural experience differed
significantly from churches in the West. Such differences only increase
over time. Later in the Middle Ages Byzantine churches appeared dramatically different from Gothic cathedrals. Just as the great religious
divide between the eastern and western churches had its origins centuries before the schism of 1054, so, too, did eastern and western church
architecture begin to diverge after Justinian I dedicated Hagia Sophia
in 537.

Hagia Sophia, Constantinople. Interior, facing east.
By permission of Dumbarton Oaks, Washington, D.C.
The interior of Hagia Sophia provides the viewer with one of the world's greatest architectural experiences. The dome, 55 meters above the floor, seems to float, as if suspended on a string, its supporting piers and pendentives not immediately apparent to the viewer. Moreover, the entire space is unclear, remaining partially hidden from the viewer until one is directly under the dome. Justinian I, in dedicating the church in 537, was aware that his architects had created a masterpiece; in fact no domed basilica on this scale was ever again constructed in Byzantium.

Theodosian land walls of Constantinople.

These walls protected Constantinople for centuries. Built in the first half of the fifth century by Theodosios II, they remain today one of Byzantium's most impressive monuments, extending six kilometers from the Sea of Marmara to the Golden Horn. In the foreground of this photograph is the first part of the triple defense, namely a ditch (filled-in in the photograph) that was some 20 meters wide and half as deep; a low wall ran along the inner side of the ditch. After the ditch are two lines of walls and towers, constructed of mortared rubble leveled by intermittent courses of brick. The exterior is faced with small limestone blocks. The outer line of walls and towers was much destroyed by Ottoman cannonry in 1453.

Theodosios I and his court viewing the races. Base of the Obelisk of Theodosios I in the Hippodrome of Constantinople.

The Hippodrome at Constantinople was more than a place where horse and chariot races occurred. It was also the focus of civic life in the capital, for it was here that the citizenry of the capital most often saw their emperors. Emperors appeared not just for horse races. It was here, adjacent to the Great Palace, where the most public display of imperial liturgy took place. It was here that emperors faced their citizenry on a regular basis, receiving their acclamations. It was also here that the citizenry could exert such expressions of public protest that were allowed. But protests could degenerate into rioting, even outright revolt, as in the case of the Nika Revolt of 532 that almost unseated Justinian I from his throne. The Egyptian obelisk that sits on this base is from Karnak, and dates from the reign of Pharaoh Tutmosis III (1490–1436 B.C.). Placed on the *spina* around which the charioteers raced, it probably commemorated the victory of Theodosios in 389 over the rebels Maximus and Victor. This side of the marble base shows Theodosios I seated in his imperial box, the *kathisma*, surrounded by members of his family and court, as well as by an imperial guard, below which are prisoners. The stylized representation conveys the liturgical formality that was required of an emperor even at a raucous sport event. The emperor's costume, his every gesture, as well as the positioning of his retinue, were rigidly programmed in a way that befitted his dignity as God's viceroy.

Shrine of Saint Symeon the Stylite the Elder in northern Syria.
In the words of Peter Brown, the holy man in Byzantium was "a man of power" (P. Brown, "The Rise and Function of the Holy Man in Late Antiquity," reprinted in *Society and the Holy in Late Antiquity* [Berkeley, 1982], 121). There is no greater example of this than Symeon the Stylite the Elder who lived and preached from high atop a pillar (*stylos*), open to the elements. Once he ascended the pillar he remained there for over 30 years until he died in 459. In doing so, the Syrian saint created a new form of asceticism (that of the stylite, meaning pillar saint) for which he gained great fame. He chose to place his pillar, which eventually reached an elevation of 16 meters, on the isolated mountaintop of Qal'at Sem'an. During his lifetime this splendid isolation was overrun by visitors and disciples, the latter forming the nucleus of a monastery that administered the huge shrine complex that the emperor Zeno built on the site after Symeon's death. From his pillar Symeon resolved local village disputes, issuing detailed commands that gained him a reputation as a champion of the oppressed. The photograph shows the interior of the ruined martyrion, an octagonal structure built around Symeon's pillar. Only the base of Symeon's pillar survives intact.

Monemvasia, the Gibralter of Greece.
Without fortifications, Byzantium could not have survived. For most of its history, Byzantium was under attack, and its preservation depended greatly on the scientific construction of walls (see C. Foss and D. Winfield, *Byzantine Fortifications, An Introduction* [Pretoria, 1986]). Indeed, the walls of Constantinople remained the most impressive urban fortifications of the entire Middle Ages, turning back numerous enemies. Much less well known are fortifications in the Byzantine countryside, many of whose defenses took advantage of natural topography. This is especially true of refuge sites, which were numerous. In Greece refuge sites appear from the late fourth century, beginning with the invasion of Greece by Alaric in 395. One famous refuge site lies along the shore of southeastern Greece (Peloponnesos) on a rocky promontory called Monemvasia ("single entrance"). It is connected to the mainland by a single causeway (seen on the right side of the photo), hence the name. The site seems to have been founded in the sixth century as a refuge from invading Slavs. Subsequently, a flourishing port developed in its fortified lower town, above which was a *kastro*. Monemvasia was the last stronghold in the Peloponnesos to surrender after the Fourth Crusade conquered Constantinople in 1204. So strong were its defenses that the Ottomans captured it (from the Venetians) only in 1540.

Dome of the Rock, Jerusalem.
Early Byzantine-Muslim relations were not restricted to warfare. The Dome of the Rock in Jerusalem, the earliest surviving Islamic monument, is a clear example of this. When it was completed in 691, Islam had triumphed in its wars against Byzantium. The monument may have been built to symbolize that victory. Inspiration was sought in the Byzantine tradition of centrally planned, octagonal martyria. Two were in Jerusalem: the Church of the Ascension and the Anastasis Rotunda. Whereas the exterior mosaic decoration has been largely replaced by Turkish tiles, the interior mosaics are original. No human or animal is shown, since such portrayals are prohibited in Islam. Instead there are vegetal motifs mixed with crowns and other symbols of the defeated Byzantine and Sassanian states. The mosaicists were doubtless Byzantine, perhaps on loan from the Byzantine court.

Katholikon at Daphni, near Athens, Greece.

The influence of Hagia Sophia on all subsequent Byzantine churches can be seen in the domed *katholikon* (i.e., monastic church) at Daphni, a suburb of Athens. The church, dedicated to the *Theotokos*, was built ca. 1100. However, unlike Hagia Sophia the dome does use pendentives, but rather an octagonal base resting on corner squinches. The plan is conventionally referred to as a Greek Cross-domed octagon, whose roots go back to the sixth century. Daphni's elaborate brickwork produces an overall effect that is both charming and dignified. Despite the difference in scale, the Daphni church provides an architectural experience that lies well within the tradition that began with Hagia Sophia. The interior of Daphni was covered with splendid wall mosaics, many of which survive. The dome at Daphni is considered to have one of the finest depictions of Christ Pantokrator. Below the dome, between the windows, are the 16 prophets of the Old Testament. In each of the four squinches is represented an important event in the life of Christ (Annunciation, Nativity, Baptism, and Transfiguration). Among the other scenes of Christ's life are the Entry into Jerusalem, Last Supper, Betrayal, Crucifixion, and Anastasis. Among the program of scenes from the life of Mary are the Prayer of Anna, the Annunciation and Dormition of the Virgin (*Koimesis*). In the apse is portrayed the *Theotokos*, seated on a throne, holding the Christ Child. The overall effect of these elegant figures on gold ground is stunning.

Christ enthroned between Zoe and Constantine IX Monomachos (1042–1055). Mosaic panel in Hagia Sophia, Constantinople. South gallery.

Many of the most memorable personalities of Byzantine history are women. They include Anna Komnene and Anna Delassene, as well as remarkable empresses like Justinian I's Theodora, and Zoe, portrayed here in her mid-sixties with her third imperial husband, Constantine IX. (The full inscription above his head reads: "Constantine in Christ God Autokrator and faithful Emperor of the Romans.") The emperor carries a bag of gold as a gift to the church of Hagia Sophia; Zoe holds a statement recording the donation. If one looks carefully, one sees that the portrait-heads of Constantine IX and Zoe are replacements of Zoe and one of her previous husbands, perhaps Romanos III; the changed name that identifies the emperor as Constantine Monomachos is quite obviously a replacement. These changes do little to alter the hidden meaning of the mosaic panel: namely, Byzantium's divine dispensation, instituted and supported by God. Nevertheless, Michael Psellus's description of court affairs makes it clear that the reality was turbulent and passionate, and quite subject to the personalities of Zoe and her imperial paramours.

Katholikon **at the Monastery of Iveron on Mount Athos, Greece.**
Mount Athos, called *Hagion Oros* ("Holy Mountain") in Greek, is a
great monastic center that has continued to flourish from Byzantine
times to the present day. It comprises a peninsula, 45 kilometers long
and up to 10 kilometers wide, in Chalkidike in northern Greece. The first
monastery founded on Mount Athos was the Great Lavra, established by
Athanasios of Athos in 963. Iveron was founded in 980 as a center for
Iberian (i.e., Georgian) monks, demonstrating how quickly Athos
became a magnet for both Greek and non-Greek monks. The *katholikon*
at Iveron, which dates from 980–983, is among the oldest surviving
churches on Mount Athos. A multiplicity of domes adorns its cross-in-
square (or *quincunx*) church and added side chapels. The drums of the
church domes have semicircular arches and colonnettes around the windows, creating an undulating roof that is charming to the eye.

***Theotokos* and Christ Child. Mosaic from the Church of the Panagia Angeloktistos at Kiti, Cyprus.**
The Virgin Mary was highly venerated in Byzantium. In art she is frequently portrayed as one sees her in this wall mosaic from Kiti: as the all-holy (*Panagia*) Mother of God (*Theotokos*, literally "God-bearing"). She stands between the archangels Michael and Gabriel (not actually shown in this photo), supporting the Christ Child on her left arm. The Virgin gazes intently at the spectator, as does the Christ Child, who blesses the viewer with his right hand. The nimbus around each head emphasizes their holiness. The inscription above identifies her as Holy Maria (*Hagia Maria*). The pose of presentation is similar to that of portable icons: the Virgin as the one who shows the way (the *Hodegetria*).

Lead Seal of Pope Honorius III from Paphos, Cyprus.
Papal involvement in Byzantium increased dramatically with the
Crusades. This lead seal (such as were commonly used in eastern and
western bureaucracies to insure the security of letters and documents;
see G. Vikan and J. Nesbitt, *Security in Byzantium* [Washington D.C.],
1982) is evidence of this. Honorius III's name is clearly seen on one
side; on the other side are portraits of saints Peter and Paul, joint
founders of the See of Rome. After the Third Crusade conquered
Cyprus in 1191, Pope Innocent III (1198–1216) urged the western military orders to defend the island against Byzantine counterattack. The
Hospitallers responded by constructing a powerful castle ca. 1200 to
defend the harbor of Paphos, Cyprus. Today the castle is referred to as
Saranda Kolones ("The Castle of the Forty Columns"). In 1204 when
the Fourth Crusade conquered Constantinople, the Byzantine threat to
Cyprus vanished. Nevertheless, Innocent III's successor, Pope Honorius
III (1216–1227), continued to be concerned with the Latin church
imposed on Cyprus, and with the rule of the island as a base of Crusader
military operations against the forces of Islam. It may have been this latter concern that prompted the pope's letter.

Saint Neophytos between archangels Michael and Gabriel. Fresco from the Monastery of Saint Neophytos, near Paphos, Cyprus.
By permission of Dumbarton Oaks, Washington, D.C. In 1159 Neophytos settled in the mountains near Paphos where he expanded a natural cave in the cliff-face of a mountain ravine into his home. It became known as the *enkleistra* ("place of seclusion"). As his fame spread he attracted disciples and visitors. In 1197 he sought seclusion higher up the cliff, where in a new cell he wrote a number of ecclesiastical works, communicating to the faithful below through a rock-cut shaft. After 1191, when the hated Crusaders conquered Cyprus, his circular letters provided comfort and advice to an increasingly demoralized populace. Thus, his power evolved within a society that esteemed asceticism and desperately needed charismatic leadership (see C. Galatariotou, *The Making of a Saint: The Life, Times, and Sanctification of Neophytos the Recluse* [Cambridge 1991]). This portrait of Saint Neophytos, commissioned by the self-proclaimed holy man himself, shows the archangels Michael and Gabriel, who normally stand beside the throne of God, attending the saint.

"Grenade" for Greek Fire from the Castle of *Saranda Kolones,* Paphos, Cyprus.

"Greek Fire" was a highly guarded secret in Byzantium's arsenal of military hardware (see E. McGeer, "Greek Fire" in A. Kashdan et al., *The Oxford Dictionary of Byzantium*, vol. 2 [Oxford, 1991], 873). Said to have been invented by a certain Kallinikos, it appears to have consisted of a petroleum mixture similar to napalm. Water could not extinguish it, which made it suitable for naval combat. Specially constructed ships could pump the substance from tubes in flaming spurts, much like modern flame-throwers. The effect on enemy ships was devastating, most notably during the Arab siege of Constantinople in 678. Greek Fire could be hurled by other means as well, including hand-thrown "grenades" suitable for attacking and defending fortifications. This likely example of a pottery "grenade" (the greatest diameter of which is 10 centimeters) was recovered from the Hospitaller castle called *Saranda Kolones* in Paphos, Cyprus. The castle was destroyed by earthquake in 1222, by which date Byzantium had long lost its monopoly on such incendiary devices.

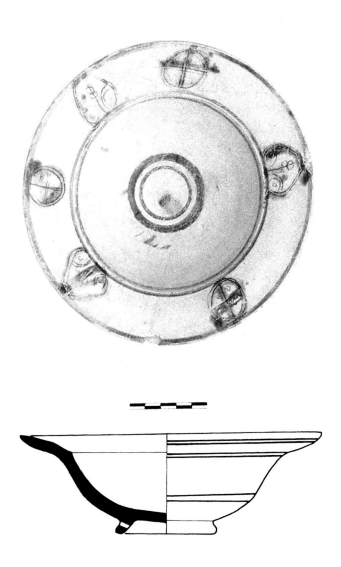

Zeuxippus Ware Bowl from Paphos, Cyprus.
Byzantine glazed pottery, which was mass-produced and exported
widely, offers information on trade and manufacturing. First excavated
at the Baths of Zeuxippus in Constantinople, varieties of this late-12th
to early-13th-century tableware are found from Italy to the Black Sea
(see A. H. S. Megaw, "Zeuxippus Ware Again," in *Recherches sur la
céramique byzantine*, ed. V. Déroche and J. M. Spieser [Athens, 1989],
259–266). This example (17 centimeters in diameter) is from the ruined
Hospitaller castle called *Saranda Kolones*, in Paphos, Cyprus.

Cathedral of the Dormition in the Kremlin, Moscow.
Byzantium profoundly influenced Russia beginning with the conversion
of Vladimir of Kiev in 989. An early example of this influence can be
found in the building program of Vladimir's son Jaroslav the Wise
(1019–1054). Jaroslav provided Kiev with a Cathedral of St. Sophia,
and built a Golden Gate for the city. Both of these recall similar monuments in Constantinople. Moscow's rise to power in the 15th century
was paralleled by the decline of Byzantium at the hands of the
Ottomans, who conquered Constantinople in 1453. Among the churches
in the Kremlin is the Cathedral of the Dormition, completed in 1479,
and shown on the left in this photograph. The façade of this five-domed
church is divided into arched bays, each with an identical window and
ornamental arcade. The use of the onion-shaped dome in Russian ecclesiastical architecture is sometimes explained as a solution to the problem of snow and ice. The church was built during the reign of Ivan III
the Great, prince of Moscow from 1462–1505, who in 1472 married
Sophia Palaiologina, niece of the last Byzantine emperor, Constantine
XI Palaiologos. Thereafter, Ivan III was viewed by his own church as a
new Constantine, and Moscow as a successor to Constantinople.

BIBLIOGRAPHY

INTRODUCTION

The bibliography is intended for an English-speaking reader. More extensive bibliographies that include works in other languages are also available. For example, some periodicals of Byzantine studies include recent bibliography with each volume, see *Byzantinische Zeitschrift* (the most complete) and *Byzantion*. A. P. Kazhdan et al. (eds.), *The Oxford Dictionary of Byzantium* (New York, 1991) includes important bibliography after each dictionary entry, although the information is current only to 1991. Annotated bibliographies of works in English on more limited topics are often less extensive than the one provided here, but nevertheless useful. For example, the recent textbook of W. Treadgold, *A History of the Byzantine State and Society* (Stanford, Calif., 1997) has such an annotated bibliography, organized by chronological period. Many of the works that follow in the bibliography below have their own bibliographies, e.g., H. C. Evans and W. E. Wixom, *The Glory of Byzantium; Art and Culture of the Middle Byzantine Era, A.D. 843–12651* (New York, Metropolitan Museum of Art, 1997).

The World Wide Web is increasingly a useful tool for information and bibliography on Byzantium. Enter "Byzantium" into a search engine to explore the Web offerings. Dumbarton Oaks Research Libraries has an extensive collection of Byzantine publications; its catalog can be accessed through its World Wide Web Home Page (http://www.ils. doaks.org).

I. GENERAL

A. Introductions (See also VII. A.)

Cavallo, G. (ed.) *The Byzantines*. Translated by T. Dunlap, T. L. Fagan, and C. Lambert. Chicago: University of Chicago Press, 1997.

Kazhdan, A. and G. Constable. *People and Power in Byzantium: An Introduction to Modern Byzantine Studies*. Washington, D.C.: Dumbarton Oaks Center for Byzantine Studies, 1982.

Laiou, A. E. and H. Maguire. (eds.) *Byzantium, A World Civilization*. Washington, D.C.: Dumbarton Oaks Research Library and Collection, 1992.

Mango, C. *Byzantium: The Empire of New Rome*. London: Weidenfeld and Nicolson, 1980.

Whitting, P. *Byzantium: An Introduction*. New York: St. Martin's Press, 1981.

B. Surveys, Textbooks

Brown, P. *The Rise of Western Christendom: Triumph and Diversity, A.D. 200–1000*. Cambridge, Mass.: Blackwell, 1996.

Browning, R. *The Byzantine Empire*. Revised ed. Washington, D.C.: Catholic University of America, 1992.

Christophilopoulou, A. *Byzantine History*. Translated by W. W. Phelps. 2 vols. Amsterdam: A. M. Hakkert, 1986–1993.

Foss, C. and P. Magdalino. *Rome and Byzantium*. Oxford: Elsevier-Phaidon, 1977.

Haussig, H. W. *A History of Byzantine Civilization*. Translated by J. M. Hussey. New York: Praeger, 1971.

Herrin, J. *The Formation of Christendom*. Princeton, N.J.: Princeton University Press, 1987.

Hussey, J. (ed.) *The Cambridge Medieval History*. 2nd ed. Vol. 4, in 2 parts. Cambridge: Cambridge University Press, 1966–1967.

Jenkins, R. *Byzantium: The Imperial Centuries, A.D. 610–1071*. London: Weidenfeld and Nicolson, 1966.

Jones, A. H. M. *The Later Roman Empire 284–602: A Social, Economic, and Administrative Survey*. Oxford: B. Blackwell, 1964. (Reprinted Baltimore: Johns Hopkins University Press, 1990.)

Mango, C. *Byzantium: The Empire of New Rome*. London: Weidenfeld and Nicolson, 1980.

Norwich, J. J. *Byzantium*. 3 vols. New York: Knopf, 1988–1995.

Ostrogorsky, G. *History of the Byzantine State*. 3rd rev. ed. New Brunswick: Rutgers University Press, 1969.

Runciman, S. *Byzantine Style and Civilization*. Harmondsworth: Penguin, 1975.

Treadgold, W. *A History of the Byzantine State and Society*. Stanford, Calif.: Stanford University Press, 1997.

Vasiliev, A. A. *History of the Byzantine Empire*. Revised ed. 2 vols. Madison: University of Wisconsin Press, 1952.

C. Reference Works

Allen, J. S. (ed.) Dumbarton Oaks Bibliographies. Series I, *Literature on Byzantine Art, 1892–1967*. Vol. I, *By Location*, Parts 1–2. Washington,

D.C.: Dumbarton Oaks Center for Byzantine Studies, 1973.

———, ed. Dumbarton Oaks Bibliographies. Series I, *Literature on Byzantine Art, 1892–1967,* Vol. II, *By Categories.* Washington, D.C.: Dumbarton Oaks Center for Byzantine Studies, 1976.

———, ed. *Author Index of Byzantine Studies.* 170 microfiches. Washington, D.C.: Dumbarton Oaks Center for Byzantine Studies, 1986.

———. *Literature on Byzantine Art.* (ed.) 2 vols. Washington, D.C.: Dumbarton Oaks Center for Byzantine Studies, 1973–1976.

Allen, J. S. and I. Ševčenko. (eds.) Dumbarton Oaks Bibliographies. Series II, *Literature in Various Byzantine Disciplines, 1892–1977.* 2 vols. Washington, D.C.: Dumbarton Oaks Center for Byzantine Studies, 1981–1994.

Glassé, C. *The Concise Encyclopedia of Islam.* San Francisco: Harper and Row, 1989.

Holt, P. M., A. Lambton, and B. Lewis. (eds.) *The Cambridge History of Islam.* 2 vols. Cambridge: Cambridge University Press, 1970.

Hussey, Joan. (ed.) *The Cambridge Medieval History.* Vol. IV. 2nd ed. Cambridge: Cambridge University Press, 1966–1967.

Kashdan, A., et al. (eds.) *Oxford Dictionary of Byzantium.* 3 vols. New York: Oxford University Press, 1991.

Strayer, J. R. (ed.) *Dictionary of the Middle Ages.* 13 vols. New York: Scribner, 1982–1989.

Van der Meer, F. and C. Mohrmann. *Atlas of the Early Christian World.* Translated and edited by M. F. Hedlund and H. H. Rowley. London: Nelson, 1958.

II. ADMINISTRATION

A. Court and Civil Bureaucracy

Bagnell R., et al. *Consuls of the Later Roman Empire.* Atlanta: Scholars Press, 1987.

Boak, A. E. R. and J. E. Dunlop. *Two Studies in Later Roman and Byzantine Administration.* London: Macmillan, 1924.

Bury, J. B. *The Imperial Administrative System in the Ninth Century.* London: H. Frowde, 1911.

Goodburn, R. and P. Bartholomew. (eds.) *Aspects of the Notitia Dignitatum.* Oxford: British Archaeological Reports, 1976.

Guilland, R. *Recherches sur les institutions byzantines.* (Studies on Byzantine Institutions.) 2 vols. Berlin: Akademie-Verlag, 1967.

———. *Titres et fonctions de l'Empire byzantin.* (Titles and Offices of the Byzantine Empire.) London: Variorum Reprints, 1976.

MacMullen, R. *Corruption and the Decline of Rome*. New Haven: Yale University Press, 1972.

Maguire, H. (ed.) *Byzantine Court Culture from 829 to 1204*. Washington, D.C.: Dumbarton Oaks Research Library and Collection, 1997.

B. Diplomacy and Foreign Policy

Blockley, R. C. *East Roman Foreign Policy: Formation and Conduct from Diocletian to Anastasius*. Leeds: F. Cairns, 1992.

Laiou, A. E. *Constantinople and the Latins: The Foreign Policy of Andronicus II, 1282–1328*. Cambridge, Mass.: Harvard University Press, 1972.

Shepherd, J. and S. Franklin. (eds.) *Byzantine Diplomacy*. Papers of the Twenty-Fourth Spring Symposium of Byzantine Studies. Cambridge, March 1990. Aldershot: Variorum, 1992.

C. Law

Ashburner, W. "The Farmer's Law." *Journal of Hellenic Studies* 32 (1912): 68–95.

———, ed. and trans. *The Rhodian Sea Law*. Oxford: Clarendon Press, 1909.

Buckland, W. W. *A Text-book of Roman Law from Augustus to Justinian*. 2nd ed. Cambridge: Cambridge University Press, 1950.

Freshfield, E. H. (trans.) *Roman Law in the Later Roman Empire: Byzantine Guilds, Professional and Commercial, Ordinances of Leo VI, ca. 895, from the Book of the Eparch*. Cambridge: Cambridge University Press, 1938.

———. *A Manual of Later Roman Law, the Ecloga ad Procheiron mutata*. Cambridge: Cambridge University Press, 1927.

Kunkel, W. *An Introduction to Roman Legal and Constitutional History*. Translated by J. M. Kelly. Oxford: Oxford University Press, 1973.

Laiou, A. E. and D. Simon. (eds.) *Law and Society in Byzantium, Ninth–Twelfth Centuries*. Washington, D.C.: Dumbarton Oaks, 1994.

Macrides, R. J. *Kinship and Justice in Byzantium, 11th–15th Centuries*. Aldershot: Variorum, 2000.

Pharr, C. (trans.) *The Theodosian Code and Novels, and the Sirmondian Constitutions*. Princeton: Princeton University Press, 1952.

Schulz, F. *History of Roman Legal Science*. Oxford: Clarendon Press, 1946.

D. Provincial Administration

Brown, T. S. *Gentlemen and Officers: Imperial Administration and Aristocratic Power in Italy, A.D. 554–800.* London: British School at Rome, 1984.

Maksimović, Lj. *The Byzantine Provincial Administration under the Palaiologoi.* Amsterdam: A. M. Hakkert, 1988.

E. Seals and Stamps

Laurent, V. *Le corpus des sceaux de l'Empire byzantin.* 2 vols. in 5 parts. Paris: Editions du Centre national de la recherche scientifique, 1963–1981.

Nesbitt, J. W. and N. Oikonomides. *Catalogue of Byzantine Seals at Dumbarton Oaks and in the Fogg Museum of Art.* 3 vols. Washington, D.C.: Dumbarton Oaks Research Library and Collection, 1991–1996.

Oikonomides, N. *Studies in Byzantine Sigillography.* 5 vols. Washington, D.C.: Dumbarton Oaks Research Library and Collection, 1987–1998.

———. *A Collection of Dated Byzantine Lead Seals.* Washington, D.C.: Dumbarton Oaks Research Library and Collection, 1986.

Vikan, G. and J. Nesbitt. *Security in Byzantium: Locking, Sealing, and Weighing.* Washington, D.C.: Dumbarton Oaks Center for Byzantine Studies, 1980.

Zacos, G. and A. Veglery. *Byzantine Lead Seals.* 2 vols. Basel: J. J. Augustin, 1972.

III. ARCHEOLOGY

A. Excavations

Avi-Yonah, M. (ed.) *Encyclopedia of Archaeological Excavations in the Holy Land.* English edition. 4 vols. Jerusalem: Israeli Exploration Society and Massada Press, 1975–1978.

Brett, G., W. J. Macaulay, and R. B. K. Stevenson. *The Great Palace of the Byzantine Emperors, being a First Report of the Excavations carried out in Istanbul on behalf of the Walker Trust.* (University of St. Andrews 1935–1938.) London: Oxford University Press, 1947.

Erim, K. *Aphrodisias, City of Venus Aphrodite.* London: Muller, Blond and White, 1986.

Harrison, R. M. *A Temple for Byzantium: The Discovery and Excavation of Anicia Juliana's Palace-Church in Istanbul.* London: Harvey Miller, 1989.

————. *Excavations at Saraçhane in Istanbul*. Vol. 1. Princeton: Princeton University Press, 1986.

Humphrey, J. H. (ed.) *The Roman and Byzantine Near East: Some Recent Archaeological Research*. 2 vols. Ann Arbor, Mich.: Journal of Roman Archaeology, 1993–1995.

Lightfoot, C. S. and E. A. Ivison. "The Amorium Project: The 1995 Excavation Season." *Dumbarton Oaks Papers* 51 (1997): 291–300.

McDonald, W. E., D. E. Coulson, and J. Rosser. *Excavations at Nichoria in Southwest Greece*. Vol. III, *Dark Age and Byzantine Occupation*. Minneapolis: University of Minnesota Press, 1983.

Redford, S. *The Archaeology of the Frontier in the Medieval Near East. Excavations at Gritille, Turkey*. Philadelphia: The University Museum, 1998.

Rice, D. T. (ed.) *The Great Palace of the Byzantine Emperors: Second Report*. Edinburgh: Edinburgh University Press, 1958.

Russell, J. "Anemurium: The Changing Face of a Roman City." *Archaeology* 33 (1980): 31–40.

Stern, E. (ed.) *The New Encyclopedia of Archaeological Excavations in the Holy Land*. New York: Simon and Schuster, 1993.

B. Historical Geography, Surveys

Bryer, A. and D. Winfield, with maps and plans by R. Anderson, and drawings by J. Winfield. *The Byzantine Monuments and Topography of the Pontos*. 2 vols. Washington, D.C.: Dumbarton Oaks Research Library and Collection, 1985.

Foss, C. *Cities, Fortresses and Villages of Byzantine Asia Minor*. Aldershot: Variorum, 1996.

————. *History and Archaeology of Byzantine Asia Minor*. London: Variorum, 1990.

————. *Survey of Medieval Castles of Anatolia*. 2 vols. Oxford: British Archaeological Reports, 1985.

French, D. H. and C. S. Lightfoot. *The Eastern Frontier of the Roman Empire*. Oxford: British Archaeological Reports, 1989.

Gregory, T. E. (ed.) *The Corinthia in the Roman Period*. Ann Arbor, Mich.: Journal of Roman Archaeology, 1994.

————. "A Desert Island Survey in the Gulf of Corinth." *Archaeology* 39 (1986): 16–21.

Hoddinot, R. F. *Bulgaria in Antiquity: An Archaeological Introduction*. London: Ernest Benn, 1975.

Lock, P. and G. D. R. Sanders. *The Archaeology of Medieval Greece*. Oxford: Oxbow, 1996.

Pringle, D. *The Defence of Byzantine Africa from Justinian to the Arab Conquest.* 2 vols. Oxford: British Archaeological Reports, 1981.
Ramsay, W. M. *The Historical Geography of Asia Minor.* London: J. Murray, 1890. (Reprinted Amsterdam: A. M. Hakkert, 1962.)
Rautman, M. L. "Archaeology and Byzantine Studies." *Byzantinische Forschungen* 15 (1990): 137–165.
Sinclair, T. A. *Eastern Turkey: An Architectural and Archaeological Survey.* 4 vols. London: Pindar Press, 1987–1990.
Tabula Imperii Byzantini (Register of the Byzantine Empire). 10 vols. Vienna: Verlag der Österreichische Akademie der Wissenschaften. 1976–1998 (in progress).
Wilson, R. J. A. *Sicily under the Roman Empire: The Archaeology of a Roman Province, 36 BC–AD 535.* Warminster: Aris and Phillips, 1990.

C. Minor Objects, Pottery

Davidson, G. R. *Corinth XII. The Minor Objects.* Princeton: American School of Classical Studies at Athens, 1952.
Hayes, J. W. *Excavations at Saraçhane in Istanbul.* Vol. 2, *The Pottery.* Edited by R. M. Harrison. Princeton: Princeton University Press, 1992.
———. *Late Roman Pottery.* London, British School at Rome, 1972.
Hill, S. *The Early Byzantine Churches of Cilicia and Isauria.* Aldershot: Ashgate, 1996.
Morgan, C. H. *The Byzantine Pottery.* Cambridge, Mass.: Harvard University Press, 1942.
Rice, D. T. *Byzantine Glazed Pottery.* Oxford: Clarendon Press, 1930.
Russell, J. "Byzantine *instrumenta domestica* from Anemurium: The Significance of Context." In R. L. Hohlfelder (ed.), *City, Town and Countryside in the Early Byzantine Era.* New York: Columbia University Press 1982, 133–163.

IV. ARMED FORCES

A. Army

Bartusis, Mark. *The Late Byzantine Army: Arms and Society, 1204–1453.* Philadelphia: University of Pennsylvania Press, 1992.
Bivar, A. D. H. "Cavalry Equipment and Tactics on the Euphrates Frontier." *Dumbarton Oaks Papers* 26 (1972): 271–291.
Burns, T. S. *Barbarians within the Gates of Rome: A Study of Roman Military Policy, ca. 375–425.* Bloomington: Indiana University Press, 1994.

Dennis, G. T. *Maurice's Strategikon: Handbook of Military Strategy*. Philadelphia: University of Pennsylvania Press, 1984.

————. *Three Byzantine Military Treatises*. Washington, D.C.: Dumbarton Oaks Research Library and Collection, 1985.

Frank, R. I. *Scholae Palatinae: The Palace Guards of the Later Roman Empire*. Rome: American Academy in Rome, 1969.

Haldon, J. F. *Recruitment and Conscription in the Byzantine Army C. 550–950: A Study of the Origins of the Stratiotika Ktemata*. Vienna: Verlag der Österreichische Akademie der Wissenschaften, 1979.

————. *Byzantine Praetorians: An Administrative, Institutional and Social Survey of the Opsikion and Tagmata, C. 580–900*. Bonn: R. Habelt, 1984.

Kaegi, Jr., W. E. *Byzantine Military Unrest, 471–843: An Interpretation*. Amsterdam: A. M. Hakkert, 1981.

MacMullen, R. *Soldier and Civilian in the Later Roman Empire*. Cambridge, Mass.: Harvard University Press, 1963.

McGeer, E. *Sowing the Dragon's Teeth: Byzantine Warfare in the Tenth Century*. Washington, D.C.: Dumbarton Oaks Research Library and Collection, 1995.

Miller, T. S. and J. Nesbitt. *Peace and War in Byzantium. Essays in Honor of George T. Dennis, S.J.* Washington, D.C.: Catholic University Press of America, 1995.

O'Flynn, J. M. *Generalissimos of the Western Roman Empire*. Edmonton: University of Alberta Press, 1983.

Thompson, E. A. (trans.) *A Roman Reformer and Inventor, Being a New Text of the Treatise De rebus bellicus*. Oxford: Clarendon Press, 1952.

Treadgold, W. *Byzantium and Its Army, 284–1081*. Stanford, Calif.: Stanford University Press, 1995.

B. Navy

Ahrweiler, Helene. *Byzance et la mer: La marine de guerre, la politique et les institutions maritimes de Byzance aux VIIe–XVe siècles*. (Byzantium and the sea: The navy, policy, and maritime institutions of Byzantium from the 7th–15th centuries.) Paris: Presses universitaires de France, 1966.

V. BIBLIOGRAPHY BY PERIOD

A. Transformation Under Diocletian and Constantine (284–337)

Barnes, T. D. *Constantine and Eusebius*. Cambridge, Mass.: Harvard University Press, 1981.

————. *The New Empire of Diocletian and Constantine*. Cambridge, Mass.: Harvard University Press, 1982.

Brown, P. *The Making of Late Antiquity*. Cambridge, Mass.: Harvard University Press, 1978.

Cameron, Averil. *The Later Roman Empire, A.D. 284–430*. Cambridge, Mass.: Harvard University Press, 1993.

————. *The Mediterranean World in Late Antiquity*. London: Routledge, 1993.

Jones, A. H. M. *Constantine and the Conversion of Europe*. 2nd ed. New York: Collier Books, 1963.

————. *The Later Roman Empire: 284–602. A Social, Economic, and Administrative Survey*. 3 vols. Oxford: B. Blackwell, 1964. (Reprinted Baltimore: Johns Hopkins University Press, 1990.)

Liebeschuetz, H. W. G. *Continuity and Change in Roman Religion*. Oxford: Clarendon Press, 1979.

Lieu, S. N. C. and D. Montserrat. (eds.) *Constantine: History, Historiography, and Legend*. London: Routledge, 1998.

Luttwak, E. *The Grand Strategy of the Roman Empire*. Baltimore: Johns Hopkins University Press, 1976.

MacMullen, R. *Roman Government's Response to Crisis, AD 235–337*. New Haven: Yale University Press, 1976.

Millar, F. G. B. *The Emperor and the Roman World, 31 B.C.–A.D. 337*. Ithaca, N.Y.: Cornell University Press, 1977.

————. *The Roman Empire and Its Neighbors*. 2nd ed. New York: Delacorte, 1967.

Williams, S. *Diocletian and the Roman Recovery*. London: Batsford, 1985.

B. Late Antiquity: Constantine to Justinian (337–527).

Barnes, T. *Athanasius and Constantius*. Cambridge, Mass.: Harvard University Press, 1993.

Bowersock, G. W. *Julian the Apostate*. Cambridge, Mass.: Harvard University Press, 1978.

Brown, P. *Authority and the Sacred: Aspects of the Christianisation of the Roman World*. Cambridge: Cambridge University Press, 1995.

————. *Power and Persuasion: Towards a Christian Empire*. Madison: University of Wisconsin Press, 1992.

————. *Religion and Society in the Age of St. Augustine*. New York: Harper and Row, 1972.

————. *The World of Late Antiquity: A.D. 150–750*. London: Thames and Hudson; and New York: Harcourt Brace Jovanovich, 1971.

————. *Augustine of Hippo*. Berkeley: University of California Press, 1967.

Browning, R. *The Emperor Julian*. Berkeley: University of California Press, 1976.

Bury, J. B. *A History of the Later Roman Empire from the Death of Theodosius I to the Death of Justinian (A.D. 395 to 565)*. 2 vols. London: Macmillan, 1923.

Cameron, Alan. *Claudian: Poetry and Propaganda at the Court of Honorius*. Oxford: Clarendon Press, 1970.

Cameron, Alan and J. Long. *Barbarians and Politics at the Court of Arcadius*. Berkeley: University of California Press, 1993.

Cameron, Averil. *The Later Roman Empire, A.D. 284–430*. Cambridge, Mass.: Harvard University Press, 1993.

———. *The Mediterranean World in Late Antiquity, AD 395–600*. London: Routledge, 1993.

Charanis, P. *Church and State in the Later Roman Empire: The Religious Policy of Anastasius the First, 491–518*. Thessalonike: Kentron Vyzantinon Ereunon, 1974.

Frantz, A., with contributions by H. A. Thompson and J. Travlos. *Late Antiquity: A.D. 267–700*. Princeton: American School of Classical Studies at Athens, 1988.

Friell, G. *Theodosius: The Empire at Bay*. London: Batsford, 1994.

Holum, K. *Theodosian Empresses: Women and Imperial Domination in Late Antiquity*. Berkeley: University of California Press, 1982.

Jones, A. H. M. *The Later Roman Empire: 284–602. A Social, Economic, and Administrative Survey*. 3 vols. Oxford: B. Blackwell, 1964. (Reprinted Baltimore: Johns Hopkins University Press, 1990.)

Kaegi, Jr., W. E. *Byzantium and the Decline of Rome*. Princeton: Princeton University Press, 1968.

King, N. Q. *The Emperor Theodosius and the Establishment of Christianity*. Philadelphia: Westminster Press, 1960.

Liebeschuetz, J. *Barbarians and Bishops: Army, Church, and State in the Age of Arcadius and Chrysostom*. Oxford: Clarendon Press, 1990.

Maenchen-Helfen, J. O. *The World of the Huns*. Berkeley: University of California Press, 1973.

Matthews, John. *The Roman Empire of Ammianus*. Baltimore: Johns Hopkins University Press, 1989.

Stein, E. *Histoire du Bas-Empire*. 2 vols. Paris: Desclèe de Brouwer, 1949–1959.

Thompson, E. A. *A History of Attila and the Huns*. Oxford: Clarendon Press, 1948.

———. *Romans and Barbarians: The Decline of the Western Empire*. Madison: University of Wisconsin Press, 1982.

C. Justinianic Expansion and Its Aftermath (527–632)

Allen, P. and E. Jeffreys. (eds.) *The Sixth Century: End or Beginning?* Brisbane: Australian Association for Byzantine Studies, 1996.

Browning, R. *Justinian and Theodora*. Revised ed. London: Thames and Hudson, 1987.

Bury, J. B. *A History of the Later Roman Empire from the Death of Theodosius I to the Death of Justinian (A.D. 395 to 565)*. 2 vols. London: Macmillan, 1923.

Cameron, Averil. *Continuity and Change in Sixth-Century Byzantium*. London: Variorum Reprints, 1981.

———. *Procopius and the Sixth Century*. Berkeley: University of California Press, 1985.

———. *The Mediterranean World in Late Antiquity, AD 395–600*. London: Routledge, 1993.

Jones, A. H. M. *The Later Roman Empire: 284–602. A Social, Economic, and Administrative Survey*. 3 vols. Oxford: B. Blackwell, 1964. (Reprinted Baltimore: Johns Hopkins University Press, 1990.)

Whitby, M. *The Emperor Maurice and His Historian: Theophylact Simocatta on Persian and Balkan Warfare*. Oxford: Clarendon Press, 1988.

D. Decline in the Seventh and Eighth Centuries (632–780)

Butler, A. J. *The Arab Conquest of Egypt and the Last Thirty Years of the Roman Dominion*. Oxford: Clarendon Press, 1978.

Haldon, J. F. *Byzantium in the Seventh Century: The Transformation of a Culture*. Revised ed. Cambridge: Cambridge University Press, 1997.

Head, C. *Justinian II of Byzantium*. Madison: University of Wisconsin Press, 1972.

Stratos, A. N. *Byzantium in the Seventh Century*. Translated by M. Oglive-Grant. 5 vols. Amsterdam: A. M. Hakkert, 1968–1980.

———. *Studies in 7th-Century Byzantine Political History*. London: Variorum Reprints, 1983.

E. Revival and Reconsolidation (780–1025)

Bury, J. B. *A History of the Eastern Roman Empire from the Fall of Irene to the Accession of Basil I (A.D. 802–867)*. London: Macmillan, 1912.

Morris, R. *Monks and Laymen in Byzantium, 843–1118*. Cambridge: Cambridge University Press, 1995.

Niavis, P. E. *The Reign of the Byzantine Emperor Nicephorus I*. Athens: Historical Publications St. D. Basilopoulos, 1987.

Runciman, S. *The Emperor Romanus Lecapenus and His Reign: A Study of 10th-Century Byzantium*. Cambridge: Cambridge University Press, 1929. (Reprinted Cambridge: Cambridge University Press, 1988.)

Tougher, S. *The Reign of Leo VI (886–912). Politics and People*. Leiden: Brill, 1997.

Toynbee, A. *Constantine Porphyrogenitus and His World*. London: Oxford University Press, 1973.

Treadgold, W. *The Byzantine Revival, 780–842*. Stanford, Calif.: Stanford University Press, 1988.

F. The Eleventh Century (1025–1095)

Angold, Michael. *The Byzantine Empire, 1025–1204: A Political History*. 2nd ed. London: Longman, 1997.

Friendly, A. *The Dreadful Day. The Battle of Mantzikert, 1071*. London: Hutchinson, 1981.

Herrin, J. "The Collapse of the Byzantine Empire in the Twelfth Century: A Study of Medieval Economy." *University of Birmingham Historical Journal* 12 (1970): 188–203.

Kazhdan, A. P. and A. Wharton Epstein. *Change in Byzantine Culture in the Eleventh and Twelfth Centuries*. Berkeley: University of California Press, 1985.

Morris, R. *Monks and Laymen in Byzantium, 843–1118*. Cambridge: Cambridge University Press, 1995.

G. The Twelfth Century (1095–1204)

Angold, Michael. *The Byzantine Empire, 1025–1204: A Political History*. 2nd ed. London: Longman, 1997.

Brand, C. *Byzantium Confronts the West, 1180–1204*. Cambridge, Mass.: Harvard University Press, 1968.

———. "The Fourth Crusade: Some Recent Interpretations," *Medievalia et humanistica* 12 (1984): 33–45.

Chalandon, F. Les Comnènes. *Etudes sur l'Empire byzantin aux XIe at XIIe siècles,* Vol. I: *Essai sur le règne d'Alexis 1er Comnène (1081–1118);* Vol. II: *Jean II Comnène (1118–1143) et Manuel I Comnène (1143–1180).* (The Komnenoi. Studies on the Byzantine Empire in the 11th and 12th centuries. Vol. I: Essay on the reign of Alexius 1st Komnenos [1081–1118]; Vol. II: John II Komnenos [1118–1143] and Manuel I Komnenos [1143–1180].) Paris: A. Picard et fils, 1900–1912.

Godfrey, J. *The Unholy Crusade*. Oxford: Oxford University Press, 1980.

Jurewicz, O. *Andronikos I. Komnenos*. Amsterdam: A. M. Hakkert, 1970.

Kazhdan, A. P. and A. Wharton Epstein. *Change in Byzantine Culture in the Eleventh and Twelfth Centuries*. Berkeley: University of California Press, 1985.

Magdalino, P. *The Empire of Manuel I Komnenos, 1143–1180*. Cambridge: Cambridge University Press, 1993.

Meyer, H. *The Crusades*. Translated by Gillingham, J. 2nd ed. Oxford: Oxford University Press, 1988.`

Morris, R. *Monks and Laymen in Byzantium, 843–1118*. Cambridge: Cambridge University Press, 1995.

Mullet, M. E. and D. Smythe. (eds.) *Alexios I Komnenos*. Belfast: Belfast Byzantine Enterprises, The Queen's University of Belfast, 1996.

Queller, D. and T. F. Madden. *The Fourth Crusade: The Conquest of Constantinople, 1201–1204*. 2nd rev. ed. Philadelphia: University of Pennsylvania Press, 1997.

Runciman, S. *A History of the Crusades*. Cambridge: Cambridge University Press, 1951–1954.

H. The Latin Empire; Byzantine States in Exile (1204–1261)

Angold, M. *A Byzantine Government in Exile: Government and Society under the Laskarids of Nicaea (1204–1261)*. Oxford: Oxford University Press, 1975.

Gardner, A. *The Lascarids of Nicaea: The Story of an Empire in Exile*. London: Methuen, 1912.

Geanakoplos, D. J. *Emperor Michael Palaeologus and the West, 1258–1282: A Study in Byzantine-Latin Relations*. Cambridge, Mass.: Harvard University Press, 1959

Jacoby, D. *Société et démographie à Byzance et en Romanie latine*. (Society and demography in Byzantium and in Latin Romania.) London: Variorum, 1975.

Kazhdan, A. P. and A. Wharton Epstein. *Change in Byzantine Culture in the Eleventh and Twelfth Centuries*. Berkeley: University of California Press, 1985.

Longnon, J. *L'empire latin de Constantinople et la principauté de Morée*. (The Latin Empire of Constantinople and the Principality of Morea.) Paris: Payot, 1949.

Miller, W. *Trebizond: The Last Greek Empire*. London: Society for Promoting Christian Knowledge, 1926. (Reprinted Amsterdam: A. M. Hakkert, 1968.)

Nicol, D. M. *The Despotate of Epiros, 1267–1479: A Contribution to the History of Greece in the Middle Ages*. New York: Cambridge University Press, 1984.

Wolff, R. L. *Studies in the Latin Empire of Constantinople.* London: Variorum, 1976.

I. Restoration, Decline, and Ottoman Conquest (1261–1453)

Babinger, F. *Mehmed the Conqueror and His Time.* Translated by R. Manheim. Princeton: Princeton University Press, 1978.

Barker, John. *Manuel II Palaeologus (1391–1425): A Study in Late Byzantine Statesmanship.* New Brunswick: Rutgers University Press, 1969.

Geanakoplos, D. J. *Emperor Michael Palaeologus and the West, 1258–1282: A Study in Byzantine-Latin Relations.* Cambridge, Mass.: Harvard University Press, 1959.

Imber, C. *The Ottoman Empire, 1300–1481.* Istanbul: Isis Press, 1990.

Laiou, A. E. *Constantinople and the Latins: The Foreign Policy of Andronicus II, 1282–1328.* Cambridge, Mass.: Harvard University Press, 1972.

Miller, W. *Trebizond: The Last Greek Empire.* London: Society for Promoting Christian Knowledge, 1926. (Reprinted Amsterdam: A. M. Hakkert, 1968.)

Nicol, D. M. *The Last Centuries of Byzantium, 1261–1453.* 2nd ed. Cambridge, Mass.: Cambridge University Press, 1993.

———. *The Immortal Emperor: The Life and Legend of Constantine Palaiologos, Last Emperor of the Romans.* Cambridge: Cambridge University Press, 1992.

———. *The Despotate of Epiros, 1267–1479: A Contribution to the History of Greece in the Middle Ages.* Cambridge: Cambridge University Press, 1984.

Runciman, S. *Mistra: Byzantine Capital of the Peloponnese.* London: Thames and Hudson, 1980.

———. *The Fall of Constantinople, 1453.* Cambridge, Mass.: Cambridge University Press, 1965.

———. *The Sicilian Vespers.* Cambridge, Mass.: Cambridge University Press, 1958.

Setton, K. M. *Catalan Domination of Athens, 1311–1388.* Revised ed. London: Variorum, 1975.

Ševčenko, I. "The Decline of Byzantium as Seen through the Eyes of Its Intellectuals." *Dumbarton Oaks Papers* 15 (1966): 167–186.

VI. CHURCH HISTORY AND THEOLOGY

A. Surveys, Reference Works

Beck, H. G. *Kirche und theologische Literatur im byzantinischen Reich.* (Church and theological literature in the Byzantine Empire.) 2nd ed. Munich: Beck, 1977.

Cross, F. I. (ed.) *Oxford Dictionary of the Christian Church.* 3rd ed. Oxford: Oxford University Press, 1997.

Geanakoplos, D. J. *A Short History of the Ecumenical Patriarchate of Constantinople (330–1990): "First Among Equals" in the Eastern Orthodox Church.* Brookline, Mass.: Holy Cross Orthodox Press, 1990.

Hamilton, J. and B. *Christian Dualist Heresies in the Byzantine World, c. 650–c. 1450.* Translated by Y. Stoyanov. Manchester: Manchester University Press, 1998.

Hussey, J. M. *The Orthodox Church in the Byzantine Empire.* Oxford: Clarendon Press, 1986.

Janin, R. *La géographie ecclésiastique de l'Empire byzantin: Les églises et les monastères des grands centres byzantins.* (The ecclesiastical geography of the Byzantine Empire: The churches and the monasteries of the great Byzantine centers.) Paris: Institut français d'études byzantines, 1975.

Meyendorff, J. *Byzantine Theology: Historical Trends and Doctrinal Themes.* 2nd ed. New York: Fordham University Press, 1987.

Prokurat, M., A. Golitzin, and M. D. Peterson. *Historical Dictionary of the Orthodox Church.* Lanham, Md.: Scarecrow Press, 1996.

Runciman, S. *The Byzantine Theocracy.* Cambridge: Cambridge University Press, 1977.

Young, F. M. *From Nicaea to Chalcedon: A Guide to the Literature and Its Background.* Philadelphia: Fortress Press, 1983.

B. Late Antiquity: 4th–7th Centuries

Brown, P. *Augustine of Hippo.* Berkeley: University of California Press, 1967.

Charanis, P. *Church and State in the Later Roman Empire: The Religious Policy of Anastasius the First, 491–518.* Thessalonike: Kentron Vyzantinon Ereunon, 1974.

Frend, W. H. C. *The Rise of the Monophysite Movement: Chapters in the History of the Church in the Fifth and Sixth Centuries.* Cambridge: Cambridge University Press, 1972.

Geffcken, J. *The Last Days of Greco-Roman Paganism.* Translated by S. MacCormack. Amsterdam: North Holland, 1978.

Gregg, R. and D. Groh. *Early Arianism. A View of Salvation.* Philadelphia: Fortress Press, 1981.

Kelly, J. N. D. *Golden Mouth: The Story of John Chrysostom.* Ithaca, N.Y.: Cornell University Press, 1995.

————. *The Athanasian Creed.* New York: Harper and Row, 1964.

————. *Early Christian Doctrines.* London: A. and C. Black, 1960.

Lane Fox, R. *Pagans and Christians.* New York: Knopf, 1987.

Lieu, S. N. C. *Manichaeism in the Later Roman Emipre and Medieval China.* 2nd ed. Tübingen: J. C. B. Mohr (P. Siebeck), 1992.

MacMullen, R. *Christianizing the Roman Empire, A.D. 100–400.* New Haven: Yale University Press, 1984.

McLynn, N. *Ambrose of Milan: Church and Court in a Christian Capital.* Berkeley: University of California Press, 1994.

Momigliano, A. (ed.) *The Conflict Between Paganism and Christianity.* Oxford: Clarendon Press, 1963.

Noble, T. F. X. *The Republic of St. Peter: The Birth of the Papal State, 680–825.* Philadelphia: University of Pennsylvania Press, 1984.

Pearson, B. and J. Goehring. (eds.) *The Roots of Egyptian Christianity.* Philadelphia: Fortress Press, 1986.

Peilkan, J. *Christianity and Classical Culture: The Metamorphosis of Natural Theology in the Christian Encounter with Hellenism.* New Haven: Yale University Press, 1993.

Trombley, F. *Hellenic Religion and Christianization, c. 370–529.* 2 vols. Leiden: E. J. Brill, 1993–1994.

Williams, R. (ed.) *The Making of Orthodoxy.* Cambridge: Cambridge University Press, 1989.

C. Iconoclastic Period: 726–843

Alexander, P. J. *The Patriarch Nicephorus of Constantinople: Ecclesiastical Policy and Image Worship in the Byzantine Empire.* Oxford: Clarendon Press, 1958.

Bryer, Anthony and Judith Herrin. (eds.) *Iconoclasm.* Ninth Spring Symposium of Byzantine Studies, University of Birmingham. Birmingham: Centre for Byzantine Studies, 1977.

Gero, S. *Byzantine Iconoclasm during the Reign of Leo III, with Particular Attention to the Oriental Sources.* (Corpus Scriptorum Christianorum Orientalium, Vol. 346, Subsidia Tomus 41.) Louvain: Secrétariat du Corpus SCO, 1973.

————. *Byzantine Iconoclasm during the Reign of Constantine V, with Particular Attention to the Oriental Sources.* (Corpus Scriptorum Christianorum Orientalium, Vol. 384, Subsidia Tomus 52.) Louvain: Secrétariat du Corpus SCO, 1977.

Martin, E. J. *A History of the Iconoclastic Controversy*. London: Society for Promoting Christian Knowledge, 1930.

D. 843 to the Reconquest of Constantinople (1261)

Angold, M. J. *Church and Society in Byzantium under the Comneni, 1081–1261*. Cambridge: Cambridge University Press, 1995.

Clucas, L. *The Trial of John Italos and the Crisis of Intellectual Values in the Eleventh Century*. Miscellanea Byzantinina Monacensia, Heft 26. Munich: Institut für Byzantinistik, Neugriechische Philologie und Byzantinische Kunstgeschichte der Universität, 1981.

Dvornik, F. *The Photian Schism: History and Legend*. Cambridge: Cambridge University Press, 1948.

Garsoïan, N. G. *The Paulician Heresy*. The Hague: Mouton, 1967.

Hussey, J. *Church and Learning in the Byzantine Empire, 867–1185*. London: Oxford University Press, 1937.

Krivocheine, B. *In the Light of Christ. St. Symeon the New Theologian (949–1022): Life, Spirituality, Doctrine*. Translated by A. P. Gythiel. Crestwood, N.Y.: St. Vladimir's Seminary Press, 1986.

Mullet, M. *Theophylact of Ochrid. Reading the Letters of a Byzantine Archbishop*. Aldershot: Ashgate, 1997.

Obolensky, D. *The Bogomils: A Study in Balkan Neo-Manichaeism*. Cambridge: Cambridge University Press, 1948.

Runciman, S. *The Eastern Schism: A Study of the Papacy and the Eastern Churches during the 11th and 12th Centuries*. Oxford: Clarendon Press, 1955.

———. *The Medieval Manichee: A Study of the Christian Dualist Heresy*. Cambridge: Cambridge University Press 1947. (Reprinted New York: Cambridge University Press, 1982.)

Smith III, M. H. *And Taking Bread: Cerularius and the Azyme Controversy of 1054*. Paris: Beauchesne, 1978.

Tougher, S. *The Reign of Leo VI (886–912): Politics and People*. Leiden: Brill, 1997.

E. Palaiologan Period: 1261–1453

Gill, J. *The Council of Florence*. Cambridge, Mass.: Cambridge University Press, 1959.

———. *Personalities of the Council of Florence*. Oxford: B. Blackwell, 1964.

Meyendorff, J. *A Study of Gregory Palamas*. Translated by G. Lawrence. London: Faith Press, 1964.

Nicol, D. *Byzantium: Its Ecclesiastical History and Relations with the Western World*. Collected Studies. London: Variorum Reprints, 1972.

Papadakis, A. *Crisis in Byzantium: The Filioque Controversy in the Patriarchate of Gregory II of Cyprus (1283–1289)*. New York: Fordham University Press, 1983.

Runciman, S. *The Great Church in Captivity*. London: Cambridge University Press, 1968.

Setton, K. *The Papacy in the Levant, 1204–1571*. 4 vols. Philadelphia: American Philosophical Society, 1976–1984.

F. Liturgy

Taft, R. F. *Beyond East and West: Problems in Liturgical Understanding*. 2nd ed. Rome: Pontifical Oriental Institute, 1997.

———. *Liturgy in Byzantium and Beyond*. Aldershot: Variorum, 1995.

———. *The Byzantine Rite: A Short History*. Collegeville, Minn.: Liturgical Press, 1992.

Walter, C. *Art and Ritual of the Byzantine Church*. London: Variorum, 1982.

VII. CIVILIZATION

A. Surveys, Introductions

Baynes, N. H. and H. St. L. B. Moss. (eds.) *Byzantium: An Introduction to East Roman Civilization*. Oxford: Clarendon Press, 1948.

Geanakoplos, D. J. *Medieval Western Civilization and the Byzantine and Islamic Worlds: Interaction of Three Cultures*. Lexington, Mass.: D. C. Heath, 1979.

Guillou, A. *La civilisation byzantine*. (Byzantine civilization.) Paris: Arthand, 1974.

Haussig, H. W. *A History of Byzantine Civilization*. Translated by J. M. Hussey. London: Thames and Hudson, 1971.

Kazhdan, A. and G. Constable. *People and Power in Byzantium*. Washington, D.C.: Dumbarton Oaks Center for Byzantine Studies, 1982.

Kazhdan, A. and A. W. Epstein. *Change in Byzantine Culture in the Eleventh and Twelfth Centuries*. Berkeley: University of California Press, 1985.

Kashdan, A., et al. (eds.) *Oxford Dictionary of Byzantium*. 3 vols. New York: Oxford University Press, 1991.

Laiou, A. E. and H. Maguire. (eds.) *Byzantium: A World Civilization*. Washington, D.C.: Dumbarton Oaks Research Library and Collection, 1992.

Magdalino, P. *Tradition and Transformation in Medieval Byzantium.* Aldershot: Variorum, 1991.

Maguire, H. (ed.) *Byzantine Court Culture from 829 to 1204.* Washington, D.C.: Dumbarton Oaks Research Library and Collection, 1997.

Runciman, S. *Byzantine Civilization.* New York: Longmans, Green and Co., 1933.

Wharton, J. A. *Art of Empire: Painting and Architecture of the Byzantine Periphery. A Comparative Study of Four Provinces.* University Park: Pennsylvania State University Press, 1988.

B. Architecture

Andrews, K. *Castles of the Morea.* Princeton: American School of Classical Studies at Athens, 1953.

Bouras, Ch. *Nea Moni on Chios: History and Architecture.* Translated by D. A. Hardy. Athens: Commercial Bank of Greece, 1982.

Ćurčić, S. Gračanica. *King Milutin's Church and Its Place in Late Byzantine Architecture.* University Park: Pennsylvania State University Press, 1979.

Deichmann, F. W. *Ravenna, Haupstadt der spätantiken Abendlandes.* (Ravenna, capital of the late antique west.) 3 vols. in 5 parts. Wiesbaden: F. Steiner, 1969–1989.

Demus, O. *The Church of San Marco in Venice: History, Architecture, Sculpture.* Washington, D.C.: Dumbarton Oaks Research Library and Collection, 1960.

Edwards, R. *The Fortifications of Armenian Cilicia.* Washington, D.C.: Dumbarton Oaks Research Library and Collection, 1987.

Foss, C. and D. Winfield. *Byzantine Fortifications: An Introduction.* Pretoria: University of South Africa, 1986.

Gregory, T. *Isthmia. V. The Hexamilion and the Byzantine Fortress.* Princeton: American School of Classical Studies at Athens, 1993.

Harrison, R. M. *A Temple for Byzantium: The Discovery and Excavation of Anicia Juiliana's Palace-Church in Istanbul.* Austin: University of Texas Press, 1989.

Hill, S. *The Early Byzantine Churches of Cilicia and Isauria.* Aldershot: Variorum, 1996.

Kähler, H. and C. Mango. *Die Hagia Sophia.* Berlin: G. Mann Verlag, 1967. Translated by E. Childs. London: A. Zwemmer, 1967.

Kleinbauer, W. E. *Early Christian and Byzantine Architecture: An Annotated Bibliography and Historiography.* Boston: G. K. Hall, 1992.

Krautheimer, R. and S. Ćurčić. *Early Christian and Byzantine Architecture.* 4th ed. Harmondsworth: Penguin, 1986.

Kuniholm, P. I. and C. L. Striker. *Dendrochronology and the Architectural History of the Church of the Holy Apostles in Thessaloniki.* Munich: Deutscher Kunstverlag, 1990.

Mainstone, R. J. *Hagia Sophia: Architecture, Structure and Liturgy of Justinian's Great Church.* New York: Thames and Hudson, 1988.

Mango, C. *Haghia Sophia: A Vision for Empires.* Istanbul: Ertug and Kocabiyik, 1997.

————. *Byzantine Architecture.* New York: H. N. Abrams, 1976.

————. *The Brazen House: A Study of the Vestibule of the Imperial Palace of Constantinople.* Copenhagen: I kommission hos Munksgaard, 1959.

————. *Materials for the Study of St. Sophia at Istanbul.* Washington, D.C.: Dumbarton Oaks Research Library and Collection, 1962.

Mark, R. and A. S. Cakmak. (eds.) *Hagia Sophia from the Age of Justinian to the Present.* Cambridge: Cambridge University Press, 1994.

Mathews, T. F. *The Byzantine Churches of Istanbul: A Photographic Survey.* University Park: Pennsylvania State University Press, 1976.

————. *The Early Churches of Constantinople: Architecture and Liturgy.* University Park: Pennsylvania State University Press, 1971.

Ousterhout, R. G. *The Architecture of the Kariye Camii in Istanbul.* Washington, D.C.: Dumbarton Oaks Research Library and Collection, 1987.

————. *The Myrelaion (Bodrum Camii) in Istanbul; with an appendix of the excavated pottery by John W. Hayes.* Princeton: Princeton University Press, 1981.

————. *The Architecture of the Kariye Camii in Istanbul.* Washington, D.C.: Dumbarton Oaks Research Library and Collection, 1987.

Pringle, D. *The Defense of Byzantine Africa from Justinian to the Arab Conquest.* 2 vols. Oxford: British Archaeological Reports, 1981.

Rodley, L. *Byzantine Art and Architecture, An Introduction.* Cambridge: Cambridge University Press, 1994.

————. *Cave Monasteries of Byzantine Cappadocia.* Cambridge: Cambridge University Press, 1985.

Scranton, R. L. *Mediaeval Architecture in the Central Area of Corinth.* Princeton: American School of Classical Studies at Athens, 1957.

Striker, C. L. and Y. D. Kuban. (eds.) *Kalenderhane in Istanbul. The Buildings, Their History and Architecture and Decoration. Final Reports on the Archaeological Exploration and Restoration at Kalenderhane Camii.* Mainz: Verlag Philipp von Zabern, 1997.

Underwood, P. A. *The Kariye Djami.* 4 vols. New York: Bollingen Foundation and Princeton University Press, 1966–1975.

Van Nice, R. L. *Saint Sophia in Istanbul: An Architectural Survey.* 2 Installments. Washington, D.C.: Dumbarton Oaks Center for Byzantine Studies, 1965–1986.

446 • Civilization

C. Art

1. Surveys

Beckwith, J. *Early Christian and Byzantine Art.* 2nd ed. New York: Penguin Books, 1970.

Buchthal, H. *Art of the Mediterranean World, AD 100 to 1400.* Washington, D.C.: Decatur House Press, 1983.

Demus, O. *Byzantine Art and the West.* New York: New York University Press, 1970.

Evans, H. C. and W. D. Wixom. (eds.) *The Glory of Byzantium. Art and Culture of the Middle Byzantine Era, A.D. 843–1261.* (Catalogue accompanying an exhibition at the Metropolitan Museum of Art from 11 March through 6 July 1997.) New York: Metropolitan Museum of Art, 1997.

Kitzinger, E. *Byzantine Art in the Making: Main Lines of Stylistic Development in Mediterranean Art, 3rd–7th Century.* Cambridge, Mass.: Harvard University Press, 1977.

———. *The Art of Byzantium and the Medieval West: Selected Studies.* Edited by W. E. Kleinbauer. Bloomington: Indiana University Press, 1976.

Lowden, J. *Early Christian and Byzantine Art.* London: Phaidon, 1997.

Mango, C. *The Art of the Byzantine Empire, 312–1453.* Sources and Documents. Englewood Cliffs: Prentice-Hall, 1972. (Reprinted Toronto: University of Toronto Press, in association with the Medieval Academy of America, 1986.)

Mathews, T. F. *The Art of Byzantium: Between Antiquity and the Renaissance.* London: Weidenfeld and Nicolson, 1998.

———. *The Clash of Gods: A Reinterpretation of Early Christian Art.* Princeton: Princeton University Press, 1993.

Milburn, R. *Early Christian Art and Architecture.* Berkeley: University of California Press, 1988.

Rice, D. T. *The Appreciation of Byzantine Art.* London: Oxford University Press, 1972.

———. *Byzantine Art.* Rev. ed. Harmondsworth: Penguin, 1968.

———. *The Art of Byzantium.* London: Thames and Hudson, 1959.

Rodley, L. *Byzantine Art and Architecture, An Introduction.* Cambridge: Cambridge University Press, 1994.

Volbach, W. F. *Early Christian Art.* Translated by C. Lygota. New York: Abrams, 1962.

Weitzmann, K. (ed.) *The Age of Spirituality.* Exhibition Catalog. New York: Metropolitan Museum of Art, 1979.

2. Specific Topics

a. Jewelry, Enamels, Glass

Ross, M. C. *Catalogue of the Byzantine and Early Medieval Antiquities in the Dumbarton Oaks Collection.* 2 vols: Vol. 1: *Metalwork, Ceramics, Glass, Glyptics, Painting.* Washington, D.C.: Dumbarton Oaks Research Library and Collection, 1962.

Weitzmann, K. *Catalogue of the Byzantine and Early Medieval Antiquities in the Dumbarton Oaks Collection.* Vol. 2: *Jewelry, Enamels, and Art of the Migration Period.* Washington, D.C.: Dumbarton Oaks Research Library and Collection, 1972.

Wessel, K. *Byzantine Enamels from the 5th to the 13th Century.* Translated by I. R. Gibbons. Greenwich, Conn: New York Graphic Society, 1967.

b. Icons

Cormack, R. *Writing in Gold: Byzantine Society and Its Icons.* London: George Philip, 1985.

Grabar, A. *Christian Iconography: A Study of Its Origins.* Princeton: Princeton University Press, 1968.

Kitzinger, E. "The Cult of Images in the Age before Iconoclasm." *Dumbarton Oaks Papers* 8 (1954): 83–150.

Maguire, H. *The Icons of Their Bodies: Saints and Their Images in Byzantium.* Princeton: Princeton University Press, 1986.

Ousterhout, R. and L. Brubaker. (eds.) *The Sacred Image East and West.* Urbana: University of Illinois Press, 1995.

Pelikan, J. *Imago Dei: The Byzantine Apologia for Icons.* Princeton: University Press, 1990.

Weitzmann, K. *Studies in the Arts at Sinai.* Princeton: Princeton University Press, 1982.

———. *Byzantine Book Illumination and Ivories.* London: Variorum Reprints, 1980.

———. *The Icon: Holy Images, Sixth to Fourteenth Centuries.* New York: G. Braziller, 1978.

———. *The Monastery of Saint Catherine at Mount Sinai: The Icons.* Vol. 1: *From the Sixth to the Tenth Century.* Princeton: Princeton University Press, 1976.

Vikan, G. (ed.) *Icon.* Washington, D.C.: Trust for Museum Exhibitions; and Baltimore: Walters Art Gallery, 1988.

c. Ivory

Cutler, A. *Late Antique and Byzantine Ivory Carving*. Aldershot: Variorum, 1998.

————. *The Hand of the Master: Craftsmanship, Ivory and Society in Byzantium (9th–11th Centuries)*. Princeton: Princeton University Press, 1994.

————. *The Craft of Ivory: Sources, Techniques, and Uses in the Mediterranean World, A.D. 200–400*. Washington, D.C.: Dumbarton Oaks Research Library and Collection, 1985.

Weitzmann, K. *Catalogue of the Greek and Roman Antiquities in the Dumbarton Oaks Collection*. Vol. 3: *Ivories and Steatites*. Washington, D.C.: Dumbarton Oaks Research Library and Collection, 1972.

d. Manuscript Illuminations

Anderson, J., P. Canart and C. Walter. *The Barberini Psalter: Codex Vaticanus Barberinianus Graecus 372*. Zurich: Belser, 1989.

Buchthal, H. and H. Belting. *Patronage in Thirteenth-Century Constantinople: An Atelier of Late Byzantine Book Illumination and Calligraphy*. Washington, D.C.: Dumbarton Oaks Center for Byzantine Studies, 1978.

Carr, A. W. *Byzantine Illumination, 1150–1250: The Study of a Provincial Tradition*. Chicago: University of Chicago Press, 1987.

Corrigan, K. *Visual Polemics in the Ninth Century Byzantine Psalters*. Cambridge: Cambridge University Press, 1992.

Cutler, A. *The Aristocratic Psalters in Byzantium*. Paris: Picard, 1984.

Galavaris, G. *The Illustrations of the Liturgical Homilies of Gregory Nazianzenus*. Princeton: Princeton University Press, 1969.

Lowden, J. *Illuminated Prophet Books: A Study of Byzantine Manuscripts of the Major and Minor Prophets*. University Park: Pennsylvania State University Press, 1988.

————. *The Octateuchs: A Study in Byzantine Manuscript Illustration*. University Park: Pennsylvania State University Press, 1992.

Nersessian, S. der. and S. Agmian. *Miniature Painting in the Armenian Kingdom of Cilicia*. Washington, D.C.: Dumbarton Oaks Research Library and Collection, 1993.

Pelekanides, S. M., P. C. Christou, C. Tsioumis, and S. N. Kadas. *The Treasures of Mount Athos: Illuminated Manuscripts, Miniatures, Headpieces, Initial Letters*. Translated by P. Sherrard. 4 vols. Athens: Ekdotike Athenon, 1974–1991.

Ševčenko, N. P. *Illustrated Manuscripts of the Metaphrastian Menologion*. Chicago: University of Chicago Press, 1990.

Spatharakis, I. *The Portrait in Byzantine Illuminated Manuscripts*. Leiden: E. J. Brill, 1976.

―――. *Corpus of Dated Illuminated Greek Manuscripts to the Year 1453*. 2 vols. Leiden: E. J. Brill, 1981.

Weitzmann, K. *The Joshua Roll: A Work of the Macedonian Renaissance*. Princeton: Princeton University Press, 1948.

―――. *Studies in Classical and Byzantine Manuscript Illumination*. ed. H. L. Kessler. Chicago: University of Chicago Press, 1971.

―――. *Late Antique and Early Christian Book Illumination*. New York: G. Braziller, 1977.

Weitzmann, K. and G. Galavaris. *The Monastery of Saint Catherine at Mount Sinai: The Illuminated Greek Manuscripts*. Princeton: Princeton University Press, 1990.

Weitzmann, K., W. C. Loerke, E. Kitzinger, and H. Buchtal. *The Place of Book Illumination in Byzantine Art*. Princeton: Art Museum, Princeton University, 1975.

e. Mosaics

Belting, H., C. Mango, and D. Mouriki. *The Mosaics and Fresoes of St. Mary Pammakaristos (Fethiye Camii) at Istanbul*. Washington, D.C.: Dumbarton Oaks Center for Byzantine Studies, 1978.

Borsook, E. *Messages in Mosaic: The Royal Programmes of Norman Sicily, 1130–1187*. Oxford: Clarendon Press, 1990.

Deichmann, F. W. *Ravenna, Haupstadt der spätaniken Abendlandes*. (Ravenna, capital of the late antique west.) 4 vols. Wiesbaden: F. Steiner, 1969–1989.

Demus, O. *The Mosaics of Norman Sicily*. London: Routledge and K. Paul, 1950.

―――. *Byzantine Mosaic Decoration: Aspects of Monumental Art in Byzantium*. London: Routledge and K. Paul, 1950. (Reprinted New Rochelle, N.Y.: Caratzas Brothers, 1976.)

―――. *The Mosaics of San Marco in Venice*. 2 vols. in 4 parts. Chicago: University of Chicago Press, 1984.

Dunbabin, K. M. D. *The Mosaics of Roman North Africa: Studies in Iconography and Patronage*. Oxford: Clarendon Press, 1978.

Mouriki, D. *The Mosaics of the Nea Moni on Chios*. Translated by R. Burgi. 2 vols. Athens: Commercial Bank of Greece, 1985.

f. Museum Catalogs (Collections, Exhibitions)

Buckton, D. (ed.) *The Treasury of San Marco, Venice*. Milan: Olivetti, 1984.

Nesbitt, J. W. and N. Oikonomides. *Catalogue of Byzantine Seals at Dumbarton Oaks and in the Fogg Museum of Art.* 3 vols. Washington, D.C.: Dumbarton Oaks Research Library and Collection, 1991–1996.

Ross, M. C. *Catalogue of the Byzantine and Early Medieval Antiquities in the Dumbarton Oaks Collection.* Vol. 1: *Metalwork, Ceramics, Glass, Glyptics, Painting.* Washington, D.C.: Dumbarton Oaks Research Library and Collection, 1962.

———. *Catalogue of the Byzantine and Early Medieval Antiquities in the Dumbarton Oaks Collection.* Vol. 2: *Jewelry, Enamels, and Art of the Migration Period.* Washington, D.C.: Dumbarton Oaks Research Library and Collection, 1965.

Weitzmann, K. *Catalogue of the Byzantine and Early Medieval Antiquities in the Dumbarton Oaks Collection.* Vol. 3: *Ivories and Steatites.* Washington, D.C.: Dumbarton Oaks Research Library and Collection, 1972.

g. Paintings

Belting, H., C. Mango, and D. Mouriki. *The Mosaics and Frescoes of St. Mary Pammakaristos (Fethiye Camii) at Istanbul.* Washington, D.C.: Dumbarton Oaks Center for Byzantine Studies, 1978.

Epstein, A. W. *Tokali Kilise: Tenth Century Metropolitan Art in Cappadocia.* Washington, D.C.: Dumbarton Oaks Research Library and Collection, 1986.

Kalokyris, K. *The Byzantine Wall Paintings of Crete.* New York: Red Dust, 1973.

Mouriki, D. "Stylistic Trends in Monumental Painting of Greece during the Eleventh and Twelfth Centuries." *Dumbarton Oaks Papers* 34–35 (1980–1981): 77–124.

Rodley, L. *Cave Monasteries of Byzantine Cappadocia.* Cambridge: Cambridge University Press, 1985.

Skawran, K. M. *The Development of Middle Byzantine Fresco Painting in Greece.* Pretoria: University of South Africa, 1982.

Underwood, P. A. *The Kariye Djami.* 4 vols. New York: Bolligen Foundation and Princeton University Press, 1966–1975.

Winfield, D. C. "Middle and Later Byzantine Wall Painting Methods." *Dumbarton Oaks Papers* 22 (1965): 61–139.

h. Silk

Muthesius, A., et al. *Byzantine Silk Weaving: A.D. 400–1200.* Vienna: Fassbaender, 1971.

i. Silver

Boyd, S. A. and M. M. Mango. (eds.) *Ecclesiastical Silver Plate in Sixth-Century Byzantium*. Washington, D.C.: Dumbarton Oaks Research Library and Collection, 1993.
Dodd, E. C. *Byzantine Silver Stamps*. Washington, D.C.: Dumbarton Oaks Research Library and Collection, 1961.
Mango, M. M. and A. Bennett. *The Sevso Treasure*. Ann Arbor: Journal of Roman Archaeology, 1994.
———. *Silver from Early Byzantium: The Kaper Koraon and Related Treasures*. Exhibition Catalog, Walters Art Gallery. Baltimore: Trustees for the Walters Art Gallery, 1986.

j. Miscellaneous

Brubaker, L. *Vision and Meaning in Ninth-Century Byzantium: Image as Exegesis in the Homilies of Gregory of Nazianzus*. New York: Cambridge University Press, 1999
Cutler, A. *Transfigurations: Studies in the Dynamics of Byzantine Iconography*. University Park: Pennsylvania State University Press, 1975.
Grabar, A. *Christian Iconography, A Study of Its Origins*. Translated by T. Grabar. Princeton: Princeton University Press, 1968.
Kartsonis, A. D. *Anastasis: The Making of an Image*. Princeton: Princeton University Press, 1986.
Kominis, A. D. (ed.) *Patmos: Treasures of the Monastery*. Translated by D. A. Hardy. Athens: Ekdotike Athenon, 1988.
Maguire, H. *Art and Eloquence in Byzantium*. Princeton: Princeton University Press, 1981.
———. *Earth and Ocean. The Terrestrial World in Early Byzantine Art*. University Park: Pennsylvania State University Press, 1987.
Manafis, K. A. *Sinai: Treasures of the Monastery of Saint Catherine*. Athens: Ekdotike Athenon, 1990.
Mathew, G. *Byzantine Aesthetics*. London: J. Murray, 1963.
Nersessian, S. der. *Armenian Art*. London: Thames and Hudson, 1977.
Vikan, G. *Byzantine Pilgrimage Art*. Washington, D.C.: Dumbarton Oaks, Trustees of Harvard University, 1982.
Walter, C. *Art and Ritual of the Byzantine Church*. London: Variorum Reprints, 1982.

D. Cultural and Intellectual Life

Browning, R. *Studies on Byzantine History, Literature and Education*. London: Variorum Reprints, 1977.

Cochrane, C. N. *Christianity and Classical Culture*. Oxford: Clarendon Press, 1940.

———. *Byzantine Books and Bookmen: A Dumbarton Oaks Colloquium, 1971*. Washington, D.C.: Dumbarton Oaks Center for Byzantine Studies, 1975.

Hussey, J. M. *Church and Learning in the Byzantine Empire, 867–1185*. London: Oxford University Press, 1937.

———. *Ascetics and Humanists in Eleventh-Century Byzantium*. London: Dr. William's Trust, 1960.

Laistner, M. L. W. *Christianity and Pagan Culture in the Later Roman Empire*. Ithaca, N.Y.: Cornell University Press, 1951.

Lemerle, P. *Byzantine Humanism: The First Phase. Notes and Remarks on Education and Culture in Byzantium from Its Origins to the 10th Century*. Translated by H. Lindsay and A. Moffat. Canberra: Australia Association for Byzantine Studies, 1986.

Mullet, M. E. *Theophylact of Ochrid*. Aldershot: Variorum, 1997.

Mullet, M. and R. Scott. (eds.) *Byzantium and the Classical Tradition*. University of Birmingham Spring Symposium of Byzantine Studies, 1979. Birmingham: Centre for Byzantine Studies, 1981.

Runciman, S. *The Last Byzantine Renaissance*. Cambridge: Cambridge University Press, 1970.

Ševčenko, I. *Byzantium and the Slavs in Letters and Culture*. Cambridge, Mass.: Harvard University Press, 1991.

———. *Ideology, Letters and Culture in the Byzantine World*. London: Variorum, 1982.

———. *Society and Intellectual Life in Late Byzantium*. London: Variorum, 1981.

Wilson, N. G. *Scholars of Byzantium*. Baltimore: Johns Hopkins University Press, 1983.

E. Influence of Byzantium on the Italian Renaissance

Geanakoplos, D. *Interaction of the Sibling Byzantine and Western Cultures in the Middle Ages and the Italian Renaissance*. New Haven: Yale University Press, 1976.

———. *Greek Scholars in Venice. Studies in the Dissemination of Greek Learning from Byzantium to Western Europe*. Cambridge, Mass.: Harvard University Press, 1962.

Kristeller, P. O. *Studies in Renaissance Thought and Letters*. Rome: Edizioni di storia e letteratura, 1969.

Monfasani, J. *Byzantine Scholars in Renaissance Italy: Cardinal Bessarion and Other Emigres*. Aldershot: Ashgate, 1995.

Wilson, N. *From Byzantium to Italy: Greek Studies in the Italian Renaissance*. Baltimore: Johns Hopkins University Press, 1992.

F. Literature

Beaton, R. *The Medieval Greek Romance*. 2nd ed. London: Routledge, 1996.

Beaton, R. and D. Ricks. (eds.) *Digenes Akrites: New Approaches to Byzantine Heroic Poetry*. Aldershot: Variorum, 1993.

Brock, S. P. *The Harp of the Spirit: Eighteen Poems of St. Ephrem*. 2nd ed. London: Fellowship of St. Alban and St. Sergius, 1983.

Browning, R. "Homer in Byzantium." *Viator* 6 (1975): 15–33.

———. *Studies on Byzantine History, Literature and Education*. London: Variorum Reprints, 1977.

———. *Medieval and Modern Greek*. New York: Cambridge University Press, 1983.

Cameron, Alan. *Literature and Society in the Early Byzantine World*. London: Variorum Reprints, 1985.

———. *The Greek Anthology: From Meleager to Planudes*. Oxford: Clarendon Press, 1993.

Cameron, Averil. *Christianity and the Rhetoric of Empire: The Development of Christian Discourse*. Berkeley: University of California Press, 1991.

Croke, B. and A. Emmett. (eds.) *History and Historians in Late Antiquity*. New York: Pergamon, 1983.

Hägg, T. *The Novel in Antiquity*. Revised ed. Oxford: B. Blackwell, 1983.

Jeffreys, E. M. and M. J. Jeffreys. *Popular Literature in Late Byzantium*. London: Variorum, 1983.

Kazhdan, A. and S. Franklin. *Studies on Byzantine Literature of the Eleventh and Twelfth Centuries*. New York: Cambridge University Press, 1984.

Kennedy, G. A. *Greek Rhetoric under Christian Emperors*. Princeton: Princeton University Press, 1983.

Kustas, G. L. *Studies in Byzantine Rhetoric*. Thessalonike: Patriarchikon Hidryma Paterikon Meleton, 1973.

Mango, C. *Byzantine Literature as a Distorting Mirror: An Inaugural Lecture Delivered before the University of Oxford on 21 May 1974*. Oxford: Clarendon Press, 1975.

Paton, W. R. (trans.) *The Greek Anthology*. 5 vols. New York: G. P. Putnam, 1925–1927.

Speck, P. *Understanding Byzantum. Studies in Byzantine Historical Sources*. Aldershot: Variorum, 2000.

Wilson, N. *Scholars of Byzantium*. Baltimore: Johns Hopkins University Press, 1983.

G. Music

Conomos, D. *Byzantine Hymnography and Byzantine Chant*. Brookline, Mass.: Hellenic College Press, 1984.

Strunk, O. *Essays on Music in the Byzantine World*. New York: W. W. Norton, 1977.

Szövérffy, J. in collaboration with E. C. Topping. *A Guide to Byzantine Hymnography*. 2 vols. Brookline, Mass.: Classical Folia Editions; and Leyden: E. J. Brill, 1978–1979.

Wellesz, E. *A History of Byzantine Music and Hymnography*. 2nd ed. Oxford: Clarendon Press, 1961.

———. *The Music of the Byzantine Church*. Cologne: Arno Volk Verlag, 1959.

H. Philosophy

Ahrweiler, H. *L'idéologie politique et l'Empire byzantin*. (Political Ideology and the Byzantine Empire.) Paris: Presses universitaires de France, 1975.

Alexander, P. J. *Religious and Political History and Thought in the Byzantine Empire*. London: Variorum, 1978.

Armstrong, A. H. *The Cambridge History of Later Greek and Early Medieval Philosophy*. Cambridge: Cambridge University Press, 1967.

Barker, E. *Social and Political Thought in Byzantium, from Justinian I to the Last Palaeologus*. Passages from Byzantine Writers and Documents. Oxford: Clarendon Press, 1957.

Wolfson, H. A. *The Philosophy of the Church Fathers*. Cambridge, Mass.: Harvard University Press, 1970.

I. Science

Haskins, C.H. *Studies in the History of Mediaeval Science*. Cambridge, Mass.: Harvard University Press, 1924.

Heath, T. *A History of Greek Mathematics*. 2 vols. Oxford: Clarendon Press, 1921.

O'Leary, De. L. *How Greek Science Passed to the Arabs*. 2nd ed. London: Routledge and K. Paul, 1951.

Patlagean, E. (ed.) *Maladie et sociétè à Byzance* (Disease and society in Byzantium). Spoleto: Centro itlaliano di studi sull'Alto Medioeveo, 1993.

Pingree, D. "Gregory Chioniades and Palaeologan Astronomy." *Dumbarton Oaks Papers* 18 (1964): 133–160.

Scarborough, J. (ed.) *Symposium on Byzantine Medicine.* Dumbarton Oaks Papers, vol. 38. Washington, D.C.: Dumbarton Oaks Research Library and Collection, 1984.

Ševčenko, I. "Remarks on the Diffusion of Byzantine Scientific and Pseudo-scientific Literature among the Orthodox Slavs." *Slavonic and East European Review* 59 (1981): 321–345.

VIII. ECONOMY

A. Surveys

Harvey, A. *Economic Expansion in the Byzantine Empire, 900–1200.* Cambridge: Cambridge University Press, 1989.

Hendy, M. F. *Studies in the Byzantine Monetary Economy c. 300–1450.* Cambridge: Cambridge University Press, 1985.

Kent, J. P. C. and K. S. Painter. *Wealth of the Roman World, A.D. 300–700.* London: British Museum Publications, 1977.

Laiou, A. E. *Gender, Society and Economic Life in Byzantium.* Aldershot: Variorum, 1992.

Lopez, R. S. *Byzantium and the World Around It: Economic and Institutional Relations.* London: Variorum, 1978.

Morrisson, C. and J. Lefort. (eds.) *Hommes et richesses dans l'Empire byzantin I, IVe–VIIe siècle.* (Men and wealth in the Byzantine Empire, 4th–7th centuries.) 2 vols. Paris: P. Lethielleux, 1989–1991.

Patlagean, E. *Pauvreté économique et pauvreté sociale à Byzance, 4e–7e siècles.* (Economic poverty and social poverty in Byzantium, 4th–7th centuries.) Paris: Mouton, 1977.

B. The Rural Economy

Bryer, A. "Byzantine Agricultural Implements: The Evidence of Medieval Illustrations of Hesiod's Works and Days." *Annual of the British School at Athens* 81 (1986): 45–80.

Dunn, A. "The Exploitation and Control of Woodland and Scrubland in the Byzantine World." *Byzantine and Modern Greek Studies* 16 (1992): 235–298.

Kaplan, M. *Les hommes et la terre à Byzance du VIe au XIe siècle.* (Men and land in Byzantium from the 6th to the 11th century.) Paris: Publications de la Sorbonne, 1992.

Laiou, A. *Peasant Society in the Late Byzantine Period: A Social and Demographic Study.* Princeton: Princeton University Press, 1977.

Lemerle, P. *The Agrarian History of Byzantium from the Origins to the Twelfth Century.* Galway: Galway University Press, 1979.

MacMullen, R. "Late Roman Slavery." *Historia* 36 (1987): 359–382.

Teall, J. "The Byzantine Agricultural Tradition." *Dumbarton Oaks Papers* 25 (1971): 35–39.

————. "The Grain Supply of the Byzantine Empire, 330–1025." *Dumbarton Oaks Papers* 13 (1959): 87–139.

C. Coinage

Bellinger, A. R. and P. Grierson. *Catalogue of the Byzantine Coins in the Dumbarton Oaks Collection and in the Whittemore Collection.* 3 vols. Washington, D.C.: Dumbarton Oaks Center for Byzantine Studies, 1966–1973.

Grierson, P. *Catalogue of the Byzantine Coins in the Dumbarton Oaks Collection and in the Whittemore Collection.* Vol. 5: *Michael VIII to Constantine XI, 1258–1453.* Washington, D.C.: Dumbarton Oaks Research Library and Collection, 1999.

————. *Byzantine Coins.* Berkeley: University of California Press, 1982.

Grierson, P. and M. Mays, *Catalogue of Late Roman Coins in the Dumbarton Oaks Collection and in the Whittemore Collection.* Washington, D.C.: Dumbarton Oaks Research Library and Collection, 1992.

Hendy, M. F. *Catalogue of Byzantine Coins in the Dumbarton Oaks Collection and in the Whittemore Collection.* Vol. 4: *Alexius I to Michael VIII, 1081–1261.* Washington, D.C.: Dumbarton Oaks Research Library and Collection, 1999.

————. *The Economy, Fiscal Administration and Coinage of Byzantium.* Northampton: Variorum Reprints, 1989.

————. *Studies in the Byzantine Monetary Economy c. 300–1450.* Cambridge: Cambridge University Press, 1985.

————. *Coinage and Money in the Byzantine Empire, 1081–1261.* Washington, D.C.: Dumbarton Oaks Center for Byzantine Studies, 1969.

D. Commerce

Heyd, W. *Histoire du commerce du Levant au moyen âge.* (History of commerce in the Levant in the Middle Ages.) 2 vols. Leipzig: O. Harrassowitz, 1936. (Reprinted Amsterdam: A. M. Hakkert, 1967.)

Jacoby, D. *Trade, Commodities and Shipping in the Medieval Mediterranean.* Aldershot: Variorum, 1997.

Lopez, R. S. *Byzantium and the World Around It: Economic and Institutional Relations*. Aldershot: Variorum, 1978.

E. Finance

Duncan-Jones, R. *Money and Government in the Roman Empire*. Cambridge: Cambridge University Press, 1994.

King, C. E. (ed.) *Imperial Revenue, Expenditure and Monetary Policy in the Fourth Century A.D.: The Fifth Oxford Symposium on Coinage and Monetary History*. Oxford: British Archaeological Reports, 1980.

Treadgold, W. *The Byzantine State Finances in the Eighth and Ninth Centuries*. New York: Columbia University Press, 1982.

IX. NEIGHBORING PEOPLES AND STATES

A. Arabs

Brooks, E. W. "The Arabs in Asia Minor (641–750), from Arabic Sources." *Journal of Hellenic Studies* 18 (1898): 182–208.

Brooks, E. W. "Byzantines and Arabs in the Time of the Early Abbasids." *English Historical Review* 15 (1900): 728–747; 16 (1901): 84–92.

Cameron, A. and L. L. Conrad. *The Byzantine and Early Islamic Near East*. 3 vols. Princeton: Darwin Press, 1992–1995.

Canard, M. *Histoire de la dynastie des H'amdanides de Jazîra et de Syrie*. (History of the Hamdanid dynasty of Algeria and Jazira.) Alger: J. Carbonel, 1951.

Donner, F. M. *The Early Islamic Conquests*. Princeton: Princeton University Press, 1981.

Honigmann, E. *Die Ostgrenze des byzantinischen Reiches von 363 bis 1071*. (The eastern frontier of the Byzantine Empire from 363 to 1071.)

Kaegi, W. E. *Byzantium and the Early Islamic Conquests*. Cambridge: Cambridge University Press, 1992.

Kennedy, H. *The Early Abbasid Caliphate*. London: Croom Helm, 1981.

Shahîd, I. *Byzantium and the Arabs in the Fourth Century*. Washington, D.C.: Dumbarton Oaks Research Library and Collection, 1984.

———. *Byzantium and the Arabs in the Fifth Century*. Washington, D.C.: Dumbarton Oaks Research Library and Collection, 1989.

———. *Byzantium and the Arabs in the Sixth Century*. 2 vols. Washington, D.C.: Dumbarton Oaks Research Library and Collection, 1995.

Vasiliev, A. A. *Byzance et les Arabes*. (Byzantium and the Arabs), vol. 3. Brussels: Institut de philologie et d'histoire orientales, 1935.

B. Armenia

Boase, T. S. R. (ed.) *The Cilician Kingdom of Armenia.* Edinburgh: Scottish Academic Press, 1978.

Der Nersessian, S. "The Kingdom of Cilician Armenia." In K. M. Setton (ed.) *A History of the Crusades.* Vol. 2. Madison: University of Wisconsin Press, 630–659.

Garsoïan, N. G. *Church and Culture in Early Medieval Armenia.* Aldershot: Variorum, 1999.

————. *Armenia between Byzantium and the Sasanians.* London: Variorum, 1985.

Garsoïan, N. G., T. F. Mathews, and R. W. Thomson. (eds.) *East of Byzantium: Syria and Armenia in the Formative Period.* Washington, D. C.: Dumbarton Oaks Center for Byzantine Studies, 1982.

Grousset, R. *Histoire de l'Arménie: Des origines à 1071.* (History of Armenia: From its origins to 1071.) Paris: Payot, 1947.

Redgate, A. E. *The Armenians.* Oxford: Blackwell, 1998.

C. The Caucasus

Allen, W. E. D. *A History of the Georgian People.* London: K. Paul, Trench, Trubner and Co., 1932.

Toumanoff, C. *Studies in Christian Caucasian History.* Washington, D.C.: Georgetown University Press, 1963.

D. Crusaders

Bon, A. *La Morèe franque.* (The French Morea.) 2 vols. Paris: E. de Boccard, 1969.

Lilie, R.-J. *Byzantium and the Crusader States, 1096–1204.* Translated by J. C. Morris and J. E. Ridings. Oxford: Clarendon Press, 1993.

Lock, P. *The Franks in the Aegean, 1204–1500.* London: Longman, 1995.

Mayer, H. *The Crusades.* Translated by J. Gillingham. London: Oxford University Press, 1972.

Ohnworge, W. *Abendland und Byzanz.* (The West and Byzantium.) Darmstadt: H. Genter, 1958.

Queller, D. E. and T. F. Madden. *The Fourth Crusade: The Conquest of Constantinople.* 2nd rev. ed. Philadelphia: University of Pennsylvania Press, 1997.

Runciman, S. *A History of the Crusades.* 3 vols. Cambridge: Cambridge University Press, 1951–1954.

Setton, K. M. (ed.) *A History of the Crusades.* 2nd ed. 6 vols. Madison: University of Wisconsin Press, 1969–1989.

E. Germanic Peoples

Burns, T. S. *A History of the Ostro-Goths*. Bloomington: Indiana University Press, 1984.
Heather, P. *The Goths*. Oxford: Blackwell, 1996.
———. *Goths and Romans, 332–489*. Oxford: Clarendon Press, 1991.
Thompson, E. A. *The Goths in Spain*. Oxford: Clarendon Press, 1969.
———. *The Visigoths in the Time of Ulfila*. Oxford: Clarendon Press, 1966.
———. *The Early Germans*. Oxford: Clarendon Press, 1965.
Vasiliev, A. A. *The Goths in the Crimea*. Cambridge, Mass.: Mediaeval Academy of America, 1936.
Wolfram, H. *History of the Goths*. Translated by T. J. Dunlap. Berkeley: University of California Press, 1988.

F. Hungary

Makk, F. *The Árpáds and the Comneni: Political Relations between Hungary and Byzantium in the Twelfth Century*. Translated by G. Novák. Budapest: Akadémiai Kiadó, 1989.
Moravcsik, G. "Hungary and Byzantium in the Middle Ages." In *Cambridge Medieval History*, IV, Part 1. Cambridge: Cambridge University Press, 1966.
———. *Byzantium and the Magyars*. Translated by S. R. Rosenbaum. Amsterdam: A. M. Hakkert, 1970.
Urbansky, A.B. *Byzantium and the Danube Frontier: A Study of Relations between Byzantium, Hungary, and the Balkans during the Period of the Comneni*. New York: Twayne Publishers, 1968.

G. Huns

Maenchen-Helfen, J. O. *The World of the Huns*. Berkeley: University of California Press, 1973.
Thompson, E. A. *A History of Attila and the Huns*. Oxford: Clarendon Press, 1948.

H. Italian States

Balard, M. *La mer noire et la Romanie génoise: XIIIe–XVe siècles*. (The Black Sea and Genoese Romania: 13th–15th centuries.) London: Variorum, 1989.
———. *La Romanie génoise: XIIe–début du XVe siècle*. (Genoese Roma-

nia: 13th-beginning of the 15th century.) 2 vols. Rome: École français de Rome, 1978.

Day, G. W. *Genoa's Response to Byzantium, 1155–1204.* Urbana: University of Illinois Press, 1988.

Matthew, D. *The Norman Kingdom of Sicily.* Cambridge: Cambridge University Press, 1992.

Nicol, D. *Byzantium and Venice: A Study in Diplomatic and Cultural Relations.* Cambridge: Cambridge University Press, 1988.

Norwich, J. J. *A History of Venice.* Vol. 1: *The Rise to Empire.* London: Allen Lane, 1977.

I. Principalities in Greece

Bon, A. *La Morèe franque. Recherches historiques, topographiques et archèologique sur la principautè d'Achaie (1205–1430).* (The Frankish Morea. Historical, topographical and archeological research on the Principality of Achaia (1205–1430).) Paris: E. de Boccard, 1969.

———. *Le Péloponnèse byzantine jusqu'en 1204.* (The Byzantine Peloponnesos to 1204.) Paris: Presses universitaires de France, 1951

Hetherington, P. *Byzantine and Medieval Greece: Churches, Castles and Art of the Mainland and Peloponnese.* London: Murray, 1991.

Longnon, J. *L'empire latin de Constantinople et la principauté de Morée.* (The Latin Empire of Constantinople and the Principality of Morea.) Paris: Payot, 1949.

Miller, W. *The Latins in the Levant: A History of Frankish Greece (1204–1566).* London: J. Murray, 1908.

J. Russia

Fedotov, G. P. *The Russian Religious Mind.* 2 vols. Cambridge, Mass.: Harvard University Press, 1946–1966.

Franklin, S. and J. Shepard. *The Emergence of Rus 750–1200.* London: Longman, 1996.

Meyendorff, J. *Byzantium and the Rise of Russia.* A Study of Byzantino-Russian Relations in the Fourteenth Century. Cambridge: Cambridge University Press, 1981.

Poppe, A. *The Rise of Christian Russia.* London: Variorum, 1982.

Thomson, F. J. *The Reception of Byzantine Culture in Medieval Russia.* Aldershot: Ashgate, 1999.

Vasiliev, A. A. "The Second Russian Attack on Constantinople." *Dumbarton Oaks Papers* 6 (1951): 161–225.

———. *The Russian Attack on Constantinople in 860.* Cambridge, Mass.: Mediaeval Academy of America, 1946.

K. Slavs

Browning, R. *Byzantium and Bulgaria*. Berkeley: University of California Press, 1975.

Dvornik, F. *Byzantine Missions among the Slavs: SS. Constantine-Cyril and Methodius*. New Brunswick: Rutgers University Press, 1970.

Fine, John. *The Early Medieval Balkans: A Critical Survey from the Sixth to the Late Twelfth Century*. Ann Arbor: University of Michigan Press, 1983.

————. *The Early Medieval Balkans: A Critical Survey from the Late Twelfth Century to the Ottoman Conquest*. Ann Arbor: University of Michigan Press, 1987.

Hoddinott, R. F. *Bulgaria in Antiquity: An Archaeological Introduction*. London: Ernest Benn, 1975.

Obolensky, D. *The Byzantine Commonwealth: Eastern Europe, 500–1453*. New York: Praeger, 1971.

Runciman, S. *A History of the First Bulgarian Empire*. London: G. Bell and Sons, 1930.

Soulis, G. C. "The Legacy of Cyril and Methodius to the Slavs." *Dumbarton Oaks Papers* 19 (1965): 19–43.

————. *The Serbs and Byzantium during the Reign of Tsar Stephen Dušan (1331–1355) and His Successors*. Washington, D.C.: Dumbarton Oaks Library and Collection, 1984.

Vlasto, A. *The Entry of the Slavs into Christendom*. Cambridge: Cambridge University Press, 1970.

Weithmann, M. W. *Die slavische Bevölkerung auf der griechischen Halbinsel*. (The Slavic population in the Greek peninsula.) (Munich: R. Trofenik, 1978.

L. Turks

Cahen, C. *Pre-Ottoman Turkey*. Translated by J. Jones-Williams. London: Sidgwick and Jackson, 1968.

Imber, C. *The Ottoman Empire, 1300–1481*. Istanbul: Isis Press, 1990.

Kafadar, C. *Between Two Worlds. The Construction of the Ottoman State*. Berkeley: University of California Press, 1995.

Savvides, A. G. C. *Byzantium and the Near East: Its Relations with the Seljuk Sultanate of Rum in Asia Minor, the Armenians of Cilicia and the Mongols, A.D. 1192–1237*. Thessalonike: Kentron Byzantinon Ereunon, 1981.

Vryonis, Jr., S. *The Decline of Medieval Hellenism in Asia Minor and the Process of Islamization from the Eleventh through the Fifteenth Century*. Berkeley: University of California Press, 1971.

M. Miscellaneous

Bachrach, A. *A History of the Alans in the West*. Minneapolis: University of Minnesota Press, 1973.

Baker, D. (ed.) *Relations between East and West in the Middle Ages*. Edinburgh: Edinburgh University Press, 1973.

Barnea, I., O. Iliescu, and C. Nicolescu (eds.) *Cultura Bizantinia in Romania*. (Byzantine culture in Romania.) Bucharest: Comiteutul de Stat pentru Cultura si Arta, 1971.

Davidson, H. R. Ellis. *The Viking Road to Byzantium*. London: G. Allen and Unwin, 1976.

Dunlop, D. M. *The History of the Jewish Khazars*. Princeton: Princeton University Press, 1954.

Hanawalt, E. A. "Scandanavians in Byzantium and Normandy." In Miller, T. S. and J. Nesbitt (eds.). *Peace and War in Byzantium. Essays in Honor of George T. Dennis, S.J.* Washington, D.C.: Catholic University Press of America, 1995, 114–122.

Morgan, D. *The Mongols*. Oxford: B. Blackwell, 1986.

Pollo, S and A. Puto. *The History of Albania: From Its Origin to the Present Day*. Translated by G. Wiseman and G. Hole. London: Routledge and K. Paul, 1981.

Winnifrith, T. J. *The Vlachs: The History of a Balkan People*. New York: St. Martin's Press, 1987.

X. REGIONS

(See also III and IX)

A. Asia Minor

Bryer, A. and D. Winfield. *The Byzantine Monuments and Topography of the Pontos*. 2 vols. Washington, D.C.: Dumbarton Oaks Research Library and Collection, 1985.

Foss, C. *Ephesus after Antiquity: A Late Antique, Byzantine and Turkish City*. Cambridge: Cambridge University Press, 1979.

————. *Byzantine and Turkish Sardis*. Cambridge, Mass.: Harvard University Press, 1976.

Miller, W. *Trebizond: The Last Greek Empire*. London: Society for the Promotion of Christian Knowledge, 1926. (Reprinted Amsterdam: A. M. Hakkert, 1968.)

Mitchell, S. (ed.) *Anatolia: Land, Men, and Gods in Asia Minor*. 2 vols. Oxford: Clarendon Press, 1993.

————. *Armies and Frontiers in Roman and Byzantine Anatolia.* Oxford: British Archaeological Reports, 1983.

Ramsay, W. M. *The Historical Geography of Asia Minor.* London: J. Murray, 1890. (Reprinted Amsterdam: A. M. Hakkert, 1962.)

————. *The Cities and Bishoprics of Phrygia.* 2 vols. Oxford: Clarendon Press, 1895–1897.

————. *The Social Basis of Roman Power in Asia Minor.* Aberdeen: Aberdeen University Press, 1941.

Sinclair, T. A. *Eastern Turkey: An Architectural and Archaeological Survey.* 4 vols. London: Pindar Press, 1987–1990.

Vryonis, S. *The Decline of Medieval Hellenism in Asia Minor and the Process of Islamization from the Eleventh through the Fifteenth Century.* Berkeley: University of California Press, 1971.

B. Balkans, Eastern Europe

Ferugla, J. *Byzantium in the Balkans: Studies on the Byzantine Administration of the Southern Slavs from the VIIth to the XIIth Centuries.* Amsterdam: A. M. Hakkert, 1976

Krivari, V. *Villes et villages de Macédoine occidentale.* (Cities and villages of western Macedonia.) Paris: P. Lethielleux, 1989.

Mócsy, A. *Pannonia and Upper Moesia.* London: Routledge and K. Paul, 1974.

Obolensky, D. *The Byzantine Commonwealth: Eastern Europe, 500–1453.* New York: Weidenfeld and Nicolson, 1971.

Wilkes, J. J. *Dalmatia.* London: Routledge and K. Paul, 1969.

C. Cyprus

Breyer, A. A. M. and G. S. Georghallides. (eds.) *The Sweet Land of Cyprus: Papers Given at the Twenty-Fifth Jubilee Spring Symposium of Byzantine Studies, Birmingham, March 1991.* Nicosia: Cyprus Research Center for the Promotion of Byzantine Studies, 1993.

Cobham, C. D. *Excerpta Cypria: Materials for a History of Cyprus.* Cambridge: Cambridge University Press, 1908.

Galatariotou, C. *The Making of a Saint: The Life, Times and Sanctification of Neophytos the Recluse.* Cambridge: Cambridge University Press, 1991.

Hackett, J. *A History of the Orthodox Church of Cyprus.* London: Methuen, 1901.

Hill, Sir G. *History of Cyprus.* 4 vols. London, Cambridge: Cambridge University Press, 1940–1952.

464 • Regions

Maier, F. G. and V. Karageorghis. *Paphos: History and Archaeology.*
Nicosia: A. G. Leventis Foundation, 1984.
———. *Cyprus from the Earliest Times to the Present Day.* Translated by
P. Gorge. London: Elek Books, 1968.

D. Egypt

Bagnell, R. *Egypt in Late Antiquity.* Princeton: Princeton University Press,
1993.
Hardy, E. R. *The Large Estates of Byzantine Egypt.* New York: Columbia
University Press, 1931.
Lallermand, J. *L'administration civile de l'Égypte de l'avènement de Dio-
clétien à la création du diocèse (284–382).* (The civil administration of
Egypt from the accession of Diocletian to the creation of the diocese.)
Brussels: Palais des Académies, 1964.

E. Greece

Bon, A. *Le Péloponnèse byzantine jusqu'en 1204.* (The Byzantine Pelo-
ponnesos up to 1204.) Paris: Presses universitaires de France, 1951.
Hetherington, P. *Byzantine and Medieval Greece: Churches, Castles, and
Art of the Mainland and the Peloponnese.* London: Murray, 1991.
Miller, W. *The Latins in the Levant: A History of Frankish Greece
(1204–1566).* London: J. Murray, 1908.
Tsougarakis, D. *Byzantine Crete from the Fifth Century to the Venetian
Conquest.* Athens: Historical Publications St. D. Basilopoulos, 1988.

F. Italy and Sicily

Brown, T. S. *Gentlemen and Officers: Imperial Administration and Aristo-
cratic Power in Byzantine Italy, A.D. 554–800.* Rome: British School at
Rome, 1984.
Guillou, A. *Studies on Byzantine Italy.* London: Variorum Reprints, 1970.
Matthew, D. *The Norman Kingdom of Sicily.* Cambridge: Cambridge Uni-
versity Press, 1992.
Runciman, S. *The Sicilian Vespers: A History of the Mediterranean World
in the Later Thirteenth Century.* Cambridge: Cambridge University
Press, 1958. (Reprinted 1992.)
Takayama, H. *The Administration of the Norman Kingdom of Sicily.* Lei-
den: E. J. Brill, 1993.

Wickham, C. *Early Medieval Italy: Central Power and Local Society 400–1000.* Totowa, N.J.: Barnes and Noble, 1981.

Wilson, R. J. A. *Sicily under the Roman Empire: The Archaeology of a Roman Province, 36 BC–AD 535.* Warminster: Aris and Phillips, 1990.

Wolf, K. B. *Making History: The Normans and Their Historians in Eleventh-Century Italy.* Philadelphia: Pennsylvania University Press, 1995.

G. Palestine and Syria

Downey, G. *A History of Antioch in Syria from Seleucus to the Arab Conquest.* Princeton: Princeton University Press, 1961.

Glucker, A. M. *The City of Gaza in the Roman and Byzantine Periods.* Osney Mead, Oxford: British Archaeological Reports, 1987.

Hirschfeld, Y. *The Judean Desert Monasteries in the Byzantine Period.* New Haven: Yale University Press, 1992.

Shereshevski, J. *Byzantine Urban Settlements in the Negev Desert.* Beersheba: Ben-Gurion University of the Negev Press, 1991.

Tchalenko, G. *Villages antiques de la Syrie du Nord: Le massif du Bélus à l'époque romaine.* (Ancient villages of north Syria: The massif of Belus in the Roman epoch.) 3 vols. Paris: P. Geuthner, 1953–1958.

H. Other Regional Studies

Dodgeon, M. H. and S. C. N. Lieu. *The Roman Frontier and the Persian Wars AD 226–363.* London: Routledge, 1991.

Johnson, S. *Later Roman Britain.* New York: Scribner, 1980.

Kennedy, D. and D. Riley. *Rome's Desert Frontier from the Air.* London: Batsford, 1990.

Lightfoot, C. S. *The Eastern Frontier of the Roman Empire.* 2 vols. Osney Mead, Oxford: British Archaeological Reports, 1989.

Malamut, Elisabeth. *Les îles de l'empire byzantine, VIIIe–XIIe siècles.* (The islands of the Byzantine Empire, 8th–12th centuries.) 2 vols. Paris: Publications de la Sorbonne, 1988.

Parker, S. T. *Romans and Saracens: A History of the Arabian Frontier.* Philadelphia: American Schools of Oriental Research, 1985.

Pringle, D. *The Defence of Byzantine Africa from Justinian to the Arab Conquest.* 2 vols. Oxford: British Institute of Archaeology, 1981.

Todd, M. *Roman Britain 55 BC–AD 400.* London: Fontana Press, 1981.

XI. SOCIETY

A. Aristocracy

Angold, Michael (ed.) *The Byzantine Aristocracy: IX to XIII Centuries.* Osney Mead, Oxford: British Archaeological Reports, 1984.

Arnheim, M. T. W. *The Senatorial Aristocracy in the Later Roman Empire.* Oxford: Clarendon Press, 1972.

Matthews, J. *Western Aristocracies and Imperial Court A.D. 364–425.* Oxford: Oxford University Press, 1975. (Reprinted 1990.)

Nicol, D. *The Byzantine Family of Kantakouzenos (Cantacuzenus), ca. 1100–1460.* Washington, D.C.: Dumbarton Oaks Center for Byzantine Studies, 1968.

B. Cities

Cameron, Alan. *Circus Factions: Blues and Greens at Rome and Byzantium.* Oxford: Clarendon Press, 1976.

Downey, G. *A History of Antioch in Syria from Seleucus to the Arab Conquest.* Princeton: Princeton University Press, 1961.

Erim, K. *Aphrodisias, City of Venus Aphrodite.* London: Muller, Blond and White, 1986.

Foss, C. *Cities, Fortresses, and Villages of Byzantine Asia Minor.* Aldershot: Variorum, 1996.

————. *Nicaea: A Byzantine Capital and Its Praises.* Brookline, Mass.: Hellenic College Press, 1996.

————. *History and Archaeology of Byzantine Asia Minor.* Aldershot: Variorum, 1990.

————. *Ephesus after Antiquity: A Late Antique, Byzantine and Turkish City.* New York: Cambridge University Press, 1979.

————. *Byzantine and Turkish Sardis.* Cambridge, Mass.: Harvard University Press, 1976.

Hohlfelder, R. (ed.) *City, Town and Countryside in the Early Byzantine Era.* New York: Columbia University Press, 1982.

Janin, R. *Constantinople byzantine: Développement urbain et répertoire topographique.* (Byzantine Constantinople: Urban development and topographical directory.) Paris: Institut français d'études byzantines, 1964.

Jones, A. H. M. *The Cities of the Eastern Roman Provinces.* 2nd ed. Oxford: Clarendon Press, 1971.

————. *The Greek City from Alexander to Justinian.* Oxford: Clarendon Press, 1940.

Kraeling, C. H. *Ptolemais: City of the Libyan Pentapolis.* Chicago: University of Chicago Press, 1962.

————. *Gerasa: City of the Decapolis*. New Haven: American Schools of Oriental Research, 1938.

Krautheimer, R. *Rome: Profile of a City, 312–1308*. Princeton: Princeton University Press, 1980.

Krekić, B. *Dubrovnik: A Mediterranean Urban Society, 1300–1600*. Aldershot: Variorum, 1997.

————. *Dubrovnik, Italy and the Balkans in the Late Middle Ages*. London: Variorum, 1980.

Liebeschuetz, J. H. W. G. *Antioch: City and Imperial Administration in the Later Roman Empire*. Oxford: Clarendon Press, 1972.

Mango, C. and G. Dagron. (eds.) *Constantinople and Its Hinterland: Papers from the Twenty-Seventh Spring Symposium of Byzantine Studies*. Aldershot: Variorum, 1995.

Roueché, C. *Aphrodisias in Late Antiquity*. London: Society for the Promotion of Roman Studies, 1989.

Runciman, S. *Mistra: Byzantine Capital of the Peloponnese*. London: Thames and Hudson, 1980.

Segal, J. B. *Edessa, "The Blessed City."* Oxford: Clarendon Press, 1970.

Velkov, V. *Cities in Thrace and Dacia in Late Antiquity*. Amsterdam: A. M. Hakkert, 1977.

C. Demography; Minorities

Ahrweiler, H. and A. E. Laiou. *Studies on the Internal Diaspora of the Byzantine Empire*. Washington, D.C.: Dumbarton Oaks Research Library and Collection, 1997.

Avi-Yonah, M. *The Jews of Palestine: A Political History from the Bark Kokhba War to the Arab Conquest*. Oxford: Blackwell, 1976.

Benjamin of Tudela. *The Itinerary of Benjamin of Tudela*. Edited and translated by M. N. Adler. London: F. Frowde, 1907.

Bowman, S. B. *The Jews of Byzantium, 1204–1453*. Alabama: University of Alabama Press, 1985.

Charanis, P. "Cultural Diversity and the Breakdown of Byzantine Power in Asia Minor." *Dumbarton Oaks Papers* 29 (1975): 3–20.

————. *Studies on the Demography of the Byzantine Empire*. London: Variorum Reprints, 1972.

————. *The Armenians in the Byzantine Empire*. Lisbon: Fudação Calouste Gulbenkian, 1963.

Jacoby, D. "La population de Constantinople à l'époque byzantine." ("The population of Constantinople in the Byzantine period.") *Byzantion* 31 (1961): 81–109.

Laiou-Thomadakis, A. E. *Peasant Society in the Late Byzantine Period: A Social and Demographic Study*. Princeton: Princeton University Press, 1977.

Morrisson, C. and J. Lefort. (eds.) *Hommes et richesses dans l'empire byzantin*. (Men and wealth in the Byzantine Empire.) 2 vols. Paris: P. Lethielleux, 1989–1991.

Russell, J. C. *Late Ancient and Medieval Population*. Philadelphia: American Philosophical Society, 1958.

Sharf, A. *Byzantine Jewry from Justinian to the Fourth Crusade*. London: Routledge and K. Paul, 1971.

Smythe, D. C. (ed.) *Strangers to Themselves: The Byzantine Outsider*. Papers from the 32nd Spring Symposium of Byzantine Studies, University of Sussex, March 1998. Aldershot: Ashgate, 2000.

Starr, J. *The Jews in the Byzantine Empire, 641–1204*. Athens: Verlag der Byzantinish-Neugriechischen Jahrbücher, 1939.

D. Education

Browning, R. *Studies on Byzantine History, Literature and Education*. London: Variorum Reprints, 1977.

Constantinides, C. N. *Higher Education in Byzantium in the Thirteenth and Early Fourteenth Centuries (1204–ca. 1310)*. Nicosia: Cyprus Research Centre, 1982.

Hussey, J. *Church and Learning in the Byzantine Empire, 867–1185*. London: Oxford University Press, 1937.

Kaster, R. *Guardians of Language. The Grammarian and Society in Late Antiquity*. Berkeley: University of California Press, 1988.

Kennedy, G. A. *Greek Rhetoric under Christian Emperors*. Princeton: Princeton University Press, 1983.

Marrou, H. I. *A History of Education in Antiquity*. New York: Sheed and Ward, 1956.

Mullet, M. and R. Scott. (eds.) *Byzantium and the Classical Tradition*. University of Birmingham Thirteenth Spring Symposium of Byzantine Studies, 1979. Birmingham: University of Birmingham, 1981.

Runciman, S. *The Last Byzantine Renaissance*. Cambridge: Cambridge University Press, 1970.

E. Gender

Boswell, J. *Same-Sex Unions in Premodern Europe*. New York: Random House, 1995.

Brock, S. P. and S. A. Harvey. *Holy Women of the Syrian Orient*. Berkeley: University of California Press, 1987.

Brown, P. *The Body and Society: Men, Women and Sexual Renunciation in Early Christianity*. New York: Columbia University Press, 1988.

Buckler, G. *Anna Comnena*. London: Oxford University Press, 1929.

Cameron, Averil and A. Kuhrt. (eds.) *Images of Women in Antiquity*. Detroit: Wayne State University Press, 1983.

Clark, G. *Women in Late Antiquity: Pagan and Christian Life-Styles*. Oxford: Clarendon Press, 1993.

Dalven, R. F. *Anna Comnena*. New York: Twayne, 1972.

Galatarioutou, C. "Holy Women and Witches: Aspects of Byzantine Conceptions of Gender." *Byzantine and Modern Greek Studies* 9 (1984 –1985): 55–94.

Garland, Lynda. *Byzantine Empresses: Women and Power in Byzantium, A.D. 527–1204*. London: Routledge, 1999.

Gouma-Peterson (ed.) *Bibliography on Women in Byzantium*. Wooster, Ohio: College of Wooster, 1995.

Harvey, S. A. "Women in Early Byzantine Hagiography: Reversing the Story." In *That Gentle Strength: Historical Perspectives on Women in Christianity*. Edited by L. Coon. Charlottesville: University of Virginia Press, 1990.

Herrin, J. "In Search of Byzantine Women: Three Avenues of Approach." In *Images of Women in Antiquity*. Edited by A. Cameron and A. Kuhrt. London: Croom Helm, 1983.

———. "Women and the Faith in Icons in Early Christianity." In *Culture, Ideology and Society*. Edited by R. R. Samuel and G. S. Jones. London: Routledge and K. Paul, 1983.

James, Liz. (ed.) *Desire and Denial in Byzantium*. Papers from the 31st Symposium of Byzantine Studies. Brighton, March 1997. Aldershot: Ashgate, 1999.

———. *Women, Men, and Eunuchs: Gender in Byzantium*. London: Routledge, 1997.

Laiou, A. *Gender, Society and Economic Life in Byzantium*. Aldershot: Variorum, 1992.

Nicol, D. *The Byzantine Lady: Ten Portraits*. Cambridge: Cambridge University Press, 1994.

Pohlsander, H. A. *Helena: Empress and Saint*. Chicago: Ares Publisher, 1995.

Salzman, M. R. "Aristocratic Women: Conductors of Christianity in the Fourth Century." *Helios* 16 (1989): 207–220.

Talbot, A.-M. *Holy Women of Byzantium: Ten Saints' Lives in English Translation*. Washington, D.C.: Dumbarton Oaks Research Library and Collection, 1996.

F. Monasticism

Brown, P. "The Rise and Function of the Holy Man in Late Antiquity."

Journal of Roman Studies 61 (1971): 80–101. (Reprinted in P. Brown, *Society and the Holy in Late Antiquity*. Berkeley: University of California Press, 1982.)

Bryer, A. and M. B. Cunningham. *Mount Athos and Byzantine Monasticism*. Aldershot: Variorum, 1996.

Charanis, P. "Monastic Properties and the State in the Byzantine Empire." *Dumbarton Oaks Papers* 4 (1948): 53–118. (Reprinted in P. Charanis, *Social, Economic and Political Life in the Byzantine Empire*. London: Variorum Reprints, 1973.)

Chitty, D. J. *The Desert a City: An Introduction of the Study of Egyptian and Palestinian Monasticism under the Christian Empire*. Oxford: Blackwell, 1966.

Dawes, E. and N. Baynes. *Three Byzantine Saints*. Crestwood, N.Y.: St. Vladimir's Seminary Press, 1977.

Hackel, S. (ed.) *The Byzantine Saint: University of Birmingham Fourteenth Spring Symposium of Byzantine Studies*. London: Fellowship of St. Alban and St. Sergios, 1981.

Harvey, S. A. *Asceticism and Society in Crisis: John of Ephesus and the Lives of Eastern Saints*. Berkeley: University of California Press, 1990.

Hirschfeld, Y. *The Judean Desert Monasteries in the Byzantine Period*. New Haven: Yale University Press, 1992.

Janin, R. *Les églises et les monastères des grands centres byzantins*. (The churches and monasteries of the great Byzantine centers.) Paris: Institut français d'études byzantines, 1975.

Mullet, M. E. and A. Kirby. *The Theotokos Evergetis and Eleventh-Century Monasticism*. Belfast: Byzantine Enterprises, Queens University of Belfast, 1994.

Nicol, D. M. *Meteora: The Rock Monasteries of Thessaly*. Revised ed. London: Variorum, 1975.

Patrich, J. *Sabas, Leader of Palestinian Monasticism: A Comparative Study in Eastern Monasticism, Fourth to Seventh Centuries*. Washington, D.C.: Dumbarton Oaks Research Library and Collection, 1995.

Rousseau P. *Pachomius*. Revised ed. Berkeley: University of California Press, 1999.

Talbot, A.-M. "An Introduction to Byzantine Monasticism." *Illinois Classical Studies* 12 (1987): 229–241.

Thomas, J. P. *Private Religious Foundations in the Byzantine Empire*. Washington, D.C.: Dumbarton Oaks Library and Collection, 1987.

Turner, H. J. M. *St. Symeon the New Theologian and Spiritual Fatherhood*. Leiden: E. J. Brill, 1990.

G. Philanthropy

Constantelos, D. *Byzantine Philanthropy and Social Welfare.* New Brunswick: Rutgers University Press, 1968. (2nd rev. edition, New Rochelle: A. D. Caratzas, 1991.)

Miller, T. S. *The Birth of the Hospital in the Byzantine Empire.* Baltimore: Johns Hopkins University Press, 1985.

Patlagean, E. (ed.) *Maladie et société à Byzance.* (Disease and society in Byzantium.) Spoleto: Centro italiano di studi sull'Alto Medioevo, 1993.

H. Popular Culture and Beliefs

Koukoules, P. *Byzantinon bios kai politismos.* (Byzantine life and civilization.) 6 vols. Athens: Ekdoseis tou Gallikou Institoutou Athenon, 1948–1957.

Maguire, H. (ed.) *Byzantine Magic.* Washington, D.C.: Dumbarton Oaks Research Library and Collection, 1995.

Maguire, E. D. and H. P., and M. J. Duncan-Flowers. *Art and Holy Powers in the Early Christian House.* Urbana: University of Illinois Press.

I. Prosopography

Jones, A. H. M., J. R. Martindale, and J. Morris. (eds.) *The Prosopography of the Later Roman Empire.* 2 vols. Cambridge: Cambridge University Press, 1971 and 1980.

Nicol, D. *Studies in Late Byzantine History and Prosopography.* Aldershot: Variorum, 1986.

————. *The Byzantine Family of Kantakouzenos (Cantacuzenus), ca. 1100–1460; A Genealogical and Prosopographical Study.* Washington, D.C.: Dumbarton Oaks Center for Byzantine Studies, 1968.

Polemis, D. *The Doukai: A Contribution to Byzantine Prosopography.* London: Athlone Press, 1968.

J. Villages

Antoniadis-Bibicou, H. "Villages déserte en Grèce, un bilan provisoire." ("Deserted villages in Greece, a provisional evaluation.") In *Villages désertés et histoire économique. Les hommes et la terre.* (Deserted villages and economic history. Men and the earth.) Vol. XI. Paris: S.E.V.P.E.N., 1965.

Kaplan, M. *Les hommes et la terre à Byzance du VIe au XIe siècle.* (Men and land in Byzantium from the 6th to the 11th century.) Paris: Publications de la Sorbonne, 1992.

Kravari, V. *Villes et villages de Macédoine occidentale.* (Cities and villages of western Macadonia.) Paris: Éditions P. Lethielleux, 1989.

Laiou-Thomadakis, A. E. *Peasant Society in the Late Byzantine Period: A Social and Demographic Study.* Princeton: Princeton University Press, 1977.

Rosser, J., W. P. Donovan, et al. "The Byzantine Occupation." In *Excavations at Nichoria in Southwest Greece.* Vol. III: *Dark Age and Byzantine Occupation, 353–424.* W. A. McDonald, W. D. E. Coulson, and J. Rosser. (eds.) Minneapolis: University of Minnesota Press, 1983.

XII. SELECTED SOURCES IN ENGLISH TRANSLATION

The following works of E. A. Hanawalt and B. MacBain offer a more complete list of translations published up to 1988.

Agathias. *The Histories.* Translated by J. D. Frendo. Berlin: DeGruyter, 1975.

(Abbasid Caliphate sources). *The Eclipse of the 'Abbasid Caliphate: Original Chronicles of the Fourth Islamic Century.* Edited and translated by H. F. Amedroz and D. S. Margoliouth. 7 vols. Oxford: B. Blackwell, 1920–1921.

Akindynos, Gregory. *Letters of Gregory Akindynos.* Edited and translated by A. C. Hero. Washington, D.C.: Dumbarton Oaks Research Library and Collection, 1983.

Ammianus Marcellinus. *The Later Roman Empire (A.D. 354–378).* Translated by Walter Hamilton. Harmondsworth: Penguin, 1988.

———. *Ammianus Marcellinus.* Edited and translated by J. C. Rolfe. 3 vols. Cambridge, Mass.: Harvard University Press, 1935–1939. (See vol. 3, 506–569, for an English translation of *Excerpta Valesiana.*)

Anna Komnene. *The Alexiad of the Princess Anna Comnena, being the history of the reign of her father, Alexius I, Emperor of the Romans.* Translated by E. A. S. Dawes. London: K. Paul, Trench, Trubner and Co., 1928.

———. *The Alexiad of Anna Comnena.* Translated by E. R. A. Sewter. Harmondsworth: Penguin, 1969.

Apophthegmata Patrum. *The Sayings of the Desert Fathers: The Alphabetical Collection.* Translated by B. Ward. Revised ed. Kalamazoo: Cistercian Publications, 1984.

Athanasios. *Athanasius: The Life of Antony and the Letter to Marcellinus.* Translated by R. C. Gregg. New York: Paulist Press, 1980.

Athanasios I. *The Correspondence of Athanasius I, Patriarch of Constantinople: Letters to the Emperor Andronicus II, Members of the Imperial*

Family, and Officials. Edited and translated by A.-M. Talbot. Washington, D.C.: Dumbarton Oaks Center for Byzantine Studies, 1975.

Baladhuri, al-. *The Origins of the Islamic State.* Translated by P. Hitti. 2 vols. New York: Columbia University Press, 1916–1924.

Barbaro, Nicolo. *Diary of the Siege of Constantinople.* Translated by J. R. M. Jones. New York: Exposition Press, 1969.

Bar Hebraeus. (Gregory Abul-Faraj). *The Chronography of Gregory Abû'l Faraj.* Translated by E. A. W. Budge. 2 vols. Oxford: Oxford University Press, H. Milford, 1932.

Benjamin of Tudela. *The Itinerary of Benjamin of Tudela.* Edited and translated by M. N. Adler. London: F. Frowde, 1907.

Book of the Eparch. In *Roman Law in the Later Roman Empire.* Translated by E. H. Freshfield. Cambridge: Cambridge University Press, 1938.

Brand, C. M. (ed.) *Icon and Minaret: Sources of Byzantine and Islamic Civilization.* Englewood Cliffs: Prentice-Hall, 1969.

Choniates, Niketas. *O City of Byzantium: Annals of Niketas Choniates.* Translated by H. Magoulias. Detroit: Wayne State University Press, 1984.

Chronicle of the Morea. *Crusaders as Conquerors: The Chronicle of the Morea.* Translated by H. E. Lurier. New York: Columbia University Press, 1964.

Chronicon Paschale. *Chronicon Paschale 284–628 A.D.* Translated by M. and M. Whitby. Liverpool: Liverpool University Press, 1989.

Claudian. *Claudian.* 2 vols. Edited and translated by M. Platnauer. London: W. Heinemann, 1922.

Codex Theodosianus. *The Theodosian Law Code.* Translated by C. Pharr. Princeton: Princeton University Press, 1952.

Constantine VII Porphyrogenitus. *De Administrando Imperio*, vol. 1. Edited by Gy. Moravcsik; translated by R. J. H. Jenkins. 2nd ed. Washington, D.C.: Dumbarton Oaks Center for Byzantine Studies, 1967.

———. *De Administrado Imperio.* F. Dvornik, R. J. H. Jenkins, et al. Vol. 2: *Commentary.* London: Athlone Press, 1962.

Dawes, E. and N. H. Baynes. *Three Byzantine Saints. Contemporary Biographies of St. Daniel the Stylite, St. Theodore of Sykeon and St. John the Almsgiver.* Translated by E. Dawes and N. H. Baynes. Crestwood, N.Y.: St. Vladimir's Seminary Press, 1977.

Dennis, G. T. *Three Byzantine Military Treatises.* Washington, D.C.: Dumbarton Oaks Research Library and Collection, 1985.

De Rebus Bellicus. *De Rebus Bellicus.* Translated by M. W. C. Hassall and R. I. Ireland. Oxford: British Archaeological Reports, 1979.

Digenes Akrites. *Digenes Akritas: The Grottaferrata and Escorial Versions.* Edited and translated by E. Jeffreys. Cambridge: Cambridge University Press, 1998.

————. Translated by J. Mavrogordato. Oxford: Clarendon Press, 1956.

Dodgen, M. H. and S. N. C. Lieu. (eds.) *The Roman Eastern Frontier and the Persian Wars (AD 226–363): A Documentary History*. London: Routledge, 1994.

Doukas. *Decline and Fall of Byzantium to the Ottoman Turks*. Translated by H. Magoulias. Detroit: Wayne State University Press, 1975.

Ecloga. *A Manual of Roman Law: The Ecloga*. Translated by E. H. Freshfield. Cambridge: Cambridge University Press, 1927.

Eunapios of Sardis. In *Philostratus and Eunapius, 317–596*. Edited and translated by W. C. Wright. New York: G. P. Putnam's Sons, 1952.

————. In *The Fragmentary Classicizing Historians of the Later Roman Empire*. Edited and translated by R. C. Blockley. Vol. 1, 1–26 (Liverpool: F. Cairns, 1981); vol. 2, 1–150 (Liverpool: F. Cairns, 1983).

Eusebios of Caesarea. Translated by G. A. Williamson. *The History of the Church from Christ to Constantine*. Harmondsworth: Penguin, 1965.

————. *The Life of the Blessed Constantine*. Translated by E. C. Richardson. In P. Schaff and H. Wace (eds.), *A Select Library of Nicene and Post-Nicene Fathers of the Christian Church*. 2nd series. Vol. 1. New York: C. Scribner's Sons, 1890. (Reprinted Grand Rapids, Mich., 1952.)

Eustathios of Thessalonike. *Eustathios of Thessaloniki. The Capture of Thessaloniki*. Translated by J. R. Melville Jones. Canberra: Australian Association of Byzantine Studies, 1988.

Evagrios Scholastikos. *Ecclesiastical History: A History of the Church in Six Books, from A.D. 431 to A.D. 594 by Evagrius*. Bohn's Ecclesiastical Library. Translated by E. Walford. London: H. G. Bohn, 1854.

Excerpta Valesiana. In *Ammianus Marcellinus*. Edited and translated by J. C. Rolfe. Vol. 3, 506–569. London: Harvard University Press, 1935–1939.

Farmer's Law. In "The Farmer's Law." W. Ashburner. Journal of Hellenic Studies 32 (1912): 68–95.

Fulcher of Chartres. *A History of the Expedition to Jerusalem*. Translated by H. S. Fink. Knoxville: University of Tennessee Press, 1969.

Geanakoplos, D. J. *Byzantium: Church, Society, and Civilization Seen through Contemporary Eyes*. Chicago: University of Chicago Press, 1984.

Genesios. *Genesios: On the Reigns of the Emperors*. Translated by A. Kaldellis. Canberra: Australian National University, 1998.

Gesta Francorum. *Gesta Francorum et aliorum Hierosolimitanorum*. Edited and translated by R. Hill. London: T. Nelson, 1962.

Gordon, C. D. *The Age of Attila: Fifth-Century Byzantium and the Barbarians*. Selections from Priskos, Malchos, Olympiodoros, and John of Antioch. Translated by C. D. Gordon. Ann Arbor: University of Michigan Press, 1960.

Greek Anthology. *Greek Anthology*. Translated by W. R. Paton. 5 vols. London: W. Heinemann, 1925–1926.

Gunther of Pairis. *The Capture of Constantinople: The Hystoria Constantinopolitana of Gunther of Pairis*. Edited and translated by A. J. Andrea. Philadelphia: University of Pennsylvania Press, 1997.

Hanawalt, E. A. *An Annotated Bibliography of Byzantine Sources in English Translation*. Brookline, Mass.: Hellenic College Press, 1988.

Ibn Batttuta. *Travels of Ibn Battuta, A.D. 1325–1354*. Translated by H. A. R. Gibb. 4 vols. Cambridge: Hakluyt Society, 1958–1971.

Ignatios the Deacon. *Correspondence of Ignatios the Deacon*. Edited and translated by C. Mango with the collaboration of Stephanos Efthymiades. Washington, D.C.: Dumbarton Oaks Research Library and Collection, 1997.

_____. *The Life of the Patriarch Tarasios by Ignatios the Deacon*. Edited and translated by S. Efthymiadis. Aldershot: Ashgate, 1998.

John Lydos. *On Powers, or the Magistracies of the Roman State*. Edited and translated by A. C. Bandy. Philadelphia: American Philosophical Society, 1983.

John Malalas. *The Chronicle of John Malalas*. Translated by E. and M. Jeffreys, and R. Schott. Melbourne: Australian Association of Byzantine Studies, 1986.

John of Ephesus. *Lives of the Eastern Saints*. Translated by E. W. Brooks. *Patrologia Orientalis* 17 (1923): 1–307; 18 (1924): 513–698; 19 (1926): 153–285.

John of Nikiu. *The Chronicle of John, Bishop of Nikiu*. Translated by R. H. Charles. London: William and Norgate, 1916. (Reprinted Amsterdam: Philo Press, 1982.)

Jones, J. R. M. (trans.) *The Siege of Constantinople 1453: Seven Contemporary Accounts*. Amsterdam: A. M. Hakkert, 1972.

Jordanes. *Gothic History*. Translated by C. C. Mierow. Cambridge: Speculum Historiale, 1966.

Joshua the Stylite. *The Chronicle of Joshua the Stylite*. Edited and translated by W. Wright. Cambridge: Cambridge University Press, 1882. (Reprinted Amsterdam: A. M. Hakkert, 1968.)

Julian. *The Works of the Emperor Julian*. Edited and translated by W. C. Wright. 3 vols. Loeb Classical Library. London: W. Heinemann (and New York: Macmillan Co.), 1913–1923.

Justinian I. *Corpus iuris civilis. The Civil Law*. 17 volumes. Translated by S. P. Scott. Cincinnati: Central Trust Co., 1932.

_____. *The Digest of Roman Law; Theft, Rapine, Damage and Insult*. Translated by C. F. Kolbert. Harmondsworth: Penguin, 1979.

Kinnamos, John. *Deeds of John and Manuel Comnenus by John Kinnamos*. Translated by C. Brand. New York: Columbia University Press, 1976.

Kosmas Indikopleustes. *The Christian Topography of Cosmas, an Egyptian Monk*. Translated by J. W. McCrindle. London: Printed for the Hakluyt Society, 1987.

Kritoboulos, Michael. *History of Mehmed the Conqueor by Kritoboulos*. Translated by C. T. Riggs. Princeton: Princeton University Press, 1954.

Lactantius. *De mortibus persecutorum*. Edited and translated by J. L. Creed. Oxford: Clarendon Press, 1984.

Leo of Synada. *The Correspondence of Leo, Metropolitan of Synada and Syncellus*. Edited and translated by M. P. Vinson. Washington, D.C.: Dumbarton Oaks, 1985.

Leontios of Jerusalem. *The Life of Leontios Patriarch of Jerusalem*. Translated by D. Tsougarakis. Leiden: E. J. Brill, 1993.

Lieu, S. N. C. and D. Montseratt. *From Constantine to Julian: Pagan and Byzantine Views. A Source History*. London, New York: Routledge, 1996.

Liutprand of Cremona. *The Embassy to Constantinople and Other Writings*. Edited by J. Norwich and translated by F. A. Wright. London: J. M. Dent: Tuttle Co., 1993.

Majeska, G. P. *Russian Travelers to Constantinople in the Fourteenth and Fifteenth Centuries*. Washington, D.C.: Dumbarton Oaks Research Library and Collection, 1984.

Mango, C. *The Art of the Byzantine Empire: 312–1453, Sources and Documents*. Englewood Cliffs: Prentice-Hall, 1972. (Reprinted Toronto: University of Toronto Press, in association with the Medieval Academy of America, 1986.)

Manuel II Komnenos. *The Letters of Manuel II Palaeologus*. Edited and translated by G. T. Dennis. Washington, D.C.: Dumbarton Oaks Center for Byzantine Studies, 1977.

Matthew of Edessa. *The Chronicle of Matthew of Edessa*. Translated by A. E. Dostourian. Ph. D. Thesis, Rutgers University, 1977. Ann Arbor, Mich.: University Microfilms, 1972.

McBain, B. "An Annotated Bibliography of Sources for Late Antiquity." *Byzantine Studies* 10 (1983): 88–109, 223–247.

Melania the Younger. *The Life of Melania the Younger*. Translated by E. A. Clark. New York: E. Mellen, 1984.

Menander Protector. *The History of Menander the Guardsman*. Translated by R. C. Blockley. Liverpool: Liverpool University Press, 1985.

Nicholas I. *Nicholas I, Patriarch of Constantinople: Letters*. Edited and translated by R. J. H. Jenkins and L. G. Westerink. Washington, D.C.: Dumbarton Oaks Center for Byzantine Studies, 1973.

———. *Nicholas I, Patriarch of Constantinople: Miscellaneous Writings*. Edited and translated by L. G. Westerink. Washington, D.C.: Dumbarton Oaks Center for Byzantine Studies, 1981.

Nikephoros I. *Short History*. Edited and translated by C. Mango. Washington, D.C.: Dumbarton Oaks Research Library and Collection, 1990.

Odo of Deuil. *De profectione Ludovici VII in orientem. The Journey of Louis VII to the East by Odo of Deuil.* Edited and translated by V. G. Berry. New York: Norton, 1948. (Reprinted 1965.)

Orosius, Paul. *The Seven Books of History against the Pagans.* Translated by R. J. Deferrari. Washington, D.C.: Catholic University of America Press, 1964.

Paul Silentiarios. Partial translation in C. Mango, *The Art of the Byzantine Empire: 312–1453, Sources and Documents.* Englewood Cliffs: Prentice-Hall, 1972, 80–96.

Philostorgios. *Sozomen; Philostorgius.* Translated by E. Walford. London: H. G. Bohn, 1855, 429–528.

Photios. *The Homilies of Photius, Patriarch of Constantinople.* Translated by C. Mango. Cambridge, Mass.: Harvard University Press, 1958.

Priskos. In *The Fragmentary Classicising Historians of the Later Roman Empire: Eunapius, Olympiodorus, Priscus and Malchus.* Edited and translated by R. C. Blockley. Vol. 1, 48–70, 113–123; vol. 2, 224–400. Liverpool: F. Cairns, 1981–1983

Prokopios of Caesarea. *Procopius.* Edited and translated by H. B. Dewing and G. Downey. 7 vols. Loeb Classical Library. London: W. Heinemann, 1914–1940.

————. *Secret History.* Translated by R. Atwater. Ann Arbor: University of Michigan Press, 1963.

————. *The Secret History.* Translated by G. A. Williamson. Harmondsworth: Penguin, 1966. (Reprinted, 1987.)

Psellos, Michael. *Fourteen Byzantine Rulers: The Chronographia of Michael Psellus.* Translated by E. R. A. Sewter. Harmondsworth: Penguin, 1953. (Reprinted 1966, 1973.)

Raymond of Aguilers. *Historia Francorum qui ceperunt Iherusalem.* Translated by J. H. and L. L. Hill. Philadelphia: American Philosophical Society, 1968.

Rhodian Sea Law. *The Rhodian Sea-Law.* Edited and translated by W. Ashburner. Oxford: Clarendon Press, 1909.

Robert of Clari. *The Conquest of Constantinople.* Translated by E. H. McNeal. New York: Columbia University Press, 1936. (Reprinted New York: Norton, 1969.)

Romanos the Melode. *Kontakia of Romanos, Byzantine Melodist.* Translated by M. Carpenter. 2 volumes. Columbia: University of Missouri Press, 1970–1973. Revisions by A. C. Bandy in *Byzantine Studies/ Etudes Byzantine* 3 (1976): 64–113; 7 (1980): 78–113.

Russian Primary Chronicle. *The Russian Primary Chronicle, Laurentian Text.* Translated by S. H. Cross and O. P. Sherbowitz-Wetzor. Cambridge, Mass.: Medieval Academy of America, 1953.

Simokattes, Theophylaktos. *The History of Theophylact Simocatta.* Translated by L. M. Whitby and M. Whitby. Oxford: Clarendon Press, 1986.

Sokrates. *Ecclesiastical History*. Translated by A. C. Zenos. In *A Select Library of the Nicene and Post-Nicene Fathers of the Christian Church.* P. Schaff and W. Wace. (eds.) 2nd Series. Vol. 2. New York: C. Scribner's Sons, 1890. (Reprinted Grand Rapids, Mich., 1952.)

Sozomen. *The Ecclesiastical History of Sozomen*. Translated by C. D. Hartranft. In *A Select Library of Nicene and Post-Nicene Fathers of the Christian Church.* P. Schaff and W. Wace. (eds.) 2nd series. Vol. III. New York: C. Scribner's Sons, 1890. (Reprinted Grand Rapids, Mich., 1952.)

Sphrantzes. *The Fall of the Byzantine Empire*. Translated by M. Philippides. Amherst: University of Massachusetts Press, 1980.

Strategikon. *Maurice's Strategikon: Handbook of Byzantine Military Strategy*. Edited and translated by G. T. Dennis. Philadelphia: University of Pennsylvania Press, 1988.

Synesios of Cyrene. *The Letters of Synesius of Cyrene*. Translated by A. Fitzgerald. London: Oxford University Press, 1926.

Synodicon Vetus. *The Synodicon Vetus*. Edited and translated by J. Duffy and J. Parker. Washington, D.C.: Dumbarton Oaks Center for Byzantine Studies, 1979.

Talbot, A.-M. (ed.) *Defenders of Images: Eight Saints' Lives in English Translation*. Washington, D.C.: Dumbarton Oaks Library and Research Library and Collection, 1998.

Theodoret of Cyrrhus. *The Ecclesiastical History, Dialogues and Letters of Theodoret*. Translated by B. Jackson. In *Select Library of the Nicene and Post-Nicene Fathers*. P. Schaff and H. Wace. (eds.) 2nd Series. Vol. 3. New York: C. Scribner's Sons, 1892. (Reprinted Grand Rapids, Mich., 1953.)

Theophanes. *The Chronicle of Theophanes the Confessor: Byzantine and Near Eastern History, A. D. 284–813*. Translated by C. Mango and R. Scott. Oxford: Clarendon Press, 1997.

Theophylact Simocatta. *The History of Theophylact Simocatta*. Translated by L. M. Whitby and M. Whitby. Oxford: Clarendon Press, 1986.

Timarion. *Timarion*. Translated by B. Baldwin. Detroit: Wayne State University Press, 1984.

Villehardouin, Geoffrey. *The Conquest of Constantinople*. In *Joinville and Villehardouin: Chronicles of the Crusades*. Translated by M. R. B. Shaw. Harmondsworth: Penguin, 1963.

William of Tyre. *A History of Deeds Done Beyond the Sea*. Translated by E. A. Babcock and A. C. Krey. 2 vols. New York: Columbia University Press, 1943.

Zosimos. *New History*. Translated by R. T. Ridley. Sydney: Australian Association of Byzantine Studies, 1982.

ABOUT THE AUTHOR

John H. Rosser (Ph.D. Byzantine History, Rutgers University) is a member of the faculty of the Department of History, Boston College. He has written numerous articles and monographs on topics related to the history and archeology of medieval Greece and Cyprus. His archeological research has included the excavation of a Crusader castle called *Saranda Kolones* (*Forty Columns*), in Paphos, Cyprus, and of the Byzantine farmstead and church at Nichoria, in southern Greece. His archeological reconnaissance in Greece has included the Grevena Project, in southwestern Macedonia. He lives in Wellesley, Massachusetts, with his wife Claire and two Siamese cats.